AIX® 5L™

Administration

Randal K. Michael

McGraw-Hill/Osborne

New York   Chicago   San Francisco
Lisbon   Londo   Madri   Mexico City
Milan   New Delhi   San Juan
Seoul   Singapore   Sydney   Toronto

McGraw-Hill/Osborne
2600 Tenth Street
Berkeley, California 94710
U.S.A.

To arrange bulk purchase discounts for sales promotions, premiums, or fund-raisers, please contact **McGraw-Hill/**Osborne at the above address. For information on translations or book distributors outside the U.S.A., please see the International Contact Information page immediately following the index of this book.

AIX® 5L™ Administration

7890 IBT/IBT 019

ISBN 0-07-222255-7

Publisher
  Brandon A. Nordin
Vice President & Associate Publisher
  Scott Rogers
Acquisitions Editor
  Francis Kelly
Project Editor
  Elizabeth Seymour
Acquisitions Coordinator
  Emma Acker
Technical Editors
  Frances Au, Terry Greenlee
Copy Editor
  Robert Campbell

Proofreader
  Linda Medoff, Paul Medoff
Indexer
  Robert J. Richardson
Computer Designers
  Carie Abrew, Michelle Galicia
Illustrator
  Michael Mueller, Lyssa Wald
Series Design
  Peter F. Hancik, Lyssa Wald
Cover Series Design
  Jeff Weeks

This book was composed with Corel VENTURA™ Publisher.

This book is dedicated to my
Wife Robin
and the girls
Andrea and Ana

ABOUT THE AUTHOR:

Randal K. Michael is a Certified AIX Specialist who has worked in the technology sector for 25 years focusing on computer systems support; he has also been a UNIX Systems Administrator for the last ten years, concentrating on AIX. Randal holds a Bachelor of Science degree in Computer Science with a Mathematics minor from the University of Alabama, School of Engineering. His broad base of experience stems from working with businesses who perform missile systems research and development, automotive electronics and control systems design, development and manufacturing, computer-aided design (both mechanical and electronic), computer-aided manufacturing, telecommunications, hospital computer support, finance, wireless communications, and beverage manufacturing. Randal has worked as a Systems Administrator for companies such as Chrysler Motors, IBM, BellSouth, Egleston Children's Hospital, Equifax, and Glenayre Electronics. Over the years Randal has worked mainly as a contract consultant. He currently works for Coca-Cola Enterprises, Incorporated, in Atlanta, Georgia.

ABOUT THE CONTRIBUTING AUTHORS:

Terry Greenlee has been an independent AIX consultant since 1992. He founded the San Jose AIX User Group in 1994 and chaired it until 1999. Terry can be contacted at Terry.Greenlee@AIXadm.org.

Charles Ritter is a Unix Systems Administrator and information technology consultant specializing in IBM's AIX operating system. Charles has eight years of experience in the industry, working for top system vendors and Fortune 500 companies, including Hitachi Data Systems, Shared Medical Systems, and Charles Schwab. He can be reached at critter@aixadm.org.

Sandor W. Sklar is a Unix Systems Administrator at Stanford University, Information Technology Systems and Services, and is an IBM Certified Specialist in AIX System Administration.

Todd Smith is an IBM Certified AIX Specialist with over 20 years of experience in the Data Processing field. He has held positions with Ciba-Vision as a programmer/analyst; with Coca-Cola Enterprises as a Systems Administrator on both iSeries (AS/400) and pSeries (RS/6000) platforms; and as Manager of Corporate UNIX Infrastructure. He currently owns A. Todd Smith Consulting (www.atoddsmith.com).

Joey Neilson is a Principal Education Specialist with Availant, Inc. (formerly known as CLAM Associates), specializing in AIX and HACMP instruction. He has more than 30 years of computer experience in hardware/software support and computer training. He is currently certified as an AIX Advanced Technical Expert and Cisco Certified Network Associate. He can be reached at joey@availant.com.

Sandy Larson is a Principal Technical Writer on the HACMP project at Availant, Inc. She has been documenting HACMP and other high availability products at Availant since 1998. She may be reached at sandy@availant.com.

Roger Fisher is a Senior Education Specialist with Availant, Inc., specializing in AIX and HACMP instruction. He has more than 30 years of computer experience in hardware/software support and computer training. He can be reached at rff@availant.com.

Judy Campos is Documentation Manager at Availant, Inc. She has been with Availant for nine years and has documented every release of HACMP since version 2.1. She may be reached at judy@availant.com.

Julia Malkin is a Technical Writer on the HACMP project at Availant, Inc. She has been documenting HACMP since 2000. She may be reached at jmalkin@availant.com.

ABOUT THE TECHNICAL REVIEWERS:

Frances Au is currently a senior technical analyst for INTRIA-HP. She has been involved in Unix Systems Administration since 1995. Apart from her extensive knowledge in legacy systems, she has in-depth working knowledge of the following Unix platforms: AIX, HP-UX, and SUN Solaris. In her spare time, she enjoys reading and travelling.

Terry Greenlee has been an independent AIX consultant since 1992. He founded the San Jose AIX User Group in 1994 and chaired it until 1999. Terry can be contacted at Terry.Greenlee@AIXadm.org.

CONTENTS

v

Part V   **Network Configuration and Customization**

ACKNOWLEDGMENTS

The knowledge I've pieced together for this work is based on the combined support and talents of computer professionals I have worked with over the years and from my contributors to this book. Each one of the contributors is an AIX expert and I want to thank each one individually. Terry Greenlee is not only a contributor, but also my technical reviewer. Terry has an attention to detail that I envy and he made this book what it is. Francis Au is another Technical Reviewer who added valuable insight into many chapters. I also want to recognize Todd Smith, with whom I worked and who is my performance guy. IBM calls Todd's disk tuning "Todd Tuned." I want to thank Kim Tran, from IBM, whose knowledge of networking stands out in this book. Charles Ritter is another talent in AIX systems administration who contributed outstanding insight into the Web and communications areas. Sandor Sklar, from Stanford University, is the person who made security a simple issue for all of us. Additionally, I'd like to thank James DeRoest for breaking ground for this book. I also must thank my editors at McGraw-Hill, Franny Kelly and Emma Acker, and the entire team of professionals who worked on this book. I need to thank Carole McClendon at Waterside Production for her efforts throughout this entire project.

On the IBM side I'd like to thank Steven Michael, who I met at IBM in Atlanta at a p690 (Regatta) seminar. Chris is the Project Manager at IBM whose ties to Austin AIX Development gave me the assistance I needed, and I want to thank him for allowing me to query my IBM contacts. These guys kept me abreast of changes in the operating system and hardware while I completed the writing of this book. I'd like to recognize my local IBM representatives, Linda Yeatman, Anna Price, Kyle Kirkman, Stuart Bailey, David Nation, Earl Mayfield Jr., Dan Hale, Steve McGill, Jake Fredrick, Sean Mea, John Rafferty, Michael Cohn, and Richard Covington. These people are always around when you need them and were extremely helpful anytime I needed assistance or had a question.

I want to especially thank Jack Renfro, who let me touch my first RS/6000 back in 1990. Jack allowed me to come into the Research and Development CAD/CAM support group at Chrysler Motors, and was my mentor for many years. I am truly grateful for everything that Jack has taught me, and especially for turning me loose on those *quickie* projects. I learned from the best!

Finally, if Mom and Gene had not helped me hang the shingle on my wall, this book would have not been written by me. Thanks to them for giving me the opportunity to finish my college education at the University of Alabama, School of Engineering for Computer Science.

PART I

System Administration Tasks and Tools

CHAPTER 1

Introduction

In the near past, UNIX primarily inhabited the dusty halls of research institutions and universities. In these environments, UNIX was used as a programmer's tool that could be built upon to meet the needs of the research community. It didn't have to be easy, it just had to be low-cost and provide standard common interfaces to support research collaboration and tool building. It is the open, standards-based face of UNIX that has brought it to the forefront of the movement toward open systems.

The proliferation of low-cost RISC processors has brought UNIX onto the desktop. The open systems, open source, and right sizing movements have brought UNIX into the commercial glass house. The time has come. UNIX has gotten a haircut, put on a suit, and gone head to head with the legacy operating systems from desktop to big iron. Vendors and standards groups are scrambling to define and implement UNIX system management and administration tools to satisfy the needs of this diverse user base that are continually changing. Are they succeeding? Well, even now a common Enterprise Management "Console" does not work for *everything* and *everybody*.

The first offerings in the realm of UNIX system management were just a set of commands encased in various user interfaces. Many of these tools take a good deal of heat from the traditional UNIX Systems Administrator crowd because of the new approaches and protocols being employed to manage standalone and distributed UNIX environments. Whether this is good or bad remains to be seen.

The Open Software Foundation (OSF) struggled with its Distributed Management Environment (DME) technology in late 1993, yet it never saw the light of day. Tivoli, Hewlett-Packard, and others have taken up the challenge and are now offering a robust multivendor OS and network management tools. Are they interoperable? The sales glossies and CD-ROM demos certainly indicate that not only are they interoperable, they also meet all the latest standards specifications. Remember standards? Everybody's got one. Rather than spending a great deal of time validating the standards issue, the best use of your time is to give each product a test drive and vote with hard-earned cash. Since you are reading this book, I can safely assume there is still some work to be done regarding development of the perfect systems management tool.

Like any multiuser operating system, UNIX requires special care to ensure that resources are distributed equitably among the user base and that these resources are secured from intrusion or failure. Our job as Systems Administrators is to guarantee that these requirements are being met. How do we do it? Read on!

AIX AND UNIX

Is AIX UNIX? It's certainly different in many respects from what might be coined legacy UNIX systems. What defines UNIX? Most vendor UNIX offerings, including AIX, pass the System V Interface Definition (SVID) tests, are POSIX compliant, and are X/Open certified. Does this make them UNIX? Before you answer that, remember: MVS, then OS/390, and now the zSeries are X/Open certified. Most of the differences found in AIX are related to system administration. As you might expect, the Systems Administrators are the most vocal when it comes to complaining or praising UNIX evolution.

AIX offers a very solid mixture of BSD and System V features. Users from either environment will find it easy to make themselves at home. The measure of an operating system should be whether it provides an environment that assists rather than hinders your ability to do meaningful work. It must also be interoperable with other architectures. AIX holds up very well under this definition.

As far as where UNIX is going, one can only hope that the vendor community is serious about maintaining a common UNIX look and feel. The Common Open Software Environment (COSE) alliance started by HP, Sun, IBM, SCO, USL, and Univel was a step in the right direction. There have been other vendor coalitions, and we have seen interfaces like the Common Desktop Environment (CDE) become a reality.

NEW FEATURES OF AIX WITH VERSION 5L

Starting with AIX 5L, a lot of commonality between AIX and other UNIX flavors gets closer. As a whole, AIX is slowly moving in the direction of System V, and IBM has embraced the open source movement by incorporating Linux Affinity into AIX 5L and AIX 4.3.3. The next sections show some of the new features and enhancements in AIX 5L.

Linux Affinity

IBM has brought Linux into the support arena and into AIX as well. With AIX 5L, and AIX 4.3.3 at maintenance level 8, you have the ability to run Linux applications, tools, and utilities, and have the same look and feel of Linux on your AIX POWER machine with KDE-2 and GNOME. You can run native Linux programs on AIX, and you can bring your Linux application source code over to AIX and recompile the application to create a new AIX application. By recompiling the application source code you add the reliability and scalability of AIX to your Linux applications. This allows you to start an e-business on small Linux and Intel servers and scale your infrastructure up with AIX.

There are three mechanisms that allow for Linux Affinity. First is the AIX Toolbox for Linux Applications. The second mechanism is through application program interface (API) code, and the third is recompiling Linux source code on AIX. Let's look at these individually. Also check out the IBM Redbook site, "*Running Linux Applications on AIX,*" at http://www.redbooks.ibm.com/pubs/pdfs/redbooks/sg246033.pdf

AIX Toolbox for Linux Applications

The AIX Toolbox for Linux Applications comes with a large assortment of native Linux applications, tools, and utilities. The GNU and Linux application development tools allow you to develop new applications for AIX. You also have two new options for your desktop environment. In addition to command line, X, and CDE, you can now have GNOME and KDE-2. Linux users also have the convenience of the Red Hat Package

Manager (RPM) for installing software, which in all gives the Linux user a familiar environment to work in.

APIs for Linux

The application program interface (API) programs and header files are Linux compatible. So this is not an environment or an additional layer of software, but a true API. Newly developed APIs on AIX for Linux are continuously being developed both by IBM and other developers. Your applications run as native AIX applications.

RPM Format

With the Red Hat Package Manager (RPM) on AIX, you can install native Linux applications using the familiar **rpm** commands used with Linux on POWER platforms. You can also install RPM format Linux programs using the new Install Wizard from IBM, **geninstall**. With the Install Wizard, you can install AIX **installp** packages as well as any of the following software package formats:

- InstallShield Multi-Platform (ISMP)
- Red Hat Package Manager (RMP)
- Uniform Device Interface (UDI)

Running KDE-2 or GNOME on Your Desktop

With Linux Affinity in AIX come the KDE-2 and GNOME desktop environments. For your Linux users they offer the look and feel of Linux with the scalability and reliability of AIX and the pSeries and RS/6000 platform. The desktop is easy to change with a few commands so everyone can work in a familiar and comfortable environment.

New Volume Group Features

Now you can have a *read-only* volume group. This is an important new feature that adds to the data protection effort for read-only and static environments. Also, the volume group identifier (VGID) has grown from 16 to 32 characters. This coincides with the physical volume identifier (PVID) character length. Hot Spare capability has also been added at the volume group level.

JFS2 Filesystem

Need a huge filesystem? You're in luck with Enhanced Journaled Filesystems, or JFS2. With JFS2 you can have a filesystem up to 4 petabytes (PB)! The 4PB limit is the theoretical limit. The actual tested filesystem size is 1 terabyte, but this is not the surprising part. You can also create a *file* up to 4PB, with 1TB being the tested file size. Also, with JFS2 you do not have to worry about i-nodes because they are now dynamically allocated. JFS2 is supported with the 32-bit kernel, but you will see a performance increase by using the 64-bit kernel.

Hot Spot Management

The new kid on the block is the **migratelp** command, which allows you to manage your storage down to the logical partition level. Got a hot spot on a disk? Move the hot disk partitions to a less active disk! Using the **migratelp** command, you can control the exact placement of specific logical partitions. To find the hot spots, you turn on statistics with the **lvmstat** command using the **-e** option.

To turn on statistic gathering:
```
# lvmstat -e -v rootvg
```

To turn off statistic gathering:
```
# lvmstat -d -v rootvg
```

View VG statistics by LV:
```
# lvmstat -v rootvg
```

View LV statistics by LP:
```
# lvmstat -l hd3
```

32-bit and 64-bit Kernel Support

When you install AIX 5L, you can choose a 32-bit or 64-bit kernel. The choice is really not a critical decision, in most cases. Both 32-bit and 64-bit kernels support 64-bit applications. Both kernels also support the new JFS2 filesystem, which allows for a large filesystem. So why the decision? It turns out that JFS2 has better performance with the 64-bit kernel. You can also support up to 96GB of memory with a 64-bit kernel.

If you are running 64-bit applications, using (or planning to use) JFS2, or have a need for 96GB of memory, you should install the 64-bit kernel. On the other hand, you may have better performance with the 32-bit kernel for 32-bit applications.

The **bootinfo -y** command shows if your system is 32-bit or 64-bit enabled. Machines since the RS/6000 H70 are 64-bit.

The **bootinfo -K** command returns the current kernel mode information for your system directly as an integer value of 32 or 64.

The **svmon -P <process_ID>** command shows if the currently running process is 32- or 64-bit and whether it is multithreaded. This information is found in the **64-bit** and **Mthrd columns**.

If your system is currently running in 32-bit mode and you want to switch to 64-bit mode, enter the following commands, provided you have already installed the **bos.mp64** fileset.

```
# ln -sf /usr/lib/boot/unix_64 /unix
# ln -sf /usr/lib/boot/unix_64 /usr/lib/boot/unix
```

```
# bosboot -ak /usr/lib/boot/unix_64
# shutdown -Fr
```

After the system reboots, the system is switched to 64-bit mode.

Resource Monitoring and Control (RMC) Subsystem

A new subsystem has been added called Resource Monitoring and Control (RMC). This subsystem is similar to the Reliable Scalable Cluster Technology (RSCT) used in the Scalable Parallel Server. It allows for system monitoring of predefined and user-created tasks and events. There are 84 predefined conditions, where you set threshold levels to respond to a trigger level. The trigger response notifies you if the event that has exceeded the threshold. You set up RMC through the Web-based System Manager (WebSM).

AIX Now Supports UNIX System V Printing

This is a centralizing effort by IBM. System V printing has a lot of advantages over the "classic" AIX printer subsystem. For example, with System V you have support for forms, and you can limit access to printers in the user community and use standard PostScript filters. However, you can have only one printer subsystem active at the same time, but you can easily switch between System V and the classic AIX printer subsystem.

System Hang Detection

The System Hang Detection feature allows you to define the action if the system is in an extreme load situation. A new **shdaemon** daemon has been added that monitors the system's ability to run processes and takes the specified action when a threshold is exceeded. Actions include these:

- Log an error in the error report.
- Send a warning message to the system console.
- Automatically reboot the system.
- Execute a command.
- Launch a recovery session login on the system console.

Dynamic CPU Deallocation

This new feature is part of Project eLiza, which is an ongoing effort by IBM to produce *self-healing* machines, among other things. Dynamic CPU deallocation enhances the availability of SMP machines by dynamically taking a failing CPU offline. This feature is not enabled by default. Configuring this option requires at least three CPUs.

To enable CPU deallocation, you can use the AIX System Management Interface Tool (SMIT) or the command shown here:

```
# chdev -l sys0 -a cpuguard='enable'
```

After making the configuration change, you can verify that it has been enabled with the following command:

```
# lsattr -El sys0
```

Beginning with AIX 4.3.3, you also have the option to deallocate CPUs on the fly from the command line. This is very useful for scalability testing. A CPU is deallocated using the logical CPU number, where the logical CPU number is an integer between 0 and $n-1$. The value of n is the total number of CPUs in the system. To deallocate CPU number 3, use the following command:

```
# cpu_deallocate 3
```

Then you can verify that the processor has been taken offline using the following command:

```
# lsattr -El proc3
```

Managing Paging Space Dynamically

New to AIX 5L is the ability to dynamically reduce the size of a paging space with the **chps -d** command without a system reboot. Before, you had to disable the target paging space so it would not be active on the next system reboot and then reboot the system, remove the paging space, and add a new paging space that was the size you wanted. This long process is not required anymore with the addition of the **swapoff** command, which dynamically frees the paging space and takes it offline.

New swapoff Command

The **swapoff** command is called by the /usr/sbin/shrinkps shell script to dynamically deactivate an active paging space. The **swapoff** command can also be used on the command line. There are two requirements for the **swapoff** command to work. The paging space must be currently active and must have been activated using the **swapon** command. The second requirement is there must be enough remaining paging space for the system to operate normally. To deallocate one or more paging spaces use the following command:

```
# swapoff paging_device [paging_device]
```

Example:
```
# swapoff paging00 paging03
```

In this example, the paging00 and paging03 paging spaces are deactivated.

Shrink Paging Space on the Fly

You can shrink the size of a paging space on the fly using the following **chps** command structure:

```
# chps -d Decrement_LVs [-a yes|no] paging_space
```

where Decrement_LVs is the number of logical partitions to remove and -a yes|no specifies whether or not to activate this paging space on the next system reboot.

The following command will shrink the paging01 paging space by four logical partitions and activate the paging space on each subsequent reboot:

```
# chps -d 4 -a yes paging01
```

This command calls the /usr/sbin/shrinkps shell script that goes through all of the previously painful steps of reducing the size of a paging space without requiring a system reboot.

Web-Based System Manager (WebSM)

The Web-based System Manager has been enhanced a lot in AIX 5L. Now WebSM can manage more than SMIT. As an example, the System V printing can only be managed from the command line or through WebSM. Also built in to WebSM is the Workload Manager, which allows you to limit resources across the system to balance the workload and ensure that applications stay within predefined limits. However, unlike SMIT, WebSM does not have a log, so you do not have an audit trail.

You can also enable WebSM to a client/server environment. In this environment you can manage the system from a remote browser. To enable WebSM as a client/server application, enter the following command:

```
# /usr/websm/bin/wsmserver -enable
```

Performance and Security Enhancements

Two new performance tools are added with AIX 5L, **truss** and **alstat**. The **truss** command allows for system call tracing, and with **alstat** you can view memory offsets. Other performance commands have new features, such as **vmstat**, which has added a timestamp with the **-t** switch.

On the security side, native Kerberos System V is standard, and IP key encryption security, PKCS support, and IBM Secure Way Directory are available.

Active and Passive Dead Gateway Detection

With Dead Gateway Detection, the system will do an adapter swap, or adapter failover, if the primary adapter gateway is unreachable and switch to the backup gateway. This configuration requires at least two network adapter cards. Dead Gateway Detection can be configured in two ways, active and passive. Passive uses TCP/IP and ARP, and active uses lost ping packets to detect a dead gateway.

Jabber Instant Messaging for AIX

Along with Linux Affinity, IBM has added support for the Jabber Instant Messenger for AIX. Jabber lets you set up instant messaging on your intranet or on the Internet. This allows you to send and receive real-time messages and have notification of other active users.

SYSTEM ADMINISTRATION ACTIVITIES

If you're new to UNIX system administration, you may be asking yourself just what a Systems Administrator does. UNIX system management involves a diverse set of skills that covers the gamut from system installation and configuration to end-user hand-holding. A large UNIX environment might be managed by a group of administrators, each responsible for a particular subsystem. A researcher might only be grappling with a UNIX workstation on the desktop. Whether acting alone or as part of a team, administrators must have a general understanding of overall UNIX system management activities to ensure that their areas of responsibility seamlessly interoperate with all the subsystems that make up the UNIX operating system. On the desktop, this responsibility often extends beyond the local system to the network and other vendor platforms that make up a distributed environment.

The text in this book is organized logically to reflect AIX administration themes and components, facilitating rapid location of the subject matter. Chapters are comprised of detailed subject descriptions, examples, and diagrams. Where appropriate, both the AIX System Management Interface Tool (SMIT), Web-based System Manager (WebSM), and command-line options are presented. Command examples are flagged with the shell prompt character (#) to distinguish them from other bullets and to remind the reader that most configuration activities are performed with superuser privileges.

```
# command
```

Each chapter culminates with a Checklist topic list that covers key points and information. DocSearch is the online manual interface for AIX and associated applications. This text is intended as a pointer to the more specific information provided in the AIX hard copy and DocSearch documents. It will also provide some insights based on practical experience with RS/6000 and pSeries hardware and the AIX operating system.

System Administration Tasks and Tools

Part I of this book overviews system administration responsibilities and identifies the base reference and management tools. Characteristics of the AIX help system DocSearch are described.

System Architecture

Part II describes the RS/6000 and pSeries hardware development history and architecture. An overview of the AIX kernel is provided to illustrate operating system principles that will assist you in understanding configuration and management issues presented in later chapters.

System Installation and Management

Part III describes the AIX management tools, including the System Management Interface Tool (SMIT) and the Web-based System Manager (WebSM), which can be used to manage most aspects of the AIX operating system.

The discussion then turns to the steps required to install and manage the AIX operating system. An overview of the AIX boot process and operation follows.

System Configuration and Customization

Part IV takes you to the point at which the operating system has been installed and must be customized to meet the needs of the application environment. This includes the runtime configuration, device configuration, and a description of the Object Data Manager (ODM) and how it is used to store and manage system configuration data. Tape solutions are discussed before the topic switches to the disk subsystem and the Logical Volume Manager (LVM), including the steps involved to add disk drives to the system. We end Part IV with terminals, modems, and AIX and System V printer subsystems.

Network Configuration and Customization

The chapters in Part V describe how to make your system accessible from a number of network architectures and topologies. TCP/IP, UUCP, and SNA are all covered in detail.

Networked File Systems

Part VI moves to network-based file systems that provide the underlying architecture for sharing information in a distributed environment. These chapters outline a number of common file system architectures, their features, and implementation requirements, as well as mechanisms for facilitating file sharing between UNIX and Windows systems, including Network File System (NFS), Distributed File System (DFS), and the desktop file system Samba.

Linux Affinity

Part VII covers Linux Affinity with AIX. This includes details on running native Linux applications on AIX and the ability to recompile Linux source code on AIX to create a new AIX application.

Distributed Services

Part VIII covers a range of distributed services. These include configuring e-mail, network news, and Web servers/browsers. X11 administration is detailed in great length. Web topics include tools for workgroup collaboration and creating a DMZ with secure servers with a touch of XML thrown in.

Managing Users and Resources

Part IX helps the Systems Administrator manage user accounts. This section outlines how to manage the user environment, do process management, and use system accounting, with ways to streamline account management and reporting.

Security

Part X is a discussion of how DCE and Kerberos can be implemented to secure and authorize principals in large networked environments. The Trusted Computer Base (TCB) is discussed as well as security tools such as COPS, Crack, and Trip Wire.

System Recovery and Tuning

In Part XI, you'll see what you do when things go bump in the night. This shows you how to keep your pSeries and RS/6000 machines running hot and lean. Backup strategies and policies are explained. System monitoring tools, problem analysis, and recovery techniques are reviewed.

Advanced Distributed Architectures

Part XII is on High Availability Cluster Multi-Processing (HACMP) and clustering techniques and implementation considerations. You are shown how to build and configure an HACMP cluster, test the failover capabilities, and keep the cluster running smoothly.

SAN, NAS, and *iSCSI Consolidated Storage*

Part XIII introduces you to storage area networks (SAN), networked attached storage (NAS), and the *i*SCSI protocol. Each storage concept is discussed and a detailed description of each technology is given. You learn how to add storage to an Enterprise Storage Server (ESS), a.k.a. The Shark, using the TotalStorage StorWatch Specialist, as well as moving storage between servers. We'll also cover the data-gathering capability of TotalStorage StorWatch Expert.

CHECKLIST

The following is a checklist for the key points in system administration tasks and tools:

- ☐ Define and implement UNIX system management and administration tools.
- ☐ Define AIX.
- ☐ Define UNIX.
- ☐ You can add AIX commands and libraries to the Application Environment Specification for the OSF/1 operating system.
- ☐ Identify AIX 5L and list why a lot of commonality exists between AIX and other UNIX flavors.
- ☐ Identify the UNIX system management diverse set of skills.
- ☐ You can run native Linux programs on AIX.
- ☐ You can bring your Linux application source code over to AIX.
- ☐ Recompile the application to create a new AIX application.

CHAPTER 2

DocSearch and the Online Manual Pages: Getting Help from the System

Starting with AIX version 4.3, IBM replaced InfoExplorer with the Web browser–based Documentation Library Service, or DocSearch. This service consists of two parts—the documentation library and a Web-based search engine.

On the command line, the **docsearch** command starts the application within a Web browser window. So, as you can imagine, the Documentation Library Service can be viewed on any external machine that has network access and a local Web browser. One of the first hurdles for new AIX users and Systems Administrators is mastering the help system; confusion over documentation locations and access mechanisms is the primary problem. The AIX DocSearch Web browser documentation system is a powerful search and retrieval tool for assistance online. DocSearch is your online rescuer when you scream "HELP!"

AIX HELP

Like any other UNIX flavor, AIX has online manual pages. The **man** command searches for reference information on commands and files. However, IBM has gone to great lengths to provide an extensive documentation library and search services that are easy and intuitive to use. The base documentation library has information on just about any topic, but there are extended documentation filesets for user and administrationguides, AIX technical references, and application development tools that can optionally be installed. IBM also has this same documentation online at the IBM Web site, www.ibm.com/servers/aix/library. Accordingly, you can skip the installation of the Documentation Library Service if you are short on disk space and have Web access.

DOCSEARCH OVERVIEW

The Documentation Library Service gives the capability to search, read, and print online HTML documents. To start the DocSearch system, type **docsearch** on the command line or in the Common Desktop Environment (CDE), click the help icon, and then select Documentation Library from the icon list. Both techniques start the Documentation Search Service in a Web browser window (an X environment is required to use the service). DocSearch is a global system library of all of the volumes that are *registered* on the documentation server. The documents can be read by clicking the hypertext link in the browser window and drilling down through the books of documentation, or by performing a keyword, or pattern, search that will display a match list of all relevant information registered in the documentation library. The search can be a simple phrase search or an advanced search using logical operators.

DOCSEARCH INSTALLATION

The Documentation Library Service is installed by default in AIX 5L, but if you did a *migration upgrade* from a previous version or release of AIX to 5L, then some problems might be encountered with DocSearch. As of this writing, 22 DocSearch problems were listed as *common* by IBM. These problems range from missing, or unset, environment variables to improper Web server configurations and a lot of little problems in between. It is straightforward to install and use the service, but it is fragile to install and everything must be completed before the Documentation Library Service will work.

Installing the Netscape Browser

Netscape is the preferred Web browser and is the first component of the search service to install. The Netscape browser software can be found on the AIX 5L Expansion Pack or the AIX 4.3.3 Bonus Pack CD-ROM; it can also be downloaded from `http:\\www.netscape.com`. However, the Netscape Web site does not provide the files in the backup file format (.bff) that SMIT and the **installp** command require, so you will have to use the installation shell script provided by Netscape. Install all of the Netscape packages for the appropriate language environment through the **smitty install_all** SMIT FastPath, the **installp** command, or the installation shell script provided by Netscape for downloaded files. There is nothing to configure at this point.

Installing the Web Server

The Web server software is the mechanism that allows the search service to work. The IBM code is based on the Apache Web Server code, but any Web server will work that can handle CGI. In this book, we will use the IBM HTTP Server package, which is really just Apache undercover. The IBM HTTP Server software is located on the AIX 5L Expansion Pack CD-ROM but is installed by default during a fresh install of the base operating system (BOS). Depending on the version of Web server code, you will install one of three filesets. For any AIX operating system shipment prior to November 1999, the HTTP Web Server code version is 1.3.3.2 or lower; the most recent versions are 1.3.6.0 for AIX 4.3.3 and 1.3.12.2 for AIX 5L, version 5.1. Install the following filesets for your particular version:

Version 1.3.3.2 (pre-AIX 4.3.3)

```
http_server.base.core
http_server.base.source
http_server.modules.ssl
```

Version 1.3.6.0 (AIX 4.3.3)

```
http_server.admin
http_server.base.rte
http_server.base.source
```

Version 1.3.12.2 (AIX 5L Version 5.1)

```
http_server.base.rte
http_server.base.source
http_server.html.en_US
http_server.man.en_US
```

DocSearch and man Pages on CD-ROM

You *can* run DocSearch and the man pages from a mounted CD-ROM, but this method is not recommended. Response time can be unacceptable; and because disk space is so cheap (in relative terms) this method is rarely used, since the desired documentation might span several CD-ROM volumes. Apart from the problem of slow response, the CD-ROM must always be mounted for the documentation service to work. The requirement for a dedicated CD-ROM drive may be a good enough reason to load the documentation onto a local hard disk.

If your system does not already have an **imnadm** user and an **imnadm** group, you need to define a new **imnadm** user and group on the system for the documentation search service. First, create a group called **imnadm** and then create a new user named **imnadm**. The **imnadm** user should have the **imnadm** group as the primary group. Ensure that the language environment variable is set to the correct value, **en_US** for United States English.

```
echo $LANG
```

Use the following SMIT fastpath to change the language variable:

```
smitty chlang
```

To start this dedicated CD-ROM configuration, you first need to create a CD-ROM filesystem to mount the CD-ROM on. A CD-ROM filesystem is accessed the same way as a standard filesystem but is mounted as read-only. As always, you need to specify three elements when creating a filesystem: the device name, the mount point, and whether or not to auto-mount the filesystem on system restart. There are three methods for creating this filesystem.

Command Line
```
# crfs -v cdrfs -p ro -d /dev/cd# -m /infocd -A yes
```

SMIT FastPath
```
# smitty crcdrfs
```

Web-Based System Management
```
# wsm
```

After you have created the CD-ROM filesystem, you need to mount the CDROM on the system with **mount /infocd** (assuming that the mount point is **/infocd**). The next step is to run the linking program located on the Base Documentation CD-ROM. First, change directory to the CD-ROM mount point— **/infocd**, in our case, and then run the **linkbasecd** command.

```
# mount /infocd
# cd /infocd
# ./linkbasecd
```

The **linkbasecd** command will create symbolic links pointing the system to the documentation on the CD-ROM. The basic operation of both DocSearch and the **man** pages is the same in this case as when the documentation is loaded onto a local hard disk. However, the response time may be very poor.

When you give up using CD-ROMs and want to install the documentation on the server disks, you first need to remove all of the previously created symbolic links. IBM thought of this and also created an unlink program. To break all of the links, run the **unlinkbasecd** command and remove the CD-ROM filesystem.

```
# mount /infocd
# cd /infocd
# ./unlinkbasecd
# umount /infocd
# rmfs [-r] /infocd
```

NOTE   The **-r** switch on the **rmfs** command will remove the mount point, or directory.

DocSearch on Fixed Disk

The entire documentation search services library should be installed on a fixed disk local to the documentation server for optimal performance. An NFS installation will work, but the availability is then dependent upon the NFS server. The extra layer of complexity is not recommended. You can also install the DocSearch core and leave the documentation CD-ROM mounted as you did in the preceding section. This method can be extremely slow, depending on the speed of the CD-ROM, and we all know that IBM has not been known for having the latest and fastest CD-ROM drives, but the servers really smoke! You could also NFS-mount the CD-ROM for even poorer performance. We will next show how to install DocSearch on both AIX 4.3.3 and 5L, version 5.1.

Installing DocSearch on AIX 4.3.3

You start by defining a new user and group on the system for the documentation search service, if the **imnadm** user and group do not already exist. First, create a group called **imnadm**, and then create a new user named **imnadm**. The **imnadm** user should have the **imnadm** group as the primary group. Ensure that the language environment variable is set to the correct value, **en_US** for United States English.

```
# echo $LANG
```

Use the following SMIT FastPath to change the language variable:

```
# smitty chlang
```

Next, install the following filesets. In each case, the residing CD-ROM is listed along with the specific filesets.

AIX 4.3.3 CD-ROM #1

```
bos.docsearch.rte
bos.docsearch.client.Dt
bos.docsearch.client.com
bos.html.en_US.topnav.navigate
bos.msg.en_US.docsearch.client.Dt
bos.msg.en_US.docsearch.client.com
```

NOTE   If your system is not running CDE, then you can omit the ***.Dt** filesets.

AIX 4.3.3 CD-ROM #2

```
IMNSearch.bld.all
IMNSearch.rte.all
```

AIX 4.3.3 Base Documentation CD-ROM

```
X11.html.en_US.all
bos.html.en_US.all
```

AIX 4.3.3 Bonus Pack CD-ROM, Volume 1

```
Netscape.communicator.com
Netscape.communicator.plugins
```

Optional installs include the AIX 4.3.3 Extended Documentation CD. The Extended Documentation CD-ROM for AIX 4.3.3 contains user and admin guides, AIX technical references, and programming guides. If you need this extended documentation, then you can install only the individual components that you need. The entire CD-ROM contents are not required.

The base documentation CD-ROM may take quite a long time to install, especially if you have an older Micro Channel machine with a slow 2X CD-ROM drive; in that case, the install could take several hours to complete. When all of these filesets are installed, you can move to the next step, configuring the Web server.

Before configuring the Web server, you first need to stop any **httpd** process:

```
# ps -ef | grep httpd
# kill <httpd Process ID>
```

Next, you need to stop the IMNSearch processes on the server:

```
# ps -ef | grep -i imn
# imnss -stop imnhelp
```

Also, if there is an entry in the **/etc/inittab** file for **httpdlite**, make sure that you comment it out with a : (colon).

NOTE   The **/etc/inittab** file uses a colon (**:**) instead of a pound sign (**#**) for comments.

Now you are ready to configure the Web server using SMIT. First, type

```
# smitty web_configure
```

and then follow these steps:

1. Select Change Documentation And Search Server.
2. Press ENTER.
3. Press F4 to select Local.
4. Press ENTER.
5. Press F4 to select IBM HTTP Web Server In Default Location.
6. Press ENTER.
7. All of the fields should automatically populate, as in the following examples.

IBM HTTP Server Version 1.3.3.2

```
DEFAULT_BROWSER = netscape
DOCUMENTATION_SERVER_MACHINE_NAME = yogi
DOCUMENTATION_SERVER_PORT = 80
CGI_DIRECTORY = /usr/lpp/HTTPServer/share/cgi-bin
DOCUMENT_DIRECTORY = /usr/HTTPServer/share/htdocs
```

IBM HTTP Server Version 1.3.6.0 and Later

```
DEFAULT_BROWSER = netscape
DOCUMENTATION_SERVER_MACHINE_NAME = yogi
DOCUMENTATION_SERVER_PORT = 80
CGI_DIRECTORY = /usr/HTTPServer/cgi-bin
DOCUMENT_DIRECTORY = /usr/HTTPServer/htdocs
```

The installation is complete.

Installing DocSearch on AIX 5L

By default, the DocSearch Library Search Services are installed as part of BOS on AIX 5L. This is new for IBM; before AIX 5L, we had to search around to find the required filesets and it was very easy to forget one or two filesets. If you did a *migration upgrade* from a previous AIX version or release, you could have a few problems getting the documentation search services working again. For each of these problems, I have found that spending one hour uninstalling and reinstalling everything was a time saver in the end.

If your system does not already have an **imnadm** user and group defined, you need to define a new user and group on the system for the documentation search service. First, create a group called **imnadm**, and then create a new user named **imnadm**. The **imnadm** user should have the **imnadm** group as the primary group. Ensure that the language environment variable is set to the correct value, **en_US** for United States English.

```
# echo $LANG
```

Use the following SMIT fastpath to change the language variable:

```
# smitty chlang
```

If you are wondering what to install on AIX 5L, version 5.1, DocSearch is installed using the following filesets found on the 5.1 media.

AIX 5.1 CD-ROM Volume 1

```
bos.docsearch.client.Dt
bos.docsearch.client.com
bos.docsearch.rte
bos.msg.en_US.docsearch.client.Dt
bos.msg.en_US.docsearch.client.com
IMNSearch.bld.DBCS
IMNSearch.bld.SBCS
IMNSearch.msg.en_US.rte.com
IMNSearch.rte.DBCS
IMNSearch.rte.SBCS
IMNSearch.rte.client
IMNSearch.rte.com
IMNSearch.rte.server
bos.man.en_US.cmds
```

NOTE   If your system is not running CDE, you can omit all of the ***.Dt** filesets to save space.

AIX 5.1 Expansion Pack CD-ROM

```
http_server.base.rte
http_server.base.source
Netscape.communicator.com
Netscape.communicator.us
```

AIX 5.1 Base Documentation CD-ROM

```
bos.html.en_US.cmds.cmds1
bos.html.en_US.cmds.cmds2
bos.html.en_US.cmds.cmds3
bos.html.en_US.cmds.cmds4
bos.html.en_US.cmds.cmds5
bos.html.en_US.cmds.cmds6
bos.html.en_US.files.files_ref
```

```
bos.html.en_US.manage_gds.install
bos.html.en_US.manage_gds.manage_bos
bos.html.en_US.manage_gds.manage_commo
bos.html.en_US.manage_gds.printers
bos.html.en_US.prog_gds.prog_bos
bos.html.en_US.prog_gds.prog_commo
bos.html.en_US.techref.base
bos.html.en_US.techref.commo
bos.html.en_US.topnav.navigate
bos.html.en_US.user_gds.user_bos
bos.html.en_US.user_gds.user_commo
dsmit.html.en_US.dsmitgd
perfagent.html.en_US.usergd
```

The previous list of filesets includes all of the available documents shipped with AIX 5L, version 5.1. When all of these filesets are installed, you are ready to start the configuration of the Web server.

Before configuring the Web server, you first need to stop any **httpd** process:

```
# ps -ef | grep httpd
# kill <httpd Process ID>
```

Next, you need to stop the IMNSearch processes on the server:

```
# ps -ef | grep -i imn
# imnss -stop imnhelp
```

Also, if there is an entry in the **/etc/inittab** file for **httpdlite**, make sure that you comment it out with a colon (:).

NOTE   The **/etc/inittab** file uses a colon (:) instead of a pound sign (#) for comments.

To configure the Web server, run the following command:

```
# smitty web_configure
```

1. Select Change Documentation and Search Server.
2. Press ENTER.
3. Press F4 to select Local.
4. Press ENTER.
5. Press F4 to select IBM HTTP Web Server In Default Location.
6. Press ENTER.

All of the fields should automatically populate, as in the following example.

IBM HTTP Web Server Version 1.3.12.2

```
DEFAULT_BROWSER = netscape
DOCUMENTATION_SERVER_MACHINE_NAME = yogi
DOCUMENTATION_SERVER_PORT = 80
CGI_DIRECTORY = /usr/HTTPServer/cgi-bin
DOCUMENT_DIRECTORY = /usr/HTTPServer/htdocs
```

As a final step, the **/etc/inittab** file needs to have an entry to start the Web server on system restart. To check the **/etc/inittab** file to ensure an entry for the Web server, enter either of the following commands:

```
# lsitab ihshttpd
```

or

```
# grep ihshttpd /etc/inittab
```

If a Web server entry is not found, then insert the following line to restart the server from the boot:

```
# mkitab ihshttpd:2:wait:/usr/HTTPServer/bin/httpd >/dev/console 2>&1 # HTTP Server
```

If you have migrated from 4.3.3 to 5.1.0, you will need to follow this procedure to get DocSearch working because of the **oslevel**-specific nature of the product.

The installation is complete.

USING DOCSEARCH

DocSearch must be executed from a graphical environment such as X Window System or CDE. Accessing the Documentation Library Service is as easy as pointing the Web browser to the documentation directory on the server.

On the documentation server, you can enter **docsearch** in an X environment and the browser will open with the collapsible tree listing each of the books registered with the Documentation Library Service. For both local and remote users with a Web browser, the URL for the documentation server should look like the following entry:

```
http://<Server-Hostname>/cgi-bin/ds_form
```

where `<Server-Hostname>` is the hostname, or IP address, of the documentation Web server.

If you do not have a local Web browser or if you have a telnet session to the remote documentation server, you will need to allow the remote system access to your X environment and export the display back to your local machine:

```
# xhost <remote_machine>
```

or

```
# xhost +
```

to allow all machines to have X access locally.

```
# export DISPLAY=<local_hostname_or_IP_address>:0.0
# docsearch &
```

The opening DocSearch windows are shown in Figure 2-1 for AIX 4.3.3 and Figure 2-2 for AIX 5L.

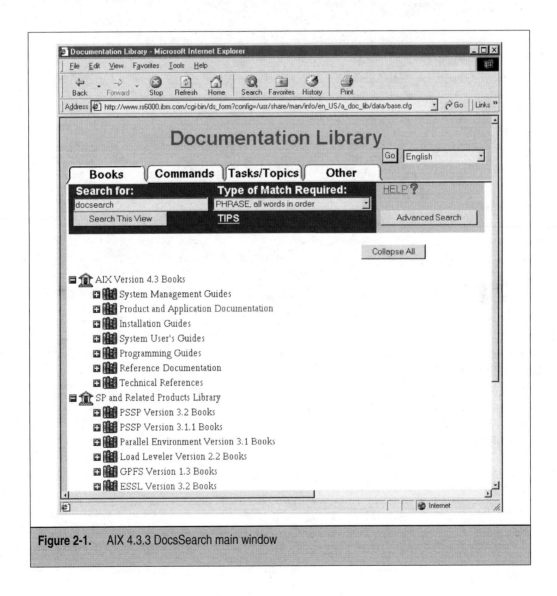

Figure 2-1. AIX 4.3.3 DocsSearch main window

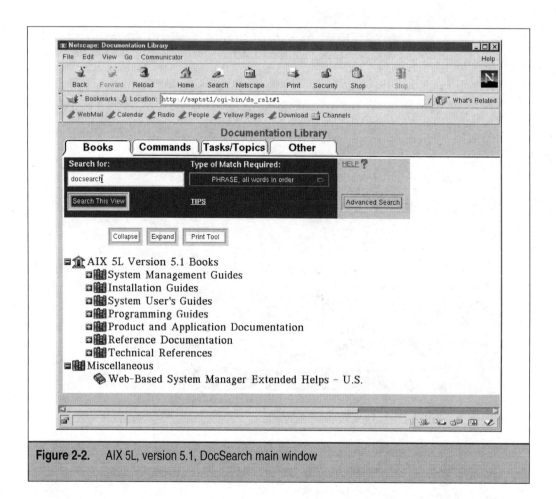

Figure 2-2.   AIX 5L, version 5.1, DocSearch main window

Documentation Library

The Documentation Library consists of all of the registered document indexes on the server. The library contents can be searched, or each separate book can be opened and viewed online. All of the library's components, except for the search engine, are installed as part of the base operating system. The search engine and documentation must be manually installed if the system is to be configured as a server. The clients can access the documentation server library remotely with a Web browser.

Searching

When you issue the **docsearch** command or point your Web browser to the documentation server, you are presented with a browser window that lists the collapsible tree and the Search For field at the top. There are also four tabs at the top that point to Books, Commands, Tasks/Topics, and Other (Other will show the programming and user guides).

To perform a search, you can enter the topic of interest in the Search For field and press the ENTER key. At this point, another browser window opens with a hypertext list of the articles matching the search criteria.

Simple Search

Your search can be a simple word or phrase match, or you can create a complex logical search using the AND, OR, and NOT logical search operators. The simple search is shown in Figures 2-3 and 2-4.

The simple search has three options for a phrase or pattern:

- PHRASE, all words in order

- ALL of these words, any order

- One or MORE of these words, any order

Advanced Search

An advanced search is performed using the logical operators AND, OR, and NOT as shown in Figures 2-5 and 2-6.

The logical AND operator specifies that *all* of the words are matched. The logical OR operator specifies that *any* of the words are matched. The NOT logical operator specifies that all of the words *except* the word that NOT negates are matched. All of these logical operators can be mixed together for a very specific search. The advanced search also enables you to specify the number of results to be displayed on a single page.

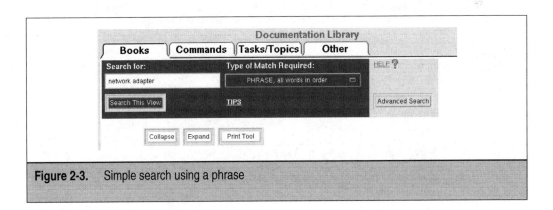

Figure 2-3.   Simple search using a phrase

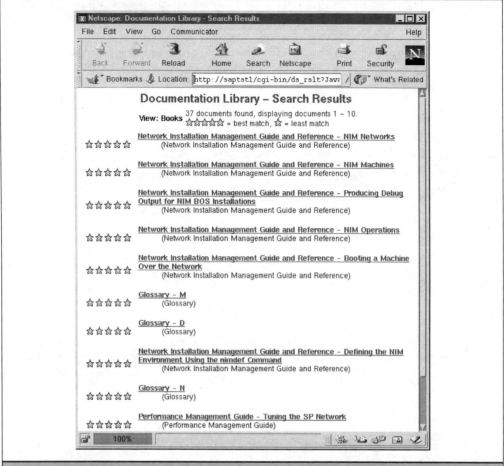

Figure 2-4. Results of a simple search

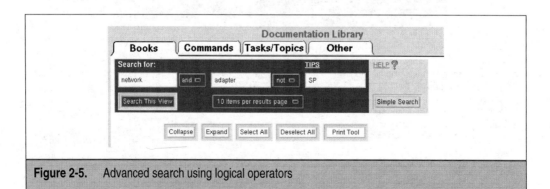

Figure 2-5. Advanced search using logical operators

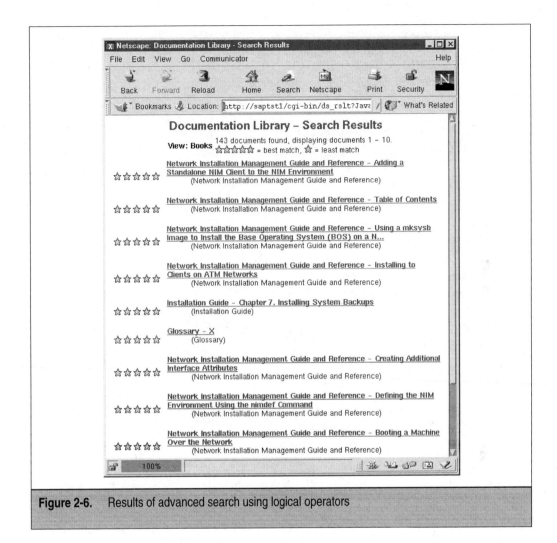

Figure 2-6.   Results of advanced search using logical operators

Registering Documents for Online Searching

Before documents on the documentation server can be searched or viewed, two things
must take place: each document and document index must be created or installed on the
DocSearch server, and each document and document index must be registered with the
library service. There are two ways you can register the documents with the server. Most
AIX applications have prebuilt indexes ready for the documentation server and will be
automatically installed with the application. Or you can make the documents known to
the server the hard way, manually creating the indexes for the documents on the server
and then manually registering the indexes. The indexing creates a compressed version of

the document, or group of documents. This new indexed file, not the original HTML file, is what DocSearch will search and display.

This section will give an overview of the steps involved to register a document and create the indexes that the Documentation Library Service requires.

1. Create the document in HTML format.
2. Create an index of the document.
3. Register the new indexes with the documentation server.

After the indexes are registered, they will be displayed in the Web browser ready for searching and viewing. You can find detailed step-by-step procedures for each of these operations in the online Documentation Library Service chapter "AIX 5L Version 5.1 General Programming Concepts: Writing and Debugging Programs." Application developers writing documentation will find this chapter especially valuable for creating auto-installed indexes when writing **installp** packages. You can also register your company's documentation with the online documentation library. This flexibility makes DocSearch a valuable enterprise-wide documentation search engine.

Common DocSearch and man Page Problems

You may experience one or more errors while using DocSearch. This is a top five list of the most common problems.

Problem 1   One of the most common problems is domain name resolution. You might have to edit the **/etc/hosts** file and add a period (.) right behind the short hostname. For example,

10.10.10.2 booboo.

Problem 2   After a 5.1 migration install, you enter **man ls** and find that there is no error or data output. You are experiencing one of the quirks that DocSearch displays. First make sure that the command's filesets are installed. The following will produce a directory listing of the filesets:

```
# lslpp -f bos.man.en_US.cmds
```

This should show you the files that were installed for the **bos.man.en_US.cmds** fileset.

If you then **cd** to **/usr/share/man/info/en_US** and run a long recursive listing (**ls -Rl * | more**) of the directory contents and most of the files are empty, then you have a problem. You have to install/reinstall the following filesets to correct the problem:

```
bos.html.en_US.topnav.navigate - Top Level Navigation
bos.html.en_US.nav            - Online Navigation
bos.html.en_US.cmds.cmds1     - AIX Commands Reference 1
```

```
bos.html.en_US.cmds.cmds2      - AIX Commands Reference 2
bos.html.en_US.cmds.cmds3      - AIX Commands Reference 3
bos.html.en_US.cmds.cmds4      - AIX Commands Reference 4
bos.html.en_US.cmds.cmds5      - AIX Commands Reference 5
bos.html.en_US.cmds.cmds6      - AIX Commands Reference 6
```

Problem 3   You get the following error message: "Error: Can't open display: XYZ." This means that you are trying to open a window defined by the DISPLAY variable that is incorrect, that the variable is unset, or that you do not have permission to use this display. Issue the following commands in sequence:

```
# xhost <remote_hostname_or_IP_address>
# export DISPLAY=<local_hostname_or_IP_address>:0.0
# docsearch &
```

Problem 4   There is no DocSearch icon on the CDE help subpanel. You have installed DocSearch, and CDE has not discovered the new icon. You need to restart the workspace manager to discover the new icon. Right-click an empty part of the screen. This will bring up the Workspace menu. In the menu, left-click Restart Workspace Manager and then click OK in the pop-up dialog box. Alternatively, you can log out and log back into the system.

Problem 5   DocSearch is starting and you receive a message that it cannot find the documentation server. In AIX 5L version 5.1, you have to manually edit the `httpd.conf` file to define the documentation server.

```
# vi /usr/HTTPServer/conf/httpd.conf
```

Search the file for the **ServerName** variable. Uncomment the line and enter the fully qualified hostname of the documentation server:

```
ServerName  yogi.mydomain.com
```

mAN PAGES

The man pages provide reference documentation about AIX commands, files, library subroutines, and system calls. The **man** command does not perform the same kind of pattern search that DocSearch provides, so you will need to know the exact command or filename for which you are seeking information. The syntax for the **man** command follows.

```
# man {command | file | subroutine | system call}
```

For example,

```
# man man
```

will display the online documentation for the **man** command. The **man** command searches and displays documents in the following order:

- Any **nroff** directories (**man?**) in the /usr/share/man directory structure.

- The formatted-version directories (**cat?**) in the /usr/share/man directory structure.

- If the previous two searches fail, the hypertext (DocSearch) database is searched. The hypertext documentation is located in the /usr/share/man/info directory structure.

Installing man Pages on AIX 4.3.3 and 5L Version 5.1

If your system only needs the man pages, then DocSearch may be overkill for you. To install the man pages on both 4.3.3 and 5L, all of the following filesets must be installed:

```
bos.html.en_US.topnav.navigate  - Top Level Navigation
bos.html.en_US.nav              - Online Navigation
bos.html.en_US.cmds.cmds1       - AIX Commands Reference 1
bos.html.en_US.cmds.cmds2       - AIX Commands Reference 2
bos.html.en_US.cmds.cmds3       - AIX Commands Reference 3
bos.html.en_US.cmds.cmds4       - AIX Commands Reference 4
bos.html.en_US.cmds.cmds5       - AIX Commands Reference 5
bos.html.en_US.cmds.cmds6       - AIX Commands Reference 6
```

Using the man Pages

The **man** command has access to information stored in DocSearch. When invoked, **man** will first search /usr/man/cat? directories, then /usr/man/man?, and, finally, DocSearch data if it is installed. The commands **man** and **catman** map man page sections 1, 2, and 8 to DocSearch commands documents, sections 2 and 3 to DocSearch subroutines documents, and sections 4, 5, and 7 to DocSearch files documents. You will need to periodically execute **catman -w** to keep the database for the **apropos** and **whatis** commands up to date.

```
# catman -w
```

From time to time, you may need to add your own custom man page information. This could be a help file explaining billing policies, backup support, locally developed software, and so on. It's a good idea to keep local man pages separate from vendor-supplied help. This keeps them from getting stepped on during installation, maintenance, and upgrade activities. Commonly used location paths for local man pages are /usr/man/manl and /usr/local/man/man?. The **$MANPATH** environment variable can be set in /etc/environment to include your local man page path. Users may also use **$MANPATH** to support their own man directories.

Here are some local man page repositories:

- /usr/man/manl
- /usr/local/man/man?
- /usr/local/cat/cat?

When creating new man pages, you can use an existing man page as a template. Try to stay within a common style so that your users know what to expect. Each man page should include a name section identifying the topic or command, a synopsis describing the command and argument options and format, a description section that describes the topic, an options section that details parameter and value information, and a section on known bugs. At the end of the man page, a "see also" section indicating related information and an optional author section identifying the author name and address can be considered.

The following is an example man page style:

```
mycommand(l)
NAME
  mycommand - Does just what I want to do.
SYNOPSIS
  mycommand [will|wont] work
  mycommand is always used as a last resort. It can
  be expected either to work or to fail. mycommand
  contains no surprises at all.
OPTIONS
  will    Completes the work at hand.
  wont    Take a vacation.
BUGS
  mycommand is always error free!
SEE ALSO
  myprogram(l), myshell(l)
AUTHOR
  Me. Who did you think it was?
```

You can include **nroff** tags in the man page to control display format. After the tags are included, you can test them using **nroff** (see Table 2-1).

```
# nroff -man mycommand.l | more
Here is a sample man page with tags inserted:
.TH mycommand l
```

```
.SH NAME
mycommand \- Does just what I want to do.
.SH SYNOPSIS
mycommand [will|wont] work
.SH DESCRIPTION
.B mycommand
is always used as a last resort. It can
be expected either to work or to fail.
.B mycommand
contains no surprises at all.
.SH OPTIONS
.TP 3
will
Completes the work at hand.
.TP 3
wont
Take a vacation.
.SH BUGS
.B mycommand
is always error free!
.SH SEE ALSO
myprogram(1), myshell(1)
.SH AUTHOR
.B Me.
Who did you think it was?
```

Tag	Purpose
.TH <name> <numw>	Man page name and section number
.SH <section>	Identifies a subsection
.B <text>	Bold or highlighted text
.I <test>	Italicized text
.PP	Blocks out a paragraph
.TP <num>	Indents paragraph <num> spaces except first line

Table 2-1.   Sample **nroff** Tags

Remember to run the **catman -w** command periodically to keep the **apropos** and **whatis** data up to date. Run the **man -k print** command both before and after the **catman -w** command to see the benefit. You might want to add it to the root cron table.

```
# catman -w
```

DocSearch

The following list is a reference to some DocSearch files and commands.

DocSearch Files/Commands	Definition
/usr/bin/docsearch	The **docsearch** command
/usr/lib/nls/msg/$LANG/docsearch.cat	The **docsearch** message catalog
/usr/bin/defaultbrowser	The **defaultbrowser** command
/usr/share/man/info	Hypertext documentation
/usr/share/man/info/$LANG	The **docsearch** installed filesets
mount -v cdrfs -r /dev/cd0 /infocd	Mount into CD-ROM

man pages

Here are the definitions of some man page files and commands.

man Page Files/Commands	Definitions
/usr/man/cat?	Formatted text; search first
/usr/man/man?	**nroff** format; search second
catman -w	Update **whatis** database for **apropos** command

CHECKLIST

The following is a checklist for the key points in Documentation Library Service and Online man Pages.

☐ To start the Documentation Library Service (DocSearch) type **docsearch** on the command line or in the Common Desktop Environment (CDE), click the help icon, and then select Documentation Library from the icon list.

☐ Local or remote users can also access the Documentation Library Service with a Web browser using the URL:

```
http://<Server-Hostname>/cgi-bin/ds_form
```

where `<Server-Hostname>` is the documentation Web server's hostname or IP address.

☐ You can run DocSearch and the man pages from a mounted CD-ROM, but this method is not recommended because response time can be unacceptable, and, the CD-ROM must always be mounted for the documentation service to work.

☐ The entire documentation search services library should be installed on a fixed disk local to the documentation server for optimal performance.

☐ To install DocSearch on AIX 4.3.3, you need to define an **imnadm** user and group if they do not already exist and ensure that the language environment variable is set to the correct value.

☐ By default, the DocSearch Library Search Services are installed as part of BOS on AIX 5L. However, if you did a *migration upgrade* from a previous AIX version or release, you could have a few problems getting the documentation search services working again and may want to uninstall and reinstall the DocSearch system.

☐ In the main DocSearch browser window, to perform a search, enter the topic of interest in the Search For field and press the ENTER key. Your search can be a simple word or phrase match, or you can create complex logical search using the AND, OR, and NOT logical search operators.

☐ You could have a problem with DocSearch domain name registration. If so, edit the `/etc/hosts` file and add a period (.) right behind the short hostname.

☐ To display reference documentation about AIX commands, files, library subroutines, and system calls, use the **man** command.

PART II

Systems and System Architecture

CHAPTER 3

POWER Processors and Systems

With IBM development teams around the world working to outrun all competitors, you can bet that these new chips pack new capabilities. There are four main advancements with the new processor technology:

- Copper technology
- Silicon on insulator
- Low *k* dielectric
- Traces with 0.18 micron and smaller technology

All of these advancements are important, and I will cover each one in turn.

Copper Technology

Copper technology allows processors to run faster and cooler. The basic idea is to use copper wires/traces instead of aluminum for such traces as those on a circuit board. With copper wire/traces, the current flows with less resistance. With a higher resistance, there is more heat, as current is restricted in its flow. With lower resistance, the current flows with less restriction, and thus the part runs cooler. The result is the ability to pack more components into a smaller space, which in turn reduces signal latency, and the result is faster clock speeds, with some processors running at 1.3 GHz. (Speeds will be faster by the time you read this!)

Silicon on Insulator

The phrase "Silicon on Insulator" sounds strange and goes against normal thinking. How can you make a fragile silicon wafer work on top of an insulator? Well, IBM has figured out a process for creating a chip on an insulator. The result is a very cool chip, which means that you need fewer cooling fans and you can leave the refrigerator at home. When things run cooler, you can place more, cooler, chips closer together. With this mix, you achieve a higher density of transistors and higher clock speeds for the CPU.

Low K Dielectric

Low k dielectric refers to the capacitance between traces within the chip. If you do not know what a capacitor is, they are the big round components inside your television. A capacitor is made of two plates and a dielectric, which is an insulator. When current flows in the plates, a charge builds up between the plates in the dielectric. When you put two wires/traces close together and run current through the wires, then you have the components to make a capacitor, with the air space between the wires being the dielectric. The measure of how well a dielectric is able to maintain a charge is known as the *dielectric constant (k)*. Material with a higher dielectric constant stores a higher charge. So we want an extremely *low k* dielectric in an integrated circuit.

When you get down to 0.18 micron, and smaller, traces inside an integrated circuit are placed as close together as possible so that you can get more stuff packed inside the chip. When the traces get too close together, you have the possibility of capacitance coupling, which is a type of "bleeding" between traces (plates) in the chip due to the charge that has built up in the dielectric, which in this case is air, an insulator. The effect is that a signal that is supposed to stay on one trace will bleed over to other traces and signals get mixed together. This effect will just not work in an integrated circuit. Accordingly, IBM came up with a method of protecting the traces from this bleeding effect with low *k* dielectric chip technology. In effect, this new chip technology is similar to placing a shield between the traces. You can think of this as like the braided wire shielding in your cable TV wiring, where the center conductor is the trace and the wire braid is the shielding. Again, the result is faster clock speeds. Of course, I am greatly oversimplifying this concept.

Small (0.18 Micron and Smaller) Traces

We have been talking about how the circuits inside today's chips are getting smaller all of the time. With all of the technological advancements that IBM has achieved with their business partners, it is no wonder that a single trace in a chip can be 0.18 microns and smaller. A trace is so small that we are getting to just a few atoms in width. Silicon cannot go much farther to reduce the trace width, but we are not quite at the lower limit yet. You will be hearing more in the near future about biological circuits that are combined by chemical or electrical manipulation. Now that's small!

THE HISTORY OF THE POWER PROCESSOR

With processor speeds doubling and tripling faster than I can read all the associated IBM announcement letters, it's difficult to keep perspective for planning purposes. The only way to make decisions requires a good understanding of the available system architectures and development directions. This advice goes for new and old equipment. Even if you have a big budget, don't dismiss older processor models or the used equipment market when planning for additional resources. In our shop, we use some older systems as a "sandbox." They can be used for noncritical support services and easily replaced at low cost if they burn out. No maintenance contract required! Just keep a few on the shelf for when you need them. With this in mind, let's make an overview of the POWER architecture and consider its history. I cringe at the thought of committing details of state-of-the-art POWER systems to the page, which most certainly will end up a fossil before the ink dries, even if I do make my copy deadline!

POWER1

The first Reduced Instruction Set Computer (RISC) was developed in 1975 at IBM's T.J. Watson Research Center as a spin-off of telephone switching research. The processor architecture, called 801, implemented a reduced instruction set of 120 instructions fused in hardware and executed one instruction per clock cycle. The IBM PC RT, first commercially available in 1986, was based on the 801 work. To improve performance, the 801 project team began working on methods to process multiple instructions per clock cycle, reducing execution wait time during branch and memory operations. This work resulted in a second-generation, three-processor architecture dubbed AMERICA. The AMERICA effort was moved to the IBM Austin development lab in 1986. Austin evolved AMERICA into what was known as RIOS and finally into the architecture we know today as *Performance Optimized with Enhanced RISC (POWER)*.

Like AMERICA, the POWER architecture married three independent functional units into a superscalar configuration with the ability to execute multiple instructions per clock cycle, leading IBM to give a new meaning to the acronym RISC, *Reduced Instruction Set Cycles*. The POWER instruction set had put on a little weight, increasing to 184 instructions; the change was probably in order. The POWER triprocessor complex, consisting of separate branch, integer, and floating-point units, is fed via a four-word-wide I/O path from separate instruction and data caches. The caches can dispatch up to four instructions per clock cycle at 20 to 30 MHz. IBM began delivering the POWER RISC System/6000 product line in February 1990. You may still be running one of the early 200, 300, or 500-series systems. I still have and use an old model 230 at work.

POWER2

The next phase in POWER architecture development incorporated additional integer and floating-point units into a custom eight-chip design that was christened POWER2. The POWER2 architecture is based on the existing POWER instruction set for upward comparability. It also incorporates a set of new instructions that capitalize on the wider data paths, and the additional processors and registers available in the new design. Using compound instructions like FMA (floating-point multiply and add), the complex is capable of executing eight instructions per clock cycle at rates from 50 to 80 MHz, but this is still slow compared to today's CPUs.

The eight-chip POWER2 complex is housed in a multichip module (MCM) set that includes an instruction cache unit (ICU), a fixed-point unit (FXU), a floating-point unit (FPU), four data cache units (DCUs), and a storage control unit (SCU). The ICU processes instructions stored in the instruction cache and dispatches non-ICU instructions to the FXU and the FPU. The FXU and the FPU each house two execution units that are responsible for doing all the numeric data crunching.

The DCU manages the four-way, set-associative, dual-ported data cache to keep information moving in and out of the processor complex. The SCU arbitrates communications between the processors, memory, and SIO bus. This includes programmed I/O and DMA processing. Greater numbers of faster processors and wider paths mean you can consume data at a higher rate, so data cache sizes were increased to 128K or 256K, depending on the configuration. The instruction cache is 32K. With a larger cache, it made sense to add a Level 2 (L2) cache to improve I/O performance between processor cache and memory. The L2 cache, which stores snapshots of recently used memory, ranges in size from 256K on smaller systems to 2MB on big RISC System/6000s. IBM announced its POWER2 systems in September 1993. The first machines included the Model 58H running at 55 MHz, the 590 at 66 MHz, and a 990 hitting 71.7 MHz. Three years later, in October 1996, the RS/6000 Model 595 appeared. This machine was the first machine to incorporate the single-chip version of the POWER2, called the P2SC (POWER2 Super Chip) processor, which runs at 135 MHz. The fastest POWER2, running at 160 MHz, can be found in some older RS/6000 SP Thin nodes and the 397 workstation.

PowerPC

In 1991, with the POWER2 work well underway, IBM began a joint development venture to consolidate the POWER architecture into a high-performance, low-cost, single-chip design that could be produced in high volume. The chip was to remain binary-compatible with other POWER architectures, support 64-bit extensions, and be multiprocessor-enabled. Target applications would include everything from PDAs and printers to personal computers and multiprocessor supercomputers. The PowerOpen development alliance of IBM, Motorola, and Apple Computer was announced in September 1993, heralding the third generation of the POWER architecture, the PowerPC.

The most notable feature of the PowerPC architecture is the extension to 64-bit addressing with dynamic switching to 32-bit mode for backward compatibility. Existing POWER binaries executed on the PowerPC but ran more slowly until recompiled under the new instruction set. Complex POWER instructions were eliminated to simplify and streamline the instruction set. Additional systems for single precision, cache management, locking operations, and support for symmetrical multiprocessing (SMP) were added to better utilize features in the new chip architecture.

The PowerPC architecture is represented by a number of microprocessor configurations through its evolution. At the low end, the PowerPC model 601 is based on a three-processor configuration similar to the original POWER implementation. The 601 processor is a bridge architecture that supports all but two of the nonprivileged POWER instructions.

Additional fixed-point units, larger data and instruction caches, and an embedded secondary cache controller allow these processors to peak at five instructions per clock cycle. Although architecture and instruction sets vary a bit across the PowerPC processor line, a common hardware reference platform (CHRP) is defined to facilitate cross-platform software development.

The PowerPC has continued to mature over the years. The more recent processors, such as the 603, 604, and 604e, are the fastest PowerPC processors out. The very common 43P desktop machine uses the 604e processor with speeds of 332 MHz and 375 MHz. The fastest PowerPC driven model is the four-way F50 running at 375 MHz.

RS64 Evolution

Pushing forward, IBM brought the POWER architecture into the 64-bit world by introducing the RS64. This processor has a 64KB L1 data cache, a 64KB L1 instruction cache, and a 4MB L2 cache. Mathematical applications benefit most from the new RS64 internals, which include one floating-point unit, a load-store unit, and two integer units. The processor runs at only 125 MHz, but the performance is good.

The SMP capacity was extended when the RS64 was released. Machines were built to support 4-way, 8-way, and 12-way SMP configurations. With these machines came more memory and disk support, badly needed as databases started getting really big, driven by business needs.

The improvements continued through 1997 up to the September 1998 release of the RS64II. Redesigned with a four-way 8MB L2 cache, the RS64II has a clock speed of 262 MHz. The L1 instruction and data caches remained at 64KB. This processor was further redesigned with the new copper technology, boosting its clock speed to 450 MHz when it was released in fall 1999. The L1 instruction and data caches were each doubled in size to 128KB. With the appearance of the RS64III, systems supported up to 24 processors.

IBM is still not finished with this processor design. With the introduction of Silicon on Insulator (SOI) into the mix, another redesign of the RS64 architecture boosted the clock speed to 600 MHz in fall 2000. This was the advent of the RS64IV processor. The latest additions include a 16MB L2 cache and clock speeds to 750 MHz.

POWER4

In our industry, we hear about the "Next-Gen" of everything. This is the hype of the moment. For IBM, the POWER4 *complex* makes up the building blocks of the "Next-Gen" for IBM. The growth in processing power is extremely aggressive, and IBM is going to pull it off. In a store near you very soon, you will be able to buy an AIX machine to sit on top of your desk that can run eight different versions of AIX and Linux at the same time on different partitions within the same desktop machine. This is Next-Gen computing from IBM, and the POWER4 complex is going to have a great deal to do with its success.

The POWER4 complex consists of multiple POWER4 microprocessors, together with an internal storage subsystem that interconnects each microprocessor for a complete SMP subsystem. The current release contains two 64-bit POWER4 microprocessors along with an integrated microprocessor interface control unit, 1.4MB of L2 cache, an L3 cache using the Merged Logic DRAM (MLD) chip, and a memory controller chip. The MLD has 32MB of L3 cache.

The POWER4 complex comes with two-, four-, and eight-way SMP modules. In the big boys, the p681 and p690, for instance, four POWER4 processors are merged into multichip modules (MCMs). To fill up a 32-way p690, four MCMs are needed.

Inside, each POWER4 chip has multiple microprocessors. The current POWER4 has two microprocessors, but IBM has very ambitious plans for the next several years. The plan is to next release a version with four microprocessors, followed by one with eight.

The goal is to have a teraflop of processing power in one 32-processor package in five years. Now that is ambitious!

Also inside the chip is a second-level cache connected to both processors through the core-interface unit (CIU). The L2 cache has three L2 cache controllers, one for each of the three L2 cache segments. A 32-bit-wide bus connects the L2 cache segments to each microprocessor in the complex. Keeping everything very tightly coupled reduces the memory latency. Amazingly, a fabric controller is implemented to control the bus network. The fabric controller provides point-to-point routes within the processor complex.

There are two L1 cache sets. One is a 64KB direct-mapped instruction cache, and the other is the L1 data cache, now 32KB. Each of the L2 cache segments is 480KB in size, making a total of 1.44MB of L2 cache.

Watch for the POWER4 to blow your doors down. Over the next few years, the machines incorporating the POWER4 will go from the high-end p690s down to the mid-range systems and finally to the desktop machines. It is going to be nice to be able to partition your machine (using LPAR) into multiple AIX and Linux machines on the fly. It will bring a whole new meaning to the word sandbox.

This gives you a high-level overview of the POWER series of microprocessors. The POWER series is going to change so quickly that you need to keep an eye on the IBM Redbooks Online Web site at this URL:

```
http://www.redbooks.ibm.com
```

SP

The Scalable Parallel (SP) product line represents the other side of IBM's architectures. A single SP complex is made up of 2 to 512 individual nodes linked via a network fabric called the *SP switch*. Each system is a separate RS/6000 or pSeries that has its own memory, I/O adapters, and copy of the AIX operating system. Discounting network-shared disks, each SP node shares nothing with its associated nodes. A single SP frame can consist of 2–16 nodes, and there may be a mixture of thin, wide, or high node types, as well as some external pSeries machines. Thin nodes take up ½ of a bay, so you can place two thin nodes next to each other. Wide nodes take up one full system bay. High nodes take up two full system bays. The processors in the thin, wide, and high nodes vary from the old microchannel architecture to the latest pSeries systems. Communication between nodes is facilitated by the network fabric of the high performance switch (HPS).

The latest selection of SP nodes are two- or four-way SMP machines using the latest 64-bit copper technology running at 375 MHz and faster. These machines support up to 8GB of memory and have four internal 72GB drives and ten available PCI adapter slots.

The HPS implements an indirect cut-through switch architecture that reduces packet buffering requirements and limits communication deadlock problems. Message packets from each node contain routing information in the packet header and can be moved across multiple paths when traversing the switch to destination nodes. The HPS is made up of one switchboard per rack, connecting an eight-element adapter board in each node and providing a 16-way connection. One node in each frame may be configured as a switch-only node for interconnection with other SP frames. I/O rates across the switch will vary with the protocol used. The speed of the SP switch is increasing to over 1 GHz.

CODE NAME REGATTA: THE P690

Currently the bad boy on the block is the p690, aka Regatta, which is an 8- to 32-way SMP server that is totally new to UNIX in many ways. The p690 has twice the processing power of its predecessor, the p680. Inside the Regatta is the latest set of the highest-end technology enhancements on the market. The building blocks of the modular design include the Central Electronics Complex (CEC) for the processors and memory, I/O drawers, and a power system including built-in battery backup power.

The CEC can currently handle up to 16 POWER4 chips, each having two microprocessors sharing L2 cache. These SMP POWER4 subsystems are packaged together into a multichip module (MCM), with each MCM having four POWER4 chips. Each POWER4 chip can have 2 or 4 processors, and soon each chip will carry 8, 16, or 32 microprocessors for a teraflop of processing power in about five years.

Single points of failure have been eliminated at the power level with redundant power supplies and battery backup to keep the system up so that an orderly emergency shutdown can occur.

The Low End Regatta (LER) system are also hitting the streets. These LER machines are the latest IBM offering to date. Each is a 1-4 way symmetrical multiprocessing (SMP) UNIX server in either deskside or high-density (4U x 24" depth) rack-mount form factor. The architecture of these 2 new models is based on a 1 GHz 64-bit POWER4 processor with 32MB Level 3 Cache. The minimum configuration includes a single 1 GHz Power4 processor (expandable to 4-way), 512MB ECC DDR (Double Data Rate) memory, (expandable to 16 GB), and one 18.2GB 10K RPM internal disk drive.

LPAR

Going back over what worked, IBM took some pieces from the mainframe world, or as they like to call them, zSeries machines. Now you can have true logical partitioning (LPAR) in a p690 machine. The LPAR lets you slice and dice your machine into up to 16 logical partitions. Each separate partition has its own set of resources. For example, you can assign processors, memory, and specific I/O ports to belong to a specific LPAR, whereas competing systems do not let you partition even at the component level. You can even create an LPAR that has a *single* microprocessor, and remember, these microprocessors are packaged in two-, four-, and eight-way POWER4 chips.

To build an LPAR, you select the resources to include. You can select specific processors, PCI slots and the exact amount of memory. There are no requirements that the resources be physically attached to the same hardware, in the same system, but many times they are. The CPUs, memory, and PCI slots can be assigned to any LPAR, no matter where they are connected.

The LPAR is a new approach in the UNIX world to the dev/test/production dilemma. Of course, IBM has been working on logical partitioning since the 1970s in the S/370 mainframes (now called the zSeries). Now you need to buy only a few p690s and slice and dice up sandboxes for developers, along with a pair of test machines for some quick testing, while you run 20 application servers at the same time. As the POWER4 makes its way into midrange and desktop machines, you will see LPAR move with it.

Project eLiza

Project eLiza is an ongoing effort by IBM to produce machines that are self-managing, self-diagnosing, and self-healing. The p690 has many aspects of project eLiza built in. As an example, the Regatta has dynamic CPU deallocation, which will take a failing microprocessor offline without bringing the entire system down. In the memory arena, the p690 will take a failed memory DIMM offline without affecting the integrity of the memory contents. IBM can do this because the memory is in a RAID-5 type configuration, where the memory contents are spread across all of the memory DIMMS with parity. These are just two examples of where IBM is going with Project eLiza.

Because of increasingly complex e-business environments, including larger and larger systems with massive user loads, IBM launched project eLiza. Project eLiza has four goals it aims to achieve:

- **Self-configuring**   Adding plug and play ability, capacity upgrades on-demand, wireless system management and setup wizards for easy customizations.

- **Self-optimizing**   Allowing the system to dynamically allocate resources, create LPARs on the fly and a self-managing performance monitoring system allowing the machine to dynamically optimize itself.

- **Self-healing** Allows the system to detect and correct problems by using Chipkill memory technology, call-home functionality, advanced clustering, multipath I/O and ECC cache memory to maximize the system's availability.

- **Self-protecting** Uses security technologies such as SSL, LDAP, Kerberos, digital certificates, encryption, and others to maximize the data and system integrity.

These advancements are not just a "vision of the future", but a real company-wide initiative that is already producing results.

System Management of the p690

The pSeries 690 is managed on the IBM Hardware Maintenance Console for pSeries, or HMC. The HMC, first introduced with the p690 to manage the system and configure LPARs, has a GUI interface system running Linux on an 32-bit Intel platform. I tend to think of the HMC as a Control Workstation for the SP and the Windows NT and Linux console for the Enterprise Storage Server (ESS).

From the HMC, you can manage the following tasks:

- **System management security**   Allows remote control on a secure network connection

- **Partition management**   A mechanism to create, manage, activate, and delete LPARs

- **System configuration**   Allows midlevel-type configurations and troubleshooting

- **Users**   Manages the user environments

- **Software maintenance**   Allows installation and maintenance of software and removable media

- **Inventory scout**   Keeps an inventory of microcode levels throughout the system

- **Service agent**   Provides automatic problem notification and call-home capability

- **Service focal point**   Provides service access to the system

- **Problem determination**   For viewing problem logs and diagnostics

We could write an entire book on the pSeries 690. But I do not need to, because there is an excellent Redbook called *IBM e@Server pSeries 690 System Handbook* that you can download in either HTML or PDF format for printing. The book, whose ID number is SG24-7040-00, can be found at the following URL:

```
http://www.redbooks.ibm.com
```

pSERIES MACHINES

The pSeries machines are the replacements for the RS/6000. Just like the RS/6000 line of machines, the pSeries machines are broken up into three classes of systems. Starting at the low end are the entry-level deskside and rack mount models. The midrange systems add a huge performance boost to application servers. At the high end of the server farm are the p680 and p690 machines that we covered in the preceding section. Then there are the Cluster 1600 machines. These machines allow interconnectivity through a high-speed SP switch and run PSSP as a communications protocol. A list of the pSeries is shown in Table 3-1.

It is getting very hard to find any more new RS/6000 models, as they are being discontinued. With the pSeries machines, you have a wide range of processor and memory options to choose from. Table 3-2 shows the current list of processors available at the IBM Web site as of this writing. Newer and faster CPUs will come rolling out, so be on the lookout for upgrades.

pSeries	610	620	630	640	660	670	680	690
Model	6C1	6F0	6C4	B80	6H0	670	S85	690
Model	6E1	6F1	6E4		6H1	671		
Model					6M1			

Table 3-1.   IBM pSeries Models

NOTE   The 6C4 and 6E4 machines are the first Low End Regatta (LER) machines, introduced in the third quarter of 2002.

COMPATIBILITY

With all the chip, system, and instruction architectures available in the POWER product line, one might be worrying about application compatibility in a mixed environment. The good news is that older binaries will likely run on newer architectures. Exceptions may include things like device drivers that have changed between releases of the AIX operating system. This should be less of a problem if all your boxes are running the same release.

I know it's difficult to remember all the details of one vendor architecture alone, so adopt a sliding window view of the computing world. Keep a bit of the old, current,

Processor Type	Clock Rate
32-bit 604e	250 MHz
32-bit 604e	375 MHz
64-bit POWER3 II	333 MHz
64-bit POWER3 II	375 MHz
64-bit POWER3 II	400 MHz
64-bit POWER3 II	450 MHz
64-bit RS64 III	450 MHz
64-bit RS64 III	500 MHz
64-bit RS64 IV	600 MHz
64-bit RS64 IV	668 MHz
64-bit RS64 IV	750 MHz
64-bit RS64 IV	1.1 GHz
64-bit RS64 IV	1.3 GHz

Table 3-2.   Available POWER Processors

and future computing technologies in the back of your head. This will keep you from repeating yesterday's purchasing and implementation mistakes or at least let you put a new twist on them. Hey, you have a big budget, so you can afford to fudge a little. Buy lots of real fast machines and no one will know the difference. At least IBM will love you.

CHECKLIST

The following is a checklist for the key points in POWER processors and systems:

- ☐ Identify the main advancements with the new processor technology:
- ☐ Define the POWER2 architecture.
- ☐ Identify the p690, aka Regatta.
- ☐ Use the pSeries machines as replacements for the RS/6000.
- ☐ Develop application compatibility in a mixed environment.
- ☐ Manage the pSeries 690 on the IBM Hardware Maintenance Console for pSeries or the HMC.

CHAPTER 4

AIX 5L Kernel

R emember the good old days when the "process" was the indivisible dispatchable unit of work under AIX V3? Each process neatly lined up by priority in serial run queues awaiting a turn on the CPU. There were parent processes, children, grandchildren, with each process generation spawning the next. All members of one big happy **init** family. As in most families, it was often difficult to get family members to talk to each other or share their belongings. When you did get them to communicate or share, everyone tried to talk or grab a resource at the same time. You had to get heavy-handed and resort to locks and semaphores to keep everyone in line. Process life could be difficult, but it was simple and understandable.

Then in AIX V4 came multiprocessing. AIX developers decided to speed up the pace of life in process city. Rather than make all processes wait on just one CPU, they added the capability to dispatch across multiple CPUs. More CPUs mean that the work gets done faster. They also decided to break up the process structure into components called *threads*. Each thread is a dispatchable unit of work. Multiple threads can be executing simultaneously on multiple CPUs. These new features improved system throughput, but they didn't come without additional complexity and some overhead.

With AIX 5L comes a scalable 64-bit kernel that can support very large application workloads that are executing on 64-bit hardware. The scalability of the 64-bit kernel is primarily due to the larger kernel address space. The kernel supports both 64-bit and 32-bit applications.

KERNEL ARCHITECTURE

The AIX kernel fundamentally started as a System V.2 kernel. However, the System V architecture represents only AIX's roots, not its whole. The AIX kernel design includes a number of features and extensions that set it apart from other SYSV-based kernels. AIX V3 introduced most of these features when the POWER architecture hit the marketplace in 1990. Now we have progressed over the years through POWER 2 and POWER 3 to the current POWER 4 processor. With the introduction of the POWER 4 chip, IBM is planning for a huge increase in processing power as the newer versions of the POWER 4 chip are released. This first rendition has dual processors in same package, with each processor having its own L1, L2, and RAM caches. The next release will have four processors, and the one to follow will have eight processors per package. The goal is to have a Teraflop of processing power in a single four-inch-square package of 32 processors.

The progression of the AIX kernel was in keeping with the progression of the hardware. We started AIX with a 32-bit kernel. Then the address space of a particular process was limited to 2^{32} bytes (4GB). With the advent of the 64-bit kernel came huge amounts of address space in the multiterabyte range. A 64-bit application can, in theory, address 2^{64} bytes of data; however, AIX is currently limited to a more realistic space of 2^{60} bytes. The largest impact of this extended address space is with mathematical applications. Now long integers are 64 bits, but integers are still 32 bits. With the 64-bit long integers, the application can make twice as many calculations in the same time frame.

However, that you have a 64-bit kernel and a 64-bit machine does not directly imply an improvement in performance of an application. The application too must support 64-bit architecture and may have to be recompiled on a 64-bit machine to take advantage of the environment. Among the advantages of the 64-bit architecture are that 64-bit data types are included, larger files can be mapped into memory, more files can be mapped into memory, and processes have access to very large address spaces. Support for 64-bit computing started with AIX version 4.3.

Along with large memory capacity, the AIX kernel can scale to supporting large numbers of running processes and open files. This feat is achieved by eliminating hard-coded table size limits such as MAXPROC that are common in other UNIX kernels. The addition of the Object Data Manager (ODM) eliminated a number of large device and configuration tables, improving operating system access to configuration information and enabling dynamic system configuration updates. The AIX kernel is dynamically extensible, meaning that new device drivers and other system extensions can be added or changed on a running system without requiring a kernel rebuild or system reboot. Additionally, a new device can be plugged into a running system and made immediately available for use by updating ODM information with the **cfgmgr** command.

```
# cfgmgr  ◄————————Update ODM information
```

Threads Versus Processes

With the introduction of AIX version 4 came the multithreaded process. Any system activity requires a process to run to execute the activity. These activities include programs, databases, shell scripts, and other system processes. Each process on a running system consists of one or more threads. Threads provide the means of overlapping, multiplexing, and parallelizing operations within a process. The process structure is separated into dispatchable components and global resources. Threads are peer entities and share global resources such as address space.

The properties of a process and the properties of a thread differ in makeup. To see this more clearly, refer to Table 4-1.

As you can see in Table 4-1, the thread has control of getting through the run queue, and the process is responsible for containing everything about the job that is executing. Multiple threads allow the system to service requests from multiple user processes at the same time. The nice thing about threads is that they can service multiple requests without the added overhead of creating multiple processes through **fork** and **exec** system calls. With processes containing the information and the thread controlling the flow, each process becomes global and each thread can have its own priority, which is a nice concept if you think about it. The overall effect is a layered environment of multiple threads, which can increase performance up to nine times over a single-threaded environment.

Signals

Signals are defined at the process level but are handled at the thread level. Each thread has a local signal mask. Synchronous signals are delivered to any thread that causes an

Process Properties	Thread Properties
pid	tid
ppid	Stack
uid	Scheduling policy
gid	Scheduling priority
cwd	Pending signals
Process environment	Blocked signals
Process statistics	Thread-specific data
Signal actions	
File descriptors	

Table 4-1.   Process and Thread Properties

exception. Asynchronous signals such as **kill()** are delivered to only one thread in a process. The signal will be delivered to a thread that has initiated a **sigwait()** for the particular signal number or to a thread that does not have it blocked. Disabling signals at the process level to protect a critical code section in a thread may not work as expected in that the signal may be delivered to a thread executing on another processor.

The AIX lock instrumentation is provided to maintain cache coherency between threads running on multiple processors. The lock state of the system can be queried using the **lockstat** command if this facility has been enabled by **bosboot** options. Since the AIX kernel is aware of its UP versus MP run mode status, MP-specific lock requests are ignored in a UP environment to shorten code paths. Application developers may then write software exclusively for MP environments that is nonetheless supported under UP configurations.

```
# bosboot -a -L   ◄────── Create a boot image with MP lock support
# lockstat -a   ◄────── Display system lock usage statistics
```

Scheduling and Dispatching

It's probably obvious by now that changes to the AIX scheduler were required to support threads. As the dispatchable units of work, threads are assigned a priority from 0 to 127. Each level is represented by a run queue. The scheduler periodically scans the run queues and recalculates priority in accordance with processor use history for those tasks not running at a fixed priority. Note that some functions such as **nice** that affect queue priority still operate on the process as a whole rather than per individual thread.

The AIX dispatcher had to be changed to facilitate the way in which threads are allocated to available processors. When a thread is bound to a processor, in what is termed *processor affinity,* the highest priority thread may not be the next one available to be dispatched. The system experiences fewer cache misses if a thread can be dispatched to the same processor on which it last ran. Conversely, overall processor utilization is improved if threads can be scheduled on any available processor. The AIX dispatcher implements what has been termed *opportunistic affinity*. An attempt will be made to run a thread on the same processor on which it last ran if that processor is available. The **bindprocessor()** routine is available for those instances when a programmer would like to enforce processor affinity for a code section.

```
# bindprocessor <proc-id> <processor>    ←——————Bind process to processor
```

The **bootinfo** command can be used in early AIX V4 systems to determine whether the platform is MP capable. Note that **bootinfo** is included but not supported starting with AIX version 4.2.

```
# bootinfo -z    ←————— Display MP capability for the current platform
```

Along with general thread support, three scheduling options are available, SCHED_RR, SCHED_FIFO, and SCHED_OTHER. The SCHED_RR enforces strict round-robin scheduling. SCHED_FIFO uses a fixed-priority, first-in, first-out ordering. SCHED_FIFO does not support preemption and is not timesliced. A thread must either block or yield the processor when running under the SCHED_FIFO scheduler. The third option, SCHED_OTHER, represents the standard AIX scheduling algorithm, where task priority degrades with CPU usage.

Run Queues

Each CPU on the system has its own set of run queues in AIX 4.3.3 and higher. For AIX 5L, an additional set of global run queues has been added. With AIX version 4, the system has 128 run queues, specified as 0–127. On a SMP machine, each processor has its own set of run queues. Having a run queue on each processor makes it easier for the scheduler to find which thread to allow to run next. The scheduler scans the bit mask to determine which bit is set for a ready-to-run state on a single run queue as opposed to a huge global run queue.

With AIX 5L, the run queues were increased from 127 run queues per processor to 255 run queues per processor. Additionally, AIX 5L has added a global run queue that can point fixed-priority threads to any processor on the system. To have all fixed-priority processes use the global run queue, you must use the **schedtune** command to set the GLOBAL attribute to 1 (one).

CPU Timeslice for a Thread to Run

Since AIX 5L uses the SCHED OTHER scheduling policy, the discussion will follow this path. Under this scheduling policy, a running thread can use the CPU for a full timeslice. By default, one timeslice is 10 ms. Not all threads get the opportunity for a full timeslice because an interrupt can cause the thread to be placed on the tail of the run queue. An interrupt can be caused by a clock interrupt, or it can arise from some other source such as disk I/O or network adapter traffic. The reason behind the thread interrupt is that interrupts always have priority over a running thread.

How a thread gets on the run queue is a complex algorithm that places a penalty on threads that have recently been running. The formula is recalculated every clock tick for the currently running thread:

Priority Value = Base Priority + Nice Value + CPU Penalty Based on Recent CPU Usage

Where:

Base Priority = 40 (PUSER)

Nice Value = 20 (Default)

CPU Penalty = CPU Usage * R (Where R is 0.5 by default)

The CPU usage for all processes is calculated once every second. The CPU penalty is calculated on every clock tick, 10 ms by default. When a thread just comes out of the CPU, it is penalized. Through all of these calculations, some work actually does get done. The threads that were penalized work their way back up to the front of the run queue and get more CPU time. The overall throughput is much higher with the SCHED_OTHER scheduling policy than with SCHED_RR or SCHED_FIFO.

MORE ABOUT THE KERNEL

In this chapter, we cover the basics of the AIX 5L kernel. At the last AIX 5L and Numa-Q conference in Atlanta, I went to an AIX 5L Kernel Internals presentation. The intensity of the discussion was at a very detailed level, and the handout was about 60 pages of eight-point type. There is a lot more to the kernel than was presented in this chapter. Please refer to the IBM Redbook Web site for details on specifics of the kernel. Here you can find some good Redpieces and white papers that go into great detail on various internal components of the AIX 5L kernel.

```
http://www.redbooks.ibm.com
```

CHECKLIST

The following is a checklist for the key points in the kernel:

- ☐ AIX 5L provides a scalable 64-bit kernel that can support very large application workloads executing on 64-bit hardware.
- ☐ The scalability of the 64-bit kernel is primarily due to the larger kernel address space.

☐ The AIX kernel is dynamically extensible, meaning that new device drivers and other system extensions can be added or changed on a running system without requiring a kernel rebuild or system reboot.

☐ A new device can be plugged into a running system and made immediately available for use by updating ODM information with the **cfgmgr** command.

☐ Any system activity requires a process to run to execute the activity. Each process on a running system consists of one or more threads. Threads provide the means of overlapping, multiplexing, and parallelizing operations within a process.

☐ Multiple threads allow the system to service requests from multiple user processes at the same time.

☐ The AIX lock instrumentation is provided to maintain cache coherency between threads running on multiple processors. The lock state of the system can be queried using the **lockstat** command if this facility has been enabled by **bosboot** options.

☐ Each CPU on the system has its own set of run queues in AIX 4.3.3 and higher. With AIX version 4, the system has 128 run queues per processor, specified as 0–127. AIX 5L has 255 run queues per processor.

☐ For AIX 5L, adds a set of global run queues that can point fixed-priority threads to any processor on the system.

PART III

System Installation and Management

CHAPTER 5

System Management Tools

UNIX has a bad reputation when it comes to system management. Most of the traditional UNIX management tools are products of necessity, built by frustrated system programmers and administrators. Historically, UNIX development efforts have focused on designing the building blocks that support this roll-your-own methodology—Perl and Tcl/Tk are cases in point.

In production enterprises, UNIX must conform to the management policies and practices that are the hallmarks of big-iron operating systems. Ad hoc tool development is not acceptable in many of these environments. A new breed of UNIX management tools are required that provide centralized control over distributed heterogeneous resources. These tools must interoperate with existing legacy tool sets. The Open Software Foundation (OSF) worked hard to define its Distributed Management Environment (DME) specification; unfortunately, DME did not achieve the wide acceptance of other OSF technologies, such as DCE.

Rather than wait for consensus on an overall platform-independent system administration strategy, many vendors began testing the waters with their own UNIX management tools. Most of these tools integrate graphical interfaces with traditional UNIX commands to streamline system installation, configuration, and management tasks. In this chapter, we will discuss three of these tools: the AIX System Management Interface Tool (SMIT), AIX Distributed SMIT (DSMIT), and the AIX Web-Based System Manager (WebSM).

SMIT

The base system administration management tool for AIX is called the System Management Interface Tool or SMIT. SMIT is an interactive interface that provides a complete administrator's toolbox that may be used to perform system management activities such as installing software, configuring devices, administering user accounts, performing system backups, scheduling jobs, and diagnosing problems. SMIT uses a menu-driven interface that streamlines and simplifies the complexity of many system management activities. SMIT does not inhibit or replace command-line access to system management; rather, it uses the same commands under the cover of the menu-driven interface. However, not all possible command and argument combinations are available under SMIT. Command and parameter selection is based on the most common use to complete a given management task. Since SMIT takes user input to build and execute commands, you must have the authority to run the commands that SMIT executes.

For novice administrators, SMIT simplifies system management through the use of task-oriented dialogs. New users can zero in on a particular task by stepping through SMIT's submenu hierarchy. Menu options for a specific task are identified with descriptive field titles and contextual help. Error checking routines validate argument type and range.

The advanced administrator may find that SMIT provides a faster interface to many management tasks than the command line. This is especially true for some configuration commands that have a multitude of switch options. When using SMIT, two files are created, the `smit.script` and the `smit.log` files. The SMIT script facility may be used to assist in creating complex administration scripts, and the logging facility keeps a log of the tasks that were performed on the system, as well as the date/time the commands were executed.

The choice is yours to use SMIT to manage AIX. As you gain experience with SMIT and the AIX environment, you may find that you prefer to use SMIT for some management activities and the command line for others. Whether you love it or hate it, SMIT is here to stay.

USING SMIT

SMIT is started by executing the **smit** command for a Motif interface or the **smitty** command for an ANSII interface from the command line. By default, SMIT will enter the top-level system management menu. To enter SMIT at a particular task submenu, you can supply the SMIT FastPath name as an argument.

```
# smit   ◄─────────── Start SMIT at the top-level menu
# smit user   ◄─────────── Start SMIT at the user admin submenu
```

SMIT allows you to take a test drive utilizing all of its features without making changes to the operating system. Invoke **smit** with the **-X** flag to kick the tires and get a feel for how it operates. SMIT will log the commands it would have executed in the `$HOME/smit.script` file.

```
# smit -X
```

You can also use the F6 key within SMIT to display the actual AIX command and arguments it will invoke before committing the update. This ability to check out the commands that SMIT will execute gives new AIX System Administrators a leg up on the command syntax and structure.

smit Versus smitty Displays

SMIT provides both ASCII and Motif-based user interfaces. The Motif interface is invoked by default on an X11 or CDE managed display and employs a point-and-click feel. The Motif display enhances the operating environment through the use of buttons, slider bars, and submenu panels. The SMIT ASCII interface is invoked using the **smitty** or **smit -C** command (see Figure 5-1 for Motif display and Figure 5-2 for the ANSII screen).

```
# smit          SMIT X11 interface
# smitty        SMIT ASCII interface
# smit -C       SMIT ASCII interface
```

Each SMIT panel is divided into three parts. At the top of the panel, the task title and instructions appear. The middle of the screen contains menu selections or input fields. Location in the set of fields is indicated by "top," "more," and "bottom." At the bottom of each panel, the set of valid function keys is listed in four columns. SMIT flags

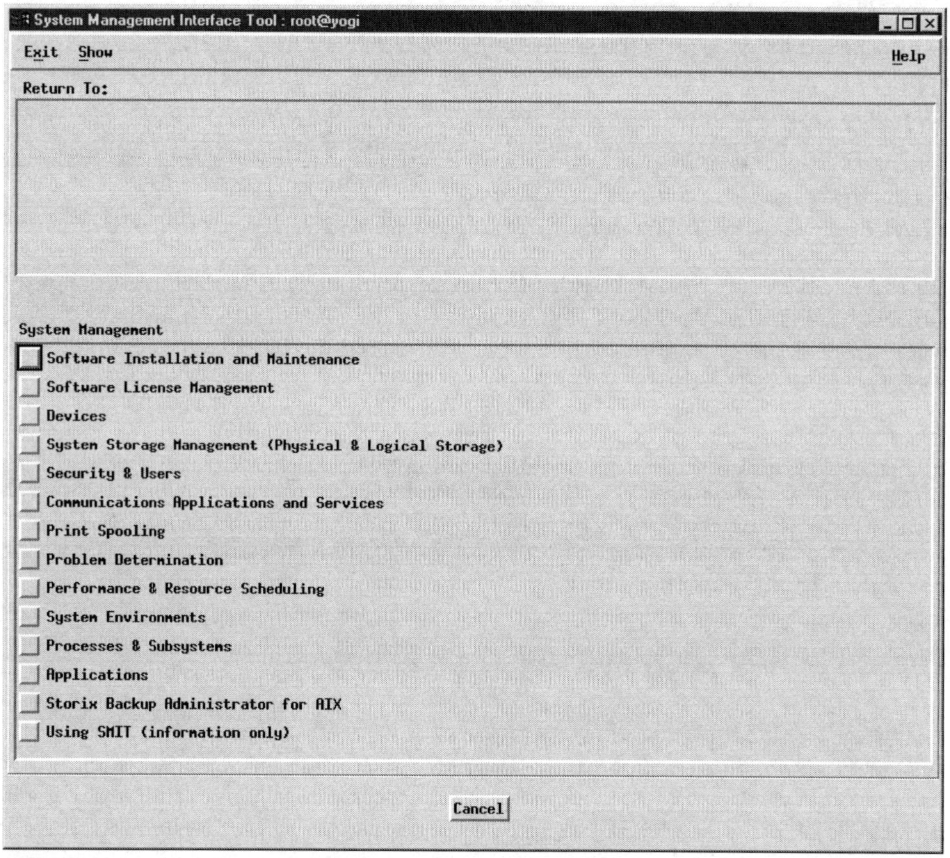

Figure 5-1.   SMIT main screen in CDE

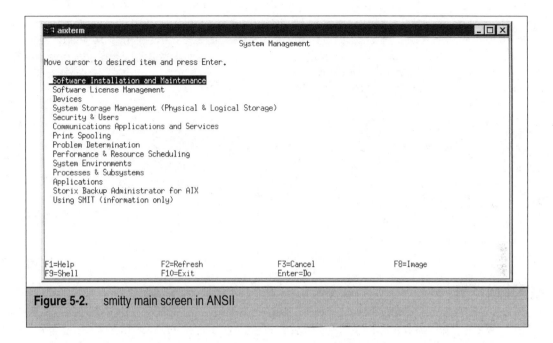

Figure 5-2.   smitty main screen in ANSII

input field types and selection lists through the use of field mark characters and buttons displayed to the far left and right of the input fields, as shown in Figure 5-3.

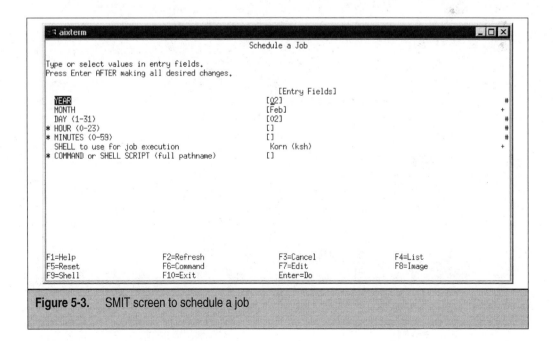

Figure 5-3.   SMIT screen to schedule a job

Notice the special symbols used in Figure 5-3. On the left side of the screen, we have the *, which specifies that a value is required for this field. On the right side, we have more symbols: #, +, and /. Table 5-1 lists each field symbol used in the SMIT panels.

Knowing the SMIT panel special symbols will let you know exactly what SMIT expects to see to perform a given task.

SMIT Keys

SMIT also has a set of keys to use while you are in the SMIT panels. Some of the keys are available only in the ANSII or the Motif display mode (see Table 5-2).

SMIT Help and Messages

You can invoke SMIT help from any menu by pressing the F1 key. Note that the message catalog is a National Language (NLS) catalog and is thus dependent on the setting of the $LANG environment variable.

SMIT Log File

SMIT creates an audit log of each SMIT session in the user's $HOME directory named smit.log. The log file indicates the SMIT submenu path traversed during the session by object class ID, panel sequence number, title, and the FastPath name. Each new SMIT session is appended to the existing log file. Take care to monitor the size of the log file over time. The location of the log file may be set using the **smit -l <PathName>** option. The level of logging verbosity may be increased using **smit -vt**.

```
# smit -l /tmp/smit.log -vt  ◄──────── Use /tmp to hold log file
```

Symbol	Meaning
*	A value is required for this field.
#	A numeric value is required for this field.
X	A hexadecimal value is required for this field.
+	A pop-up list is available for this field using F4 (or ESC-4).
[ ]	A field can be typed in.
< >	Data displayed is larger than the field display. The < and > indicate the overflow direction.
/	A file/directory pathname is required for this field.
?	Any value entered will not be displayed.

Table 5-1. Special Symbols Used in SMIT Panels

Keystroke	Function
F1 (or ESC-1)	Help—for the specific task
F2 (or ESC-2)	Refresh—or redraw the screen (ANSII)
F3 (or ESC-3)	Cancel—the current function, returns to the previous screen (ANSII)
F4 (or ESC-4)	List—for pop-up field options (ANSII)
F5 (or ESC-5)	Reset—field value to the original value
F6 (or ESC-6)	Command—shows the actual command that SMIT will execute
F7 (or ESC-7)	Edit—allows you to edit a pop-up field or select from a multiselectable pop-up list
F8 (or ESC-8)	Image—saves the current SMIT panel to the `smit.log` file if followed by the ENTER key and shows the SMIT FastPath for the current SMIT panel
F9 (or ESC-9)	Shell—starts a subshell. Typing **exit** returns to SMIT (ASCII). Resets all SMIT fields (Motif)
F10 (or ESC-0)	Exit—exits SMIT immediately back to the command line (ASCII) or skips to the command bar (Motif)
F12	Exit—exits SMIT immediately (Motif)
CTRL-L (ell)	List—for pop-up field options (Motif)
PGDN (or CTRL-V)	Scrolls down one page at a time
PGUP (or ESC-V)	Scrolls up one page at a time
ESC-<	Moves to the top of the scrolling screen area (ASCII)
ESC->	Moves to the bottom of the scrolling screen area (ASCII)
ENTER	Executes the current SMIT command or selects the current pop-up selection
/text	Searches for the string specified by the *text* parameter
N	Searches for the next occurrence of *text*

Table 5-2. Special Keys Used by SMIT

For example, removing the **paging00** paging space:

```
[Jul 26 2001, 22:43:35]
    Starting SMIT
(Menu screen selected as FastPath,
        id           = "storage",
        id_seq_num   = "010",
        next_id      = "lvm",
        title        = "Logical Volume Manager".)
(Menu screen selected,
        FastPath     = "lvm",
        id_seq_num   = "010",
```

```
        next_id      = "lvm",
        title        = "Logical Volume Manager".)
(Menu screen selected,
        FastPath     = "lv",
        id_seq_num   = "020",
        next_id      = "lv",
        title        = "Logical Volumes".)
(Dialogue screen selected,
        FastPath     = "rmlv",
        id           = "rmlv",
        title        = "Remove a Logical Volume".)
[Jul 26 2001, 22:43:50]
    Command_to_Execute follows below:

>> rmlv -f 'paging00'

    Output from Command_to_Execute follows below:
---- start ----
rmlv: Logical volume paging00 is removed.
---- end ----
[Jul 26 2001, 22:44:00]
```

SMIT Script File

Along with the log file, SMIT appends the AIX commands invoked during the session to a local $HOME/smit.script file. The script file information can be used to create complex management scripts or review the commands invoked during a previous session. For example, say you use SMIT to configure the first of a set of 64 TTY devices. Edit the $HOME/smit.script file and, duplicating the **mkdev** command 62 times for the remaining devices, change each device name and attributes as required. The script file can be executed from the command line to complete the definition for the remaining devices. Use the **smit -s** <**PathName**> option to create a script file in a location other than your home directory.

```
# smit -s /tmp/smit.script   ◄──────── Create a script file in /tmp
```

For example, the smit.script entries surrounding the removal of the **paging00** paging space:

```
#       [Jul 26 2001, 22:43:50]
#
rmlv -f 'paging00'
#
#       [Jul 26 2001, 22:44:23]
#
lsvg -o|lsvg -i -l
```

```
#
#      [Jul 26 2001, 22:44:57]
#
rmlv -f 'loglv00'
#
#      [Jul 26 2001, 22:47:20]
#
chdev -l sys0 -a maxuproc='128'
#
```

As you can see, we were doing a lot more than removing the **paging00** paging space on July 26. We began by removing the **paging00** paging space but then went on to display a listing of all currently active logical volumes, removing the **loglv00** log logical volume and setting the maximum number of processes per user to 128. The `smit.script` file is extremely valuable when you want to create shell scripts to automate systems changes and reconfigurations.

SMIT FastPaths

SMIT allows you to bypass dialog and menu screens and enter a task directly through the use of a FastPath name (see Table 5-3). A FastPath name is an identifier for a particular SMIT panel. FastPath names are recorded as part of the `$HOME/smit.log` information. The FastPath name is included as an argument to the **smit** command to enter a task panel directly.

```
# smit nfs  ◄───────── Access SMIT NFS management
```

Remembering all the FastPath names and management commands can be a real challenge. Fortunately, the AIX developers implemented an easy-to-remember rule for the FastPath and command names. A set of four prefixes, **ls**, **mk**, **ch**, and **rm**, are appended to a root task name in the **list**, **make**, **change**, and **remove** operating system objects. For example, to make a TTY device, the FastPath or command name is **mktty**.

FastPath and Command Operations and Objects

AIX administration commands are made up using two parts: the operation followed by an operation object, as shown here:

Operation	**mk**, **ls**, **ch**, **rm**
Objects	**dev**, **user**, **fs**, **vg**, **pv**, **tty**, **cd**, **tape**, etc.

Putting the operation with the object will produce a direct SMIT FastPath, in most cases, as shown in Table 5-3.

Many more SMIT FastPath options are available for most every other system management task that has a lower-level submenu. As an example, if you want to go directly to adding a user to the system, the SMIT FastPath is **smitty mkuser**.

Task	SMIT FastPath
Software installation and maintenance	install
Software license management	licenses
Device management	dev
System Storage management (physical and logical storage)	storage
Journaled filesystem management	jfs
Logical volume management	lvm
NFS management	nfs
Security management	security
User management	user or users
Communications applications and services	commo
TCP/IP management	tcpip
Print queue management	spooler
Problem determination	problem
System diagnostics	diag
Performance and resource scheduling	performance
System environments	system
Processes and subsystems	src

Table 5-3.   SMIT FastPath for Application Submenus

Customizing SMIT

SMIT is composed of a hierarchical set of menu panels, an NLS message catalog, a command interface, and a logging and scripting facility. These components are integrated to provide a seamless interface for managing the operating system and system resources.

Three types of SMIT display panels are used to manage the dialog between the user and management tasks: Menu, Selector, and Dialog. Menu panels display management task selections. Selector panels (see Table 5-4) present a range of values from which you

Type	Function
Menu	List of task options
Selector	Request additional input before proceeding
Dialog	Request values for command arguments and options

Table 5-4.   SMIT Panel Types

must choose before proceeding with the management task. You may choose more than one. Dialog panels provide input fields for specifying command arguments and values.

SMIT objects are generated with the ODM generation facility and then stored in files in a designated database. By default, they reside in the `/usr/lib/objrepos` directory. The SMIT database consists of the following files, by default:

```
sm_menu_opt
sm_menu_opt.vc
sm_name_hdr
sm_name_hdr.vc
sm_cmd_hdr
sm_cmd_hdr.vc
sm_cmd_opt
sm_cmd_opt.vc
```

These eight files should always be maintained together, including saving and restoring. After becoming experienced with the ODM (see Chapter 9 for more on the ODM) and SMIT architectures, you may use ODM commands to customize SMIT. SMIT object class names and object identifiers are listed in the SMIT log file when SMIT is invoked with the verbose trace **-vt** option.

```
# smit -vt    ◄——————SMIT verbose tracing
```

WEB-BASED SYSTEM MANAGER

For those of you who prefer a bit more flash in system management tools, Web-Based System Manager (WebSM) is the tool for you. WebSM provides a comprehensive set of system management tools for AIX 5L. Because of the mouse-driven, point-and-click, drag-and-drop Web-based desktop environment, WebSM is intuitive to use. It is more colorful than SMIT, and it prevents you from wallowing in the muck of the AIX command line. AIX 5L leans heavily toward the WebSM, and it appears that some new features may be available only via the WebSM in coming AIX releases. Managed objects and associated tasks are displayed as icons with a Web browser look and feel (see Figure 5-4). To perform an action, double-click on the desired object. If additional information is required, a WebSM dialog panel is displayed to accept configuration information.

The AIX 5L release of WebSM has the ability to manage numerous AIX 5L host machines on both Power and IA-64 hardware. Also new to the 5L release of WebSM is the support for dynamic monitoring of system events through the Resource Monitoring and Control (RMC) software originally created for the IBM RS/6000 SP frames. Now you do not have to write all of those shell scripts to monitor your systems for problems like full filesystems.

WebSM can run in stand-alone or client/server modes. In the stand-alone mode, WebSM manages the local AIX system. In the client/server mode, WebSM can manage AIX systems from a remote PC or from another AIX system that uses a graphical user

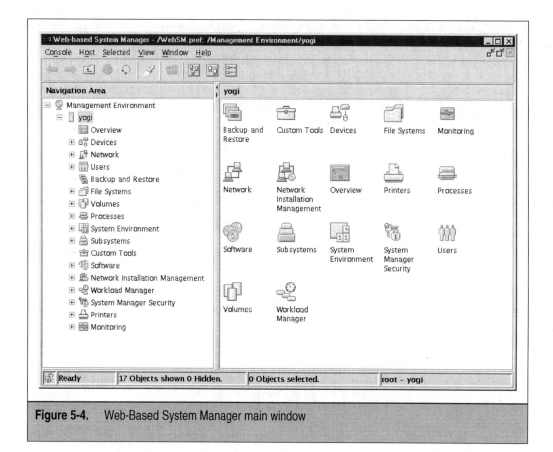

Figure 5-4. Web-Based System Manager main window

interface. In this environment, the AIX system that is managed remotely is the *server* and the system from which you perform the administration is the *client*. WebSM has been tested with both Netscape Navigator and Microsoft Internet Explorer.

WebSM can be run from any operating system platform that uses a Java 1.3, and above, enabled browser. To date, WebSM has been tested only on AIX 5L versions 5.0 and 5.1 and on Microsoft Windows NT, 98, ME, and 2000.

WebSM can be started from the AIX Common Desktop Environment (CDE) application manager System_Admin window or from the command line using the **wsm** command.

DISTRIBUTED SYSTEMS MANAGEMENT

Distributed system management tools seem to come and go. Distributed SMIT is available as part of IBM's system management products, which provide a SMIT interface for managing distributed UNIX platforms. References to DSMIT began to disappear after the announced merge of SystemView with Tivoli's Tivoli Management Environment (TME).

DSMIT

Distributed System Management Interface Tool (DSMIT) is installed as a separate product on AIX V3.2.5 and AIX V4. Functionally, it is the same as single-system SMIT, but it goes a step further in allowing remote management of a number of vendor UNIX products including the following:

- AIX 3.2.5, AIX V4
- Sun OS 4.1.3
- Solaris 2.3, Solaris 2.4
- HP-UX 9.0

As you might expect, DSMIT is broken up into clients (managed systems) and servers (managing systems). Machines managed by DSMIT are grouped into domains. Subsets of machines within a domain are called the working collective. Table 5-5 shows the breakdown of systems and various configuration information stored in the `/usr/share/DSMIT` directory.

As you might imagine, security in a distributed management environment is a critical issue. DSMIT uses MIT Kerberos V5 security services for authenticating DSMIT servers and clients. Commercial masking data facility (CMDF) and message authentication code (MAC) protocols are used to ensure data integrity and guard against message tampering. The nice thing about this is that, after you have validated yourself to Kerberos as a System Administrator, you don't need to log into each system you will be managing.

DSMIT allows you to select sets of systems for management functions. When an update is to be made, you can choose to send the command to all machines in the set at once (concurrent mode) or one at a time (sequential mode). You can bail out in the latter case if problems with an update are indicated. To make things easy or confusing

File	Purpose
domains	Client groups
dsmitos	Operating systems managed
clients	Managed hosts
security/v5srvtab	Principal key
security/admin.cfg	Administrator keys
security/managing.cfg	Managing systems keys
security/managed.cfg	Managed systems keys
security/dsmit.ptr	DSMIT config file server

Table 5-5. `/usr/share/DSMIT`

(depending on your point of view), a shell environment variable can be set to indicate that DSMIT should be run when a user or administrator types **SMIT**.

```
SMIT=d  ◄────────Invoke DSMIT instead of SMIT
```

This is about all we're going to say about DSMIT, since bets are being placed on a replacement from Tivoli. The following section describes the OSF's Distributed Management Environment (DME) specification to give you some background on Tivoli's systems management technology. Tivoli was one of the principle technology providers for the DME specification.

DME History

In the early 1990s, the Open Software Foundation defined a management standard for distributed systems called the Distributed Management Environment (DME). The DME technology specification defines a uniform and consistent set of tools and services that may be used to manage both standalone and distributed heterogeneous systems, applications, and networks.

DME combines a select set of vendor management technologies into a consistent framework based on a three-tier model. The lowest tier supports single-host management activities. The second level provides cell naming and security management in distributed environments. The top level encompasses enterprise-wide management via Motif-based GUI interfaces. DME routines communicate with managed objects using DCE, SNMP, and OSI CMIP. Table 5-6 lists the DME technology selections by the developing entity.

The DME Request for Technology (RFT) was first issued in July 1990. After evaluation by OSF's Munich Development Office, a selection was made in September 1991. The selected technologies went through a period of integration testing, during which time code snapshots were made available to interested parties. DME license fees were set, and the first code release was scheduled for the fourth quarter of 1993.

IBM	Data Engine, System Resource Controller
MIT Project Athena	Palladium Print Services
Tivoli	WIzDOM Object Oriented Framework
Banyan	Network Logger
HP	Open View Network Management Server
	Software Distribution/Installation Utils
	Network License Manager
Groupe Bull	Consolidated Management API
Gradient	PC Ally and Client Lib for Net License Server
	PC Agent and Event Components

Table 5-6. DME Technology Selections

SMIT

- **smit**   Motif interface
- **smit -C, smitty**   TTY interface
- **smit -X**   Inhibit updates, test drive SMIT
- **F6-key**   Display command to be executed by SMIT
- **smit <fast-path-name>**   Display SMIT submenu
- **$HOME/smit.log**   SMIT transaction log
- **$HOME/smit.script**   SMIT command log
- **/usr/lib/objrepos/**   SMIT ODM panel database sm_xxxx_xx
- **DSMIT**   Distributed SMIT
- **SMIT=d**   Invoke DSMIT instead of SMIT

WSM

- **wsm**   Start the Web-based System Manager Interface

CHECKLIST

The following is a checklist for the key points in system management:

- ☐ Execute the System Management Interface Tool or SMIT, the base system administration management tool for AIX, with the **smit** command for a Motif interface or the **smitty** command for an ANSII interface.

- ☐ Press the F6 key within SMIT to display the actual AIX command and arguments it will invoke before committing the update.

- ☐ Invoke SMIT help from any menu by pressing the F1 key.

- ☐ SMIT creates an audit log of each SMIT session named smit.log in the user's $HOME directory.

- ☐ SMIT appends the AIX commands invoked during the session to a local $HOME/smit.script file.

- ☐ You can use the smit.script file to create shell scripts to automate systems changes and reconfigurations.

- ☐ You can bypass SMIT dialog and menu screens and enter a task directly through the use of a FastPath name.

- ☐ Remember FastPath command names by appending one of four prefixes , **ls**, **mk**, **ch**, and **rm**, to a root task name in the **list**, **make**, **change**, and **remove** operating system objects.

- ☐ SMIT uses three types of display panels, Menu, Selector, and Dialog, to manage the dialog between the user and management tasks.

- ☐ SMIT objects are stored in eight files in a designated database found in the /usr/lib/objrepos directory by default. These eight files should always be maintained together, including saving and restoring.

- ☐ AIX 5L's Web-Based System Manager (WSM) provides mouse-driven, point-and-click, drag-and-drop system management tools.

- ☐ Start WebSM from the AIX Common Desktop Environment (CDE) application manager System_Admin window or from the command line using the **wsm** command.

- ☐ In the client/server mode, WSM can manage AIX systems from a remote PC or from another AIX system that uses a graphical user interface

- ☐ Distributed SMIT, DSMIT, goes a step further than SMIT by allowing remote management of multiple vendors' UNIX products.

- ☐ When you make an update with DSMIT, you can choose to send the command to all machines in the set at once (concurrent mode) or one at a time (sequential mode).

CHAPTER 6

AIX Installation and Maintenance

As we all know, IBM is well known for changing the maintenance and installation procedures with each new release. IBM might claim otherwise, but I've been upgrading systems for a very long time, and that has been my experience. Each time you install AIX, I recommend that you follow the installation guide *carefully,* even when you feel like you can do it in your sleep. (Especially, read the release notes!) I can tell you from experience that cutting corners can have catastrophic results. Follow the install path that fits your environment and you'll keep surprises at a minimum. Our starting point is keeping the existing environment isolated from the install and maintenance process.

Along with procedure changes, you will also see that IBM has given in to the licensing pressure like every other OS vendor and now requires in AIX 5L that you accept the electronic license agreements as you install new software on the AIX system. These licensing agreements can be set to be automatically accepted and should not pose a problem with nonprompting installations (see ACCEPT_LICENSE in the section "Complete Overwrite," later in this chapter). Gone are the days when just installing the product implies acceptance of the license agreement.

As of this writing, AIX 5L version 5.1 is the current release. AIX 5L version 5.2 is due out in the third quarter of 2002, with subsequent releases of versions 5.3 and 5.4 due about every year in the third or fourth quarter. I recommend staying as close to the current release as is comfortable for your environment. Keeping current will get you the best support from IBM when questions or problems occur (the AIX support number is 1-800-CALL-AIX). I will concentrate on installation and maintenance functions at the AIX 5L version 5.1 level in this chapter. Also study the IBM publication *AIX 5L Version 5.1 Installation Guide* (SC23-4374) found on `http://www.redbooks.ibm.com`.

INSTALLATION AND MAINTENANCE PLANNING

Installing a brand new operating system or application on a new computer is like painting on clean canvas. You're not encumbered with preserving or working within any existing paradigm. You have the freedom to plan your environment from scratch. Planning is the key word here. Operating system and production filesystem configuration should be configured to get the best performance from the disk space. Always strive to implement a configuration that facilitates future product upgrades and allows for easy maintenance tasks. Reserve disk space for non-rootvg volume groups to hold your user and local production filesystems. If you are installing multiple machines, consider installing one system as a reference system that can then be cloned from a Network Install Manager (NIM) system image, or mksysb. There are other, less complicated methods of installing **mksysb** images that you may want to look into, for example, Alternate Disk Installation (see the section "Alternate Disk Install Procedure," later in the chapter). Make use of the worksheets provided in the planning section of the installation guide. The planning sheets make a good reference set when you need to review your installation plan at some time in the future.

Here are some installation considerations.

Memory   The base memory requirement for AIX 5L version 5.1 is 64MB of RAM.

Installation Media   A CD-ROM is the only IBM offering other than preinstallation. Network Install Manager (NIM) is also available over Token Ring, Ethernet, and FDDI.

BOS Disk Space   The disk space required varies dramatically depending on your environment. I would always have as a bare minimum 4GB (9GB is even better!) of unmirrored disk space available, then mirror rootvg. It is just stupid *not* to mirror the root volume group on a production system.

Licensed Program Product Disk Space   What do you want to install? Look at the documentation provided with the software and pad the requirements by 50 percent. Disk space is cheap!

Paging Space   The paging space requirements differ depending on the application running on the system. If you are running a database, then create several "large" paging spaces, *all* in rootvg, of approximately equal size. Here, the word *large* is a relative term. Typically, total paging space should start at twice real memory, even for systems with a large amount of RAM. If you are running SAP with Oracle, the vendors want tens of GB of paging space, just in case (in case of what, they do not say!).

CAUTION   Never put more than one paging space on a single disk!

Since VMM uses paging space in a round-robin technique, it evenly uses all of the system paging spaces. If you have more than one paging space on a single disk, you may be overworking this single disk and defeating the purpose of the round-robin technique.

/tmp Space   Start out with a minimum of 100MB of /tmp space, just in case.

Create Separate Volume Groups for Local User and Production File Systems   Reserve rootvg for the operating system, and place applications and other *shared* data on non-rootvg disks.

Reference System and Network Install Manager   If you are installing a large number of systems or want to set up a standard, consider using Network Install Manager (NIM) to set up a reference machine. Using NIM can greatly simplify and streamline repetitive installs over the network, either locally or worldwide.

Network Parameters   Talk to your network administrator about the best networking options for your system; whether this is a new or old machine, the network admin may have some new equipment that you are not aware of. Consider everything when setting network options. Most sites can handle at least 100MB full duplex. When possible, do not configure the Ethernet card or the router port to *autonegotiate,* which means it will change network settings depending on the network. One common problem occurs when a CISCO router is set to autonegotiate 10/100 *half* duplex. The adapter will switch to 100MB, but it cannot autonegotiate to *full* duplex. The result is that the system will have very poor performance.

Machine Support for AIX 5L   Support for Micro Channel Architecture (MCA) and POWERPC Reference Platform (PReP) will no longer be supported after AIX 5L, version 5.1. Starting with AIX 5L, version 5.2, which is set to GA in the fourth quarter of 2002, will no longer support the MCA models in the following Machine Type list:

  7006, 7007, 7008, 7009, 7010, 7011, 7012, 7013, 7015, 7030, and 7202.

The following PReP-based systems, specified in the following Machine Type list, will no longer be supported starting with AIX 5L, version 5.2:

  6015, 6042, 6050, 6070, 7020, 7024, 7025, 7026, 7043, 7247, 7248, 7249, and 7317.

Unfortunately, this list includes the popular 43-P models.
The following SP nodes (all MCA-based) will no longer be supported in AIX 5L, version 5.2:

  2001, 2002, 2003, 2004, RPQ (66MHz Wide 59H), 2005, 2006, 2007, 2008, 2009, 2022.

The following PCI Adapters (specified by feature code) are no longer supported starting with AIX 5L, version 5.2:

  2408, 2409, 2638, 2648, 2657, 2837, 2854, 2855, 2856, 8242.

The following ISA Adapters (specified by feature code) are no longer supported starting with AIX 5L, version 5.2:

  2647, 2701, 2931, 2932, 2933, 2961, 2971, 2981, 8240, 8241.

Carefully check the machine type and adapter feature codes to confirm compatibility before starting your AIX 5L installation.

Product Packaging

First, the AIX 5L operating system is shipped only on CD-ROM. To simplify the installation and maintenance process and group products by intended service profile more accurately, software is grouped as products, packages, bundles, and filesets. At the lowest level, a *fileset* identifies software that provides a specific function. A fileset is the smallest installable and updatable unit for maintenance purposes. You'll get to know filesets very well. Filesets that have been grouped to provide a common service set are called *packages*, like the collection of filesets that make up BOS networking. Licensed products represent a collection of packages that are distributed as a set on installation media. Groups of packages, filesets, and associated maintenance that are combined for a specific service profile are called *bundles*. Examples would include App-Dev, CDE, GNOME, KDE, Client, Server, or Device profiles on AIX 5L. You can create your own custom bundles using SMIT to capture a particular application level or to group filesets and packages the way you think they should have been grouped in the first place.

Three levels of software packaging

- **Fileset** Specific function software set
- **Package** Common function filesets
- **Bundle** Group of filesets, packages, and maintenance

There are three parts to the installed software product:

- **usr Part** Contains the part of the product that can be shared by machines of the same hardware architecture
- **root Part** Contains the part of the product that cannot be shared. The root part is specific to a particular machine
- **share Part** Contains the part of the product that can be shared with other machines; this part of the software is not machine dependent in any way

You will see **usr**, **root**, and **share** referred to when you install software and the commit process executes within SMIT.

Support Information

Before jumping in with both feet, read any product-related README files. Contact IBM support representatives concerning the latest maintenance level (ML) patch set for your operating system version, release, and modification, and ask for any planning information for the release level being installed. Before you contact an IBM service representative or software manufacturer, make sure you have your AIX version and release numbers, your service modification level, your machine serial number and model number, and your customer number. To identify the version and release numbers for an existing system, use the **oslevel** command. The **oslevel** command reports the current level of the operating system by using a subset of the filesets installed on the system. The **oslevel -q** command will display any base migration upgrades that are installed. If **oslevel** shows only 4.3.2.0 and the **-q** option shows 4.3.3.0 is present, then

oslevel -l 4.3.3.0 will help identify the missing filesets. The filesets used to determine the current AIX level are the BOS, base devices, base printers, and X11.

Note that if you run the **oslevel** command after an ML update, the system will not report the ML in the **oslevel** command output. This output differs because the ML filesets are usually only a small subset of the operating system. The **instfix** command is a good tool for ML analysis. For example, the command **instfix -i | grep AIX_ML** will display *all* maintenance levels that have been installed on your system. To list only the *latest* maintenance level, you can use the **oslevel -r** command.

Another command that is useful for system information is the **uname** command. Issue the **uname -a** command to display the UNIX flavor, the system hostname, the operating system release, the operating system version, and the machine ID number. You can also get the version and release of the operating system with the **uname -vr** command. Note that **uname** will give the release level first, regardless of the argument order. Thus, "1 5" indicates version 5, release 1. The command **uname -m** displays machine ID in the form *xxyyyyyymmss*, which breaks down as follows:

xx	00 for RS/6000
yyyyyy	CPU ID
mm	Model identifier
ss	Submodel identifier

The command **oslevel** returns the AIX product level. Mine reads 5.1.0.0. Please refer to the man page for **uname** to help identify different machine models.

Your system maintenance level can be obtained from **bos.rte** history. Use the **lslpp -h** command to display the maintenance history and state. The -h option is best for reviewing what older filesets were installed and on what date the installation took place. The -l option will display the current patch level as updated to the /usr/lib/objrepos database. Please note that old filesets like DB2 version 2 will still need the -h option to see the current updates (this problem was fixed with DB2 version 5).

```
# lslpp -h bos.rte    ◀────────── Short listing

Fileset       Level   Action  Status  Date    Time
------------------------------------------------
Path: /usr/lib/objrepos
bos.rte
     5.1.0.0  COMMIT      COMPLETE  07/27/01  14:43:24
Path: /etc/objrepos
     5.1.0.1  COMMIT      COMPLETE  07/27/01  14:43:24
```

A quick snapshot of maintenance level and state can be obtained using the **-L** option to **lslpp**.

```
# lslpp -L bos.rte
```

```
  Fileset                     Level   State  Type  Description (Uninstaller)
  ------------------------------------------------------------------------
  bos.rte                     5.1.0.0   C     F     Base Operating System Runtime
State codes:
 A -- Applied.
 B -- Broken.
 C -- Committed.
 O -- Obsolete.  (partially migrated to newer version)
 ? -- Inconsistent State...Run lppchk -v.

Type codes:
 F -- Installp Fileset
 P -- Product
 C -- Component
 T -- Feature
 R -- RPM Package
```

The fix level, or the last field, of a fileset is incremented until a new cumulative fileset maintenance or base level is available. Fileset levels are identified using the *version.release.modification.fix* numbering scheme, for example, 5.1.0.1. If you experience problems, do not hesitate to call IBM Support for help.

Phone Support:	1-800-CALL-AIX

You can review the problem and service the database yourself if you have network access to IBMLink or Support Line sites. If you don't have network access to these sites, IBM provides periodic snapshots of the IBMLink question and service databases on CD-ROM. Order AIX Technical Library/6000 CD-ROM. See Appendix A for additional information on AIX help sites and archives on the Internet. A few key sources are listed here:

Web sites:	http://www.ibm.com/server/support (Needs JavaScript and cookies enabled)
	http://www.ibmlink.ibm.com/
	http://www.austin.ibm.com/services/
FTP site:	ftp://services.software.ibm.com/aix/fixes

You can download patches and fixes over the Internet using IBM's Web-based fix distribution support at http://www.ibm.com/server/support. On December 31, 2001, IBM withdrew the **FixDist** tool from service worldwide and replaced it with the Web-based fix distribution support. You can select maintenance by ML, PTF, and APAR numbers.

If you have access to a Usenet news service, check out the comp.unix.aix newsgroup, or browse its archives at http://groups.google.com/. The best help information comes from peers who are using AIX in the field. IBM support personnel and developers also watch these groups and may lend assistance.

Choosing an Installation Method

AIX can be installed using one of three methods: complete overwrite install, preservation install, or migration install. A complete overwrite install is used to install AIX on new computers or to overwrite a previous installation of the operating system without saving anything in the previous installation. A preservation install will attempt to preserve existing user directories in the root volume group (rootvg) by overwriting only the /, /usr, /var, and /tmp filesystems. As I will explain later in the chapter, a much safer strategy is to keep any user or local data in filesystems that do not reside in rootvg. The migration install option is used to retain the root volume group layout and system configuration files. This is the default installation option for AIX 5L version 5.1.

With any of these installation methods, you need to make sure that you have a good **mksysb**, or **sysback**, **rootvg** backup image. You may need to go back and retrieve a font file, or something, if you have a heavily customized system. Application fonts are the only things that I have ever lost with a migration upgrade. Having the backup tape makes it very easy to put the lost files back in place.

For an easy way out of a bad installation or upgrade, you should consider using the Alternate Disk Installation utility. Alternate Disk Install allows you to clone **rootvg** to an alternate set of disks. This technique can give you an easy way to recover from a failed migration (see "Using Alternate Disk Install," later in this chapter).

APPLY and COMMIT

Before installing new software or undertaking maintenance on an existing system, you need to have a back-out strategy in the event that problems occur during or after the installation. The AIX default is to add new software and maintenance to the system using the COMMIT option as opposed to the APPLY state. The APPLY option keeps a history file and a backup copy of each object replaced by the software update. If you are not happy with the update, you can REJECT the filesets and restore the previous version. When using SMIT to install software updates, set the COMMIT Software? options to No and the Save Replaced? option to Yes. These two SMIT options are mutually exclusive, meaning they must have opposite values. The command-line options are listed here:

```
# installp -qa -d /usr/sys/inst.images -X all    ◄──────── APPLY updates
# installp -rB -X all    ◄──────── REJECT updates
```

Once satisfied with the update, you can COMMIT the update to remove the backup copy of the previous version.

```
# installp -c -g -X all    ◄──────── COMMIT updates
```

or

```
# smitty install_commit    ◄──────── SMIT FastPath
```

The caveat to installing using the APPLY option is that additional disk space is required to hold the old version. If you don't have the disk space to spare, you must install the update with COMMIT. This option will save on disk space, but it does not provide a simple back-out mechanism. Make a full backup of your root volume group file systems prior to installing with COMMIT. In the event of a problem, you can restore the backup.

Install with COMMIT

```
# installp -qa -d /cdrom/usr/sys/inst.images -c -N all   ◄───┘
```

In the event that you must remove a committed lpp, you can invoke the deinstall function of the **installp** command. This **-u** option will remove product files, associated maintenance, and vital product data (VPD) from the system regardless of the product installation state.

```
# installp -u   ◄─────────────── fileset_name Remove software
```

As with all **installp** command options, it is always a good practice to add the **-p** option to *preview* the results first! As an example:

```
# installp -up fileset_name 1>/tmp/output 2>&1
# view /tmp/output
```

Filesystem Expansion On-the-Fly

To ensure that sufficient filesystem space is available, you can elect to have filesystem size automatically increased during the installation. Unfortunately, this process will sometimes overallocate filesystem space, the result being wasted disk space at the end of the installation. Automatic filesystem expansion can also cause the installation to abort if the requested increment in logical partitions is not available in the volume group. In most cases, you will be better off calculating the space required for the update and allocating the space manually before starting the install process. Remember you cannot easily shrink a filesystem once it is overallocated, but this is usually not a big problem with the large disks being produced today.

```
# installp -qa -d /cdrom/usr/sys/inst.images -X all
# installp -qa -d   ◄─────────────────── Auto expansion
/cdrom/usr/sys/inst.images all   ◄─┐
                                   └ No auto expansion
```

System State

When installing a new product release or maintenance, limit the activity on your system. For some products, this involves shutting down the application being updated and stopping any related subsystems and subservers. If it is controlled by the System

Resource Controller (SRC), use the **stopsrc** command to shut down subsystems and subservers. For example,

```
# stopsrc -g tcpip◄————— Stop the TCP/IP subsystem group
```

When updating your operating system or a group of products, it is easier to reduce system activity by shutting down to maintenance mode. This will stop all applications and subsystems and restrict access to the system other than from the system console.

```
# shutdown -m◄————— Shut down to maintenance mode
```

If maintenance mode is not required, you can temporarily inhibit nonroot login access by creating a /etc/nologin file. Each time a nonroot user attempts to log in, the contents of the /etc/nologin file are displayed. For example,

```
Login access is temporarily inhibited due to system maintenance
activities. Please try again after 7:30AM.
```

The /etc/nologin file can be an empty file. It is not the *contents* of the file but the very *existence* of the /etc/nologin file that prohibits nonroot logins. The /etc/nologin file, if it exists, is removed from the system as a normal part of the third phase of the boot process. Remember, if you have disabled remote root logins on the system (which is highly recommended) you must be on the console to log into the system if an /etc/nologin file exists! If you do not need to reboot your machine, then do not forget to remove this file, or all of the users will continue to be locked out when your maintenance window is complete.

Updating Existing AIX Systems

Installing an upgrade or maintenance to an existing AIX system is much easier if you have kept your user filesystems and local product data on non-rootvg volume groups. Before installing the upgrade or maintenance, the non-rootvg volume groups may be exported, protecting them from update problems.

CAUTION   It is extremely important to record the ownership of all of the /dev devices for logical volumes before you export the volume group. It is common for a nonroot user (db2adm) to own /dev devices for logical volumes. When you import a logical volume, all of the /dev logical volumes will be owned by root. To record the ownerships, run the command **ls -l /dev > /usr/local/etc/dev.list**.

After importing the volume group(s), you will have to restore the ownerships manually or with a script.

You can use the following command to export volume groups after unmounting all of the filesystems:

```
# exportvg <VGname>
```

Once the update is complete, the volume groups can be imported back into the system using

```
# importvg -y <VGname>  PhysicalVolume
```

For example,

```
# importvg -y appvg  hdisk10
# mount -a
```

If you need to specify the volume group *major number* for this volume group import, for example in an HACMP cluster, you can add the **-V *major_number*** command parameter as in the following example:

```
# importvg -V 46 -y appvg hdisk10
```

The preceding command specified that 46 is the major number for the **appvg** volume group.

To find the next available major number on the system, use the following command:

```
# lvlstmajor
```

If you have systems in an HACMP cluster, you must keep the device major numbers consistent so that both machines know what the major number of each shared volume group is.

NOTE   On a multidisk volume group, you need to specify only one disk in the volume group when using the **importvg** command.

There are two ways to perform an upgrade. If the AIX version and revision remain the same and you are going to a new modification and fix level (as an example, if you are currently at 4.3.2.0 and you want to upgrade to 4.3.3.0), there is a quick upgrade path. For this situation only, you can just stop all of the applications, lock out all of the users and export all of the non-rootvg volume groups, and then run **smitty update_all**. If you have the disk space available, you may want to APPLY the updates instead of using COMMIT. Using APPLY, you have the ability to reject the updates if things do not work as expected. This method works only if the AIX version and revision remain the same. However, if you are going to use the APPLY installation option, you first need to COMMIT everything currently on the system. On the command line, run the command **smitty install_commit**. Take all of the defaults and press ENTER twice. Once all of the previously APPLIED filesets are in the COMMIT state, you can proceed with the upgrade.

If you are upgrading to a new AIX version or release (if, for example, you are upgrading from AIX 4.3.3.0 to AIX version 5.1.0.0), you are required to boot the system into maintenance mode using the new installation CD-ROM. In this case, we are upgrading both the version and release levels. You must also boot from the installation CD-ROM if you are upgrading to a different version, for example, upgrading from 5.1.0.0 to 5.2.0.0.

- **If you have a PCI bus machine,** boot from the installation medium (CD-ROM is the only option for AIX 5.1 shipped from IBM). Insert the CD-ROM in the drive, turn on the power if necessary, and press the appropriate function key (refer to Chapter 7) as soon as the keyboard is initialized and the beep is sounded.

NOTE   Not all machines support a service mode boot list (see Appendix A).

- **If you have a Micro Channel machine with a key switch,** turn the key to service, insert the CD-ROM in the drive, reboot or turn the power on, and follow the prompts to identify the console and select the language and installation method.

Before starting a migration installation, run the **bootinfo -b** command to find the last boot device and write the **hdisk#** down for later reference. Before initiating a preservation install, record the location, layout, and space on each of the physical volumes to be used by the install process. Begin by displaying the physical volume names.

```
# lspv
hdisk0          000b8a3d84178021      rootvg
hdisk1          000b8a3d1384358b      rootvg
hdisk2          000b8a3d1382b3f9      appvg
hdisk3          000b8a3d1382b821      appvg
hdisk4          000b8a3d1382bb65      appvg
hdisk5          000b8a3d1382beac      appvg
hdisk6          000b8a3d1382c1e3      appvg
hdisk7          000b8a3d1382c512      appvg
```

For each physical volume, display the location information.

```
# lsdev -C -l hdisk0
hdisk0 Available 10-60-00-8,0 16 Bit SCSI Disk Drive
```

Use **df** and **lsvg** to total the used and free space making up the root file systems and the root volume group.

```
# df -v / /usr /tmp /var
Filesystem   Total KB   used   free    $used iused  ifree  %iused Mounted
/dev/hd4     32768      29796  2972    90$   1864   6328   22%    /
/dev/hd2     499712     456704 43008   91$   17438  107490 13%    /usr
/dev/hd3     323584     21068  302516  6$    103    81817  0%     /tmp
/dev/hd9var  1048576    227520 821056  21$   1635   260509 0%     /var
```

```
# lsvg rootvg
VOLUME GROUP:    rootvg              VG IDENTIFIER:    000b8a3db1056b23
VG STATE:        active              PP SIZE:         16 megabyte(s)
VG PERMISSION:   read/write          TOTAL PPs:       1084 (17344 megabytes)
MAX LVs:         256                 FREE PPs:        710 (11360 megabytes)
LVs:             9                   USED PPs:        374 (5984 megabytes)
OPEN LVs:        8                   QUORUM:          1
TOTAL PVs:       2                   VG DESCRIPTORS:  3
STALE PVs:       0                   STALE PPs:       0
ACTIVE PVs:      2                   AUTO ON:         yes
MAX PPs per PV:  1016                MAX PVs:         32
LTG size:        128 kilobyte(s)     AUTO SYNC:       no
HOT SPARE:       no
```

Cloning AIX Systems

When you clone AIX systems on *identical* hardware (exact same hardware!), you can just use a **mksysb** bootable backup image. To clone a system to *different* hardware, you have to follow a special procedure and boot from the installation medium provided by IBM. The problem with booting from a **mksysb** tape on different hardware is that you will not have all of the necessary drivers for any different hardware architecture on the backup tape. To get around this little problem, we boot from the installation CD-ROM, with the new **mksysb** tape in the tape drive. When we get to the Options menu, we select **Start Maintenance Mode For System Recovery** and then select **Install From A System Backup** at the bottom of the list. Then the menu will prompt you to select the tape drive that holds the **mksysb** tape. The system will install the system from the tape and use the CD-ROM to get the proper drivers and filesets for the particular machine. This is equivalent to running **smitty cfgmgr** with the Base Operating System CD-ROM in the CD drive to automatically add drivers to the system.

INSTALLING AIX

If you are installing a brand new pSeries or RISC System/6000, parts of the base operating system (BOS) and product runtime environments may be preinstalled on the system. Note that the preinstalled system does not represent the full product or maintenance set. You must complete the installation of the remaining products and maintenance before configuring the system for use.

If you will be using a serial-attached TTY as the console, use the following settings on the TTY:

- 9600 bps
- 8,1,none
- 24 × 80 Display

- Auto LF off
- Line Wrap on
- New Line CR

Follow this ten-step list to install AIX:

1. Complete installation planning.
2. Turn on all attached devices.
3. Set the key switch (if present) to the Service position.
4. Insert the installation media or **mksysb** bootable tape (you may need to power on).
5. Turn on system power. (Don't worry, you have plenty of time!)
6. For PCI-bus systems only: press the appropriate function key for your model *just after* the keyboard is initialized and the beep sounds (usually F5).
7. Select console and *installation* language when prompted.

```
******* Please define the System Console. *******

Type a 1 and press Enter to use this terminal as the
    system console.
Pour definir ce terminal comme console systeme, appuyez
    sur 1 puis sur Entree.
Taste 1 und anschliessend die Eingabetaste druecken, um
    diese Datenstation als Systemkonsole zu verwenden.
Premere il tasto 1 ed Invio per usare questo terminal
    come console.
Escriba 1 y pulse Intro para utilizar esta terminal como
    consola del sistema.
Escriviu 1 1 i premeu Intro per utilitzar aquest
    terminal com a consola del sistema.
Digite um 1 e pressione Enter para utilizar este terminal
    como console do sistema.
```

```
>>>  1 Type 1 and press Enter to have English during install.
     2 Entreu 2 i premeu Intro per veure la installaci en catal.
     3 Entrez 3 pour effectuer l'installation en franais.
     4 Fr Installation in deutscher Sprache 4 eingeben
       und die Eingabetaste drcken.
     5 Immettere 5 e premere Invio per l'installazione in italiano.
     6 Digite 6 e pressione Enter para usar Portugus na instalao.
     7 Escriba 7 y pulse Intro para la instalacin en espaol.

                                               |

     88  Help ?

>>> Choice [1]:
```

8. When the Welcome To Base Operating System Installation And Maintenance screen is displayed, you must decide whether to proceed with installation defaults or to verify and/or modify settings before continuing. Enter **88** at any time to display help information.

```
                    Welcome to Base Operating System
                       Installation and Maintenance

Type the number of your choice and press Enter.  Choice is indicated by >>>.

>>> 1 Start Install Now with Default Settings

    2 Change/Show Installation Settings and Install

    3 Start Maintenance Mode for System Recovery




    88  Help ?
    99  Previous Menu
>>> Choice [1]: _
```

Installation modifications include

- **Installation method**
  - New and complete overwrite install
  - Preservation install
  - Migration install
- **Primary language environment**   en_US for United States English

```
                      Installation and Settings

Either type 0 and press Enter to install with current settings, or type the
number of the setting you want to change and press Enter.

    1  System Settings:
         Method of Installation............Preservation
         Disk Where You Want to Install.....hdisk0...

    2  Primary Language Environment Settings (AFTER Install):
         Cultural Convention...............English (United States)
         Language .........................English (United States)
         Keyboard .........................English (United States)
         Keyboard Type.....................Default

    3  Advanced Options

>>> 0  Install with the current settings listed above.

                      +----------------------------------------------------
    88  Help ?        |  WARNING: Base Operating System Installation will
    99  Previous Menu |  destroy or impair recovery of SOME data on the
                      |  destination disk hdisk0.
>>> Choice [0]: _
```

- **Installation disks**   Normally hdisk0 and possibly hdisk1. (Specify all of the disks in rootvg, even the mirrored drives!) It is important to know he actual location code of the disk you found using the **lsdev -C -l hdisk#** command. Note that hdisk0 on the old system may be hdisk2 after booting from the install disk.

- **File system sizing**   There is an option to resize logical volumes for an exact fit if overallocated.

- **Trusted computing base**   Turn on high-level system security. TCB cannot be removed without reinstallation of AIX, and TCB can be installed on the system only at initial system installation time. TCB performs a checksum on critical system files to ensure they have not been hacked.

9. Turn the key (if present) to the normal position.

10. After the installation is complete, the system will reboot and the SMIT Installation Assistant screen will be displayed. The SMIT Installation Assistant will help you finish the system configuration. This will include setting the date and time, setting the root password, setting up the network interface, and so on. The Installation Assistant will be displayed at each system boot until you have selected Tasks Completed—Exit To AIX Login to signal that your configuration changes have been completed.

```
                          Maintenance

          Type the number of your choice and press Enter.

          >>> 1  Access a Root Volume Group
              2  Copy a System Dump to Removable Media
              3  Access Advanced Maintenance Functions
              4  Install from a System Backup













             88   Help ?
             99   Previous Menu

          >>> Choice [1]:
```

```
                    Choose mksysb Device
     Type the number of the device containing the system backup to be
     installed and press Enter.

          Device Name                        Path Name

     >>>   1 tape/scsi/8mm5gb                /dev/rmt0
           2 cdrom/scsi/scsd                 /dev/cd0




          88   Help ?
          99   Previous Menu
     >>> Choice [1]: _
```

Complete Overwrite

A complete overwrite does just what the name implies: it overwrites everything on the target disks. Use this method to install AIX 5L on a new machine or to completely overwrite an existing system. If a graphics adapter is present, the BOS installation will automatically install all of the runtime filesets along with any other filesets required for the installed hardware on the system.

You will again notice that you now have to accept the electronic license agreements before the installation will continue. Failure to accept the license agreement will cancel the installation. If you are using a modified bosinst.data file for an unattended installation, then you will need to set the ACCEPT_LICENSES field, in the control_flow stanza, to accept the licenses and prevent a user prompt at the first system reboot.

At the first system reboot, you will be presented with the Configuration Assistant if you have a graphics console and the Installation Assistant if you have an ASCII console. The Installation and Configuration Assistants are both used for the same purpose, to customize the newly installed system. These are SMIT panels that will guide you through setting up the following items:

- Setting the system date, time, and time zone
- Setting the root password
- Managing system storage and paging space
- Configuring network communications (TCP/IP)
- Configuring a Web server to run the Web-based System Manager in a browser
- Configuring the Online Documentation Library service

The final option is to exit the Configuration Assistant. When you exit the Configuration Assistant or the Installation Assistant, the "first boot" flag is cleared and these screens will not appear on any subsequent reboots. If you need to access either of these configuration tools again, you can enter **install_assist** or **configassist** on the command line.

Migration Upgrade

The migration upgrade is the default installation path to get to AIX 5.1, including version 3.2.5 and any version of AIX 4. You can upgrade directly to 5L from any previous AIX version. The migration installation looks at all of the filesets currently on the system and determines which filesets need to be updated and replaced. The following filesets are automatically installed or updated:

- BOS commands
- BOS libraries
- BOS curses and termcap
- BOS networking
- BOS directories, files, and symbolic links
- Messages
- X11R3
- X11R4
- X11 fonts

The migration procedure consists of the following four steps:

1. Completing the installation prerequisites
2. Readying the system for OS upgrade
3. Booting into maintenance mode with the installation media
4. Completing the BOS installation after an initial reboot

The prerequisites include connecting any external devices and ensuring each device is powered on. Make sure that the root user has a primary authentication method of SYSTEM. To check this, enter the following command:

```
lsuser -a auth1 root
```

The command should return the following:

```
root auth1=SYSTEM
```

If you get any other response, change the value with the following command:

```
chuser auth1=SYSTEM root
```

Make sure that you get everyone off the system, and it is a good idea to disable all nonroot logins by creating a /etc/nologin file. Put a message in the file, something like System is down for upgrade. . . Try again later. . ..

The system must have a minimum of 64MB of RAM. You can list the real memory with either of the following commands:

```
bootinfo -r
lsattr -El sys0 | grep realmem
```

Both of these commands list the memory in kilobytes.

Run a system backup, preferably a **mksysb** or **sysback** image. You may lose a file or two that you want during the upgrade, and a backup tape can save a lot of trouble. The only file I have ever lost was a special font file for an application, which was easily retrieved from the tape.

After the prerequisites are complete, we need to prepare the system for installation. First, power the system down if it is running. If your system has a key, turn the key to the service position. Either the word "Service" or a diagram or a wrench specifies the service key position. Turn on all external devices, and allow all external disk drives time to spin up and devices to complete self-tests.

Next, we are ready to boot from the installation medium, which is a CD-ROM for AIX 5.1. Insert the CD-ROM and power on the system (you may need to power on the system and insert the CD-ROM—you have plenty of time to do both). If you have a PCI-bus machine (no key switch!), then *just after* the beep sounds and the keyboard is initialized, press the appropriate function key (usually F5). Pressing the function key tells the system to boot into maintenance mode. After a few minutes, you will see c31 appear in the LED display. On the console, type 1 or press F1 and then ENTER to define the console. Next you are asked to select a language for the *installation*.

NOTE   The installation and production languages can differ.

Then we get to the welcome screen. Always select **Change/Show Installation Settings** to verify the installation disk(s) and language environment. When everything looks good, enter **0** (zero) and then press ENTER to start the installation. If your system has a key switch, you can turn it back to the "Normal" position at any time before the installation completes.

Install the ML Patches

After the installation completes, make sure that you install the latest maintenance level (ML) patches. You can download these from IBM or call 1-800-CALL-AIX to order the latest set on CD-ROM. Use the SMIT FastPath **smitty update_all** to install the latest ML filesets and reboot the system one more time. You are ready to go!

Preservation Installation

A *preservation installation* is intended for use when you want to save only the user-defined filesystems and the /home filesystem but not the system configuration as in a migration installation. The preservation installation will also preserve the page and dump devices. The preservation installation will completely overwrite /usr, /var, /tmp, and / (root) filesystems. You may want to pay particular attention to the **/usr/local** directories, if you have anything there. AIX 5L installs links in /usr/local/apache/htdocs and creates two files in /usr/local/LUM/en_US by default. If you have not created a separate filesystem for /usr/local you should think about making this directory structure a separate filesystem before any upgrade.

Using Alternate Disk Install

If your environment is like mine, then you are not allowed *any* down time! Even reboots are moving to a need-to-have basis. I am guessing that "need to have" is when the applications and databases start acting screwy. Since our environment is driven by the business, which we have no control over, using Alternate Disk Install can greatly simplify maintenance procedures and system upgrades, as long as the AIX upgrade is not a new release or version, which requires booting into maintenance mode from the installation media.

Alternate Disk Install is a very nice tool that allows you to do system upgrades and maintenance on a live system, to a different disk set, without interruption. The requirement for Alternate Disk Install is an equal number of disks currently in the rootvg volume group dedicated as *alternate disks.* You first add these alternate disks to the rootvg volume group, and then you can clone your system to the alternate disk(s) as a backup or do your maintenance upgrade as the system is cloning to the alternate disk(s) in a single procedure. When the process is complete, the system's boot list is changed automatically so that the system will boot into the new environment, on the alternate disks, on the next system reboot. Let's set it up.

Alternate Disk Install Procedure

The **bos.alt_disk_install** fileset must be installed on the system. We are going to look at two options for using alternate disk install. The first is an alternate **mksysb** disk installation, and next we will look at alternate disk **rootvg** cloning.

An alternate **mksysb** installation allows installing a **mksysb** image that was created on another system onto an alternate rootvg disk on a target system. The command to execute is:

```
# alt_disk_install -d /dev/rmt0 hdisk1
```

This assumes that the **mksysb** tape is loaded in the **/dev/rmt0** tape drive and hdisk1 is your alternate **rootvg** disk. The system will now contain two root volume groups, the original **rootvg** and a second volume group called **altinst_rootvg**. After this procedure completes, the system's boot list is automatically changed to boot onto the new

atlinst_rootvg disk(s) on the next system reboot. At this point, **atlinst_rootvg** will become **rootvg** and the original **rootvg** will be called **old_rootvg**. You can see this transition using the **lspv** command before and after. To go back to the original **rootvg**, change the boot list and reboot the system.

You can do the same task using the SMIT FastPath **smitty alt_mksysb**, as shown in Figure 6-1.

We can also clone **rootvg** to another disk, or disk set. This procedure is called *alternate disk rootvg cloning*. Cloning the root volume group to an alternate disk, or disk set, has some nice advantages. You can just clone **rootvg** and have an online backup copy available, just in case.

You can also clone **rootvg** and at the same time install ML upgrades on the system. Then the next time you reboot, you will be running on the new ML and you can test it with the ability to go back in time by just changing the boot list and rebooting the system. There are two command options, one for each task.

To only clone rootvg to have a backup copy, issue the following command:

```
# alt_disk_install -C hdisk1
```

assuming `hdisk1` is your alternate disk.

To clone **rootvg** and also install maintenance updates, issue the following command:

```
# atl_disk_install -C -F update_all -l /dev/cd0 hdisk1
```

assuming `/dev/cd0` holds the maintenance updates and `hdisk1` is your alternate disk.

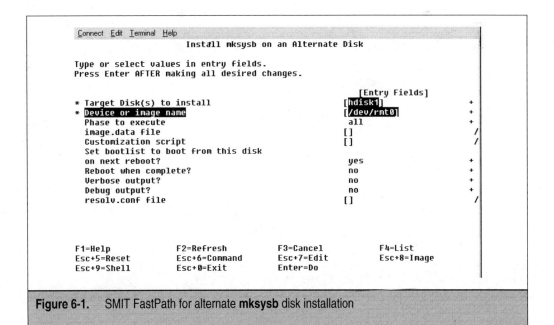

Figure 6-1. SMIT FastPath for alternate **mksysb** disk installation

The SMIT FastPath is **smitty alt_clone**, as shown in Figure 6-2.

If you want to remove your alternate rootvg, *do not* use the **exportvg** command. Instead, use the command

```
# alt_disk_install -X
```

This command removes the alternate disk definition, **altinst_rootvg**, from the ODM. If you exported the volume group, then you have to create a new /etc/filesystems file before the next system reboot.

It might be helpful to note that, even though the **altinst_rootvg** is removed from the ODM on the hdisk0 rootvg, the cloned image on hdisk1 remains intact and can still be booted from by changing the **boot list**. To see the detail of hdisk1, run the following command:

```
# lqueryvg -Atp hdisk1
```

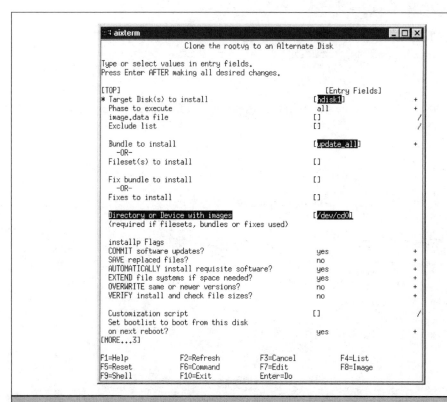

Figure 6-2.   SMIT FastPath for alternate disk rootvg cloning

Cloning AIX Systems to New Hardware

We are getting a lot of new machine upgrades. Most of our H-50 and below RS/6000 machines are being replaced by either H-80 RS/6000s or 6H1 pSeries machines (some of these machines have the same CPU). Each system changeover requires using the cloning procedures to different hardware. This is really very straightforward and easy to do once you get the procedure down.

The first thing that you want to do is run a fresh **mksysb** on the current machine. Make sure that all of the applications are stopped. Bring down all of the databases. Get all of the users off the system and then lock out all nonroot users by creating an **/etc/nologin** file. I think you get the picture: we want a completely idle system before running the **mksysb** backup. You should also extract a file from the **mksysb** tape using the following procedure to ensure that the backup is good. This procedure assumes the rmt0 tape drive is used. Restoring a single file from a **mksysb** tape requires the nonrewinding tape mode (**/dev/rmt0.1**). This can be time-consuming, so it may help to also make an online **mksysb** backup to a non-rootvg or NFS filesystem. If you use this method, make sure that the root users on both systems can write large files and the filesystem is large file enabled. Insert the newly created **mksysb** tape in the tape drive and run the following commands:

- `# tctl -f /dev/rmt0 rewind` ◄——— Rewind the tape
- `# tctl -f /dev/rmt0.1 fsf 3` ◄—— Fast forward 3 records (/dev/rmt0.1 = no rewind)
- `# restore -xvpf /dev/rmt0.1 ./etc/hosts` ◄—— Extract the /etc/hosts file from tape

NOTE Do not forget the dots. If you omit the dot before `/etc/hosts`, the file will not be installed.

If this procedure is successful, then we most likely have a good backup. The only way to really know if you have a good **mksysb** backup is to restore the system!

The next steps will guide you through the cloning process:

1. Insert the current AIX release CD-ROM, the same AIX version that the **mksysb** backup was done on, into the CD-ROM drive.

2. Insert the **mksysb** tape into the tape drive.

3. Power down the system.

4. Ensure that all of the external devices, if any, are powered on.

5. Turn the key mode switch, if present, to the "Service" position (Micro Channel machines).

6. Turn the power on.

7. (If you have a key mode switch, skip this step.) Just as the keyboard is initialized and the beep sounds (PCI-bus machines only), press the appropriate function key, usually F5. This tells the PCI-bus machine that you want to enter service mode.

8. After a few minutes, you will be prompted to define the console by entering **1** and pressing ENTER.

9. At the next prompt, select **Start Maintenance Mode For System Recovery**.

10. Then select **Install From A System Backup**.

11. The next option allows you to point to the tape drive that holds the **mksysb** tape.

12. At this point, the tape header information is read, and after a minute or two you will have the option to start the restore or to **Change/Show The Installation Settings**. Always select the **Change/Show** option to verify that the system is planning to do what you are expecting it to do. Verify the installation disk(s) and the language environment.

13. Then start the restore. You can turn the key mode switch to normal at any time, if present.

14. After the installation is complete, the system will automatically get any new drivers and filesets it needs for the new hardware from the installation CD-ROM.

15. Next, install the latest maintenance-level patches for your AIX version from IBM. Even if you had previously installed the ML patches on the old hardware, you will need to go through the process again. From the command line, enter **smitty update_all**, point to the ML patch media, and press ENTER twice. You need another reboot after the ML patches are installed.

INSTALLING LICENSED PROGRAM PRODUCTS (LPP)

Installing Licensed Program Products (LPP) can be managed using the SMIT install FastPath or by using the **installp** command. It's much easier to do this with SMIT in that SMIT will remind you of all the options associated with performing an install or updates.

You can also preview your installations and create your own bundle lists at the same time. Running **installp** in the preview mode outputs important details to standard error.

```
# installp -Xqap -d /cdrom/usr/sys/inst.images all
```

The preceding command will send standard error and standard output to the screen, so let's save this output to the file /tmp/output with the following command:

```
# installp -Xqap -d /cdrom/usr/sys/inst.images all 1>/tmp/output 2>&1
```

Now we can **vi** the /tmp/output file and trim the file to a simple list of needed filesets found under SUCCESS in the list. Give the new list file a name like /tmp/

mylist. Cut out any fileset that you do not need, including devices (most devices are already installed by the migration). Now preview your installation using your new list file.

```
# installp -Xqap -d /cdrom/usr/sys/inst.images -f /tmp/myfile 1>/tmp/output 2>&1
```

Next view the /tmp/output file for details. When the install previews with no errors, then you can remove the **-p** option and run the installation for real.

To install everything on the CD-ROM, you can run the following command:

```
# installp -qa -d /cdrom/usr/sys/inst.images -X all
```
◄──── Install *all* on CD-ROM

Products and maintenance will usually be installed into the LPP directory, /usr/lpp. A separate subdirectory is created for each product, package, and fileset.

The contents of the installation CD-ROM may be reviewed by selecting List Software And Related Information from the SMIT Software Installation And Maintenance menu or by executing **installp** with the **-l** option.

In the event that one or more of the applications will be installed on multiple machines, you might want to copy the contents of the installation CD-ROM to disk for use with an install server. Select Copy Software To Hard Disk For Future Installation from the **smitty bffcreate** FastPath menu. You may also use the **bffcreate** command to copy the software update to disk.

```
# bffcreate -qv -d'/dev/rmt0' -t'/usr/sys/inst.images' '-X' all
# smitty maintain_software
```

It is a good practice to make /usr/sys/inst.images a separate filesystem from /usr so that you can recover the disk space later if needed. The filesystem can still be mounted on /usr/sys/inst.images. Just make sure that you do not mount it over files that you need (see the end of the section "Creating New Bootable Media and Backups," later in this chapter).

To install *all* software on the media, invoke SMIT with the **install_all** FastPath name. You will be prompted for the media type, and installation will proceed using default options. If you want to select other update options or install a subset of the updates on the media, start SMIT using the **install_latest** FastPath. Use the F4 key to list the products available on the media. Individual entries may be tagged for installation using the F7 key.

```
# smit install_latest
```

In the previous section on installation planning, I discussed the pros and cons of installing with COMMIT and automatically extending the filesystem. The same arguments relate to product and maintenance updates. If you have extra disk space to play with, electing not to COMMIT and allowing filesystem extension will make the install smoother.

During the installation and update process, progress information is displayed by SMIT and the **installp** command. SMIT will log this information to the $HOME/ smit.log file. You may wish to redirect output (both standard error and standard output) from **installp** to a file if it was invoked from the command line. Once the install has completed, verify the status of the update.

ifor Licensing

The proper name for the licensing system is LUM, but I still refer to the license system as ifor/LS. Anytime you install a new LPP application, you will have to deal with the license. Examples are C and C++ for AIX. Both of these products have the license files on the installation CD-ROM, but you must register the license with the ifor/LS server.

The first step is to ensure that you install the license fileset. If you do not, it will be intuitively obvious when you cannot find the license file. Always refer to the installation documentation for the procedure to install and license the product and the full path to the license file.

The LUN, as it's called, requires a couple of filesets for the basics and a few more optional filesets are available:

The Basics

```
ifor_ls.base.cli
ifor_ls.msg.en_US.base.cli
```

The Optional Filesets

```
ifor_ls.compat.cli
ifor_ls.html.en_US.base.cli
ifor_ls.java.gui
ifor_ls.msg.en_US.compat.cli
ifor_ls.msg.en_US.java.gui
```

To configure a license server, you have two options. If you are running CDE, open a window and type in **i4cfg**, and a GUI interface will appear after a minute or two (slow Java). For an ASCII display, use the command **i4cfg -script**. Both commands ask the same questions. Just follow through the questions and register your product with the newly configured license server. There are five types of licenses: node-lock, concurrent node-lock, concurrent-use, use-once, and compound.

Node-Lock License

A *node-lock* license is machine specific. In a node-lock license environment, each machine must have its own unique license key. For this option, it does matter *where* the licensed application runs; thus it *cannot* execute via an NFS-mounted filesystem *unless* the NFS client has a node-lock license. However, if the NFS server has a node-lock license, then none of the NFS clients will be able to run the licensed product unless also locally licensed.

Concurrent Node-Lock License

A *concurrent node-lock* license allows a fixed number of concurrent users to execute the licensed product at the same time on a single machine. The same NFS client restrictions apply as for a node-lock license.

Concurrent Use License

A *current use* license allows the license to *float* within the network, and thus to each of the NFS clients. One or more license servers control access to the application throughout the network.

Use-Once License

A *use-once* license is used up as soon as it is consumed. One time, that's it!

Compound License

A *compound* license contains a password that allows it to create more licenses as required. This type of license is primarily used for license redistribution.

Verifying Installation with lppchk

After a new installation or a maintenance-level upgrade (and just periodically!), you should run **lppchk -v** from the command line to verify that all of the system's filesets are installed properly. If you run this command and you receive any message about BROKEN or OBSOLETE filesets, then further investigation needs to be performed to determine the cause. The OBSOLETE state is usually because mixed AIX versions of a fileset are installed. A BROKEN fileset could indicate a serious problem, and you may need to deinstall and reinstall the application filesets.

INSTALLING NON-LPP PRODUCTS

It's a good idea to keep local, public domain, and vendor products separate from BOS directories. This will ensure that they will not be clobbered by BOS upgrades and installations. A common practice is to create a local product filesystem called /usr/local. Within /usr/local, create subdirectories bin, lib, etc, and src. You can add these directories to the default command PATH and create symbolic links from BOS directories, if required.

REMOVING INSTALLED SOFTWARE

When you do not need an application on the system, you can remove it through the SMIT software maintenance utilities. Using SMIT is the easiest method. One thing to be careful of is the requisite software for each of the filesets. I recommend that you *never* set the Remove Requisite Software option to Yes. You just might have to reinstall the entire system from a backup tape, if you have one. Always select No for Remove Requisite Software so if you get any kind of error, you can remove the filesets one at a time. This is an easy process because SMIT will tell you each fileset that has a requisite dependency and you can independently determine if your system requires the fileset(s) for anything other than the piece of software that you are removing.

To remove installed software, just run **smit,** or **smitty** for ASCII, from the command line. Select the first option, Software Installation And Maintenance. Next, select the third option, Software Maintenance And Utilities. The third option in the next panel is Removed Installed Software. The SMIT panel will be sitting at the Software Name prompt. Press F4 to get a listing of all of the installed software on the system, or, if you know the fileset name, enter the name of the fileset in the input field.

CAUTION   The third option is Remove Dependent Software? and has a default of No. Use caution in setting this field to Yes!

Always start out by setting the Preview Only? option to Yes and looking at what the SMIT procedure is going to do to your system. The main point is to be *very* careful removing software from your system.

APPLYING MAINTENANCE LEVEL (ML) PATCHES

The first and foremost rule of system maintenance: "If it isn't broken, don't fix it!" If only it were that easy! The AIX operating system and product set is made up of a large number of subsystems. Each subsystem contains hundreds or thousands of components. In this not-so-perfect world, problems will crop up in many of these objects. Try to stay as current as possible. Sometimes an ML release does not go as planned, such as ML 7 for AIX 4.3.3. ML 8 was close to follow, and ML 9 was the last ML release for AIX 4.3.3 as of this writing.

All the operating system and applications vendors are doing their best to drive product error rates down. This is a very difficult task that is complicated in shared-library environments. Think of the number of commands and subsystems that depend on libc.a! IBM has addressed the problems encountered with the old selective-fix strategy by packaging fixes by fileset into maintenance levels.

The AIX 5L maintenance strategy packages prereq and coreq fixes together by fileset. A fileset is the smallest updatable unit and represents a specific function. Maintenance levels are packaged and shipped at a frequency of three or four times a year. AIX 5L also provides **installp** options. Most notable are the flags **-V**, which adjusts the verbosity of status messages; **-u**, which provides deinstall capability for COMMITED products; **-L**, which indicates which products are already installed; and **-g**, which automatically installs, commits, or rejects requisite software (**-g** can be dangerous!). The preferred ML installation method is **smitty update_all** or using **smitty alt_clone** if you have alternate **rootvg** disks.

The rules for installing maintenance are the same as described in the previous section on installing program products. For distributed environments, you may wish to copy the maintenance set to disk for access from an install server. You might also choose to build a reference system image accessible from a network install server.

Read the maintenance documentation carefully before beginning the update. A short description of maintenance levels or supplemental information on the media may be displayed from **smitty list_media** or by using **installp** with the **-i** or **-A** options.

```
# installp -iq -d /dev/cd0 all    ◄─────── Display supplemental information
# installp -qA -d /dev/cd0 all    ◄─────── Display APAR information
```

Applying Versus Commiting

You do have two options for installation. You can keep a backup copy of the old stuff by only installing the ML in an APPLIED state. However, it is *extremely* important that you commit everything already on the system first!

Before installing a new ML, always run the following command:

```
# smitty install_commit
```

Take the default of ALL filesets and press ENTER twice. The COMMIT process removes the old copies of the APPLIED product and will give you back some /usr filesystem space, maybe not much.

Now you can install the ML patch set and reboot the system—yes, you *must* reboot!

```
# smitty update_all
```

Since the default is to COMMIT, you must manually set the options to install the ML package in an APPLIED state.

- Select **COMMIT Softare Updates?** | **No**
- Select **SAVED Replaced Files?** | **Yes**

These two options are mutually exclusive and must have opposite values.

Testing Period

Test? Why test? Have you ever heard this before? Any time you are going to install a new ML at your site, get a test/development box and install the ML patches in the APPLIED state. Then test it for several weeks. This should give you time to find any obvious bugs in the software update. Of course, it may not be a bug; it could be a feature! Just having the code on the box for a few weeks does not constitute "tested." You have to exercise the system and all of the applications to ensure that everything not only works but causes no additional system load or problems.

Why smitty install_commit Is So Important

Before installing any software in an APPLIED state, you should always COMMIT everything already installed. The reason we use the APPLIED state in the first place is to have a means of backing out of the mess created by the newly APPLIED software.

To cleanly back out, we just reject the updates using SMIT software maintenance utilities. However, if you have other software in an APPLIED state and you need to reject updates, and you do the deed, you may end up in a very unstable system state. I saw a guy reject ALL updates after a screwy upgrade and he had *not* previously committed everything on the system. The result was not pretty! He removed a large portion of the operating system and application updates and went back in time two years! Needless to say, the backup tapes were called back and he updated his resume.

Always run this before installing new software in an APPLIED state:

```
# smitty install_commit
```

Using smitty update_all

The IBM-recommended method for installing ML patch updates is to use **smitty update_all**. When you use this method, the system is queried for installed filesets that require updating and each one is automatically installed. I recommend that you first commit everything with **smitty install_commit** and then use **smitty update_all** to install the new updates in an APPLIED state. If you have a problem, then reject the updates and go back to the old code. This is an easy way to keep your job.

Installing Individual APARs and PTFs

You install individual APARs and PTFs the same way you install individual filesets. Put the installation CD-ROM in the drive and run **smitty install_latest**. Then press F4 to get a list of the filesets on the installation CD-ROM. The F7 key selects each fileset and pressing ENTER performs the install. You should always install APARs and PTFs in an APPLIED state, just in case.

Rejecting Updates

When things go bump after an update, you can easily back out if you followed our procedure. The first thing you should do after you install the latest ML and find a new problem is to call IBM AIX Support at 1-800-CALL-AIX and let them help you debug the problem before you reject any updates.

If IBM could not fix the problem, your last course of action is to reject the updates. If, and I mean *if*, you previously committed all of the software before updating the system, we can just reject the new updates and the old version will be put back in place. If you did not previously commit everything, you may still be able to recover, but you will have to pick out exactly the fileset(s) that you want to reject. Having to pick and choose can be a nightmare, and you should probably go ahead and call back the backup tapes, just in case.

To reject updates, enter **smitty software_maintenance** on the command line. Select the second option, Reject Applied Software Updates. You will be prompted for Software Name. You have two options: press F4 for a list and use the F7 key to select each software component to reject, or just enter **ALL** to reject all software in an APPLIED state.

POST INSTALLATION AND MAINTENANCE TASKS

With the installation or maintenance process complete, there is still a bit of tidying up to be done before making the system available for use. A new installation requires that you set default system and environment variables. If you installed over an existing system, you will need to restore the previous environment. Product updates or maintenance will require testing before committing or rejecting the update. Finally, create new stand-alone media and take a fresh backup of the new system. A clean snapshot can be used as a reference point for installing additional machines or as a fallback should problems arise in the future.

Review Install / Update Status

Review the status of software product and maintenance updates using List All Applied But Not Committed Software from the **smitty installp** menu or by invoking **lslpp** from the command line.

```
# lslpp -h bos.rte       ◄───────── Display LPP history


Fileset     Level  Action  Status  Date   Time
---------------------------------------------
Path: /usr/lib/objrepos
bos.rte
   5.1.0.0  COMMIT    COMPLETE  07/26/01  17:52:34
Path: /etc/objrepos
bos.rte
   5.1.0.0  COMMIT    COMPLETE  07/26/01  17:52:34
```

LPP software can be in one of the following states:

- **APPLY**   Fileset was being applied.
- **COMMIT**   Fileset was being committed.
- **REJECT**   Applied fileset was being rejected.
- **DEINSTALL**   Fileset was being removed from the system.
- **CLEANUP**   Fileset cleanup follows failed APPLY or COMMIT.

In the event of problems with the update, invoke cleanup and reinstall. LPP cleanup can be executed from **smitty cleanup** or via the **installp -C** option. Installations using

SMIT or the **installp** command will normally perform any cleanup automatically in the event of a failure.

```
# smitty cleanup
# installp -C <Fileset>
```

Restoring Your Environment

Setting default system environments is a final step for the installation paths described thus far. This involves setting or validating the default language, time zone, console type, number of licensed users, and number of virtual terminals. IBM has kindly provided a SMIT FastPath that addresses each of these variables. With root permissions, invoke the SMIT system FastPath.

```
# smitty system
```

In a networked environment, you will also need to set your network interface address and characteristics.

Set the root account password. The default installation does not provide a password for root. Need I say more?

Restore any configuration tables from the previous system, and reimport any volume groups exported as part of the preliminary installation planning.

```
# importvg -y <VGname> -V <MajorNumber> <PhysicalVolume>
```

You can also use the SMIT FastPath **smitty importvg** and remember to restore the ownership of the logical volume devices if needed. The Major Number will be assigned by the system if it is omitted. You will need to supply a Major Number if you are running HACMP and servers share the same disk(s).

Creating New Bootable Media and Backups

Next, make sure you have multiple copies of stand-alone bootable media that reflect the new system's install and maintenance level. Notice I said *multiple copies*. I must admit that I have been bitten more than once having only a single copy of some crucial bit of data. Create a backup image of the new rootvg on tape using the **mksysb** command. These tapes can be used to recover from a disk failure or be used to install additional machines. Begin by using the **mkszfile** command to create an /image.data file. This file contains descriptive information about the filesystems in the rootvg. Edit this file so that it contains only those filesystems you wish to include in your reference set. Use the following procedures to create the backup and bootable images. When booting from the stand-alone tape, the AIX Install/Maint shell is executed, which will guide you through the restoration process.

To create a bootable backup tape:

1. `# mkszfile` ◄——— Create a new /image.data file
2. `# tctl -f /dev/rmt0 rewind` ◄——— Rewind tape

3. # mksysb /dev/rmt0   Create backup.

4. # chdev -l rmt0 -a block_size=<blocksize>   Reset tape block size.

DISTRIBUTED SYSTEM INSTALLATION

If installing or updating a single system isn't problem enough, think about repeating the process over and over again in a multisystem environment! In many cases, these systems represent both disk and nondisk configurations.

NFS Installation Support

In networked environments with existing AIX systems, copy product and maintenance images to a file system, /inst.images. NFS export this filesystem to each of the remote sites. This method requires repeating the installation process on each machine. It provides the capability of individually tailoring the update on each system.

Creating a Reference System

To minimize the amount of time and work required to update multiple disk systems, create a single reference system image that can be cloned on each machine.

1. Update and tailor one system that represents your base configuration.

2. List the filesystems that you do not want to back up in the /etc/exclude .rootvg file and run the **mksysb** with the **-i** and **-e** options.

    ```
    # echo /inst.images >> /etc/exclude.rootvg
    # mksysb -i -e /inst.images/image_name
    ```

3. In nonnetworked environments, direct **mksysb** output to portable media. If network access is available, direct the output image to a filesystem, /inst.images.

4. Create a Network Install Manager in networked environments with NFS and TCP/IP support.

Network Install Manager (NIM)

Network Install Manager (NIM) facilitates central management of software installation and maintenance across all AIX machines participating in a distributed networked environment. How was that statement for an intro? NIM can also customize, boot, and run diagnostics remotely on each of the NIM-managed workstations. NIM is TCP/IP-based, using the BOOTP, TFTP, and NFS protocols to distribute boot images and software to each NIM client. NIM can be used over any network that supports the TCP/IP protocol and can support multiple network interface types on the central server. As you might guess, NIM is a very complex tool, but there is an Easy Setup SMIT option that uses the most common setup for configuration, **smitty nim_config_env**. The Easy Setup is great, but we need to add in more details for the novice to get started.

1. First, create a /tftpboot filesystem before running smitty **nim_config_env**. To create the /tftpboot filesystem and install the NIM software, use the following command sequence:

```
# mklv -y 'lvtftp' rootvg 1
# crfs -v jfs -d lvtftp -m /tftpboot -A yes
# mount /tftpboot
# chfs -a size=120000 /tftpboot
# df -k /tftpboot
# installp -qaX -d <device> bos.sysmgt..nim.master
bos.sysmgt.nim.spot
# smitty nim_config_env
```

2. Create a /tftpboot filesystem and install the NIM filesets using the preceding command sequence.

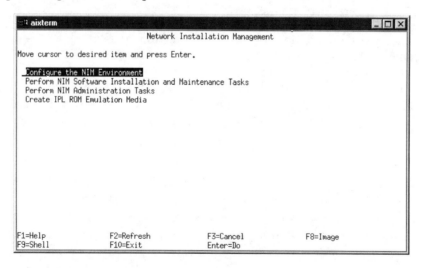

3. Configure the NIM Master from CD-ROM using **smitty nim_config_env**.

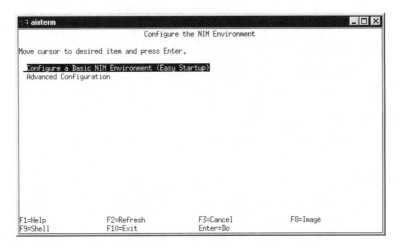

4. Define the client machine(s) using **smitty nim_mac**.

5. Create a **mksysb** image and define a **mksysb** resource using **smitty nim_res**.

6. Install a stand-alone client from the **mksysb** image using **smitty nim_bosinst**.

7. Boot the client.

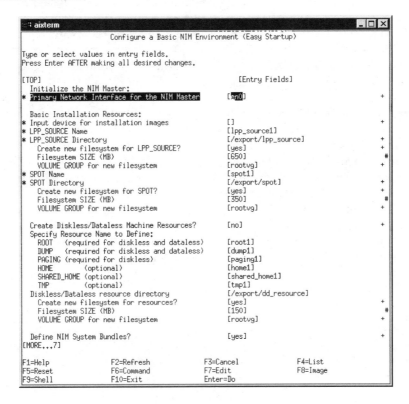

An NIM environment is composed of two system types: an NIM master and one or more NIM clients. An NIM master centrally orchestrates all the management functions for the NIM clients in the network. The master server must be a stand-alone workstation with sufficient storage resources to provide boot images and shared product object trees (SPOT) for all managed clients. The NIM master server must be installed with the AIX network and **sysmgt** filesets required for NIM operation. There is only one NIM master per set of clients. NIM clients may be any mixture of diskless, dataless, and stand-alone workstations with network connectivity to the NIM master.

NIM supports three types of clients:

- **Stand-alone**   Machines with local copies of AIX and LPPs

- **Diskless**   Network filesystems, paging, and dump; bootstrap ROM for network boot

- **Dataless**   Network filesystems; local paging and dump; bootstrap ROM for network boot; better performance than diskless configuration

The AIX filesets that make up NIM support are bundled in **bos.sysmgt**. The **bos.sysmgt.nim.master** fileset is used to build the NIM master server. The **bos.sysmgt.nim.client** fileset is installed on each of the stand-alone NIM clients. The fileset **bos.sysmgt.nim.spot** is used to create SPOT filesystems for NIM diskless and dataless client types.

The NIM master stores information required to identify each managed client and network type as an object in an ODM database. This is where most of the difficulty comes in managing a NIM environment. Commands are supplied to list, update, and verify NIM ODM objects and relationships; but in practice, fencing with the ODM is not quite as straightforward as working with human-readable tables. The NIM master must maintain relationships that link machine objects to network objects, network objects to network objects (routing), and machine objects to machine objects. Common NIM commands used to update and verify NIM ODM objects and relationships include **nim**, **nimconfig**, **nimclient**, and **lsnim**.

My recommendation is that you use SMIT to configure and manage NIM; you can use the Web-based System Manager, but it is a Java pig and is very slow to use. The SMIT panels do a much better job in reminding you of all the attributes that must be associated with NIM objects to ensure that proper object-to-object relationships are maintained. Go ahead and use **lsnim** to do a quick check of ODM contents, but use SMIT to do the rest. I'll use SMIT in the following treatment of setting up an NIM environment.

For Information and Support

- 1-800-CALL-AIX
- 1-800-IBM-4FAX
- 1-800-237-5511

For Problem Support

IBMlink.advantis.com	Internet telnet IBMLink

For Maintenance Level and History

`oslevel`	AIX 3.2.4+ version and release level
`uname -v -r`	Display version and release level
`lslpp -a -h <product>`	List maintenance history

For Packaging

Fileset	Specific function software set
Package	Common function filesets
Licensed product	Distribution package sets
Bundle	Group of filesets, packages, and maintenance

For Backup rootvg

`mkszfile`	Create `image.data` file for mksysb
`mksysb /dev/rmt0<<t>>`	Back up rootvg to tape

For Maintenance Installation

`smit install`	Base install panel
`smit install_latest`	Selective install panel
`smit install_all`	Install ALL products
`bffcreate -qv -d <media> -f <disk-path>`	Copy maint to disk
`installp -qa -d <media-path> -X all`	APPLY updates
`installp -rB -X all`	REJECT updates
`installp -c -g -X all`	COMMIT updates
`Installp -u <fileset>`	DEINSTALL a fileset
`installp -C <fileset>`	CLEAN UP failed install

For NIM

`smit nimconfig`	Configure and start NIM master
`smit nim_mknet`	Create NIM network objects
`smit nim_mkroute`	Define NIM network routes
`smit nim_mkmac`	Create client network object
`smit nim_mkres`	Create lpp_source
`smit nim_alloc`	Create bos.inst resources
`lsnim`	List NIM-defined objects
`bootinfo -q`	Check IPL ROM emulation
`bosboot -r`	Create IPL ROM media

smit nim_alloc	Create bos_inst resource on client
smit nim_perms	Set master push permission
smit nim_mac_op	Select client and resource
smit nim_mkgrp	Create a NIM client group
smit bos_inst	Push install stand-alone client
smit nim_install	Pull install from client
smit dksl_init	Initialize diskless client
smit nim_mac_opp lppchk	Verify installation
smit nim_backup_db	Back up NIM configuration
smit nim_restore_db	Restore NIM configuration
smit nim_client_op	Remotely operate a NIM client
smit nim_unconfig	Unconfigure NIM master

CHECKLIST

The following is a checklist for the key points in installation and maintenance:

- ☐ Follow the installation guide carefully each time you install AIX.
- ☐ Configure operating system and production filesystem configuration to get the best performance from the disk space.
- ☐ Preinstall parts of the basic operating system (BOS) and product runtime environments on the system, if you are installing a brand new P-Series or RISC System/6000.
- ☐ Manage the installation of the Licensed Program Products (LPP) by using the SMIT install FastPath or by using the **installp** command.
- ☐ Monitor the installation of non-LPP products.
- ☐ When you do not need an application on the system, you can remove it through the SMIT software maintenance utilities.
- ☐ Apply maintenance level (ML) patches.
- ☐ Set default system and environment variables for a new installation.
- ☐ Identify distributed system installation procedures.
- ☐ Identify DocSearch keywords.
- ☐ Identify software install/maintenance information and support procedures.

CHAPTER 7

AIX System Boot and Shutdown

Each time you power up your pSeries, RS/6000, or Itanium-based system, a complex series of system checkouts and initialization tasks are executed. The only outward sign of this activity is the play of numbers across the console or the LED display on the front panel. This system startup process is what you might be familiar with on other UNIX systems as bootstrapping. Bootstrapping a POWER AIX system involves a hardware initialization phase followed by AIX kernel initialization. IBM refers to the hardware phase as *Read Only Storage Initial Program Load (ROS IPL)* or *Read Only Memory IPL (ROM IPL)*. In the discussion that follows, you can interchange *ROM* for *ROS* if you find it confusing. You may find that the terms *IPL* and *boot* are often used interchangeably in many of the IBM documents. Since *IPL* conjures images of 370/390 MVS or VM architectures and *boot* is more common in UNIX circles, I'll tend to use boot in the remainder of the chapter.

It's important that the system administrator be familiar with the sequence of events that are taking place under the system unit cover at boot time. Understanding the system startup flow of control will assist you in diagnosing hardware and configuration problems when they occur. Notice that I said, "when they occur!"

BOOTING THE SYSTEM

AIX may be started in one of three ways:

1. Normal boot
2. Stand-alone boot
3. Network boot

The normal boot is a boot from a local disk, or set of local disks. The system is initialized with runtime kernel. Set the key mode switch in normal position (if present) and boot the machine. When booted, the multiuser normal mode of operation is resumed.

The standalone boot is similar to the normal boot, but the system is brought up with a single-user maintenance, install, or diagnostic mode kernel. The system is booted from local disk, CD-ROM, or tape. Set the key mode switch to the service position (if present). If your machine does not have a key mode switch, you must press the appropriate function key (usually F5 or F6) just after the keyboard is initialized and the beep is sounded. Standalone boot is used when installing software or performing maintenance or diagnostics (see the section "Standalone Boot" immediately following this section).

With the network boot, the boot information and kernel are provided by a network-based file server. ROS broadcasts a boot request packet to locate a boot server. The reply packet from the server indicates how to load the boot image from the server. The boot kernel and filesystem are copied from the server via TFTP. Note that the network boot on older Micro Channel systems may require IPL ROM emulation.

Once the boot kernel and file system are loaded, generally the same steps are followed in all three modes to initialize a runtime AIX kernel. Assuming that the system is configured correctly, normal and network boot proceed with bringing AIX up to multiuser mode after power-on without additional intervention, the exception being boot for installation or maintenance purposes. The boot sequence of events is outlined in "Boot Sequence of Events" later in this chapter.

Standalone Boot

In the event of a system problem, or when required for AIX installation or maintenance, you may need to start the system in standalone mode. In standalone mode, the system runs the boot kernel and provides minimal access to the volume groups and file systems on disk. Booting the system in standalone mode will assist you in recovering corrupted system configuration files and file systems.

Here is the standalone boot procedure:

1. Set the system key in the service position if it is a Micro Channel machine. For PCI-bus machines, press the appropriate function key for your model, usually F5 or F6 (or 5 or 6 on ASCII terminals)..

2. Insert a CD-ROM or tape containing a boot image and power on the system.

3. When prompted, select the console display.

4. Select Start Maintenance Mode For System Recovery.

5. Select Access A Root Volume Group.

6. Select the volume group number.

7. Select Access This Volume Group and Start A Shell.

CREATING BOOTABLE MEDIA

In order to boot AIX, a boot image or bootstrap kernel must be available on one or more boot devices specified by the boot list stored in nonvolatile system RAM (NVRAM). ROS boot code will attempt to access each device in the list until a valid boot device is found from which to load the boot image. The machine will boot using the first boot image found in the boot list.

The boot device characteristics and the location and size of the boot image on the device are described by a boot record. The boot record may be added to the beginning of the boot image, or in the case of a disk device, the boot record is written to the first sector of the disk. The boot image and file system may or may not be compressed to save space and access speed.

Configuring the Bootlist on Micro Channel Machines

At system startup, the ROS boot code will attempt to access boot devices from a list of boot devices stored in NVRAM. The boot list can be tailored or recovered by invoking the **bootlist** command. Here are some examples:

```
# bootlist -m normal -o          ◄──────── To see the current boot list before you change it
# bootlist -m normal hdisk0 hdisk1     ◄──────── Change boot list for a mirrored rootvg
```

```
# bootlist -m normal ent0 bserver=128.95.132.1 \
  gateway=128.95.135.100 client=128.95.135.10 cd0
# bootlist -m normal hdisk0 hdisk1
```

NOTE   When the boot server and the client are on the same subnet, the gateway can be identified as `gateway="`.

Separate lists are maintained for normal boot, service boot, and previous boot. Valid AIX 5L boot device types are listed in Table 7-1. Device drivers for each of these device types are available in NVRAM.

Configuring the Boot-List on PCI-Bus Machines

Not all PCI-bus machines support setting a service mode boot list. To check if your PCI-bus system supports setting the service mode boot list, run the following command:

```
# bootlist -m service -o   ◀━━━━━━━━  Check current boot list before you change it
# bootlist -m service -o cd0 rmt0 hdisk0   ◀━━━━━━━━ Change to boot list
```

If you receive the following error message, then your machine does not support this **bootlist** command option:

```
bootlist: Invalid mode (service) for this model
```

There are three methods you can use to set the boot list. The **bootlist** command is the easiest method. You can also use the System Management Services (SMS) programs by pressing the F1 key during the initial boot process. The **diag** facility, which is part of the **bos.rte.diag** package, has an option to set the boot list also.

The older RS/6000 machines that do support setting a service mode boot list have two separate boot lists, default and custom. The default boot list is for normal booting. This default boot list is used when you press F5 or F6 just after the keyboard is initialized and the beep is sounded. The custom boot list is a device list created by using the

Boot Device	Medium
fdXX	Diskette
hdiskXX	Disk
cdXX	CD-ROM
rmtXX	Tape
entXX	Ethernet
tokXX	Token ring
fddiXX	FDDI

Table 7-1.   Boot Device Types

bootlist command, the **diag** facility, or the SMS menu during boot. All other PCI-bus machines have an additional customized service boot list. You set up this boot list using the **bootlist** command with the **-m service** option. After you set up the service boot list, you use the F5 and F6 functions keys during the boot process. Use F5 to use the default service boot list and use F6 to boot from the customized service boot list. You will also see some differences with various models. As always, refer to the User's Guide for your particular model. You can find this information online at the following URL:

```
http://www.ibm.com/servers/eserver/pseries/library/hardware_docs/
```

Service Processor

On pSeries and newer RS/6000 models there is an extra processor known as the *Service Processor*. In reality, the Service Processor is firmware that is not part of the AIX operating system. The purpose of the Service Processor is to continuously monitor the system for failures and allow for system reconfiguration. The Service Processor provides the following functions:

- Access from local or remote ASCII terminals
- Console mirroring for dual support
- Control menus call-out failure reporting, aka, Call Home
- Remote power on
- Unattended start after power failure
- Remote power off/reboot
- Mutual surveillance with the system processor
- Updatable control firmware
- Extended progress and error indicators

The Service Processor menu provides the following top-level options:

Main Menu

```
1. Service Processor Setup Menu
2. System Power Control Menu
3. System Information Menu
4. Language Selection Menu
5. Call-In/Call-Out Setup Menu
6. Set System Name
99. Exit from Menus
```

To gain access to the service menu, you power the system on and press ENTER twice, or you can access most functions through the **diag** command.

When you initially power on a system with a Service Processor, it will not automatically boot. You first need to press ENTER twice to gain access to the Service

Processor menu. Select option 2 from the menu, System Power Control Menu, and select Power On The System. After this step, the boot procedure is just like for any other system.

There are other options for the Service Processor. You can set up the Call Home functionality that will dial out to IBM support in the event of a detected system failure.

BOOT SEQUENCE OF EVENTS

What happens when you boot an AIX machine? There are five basic steps that take place during the boot process:

1. POST—Hardware is checked and initialized.

2. The Boot Logical Volume (BLV) is located using a boot list.

3. The BLV is loaded, and control is passed to the kernel.

4. The system devices are configured using different options to the **cfgmgr** command.

5. The **init** process (PID = 1) is started, and the /etc/inittab file is processed.

Entering into Maintenance Mode

There are several ways to get into maintenance, and the task you want to accomplish determines the process required. Running a filesystem check or some network adapter reconfigurations requires maintenance mode at the local disk boot level. For major system diagnostics, you need to boot into maintenance mode using the diagnostic CD-ROM supplied with your system. To clone your system or to upgrade your system to a newer AIX version or release, you need to boot the system using the installation media.

Key Switch on Micro Channel Machines

All Micro Channel RS/6000 machines have a key switch that has three switch selections. The *normal* position is for normal multiuser operation. The *secure* position is used to lock down a running system or to disable booting a powered-down system. If the system is running, you can place the key switch in the secure position and disable accidentally rebooting the system by disabling the reset and power buttons. If the key switch is in the secure position when the system is powered on, then the boot process will quickly stop at the LED code 200. The system will not boot until the key switch in moved to the normal or service position.

The service position is used to boot the system into maintenance/diagnostics mode and to unlock the internal lock that prevents you from opening the chassis case to access the hardware on some models. If you do not have the key to the system, you cannot upgrade the operating system, open the chassis to work on the hardware, or run diagnostics on the system. If you lose the key, your only option is to call IBM support at 1-800-IBM-SERV and have a CE come to your site and replace the entire assembly. By the way, replacing the key switch is not cheap!

Entering Maintenance Mode on PCI-Bus Machines

The PCI-bus pSeries and RS/6000 machines do not have a key switch. You enter maintenance mode on a PCI-bus machine using the appropriate function key for your model. The function keys that control the boot process are F1 to get to the System Management Services (SMS). In SMS you can change the system bootlist and control other boot options and query the hardware configuration. Function keys F5 and F6 control booting into maintenance mode. (Not all RS/6000 machines support a service mode boot list; see Appendix A.)

The trick is in the timing. The appropriate function key must be pressed *just after* the keyboard is initialized and the beep is sounded and before the icons disappear from the screen. The timing presents a problem on machines that have energy-saving monitors that power down to save the screen and to save power. If you have one of these monitors, do not wait for screen to come alive and the icons to appear. Just start pressing the F1, F5, or F6 key from a graphics console or the 1, 5, or 6 key from a **tty** console (do not press a following ENTER key) as soon as the beep is sounded. If you miss the timing window, then you will have to reboot the system and start over.

THE AIX BOOT PROCESS

The boot process in AIX is an extensive and complex process. All of the hardware is check out and initialized. The system first does a power-on self-test (POST). Next the bootstrap image is located. Then the boot list is searched for a valid boot image. The boot logical volume (BLV) is loaded into memory and a RAM disk is created with the root filesystem mounted on the RAMDISK. The Configuration Manager (**cfgmgr**) executes different boot phases, and finally the **init** process is started and the /etc/inittab file is processed.

One of two types of boot is performed depending on the value of the system-reset count: cold boot and warm boot.

Built-in Self Test—BIST

The BIST is for older Micro Channel machines. A cold boot is started each time the computer is turned on. If the model is equipped with an on-card sequencer (OCS), the OCS performs a built-in self test (BIST) of the processor complex. The OCS fetches seed and signature patterns from ROM to test and validate each processor component. The seed pattern is sent to a common on-chip processor (COP) resident on each of the processor chips. Test results are compared with the signature data. The BIST performs the following functions:

1. Initializes and tests COPs and embedded chip memory
2. Tests AC/DC logic
3. Initializes and resets hardware for ROS IPL

A warm boot occurs when the reset button is pressed on a running system or initiated via software control. For example, a warm boot results when the **reboot** command is executed at runtime. The BIST phase is bypassed during a warm boot. Processor memory, cache, and registers are reset, and the system branches to the warm boot entry point in ROS.

Power-On Self Test—POST

When the machine is powered up, the hardware is verified and the system hardware is initialized. This hardware checking and initialization process is called power-on self-test (POST) and is the first task in starting a PCI-bus machine. During the POST process, we initialize memory, keyboard, communications, and the audio. During this process, you will see the icons appear across the screen. This is the same part of the boot sequence when you press the appropriate function key to activate a different boot list.

ROS Initialization

After the POST processing, the bootstrap code is located and loaded. The first 512 bytes of the boot sector contain the bootstrap code. The bootstrap code is loaded into RAM during the boot process. This part of the boot sequence is controlled by the System Read Only Storage (ROS) stored in firmware. The ROS Initialization process is invoked when hardware events trigger a system reset. Normally, this occurs when you turn the system on or press the reset button. Resets also occur in the event of a hardware failure or machine check. Since you can run other operating systems on a pSeries or RS/6000 platform, the System ROS is not part of AIX because you may be running Linux. The System ROS just brings the hardware to life.

Bootstrap Startup

After POST the System ROS loads the bootstrap code, this code takes control of the boot process. Booting into AIX, the bootstrap code next locates the boot image, or Boot Logical Volume (BLV), in the boot list and loads the BLV into memory. The BLV is compressed, so it is mostly referred to as a boot image. In normal operation the BLV will reside on a local hard disk. In a NIM boot sequence, the BLV is loaded over your network. The network can be a local LAN or a distant WAN. At this point, control is passed to the BLV, and the AIX kernel takes over the control of the boot process.

AIX Kernel Boot Control

The BLV contains four components: the AIX kernel, an reduced ODM, a `rc.boot` file, and all of the required boot commands. The AIX kernel, which manages memory, processes, and devices, is loaded from the BLV.

The AIX kernel first creates a RAM filesystem with mount points /, /usr, and /var. The /etc, /dev, and /mnt directories are subdirectories in the root "/" filesystem. The root volume group is not yet accessible at this point, and the AIX kernel is still using the BLV loaded in RAM. In the next step, the kernel starts the **init** process (PID = 1), which is retrieved from the BLV. At this point, the **init** process takes over control of the boot process.

Steps to get to Kernel Control

- Retrieve boot device list from NVRAM.
- Locate boot device from list.
- Load and validate boot record.
- Load boot image into reserved RAM.
- Pass control to boot kernel.

Boot Sequence for the init Process

The **init** process is now in control of the boot process. The **init** process executes three phases of the boot process by invoking the **rc.boot** command with **1, 2,** and **3** as command augments. Each of these three phases takes on certain responsibilities. The first phase initializes the hardware to get the system booted. The second phase mounts the filesystems as a RAMFS, or RAM filesystem. The third phase completes the hardware configurations and starts the **init** process, and then the `/etc/inittab` file is read and processed.

Phase 1 of rc.boot

The first **rc.boot** phase is with the command **rc.boot 1**. This first phase initializes only the devices required to get the system booted, but not all devices are configured during the first phase. The **restbase** command is executed and copies the ODM in the BLV to the RAM filesystem. If **restbase** completes without error, the LED display will show 510. If the **restbase** command fails, the LED display will show 548. In the next step, the Configuration Manager (**cfgmgr**) is run for phase 1, **cfgmgr -f**. The **cfgmgr** command queries the ODM for the objects in the Config_Rules class and executes anything under the Phase 1 stanza. This step configures only the devices needed to get the system booted.

Phase 2 of rc.boot

The **init** process next starts **rc.boot** phase 2 by executing **rc.boot 2**. During this boot phase, the LED display will show 551. In this second phase, the root volume group (rootvg) is varied online with the **ipl_varyon** command. If the **ipl_varyon** command completes successfully, the LED display will show 517. If the **ipl_varyon** command fails, then the LED code will show 552, 554, or 556 and the system stops. If the **ipl_varyon** command succeeds, then a filesystem check (**fsck**) is performed on the root filesystem, which is the **hd4** logical volume. If the **fsck** fails, the LED display will show 555. After a successful filesystem check, the `/dev/hd4` logical volume is mounted on the RAM root filesystem. If the mount fails, the LED display will show 557 and the system stops. This LED code usually indicates a corrupted JFS log.

Next, in order, filesystem checks and mounting are done on **hd2** (/usr), **hd9var** (/var) and paging (**hd6**). If the hd2 mount fails, the LED display will show 518, the boot process ends, and the system stops. When the /var filesystem is mounted, the **copycore** command checks the system to see if there has been a system dump since the last reboot. If a system dump is found, the **copycore** command copies the dump from **hd6** (paging space) to /var/adm/ras. If there is not enough filesystem space, you will be prompted to copy the dump to a tape device. However, the system can be configured so that this will not stop the boot process to prompt for the dump tape (see **sysdumpdev** command). At this point the paging space, **hd6**, is ready for mounting.

In the **rc.boot** phase 1, **rc.boot 1**, all of the base devices needed to get the system started were configured in the ODM of the RAM filesystem. We need to copy these device configurations to disk. The **cp Cu* /mnt/etc/objrepos** command copies the ODM data to disk. At this point, both copies of the ODM, **hd4** and **hd5**, are synced.

Up to now, there has not been a console available to view the boot progress, only LED display codes. All of the boot information has been written to a special boot log file. To view the system boot log, you must use the **alog** command.

```
# alog -t boot -o
```

Using this command, you can view the entire boot process log.

All of this has been done in the RAM filesystem so far. In AIX 5L, the access to the RAM filesystem was changed. To access the RAM filesystems, the prefix /../ is added, for example /../usr to access the /usr mount point in the RAM filesystem.

The RAM filesystem is no longer needed, so the kernel replaces the **init** in the BLV with the **init** in / (the **hd4** logical volume is mounted as the root filesystem), then clears the RAMDISK from memory.

Phase 3 of rc.boot

In this final step, the **/etc/init** is started and **init** goes through the /etc/inittab file and executes each entry for the run level for which we are booting, the default is specified on the first line of the /etc/inittab file. The default run level in AIX is run level 2. The LED display will show 553 while the /etc/inittab file is being processed. While processing the /etc/inittab file, **rc.boot** is called for a third time (**rc.boot 3**).

In **rc.boot** phase 3, **fsck** is run on the /tmp filesystem and is mounted. Next the root volume group is synchronized using **syncvg roovg**. In the final part of **rc.boot 3**, the **cfgmgr** command is executed again and configures all of the remaining devices on the system that were skipped in **rc.boot** phase 1. For a normal boot, **cfgmgr** runs with the **-p2** switch, for Configuration Manager phase 2. For a service boot, the **cfgmgr** command runs with the **-p3** switch for Configuration Manager phase 3. Depending on the command switch provided to the **cfgmgr** command, the ODM is queried for the **Config_Rules** ODM class. For **cfgmgr -p2**, the methods under the **phase=2** stanza are executed. For **cfgmgr -p3**, the methods under the **phase=3** stanza are executed. After the methods are executed, all of the remaining system devices that were skipped in **rc.boot** phase 1 are configured.

The system console is defined and activated in the next step with the **cfgcon** command. There are four possible LED display values associated with the console definition. If the console is not configured or there are multiple **tty** definitions, then c31 is displayed and a menu is displayed for you to define the console. If the console is found to be a low-function terminal, **lft** (graphic), the LED display will read c32. If the console is found to be a **tty**, the LED will display c33, and if the console is a file, then c34 is displayed.

If your system is set to use the Common Desktop Environment (CDE), then CDE is started and you will see a graphical boot. You can also configure CDE so that the boot process is not graphical, but the operation mode is graphical. This is the way I always configure a machine running CDE. I run CDE this way because I have had machines act strangely and for various reasons the graphical boot did not start. To get around this, I just configure CDE to start only at the login prompt and with an ANSII boot.

The final step is synchronizing the ODM in the BLV with the ODM in the root filesystem, /etc/objrepos. The **savebase** command accomplishes this task.

We still have a few more steps. The **syncd** daemon is started, and all of the data in memory is written to disk. Next the **errdemon** daemon is started. This is the process that writes to the system error log. After this, you will not see any more LED display, unless the system crashes, and then you see flashing 888!

The /etc/nologin file is removed from the system, if it exists. This is a nice tool to lock out all nonroot users from the system. If you forget to remove the /etc/nologin file, it will be removed for you. However, you may want to keep users locked out if you are doing maintenance, so remember to create another one after the reboot. If the hardware configuration has changed or is out of sync with the ODM, then you will see a message during the boot to run **diag -a**. You can run this on a live and active system, since it is just cleaning up the ODM.

The final message on the console is System Initialization Completed. At this point, **rc.boot 3** ends execution, and the rest of the /etc/inittab file is processed.

FAST BOOT ON MP MACHINES WITH MPCFG COMMAND OPTION

Booting a multiprocessor machine with a large amount of memory and a bunch of devices can take a very long time. I have a pair of J-50s with about 350 SSA disks in an HACMP cluster. It takes 45 minutes to do a fast boot, and that is not even counting the time it takes to start the HACMP-controlled applications. That time is doubled if the fast boot is not set. IBM knows about this and has supplied the **mpcfg** command. (The **mpcfg** command works only with multiprocessor machines that have Micro Channel I/O.) To always have a multiprocessor system fast boot (in relative terms), add the following command to the /etc/inittab file:

```
fastboot:2:once:/usr/sbin/mpcfg -cf 11 1 >/dev/console2>&1 # Fast boot
```

or from the command line, you can run this command:

```
# mpcfg —cf 11 1   ◄————— (That's eleven space one)
```

The **mpcfg** command is good for only one reboot, so I make an entry in the system's /etc/inittab file.

STOPPING THE SYSTEM

Like all things in life, runtime must come to an end, but the business will never understand. To restart the system, you can use the **shutdown** or **reboot** command to bring services and the system offline gracefully. First stop all of your databases and applications! In AIX, you can create a file called /etc/rc.shutdown. If you have applications that you want to always stop before a system shutdown or reboot, put the commands or script names in this file. However, if any command in the /etc/rc.shutdown returns a nonzero exit code, the shutdown is aborted! This is a nice tool to gracefully bring the system down, but just one little failure, or nonzero exit code, will cause the system to abort the shutdown and continue running. This can cause some problems, especially for automated reboots. You may also end up with a partially stopped application that is not usable. So use caution! However, you can add an **exit0** to the end of the **rc.shutdown** script.

The **shutdown** command supports a number of flags to control how the system is to be brought down. By default, it will warn users, wait one minute, terminate active processes, sync the file systems, and halt the CPU. You may indicate that the system is to be immediately restarted after shutdown by using the **-r** flag or by invoking the **reboot** command.

```
# shutdown —m +5    ◄——————— Shut system down to single user in 5 minutes
# shutdown -r       ◄——————— Shut down and reboot
# shutdown now      ◄——————— Shut down immediately without rebooting
# shutdown -r       ◄——————— Reboot now
# shutdown -Fr      ◄——————— Reboot now without any user warning
# shutdown -r now   ◄——————— Reboot now and warn the users
# shutdown -k       ◄——————— Avoid shutting down the system
```

TROUBLESHOOTING

The RS/6000 is very good about checking its hardware during the power-on self-test (POST) at power-up time. Keeping track of the LED information during system power-up will assist you in debugging hardware problems. If the system boots up, check the error report first! If you suspect hardware problems or the system won't boot, use the pSeries or RS/6000 diagnostic programs to assist in determining the failure. The diagnostic programs may be run in standalone mode or in concurrent mode with AIX online using the **diag** command. For concurrent mode operation, as superuser enter the **diag** command and follow the menu instructions. Standalone mode is similar to booting from tape or CD-ROM as described previously.

1. Set system key in service position (if present).

2. Insert a CD-ROM disc or a tape containing a boot image and power on the system.

3. When prompted, select the console display.

4. Select Start Maintenance Mode For System Recovery.

5. Select Access Advanced Maintenance Mode Functions.

ITANIUM-BASED SYSTEM BOOT

New to AIX 5L is the ability to run on Itanium-based machines, which are 64-bit Intel processors. There are four differences between the boot processes on the POWER systems and on the Itanium-based machines.

1. The Read Only Storage (ROS) on the POWER systems is replaced by a common PC BIOS and an Extensible Firmware Interface, or EFI, which provides a common standard interface between the system firmware and the operating system. This new standard was created by Intel.

2. The firmware on the POWER systems provides the System Management Services (SMS) and gives you several ways to change the boot device list. The Itanium-based allows you to change the boot device list by way of an EFI Boot Manager. You can also change the hardware configuration using the Setup tool menu during the boot process.

3. The POWER systems use a Boot Logical Volume (BLV), or boot image, and ROS controls loading the RAM filesystem. On the Itanium-based systems, the boot disk contains two partitions. The Physical Volume Partition contains **rootvg** and the BLV, and the EFI System Partition is a small "boot loader sector" that contains the boot loader program, **boot.efi**. The **boot.efi** program loads the BLV into the RAM disk.

4. Most every POWER machine has an LED display to show you the progress of the boot process. The Itanium-based systems do not (at least currently) have LED displays. Instead, all of the messages are sent to the system console.

For more information on the Itanium-based system boot process and the Extensible Firmware Interface (EFI), check out this Intel Web site:

```
http://www.intel.com/design/itanium/index.htm
```

You should also read the Redbook *AIX 5L Differences Guide Version 5.1 Edition,* SG24-5765. You can download the Redbook in a PDF or HTML format from this IBM Web site:

`http://redbook.ibm.com/redbooks/SG245765.html`

CHECKLIST

The following is a checklist for the key points about system boot and shutdown:

- ☐ AIX may be booted in one of 3 ways: normal boot, standalone boot, network boot

- ☐ To boot the system into standalone mode for AIX installation or system maintenance, set the system key (if present) in the service position or press the F5 or F6 just after the keyboard is initialized.

- ☐ Run the **bootlist** command to tailor or recover the list of boot devices stored in NVRAM.

- ☐ With an Itanium-based system, change the boot device list using the EFI Boot Manager.

- ☐ On models with a Service Processor and firmware that continuously monitors the system for failures and allows for system reconfiguration: To access the service menu, power the system on and press ENTER twice, or use the **diag** command to access most service functions

- ☐ For major system diagnostics, you need to boot into maintenance mode using the diagnostic CD-ROM supplied with your system.

- ☐ To clone your system or to upgrade your system to a newer AIX version or release, you need to boot the system using the installation media.

- ☐ To view the special boot log file the system writes all the boot information to, use the **alog -t boot -o** command.

- ☐ To configure CDE so the boot mode is not graphical but the operation mode is graphical, configure CDE to start only at the login prompt.

- ☐ To configure multiprocessor machines with Micro Channel I/O to use the fast boot, use the **mpcfg** command either in the `/etc/inittab` file to make the change permanent or run it from the command line to affect the next boot only.

- ☐ Use the **shutdown** or **reboot** command to bring services and the system offline gracefully after stopping all your databases and applications.

☐ If you have applications that you want to always stop before a system shutdown or reboot, put the commands or script name in the `/etc/rc.shutdown file.`

☐ To restart the system immediately after shutdown, shut the system down with the **shutdown -r** command or **reboot**.

☐ If you suspect hardware problems or the system won't boot, use the pSeries or RS/6000 diagnostic programs using the **diag** command to assist in determining the failure.

PART IV

System Configuration and Customization

CHAPTER 8

AIX Runtime Configuration

Here's a short and sweet chapter on defining your runtime settings. All but one of these tasks are available from a single SMIT environment screen. The reason that I'm making it a separate chapter is that, more often than not, administrators forget to take care of some, or all, of these steps after completing an installation or upgrade. It's just too tempting to select Tasks Completed—Exit to AIX at the end of a long day of installs. A week later, we're standing around scratching our heads trying to figure out why we can't run just one more process or why there seem to be only two active licenses on the system.

The other reason for making this a separate chapter is that most of the coarse system tuning can be done from these screens—things like setting maximum I/O buffers and pacing. In a mixed workload environment, a small change in some of these numbers can make a big difference in system throughput.

SYSTEM ENVIRONMENTS

To get to the SMIT catchall runtime setting panel (see Figure 8-1), enter the SMIT FastPath **smit system**.

```
# smit system
```

Stop the System

The first selection in the System Environment panel is an option to stop the system. If you are not comfortable with using the command-line options, you can use the SMIT FastPath **smit shutdown** (see the following illustration). You can enter a message to send out to all users, select the reboot option, and set the time delay before shutdown or reboot.

```
# smit shutdown
```

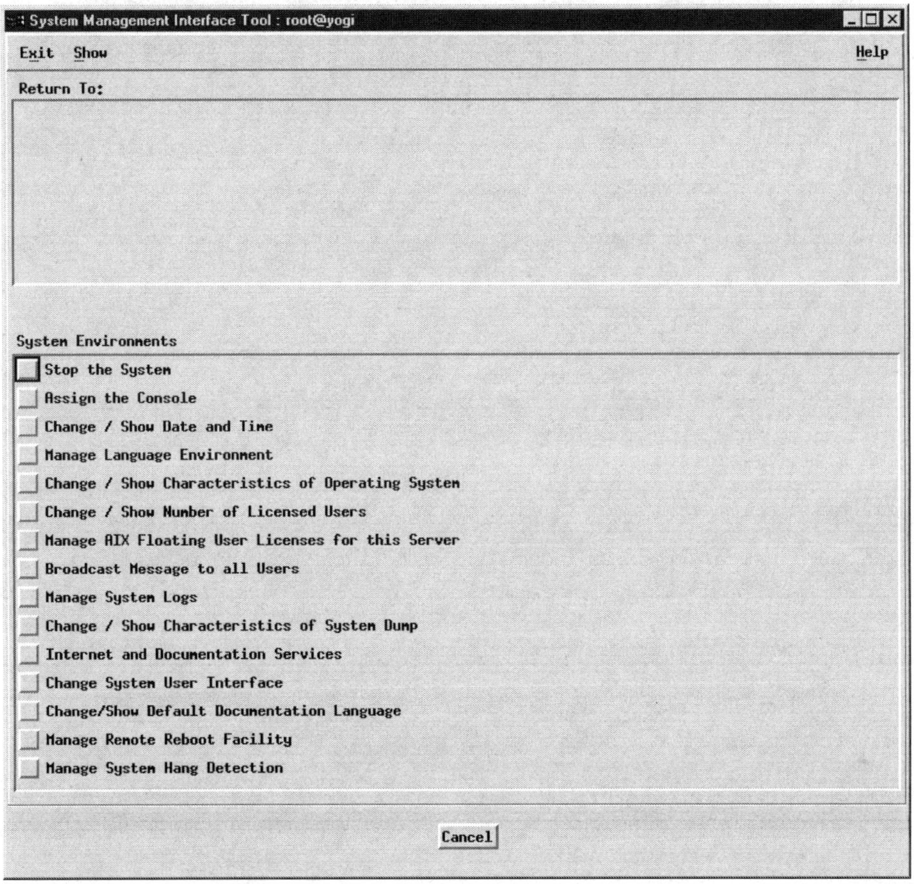

Figure 8-1. System Environments SMIT panel

Assign the Console

The next menu option enables you to assign or reassign the system console device as shown in the next illustration. Sure, it worked fine during installation when you had a terminal plugged into the serial port. Then you unplugged the tube without resetting console support. You don't need to have a terminal plugged into a pSeries or RS/6000 machine for operation, but you may want to direct console output to another device or file. You can do console assignments from the SMIT FastPath **smit chcons**.

```
# smit chcons
```

Time Settings

Two easy settings that should have been handled at the end of the installation process are time and language settings (see Figure 8-2). Aha! Now you know why the date/time

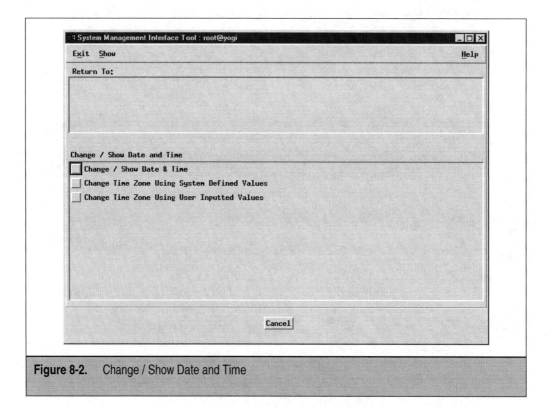

Figure 8-2. Change / Show Date and Time

stamps in the mail headers have been off by a few time zones. You can set the correct date and time zone by invoking the SMIT FastPath **smit chtz_date**.

```
# smit chtz_date
```

Language Environment

Most likely, you got the correct language set during installation, but did you know that you can add other languages to the set? AIX will enable you to configure a hierarchy of language environments (see Figure 8-3). This may be helpful in multilingual communities. You can also use SMIT to translate messages, and flat files, into a new base language.

```
# smit mlang
```

Set Characteristics of the Operating System

From just one panel in SMIT (see Figure 8-4), you can alter AIX kernel characteristics that hit most of the critical subsystems, including the virtual memory manager, the scheduler, and the dispatcher. It's a great screen for wreaking havoc on a system. Open the AIX Pandora's box by using the SMIT FastPath **smit chgsys**.

```
# smit chgsys
```

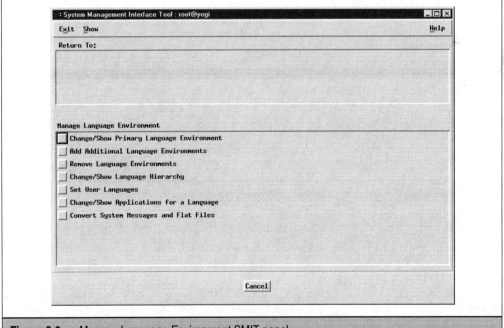

Figure 8-3.   Manage Language Environment SMIT panel

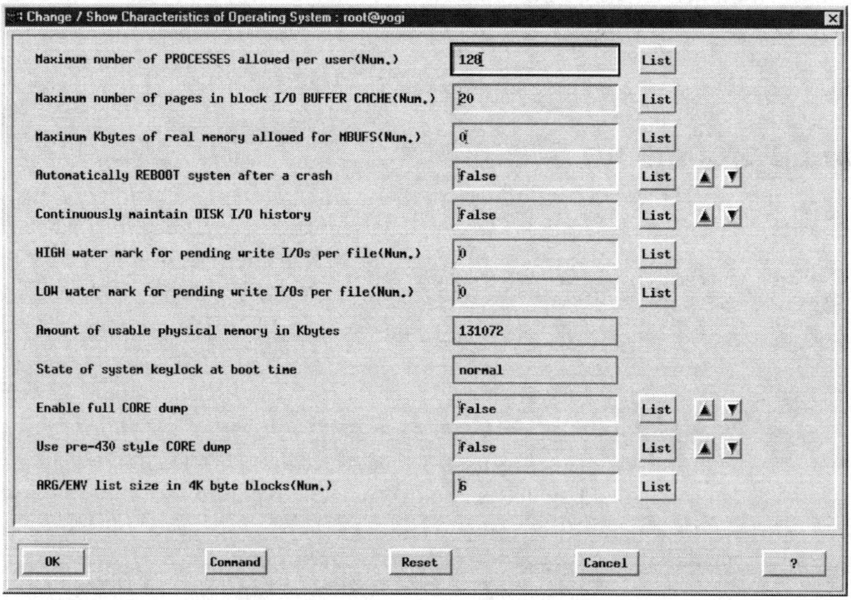

Figure 8-4.   Change/Show Characteristics Of Operating System SMIT panel

Be careful making changes to the system on this panel. Just change one thing at a time; if the change does not help, change it back! Some changes made in this SMIT panel may require a reboot to set or reset a value.

The first entry in the panel is for the maximum number of processes allowed per user. Maybe this is why you can't start one more process. There are trade-offs in making this parameter too large or too small. Making it too large can cause you grief during situations when you have a runaway process that is forking new copies of itself. It seems like every year we get a new batch of programmers who like to try out a tight **fork()** and **exec()** loop. Setting the maximum number of processes too low means frustration when you try to start that one process too many.

Next in the list is the maximum number of pages in block I/O buffer cache. This setting is used as a buffer for I/O to block special files. Basically, it mimics a BSD or System V buffer cache. It's not heavily used by the system and takes away from real memory.

The next entry controls the amount of real memory that can be pinned for network MBUFS. Again, this is another parameter that takes away from real memory. To enable the collection of MBUF statistics, you need to change the following entry at the bottom of the /etc/rc.net file (change the extendednetstats value from 0 to 1).

```
/usr/sbin/no -o extendednetstats=1 >/dev/null 2>&1
```

If the system is collecting MBUF statistics, you can use the **netstat -m** command to see if you are running out of MBUFS before making the value larger.

You might want to set the switch for automatically rebooting the system after a crash to true for systems that are left unattended in order to maintain system availability.

If you regularly use the **iostat** command to check statistics on disk I/O rates, you will want to leave Disk I/O History set to true. It's not that much overhead, but you could elect to turn it off until you want to do I/O monitoring.

The next two entries control the high- and low-water marks that control pending I/Os. These parameters can have a dramatic effect on system throughput and are primarily geared toward the type of work being done by the machine. When a process writing to a file hits its high-water mark for pending I/Os, that process is suspended until the I/O queue drops to or below the low-water mark. This can keep big database load processes from holding up a user trying to open an e-mail inbox. Conversely, you could set these to favor a big writer to speed up building a large file.

Skipping to the third from last entry, Enable Full CORE Dump: this may be important when you are debugging applications for which you need to see memory locations outside of kernel structures and space. Note that enabling this will result in large program core dump files that may require more space in the filesystems affected, and user limits will need to be adjusted. This has nothing to do with the system dump detailed in an upcoming section, "Dump Device."

There are other selections in this panel that you may want to investigate further.

Number of Licensed Users

Back to the System Environments panel. Select Change/Show Number Of Licensed Users or run the SMIT FastPath **smit chlicense** to alter the number of licensed users as shown in the next illustration. The default is a two-user license and no floating licenses. This might be another reason why you can't start one more instance of an application.

```
# smit chlicense
```

Manage Floating User Licenses

This option enables you to add floating user licenses for specific versions of AIX including 4.1, 4.2, 4.3, and 5L (see Figure 8-5). You must supply the AIX level of the user licenses and the number of floating user licenses you want to add to the system. For direct access, use the SMIT FastPath **smit netls_server**.

```
# smit netls_server
```

Broadcast Message to All Users

You can broadcast a message to all logged-on users using the SMIT FastPath **smit wall** command (see the illustration), which performs the same function as the **wall** command itself. You need to understand that only users who are logged into AIX will see the message. If a user logs into an application and not into the operating system, then no message can be received using **wall**. The user must also have an open window if he or she is running in an X Window System environment.

```
# smitty wall
```

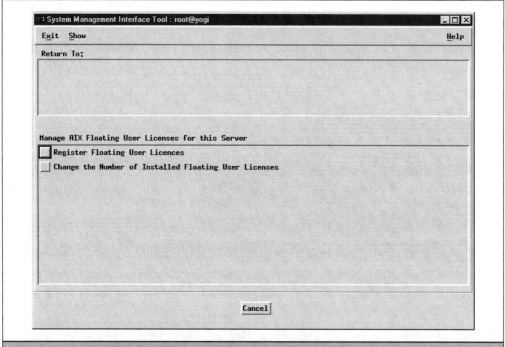

Figure 8-5.   Manage AIX Floating User Licenses SMIT panel

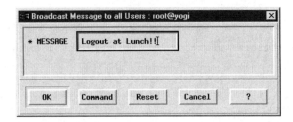

System Logs

The system error log (ErrLog) is a very nice facility when it comes to tracking system hardware and applications problems. Unfortunately, it is one of the most ignored features in AIX. Without active housecleaning, the error log `/var/adm/ras/errlog` is usually missing the critical history information that leads up to a system problem. The log should be monitored regularly to scan for intermittent system problems. The companion `alog` screens are used to control logs produced by the **alog** command. This command is used in conjunction with other command output piped to the **alog** standard input. You can manage the system logs from the SMIT FastPath **smit logs**, as shown in Figure 8-6.

```
# smit logs
```

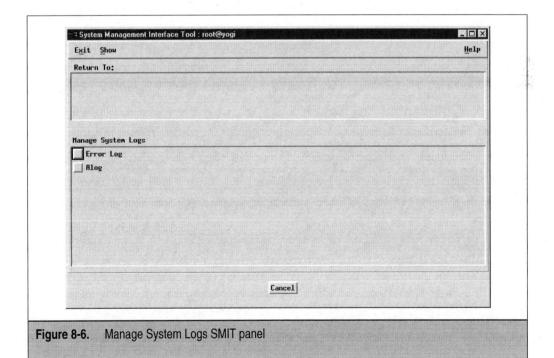

Figure 8-6.   Manage System Logs SMIT panel

Dump Device

Like the log screens, the System Dump menu (see Figure 8-7) is critical to managing problem information. By default, AIX 4.3 and 5L use the /dev/hd6 paging space as the primary dump device. In most large environments, a dedicated dump device should be defined, other than paging space. In previous releases, there was a problem with systems that had mirrored paging space and in which a dump occurred. In a kernel panic, confusion arose about which *side* of the mirror to use as the dump device. This problem has been corrected in AIX 4.3.3 with ML 6. However, the main reason for a dedicated dump device is to allow an automatic reboot after a system dump that preserves the dump image without having to save it to a tape or disabling a paging device.

Access the SMIT dump menu with the SMIT FastPath **smit dump**.

```
# smit dump
```

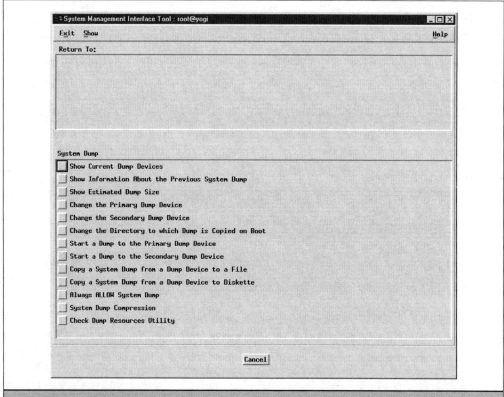

Figure 8-7. System Dump SMIT panel

Internet and Documentation Services

Before you can use the DocSearch (Documentation Search Service), Netscape, or a search server, you must configure the access mechanisms (see Figure 8-8). Using the SMIT FastPath **smit web_configure** is the quickest way to set everything up. Normally, you can take the defaults except for the Search/Web Server. If you press F4, or ESC-4, you can see the list of installed products. Read your documentation for setting up these services and read Chapter 2 for details on setting up DocSearch. There is also an entry for the Web-Based System Manager (WebSM).

```
# smit web_configure
```

Change the System User Interface

You have at least three options for a user interface, depending on the software installed on the server. I have the Common Desktop Environment installed, as well as all of the Linux desktops (KDE and GNOME). You can use the SMIT FastPath **smit dtconfig** to select between ASCII, CDE, and CDE with ASCII during boot.

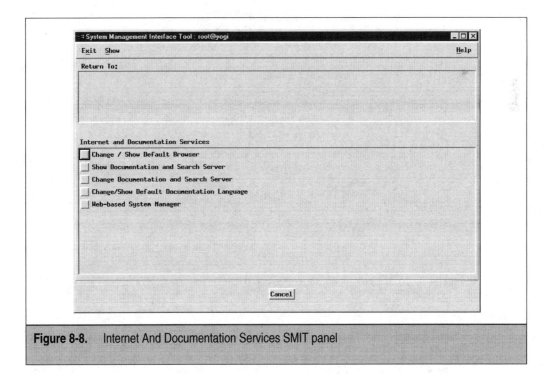

Figure 8-8.   Internet And Documentation Services SMIT panel

The Linux options are currently not available as SMIT or WebSM options. You can see more information on the Linux Affinity with AIX 5L in Chapter 21.

```
# smit dtconfig
```

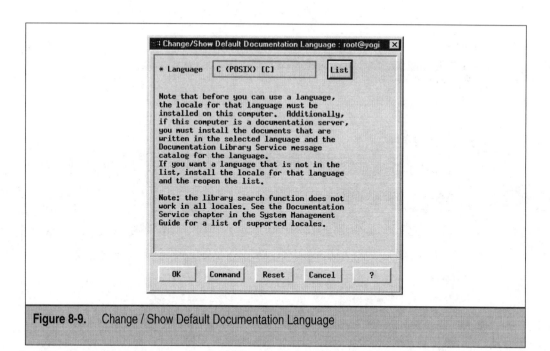

Default Documentation Language

You have the ability to change the default documentation language using the SMIT FastPath **smit chdoclang** (see Figure 8-9). Not all languages are supported for the library search function. You must install the locale for the language before you can

Figure 8-9. Change / Show Default Documentation Language

use it. For a documentation server, you not only have to install the language locale, but you also must install the documents written for that specific language.

```
# smit chdoclang
```

Manage Remote Reboot Facility

You can, if you desire, remotely reboot your systems as shown in the next illustration. I never use this facility because it is a security violation at my shop. However, there is a place for it. If you are doing remote installation and updates that require a reboot, then this facility can save a lot of time. The Remote Reboot Facility is activated by using the SMIT FastPath **smit rrbtty**. Once you activate a port for this purpose, you must not use it for anything else.

```
# smit rrbtty
```

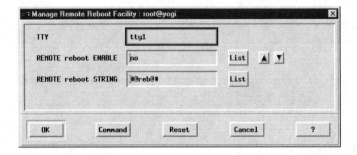

Manage System Hang Detection

This is new to AIX 5L. If your system *hangs*, this facility gives you the ability to take some kind of action. By default, it will not do anything. It is up to you to specify what corrective measure you want the machine to take. A shell script can be used to instruct the system how to react to a system hang condition. This is part of IBM's *self-healing* Project eLiza strategy that is an ongoing development effort. Use the SMIT FastPath **smit shd** to set up hang detection, as shown in Figure 8-10.

```
# smit shd
```

PTY

The AT&T-style pseudo-TTYs (PTYs) are not allocated automatically under AIX 4 or 5L. The number of PTYs must be specified for both AT&T and BSD-style devices as

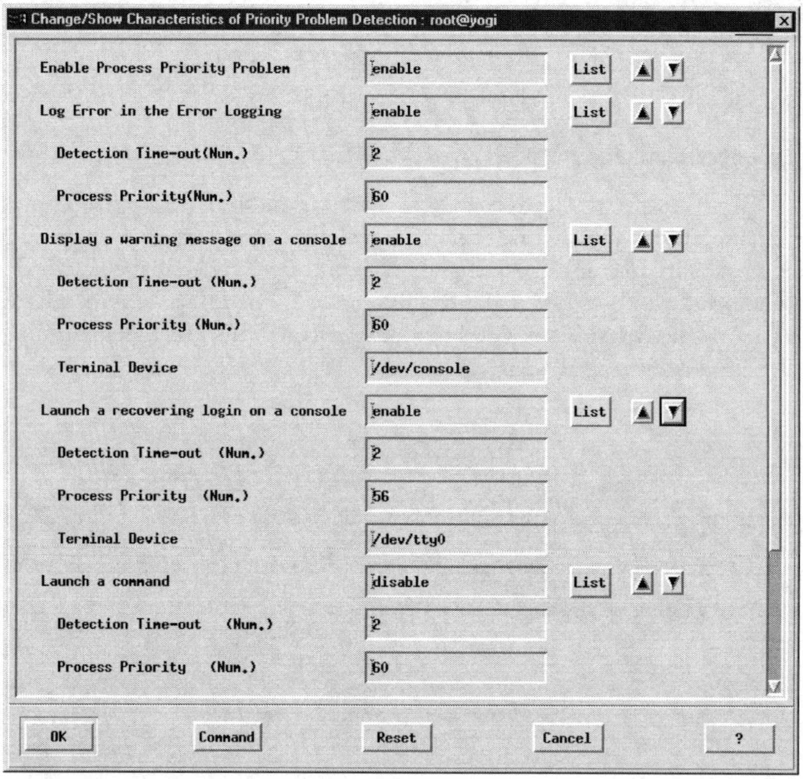

Figure 8-10. Change/Show Characteristics Of Priority Problem Detection SMIT panel

shown in the next illustration. This is the likely cause of not being able to start additional X11 applications. Change the number of PTYs using the SMIT FastPath **smit chgpty**.

```
# smit chgpty
```

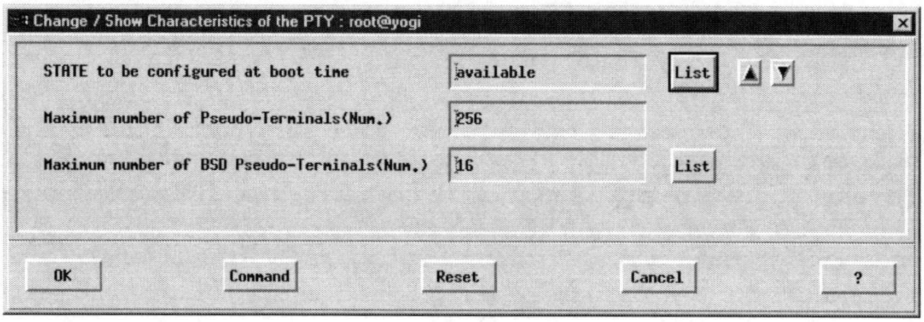

CHECKLIST

The following is a checklist for the key points in AIX Runtime Configuration:

☐ If you are not comfortable using the command-line options, you can use the SMIT FastPath **smit shutdown** to stop the system and send a message to all users.

☐ Set the correct date and time zone by invoking the SMIT FastPath **smit chtz_date**.

☐ You can add more languages to the set with the **smit mlang** command.

☐ You can alter AIX kernel characteristics for the maximum number of processes allowed per user, the maximum number of pages in block I/O buffer, the amount of real memory that can be pinned for network MBUFS, and other memory and scheduler subsystems using the SMIT FastPath **smit chgsys**. Be careful making changes to the system on this panel!

☐ To alter the number of licensed users, run the SMIT FastPath **smit chlicense**.

☐ You can broadcast a message to all logged-on users using the SMIT FastPath **smit wall** command.

☐ Monitor the /var/adm/ras/errlog log file regularly to scan for intermittent system problems using the **errpt** command..

☐ Manage the system logs from the SMIT FastPath **smit logs**.

☐ In most large environments, you should define a dedicated dump device as the primary dump device rather than the AIX 4.3 and 5L default of the /dev/hd6 paging space. Access the SMIT dump menu with the SMIT FastPath **smit dump**.

☐ You have at least three options for a user interface, depending on the software installed on the server. You can use the SMIT FastPath **smit dtconfig** to select between ASCII, CDE, and CDE with ASCII during boot.

☐ To activate the Remote Reboot Facility, use the SMIT FastPath **smit rrbtty**.

☐ In AIX 5L, Use the SMIT FastPath **smit shd** to set up hang detection to determine how the system will react to a hang condition.

CHAPTER 9

AIX Device Configuration Manager (*cfgmgr*) and the Object Data Manager (ODM)

Unlike many traditional UNIX systems, AIX supports dynamic device configuration and management. In most cases, you can connect external devices to a running system, configure the device attributes, and begin using the new device. No kernel rebuild! No system reboot! How this works is that AIX allows dynamic kernel extensions and device driver installation to a running kernel and dynamic device configuration through the object data manager (ODM). If you spend much time with AIX, it's essential that you develop a good understanding of ODM structure and operation. Since device management and the ODM are so tightly coupled, it makes sense to begin the discussion on devices by outlining the functional characteristics of the ODM.

ODM OVERVIEW

In the beginning, there were UNIX system configuration tables. They were sent forth to the BSD and System V masses, bringing all into a common fold of administration. But then, workstations multiplied and prospered. Configuration tables became large and unwieldy. Out of this mire of table parsing, a new doctrine was prophesied that would reduce the waiting and gnashing of teeth during login processing and password updates. It was called **dbm** and it was good. **dbm** routines reduced large configuration tables into a database of key-content pairs. Items in a database are retrieved in one or two file I/Os, while **dbm** databases are represented as an index file, `*.dir`, and a data file, `*.pag`. A common example of a **dbm** database is the password `passwd.dir` and `passwd.pag` file.

IBM decided to take the **dbm** doctrine one step further by introducing a hierarchical object-oriented database for configuration data called the object data manager, or ODM. The ODM centralizes a number of the standard configuration tables into a single management structure with update validation. AIX commands and kernel routines access ODM objects using SQL-like semantics.

ODM COMPONENTS

The ODM is comprised of a database of *object classes*, for example, the **tape** class. Within each object class is a list of *objects*, for example, 4 mm and 8 mm tape drives. Each object within each object class has a set of *object descriptors* that describes that particular object, for example, the tape block size and the SCSI ID on each tape drive. Example **object descriptors** are **uniquetype (tape/scsi/4mm4gb)**, **attribute (block_size)**, **default value (1024)** and **possible values (0-16777215,1)**. The object descriptors are commonly referred to as the attributes of the object.

Each component of the ODM—object class, object and object descriptor— has one or more commands that control adding, deleting, changing, or querying the component.

To add or delete object classes, we use the **odmcreate** and **odmdrop** commands. The **odmdrop** command is a *very dangerous* command! The **odmdrop** command deletes the *entire* object class and can leave your system useless—for example, with *no* tape drives, or, even worse, *no disks!*

To add, change, delete, and query an object, within an object class, we use the **odmadd, odmchange, odmdelete,** and **odmget** commands. Most of the time, you will use (I hope!) the **odmget** command. Use **odmget** to query the database for either predefined or customized objects.

To look at the object descriptors that show individual attributes of the object, use the **odmshow** command. The **odmshow** command allows you to look at how the object class is put together.

Some handy **odmget** commands are listed here:

Some handy odmget commands	Function
`odmget -q name=hdisk0 CuDv`	ODM object that describes hdisk0
`odmget -q name=hdisk0 CuAt`	ODM object that stores the PVID of hdisk0
`odmget -q type=osdisk PdDv`	ODM object that describes the predefined disk type **osdisk**
`odmget -q parent=scsi0 CuDv`	ODM objects within CuDv attached to parent device scsi0

You can also use the **like** operator with the **odmget** command:

`odmget -q "name like hdisk?" CuDv`   ◄——— All ODM customized disk devices

ODM Database

The ODM database manages almost everything on the system. The ODM manages the data associated with all of the devices on the system, some of the software on the system, the System Resource Controller, Error Logging and System Dump Facilities, the SMIT menus, Network Install Manager (NIM), and the configuration of TCP/IP. However, the ODM does *not* manage the print queues, filesystems (filesystems are controlled by the Logical Volume Manager—LVM), system security, or users and user passwords. All of these components are controlled by files under /etc and /etc/security.

Object classes are implemented as standard UNIX files in a directory that represents the ODM database. AIX versions 4 and 5L use three default ODM directories. The /etc/objrepos directory holds all of the *customized devices,* or devices that have been found and configured on the system. The /usr/lib/objrepos directory contains all of the *pre-defined device* object classes, or devices that are supported but not currently installed or active on the system, as well as the LPP updates as they are applied. The /usr/share/lib/objrepos directory holds the *share* part of each LPP, the four object classes used by the Software Vital Product Data (SWVPD), which are **lpp, history, inventory,** and **product**. This also allows for diskless, dataless, and other workstations.

The **ODMDIR** environment variable defines the directory path used as the default ODM database directory. The default **ODMDIR** path is set to /etc/objrepos by the

/etc/environment file. The **ODMDIR** environment variable may be manipulated to designate custom application databases.

`/etc/objrepos` ◄——————— Default object class directory

CDiagAtt	CDiagAtt.vc	CDiagDev	Config_Rules	CuAt
CuAt.vc	CuDep	CuDv	CuDvDr	CuPath
CuPath.vc	CuPathAt	CuPathAt.vc	CuVPD	DAVars
DSMOptions	DSMOptions.vc	DSMenu	FRUB	FRUs
MenuGoal	PDiagAtt	PDiagAtt.vc	PDiagDev	PDiagDev.vc
PDiagRes	PDiagRes.vc	PDiagTask	PDiagTask.vc	PdAt
PdAt.vc	PdAtXtd	PdAtXtd.vc	PdCn	PdDv
PdDv.vc	SRCextmeth	SRCnotify	SRCodmlock	SRCsubsvr
SRCsubsys	SWservAt	SWservAt.vc	TMInput	config_lock
crypto_module	crypto_module.vc	diag_lock	diag_log_lock	errnotify
history	history.vc	inventory	inventory.vc	lpp
lpp.vc	nim_attr	nim_attr.vc	nim_object	nim_object.vc
nim_pdattr	nim_pdattr.vc	pmmi_data	product	product.vc

`/usr/lib/objrepos` ◄——————— Additional ODM directory

CC	CC.vc	DSMOptions	DSMOptions.vc	DSMenu
FONT	FONT.vc	GAI	GAI.vc	KEYBOARD
KEYBOARD.vc	MESSAGES	MESSAGES.vc	PDiagAtt	PDiagAtt.vc
PDiagDev	PDiagDev.vc	PDiagRes	PDiagRes.vc	PDiagTask
PDiagTask.vc	PdAt	PdAt.vc	PdAtXtd	PdAtXtd.vc
PdCn	PdDv	PdDv.vc	XINPUT	XINPUT.vc
crypto_module	crypto_module.vc	fix	fix.vc	fix_lock
history	history.vc	inventory	inventory.vc	lag
lag.vc	lpp	lpp.vc	product	product.vc
sm_cmd_hdr	sm_cmd_hdr.vc	sm_cmd_opt	sm_cmd_opt.vc	sm_menu_opt
sm_menu_opt.vc	sm_name_hdr	sm_name_hdr.vc	vendor	vendor.vc

Objects and Object Classes

ODM objects are the data items that make up the object classes. Object attributes are mapped to a C language structure that represents the object class definition in a stanza format. The object class definition describes the descriptor-value pairs that make up an object. Object classes may be relationally joined to other object classes using a special link descriptor.

Initially, the object class definition is constructed as an **ASCII text file** identified by the * . cre extension. This description file is read by the **odmcreate** command to create the object class. The result is an empty **object class** and an * . h header file that may be used by application programs to populate and manipulate members in the object class. As an example, consider the generic attributes of an **inventory object class** for a music store, such as the inventory.cre file:

```
class Inventory {
    char item[20];
    char description[80];
    char color[20];
    short unit_number;
    char manufacturer[20];
    long quantity;
    long unit_price;
    method order_more;
}
```

To add the new object class, **Inventory,** to the ODM, we use the **odmcreate** command.

```
# odmcreate inventory.cre   ◄──────── Creates an empty object class called Inventory
```

The next step is to add some data to the **Inventory** object class. We again create an ANSI text file to store the entries and then we use the **odmadd** command to populate the **Inventory** object class.

For the **Inventory** object member, we create the following text file:

Inventory
```
item = "Drum_Sticks"
description   = "Rudimental drum sticks, plastic tip."
color   = "black"
unit_number   = 293
manufacturer = "Prehistoric Logs"
quantity = 20
unit_price = 2050
order_more = /usr/local/bin/check_inventory
```

Let's save the previous data in a file called NewInventory. To populate the **Inventory** object class with the data stored in the NewInventory file we use the **odmadd** command.

```
# odmadd NewInventory
```

To query the **Inventory** object class, we can use the **odmget** command. To query the ODM **Inventory** object class for color=black, we use the following command:

```
# odmget -q color=black Inventory
```

The command will return the stanza formatted output listed here.

Inventory

```
item = "Drum_Sticks"
description = "Drum Sticks - Plastic tip"
color = "black"
unit_number = 293
manufacturer = "Prehistoric Logs"
quantity = 20
unit_price = 2050
order_more = "/usr/local/bin/check_inventory"
```

To change the quantity from 20 to 50, we need to extract the object and store it in a file. We can use the preceding command and redirect output to a file and then edit the file.

```
odmget -q quantity=20 Inventory > /tmp/Inventory.out
```

Now, we just edit the /tmp/Inventory.out file, change the quantity stanza from 20 to 50, and save the file.

Next, we remove the old record using the **odmdelete** command.

```
odmdelete -q quantity=20 -o Inventory
```

Now we can add the modified record using the **odmadd** command.

```
odmadd /tmp/Inventory.out
```

To verify that the quantity was indeed changed, we can query the **Inventory** object class using the **odmget** command again.

```
odmget -q quantity=50 Inventory
```

The output reveals that our changes were made as we expected.

Inventory

```
item = "Drum_Sticks"
description = "Drum Sticks - Plastic tip"
color = "black"
unit_number = 293
manufacturer = "Prehistoric Logs"
quantity = 50
unit_price = 2050
order_more = "/usr/local/bin/check_inventory"
```

Finally, let's remove the **Inventory** object class that we created. To remove an object class, we use the **odmdrop** command.

CAUTION   Know exactly what you are doing when using the **odmdrop** command! You can easily make your system unusable if you make a mistake.

```
odmdrop -o Inventory
```

The object class definition may specify a method descriptor. The method defines a program that is to be invoked by the **odm_run_method** routine. The method updates the state of the object. In the previous example, the method would check the inventory and change state when the inventory was exhausted. Each object in the object class may specify a unique method program. Methods are represented as null-terminated, 255-character strings. The ampersand (&) may be appended to the method for asynchronous execution.

Command and Library Interface

Users and applications manipulate ODM data via commands and library routines. The list of commands and library routines in Table 9-1 will give you a feeling for types of operations permitted on ODM data.

DEVICE CONFIGURATION

Device interface definitions and configuration attributes are stored as objects in the ODM database. Each time the system is booted, the **cfgmgr** command walks the I/O bus and identifies all devices present on the system. Device location and type information is stored in the ODM, and the associated configuration rules and initialization methods are run to make the devices available for use (see Chapter 7).

Configuration Manager can also be invoked on a running system from the SMIT devices menus or by executing **cfgmgr**, **mkdev**, **chdev**, or **rmdev** from the command line. The same dynamic device configuration activities preformed at boot time are invoked while the system is up and available for use. This feature allows you to make new devices available without requiring a system reboot. The commands in Table 9-2 are some of the more common commands that act directly on the ODM.

PREDEFINED AND CUSTOMIZED DEVICES

Device configuration information is separated into predefined and customized object classes. Predefined object class information represents default configuration information

Library routine	Command	Use
odm_set_path		Set ODM database location (ODMDIR represents a shell environment variable)
	RESTBASE	Retrieve customized objects from boot image and store in ODM
	SAVEBASE	Store ODM-customized objects in boot image
odm_rm_class	ODMDROP	Remove an object class
	ODMSHOW	Display object class definition
odm_create_class	ODMCREATE	Create empty object class with associated C headers for applications
odm_add_obj	ODMADD	Add an object to an object class
odm_change_obj	ODMCHANGE	Modify object attributes
odm_rm_obj	ODMDELETE	Delete object from an object class
odm_get_obj	ODMGET	Retrieve an object in odmadd format
odm_get_by_id		Retrieve an object by its ID
odm_rm_by_id		Remove an object by its ID
odm_get_first		Retrieve first object that matches criteria
odm_get_next		Retrieve next object that matches criteria
odm_get_list		Retrieve a list of objects that match criteria
odm_mount_class		Retrieves the class symbol structure
odm_open_class		Opens an object class
odm_free_list		Free memory allocated for odm_get_list
odm_run_method		Execute method associated with an object
odm_close_class		Close object class
odm_err_msg		Retrieve error message string
odm_lock		Lock object for update
odm_unlock		Unlock object
odm_initialize		Initialize ODM session
odm_terminate		Terminate an ODM session

Table 9-1. ODM Commands and Library Subroutines

Command	Action
# smitty devices	SMIT FastPath
# mkdev -l tty0	Add a TTY device
# lsdev -C -s scsi -H	List existing SCSI devices
# chdev -l rmt0 -a block_size=0	Change tape block size
# lsattr -D -l rmt0	List tape attributes
# rmdev -l rmt0	Turn off the tape device but keep the definition
# rmdev -l rmt0 -d	Remove a tape device
# cfgmgr	Update ODM and kernel

Table 9-2. Most Common ODM Commands

for all devices supported by AIX. Customized object classes represent the devices actually present on the system.

`/etc/objrepos/Pdxxx` ODM predefined Attributes, Connections, and Devices:

PdAt   PdCn   PdDv

`/etc/objrepos/Cuxxx` ODM customized Attributes, Dependencies, Device Drivers and Vital Product Data:

CuAt   CuDep   CuDv   CuDvDr   CuVPD   Config_Rules   CuOD (New to 5L!)

`/usr/share/lib/objrepos` Components of the SoftWare Vital Product Data (SWVPD)

lpp   history   inventory   product

Device object classes are linked hierarchically into subclasses. For example, 7207 and 3590 tape devices represent subclasses under the **tape** object class. The **tape** object class, in turn, is a subclass of the **SCSI** object class. This hierarchy enforces configuration relationships.

- Parent object class information must be configured before child subclass configuration.
- Parent object class information may not be modified if child subclasses exist.
- Parent object classes may not be removed if child subclasses exist.

New ODM Class for AIX 5L (CuOD)

New to AIX 5L are a number of new technologies that require new ODM control, so IBM created a new ODM class, **CuOD**, or Customized On-Demand object class. One of IBM's new offerings is Dynamic CPU Allocation. The **CuDD** class allows you to order a new pSeries machine with extra CPU capacity, and you can dynamically allocate these new CPUs on-the-fly. The processors are ordered by the Feature Code (FC) for the target system. Basically, all you are doing is ordering a system with extra CPUs with the ability to activate the extra CPUs at a later date, thus reducing front-end costs and not giving all of the extra power to the users and applications at once. Shops that charge for CPU time will like this feature.

Another part of this same technology thinking is Dynamic CPU Deallocation, which will bring a failing CPU offline and out of service without bringing the system down. Memory technology, including Memory ChipKill, Bit Scattering, and Bit Steering, are part of a RAID 5–type technology for the memory subsystem. In case a memory DIMM fails, the system will automatically disable access to the chip and the system will keep running. This is a hardware feature, not part of the **CuOD** ODM class.

While we are on the subject of new things, Logical Partitioning (LPAR) starting with AIX 5L, version 5.2, allows you to create 1–16 logical systems within a single machine. These *logical system partitions* are considered independent systems to the outside world and can be managed as independent systems. IBM allows you to create these LPARs by specifying the exact number of processors and memory for the logical system, and allows different OS (AIX and Linux!) versions to run within the same machine. This is an incredible break through tool for development shops! When they need a sandbox to play in, just create one on-the-fly.

The ODM class **CuOD** is responsible for the dynamic mechanisms that make some of these technologies work; of course, the POWER 4 processor is required also.

NOTE   A POWER 4 CPU chip is really a 2-way SMP on a single chip that can be independently controlled!

A Sampling of ODM Object Classes

A special object class, predefined connections (**PdCn**), defines the hierarchy of device classes and subclasses. Device attributes are maintained as separate attribute object classes. See Table 9-3 for a sampling of AIX object classes.

You can display object class definitions using the **odmshow** command.

```
# odmshow <ObjectClassName>
```

Tables 9-4 through 9-7, representing the predefined and customized device and attribute descriptors, will give you some idea as to how device information is represented and linked.

Class Object	Contents of the Object Class
PdDv	Predefined devices supported by AIX
PdAt	Predefined device attributes
PdCn	Predefined device subclass connections
CuDv	Customized devices attached to the system
CuDvDr	Customized device drivers
CuAt	Customized device attributes
CuDep	Custom device dependencies
CuVPD	Customized vital product data
Config_Rules	Configuration rule sets

Table 9-3.   Sampling of AIX Object Classes

Descriptor Name	Descriptor Definition
Type	Device type
Class	Device class
Subclass	Device subclass
Prefix	Prefix name
Devid	Device ID
Base	Base device flag
has_vpd	VPD flag
Detectable	Device detectable flag
Chgstatus	Change status flag
bus_ext	Bus extender
Fru	FRU flag
Led	LED value
Setno	Set number
Msgno	Message number
Catalog	Catalog number
DvDr	Device driver name
Define	Define method
Configure	Configure method
Change	Change method
Unconfigure	Unconfigure method
Undefine	Undefine method
Start	Start method
Stop	Stop method
inventory_only	Inventory only flag
Uniquetype	Unique type

Table 9-4.   PdDv Descriptors

Descriptor Name	Descriptor Definition
Uniquetype	Unique type
Attribute	Attribute name
Deflt	Default value
Values	Attribute values
Width	Width
Type	Type flags
Generic	Generic flags
Rep	Representative flags
nls_index	NLS index

Table 9-5.   **PdAt** Pre-defined Attribute Descriptors

Descriptor Name	Descriptor Definition
Name	Device name
Status	Device status flag
Chgstatus	Change status flag
Ddins	Device driver instance
Location	Location code
Parent	Parent device
Connwhere	Where connected

Table 9-6. (CuDv) Customized Device Descriptors

DEVICE STATES

The **cfgmgr** routine is responsible for updating custom device information using the configuration rule sets, **cfgmgr** invokes the method specified for each attached device and updates the devices state. After the device method is complete, the device is set to one of three states: defined, stopped, or available, as shown in Table 9-8.

BOOT DEVICES

A small ODM database representing device configuration information is maintained as part of the AIX boot images. This information can be updated from the master ODM database using the **savebase** command. Likewise, ODM information from the boot image can be restored to the master ODM database by invoking the **restbase** command (see Chapter 7).

```
# savebase
```
◄─────── Save master ODM custom device data to the boot image

```
# restbase
```
◄─────── Restore custom ODM data from the boot image to the master ODM databababse

Descriptor Name	Descriptor Definition
Name	Device name
Attribute	Attribute name
Value	Attribute value
Type	Attribute type
Generic	Generic flags
Rep	Representative flags
nls_index	NLS index

Table 9-7. (CuAt) Customized Attribute Descriptors

Device State	State Definition
Defined	Device defined but not available for use
Stopped	Device configured but not available
Available	Device configured and available

Table 9-8.   Device States

SMALL COMPUTER SYSTEM INTERFACE

The most common device interface for the pSeries and RISC System/6000 is the small computer system interface (SCSI). The SCSI standard defines a generic interface and command protocol that will support most device types. Devices are attached in a daisy-chain fashion to the host adapter. The total chain length cannot exceed the distance maximum for the adapter type.

SCSI-1 and SCSI-2

The RISC System/6000 supports both SCSI-1 and SCSI-2 adapters and devices. Both SCSI-1 and SCSI-2 devices may be mixed on either adapter type; however, throughput to the device will be limited to SCSI-1 speeds. The **cfgmgr** queries the device type during SCSI device configuration and records the SCSI type. This eliminates the need for device drivers to continually query the SCSI type to determine whether extended SCSI-2 commands are supported. SCSI-1 support provides transfer rates up to 4 megabytes per second. The SCSI-2 Fast SCSI mode extends synchronous transfer rates to 10 megabytes per second. SCSI-2 signal control is also two to three times faster than SCSI-1. A maximum of 8 devices can be on a single SCSI-1 or SCSI-2 bus.

Single-Ended and Differential SCSI

Single-ended SCSI connections have a combined distance limitation of 6 meters. The logic level of each wire is based on the voltage difference with a common ground. Differential SCSI connections can run up to 25 meters. Logic levels on differential connections are based on the potential difference between two signal wires.

Single-ended connections can be a real problem with some RS/6000-9XX systems. The SCSI cable management arms in early 9XX racks eat up approximately 4.75 meters of the total 6-meter cable length. A single-ended SCSI to a differential SCSI adapter can be used to get around the problem.

Fast SCSI

The SCSI Fast-20 supports up to 8 devices but only a cable length of 3 meters for single-ended. Fast differential SCSI can reach a cable length of 25 meters with a maximum bus speed of 20MB/Sec.

Wide SCSI

If the word is not preceded with "Wide," then it is narrow. The Wide SCSI specification has a 16-bit bus width, as opposed to the normal 8-bit bus. Wide SCSI will sometimes allow up to 16 devices on the SCSI bus instead of only 8 devices, but look at your device specification for your hardware.

Fast and Wide SCSI

Fast and Wide SCSI can have up to 16 devices with a cable length up to 25 meters for differential but only 3 meters for single-ended. The bus speed can reach 20MB/Sec.

Ultra SCSI

Ultra SCSI doubles the bus speed to 40MB/Sec but cuts the maximum number of devices down to 4 on a short 3 meter cable.

Ultra-Wide, Wide and Narrow Ultra-2, Ultra-3, and Ultra-320 SCSI

Yes, there are more. Ultra-Wide SCSI has a maximum bus speed of 40 MB/Sec with 16 devices on a 25-meter cable. Ultra-2 SCSI has an 8-bit bus with a maximum bus speed of 40MB/Sec and allows a maximum of 8 devices on a 25-meter cable. Wide Ultra-2 doubles the bus speed to 40MB/Sec with a 16-bit-wide bus and can support up to 16 devices. Ultra-3 SCSI is also called Ultra160 SCSI. Ultra-3 SCSI again doubles the bus speed, this time to 160MB/Sec on a 16-bit-wide bus. Up to 16 devices are supported with a maximum cable length of 12 meters. The Ultra-320 SCSI brings the bus speed up to 320 MB/Sec and supports up to 16 devices. The bus width is 16-bit and the maximum cable length is 12 meters.

Cables and Adapters

Be very careful with your SCSI cable lengths. Strange things start to happen when the cables exceed the maximum cable length for the particular SCSI type you are working with. The most common device operation errors come from mixing SCSI device types on the same bus and forgetting to measure *all* of the SCSI cable. Always measure the cable from SCSI terminator to SCSI terminator, which brings up another point. The SCSI bus *must* be terminated! In newer equipment and on most internal SCSI adapters, the terminators are installed internally.

If you are running HACMP and are using external SCSI disks as your shared disks, remember to *twin-tail* your SCSI bus. When you twin-tail the bus, you remove all of the internal SCSI terminators from the SCSI adapter. Then, on the SCSI bus cable, you add a twin-tail connector on the cable and terminate the bus on the external cable. With the external SCSI termination, you do not have to worry about a dead system bringing down your entire HACMP cluster. You also need to change the SCSI address of one of the adapters, but this is covered in the next section.

SCSI Addressing

Each SCSI string supports either 8 or 16 addresses (0–7 or 0-16) that must be divided up between the devices and the adapter. Some device controllers support multiple devices from a single SCSI ID using logical unit numbers (LUNs)—an example is a SCSI RAID 5 disk array. In most cases, you are only going to have either 7 or 15 addresses that may be assigned to the devices on the SCSI chain. The SCSI adapter requires one of the addresses—normally, SCSI ID 7. Arbitration on a SCSI chain begins with the high address numbers, so better response is provided to devices with larger SCSI IDs. Device SCSI IDs are commonly selectable via jumpers or from a selector wheel on the device frame or housing.

The SCSI address format is

AB   Two-digit SCSI address where *A* represents the SCSI ID and *B* represents the logical unit number

Devices are identified by a location code. Verify that the location code matches the actual hardware slot and interface using the **lsdev** command.

The device location codes are as follows:

AA-BB-CC-DD

where

AA = Drawer location or planar
BB = I/O bus and slot
CC = Adapter connector number
DD = SCSI ID or port number

SCSI Over IP (*i*SCSI)

What is this? Yes, SCSI over IP, or *i*SCSI, has emerged as the standard for Networked Attached Storage (NAS). The most common use of NAS is for file sharing. The *i*SCSI standard allows SCSI devices to communicate on the IP network. Normally, *i*SCSI is implemented over a gigabit IP network. If you really think about it, NAS is nothing more than NFS on steroids! It is cost effective and an excellent solution when you have a small number of machines that need access to the same data. For larger environments, a Storage Area Network (SAN) is more appropriate. You can reduce access time to the shared data more than ten times over traditional NFS mounts by removing the I/O from a single machine and moving the traffic to the network. Of course, your network needs to be able to handle the traffic, and a SAN should be considered for heavier traffic needs. There is more on SANs and NAS in Chapter 29.

USING SMITTY CFGMGR TO AUTOCONFIGURE YOUR SYSTEM

If you install new devices in you systems that are not in the predefined or customized ODM object classes, you can do a little trick. We just let the system get the device drivers and other device information directly from the operating system CD-ROM. It is a good idea to run this procedure after any type of upgrade, too.

Insert the base operating system CD-ROM for your current OS level, and use the **oslevel** command to query the system. After the CD is inserted in the drive, issue the following command:

```
# smitty cfgmgr
```

When the menu pops up, press the F4 key to select the **Installation Device**, probably /dev/cd0. Then press the ENTER key twice, and the system will automatically load any device code that it needs and update the ODM. This is a very useful and foolproof tool! Remember to apply your ML code updates again in case any of the device code has been updated.

UPDATING THE PRODUCT TOPOLOGY DISKETTE

It's a good idea to update the topology diskette supplied with your system each time you add a new device. These diskettes are used by IBM service and support representatives to keep a record of your system configuration. These are especially helpful for sites that have a number of machines. After updating the diskette, send a copy to IBM hardware support using the mailer and address label supplied with the update diskette.

Here is the topology update procedure:

1. Shut down the system.
2. Set the key switch to the service position.
3. Boot the system.
4. At the **Diagnostics Operating Instructions** display, press ENTER.
5. At the **Function Selection** menu, select the **Service Aid** option.
6. At the **Service Aids Selection** menu, select the **Product Topology** options.
7. Follow the instructions displayed. When prompted, "**Do you have any update diskettes that have not been loaded?**", answer yes and insert

the Product Topology Update diskette. Follow the instructions to update the Product Topology System diskette. If the **EC And MES Updates** screen is displayed, select the F7 key to commit updates.

8. Repeatedly press F3 to exit all diagnostics menus.

9. Reset the key switch to the normal position (if present).

10. Reboot the system.

CHECKLIST

The following is a checklist for the key points in the AIX Device Configuration Manager and the Object Data Manager:

☐ IBM's object data manager, ODM, is a hierarchical object-oriented configuration database manager.

☐ To add, change, delete, and query an object within an object class, use the **odmadd, odmchange, odmdelete,** and **odmget** commands.

☐ You can manipulate the directory path used as the default ODM database directory, /etc/objrepos, using the **ODMDIR** environment variable in the /etc/environment file.

☐ To add a new object class to the ODM, use the **odmcreate** command.

☐ To add data to a new object class, use the **odmadd** command.

☐ Device interface definitions and configuration attributes are stored as objects in the ODM database, and you can invoke Configuration Manager on a running system by executing **cfgmgr, mkdev, chdev,** or **rmdev** from the command line to make new devices available without a system reboot.

☐ You can use the new Dynamic CPU allocation feature in AIX 5L to dynamically allocate extra CPU capacity in a pSeries machine on-the-fly.

☐ You can use Dynamic CPU Deallocation to bring a failing CPU offline without bringing down the system.

☐ With Logical Partitioning (LPAR) in AIX 5L version 5.2, you can create 1–16 logical systems on a single machine with each logical system partition seen and managed as an independent system.

☐ You can update the small device configuration ODM database, maintained as part of the AIX boot images, from the master ODM database using the **savebase** command.

☐ If you mix SCSI-1 and SCSI-2 adapters and devices on an RISC System/6000, throughput to the device will be limited to the slower SCSI-1 4 MB/Sec speed.

☐ Limit your single-end SCSI chains to a combined distance of 6 meters and your differential SCSI chains to a combined distance of 25 meters.

- [ ] Limit single-ended SCSI Fast-20 chains to a 3-meter cable length and fast differential SCSI to 25 meters.

- [ ] You must terminate the SCSI bus.

- [ ] Assign unique SCSI addresses to each device on a chain and use higher address numbers for devices that will benefit from faster response.

- [ ] To easily install new devices in your system that are not in the predefined or customized ODM object classes, insert the base operating system CD-ROM for your current OS level, and then run the **smitty cfgmgr** command, press **F4** and select the installation device, and press **ENTER** twice.

- [ ] Update your topology disk each time you add a new device, and send a copy to IBM using the supplied mailer.

CHAPTER 10

Tape Systems

Magnetic tape, because of its large storage capacity, low cost, and long storage life (usually in excess of two years), has been the secondary storage media of choice for many years. The RS/6000 and pSeries machines support most any type of tape drive, and IBM is always working on increasing the storage capacity.

Before we look at the attributes of the individual device types and tape formats, it will be helpful to do a review of general tape characteristics. An understanding of how data is represented on the physical media will assist you in making better use of the resource.

Physical Characteristics

The earliest use of magnetic tape was in the German magnetophon. This device used a plastic tape doped with iron oxide. Later, the United States experimented with paper tape coated with iron oxide. This was followed by acetate and finally polymer-based tape. The thickness of the oxide coating, the particle density, and the particle distribution on the tape surface determine the signal strength that may be encoded. A thicker and denser oxide layer improves the signal strength but reduces high-frequency response for audio tape. If the layer is too thin, print-through may occur. Print-through is the transfer of the recorded magnetic signal between tape layers on the reel. Tape thickness and base substrate also determine transport friction, media durability, and shelf life. Data-grade tape employs a thicker and denser oxide coating than standard audio tapes and is usually more expensive. This is changing somewhat with digital audio tape (DAT), which has a denser coating than other audio tapes. The same relationship holds true for data and video 8 mm tape. Good quality videotape may work in your 8 mm tape drive, but I wouldn't recommend it! I learned the hard way!

Over the last few years we have also seen improvements in mechanical transport and head technologies. Helical-scan heads are replacing fixed-head configurations for digital recording (see the illustration). Helical-scan heads spin as the tape moves across the head surface. This reduces the transport speed requirements for the tape moving from spindle to spindle. Data is written diagonally across the tape surface. This will be an important point to remember when we talk about block sizes in the next section.

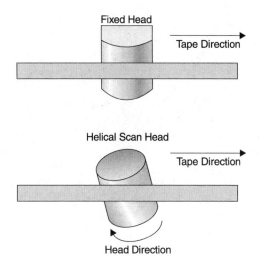

Data Format

Data is recorded on tape in blocks. Each block of data is separated from the next by an interrecord gap. Files on a tape are delimited by tape marks or file marks. A tape mark indicates the beginning of tape (BOT). Two tape marks in succession indicate the end of tape (EOT). BOT may also be followed by a special file called a tape label. The label indicates the volume name, size, and sequence number in a multivolume set.

Blocks are either fixed or variable in length (see the following illustration). Fixed-block format means that data is read and written in chunks that are all the same size. Data must be read from and written to the media in multiples of the block size. Variable-block format leaves it up to the application to determine the length of each block of data. A request to read more data than is available in the next tape block will result in a short read when using variable format. This feature is useful for commands like **dd** that will support short reads, but it is detrimental to less-forgiving commands such as **tar**, **cpio**, **pax**, **backup**, and **restore**. The good news is that, when using variable block size, the **dd** command can be employed with an excessive block size to buffer input to **tar**, **cpio**, **backup**, and **restore**.

```
# dd if=/dev/rmt0.1 ibs=64k obs=512  | restore -xvf-
# dd if=/dev/rmt0.1 ibs=64k obs=5120 | tar -xvBf-
# dd if=/dev/rmt0.1 ibs=64k obs=5120 | cpio -ivB
# dd if=/dev/rmt0.1 ibs=64k obs=5120 | pax -rf-
```

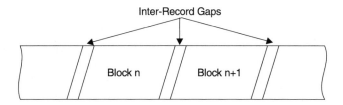

Block Size

Block size is an important consideration and will affect the total media capacity and the time required to read or write data on the device. Larger block sizes reduce the number of interrecord gaps and make better use of the tape. The block size should also reflect the physical block size written by the device. For example, an 8 mm tape drive writes 1024 bytes per block diagonally across the width of the tape. If the block size defined to AIX for the device is fixed at 512 byte blocks, then the device will write out 512 bytes of data and pad the remaining 512 bytes in the physical 1024-byte block. This effectively reduces the media capacity by half, and restores will take twice as long. When variable-length blocks are defined in AIX for the example 8 mm device, block sizes larger than 1024 will fill each physical block on the tape. If the block size used by the application is not a multiple of 1024, then the last physical block written will be padded.

Block size is application dependent. Selecting the wrong block size can inhibit the ability to read backup media and cause portability problems. IBM's **mksysb** script changes the block size to 512 bytes for the first three images (boot, bosinst, and toc) of a bootable system backup tape and then restores the previous block size before backing up the rootvg volume group to the fourth image. The **savevg** command is a symbolic link to the **mksysb** script that will not change the tape device block size or create the boot, bosinst, and toc images when backing up non-rootvg volume groups.

You can change the default block size defined to AIX for a tape device using the **chdev** command or through SMIT, as shown in the following listing. Remember that this does not alter the physical block size used by the device!

```
# chdev -1 rmt0 -a "block_size=0"      ◄──────────Variable block size
# chdev -1 rmt0 -a "block_size=512"    ◄──────────Fixed 512-byte block size
# chdev -1 rmt0 -a "block_size=1024"   ◄──────────Fixed 1024-byte block size
```

Or you can use the SMIT FastPath **smit chgtpe**.

```
# dd if=/dev/rmt0.1 ibs=64k obs=512  | restore -xvb
# dd if=/dev/rmt0.1 ibs=64k obs=5120 | tar -xvBf-
# dd if=/dev/rmt0.1 ibs=64k obs=5120 | cpio -ivB
```

If portability is an issue, you will want to define a default block size of 0, which indicates a variable block size. Byte ordering and ASCII/EBCDIC conversion can be handled by the **conv** option to the **dd** command.

```
# dd if=/dev/rmt0 conv=swab    ◄──────────────────Swap byte pairs
# dd if=/dev/rmt0 conv=ascii   ◄──────────────────Convert EBCDIC to ASCII
# dd if=/dev/rmt0 ibs=512 obs=1024 conv=sync  ◄──Pad blocks
```

Table 10-1 provides a few hints when using **tar** to move data from an RS/6000 or pSeries machine to one of the listed vendor types.

Vendor	Hint
DEC	OK. Check for compatible tape type/density.
Sun	Sun uses 512-byte blocks by default. On RS/6000, set block size to 512 or use **dd conv=sync** to pad blocks when reading Sun tapes.
HP	OK. Check for compatible tape type/density.
SGI	Swap byte pairs using **dd conv=swab**.

Table 10-1. RS/6000 and pSeries Tape Conversions Using **tar**

Device Names

Along with the block size, you must also be aware of the implicit tape **ioctl** operations associated with the device special filenames. Device special filenames are associated with a unique major number that identifies the tape device driver location in the device switch table. A per-device unique minor number identifies entry points in the tape device driver that correspond to various density and tape control operations. If you are familiar with other UNIX tape systems, you know that nearly everyone uses his or her own scheme for naming device special files. Table 10-2 represents the AIX default device names and the corresponding control operations and densities.

The high and low density values are dependent upon the device. Consult the vendor documentation concerning the device characteristics.

Make sure you take a close look at the **rmt** man page information on how BOT, EOF, and EOT are handled for both reading and writing. You may be in for a surprise if you do not select the correct device name for your application's requirements. This can be especially true for EOT handling on nine-track tape drives. UNIX generally does

Filename	Rewind on Close	Retention on Open	Density
/dev/rmt*	Yes	No	High
/dev/rmt*.1	No	No	High
/dev/rmt*.2	Yes	Yes	High
/dev/rmt*.3	No	Yes	High
/dev/rmt*.4	Yes	No	Low
/dev/rmt*.5	No	No	Low
/dev/rmt*.6	Yes	Yes	Low
/dev/rmt*.7	No	Yes	Low

Table 10-2. Tape Device Name Implicit Options

not sense EOT before reaching it. Improper tape positioning at EOT can cause the application to run the tape off the end of the reel. You will make few friends in the operations staff if you do this very often.

Tape Positioning

The tape device driver supports a somewhat standard set of **ioctl** operations used to control tape positioning. These operations can be invoked from the local command line, remotely, or within a program. Local and remote positioning is handled by the **tctl** and **rmt** commands, respectively. If you are familiar with the **mt** command on other UNIX platforms, both **mt** and **tctl** are now supported by the same hard-linked runtime, as can be seen by executing the command **what /usr/bin/mt**.

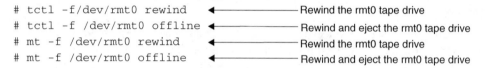

```
# tctl -f/dev/rmt0 rewind        ──────── Rewind the rmt0 tape drive
# tctl -f /dev/rmt0 offline      ──────── Rewind and eject the rmt0 tape drive
# mt -f /dev/rmt0 rewind         ──────── Rewind the rmt0 tape drive
# mt -f /dev/rmt0 offline        ──────── Rewind and eject the rmt0 tape drive
```

For remote operation, be aware that AIX **ioctl** call numbers don't necessarily map one-for-one with those on the remote system (see Table 10-3). You can fix the mapping problem by creating a wrapper for **rmt** to remap the command-line parameters to those in use by the remote system.

AIX	ioctl Number	Remote	ioctl Number	Comment
STOFFL	5	MTOFFL	6	Rewind unload tape
STREW	6	MTREW	5	Rewind tape
STERASE	7	MTERASE	9	Erase tape
STRETEN	8	MTRETEN	8	Retention tape
STWEOF	10	MTWEOF	0	Write end-of-file marker
STFSF	11	MTFSF	1	Forward space file
STRSF	12	MTBSF	2	Back space file
STFSR	13	MTFSR	3	Forward space record
STRSR	14	MTBSR	4	Back space record
N/A	N/A	MTNOP	7	NO-OP
N/A	N/A	MTEOM	10	End-of-media
N/A	N/A	MTNBSF	11	Back space to BOF

Table 10-3. AIX to UNIX ioctl Mapping

Be aware of where you are during tape operations. After each program **read()** or **write()** operation, the tape head is positioned at the beginning of the next block or the beginning of blank space. Tape marks are treated exactly like a file, so they must be accounted for when skipping from file to file on a tape.

Permissions

Restricting access to tape devices tends to be a problem on many UNIX systems. The device special files are commonly set read/write by the world. In the absence of additional tape allocation software, you can easily create your own drive reservation application using the following algorithm:

1. Check for a free device (absence of device lock files). If all devices are in use, exit. If not, continue.

2. Fork and spawn a new shell. Wait until process exit to release the device.

3. Create a lock file for the selected device.

4. Set permissions and ownership to the requester.

The following are the default device permissions:

```
# ls -l /dev/rmt*
crw-rw-rw-   1 root      system    19,   0 Feb 17 23:58 /dev/rmt0
crw-rw-rw-   1 root      system    19,   1 Feb 17 22:58 /dev/rmt0.1
crw-rw-rw-   1 root      system    19,   2 Jul 26 2001  /dev/rmt0.2
crw-rw-rw-   1 root      system    19,   3 Jul 26 2001  /dev/rmt0.3
crw-rw-rw-   1 root      system    19,   4 Jul 26 2001  /dev/rmt0.4
crw-rw-rw-   1 root      system    19,   5 Jul 26 2001  /dev/rmt0.5
crw-rw-rw-   1 root      system    19,   6 Jul 26 2001  /dev/rmt0.6
crw-rw-rw-   1 root      system    19,   7 Jul 26 2001  /dev/rmt0.7
```

TAPE TOOLS

AIX provides a limited set of tape utilities. The following set of commands supports tape manipulation:

- **dd**   Read/write variable block sizes and perform data conversion
- **tcopy**   Display tape directory or copy tape to tape
- **tar, cpio, pax, backup/restore**   Archive; may use tape as a media
- **rdump, rrestore**   Remote archive and restore; may use tape as a media

LINEAR OPEN TAPE (LTO) ULTRIUM TAPE DRIVES

In 1997, a consortium was formed between IBM, HP, and Seagate for a new open tape standard. Ultrium is the first LTO offering from IBM. With Ultrium LTO, you get high capacity at 100GB per tape and high performance at 10–20 MB/second.

The LTO tape drive uses an open industry standard and has improved reliability over DLT, improved capacity (by 250 percent) over DLT, and improved performance (by 250 percent) over DLT. Since LTO is an open format, there are multiple manufacturers of media and drives, and the cartridges are interchangeable. There are four generations in the works for LTO Ultrium tape drives as shown in Table 10-4.

For a complete list of all of the tape cartridge, tape drives, and tape library specifications, refer to the IBM Web site at http://www.storage.ibm.com/ssg.html. From this Web page, select the TotalStorage Solutions product guide to view the PDF file.

IBM's Four LTO Ultrium Options

- Ultrium Tape Drive—Models 3580-L11 and 3580-H11

- Ultrium Tape Autoloader—Models 3581-L17 and 3581-H17

- Ultrium Scalable Tape Library—Model 3583

- UltraScalable Tape Library—Model 3584 L32 or D32

You can get more information on each of these IBM offerings at http://www.ibm.com/storage/lto.

New to the LTO Ultrium Scalable Tape Library and the UltraScalable Tape Library is the capacity for Native Fibre Channel connectivity through the internal SAN Data Gateway Module.

At the high end of the Ultrium LTO offerings is the IBM UltraScalable Tape Library 3584-L32. This machine uses an exclusive multipath architecture with up to 12 logical library partitions, supports both Native Fibre Channel and SCSI LTO drives, is

Generation	First	Second	Third	Fourth
Capacity	100GB	200GB	400GB	800GB
Transfer rate	10–20 MB/sec	20–40 MB/sec	40–80 MB/sec	80–160 MB/sec
Media	Metal particle	Metal particle	Metal particle	Thin film

Table 10-4.   LTO Ultrium Present and Future

autocalibrating, has Dual Picker Robotics, supports redundant power supplies, and can hold 141 to 281 Ultrium tape cartridges.

The LTO Ultrium Scalable Tape Library supports enhanced management capabilities using StorWatch Expert ETL, which is a different StorWatch product than the version used on the Enterprise Storage Server (ESS, a.k.a. the Shark). StorWatch Expert ETL provides remote management capability by way of your Web browser, which allows all of the operator control panel functions to be handled through the network, including microcode downloads. This functionality also allows for SNMP monitoring of the tape library.

The following operating systems are supported for LTO Ultrium attachment:

- AIX 4.3.2 or later

- OS/400 V4R4 or later

- Microsoft Windows NT 4.0 with service pack 6

- Microsoft Windows 2000 for build 2195 or later

- Sun Solaris 2.6, Solaris 7, and Solaris 8

- HP-UX 11.0

Most backup software is supported in the LTO Ultrium tape systems, but Tivoli Storage Manager (TSM) is preferred by IBM.

IBM 3494 ENTERPRISE TAPE LIBRARY

The IBM 3494 Enterprise Tape Library is the workhorse for backup and recovery in many large enterprises. The 3494 can store over 6000 tape cartridges and supports up to 76 Magstar tape drives. The nice thing about the 3494 Tape Library is that it is expandable to up to 16 library frames, which can store up to 748TB of stored data.

The Tape Library Base Frame holds the brains of the 3494 tape subsystem. The control mechanism is a PC running OS/2, which runs the tape and robotic subsystems. Each Tape Library Base Frame consists of the Tape subsystem, which supports IBM 3590 and 3490E tape drives, the Library Manager, a single- or dual-gripper tape cartridge accessor, cartridge storage cells, which run across the front and back of the frame, and an optional I/O station.

There are three types of expansion frame options to extend the capacity of the 3494 Tape Library:

- **Tape drive expansion frames**   This type of frame is used to provide additional tape drives and cartridge cells. Three types of drive frames allow for flexibility in choosing the tape drive technology to suit your particular needs.

- **Tape storage frames**   This type of expansion frame is used to add additional tape storage cells. Each storage frame supports up to 400 additional tape cartridges.

- **High-availability frames**   This type of frame adds an additional Library Manager and a second cartridge accessor with either single or dual grippers mounted at each end of the library. Having a second Library Manager provides seamless continuation of service to keep running in the unlikely event of the primary Library Manager or cartridge accessor failing. Both of the cartridge accessors can operate at the same time by enabling the dual active accessor feature.

You can combine various models of the Enterprise Tape Library to support up to 16 frames, which can hold over 6000 tape cartridges and up to 748TB of data.

LINUX TAPE SUPPORT

IBM's support for the Open Source platform of Linux has extended to the tape systems. This support has produced an IBM Linux tape driver for the 32-bit Intel-based platforms starting with Red Hat Linux version 7.1. This new tape subsystem driver adds extended tape operation capabilities, including better error recovery and a suit of tape utilities for the lineup of IBM tape products. The following is a list of the Linux supported tape drives and autoloaders tape systems.

- Ultrium External Tape Drive—Model 3580

- Ultrium Tape Autoloader—Model 3581

- IBM Enterprise Tape Drive—Model 3590 and E11/B11 and E1A/E1B tape systems

- IBM Enterprise Tape Library—Model 3494

- Ultrium Scalable Tape Library—Model 3583

- UltraScalable Tape Library—3584

PUBLIC DOMAIN TAPE TOOLS

Many public domain and commercial software packages are available for download, as in Table 10-5 although, of course, the commercial packages come at a cost. You can search the Web for software products, but two useful ones can be found at the following URLs:

```
http://www.stokely.com/ unix.sysadm.resources/backup.html
http://www.rootvg.net/
```

Amanda	Extremely flexible backup tool that supports network and local backups, kerberos security, and almost any tape subsystems including tape libraries.
magtapetools	Package of tape tools supporting interrogation of tape contents, tape copy, reading random blocks, and reading/writing ANSI labels.
tapemap	Map a tape. Reports min/max block size and block count for each file on the tape.
fsbackup	Incremental backup utility that supports compression and encryption.
storix	Complete backup management for all RS/6000s, pSeries, SPs, and Intel IA-64 systems running AIX. Supports local and network backups.

Table 10-5.   Additional Tape Tools

CHECKLIST

The following is a checklist for the key tape system points:

- [ ] Data is recorded on tape in blocks. Each block of data is separated from the next by an interrecord gap.

- [ ] Files on a tape are delimited by tape marks or file marks. A tape mark indicates the beginning of tape (BOT). Two tape marks in succession indicate the end of tape (EOT).

- [ ] BOT might be followed by a special file called a tape label. The label indicates the volume name, size, and sequence number in a multivolume set.

- [ ] To maximize tap use efficiency and minimize restore time, use the **chdev** command to change the AIX default block size for a tape device so it matches the device's physical block size.

- [ ] If portability is an issue, define a default block size of 0, which indicates a variable block size.

- [ ] Device special filenames are associated with a unique major number identifying the tape device driver location in the device switch table.

- [ ] Handle local and remote positioning with the **tctl** and **rmt** commands respectively.

- [ ] Because the device special files are commonly set read/write by the world, if you want to restrict access to tape drives in the absence of additional tape allocation software, you can easily create your own drive reservation application.

- ☐ Use the **tcopy** command to display a tape directory or copy tape to tape.
- ☐ The standard **tar, cpio, pax, backup/restore** commands can use tape as a media.
- ☐ The remote archive and restore commands `rdump`, **rrestore** can use tape as a media.

CHAPTER 11

The AIX Logical Volume Manager (LVM)

Since you are reading this book, you are without a doubt going to manage AIX systems. The most important chapter in this book is this chapter. A thorough understanding of the storage hardware and the Logical Volume Manager (LVM) and its components is vital to effective AIX system management. I want to start this chapter with the hardware components and then move into the components of the Logical Volume Manager (LVM) and the terminology that we use.

DISK EVOLUTION

Are your filesystems half full, or are they half empty? It doesn't matter how much disk space you throw into a system. They are always half full and growing fast! A typical AIX 5L installation with DocSearch installed is about 2.75 gigabytes (GB) for a base installation. A more valid size for all of the extra toys is on the order of 4GB of unmirrored space. (Always mirror the *root volume group!*) If you have been around computer systems for a long time like I have, you may remember when 10MB hard drives on an IBM PC/XT seemed like more storage than you could ever use. Today the IBM pSeries machines ship with 32GB and 72GB hard drives, and 128GB and 256GB drives are coming fast.

DISKS ARE DOUBLING EVERY SIX MONTHS

As I stated in the previous section, the IBM pSeries machines are shipping with 32GB and 72GB drives. This transition to twice the disk space occurred in only six months! Of course this disk technology has been in the works for years. The evolution is possible because of two main factors: The disk drive head is getting much smaller, and the platter technology keeps getting better. The disk drive heads are getting as small as the surface mount electronic components that you see on circuit boards.

A drive head in the 1980s was the size of your fingernail, but the disk drive could only hold about 10MB of data. The smaller and smaller heads allow for finer granularity of the disk platter. The disk platter technology is moving to better platter material, and many companies are doing research and development on plastic disk drives. The plastic platter is coated with a magnetic substrate to give the plastic magnetic properties. As these new technologies are perfected, the disk drives are doubling in capacity every six month while keeping the same footprint.

DISK HARDWARE

Workstation and personal computer disk drives have primarily been either Integrated Drive Electronics (IDE) drives or Small Computer System Interface (SCSI) drives. IDE drives integrate all the controller functions into the disk housing. SCSI drives also integrate controller functions in the disk assembly but require a more complex adapter card on the I/O bus. The IBM pSeries and RISC System/6000 support internal SCSI disks, as well as Micro Channel or PCI adapters (depending on model) for attaching external single-ended, differential, fast, narrow, wide SCSI, SCSI-2, and Ultra-SCSI disk devices. However, you are not going to see an IDE drive in a pSeries machine, only SCSI, SSA, ESS (The Shark!), and optical storage.

Be on the lookout for solid state storage! You may have noticed that memory prices have come down quite a bit during the last few years. Researchers are working to use this same type of technology to developt solid state disk drives. A few companies are offering these "disk drives" already, but some more work needs to be done for these to be mainstream. Of course, these chips do not lose your data when the machine is turned off! The technology is a type of nonvolatile RAM (NVRAM) that can be dynamically updated.

Serial Storage Architecture (SSA)

A recent option for connecting disk devices is IBM's Serial Storage Architecture (SSA). SSA uses a loop configuration for connecting devices to one or more pSeries or RS/6000 computers. The loop architecture is akin to token ring or dual-ring FDDI in that the loop can be broken and traffic will be rerouted using the remaining link, thus allowing you to add disks to an SSA loop on a running system. It provides fault tolerance in the machine to device connection that is not available with SCSI or IDE-type attachment. There is also no bus arbitration protocol like that required in SCSI configuration. SSA supports concurrent full-duplex 80 MB/sec I/O between the host and disk device. This capability is called spatial reuse.

Using diag to Troubleshoot SSA Disks

The **diag** facility is used to troubleshoot the SSA subsystem. The most valuable task is to verify the SSA loop. Given a visual representation of the loop, it is very easy to troubleshoot the SSA subsystem. At the command line, enter **diag**. This command will start a query of the system, and then a screen is displayed. Press the ENTER key to continue with **diag** or press F3 to exit. In the next panel, use the arrow keys to move down and select Task Selection. Page down the Task Selection list to close to the bottom where the SSA disk utilities are located. One of the selections is Loop Verification. Select which SSA loop you want to verify and press ENTER. The output will vary depending on how the SSA loop has been configured, but a broken or open loop will stand out with the specific disk marked.

RAID

A Redundant Array of Independent Disks (RAID) brings additional fault tolerance into storage support through the use of data mirroring and striping technologies. In addition to data fault tolerance and availability, RAID can maximize read I/O performance by spreading access across multiple disk devices, which allows more spindles to get into action to read and write data.

Essentially, RAID is a group of drives (stripe or mirror set) that are linked by a special-purpose bus, processor, and cache memory structure to distribute file data across all the drives in the set. The type of mirroring or striping performed is designated by the RAID levels 0–5. RAID level 0 is used to stripe data across disks without any parity recovery support. RAID level 1 is what we have come to know as mirroring. RAID level 2 is a technique originally patented by Thinking Machines, Inc. In a RAID 2 configuration, data is bit- or byte-striped across multiple drives along with parity information that can be used to reconstruct the data on any individual driver in the event of a failure. Like RAID 2, RAID level 3 synchronously stripes data across all of the drives, but it uses a single drive to store the parity information for the stripe set.

RAID level 4 stripes data like RAID levels 2 and 3 and records parity. It differs from the other two in that data can be read asynchronously across the drives in the stripe set, improving concurrent read access. Writes must occur synchronously, so an I/O is not complete until all drives in the set have been updated. RAID level 5 is similar to the previous three with the exception of parity data. Parity is striped across the drive set to eliminate the problem created if a single parity drive should fail.

Many shops I have worked at use RAID 0+1, which is commonly referred to as RAID 10. Using RAID 10 increases performance and reliability by taking the RAID level 0 stripped disks and mirroring them with RAID level 1 technology. I mostly see the RAID 0+1 configuration done with SSA 7133 drives. The various RAID levels are outlined in Table 11-1.

RAID and a Storage Area Network (SAN)?

Configuring the Enterprise Storage Server (ESS), which is commonly referred to as "The Shark," is a little different than you might expect. All of the disks that are zoned and configured for your machine to see are presented to your system one time for each *fibre channel adapter* that is connected in this disk zone. As an example, if you have ten disks, hdisk10 through hdisk19, and you have four fibre channel adapters, you will see each disk four times! This can be very confusing to look at, but the system really converts these multiple disks into what is called a V-Path.

Level	Description
RAID 0	Striped data, no parity
RAID 1	Mirrored data
RAID 2	Striped data with parity
RAID 3	Striped data with parity drive
RAID 4	Striped data with parity and asynchronous read access
RAID 5	Striped data with striped parity

Table 11-1. RAID Levels

The V-Path is a virtual path to the disk drive that the system can see. So when you create a volume group of a logical volume, you specify which disk by using the V-Path definition. The trick to make the disks "RAID" is that we stripe each logical volume across *all of the fibre channel adapters*, which is done by the load balancing software. The performance gain is big with four paths into the same internal RAID level 5 array. The ESS uses RAID level 5 internally, so this configuration really smokes! You can also use JBOD (Just a bunch of disks) in a Shark, but you lose automatic recovery in case of a disk failure. There is much more on storage area networks in Chapter 29.

Fixed Disk Architecture

The disks themselves are multiple platters stacked like records on a hub (see Figure 11-1). Each platter is coated with a magnetic substrate. One or more electromagnetic heads may be moved back and forth across a platter from outer edge to inner edge. The heads react to the polarization of the magnetic particles formatted in circular tracks around the surface of the platter. The heads are positioned on the platters by a disk controller circuit that receives its instructions from the operating system.

Most disks come preformatted with a bad-sector map allocated. If you have to format a disk, invoke the **diag** command or reboot the system in single-user maintenance mode. From the **diag** function selection, select **Task Selection** followed by **Media Format** and **Media Certify**.

```
# diag
```

Function selection
Task selection (Diagnostics, Advanced diagnostics, Service aids, etc.)
  Service aids
Format media
  Certify media

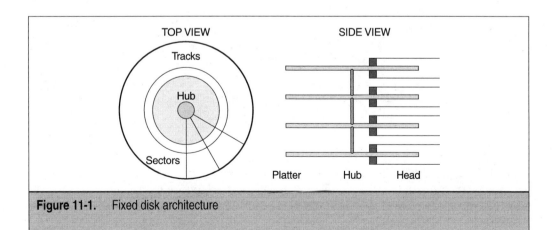

Figure 11-1.   Fixed disk architecture

Formatted space on the disk is made up of sectors or blocks. The sector size will vary with make and model and may be either fixed or variable. Tracks are made up of sectors aligned in circles on each platter. Stacked tracks on the platters make up a cylinder. All of these huge disks today are the result of technology that has dramatically reduced the size of the head that rides on the platter. If you open up a disk drive (only do this with a bad disk!) and remove the head from the actuator arm, you can see that the head is only a tiny speck. Before this new technology, the head was about the size of a pinky fingernail.

DISK INSTALLATION

To add a new SCSI disk to the system, plug the disk onto one of the SCSI adapters on the back of the system unit. This is best done with the system powered down, but it can be done online if your disks and the subsystem are hot-swappable. Multiple SCSI devices may be daisy-chained from a single SCSI adapter. Each disk must represent a unique SCSI ID and logical unit number (LUN) in the chain. The SCSI ID is jumper or switch selectable on the drive assembly or casing. SCSI IDs range from 0 through 7 for older SCSI drive and 0–15 for the wide and Ultra SCSI, with 7 usually assigned to the adapter. When the system is booted, the new disk is automatically identified and recorded in ROS and the ODM database. You can update device information online by invoking **cfgmgr** or using the **mkdev** command. The new disk is assigned the next available **hdisk<*nn*>** label.

```
# mkdev -c disk -s scsi -t osdisk -p scsi2 -w 8,0 -l hdisk10 -a pv=yes
# cfgmgr -vl scsi2
```

(or)

```
# cfgmgr -v
```

(or)

```
# smitty cfgmgr
# lspv
# lsdev -Cc disk
```

Use the **lspv** and **lsdev** commands shown here to make sure that the disk has a PVID and is in an available state.

Managing Physical Volumes

The physical disk volumes in AIX are given the name hdisk#, where # is an integer number starting with 0, zero. The disks are detected, configured, and given a name by the Configuration Manager, with the **cfgmgr** command. The actual name of the disk is dependent upon where it is physically installed in the system, since **cfgmgr** walks the bus and assigns hdisk numbers as each disk is found. In most systems, the **cfgmgr** will walk the bus in a parallel mode, but you can override this method by adding the **-s** flag to the **cfgmgr** command to specify serial mode.

There are some tricks that will influence the hdisk number assignments that you may need to use at one point or another. An example is HACMP clustered systems (see Chapter 28 for more details), where it is extremely important that the hdisk numbers for shared disks are in sync. One way of getting the hdisk numbers in sync is to power on the external disk sets one at a time and run **cfgmgr** multiple times, one for each disk set power on. The trick is to duplicate the efforts on each machine at each step through the process.

The procedure would look something like the following:

1. Stop all applications on both systems.

2. Remove the hdisk definitions for all of the disks that you want to sync that are *not* in rootvg. Use the **rmdev -dl hdisk#** command for each disk. Repeat for all systems in the shared disk cluster.

3. Run the **lspv** command to ensure that the all of the disks have been removed.

4. Power down all of the disks for which you want the hdisk numbers to be in sync.

5. Power on the first set of disks. These disks will receive the lowest hdisk numbers.

6. Run **cfgmgr -v** on each system. If you know the parent adapter for the disks, you can execute the **cfgmgr -vl** *adapter* command.

7. Run **lsp** to ensure that the disks are numbered as you want them on each system and to ensure that the disk numbers are in sync. You will need to refer to the PVID to ensure that the PVID and the hdisk numbers match on all systems.

8. Repeat steps 5, 6, and 7 for the remaining disk sets.

An Easier Way to Rename Disks

If the preceding section just lost you, try the exercise in this section. The scenario goes like this: We have three disks on the scsi1 controller named hdisk2, hdisk3, and hdisk4. We need to remove these disks and add them back to the system as hdisk10, hdisk12, and hdisk14.

The first step is to list the disk locations within the system:

```
# lsdev -Cc disk

    hdisk0 Available 04-B0-00-0,0  Other SCSI Disk Drive
    hdisk1 Available 04-B0-00-1,0  Other SCSI Disk Drive
    hdisk2 Available 04-03-00-8,0  Other SCSI Disk Drive
    hdisk3 Available 04-03-00-9,0  Other SCSI Disk Drive
    hdisk4 Available 04-03-00-10,0 Other SCSI Disk Drive
```

Next we need to list the adapter locations within the system:

```
# lsdev -Cc adapter | grep scsi

    scsi0  Available 04-B0 Wide SCSI I/O Controller
    scsi1  Available 04-03 Wide SCSI I/O Controller
```

We now need a list of the volume groups involved in this disk reassignment:

```
# lspv

    hdisk0        000400434b33e6eb    rootvg
    hdisk1        000400434a771e22    rootvg
    hdisk2        000400439e42cd74    appvg
    hdisk3        000400439a5deff0    appvg
    hdisk4        000400439a5e07e9    appvg
```

Before we make any changes, we first need to make the target volume group unavailable:

```
# varyoffvg appvg
```
◄——— See the section "Varying On and Varying Off Volume Groups" later in this chapter for more details.

Now we can remove the target devices on **scsi1** (2@8,0 3@9,0 4@10,0). From the command prompt, enter the following command sequence. Basically, this is like writing a shell script on the command line:

```
# for N in 2 3 4
> do
> rmdev -dl hdisk$N
> done
```

NOTE   Do not type the greater than signs (>), because these are prompts. Press ENTER after each line.

Preview the commands to add the devices with new names:

```
# for NA in 10@8,0 12@9,0 14@10,0
> do
> N=$(echo $NA | awk -F@ '{print $1}')
> A=$(echo $NA | awk -F@ '{print $2}')
> echo "mkdev -c disk -s scsi -t osdisk -p scsi1 -w $A -l hdisk$N -a pv=yes"
> done
```

The preview output will show these commands:

```
mkdev -c disk -s scsi -t osdisk -p scsi1 -w 8,0 -l hdisk10 -a pv=yes
mkdev -c disk -s scsi -t osdisk -p scsi1 -w 9,0 -l hdisk12 -a pv=yes
mkdev -c disk -s scsi -t osdisk -p scsi1 -w 10,0 -l hdisk14 -a pv=yes
```

Now remove the **echo** around the **mkdev** command to actually execute the commands:

```
# for NA in 10@8,0 12@9,0 14@10,0
> do
> N=$(echo $NA | awk -F@ '{print $1}')
> A=$(echo $NA | awk -F@ '{print $2}')
> mkdev -c disk -s scsi -t osdisk -p scsi1 -w $A -l hdisk$N -a pv=yes
> done
```

The resulting output is shown here with our new hdisk numbers:

```
hdisk10 Available
hdisk12 Available
hdisk14 Available
```

List the new device names:

```
# lsdev -Cc disk
```

```
hdisk0  Available 04-B0-00-0,0  Other SCSI Disk Drive
hdisk1  Available 04-B0-00-1,0  Other SCSI Disk Drive
hdisk10 Available 04-03-00-8,0  Other SCSI Disk Drive
hdisk12 Available 04-03-00-9,0  Other SCSI Disk Drive
hdisk14 Available 04-03-00-10,0 Other SCSI Disk Drive
```

List the hdisks numbers, PVIDs, and the associated volume groups:

```
# lspv
```

```
hdisk0          000400434b32e6eb     rootvg
hdisk1          000400434a781e22     rootvg
hdisk10         000400439e42cd74     appvg
hdisk12         000400439a5deff0     appvg
hdisk14         000400439a5e07e9     appvg
```

Note that the physical disks in a volume group are identified by the PVID and not by the hdisk number. We do not have to import the volume group again before we vary it on.

```
# lqueryvg -Atp hdisk10

        Max LVs:        256
        PP Size:        25
        Free PPs:       504
        LV count:       3
        PV count:       3
        Total VGDAs:    3
        Conc Allowed    0
        MAX PPs per     1016
        MAX PVs:        32
        Conc Autovar    0
        Varied on Co    0
        Logical:        000400439a5df5d2.1    lv1ac1 1
                        000400439a5df5d2.2    loglv00 1
                        000400439a5df5d2.3    lv01 1
        Physical:       000400439a5deff0 1    0
                        000400439a5e07e9 1    0
                        000400439e42cd74 1    0
        Total PPs:      813
```

Make the volume group available again by varying appvg back online:

```
# varyonvg appvg  ◄─────── No need for importvg in this case
```

Configuring a Hot Spare

In this hot spare example, appvg is mirrored from hdisk1 to hdisk2, and hdisk3 and hdisk4 will be the hot spares:

```
# lsvg appvg
VOLUME GROUP:    appvg          VG IDENTIFIER:   00002248000049000000000ebab4aefe2
VG STATE:        active         PP SIZE:         32 megabyte(s)
VG PERMISSION:   read/write     TOTAL PPs:       2184 (69888 megabytes)
MAX LVs:         256            FREE PPs:        2184 (69888 megabytes)
LVs:             0              USED PPs:        1092 (34944 megabytes)
OPEN LVs:        0              QUORUM:          1
TOTAL PVs:       4              VG DESCRIPTORS:  3
STALE PVs:       0              STALE PPs:       0
ACTIVE PVs:      4              AUTO ON:         yes
```

```
MAX PPs per PV: 1016              MAX PVs:        32
LTG size:        128 kilobyte(s) AUTO SYNC:      no
HOT SPARE:       no
```

Check for the volume groups associated with the disks:

```
# lspv
hdisk0            0000468644af1894            rootvg
hdisk1            00003095a330a867            appvg
hdisk2            00003095a330baa8            appvg
hdisk3            00003095a330bca2            appvg
hdisk4            00003095a330c825            appvg
```

The **chpv** command has a **-h** flag the sets the characteristics and the allocation permissions of the physical volume so that it can be used as a hot spare. The **-h** flag has no effect for nonmirrored logical volumes. The **-h** flag can take either **y** or **n** as a parameter to add or remove the disk to or from the hot spare pool.

Set up the hot spare disks:

```
# chpv -h 'y' hdisk3 hdisk4    #  -h [y|n]
```

Check the hot spare disks:

```
# for N in a867 baa8 bca2 c825
> do
> lquerypv -g 0000224800004900000000ebab4aefe2 -p 00003095a330$N -S
> done
0
0
32
32
```

NOTE   Do not enter the greater-than (>) signs; these are prompts.

Just like the **chpv** command, the **chvg** command uses the **-h** flag to set the sparing characteristics for the volume group, which is specified by the VolumeGroup parameter. The **-h** flag has four parameters that may be used:

- **y**   Allows for automatic migration of failed disk partitions from one failed disk to one hot spare.
- **Y**   Allows for automatic migration of failed disks and can migrate to the entire hot spare pool. This is different than a one-to-one partition migration.
- **n**   Prohibits failed disk migration. This is the default.
- **r**   Removes all of the disks from the hot spare pool for the volume group.

Next we will enable a hot spare for the volume group:

```
# chvg -h'y' -s'y' appvg
```

We use the **-s** flag to sync the mirrors in the previous command.
View the volume group changes,

```
# lsvg appvg
VOLUME GROUP:     appvg             VG IDENTIFIER:
00002248000049000000000ebab4aefe2
VG STATE:         active      PP SIZE:          32 megabyte(s)
VG PERMISSION:    read/write  TOTAL PPs:        2184 (69888 megabytes)
MAX LVs:          256         FREE PPs:         2184 (69888 megabytes)
LVs:              0           USED PPs:         1092 (34944 megabytes)
OPEN LVs:         0           QUORUM:           1
TOTAL PVs:        4           VG DESCRIPTORS:   3
STALE PVs:        0           STALE PPs:        0
ACTIVE PVs:       4           AUTO ON:          yes
MAX PPs per PV:   1016        MAX PVs:          32
LTG size:         128 kilobyte(s) AUTO SYNC:    yes
HOT SPARE:        yes (one to one)
```

check for errors,

```
# errpt | head -3
IDENTIFIER TIMESTAMP  T C RESOURCE_NAME   DESCRIPTION
A6DF45AA   0127191502 I O RMCdaemon       The daemon is started.
7F88E76D   0127184302 P S console         SOFTWARE PROGRAM ERROR
```

check the daemon,

```
# lssrc -s ctrmc
Subsystem          Group          PID       Status
 ctrmc             rsct           13934     active
```

check the process tree:

```
# pstree -p 13934
-+- 00001 root /etc/init
 \-+= 03150 root /usr/sbin/srcmstr
   \--= 13934 root [3]/usr/sbin/rsct/bin/rmcd -c
```

or just use the AIX **ps** command:

```
# ps -ef | grep rmcd
 root 13934 3150   0 10:02:00   -  0:00 /usr/sbin/rsct/bin/rmcd -c
```

If you like using the **pstree** freeware program, you can get the source code at either of the following URLs:

```
http://freshmeat.net/projects/pstree/
ftp://ftp.thp.Uni-Duisburg.DE/pub/source/
```

INTRODUCING THE LVM

If you plan to work with AIX, you *must* learn and understand the Logical Volume Manager (LVM) and how it works. I want to start with the makeup of the LVM. We start with the largest structure, which is one or more disks grouped together to make a *volume group (VG)*. Within the VG, we create *logical volumes (LVs)*. The LV is made up of *logical partitions (LPs)* that are mapped to actual disk partitions called *physical partitions (PPs)*. On top of the LV, we can create *filesystems,* which have a mount point or directory. We can also have *raw logical volumes,* which are nothing more than an LV without a mount point that is accessed through its raw device name. Databases like to use raw LVs, but it is a big no-no to pair raw LVs with High Availability Cluster Multi-Processing (HACMP)! For details on HACMP, see Chapter 28.

The LVM consists of the following components:

- Volume groups (VGs)
- Physical volumes (PVs)
- Logical volumes (LVs)
- Logical partitions (LPs)
- Physical partitions (PPs)

Notice the acronyms for each component: VG, PV, LV, LP, and PP. You will see these often, so please learn each acronym. If you understand the concepts of the preceding five LVM components and how they interrelate, you have it licked. We are going to take these components one at a time and explain how they interrelate.

A *physical partition (PP)* is a section of disk space that can be used for *logical volumes (LVs)*. Typically, logical volumes are for filesystems and for paging space. Traditional legacy UNIX systems restrict partitions to contiguous space on a single disk such that a single filesystem cannot be any larger than the size of available contiguous space on a single disk. However, AIX uses the concept of *logical volumes (LVs)* to map to physical disk space. A logical volume is represented by a mapping of *logical partitions (LPs)* to *physical partitions (PPs) residing on one or more physical disks* within the same *volume group (VG)*.

Each physical disk may contain up to 1016 physical partitions (PPs) ranging in size from 1 to 256 megabytes, in powers of 2. Starting in AIX 4.3, you can increase the number of PPs, but you will decrease the maximum number of disks for the VG. There are mathematical limits to addressing that require this give and take. The default physical partition size is four megabytes. However, the size of the PP depends on the size of the disk. The PP size is the same for the entire VG! One to three physical partitions may be mapped to a logical partition, which is called mirroring. Logical volumes are allocated from logical partitions within a single volume group (VG).

The LVM Components

The Logical Volume Manager consists of a hierarchy of components from the smallest piece called the Physical/Logical partition (PP and LP), to the Volume Group being the largest. The LVM components are described in the following five items.

1. A *physical volume (PV)* is a single piece of disk storage. A PV may be a single disk drive, or it may be a single RAID multidisk array. As an example, if I create an eight-disk RAID level 5 SSA disk array, it is presented to the system as a single hdisk<#>, maybe hdisk5. Individual disks, which are not part of an array, are also presented to the system as a single hdisk<#>, maybe hdisk1. So a *physical volume (PV)* is exactly what you would expect, a physical piece of storage hardware. The disk(s) can be attached internally in the machine or can be attached as an external hardware component.

2. A *volume group (VG)* is a collection of one or more *physical volumes (PVs)*. All of the PVs added together make up the total size of the VG. As an example, if I create a VG, maybe I call it **appvg**, and with ten 32GB individual disk drives, the total size of the VG is 320GB. A VG is the largest unit of storage that AIX can allocate. Within the VG, we create smaller structures like logical volumes (LVs) and filesystems, which are discussed later. A nice thing about a VG is that it can be moved from one machine to another machine and *imported* to be a resident VG. Since a VG is made up of PVs, we break up a VG into physical partitions (PPs), which are the smallest unit of measurement within a VG.

3. A *physical partition (PP)* is a small block of a PV, or physical volume. A PP is the basic building block unit of storage. So a PV is split up into equal-sized blocks of storage called PPs, or physical partitions. The size of the PP is referred to as the *PP size*. The default PP size is 4MB. However, this default was created when a 4GB disk was the standard, and now we have huge disks shipped with the machines. All PPs within a VG are the same size, and you cannot change the PP size dynamically. Since a PV is split up into equal-sized PPs, there is a standard maximum number of PPs of 1016. For larger disk drives, and disk arrays, you have two options: 1) increase the size of the volume group PP to larger than 4MB, in powers of 2, which you *cannot* do on the fly. The second option is to allocate more PPs to each PV, which you *can* do on the fly. The maximum number of PPs is extended by multiples of 1016. Since a VG has a maximum number of PPs, each time you double the maximum number of PPs per PV, you cut in half the maximum number of PVs within the VG. We will cover this topic more later in the chapter, so just keep reading.

4. A *logical partition (LP)* is a map to a *physical partition (PP)* on a disk drive. The LPs are allocated in contiguous units. However, the PP that each LP maps to can be any PP within the same VG, or volume group. This is the mechanism that allows a filesystem to span multiple disks in AIX.

5. A *logical volume (LV)* is a collection of one or more *logical partitions (LPs)* within the same volume group (VG). The PPs that each LP is mapped to can be any PP within the same VG. This LP mapping allows the disk space to be *presented* to the system as contiguous disk space when in reality it is the LP *map* that is contiguous. On top of these logical volumes, we can build filesystems that can be accessed through a mount point, or directory. Each logical partition (LP) that makes up a logical volume is the same size as the PP size (4MB by default); they are one and the same, with each LP mapping to a PP.

Putting the LVM Together

Each VG is made up of 1 to 32 physical disks for normal VGs and 128 disks for *big volume groups.* Partition mapping, volume management, and interfaces are implemented through a pseudo–device driver and manager called the Logical Volume Manager or LVM. There is a lot to the LVM, so let's start out slow, and I hope I have not lost you already. Look at Figures 11-2 and 11-3 to see how the LVM components go together.

Using the abstraction of logical to physical partition mapping, AIX is able to dynamically increase the size of volume groups, logical volumes, and ultimately filesystems without service interruption! Prior to LVM support, you were required to back up the filesystem to disk or tape, destroy the data structure, rebuild the structure with the new allocation sizes, and restore the backup. LVM allows you to manage disk space online *dynamically* rather than requiring hours of filesystem downtime, and for paging space, you can also reduce the size of a paging space volume on the fly with AIX 5L!

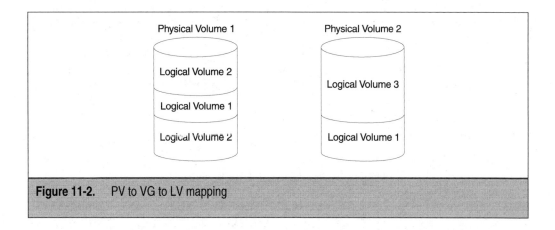

Figure 11-2.   PV to VG to LV mapping

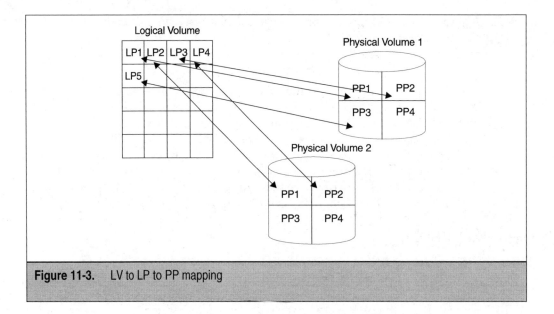

Figure 11-3.   LV to LP to PP mapping

Tailoring the logical partition mapping allows you to optimize filesystem placement. Busy filesystems should be located in the center of the physical disk (referred to as intradisk policy) and spread the data across multiple physical disks, or PVs. The LVM also supports mirroring, making duplicate copies of a logical volume available for concurrent read access. Mirroring also improves data availability.

AIX 4.3 LVM and above supports RAID 0 striping. As you may already know, striping is a mechanism that allows you to distribute a file or filesystem's data blocks evenly across multiple disks to improve I/O performance. Striping is specified when you create the logical volume. There are a few restrictions when using striped volumes. Physical partitions must be allocated evenly between the disks included in the stripe set. You can't combine other LV features like mirroring with striping (RAID 0+1 is done within the SSA configuration and is detached from the LVM), and you can't move a striped LV after creation. Do your homework up front before settling on a striped configuration. A striped LV does not like to be unstriped, but you can do it by creating a new LV and run a **migratepv** command to move the data to the new area. A new feature in AIX 5L is the options for mirror write consistency (off, active, or passive).

Hot Spot Management

New to 5L is the ability to for *hot spot management*. With hot spot management, you can move individual hot LPs between disks, of course within the same VG. Hot spot management is a very useful tool to fine-tune the disk performance within a volume group. The ability to move a single LP from one disk to another is only available in AIX 5L and presents a huge advantage over any other operating system for disk tuning.

Here is how AIX 5L hot spot management works. A hot spot problem exists when one or more logical partitions on a disk have so much disk I/O activity that the system performance is degraded. AIX 5L has provided two new commands, **lvmstat** and **migratelp**, that enable you to identify and resolve hot spot problems in each logical volume.

Gathering Statistics

Before you can monitor for hot spots, you must enable the gathering of statistics using the **lvmstat** command.

```
# lvmstat -e -v rootvg
```

The previous command will enable statistic gathering for the rootvg volume group. You can also enable gathering of statistics on a single logical volume by using the **-l** flag and specifying the logical volume name as shown in the next command:

```
# lvmstat -e -l hd2
```

By default, statistics gathering is turned off. Enabling statistics at the volume group level allows you to monitor all logical volumes in the volume group, as opposed to a single logical volume.

The **lvmstat** command will produce reports at the logical volume level. The first report produced by the **lvmstat** command shows statistics since the last system reboot. The succeeding reports show the statistics since the previous report. See the **lvmstat** output listed here:

```
# lvmstat -v rootvg
Logical Volume      iocnt    Kb_read    Kb_wrtn      Kbps
   hd2               9358      21548      25520      0.01
   hd9var            6098        538      23714      0.00
   hd4               4418       1908      15980      0.00
   hd8               3261          0      13044      0.00
   lvscripts         2073       3044       1244      0.00
   hd3                170        112        616      0.00
   hd6                118        456         16      0.00
   hd10opt             93        324         68      0.00
   lv00                30         35          8      0.00
   hd1                 11          8          8      0.00
   hd5                  0          0          0      0.00
```

As you can see, the report is produced in descending order or activity. This output for the rootvg volume group shows the I/O activity for each logical volume including the number of I/O requests (iocnt), the KB of data read (Kb_read), the KB of data written (Kb_wrtn), and the KB/second of data transferred (Kbps). If the **-l** flag is specified, then the statistics are for the physical partition partitions of the logical volume named. The mirrored copies of each logical partition are considered to be independent for reporting purposes. This independence allows you to fine-tune the mirrors for hot spots.

The **lvmstat** also allows reporting over an interval, specified in seconds. Each interval produces a separate report. The first report in the series contains statistics since the volume group was last varied on, and each subsequent report contains the statistics since the last report. The count parameter allows you to specify how many partitions to report on if the **-l** flag is used to specify a single logical volume, or how many logical volumes to report on if the **-v** flag is used to specify a volume group. If the count is 5, then the five busiest partitions are reported for logical volumes (**-l**) or the five busiest logical volumes are reported for a volume group (**-v**). As an example, to display the top three logical volumes in the rootvg volume, use the following command:

```
# lvmstat -v rootvg -c 3
Logical Volume       iocnt    Kb_read    Kb_wrtn      Kbps
   hd2               9682      23016      25920      0.01
   hd9var            6258        564      24366      0.00
   hd4               4536       1960      16412      0.00
```

To display the top ten logical partitions for the hd2 logical volume, use the following command:

```
lvmstat -l hd2 -c 10
Log_part  mirror#  iocnt    Kb_read    Kb_wrtn      Kbps
       5        1   1207        652       8084      0.00
       1        1   1047         72       4116      0.00
     107        1    754        508       2520      0.00
       9        1    427        156       2796      0.00
      55        1    412        348       1328      0.00
      23        1    401        304       1304      0.00
      37        1    392        296       1276      0.00
      57        1    376        228       1276      0.00
      11        1    334         76       1260      0.00
      15        1    245        440        552      0.00
```

To display reports continuously every five seconds for the hd2 logical volume, issue the following command:

```
# lvmstat -l hd2 5
```

To display ten reports every five seconds, run the following command:

```
# lvmstat -l hd2 5 10
```

To reset the all of the statistics counters for the rootvg volume group, run the following command:

```
# lvmstat -v rootvg -C
```

To disable statistics gathering for the rootvg volume group, use the following command:

```
# lvmstat -d rootvg
```

Migrating Physical Partitions

Using the output of the **lvmstat** command, it is very easy to identify the hot logical partitions (LPs). These heavily used LPs will stand out and will be listed at the top of the report output. If you have a disk with several hot LPs and you want to balance the load across the available disks, you can use the **migratelp** command to move the LPs between disks.

The **migratelp** command uses the logical partition number (*LPartnumber*), the logical volume name (*LVname*), the logical volume copy number (*Copynumber*), and if the LV is mirrored, the destination physical volume (*DestPV*) and the physical partition number (*PPartNumber*) to control how the copy service will be used. The syntax of the **migratelp** command is listed here:

```
migratelp LVname/LPartnumber[/Copynumber] DestPV[/PPartNumber]
```

If the destination *PPartNumber* is specified, it will be used; otherwise, a destination *PPartNumber* will be generated using the interregion policy of the logical volume. For mirrored LVs, the first mirror copy of the LP will be moved. If you want to specify which LP copy to migrate—and you will want to do this—you must use 1, 2, or 3 for the Copynumber parameter to the **migratelp** command. Some manual page examples are listed here for using the **migratelp** command:

1. To move the first logical partitions of logical volume lv00 to hdisk1, type

   ```
   # migratelp lv00/1 hdisk1
   ```

2. To move second mirror copy of the third logical partitions of logical volume hd2 to hdisk5, type

   ```
   #  migratelp hd2/3/2 hdisk5
   ```

3. To move third mirror copy of the twenty-fifth logical partitions of logical volume testlv to hundredth partition of hdisk7, type

   ```
   #  migratelp testlv/25/3 hdisk7/100
   ```

These new features to AIX 5L are included in the standard **bos.rte.lvm** fileset. This LVM fileset also includes some other new commands for you to investigate:

Intermediate level command that migrates a missing disk
with the hot spare and syncs the stale partitions

```
/usr/sbin/hotspare ◄─────┐
/usr/sbin/lvmstat ◄──────────────── Reports on the status of a VG or LV
/usr/sbin/migratelp ◄────────── Allows relocation of LP between disks
/usr/sbin/readvgda ◄────────── Directly reads data from the VGDA
/usr/sbin/shrinkps ◄────────── Reduces the size of a paging space
```

One fileset that is missing from the AIX 4.3.3 **bos.rte.lvm** fileset is the **/usr/sbin/updatelv** command.

CONFIGURING VOLUME GROUPS

In order for a new disk to be made available to the LVM, the disk must be designated a physical volume and assigned a physical volume identifier (PVID). The PVID is a 16-digit hexadecimal number on older AIX versions and is a 32-digit hexadecimal number in AIX 5L. Both AIX 4.3 and AIX 5L show only 16-digit numbers with the **lspv** command. The **lsattr -El hdisk0** command will show the 32-digit number with AIX 5L and AIX 4.3.3 (with Maintenance Level 8 and above installed). It is interesting to note that all of the extra 16 characters are "0." You create a PVID on a new disk with the following command:

```
# chdev -l hdisk<n> -a pv=yes
```

You can list physical disks on your system using **lsdev**:

```
# lsdev -C -c disk
hdisk0 Available 00-00-0S-00 4.2 GB SCSI Disk Drive
hdisk1 Available 00-00-0S-10 4.2 GB SCSI Disk Drive
hdisk2 Available 00-04-00-30 Other SCSI Disk Drive
hdisk3 Available 00-04-00-40 Other SCSI Disk Drive
hdisk4 Available 00-04-00-50 Other SCSI Disk Drive
hdisk5 Available 00-04-00-00 Other SCSI Disk Drive
hdisk6 Available 00-04-00-10 Other SCSI Disk Drive
hdisk7 Available 00-04-00-20 Other SCSI Disk Drive
```

To list the PVIDs associated with these disks, use the **lspv** command:

```
# lspv
hdisk0 000008870001c7e1 rootvg
hdisk1 00001508fce5bbea rootvg
```

```
hdisk2 00004060c388efc4 vg00
hdisk3 000015082c6e92df vg00
hdisk4 0000150837cc1a85 vg01
hdisk5 000015082c28f5c7 vg01
hdisk6 000015082c2931f5 vg01
hdisk7 000015082c296d8f vg01
```

To add the new disk to a new or existing volume group, use SMIT or the **mkvg** and **extendvg** commands (see Figure 11-4):

```
# mkvg -f -y vg10 hdisk10 hdisk11 ◄── Create a volume group vg10 using hdisk10 and hdisk11
# extendvg -f rootvg hdisk8 ◄──────── Add hdisk8 to the rootvg volume group

# smit mkvg
```

A volume group identifier (VGID) is assigned to each volume group. The VGID is a sixteen-digit hexadecimal number in older AIX versions and is a 32-digit hexadecimal number in AIX 5L. Each VGID in the system is represented by an entry in the /etc/vg directory.

```
# ls /etc/vg
vg00012560841690B0   vg000125608A48C772
vg00012560841690B00000000000000000
```

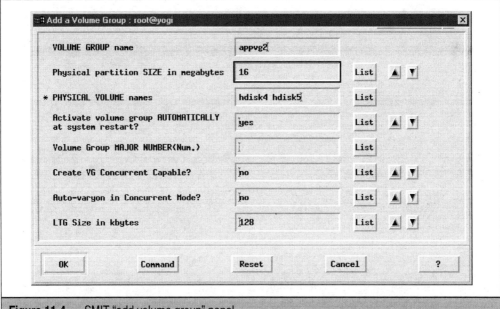

Figure 11-4.   SMIT "add volume group" panel

To display the configuration of the existing volume groups on your system, use the **lsvg** command:

```
# lsvg ◄───────────────── List volume groups
rootvg
vg01
vg02
vg03
# lsvg -l rootvg ◄───────── List the contents of the rootvg volume group
```

rootvg:

LV NAME	TYPE	LPs	PPs	PVs	LV STATE	MOUNT POINT
hd5	boot	2	2	1	closed/syncd	N/A
hd6	paging	84	84	1	open/syncd	N/A
hd8	jfslog	1	1	1	open/syncd	N/A
hd4	jfs	8	8	1	open/syncd	/
hd2	jfs	296	296	2	open/syncd	/usr
hd9var	jfs	13	13	2	open/syncd	/var
hd3	jfs	26	26	1	open/syncd	/tmp
hd1	jfs	1	1	1	open/syncd	/home
hd10opt	jfs	156	156	2	open/syncd	/opt
lvscripts	jfs	25	25	1	open/syncd	/scripts
lv00	jfs	10	10	1	open/syncd	/storix

```
# lsvg -p rootvg ◄───────── List physical volumes in the root volume group
```

rootvg:

PV_NAME	PV STATE	TOTAL PPs	FREE PPs	FREE DISTRIBUTION
hdisk0	active	479	0	00..00..0000..00
hdisk1	active	479	336	96..48..00..96..96

Quorum

Each physical volume in the volume group is marked with a volume group descriptor area (VGDA) and a volume group status area (VGSA). The VGDA and the VGSA are the most important components of a volume group! The VGDA contains identifiers for all logical and physical volumes and partitions that make up the volume group. The VGSA is a bitmap used to indicate which physical partitions on the disk are stale and require synched update.

When a volume group is activated using the **varyonvg** command or SMIT, the LVM verifies that it has access to *at least 51 percent of the VGDA and VGSA* copies before going online. This majority, called a *quorum,* is required by the LVM to ensure data integrity. Any physical volume not available is reported. The system administrator must decide whether to continue if a device is not accessible. If a majority quorum is not established for the volume group, it is not activated. However, believe it or not, you can force it to vary online with the **-f** switch to the **varyonvg** command.

```
# varyonvg <VGname>  ◄──────────── Vary a volume group online
# varyonvg -f <VGname> ◄─────────── Force vary on a volume group
```

You can take a volume group offline using the **varyoffvg** command or via SMIT. Note that all access to logical volumes in the volume group must be terminated. Any filesystems located in the volume group must be unmounted, and any paging space must not be active.

```
# varyoffvg <VGname>
# smit varyoffvg
```

To remove or replace physical volumes in a volume group for maintenance purposes, use SMIT or the **chpv** command.

```
# reducevg <VGname> <PVname> ◄────── Remove the disk from VG
# rmdev -dl hdisk<n> ◄────────────── Remove the hdisk definition
```

Replace the disk...

```
# cfgmgr -v ◄──────────────────────── Let the system discover the disk
# lspv ◄───────────────────────────── Find the newly found disk and write down the hdisk #
# chdev -l hdisk<n> -a pv=yes ◄────── Create a PVID for the new hdisk
  extendvg <VGname> <hdisk<n> ◄────── Add the new disk into the volume group
```

NOTE   When you remove all of the physical volumes from a volume group, the volume group is deleted from the system (**reducevg** command).

An entire volume group may be moved as a unit from one system to another. When the volume group is exported, all references to it are removed from the ODM. When the volume group is imported on the new system, all device table, special file, and /etc/filesystem entries are added automatically to the ODM. You can export and import a volume group on the same system to resynchronize the VGDA and ODM information.

```
# exportvg <VGname>
# importvg <VGname> <PVname>
```

Root Volume Group—rootvg

A special VG called rootvg is used by AIX for the operating system's root filesystems and the default paging areas. It's a good idea to use separate volume groups for user and local application filesystems. This way, you can export and import these volume groups before and after operating system upgrades. Each AIX BOS installation destroys all or part of rootvg.

Mirroring rootvg

If you do not mirror the root volume group, you have a single point of failure. Always mirror rootvg! I have seen too many unnecessary system rebuilds because rootvg was not mirrored. Mirroring rootvg is a straightforward process and consists of the following steps, in which we are going to mirror rootvg to a new disk called **hdisk1**:

1. Add hdisk1 to the rootvg for mirroring:

   ```
   # extendvg rootvg hdisk1
   ```

2. Use this command if all the rootvg logical volumes were created properly:

   ```
   # mirrorvg rootvg  ◄────────── This command will do it all if no errors occur
   ```

3. Or (if a problem was encountered) manually mirror rootvg and do not mirror the dump device (lv00 in example):

   ```
   # lsvg  ◄──────────────── To make sure there are two drives in rootvg
   # lsvg -l rootvg  ◄─────── To see if anything is mirrored already
   # lsvg rootvg  ◄────────── To check available space
   ```

4. Mirror each logical volume:

   ```
   # for N in $(lsvg -l rootvg | grep syncd | awk '{print $1}' | grep -v lv00)
   > do
   > echo $N
   > mklvcopy $N 2
   > done
   ```

5. Sync the volume group:

   ```
   # syncvg -v rootvg
   # lsvg -l rootvg
   ```

6. Configure the boot devices:

   ```
   # ipl_varyon -i

   PVNAME          BOOT DEVICE     PVID                    VOLUME GROUP ID
   hdisk0          NO              00001047375ac230        000010472822f021
   hdisk1          YES             000010472822e532        000010472822f021

   # bosboot -a -d /dev/hdisk0

   bosboot: Boot image is 6955 512 byte blocks.

   # ipl_varyon -i
   ```

```
PVNAME           BOOT DEVICE      PVID                      VOLUME GROUP ID
hdisk0           YES              00001047375ac230          000010472822f021
hdisk1           YES              000010472822e532          000010472822f021

# chvg -a'y' -Q'n' -x'n' rootvg  ◄────────── A QUORUM of disks required = no

# bootlist -m normal -o

hdisk1

# bootlist -m normal hdisk0 hdisk1
# bootlist -m normal -o

hdisk0
hdisk1

# lsvg rootvg | grep -i QUORUM

OPEN LVs:        14                        QUORUM:          1
```

The **mirrorvg** command does all of the **mklvcopy** commands under the covers for you.

Since disk quorum was disabled, we must reboot the system for the changes to take effect.

```
# shutdown -r now
```

Adding a Volume Group

As we previously discussed, a volume group consists of one or more disks, or physical volumes. We have two options when creating a new volume group, *normal* and *big* volume groups. A big volume group extends the maximum number of logical partitions from 256 up to 512. Tables 11-2 and 11-3 show the difference between normal and big volume group limits.

Maximum Number of Disks in the VG	Maximum Number of Partitions for Each Disk
1	32512
2	16256
4	8128
8	4096
16	2032
32	1016

Table 11-2.   Normal Volume Group Limits

Maximum Number of Disks in the VG	Maximum Number of Partitions for Each Disk
1	130048
2	65024
4	32512
8	16256
16	8128
32	4096
64	2032
128	1016

Table 11-3.   Big Volume Group Limits

To specify a big volume group, add the **-B** switch to the **mkvg** command. If the **-B** switch is omitted, the volume groups will be a normal volume group. To specify the number of disks and the maximum number of partitions per disk, you use the t-factor. The *t-factor* is a multiple of 1016. For each t-factor increase, you double the number of physical partitions but cut in half the maximum number of disks allowed in the volume group.

To create a normal volume group called **appvg** using hdisk4 that has 16MB PP size and can have up to 16 disks, issue the following command:

```
# mkvg -s 16 -t2 -y appvg hdisk4
```

The **-s 16** specifies a 16MB PP size, and the **-t2** specifies a t-factor of **2**. The **-y** switch specifies the name of the volume group, **appvg**. In Table 11-2, you can see that we can have up to 16256 partitions per disk and up to 16 disks in this *normal* volume group.

To create a big volume group called **bigappvg** that can have up to 16 disks and 8128 partitions per disk and that uses hdisk5 through hdisk10, issue the following command:

```
# mkvg -B -t8 -y bigappvg hdisk5 hdisk6 hdisk7 hdisk8 hdisk9 hdisk10
```

We can also change our normal **appvg** volume group to be a big volume group with the following command:

```
# chvg -B appvg
```

Importing and Exporting Volume Groups

One of the nice things about a volume groups is that they are portable. You can export a volume group on one machine, recable the disks to a different system, and import the volume group. The two commands that export and import volume groups are **exportvg** and **importvg**. When you export a volume group, you completely remove it from the ODM, and when you import a volume group, you add it to the ODM. As an example, we want to use our **bigappvg** volume group on another machine. The following commands will export the volume group and import the volume group.

On machine A:

```
# exportvg bigappvg
```

On machine B:

```
# importvg -y bigappvg hdisk5
```

A lot is assumed in the previous example. You need to use the PVID of one of the disks in the volume group as the target disk set that contains the exported VG. (Remember the VGDA?) In this example, we found that the PVID was on hdisk5 by examining the output of the **lspv** command. Volume groups also have a *major number* that is unique to the system. To find the next available major number on a system, issue the following command:

```
# lvlstmajor
```

To specify a major number, we use the **-V** switch. On my machine, the next available major number is 27. So we change our **importvg** command to use major number 27:

```
# importvg -V 27 -y bigappvg hdisk5
```

NOTE   If the **-V** switch is omitted from the **importvg** command, the next available major number will be assigned.

Varying On and Varying Off Volume Groups

Before a volume group can be accessed, it must be varied on. Also, before you can export a volume group, it must be varied off. The commands that vary on and off volume groups are **varyonvg** and **varyoffvg**. To vary off and vary on the **bigappvg** volume group, we use the following commands:

```
# varyoffvg bigappvg
# varyonvg bigappvg
```

Reorganizing a Volume Group with reorgvg

The **reorgvg** command is used to reorganize the PP allocation within the volume group. This reorganization is an attempt to meet the in*tra*disk policy (refer to the section "Configuring Logical Volumes" later in this chapter for details on policy) of each LV in the volume group. There must be at least one free PP in the volume group for the **reorgvg** command to complete successfully. When using the **reorgvg** command, you can specify individual LVs in the VG that you want to reorganize; otherwise, all of the LVs are reorganized in the VG.

As an example, we want to reorganize the **dat01**, **dat02**, and **idx01** in our **bigappvg** volume group:

```
# reorgvg bigappvg dat01 dat02 idx01
```

To reorganize every LV only on **hdisk5** in the **bigappvg** volume group, we can use the following compound command:

```
# echo "hdisk5" | reorgvg -i bigappvg dat01 dat02 idx01
```

HACMP and Synchronizing Volume Groups

We are getting a little ahead of the game in this section. HACMP is an acronym for High Availability Cluster Multi-Processing. HACMP is used to make your application servers fault resilient by *failing over* to a standby machine if the primary machine fails. To do this, the disks that holds the application, or anything that must be highly available, must be shared between the machines in the cluster. Usually the disks are twin-tailed between two machines and the controlling machine has the VG imported and varied on. In case of failure, the standby machine must import the shared volume group, vary it on, and start the application on the new node.

The problem arises when you make changes to the VG and the other machine does not know about the changes. To synchronize the VG, we need to vary off the VG only on the primary node and import the volume group on the standby node. After this process, the volume group is varied off from the standby node and varied on the VG to the primary node.

NOTE   By default, all of the raw devices are owned by **root** user and the **system** group.

There is also the **-L** option to the **importvg** command for a system to learn about changes to a known VG. The following process will accomplish the same task as exporting and importing the volume group.

- **Primary node**   `varyonvg -b -u bigappvg`
- **Standby node**   `importvg -L bigappvg hdisk10`
- **Primary nod:**   `varyonvg bigappvg`

CONFIGURING LOGICAL VOLUMES

To make use of the disk space available in a volume group, you will need to create a logical volume. Logical volumes are analogous to partitions on other UNIX systems but provide some significant enhancements. The structure and features provided by logical volumes should be well understood before proceeding with allocating space for filesystems or paging areas. In other words, you should be able to determine the following:

- Logical volume type
- Size in logical partitions
- Inter disk partition layout (as opposed to the intra disk policy)
- Write scheduling policy
- Intra disk partition layout (as opposed to the inter disk policy)
- Whether it will be mirrored
- Whether it will be striped

Logical Volume Types

The LVM basically manages all logical volume types the same way. A logical volume may warrant special consideration when defining some of the other attributes. For example, you may wish to locate paging logical volumes in the center of the disks to reduce head movement. There are five logical volume types used by AIX:

- **Filesystem**   Holds filesystem data and metadata
- **Log**   Holds JFS metadata update log
- **Paging**   Paging areas
- **Boot logical volume**   Boot block and RAM filesystem code
- **Dump area**   Holds panic dumps

Logical Volume Size

When you create a new logical volume or add space to an existing logical volume, you will be working in logical partition (LP) units. As an example, if you accepted the default 4-megabyte partition size, then a 512-megabyte logical volume will require 128 logical partitions (512 MB logical volume divided by 4 MB logical partition size equals 128 logical partitions). When you create a LV, you may define a maximum number of logical partitions that can be used for the logical volume (the default is 512). This value limits the size to which this logical volume may grow within the volume group. The maximum limit may be increased if additional logical volume space is required at a later date.

You may notice that, when you add up the number of partitions represented by the physical volumes in a volume group, you have lost somewhere between 7 to 10 percent of the total formatted space. This is due to space overhead required by the LVM to manage the volume group. Remember the VGDA and VGSA structures described in the previous sections?

Interdisk Policy

The interdisk layout policy determines the range of physical disks that may be used to allocate partitions for the logical volume. The interdisk policy may be either minimum or maximum, along with a range limit governing the number of physical disks that may be used.

- **Minimum** Provides highest availability. All partitions are allocated on a single physical volume. For mirrored logical volumes, the first copy will be allocated on a single physical disk. The second copy can be allocated across multiple physical volumes up to the range limit unless the Strict option is selected.

- **Maximum** Provides the best performance. Each logical partition in the logical volume will be allocated sequentially across up to the range limit of physical volumes. If one of the physical disks fails, then the entire logical volume is unavailable.

Intradisk Policy

The intradisk layout policy (see Figure 11-5) defines where partitions will be allocated within a physical disk. One of five regions may be selected: *inner edge, inner middle, center, outer middle,* and *outer edge.* Inner edge and outer edge have the slowest seek times. Average seek times decrease toward the center of the disk, which is where the "sweet spot" on the disk is located.

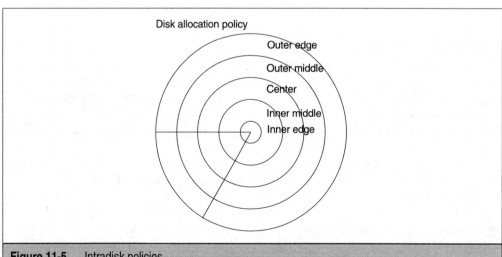

Figure 11-5. Intradisk policies

Use the **lsvg** command to display the layout of existing logical volumes and the number of free partitions:

```
# lsvg rootvg
VOLUME GROUP:    rootvg              VG IDENTIFIER:  00012560841690b0
VG STATE:        active              PP SIZE:        4 megabyte(s)
VG PERMISSION:   read/write          TOTAL PPs:      958 (3832 megabytes)
MAX LVs:         256                 FREE PPs:       336 (1344 megabytes)
LVs:             11                  USED PPs:       622 (2488 megabytes)
OPEN LVs:        10                  QUORUM:         2
TOTAL PVs:       2                   VG DESCRIPTORS: 3
STALE PVs:       0                   STALE PPs:      0
ACTIVE PVs:      2                   AUTO ON:        yes
MAX PPs per PV: 1016                 MAX PVs:        32
LTG size:        128 kilobyte(s)     AUTO SYNC:      no
HOT SPARE:       no
```

```
# lsvg -l rootvg
rootvg:
LV NAME          TYPE      LPs    PPs    PVs   LV STATE      MOUNT POINT
hd5              boot      2      2      1     closed/syncd  N/A
hd6              paging    84     84     1     open/syncd    N/A
hd8              jfslog    1      1      1     open/syncd    N/A
hd4              jfs       8      8      1     open/syncd    /
hd2              jfs       296    296    2     open/syncd    /usr
hd9var           jfs       13     13     2     open/syncd    /var
hd3              jfs       26     26     1     open/syncd    /tmp
hd1              jfs       1      1      1     open/syncd    /home
hd10opt          jfs       156    156    2     open/syncd    /opt
lvscripts        jfs       25     25     1     open/syncd    /scripts
lv00             jfs       10     10     1     open/syncd    /storix
```

Mirrors

For high-access filesystems, mirrors provide a mechanism that improves availability (a copy of the primary logical volume is maintained) and access time (multiple paths to the data). You may choose to keep two mirrored copies in environments that require higher levels of availability and fault tolerance. Three mirrored copies are the maximum.

When reading a mirrored logical volume, if the primary path is busy, the read can be satisfied by the mirror. Writes are sequential to logical volumes confined to a single physical disk. If mirrors occupy more than one physical disk, write scheduling can be either sequential or parallel.

- **Sequential writes**   Writes are ordered in the sequence that they occur. Each write operation is scheduled sequentially to each copy and returns when both updates are completed.

- **Parallel writes**   Writes are scheduled across the multiple disks at the same time. The write returns after the longest write completes.

Mirrors can be created when the logical volume is created by requesting more than one copy (see Figure 11-6). To mirror an existing logical volume, use the SMIT FastPath **smitty mklvcopy**.

```
# smit mklvcopy ◄─────── Start SMIT and select logical volume to be mirrored
```

Adding a Logical Volume

After selecting the volume placement characteristics for the new logical volume, you can create it using the SMIT FastPath **smitty mklv** (see Figure 11-7).

```
# smitty mklv
```

Logical Volume Maps

To look at how the LVs are mapped to the PPs, you can use the **lslv -m** *<LVname>*. From the output, you can see how each logical partition is mapped to a physical partition and which disk drive(s) the physical partitions reside on. For mirrored logical volumes, a single logical partition is mapped to either two or three physical partitions, hopefully on different physical volumes!

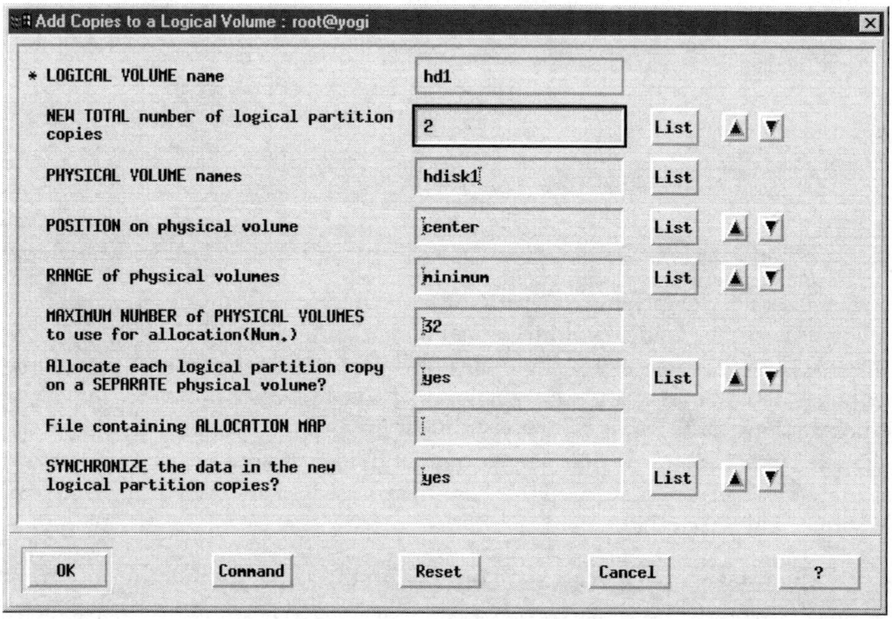

Figure 11-6.   SMIT "mirror-logical volume" panel

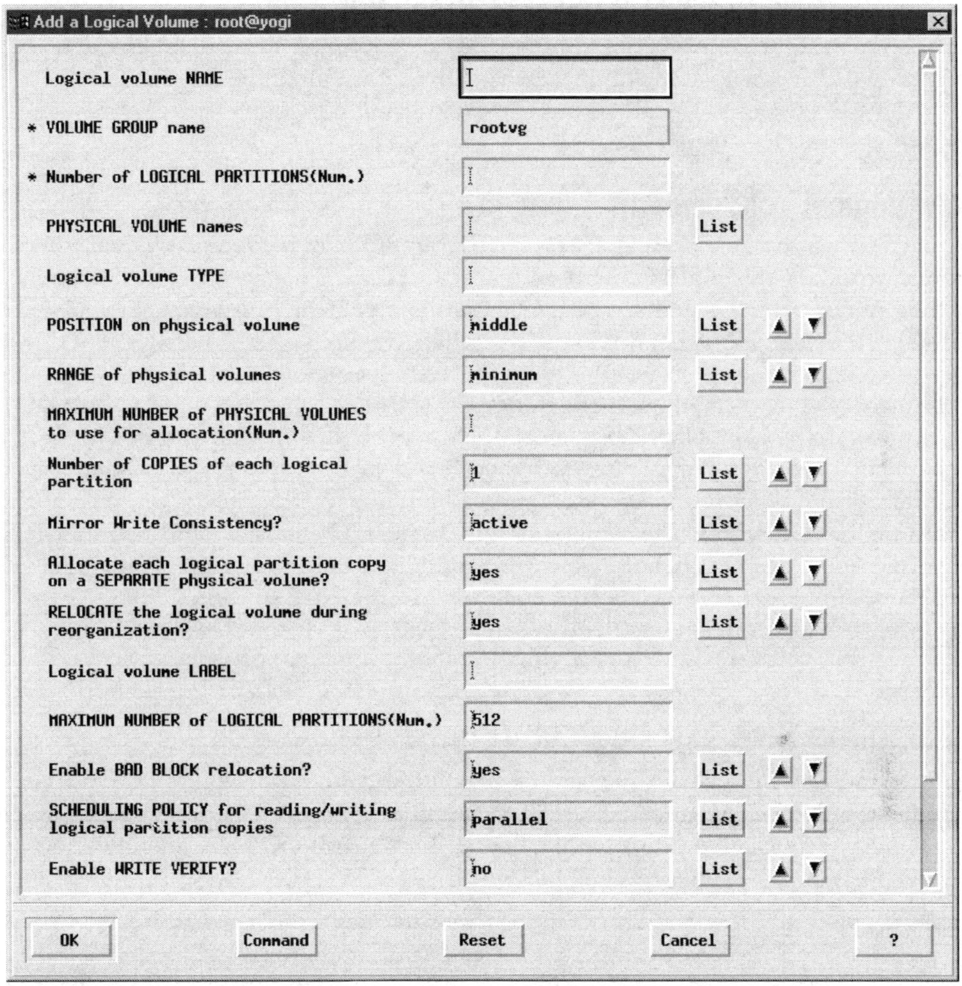

Figure 11-7.   SMIT "add logical volume" panel

Raw Logical Volumes

Database applications are notorious for requiring raw logical volumes. A raw logical volume is a logical volume without a filesystem. Paging space is also a raw logical volume. The access to raw logical volumes is done by way of the *raw device* in /dev/r*. Each of these raw devices is a character special file, and most disk devices have multiple raw devices associated with them. The application usually sets up soft links to each raw device for access.

File Ownership of Raw LV Devices and Links

You can run into trouble when adding raw logical volumes for the DBA if you forget to change the file ownership and group. My DBAs need all of the raw devices to be owned by **dba** user and the **dba** group. By default, all of the raw devices are owned by **root** user and the **system** group.

Raw Logical Volumes and Async I/O

Now you are asking for trouble! If you have a requirement for Async I/O, then you should never use raw logical volumes. Instead opt for JFS filesystems. The problem with combining raw LV and Async I/O is that Async I/O is running along and throwing the data over the fence to the operating system to store to disk. All of this unwritten data is cached in a buffer, thus the term *Asynchronous I/O*. If the machine fails, then all of the data in the cache buffer is lost forever, and you end up with a corrupted database! However, if you use Async I/O with a JFS filesystem and the system fails, you should never lose any data. This is because the JFS filesystem has its journal log, and when the machine is rebooted it will know to *replay* the journal log to complete the disk writes. The combination of Async I/O and raw logical volume is a particularly big problem in an HACMP cluster. If a machine detects a problem it can trip the *dead-man switch,* and a **halt -q** command is immediately issued. Just remember to always use JFS or JFS2 filesystems when Async I/O is required (see the section "Filesystems (JFS and JFS2)" later in this chapter for more details).

Increasing the Size of a Logical Volume

You can increase the size of a logical volume on-the-fly in AIX using the **extendlv** command or by the SMIT FastPath **smitty extendlv**.

To add five logical partitions to the hd9var logical volume, issue the following command:

```
# extendlv hd9var 5    ◄──────── This is done for you with the chfs command
```

It is important to note that the **extendlv** command will not automatically make any of this new space available to a JFS or JFS2 *filesystem* on the target logical volume. The **chfs** command will add the needed partitions and extend the *filesystem* both with one command:

```
chfs -a size=SIZE_IN_512_BYTE_BLOCKS   MOUNT_POINT
```

Decreasing the Size of a Logical Volume

This is a problem with AIX. It is possible to remove logical partitions from a logical volume with the unsupported command **lreducelv** and other unsupported LV commands to build the needed LV map file. These commands are used in the **rmlv** script to remove all the logical partitions in order to remove the entire logical volume.

This process is beyond the scope of this chapter, but I feel confident that someone could someday write a **reducelv** wrapper script to make it useful. Another problem comes when you have a filesystem on top of the logical volume you want to reduce. There are no supported or unsupported commands to deal with this that I know of. So please do not try it unless you have a system you can destroy. *Use at your own risk* and for more details read *AIX Logical Volume Manager from A to Z: Troubleshooting and Commands* from Redbooks and IBM: http://www.redbooks.ibm.com/pubs/pdfs/rebooks/sg245433.pdf.

Defragment a Filesystem with defragfs

The **defraglv** command attempts get more contiguous PP for the filesystem. If your filesystems consist of PPs scattered over the disk, you will see some benefit, but it is usually negligible. To defrag the /bigdata01 filesystem issue the following command:

```
# defragfs /bigdata01
```

synclvodm Command

The **synclvodm** command synchronizes or rebuilds the logical volume control block (LVCB), the device configuration database in the ODM, and the volume group descriptor areas on each of the physical volumes in the specified volume group.

Remember that if you run this command on a system that is running raw logical volumes, all of the raw devices in the /dev/r* directory will be owned by the **root** user and the **system** group! If you are running a database under raw logical volumes, just remember to go back and change the raw device file ownership accordingly.

NOTE In AIX 4.3 IBM added the **-P** flag to the **synclvodm** command that preserves the ownership and permissions of the logical volume raw devices. Always use the **-P** flag to preserve raw device settings!

It is rare that you need to run this command, but if for some reason the device configuration database becomes inconsistent, you can run the following command:

```
# synclvodm -v -P rootvg
```

(or)

```
# synclvodm -v -P rootvg lv01 lv02 hd1
```

FILESYSTEMS (JFS AND JFS2)

The most common use of logical volumes is to contain filesystems. A *filesystem* is the structure that supports a UNIX directory and file tree. A filesystem tree begins with the root directory at the top, with subdirectory branches proceeding down from the root.

Each directory level in the tree may contain files and directories. The primary structures that make up the filesystem are the super block, inodes, and data blocks.

New enhancements to the Logical Volume Manager (LVM) in AIX 5L include the 64-bit JFS2 filesystem, which is the only filesystem available on the Itanium-based machines. The JFS2 filesystem is an expanded JFS filesystem capable of 1 Terabyte (TB) files and 4 Petabyte (PB) filesystems! The 4PB filesystem is a theoretical size, since no one, to my knowledge, has ever bought 4PBs of disk drives to connect to a machine, but the math works. Another enhancement in JFS2 is dynamic inode allocation.

It is important to note that some C compilers still have a 2GB limit on file size. You will need to learn the proper compiler flag (-D_LARGE_FILES) to enable large access from your compiled code.

Super Block

The super block describes the overall structure of the filesystem within the logical volume. It contains the filesystem name, the size, the pointer to the inode and free block lists, and so on. The super block is used to keep track of the filesystem state during operation. Super block information is also used to verify the integrity of the filesystem as part of the boot process and in the event of a failure.

Each directory and file in the filesystem is represented by an inode. The inode can be thought of as an index entry. Each inode is sequentially numbered from 1 up to the maximum number of inodes defined for the filesystem. JFS2 filesystems, which are new to AIX 5L, dynamically allocate inodes as they are needed. The inode identifies the attributes of the file or directory it represents:

- File mode
- File type
- Owning UID and GID
- Date and time stamps
- Number of links
- Pointer to data blocks
- Size in bytes
- Size in blocks

Inodes

The number of inodes created for filesystems are based on the size of the filesystem. The native AIX V5 JFS filesystem permits limited control over the number of inodes allocated. This means more wasted space for filesystems that will contain a small number of very large files; for example, databases. The numbers of inodes allocated is no longer directly fixed to the number of filesystem blocks allocated. The number of inodes to be created is controlled using the Number Of Bytes Per Inode (NBPI) option at filesystem creation time. This value allocates one inode per number of filesystem bytes as specified by NBPI. The NBPI value is a multiple power of 2 ranging from 512 to 16,384. To reduce the number of inodes for a filesystem, select a large NBPI value. For more inodes, pick a small value. Note that you can't change the NBPI value for an existing filesystem.

New to AIX 5L is the JFS2 filesystems and inodes that are allocated dynamically instead of being created when the filesystem is created.

Information for a particular inode can be displayed using the **istat** command:

```
# istat 25 /dev/hd6
Inode 25 on device 10/8      File
Protection: rw-r--r--
Owner: 0(root)        Group: 0(system)
Link count:    1        Length 4005888 bytes
Last updated:     Thu Nov 22 07:20:23 2001
Last modified:    Thu Nov 22 07:20:23 2001
Last accessed:    Thu Nov 22 07:19:58 2001
Block pointers (hexadecimal):
58         60        68        70        82        8a        92        9a
```

To find the i node for a particular file, use **istat** *filename*.

To find the filename associated with the **inode** number, use the **-inum** flag with the **find** command:

```
# find /home -xdev -inum 25 -print
/home/rmichael/.forward
```

Data Blocks

Data blocks are used to store the actual file data in the filesystem. Each inode contains 13 data block address slots. The first eight address slots point at the first eight file data blocks of the file. The ninth address points to an in-core inode structure. The disk inode information is copied to this structure when the file is opened. The tenth through thirteenth addresses point to indirect data blocks, which are used to address data blocks for large files. Each indirect block supports 1024 addresses. Because file addressing is restricted to 32 bits, third-level indirection is not used.

Fragments

AIX V4 JFS introduced BSD-like disk fragmentation. Fragments are small filesystem blocks based on a division of a power of 2 of the full 4KB block size. The fragment size is defined at filesystem creation time and may take a value of 512 bytes, 1KB, 2KB, and 4KB (default). Individual filesystems may have different fragment sizes specified.

Fragment sizes are specified on a per-filesystem basis. You can define small fragment sizes for filesystems that support small files and larger fragment sizes for those with large files. Fragments provide a means for using the unallocated space left in partially filled 4KB blocks. The only reason to change the fragment size is if you have a huge number of small files.

There are some restrictions and a downside, too, when using fragments. First of all, fragments are only supported in inode direct blocks. JFS inodes have eight direct block addresses. The ninth is used for indirect addressing. The upper nibble of an inode direct block address is used to store the fragment ratio for the block. Thus fragments are only supported for file sizes up to 32KB. Files that are larger than 32KB use the full 4KB block sizes. Note that large files do not use fragments for the first 32KB and full block sizes for the remainder. Also, you may have already guessed that by using small fragment sizes, you increase the fragmentation of your overall filesystem space. To address this, we use the **defragfs** command to defragment filesystems:

```
# defragfs /usr  ◄────────── Defragment /usr filesystem
# defragfs -r /usr  ◄────────── Report /usr fragment state

statistics before running defragfs:
number of free fragments 43107
number of allocated fragments 199581
number of free spaces shorter than a block 0
number of free fragments in short free spaces 0
statistics after running defragfs
number of free spaces shorter than a block 0
number of free fragments in short free spaces 0
other statistics:
number of fragments moved 2285
number of logical blocks moved 2285
number of allocation attempts 635
number of exact matches 136
```

Compression

JFS compression is an installable BOS fileset option. Compression support is selected on a per-filesystem basis at filesystem create time. AIX applies compression at the logical block level rather than at the file level. This improves random I/O performance in that the entire file does not have to be decompressed. Compression is also only applied to regular files and long symbolic links.

Space allocation can be a problem for compressed filesystems. It is always difficult to tell how much space will be required by a file after compression. To avoid overallocation problems, AIX allocates the full block requirement for the uncompressed file. The assumption being that after compression the file won't be larger than the original.

For regular files, you can use the standard **compress** command, which can achieve compression rates as high as 50 percent. I like to use **gzip** for file compression. The **gzip** command has nine levels of compression, 0–9, with 9 being the most compression. Depending on the file you can get up to 70 percent compression or so. Try this command on a large file:

```
# gzip -9 my_huge_file
```

Large Files

AIX 5L supports files up to 64GB for standard JFS filesystems and file sizes up to 1TB for JFS-2 filesystems. The filesystem limits for AIX 5L is 64GB for standard JFS and up to 4 Petabytes for JFS2! Be thankful for the 64-bit addressing.

Virtual Filesystem

AIX 5L supplies a generic filesystem interface called the Virtual Filesystem (VFS) that permits it to support a number of filesystem types. VFS is an abstraction of the underlying physical filesystem mount structure, inodes, and operations.

The underlying physical filesystem is represented in VFS by a generic mount structure and an array of operations permitted on the physical filesystem called **vfsops**. VFS uses a paired abstraction of **vnodes** and **gnodes** to reference the underlying filesystem inode structures. One or more **vnode** structures reference a **gnode** that is linked to the real inode. VFS operates on the underlying inodes using **vnode** operations called **vnodeops**. VFS-supported filesystem types are defined in /etc/vfs:

```
%defaultvfs     jfs nfs
#
cdrfs      5     none none
procfs     6     none none
jfs        3     none /sbin/helpers/v3fshelper
jfs2   0    /sbin/helpers/jfs2     none
nfs    2    /sbin/helpers/nfsmnthelp     none remote
sfs    16   none  none
nfs3   18   /sbin/helpers/nfsmnthelp     none remote
cachefs    17    /sbin/helpers/cfsmnthelp     none remote
autofs     19    /sbin/helpers/aufsmnthelp    none
dfs    7    /sbin/helpers/dfsmnthelper none
```

Journaled Filesystem Configuration

The native filesystem in AIX is a log-based filesystem called the Journaled Filesystem (JFS). Log-based filesystems like JFS improve recovery by maintaining a circular update log. In the event of a failure, the JFS log is replayed to recover the filesystem state. Log recovery of a filesystem is completed hours faster than a full **fsck** walk of a filesystem. AIX provides the **fsck** to assist in disaster recovery; however, it is not invoked as part of the standard boot procedure.

When a JFS or JFS2 filesystem is created, a *log logical volume* is also created if it does not already exist. A log logical volume can support several filesystems within a volume group.

Create or update a JFS filesystem using the SMIT fast path or the **crfs** and **chfs**. A new JFS filesystem may be created in an existing empty logical volume, or a new logical volume will be built to hold the new filesystem (see Figure 11-8.) Be careful when specifying the size of the filesystem! Filesystem blocks are 512 bytes in size. Table 11-4 gives general rules of thumb.

*Default Logical Partition Size   If it was any clearer than this, it wouldn't be UNIX, and it sure wouldn't be AIX.

```
# crfs -v jfs -g uservg1 -m /u4 -a size=1048576
# smitty crjfs
```

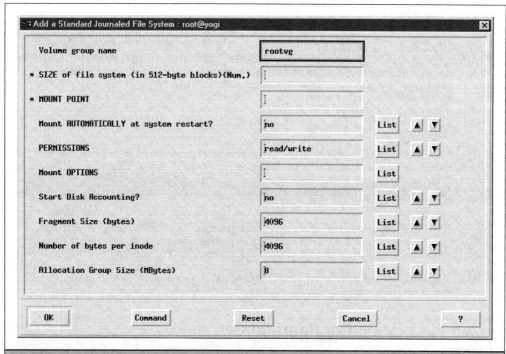

Figure 11-8.   SMIT "add journaled filesystem" panel

Block Size	Action
512	Updating new or existing filesystem size
1024	AIX commands that report filesystem use. Normally the **-k** flag (**df -k**)
512–4096	AIX fragment sizes
4096*	Managing logical partitions for logical volumes

Table 11-4.   Block size actions

The filesystem attributes are recorded in the ODM custom databases and the /etc/filesystems file. Do not edit the /etc/filesystems file. Use SMIT or the Web-Based System Management (wsm).

```
/:
  dev = /dev/hd4
  vfs = jfs
  log = /dev/hd8
  mount = automatic
  check = false
  type = bootfs
  vol = root
  free = true
/home:
  dev = /dev/hd1
  vfs = jfs
  log = /dev/hd8
  mount = true
  check = true
  vol = /home
  account = true
  free = false
  quota = userquota
/usr:
  dev = /dev/hd2
  vfs = jfs
  log = /dev/hd8
  mount = automatic
  check = false
  type = bootfs
  vol = /usr
  free = false
```

```
/var:
  dev = /dev/hd9var
  vfs = jfs
  log = /dev/hd8
  mount = automatic
  check = false
  type = bootfs
  vol = /var
  free = false
/tmp:
  dev = /dev/hd3
  vfs = jfs
  log = /dev/hd8
  mount = automatic
  check = false
  vol = /tmp
  free = false
/mnt:
  dev = /dev/hd7
  vol = "spare"
  mount = false
  check = false
  free = false
  vfs = jfs
  log = /dev/hd8
```

You may remove a filesystem using the **rmfs** command:

```
# rmfs /n5 ◄─────────── Remove filesystem /n5
```

or SMIT:

```
# smitty rmjfs
```

NOTE   The **rmfs** command will remove the filesystem and logical volume at the same time.

Large Filesystems (JFS-2)

In AIX 5L IBM introduced the Enhanced Journaled Filesystem (JFS-2). The JFS-2 filesystem is based on standard JFS. The new JFS-2 filesystem is the standard filesystem for the Itanium-based systems. JFS-2 uses an extended base allocation, which is a way to address multiple disk block addresses at the same time. The result is a high-performance filesystem that supports huge files up to 1TB and filesystems up to 4 Petabytes. The inodes in a JFS-2 filesystem are allocated dynamically, so you do not have to worry about running out of inodes any more. You have to specify a JFS-2 filesystem at creation time. You cannot change a filesystem on the fly. The proper way to change a filesystem from JFS to JFS-2 is to back up the JFS filesystem, create a new JFS-2 filesystem, and restore the JFS data in the new JFS-2 filesystem.

Mounting and Unmounting Filesystems

Filesystem data is made accessible by mounting the filesystem on a mount point. The *mount point* is a directory in a previously mounted filesystem like the root filesystem. You might think that this is a chicken-and-egg problem; however, the boot procedure handles the special case of mounting the root filesystem. The mount point is usually an empty directory, but that is not a requirement. If you mount a filesystem over a populated directory, the previous subdirectory tree is not harmed, but it is no longer accessible until the filesystem has been unmounted (see Figure 11-9.)

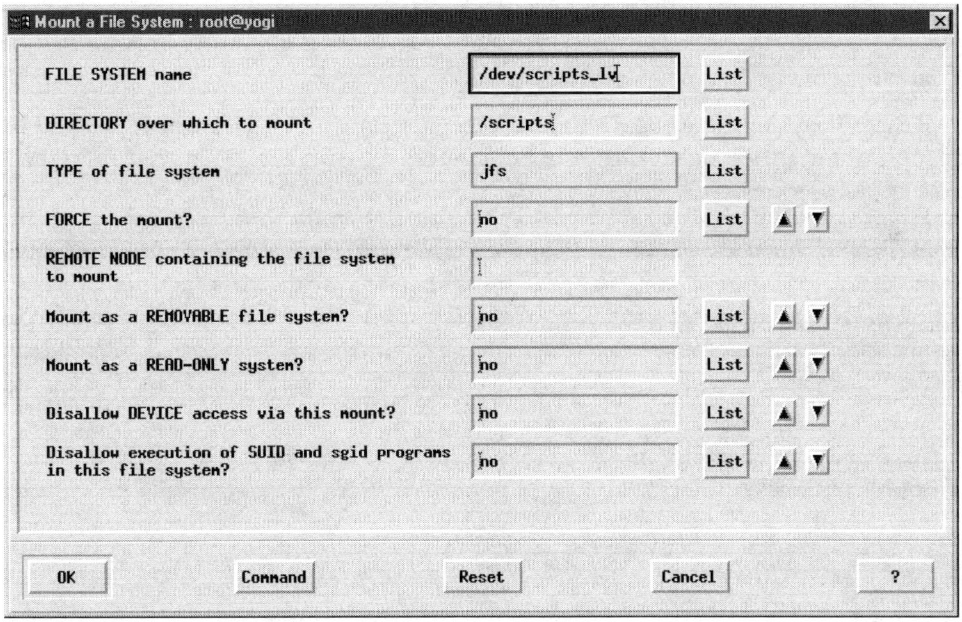

Figure 11-9.   SMIT "mount a filesystem panel"

Filesystems may be mounted or unmounted with the mount and umount commands:

```
# mount /dev/hd5 /n5  ◄─────── Mount /dev/hd5 on /n5
# umount /n6  ◄─────── Unmount filesystem /n6
```

or by using SMIT:

```
# smit mountfs
```

You cannot unmount a filesystem that is busy. A filesystem is busy if any application has a file or directory open. This can be caused by an executing process or a user whose current directory path is within the filesystem. Use tools like **fuser** and the public domain **lsof** commands to identify which processes and users have files open:

```
# fuser -u /dev/hd1  ◄─────── AIX open file lister
/dev/hd1: 32605c(deroest) 43100c(deroest) 47029(root)
```

```
# lsof /dev/hd1  ◄─────── Public domain program to list open files
COMMAND    PID USER   FD   TYPE  DEVICE      SIZE/OFF   INODE/NAME
ksh     32605 deroest  cwd  VDIR  10, 8 1536    18 /home    (/dev/hd1)
aixterm    43100  deroest    cwd VDIR  10, 8 1536    18 /home (/dev/hd1)
ksh    47029 root      63u   VREG  10, 8 2678    78 /home    (/dev/hd1)
```

Which filesystems are to be mounted automatically at boot time are specified by the **mount=automatic** or **mount=true** parameters for each filesystem stanza in the /etc/filesystems file. To change a filesystem to automatically mount at system restart, use either the **smitty chfs** or **chfs -A yes** *filesystem* command.

Filesystems may also be identified as a group by adding a **type=**<*name* parameter for the group in /etc/filesystems. This is specified by the **chfs -u** *groupname flesystem*. The group name can then be used to mount or unmount all the filesystems in the group from a single command:

```
# mount -t nfs  ◄─────── Mount all filesystems in /etc/filesystems with type=nfs
```

To display the currently mounted filesystems and their state, use the **df** and **mount** commands:

```
# df -k
Filesystem    1024-blocks      Free %Used    Iused %Iused Mounted on
/dev/hd4           32768     15772   52%     1727    11% /
/dev/hd2         1212416     27084   98%    37639    13% /usr
/dev/hd9var        53248     26812   50%      580     5% /var
/dev/hd3          106496     99872    7%      139     1% /tmp
/dev/hd1            4096      3916    5%       25     3% /home
```

```
/proc                    -              -    -           -      -  /proc
/dev/hd10opt       638976          22388  97%       15603    10%  /opt
/dev/lvscripts     102400          75296  27%         651     3%  /scripts
/dev/lv00           40960          30612  26%          72     1%  /storix


# mount
  node        mounted        mounted over    vfs      date         options
--------  ---------------  ---------------  ------  ------------  ---------------
          /dev/hd4         /                jfs     Nov 25 11:33  rw,log=/dev/hd8
          /dev/hd2         /usr             jfs     Nov 25 11:33  rw,log=/dev/hd8
          /dev/hd9var      /var             jfs     Nov 25 11:34  rw,log=/dev/hd8
          /dev/hd3         /tmp             jfs     Nov 25 11:34  rw,log=/dev/hd8
          /dev/hd1         /home            jfs     Nov 25 11:34  rw,log=/dev/hd8
          /proc            /proc            procfs  Nov 25 11:34  rw
          /dev/hd10opt     /opt             jfs     Nov 25 11:34  rw,log=/dev/hd8
          /dev/lvscripts   /scripts         jfs     Nov 25 11:34  rw,log=/dev/hd8
          /dev/lv00        /storix          jfs     Nov 25 11:34  rw,log=/dev/hd8
```

Problems with Unmounting a Filesystem

If you cannot unmount a filesystem, then it is being used. Even if someone has changed directory to the filesystem you want to unmount, it is in use and cannot be unmounted. I also see people confused when they try to remove a CD-ROM from a drive and the door will not open—this is because the CD-ROM is mounted.

If you need to immediately unmount a filesystem and it is in use, you can use the **fuser** command with the **-k** switch option, for kill. As an example if you want to unmount /data01 and it is busy, try the following commands:

```
# fuser -k /data01
# umount /data01
```

Increasing the Size of a Filesystem

Filesystems can be increased on the fly with the SMIT FastPath **smitty chfs** or the **chfs** command. To increase the size of the /home filesystem to 40960 512-byte blocks, issue the following command:

```
# chfs -a size=40960 /home
```

NOTE   The number for the **size** parameter does not have to be exact. The system will round up to the next partition size.

To add 40MB to the /home filesystem, issue the following command:

```
# chfs -a size=+81920 /home
```

Decreasing the Size of a Filesystem

Increasing the size of a filesystem, logical volume, or volume group can be done on the fly with SMIT as described in the previous sections. To decrease the size of a filesystem requires doing things the old-fashioned way: back up the filesystem, re-create it, and restore the backup. It gets even trickier if you are resizing one of the operating system filesystems like /usr. Let's use /usr as an example because it's a worst-case scenario.

1. Export any non-rootvg volume groups. Makes for peace of mind.

   ```
   # exportvg <VGname>
   ```

2. Invoke **mkszfile** to create an **image.data** map file of the current filesystem attributes:

   ```
   # mkszfile
   ```

3. Create a rootvg backup using **mksysb**.

   ```
   # mksysb /dev/rmt0
   ```

4. Reboot the system from stand-alone media, in this case consisting of the AIX 5L installation CD #1.

5. Choose Change/Show Installation Settings And Install from the Welcome To Base Operating System Installation And Maintenance menu.

6. Toggle the Shrink Filesystems selection to Yes. You will then be prompted to select a new size. Note that changing the filesystem size will override the map created in step 3. *Make sure you leave enough space to restore your backup image!*

7. Insert the **mksysb** backup media and select Continue with choices indicated above.

8. Reboot the system after the restore is complete and import the non-rootvg filesystems that were exported in step 1.

   ```
   # importvg <VGname>
   ```

For more information on backup and restore methods, refer to Chapter 25.

PAGING SPACE

Paging (swap) space is used by AIX to support virtual memory services. When free memory becomes low or exhausted, AIX moves data pages from primary memory storage to the paging areas according to a least recently used algorithm. A threshold is maintained for virtual memory usage by the operating system. When the threshold is exceeded, a SIGDANGER signal is sent to all processes. If a second threshold, called the kill level, is exceeded, then the operating system sends SIGKILL signals to the biggest memory offenders. This process continues until memory utilization falls below the threshold levels.

In order to keep this kind of trouble from occurring, you need to make sure that sufficient paging space is available. How much is going to depend on your system use profile. What are the average working set sizes required by your workload? Multiuser systems running a number of processes with large working sets may require two or more times the available real memory as paging space. A single-user workstation can get away with far less depending on available real memory and disk. Paging space is allocated as paging logical volumes. You can split up paging space as separate logical volumes on separate physical disks to improve paging performance. Always limit paging partitions to one per physical disk!

Paging Space Best Practices

Paging space is disk storage that is used to temporarily store memory pages when the system real memory is running low. Some people may refer to paging space as *swap* space. A paging space is a logical volume that has the LV attribute set to paging. We refer to this type of logical volume as a paging space logical volume (or just paging space). All paging space is controlled by the Virtual Memory Manager (VMM). For a process to run, it must be loaded into real memory, but not all of the processes residing in memory are active. The VMM is always scanning the memory for the oldest and least used processes in memory. When real memory runs low, the VMM will *page out* this least used memory page to the paging space on disk. When this page frame is needed again, it is *paged in* by the VMM and is made ready to run again.

The VMM partitions all of the address space into segments that are 256MB of contiguous virtual memory address space. Each of these virtual memory segments is further partitioned into 4096-byte *pages,* or 4KB page frames. You will often here the term *page fault.* A page fault can be either a new page fault or a repage fault. A new page fault occurs when a page that is needed in memory has not yet been referenced or has not recently been referenced. A repage fault occurs when a recently referenced page is not found in memory, which is usually because it has been paged out to disk paging space.

The first thing to always keep in mind is that paging space is a holding area for inactive processes. Paging space is *not* a substitute for real memory! The more processes that are active on your system, the more real memory your system needs. If your machine has too little memory, it will reach a point where it is constantly paging, a state that is called *thrashing.* Thrashing is a process where the VMM attempts to make room in real memory by paging out and as soon as a process is paged out, it is immediately needed again and the VMM pages in the frame back into memory. This process is repeated continuously, and the machine is not getting any work done. Adding more paging space will not solve the problem. The only solution is to add more real memory. Another problem with thrashing is that eventually your machine will crash! The first sign that you are running out of paging space consists of a bunch of weird errors, for example:

```
Fork failure - not enough memory available
Fork function not allowed. Not enough memory available
fork () system call failed
Unable to fork, too many processes
ksh: cannot fork not enough swap space
INIT: Paging space is low
Not enough memory
```

Adding a Paging Space

Paging space requirements depend on the amount of real memory in your system. During the BOS installation process, paging space is created automatically; however, it is never enough to do any heavy work. If real memory is greater than or equal to 64MB (the minimum for AIX5L!) the system will create a single paging space equal to real memory plus 16MB. This is not enough paging space! The actual amount of paging space required depends on the applications you are running and how much real memory is in the system. Any database (DB2, Oracle, or Sybase) needs a lot of memory *and* paging space. On our SAP systems, the requirement for memory is 4GB *as a minimum* and the paging space requirement is in the *tens of gigabytes!* You need to do some research on your application requirements before setting up your paging space.

There are two commands that will display the amount of real memory in your system. Both commands report resident memory in kilobytes:

```
lsattr -El sys0 | grep realmem
bootinfo -r
```

You need to monitor how your system is using paging space to know if you have enough. You can monitor each paging space with the **lsps -a** command, and you can get a summary of all paging spaces put together using the **lsps -s** command. The default system paging logical volume is hd6. Each additional paging space logical volume will be assigned paging00, paging01, and so on.

Here is a listing of paging space best practices:

1. Each paging space should be pretty close to the same size. The VMM uses a round-robin technique to attempt to balance paging space usage.

2. It is not advisable to put more than one paging space on a single disk! Placing each paging space on a separate disk helps to minimize any disk I/O bottleneck and ensures that the round-robin technique used for paging space is not defeated. However, your paging space should be mirrored just as you should mirror the root volume group.

3. Never extend a paging space to span multiple disks. Since the VMM is using a round-robin technique, the disk activity will be unbalanced.

4. Always place paging space logical volumes on disks with the lowest disk activity. You never want the system paging space and an application competing for disk I/O: the paging space will always win and the application will suffer tremendously.

5. Place paging space on disks that are on different disk adapters, or controllers. Using multiple disk controllers will give you much better throughput and will improve performance.

To add paging space to the system, you can use **smitty mkps** SMIT FastPath or the **mkps** command. You can also change the current paging space allocations using **smitty chps** SMIT FastPath or the **chps** command. Paging space is allocated in logical partitions (LPs). The following command will create a paging space on hdisk1 that is 8 LPs in the rootvg volume group and will be *activated immediately* and on *all subsequent system restarts*:

```
mkps -a -n -s8 rootvg hdisk1
```

You can also use SMIT to add paging space as shown in Figure 11-10.

Activating and Deactivating a Paging Space

For a paging space to be used, it must be activated. All paging spaces are defined in the /etc/swapspaces file. You can activate the paging spaces dynamically by using the **swapon** command. To activate the **paging03** paging space, issue the following command:

```
swapon /dev/paging03
```

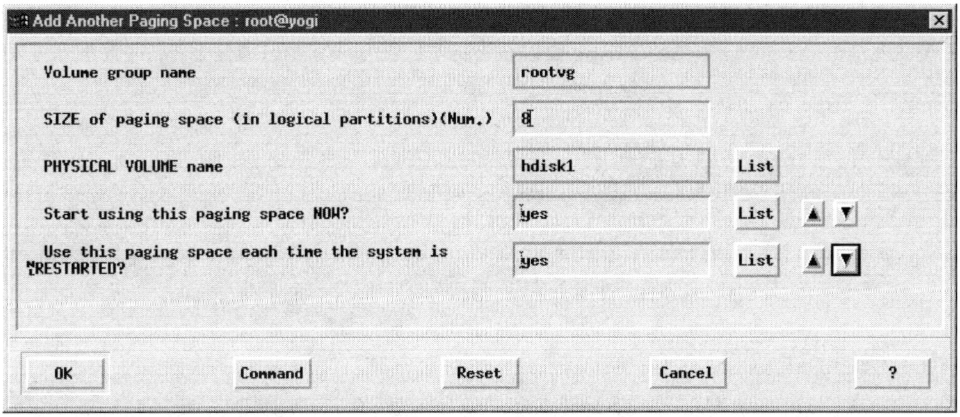

Figure 11-10.   SMIT "Add Paging Space" panel

To activate all paging spaces at once, issue the following command:

```
swapon -a
```

New to AIX 5L is the **swapoff** command. The **swapoff** command will enable you to deactivate a paging space on the fly! In the previous AIX versions, we had to set the paging space not to activate on a system restart and reboot the system. IBM is moving closer and closer to no downtime!

To deactivate the **paging03** paging space, issue the following command:

```
swapoff /dev/paging03
```

Removing an Active Paging Space

Before you can remove a paging space from the system, the paging space must be deactivated, as shown in the section immediately preceding this. To remove the **paging03** paging space from the system, issue the following commands:

```
swapoff /dev/paging03
rmps paging03
```

Reducing the Size of an Active Paging Space

Also new to AIX 5L is the ability to reduce the size of a paging space on a running system (see Table 11-5). IBM added another switch to the **chps** command, **-d**. This command will execute the shrinkps shell script that will jump through all of the extra hoops for you. If you want to look at the shell script, it is in /usr/sbin/shrinkps. The SMIT FastPath is **smitty chps**.

To reduce the size of the **paging03** paging space by two logical partitions, issue the following command:

```
chps -d2 paging03
```

VOLUME MAINTENANCE

Other than the cases of reducing the size of existing filesystems or paging areas, the AIX LVM and JFS and JFS-2 systems make disk management a breeze. It's the "other than" cases that still require a bit of work.

Moving Filesystems

There are several reasons why you may want to move a filesystem around on your system. You always want to separate heavily used filesystems to separate disks. A good example of this is separating your indexes and data in a database. Filesystems

Command	Description
mkps	Adds an additional paging space
rmps	Removes an inactive paging space
chps	Changes the attributes of a paging space
lsps	Displays paging space statistics
swapoff	Deactivates paging space on a running system
swapon	Activates paging space
chps –s	Increases the size of a paging space
chps –d	Dynamically decreases the size of a paging space on a running system
shrinkps	Shell script that **chps -d** executes to shrink paging space
svmon	Takes a snapshot of virtual memory usage. Part of the perfagent.tools fileset
topas	IBM's top/monitor clone
vmstat	Reports virtual memory statistics
sar	System Activity Report
istat	Status of inodes
slibclean	Removes any currently unused modules in kernel or library memory
ps	Displays the current status of processes

Table 11-5.   Handy Commands for Paging Space

may be moved within a machine provided there is sufficient free disk space. If you are short on disk space, follow the procedure described in the section "Increasing the Size of a Filesystem" in this chapter.

Moving Logical Volumes Within the Same Volume Group

To migrate the filesystem logical volume to another physical volume within the same volume group, use the **migratepv** command or the **smitty migratepv** SMIT FastPath.

- Use **lslv** to identify the current logical volume location and produce a physical disk map.
- Use the **migratepv -l** command to move the logical volume to its new location.

For example, to move the paging03 paging space from hdisk1 to hdisk2 in rootvg, issue the following command:

```
# migratepv -l paging03 hdisk1 hdisk2
```

Moving Logical Volumes Between Volume Groups

To move a logical volume to a different volume group, we use the copy LV command, **cplv**. For example, to move the dat01 LV from rootvg to appvg, issue the following three commands:

```
# cplv -v appvg -y new01 dat01
# chlv -n old01 dat01
# chlv -n dat01 new01
```

Moving Volume Groups

You can also move a volume group from one system to another using the **exportvg** and **importvg** commands or the **SMIT vg** FastPath.

1. Unmount all the filesystems and deactivate any paging areas contained in the volume group to be moved.

2. Export the volume group using **exportvg**.

3. Move the physical disks containing the volume group to the new system and run **cfgmgr** to detect and configure the disks.

4. Import the volume group on the new system using **importvg**. All table references will be updated automatically.

5. Mount the filesystems and active paging space on the new system.

TROUBLESHOOTING

Troubleshooting disk hardware, LVM, and filesystem problems usually requires intimate knowledge of the event history leading to the problem. For hardware problems:

- Check error log with the **errpt** command.
- Check cabling.
- Check SCSI terminator.
- Check SCSI ID jumpers or switch settings.
- Verify SSA loops.
- Run diagnostics from a stand-alone CD-ROM or the **diag** program.

For LVM-related problems, try resynchronizing the ODM and configuration table entries by exporting the problem volume group followed by an import. You can narrow down the problem area by using **lslv** to display logical volume attributes and maps.

If a filesystem has become corrupted, take the filesystem offline and run the **fsck** command, which will walk the filesystem structures and identify problem entries or chains. Occasionally a volume group–related ODM update may abort, leaving the volume group locked. To unlock a volume group, issue a **getlvodm**/**putlvodm** sequence using the volume group name as an argument.

```
# chvg -u rootvg ◀─────── Unlock rootvg
```

CHECKLIST

The following is a checklist for the key points in Storage Hardware and the Logical Volume Manager

☐ Use the **diag** command to troubleshoot the IBM Serial Storage Architecture (SSA) subsystem.

☐ A physical volume (PV) is a single piece of disk storage. A PV may be a single disk drive, or it may be a single RAID multidisk array.

☐ A volume group (VG) is a collection of one or more physical volumes (PVs).

☐ A physical partition (PP) is a small block of a PV, or physical volume. A PP is the basic building block unit of storage.

☐ A logical partition (LP) is a map to a physical partition (PP) on a disk drive.

☐ A logical volume (LV) is a collection of one or more logical partitions (LPs) within the same volume group (VG).

☐ Busy filesystems should be located in the center of the physical disk (referred to as intradisk policy) and spread the data across multiple physical disks, or PVs.

☐ AIX 5L provides hot spot management, the ability to identify a logical partition with so much I/O activity that it is degrading system performance and move a single LP from one disk to another.

☐ Enable gathering of statistics for hot spot monitoring with the **lvmstat** command.

CHAPTER 12

*Printers and the
Print Subsystem*

New to AIX 5L is the support for System V printer services. To support System V, IBM added a new user (**lp** user) and a new **lp** group to the AIX operating system. The System V version that IBM uses in AIX 5L is release 4 (SRV4) of the System V print subsystem. You can run either the classic AIX or the System V printer subsystem on POWER systems. You must select one because they will not run concurrently, but you may switch between AIX and SRV4. For Itanium-based systems, the classic AIX printer subsystem is not available. The default printer subsystem is the System V, SRV4 release. On POWER systems, both the AIX and SRV4 subsystems are available, but the AIX printer subsystem is the default. The long-term goal for AIX is to make System V the default print subsystem for all platforms. Before we go into the System V printer subsystem, a review of AIX printing is in order.

The classic AIX printer subsystem provides a rich set of commands and configuration options that go far beyond the printing facilities offered by many other UNIX implementations. When the AIX printer subsystem was developed, it was created using a combination of System V and BSD standards. Then IBM added some unique features available only in AIX. Since the AIX printer subsystem was designed with a combination of standards, there is an easy transition to AIX because most of the commands for both System V and BSD are provided. If you are familiar with the traditional BSD or System V printing environments, you will find that the AIX printing subsystem is not only interoperable with these environments, but that it also involves some significant differences.

The printing subsystem in AIX comprises commands designed to meet the demands of the distributed printing technologies found in most network landscapes. Most of these commands are provided to support compatibility at the user interface level with BSD, System V, and older versions of AIX. Users familiar with BSD printing commands will be able to use the same commands and options when printing files on an AIX system. The same holds true for System V commands. What's even better is that AIX also provides one command, **enq**, that will do most everything the other commands can do.

General spooling configuration has been reduced to two steps starting in AIX 4. You define a printer model that represents the print device attached to the system. Next, you add a print queue to hold files waiting to be output to the device. All of this can be done in one step using either SMIT or WebSM. Both management interfaces walk you through the steps for adding the printer and print queue. This will be covered in the following sections.

DATA FLOW OF A PRINT JOB

Each time you submit a job for *local printing,* the job goes through a queue, just like people standing in a line. Users and applications submit jobs for printing using one of the following commands: **qprt**, **lp**, **lpr**, or **enq**. Whichever command is used, the job is submitted to the spooler by the **enq** command. The **enq** command is responsible for processing the job. So any of the previously listed commands are translated to the **enq** command with the proper command parameters. The **enq** command creates a job description file, or JDF, and then sends notification to the **qdaemon** that a new job has been submitted.

The **qdaemon** does what you would expect: it runs at all times to manage the queues. The **qdaemon** is started at boot time from the /etc/inittab file. Also, the **qdaemon** is under the control of the System Resource Controller (SRC), so you can manually start, stop, and refresh the **qdaemon** at any time using the following commands:

```
# startsrc -s qdaemon
# refresh -s qdaemon
# stopsrc -s qdaemon
```

The **qdaemon** maintains the print queues by maintaining a list of all of the defined queues and is responsible for monitoring the queues for new print jobs. When a new job is submitted, the **qdaemon** attempts to process the job if the printer resource is currently available. If the resource is not available, the job is queued and the **qdaemon** will attempt to print the job later.

The classic AIX printer subsystem has a specific flow to the queuing system. The following eight steps are followed each time a new job is submitted:

1. Whichever print command is used calls the **enq** command, which checks the validity of the queue name and makes sure that the command parameters are correct. If everything passes the test, the job continues; if a problem is found, the job is rejected and the user receives an error message.

2. Next the /var/spool/lpd/qdir directory receives an entry to identify the new print job. Some command options allow a copy of the print file to be made, which is a good idea if you want to capture a point-in-time snapshot of a file. If a copy of the source file is to be made, then the copy of the file is placed in the /var/spool/qdaemon directory.

3. At this point, the **qdaemon** is notified that a new job exists in the /var/spool/lpd/qdir directory.

4. When the job reaches the top of the queue, or the front of the line, the /etc/qconfig file is read by the **qdaemon** to get a description of the queue. The /etc/qconfig file has a description of each queue on the system.

5. When the queue starts working on the job, the **qdaemon** sends an update to the /var/spool/lpd/stat file showing that the job is active.

6. The *backend* program for the queue is started by the **qdaemon** and receives the filename and the print options for the job, which is turned into a command-line statement.

7. The backend puts all of the pieces together. The files with the attributes are assembled together into a data stream, which is stored in virtual printer definitions in the `/var/spool/lpd/pio/@local` directory.

8. Finally the data stream is sent to the printer device driver by the backend program for printing.

If a file is *spooled*, a copy of the file remains in the `/var/spool/qdaemon` directory until the job has completed printing. This ensures that the file that is spooled to the printer is the same as it was when you issued the print command. This allows you to change or edit the original file. It will not affect the printer output.

When a file is *queued*, however, a pointer to the original file is placed in the `/var/spool/lpd/qdir` directory. If the original file is changed before the file is printed, then the *updated* file is printed.

NOTE   All of this spooling in the `/var` filesystem can fill it up. So keep an eye on `/var` to ensure that you do not run out of filesystem space.

Important Files and What They Do

Six files are used in the classic AIX print subsystem. Each has a responsibility to keep the queue flowing. See Table 12-1 for details.

File or Directory	Function
`/etc/qconfig`	Queue configuration file that describes the queues and devices available for each queue.
`/var/spool/*`	Directory that contains spooling directories and files used by daemons and programs.
`/var/spool/qdaemon`	Directory that contains copies of files that have been spooled.
`/var/spool/lpd/stat/*`	Directory that contains status information of print jobs.
`/var/spool/lpd/qdir/*`	Directory that contains queue requests and information about queued files.
`/var/spool/lpd/pio/@local`	Directory that contains virtual printer definitions. This is the merging point for printer attributes and data stream type attributes.

Table 12-1.   Printing Files and Directories

What Is a qdaemon?

The **qdaemon** schedules jobs and manages queues. It is started a boot time from the /etc/inittab file using the **startsrc** command and can be started, stopped, and refreshed using the System Resource Controller (SRC) commands **startsrc**, **stopsrc**, and **refresh** on the command line.

The **qdaemon** uses the /etc/qconfig file to control its activities. The /etc/qconfig file contains queue definitions, in stanza format, for every queue defined on the system. Each stanza in the /etc/qconfig file controls different aspects of a print queue, such as defining the queue device that points to a particular printer, the backend program, and any management options that are available for the print queue.

To process each print request, the **qdaemon** calls the backend program specified in the /etc/qconfig stanza for the target print queue. Two backend programs are used. For local print jobs, ones to locally attached printers, the **/usr/lib/lpd/piobe** backend program is used. For remote printers, the **/usr/lib/lpd/rembak** backend program is used.

The backend program gets the printer ready to print by setting the printer attributes. If header and trailer pages are enabled, the backend program prints them too.

The /etc/qconfig file is the mechanism used in customizing queues. Each entry is in stanza format, and there are two types of stanzas. First is the queue stanza, which starts with the queue name. Each queue stanza can be up to 20 characters and must be terminated with a colon. The queue stanza points to the printer device for the queue. The default print queue for the system is defined to be the first entry is in the /etc/qconfig file. When you use SMIT or WebSM to set a default queue, the only thing that is done is to shuffle the queue stanza to the top of the file.

File Listing of the /etc/qconfig Stanzas on My Machine

```
hp4:
        device = lp0
lp0:
        file = /dev/lp0
        header = never
        trailer = never
        access = both
        backend = /usr/lib/lpd/piobe
hp4-ps:
        device = lp0
lp0:
        file = /dev/lp0
        header = never
```

```
        trailer = never
        access = both
        backend = /usr/lib/lpd/piobe
hp4-gl:
        device = lp0
lp0:
        file = /dev/lp0
        header = never
        trailer = never
        access = both
        backend = /usr/lib/lpd/piobe
```

Any user can define a default printer that overrides the first entry in the /etc/ qconfig file. The environment variable used to define a different default printer is—you guessed it—PRINTER. This variable must be set by each user who wishes to define a default printer. A .profile entry is the easiest way. To define the hp4-ps print queue to be the default, enter the following command:

```
# export PRINTER=hp4-ps
```

CONFIGURING AIX PRINTERS

The first place to look is the SMIT menus. Using the SMIT FastPath **smit spooler** is a good place to start (see Figure 12-1).

You can add a printer from the SMIT panel by selecting the SMIT option **Add A Print Queue**. SMIT will display a panel from which you select a printer attachment type (seeFigure 12-2).

For this example, you are going to select a locally attached printer, so select **Local** from the **Add A Print Queue** panel. This will bring up the next SMIT panel; select the Printer Type **IBM**, shown in Figure 12-3.

The next SMIT panel is the list of predefined IBM printer drivers, which are defined as printer models (see Figure 12-4). If the software for the printer model you selected is not installed on your system, you will be prompted to insert the installation media to install the printer driver before you can continue with the printer configuration, shown in Figure 12-5. If, however, you do not select the **List** option during printer driver installation, you will install every printer model on the installation media, which is a huge waste of disk space! For this example, select the **IBM 4039 Laser Printer**.

Next you will be prompted for the **Printer Interface Selection**, shown in Figure 12-6.

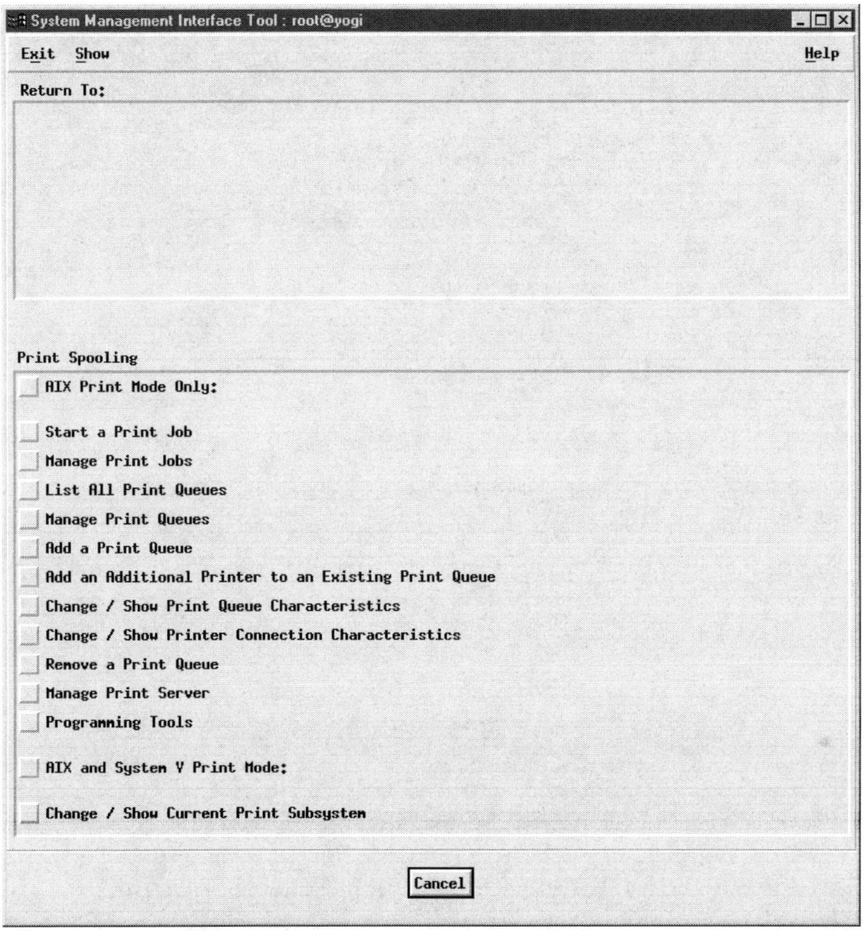

Figure 12-1. Print Spooling SMIT panel

This SMIT panel is followed by the **Parent Interface Selection** panel, shown in Figure 12-7.

Now the final SMIT panel is displayed, **Add A Print Queue**. In this panel, you add the print queue name(s) that you want to add. For the IBM 4039 printer, there are two print queue options, PCL and PostScript. I am adding a queue for both types of printing, shown in Figure 12-8.

When you enter the print queue names and click **OK**, SMIT will create the print queue(s) and set the queue to an enabled state.

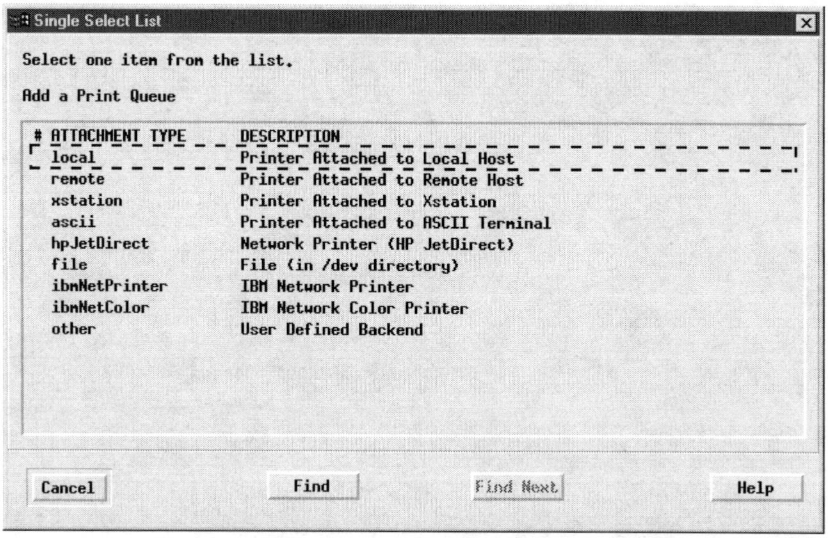

Figure 12-2. Add A Print Queue SMIT panel

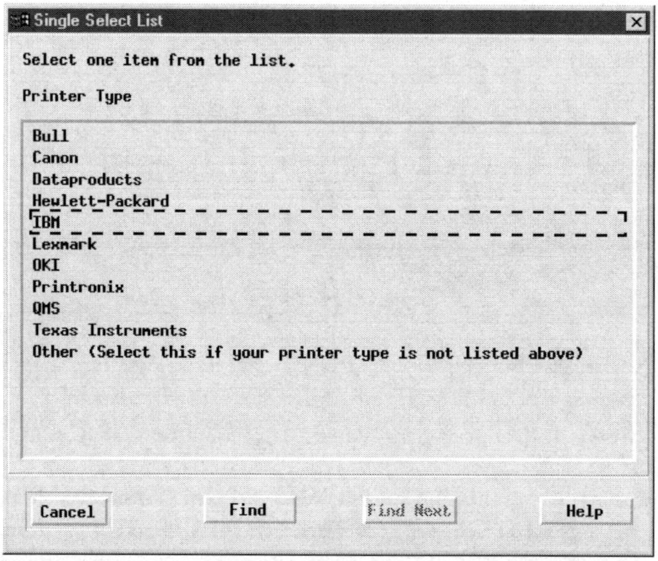

Figure 12-3. Select Printer Type SMIT panel

Figure 12-4.   Select Printer Model SMIT panel

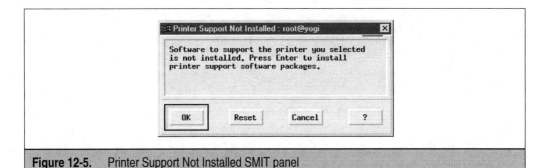

Figure 12-5.   Printer Support Not Installed SMIT panel

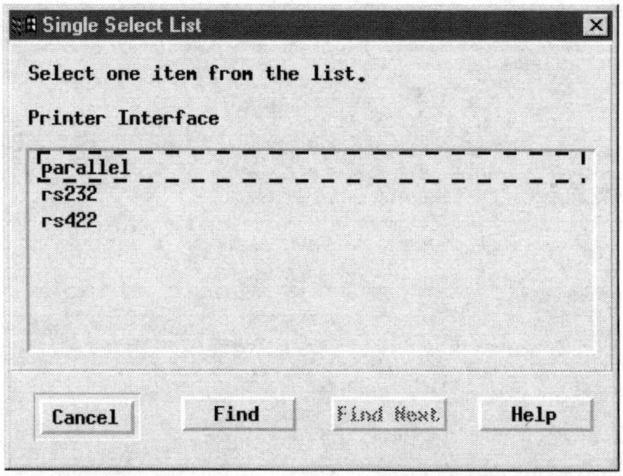

Figure 12-6. Printer Interface Selection SMIT panel

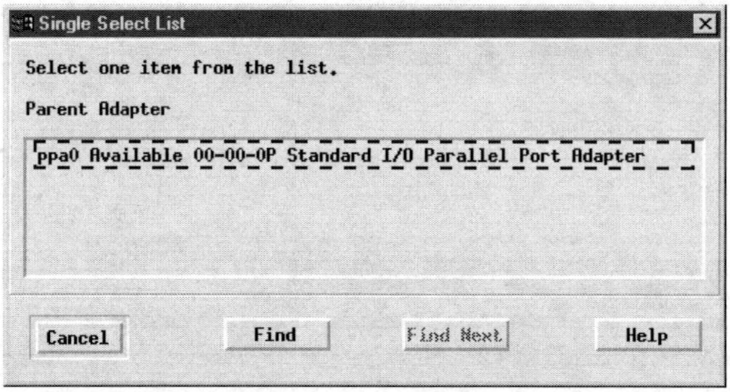

Figure 12-7. Parent Interface Selection SMIT panel

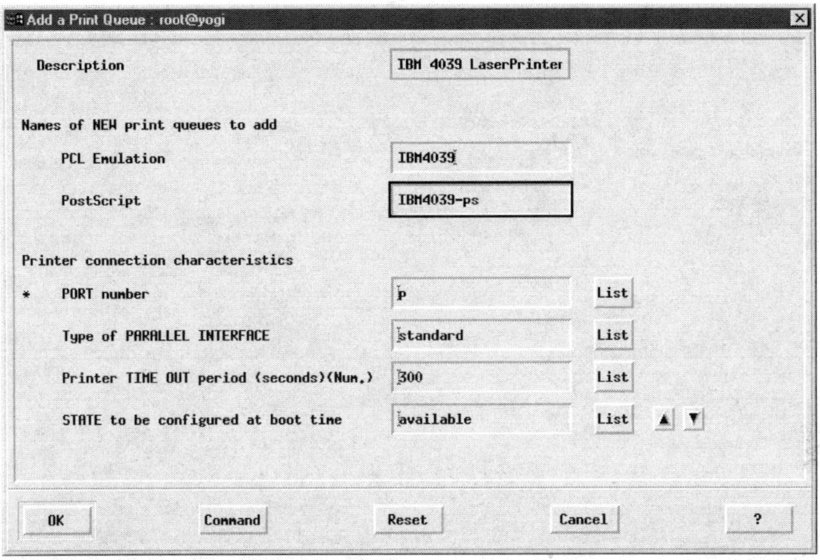

Figure 12-8. Add A Print Queue SMIT panel

You can also use the Web-Based System Manager, using the **wsm** command, to configure printers. The main WebSM printer window is shown in Figure 12-9.

LPD DAEMON

Inbound print requests from a TCP/IP-based network are managed by the **/usr/sbin/lpd** daemon. The **lpd** daemon manages incoming job requests from the network and deposits them into the appropriate queues for subsequent processing by **qdaemon**. Like **qdaemon**, the **lpd** daemon is a subsystem that can be started as part of system boot and shutdown processing by adding it to /etc/inittab, or as required from the command line. The /var/spool/lpd/stat/pid file contains the PID of the currently running **lpd** daemon.

```
# startsrc -s lpd  ◄──────── Start lpd daemon
# refresh -s lpd  ◄──────── Refresh lpd daemon
# stopsrc -s lpd  ◄──────── Stop lpd daemon
```

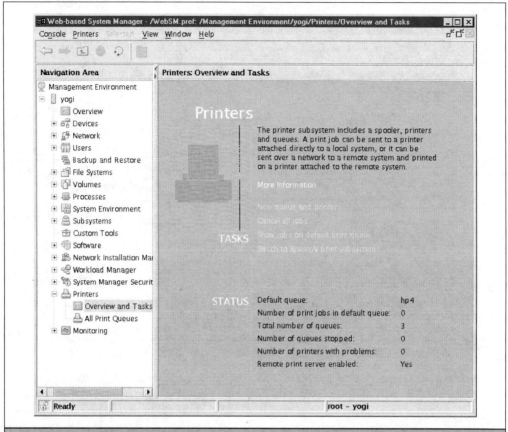

Figure 12-9.   Web-Based System Manager printer manager window

To control which remote systems may communicate with **lpd** and access your local queues, you must add the hostname of each remote system into the /etc/hosts.lpd file. A single plus ( ) character in the hosts.lpd file indicates that *any* remote system may have access to your local queues.

The following is an example of /etc/hosts.lpd:

```
#
# /etc/hosts.lpd
#
# This file, along with the /etc/hosts.equiv file, defines which foreign
# hosts are permitted to remotely print on your host. To allow a user
# from another host to print on your host, that foreign hostname must be
# in this file or in /etc/hosts.equiv. The lpd daemon searches
```

```
# /etc/hosts.equiv before this file, so the definitions in it take
# precedence.
#
# The format of this file is as follows:
#
# [-]hostname
#
# The hostname can be preceded by a '-' character to deny access. If you
# are using NIS, the hostname may be in the form:
#
# +@netgroup
# -@netgroup
#
# where "netgroup" is an NIS netgroup defined in the netgroup map. The
# '+' form allows access to any host in the netgroup, while the '-' form
# denies access to any host in the netgroup.
#
# Lines beginning with a '#' character and blank lines are ignored.
#
# Examples:
#
# host
# -host
# +@group
# -@group
wilma
dino
booboo
bambam
daffy@mydomain.com
```

Communication with remote **lpd** daemons is handled by the **writesrv** subsystem. If you have trouble communicating with a remote system that is responding to other network services, make certain that the **writesrv** subsystem is running and that it is listening to a socket.

```
# lssrc -s writesrv  ◄──────────── Verify subsystem is operative
# ps -ef | grep writesrv  ◄──────── Verify process is running
# netstat -a | grep writesrv  ◄──── Verify socket connection is listening
```

Configuring a Print Server

Since your machine now has a local printer attached to a print queue, it is an easy process to make this server into a print server. The only things that need to be done on the print server side are to add the client machines into the /etc/hosts.lpd file and to start the **lpd** daemon. You can add entries into the /etc/hosts.lpd file as hostnames, or you can use the IP address. I prefer not to hard-code any IP addresses into anything. It is always better to use the hostname, since the IP address of a machine may change at some point.

The easiest method to add the client machines to the /etc/hosts.lpd file and to start the **lpd** daemon is through SMIT. The SMIT FastPath to add the hosts to the /etc/hosts.lpd file is **smit mkhostslpd,** which is executed on the print server side (see the illustration).

The last step on the print server is to start the **lpd** daemon. Using SMIT is the preferred method because SMIT will make the required entry in the /etc/inittab file so that the daemon is started automatically on subsequent system reboots. Since the **lpd** daemon is under the control of the System Resource Controller (SRC), you can also use the following commands to manually start, stop, and refresh the **lpd** daemon.

```
# startsrc -s lpd
# stopsrc -s lpd
# refresh -s lpd
```

The SMIT FastPath to start the **lpd** daemon and have SMIT add an entry to the /etc/inittab, **smit mkitab_lpd,** is shown in Figure 12-10.

Adding a Remote Print Queue

On the client side, we need to define the remote print queue. We use a lot of the same techniques for a remote print queue as is used to define a local print queue. The main difference is that we select the **Printer Attachment Type** to be **Remote** instead of **Local.** We also define the print server on the client side. In Figure 12-11, the remote printer attachment is selected.

Selecting **Remote** will bring up the next panel, where you can define the type of filtering, if any, that you want to use for this remote printer. For most configurations, **Standard Processing** will do what you need to do. The filter panel is shown in Figure 12-12.

I selected Standard Processing, which brought the SMIT panel to define the remote queue, as shown in Figure 12-13. One thing to notice is that AIX supports remote queuing not only for AIX but also for BSD and System V print subsystems. To select a different print subsystem, select the **List** button next to the **Type Of Spooler On The Remote System** line.

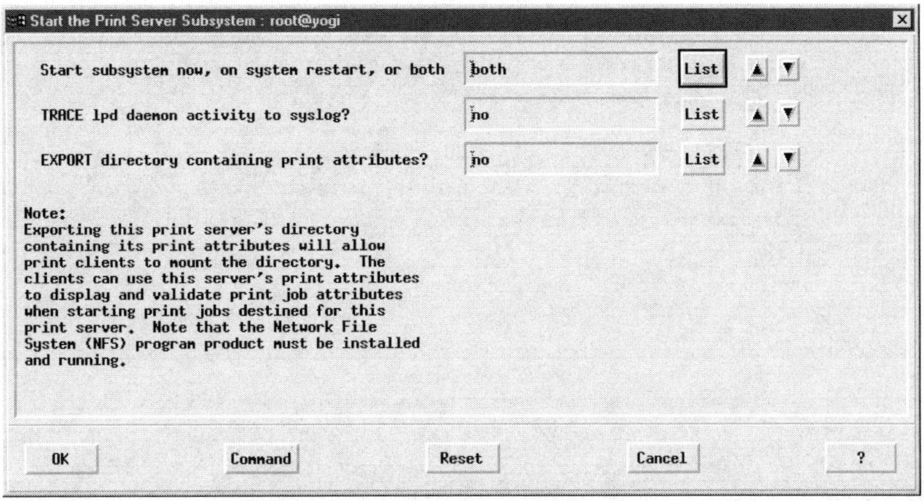

Figure 12-10. Start The Print Server Subsystem SMIT panel

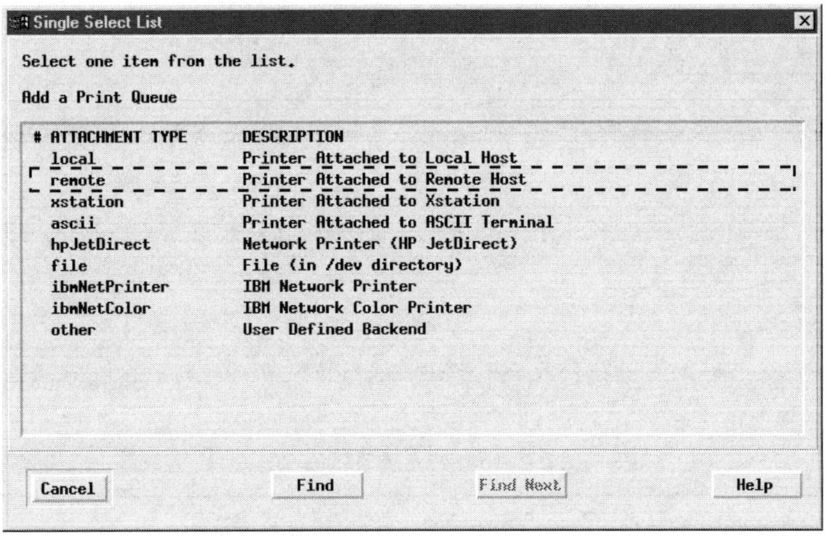

Figure 12-11. Printer Attachment Type SMIT panel

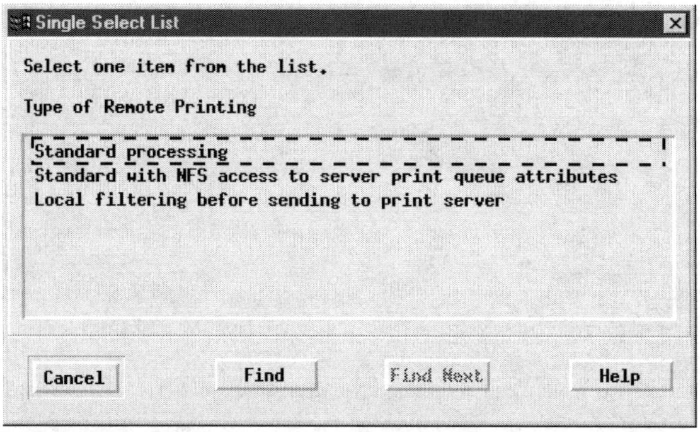

Figure 12-12.   Type Of Remote Printing SMIT panel

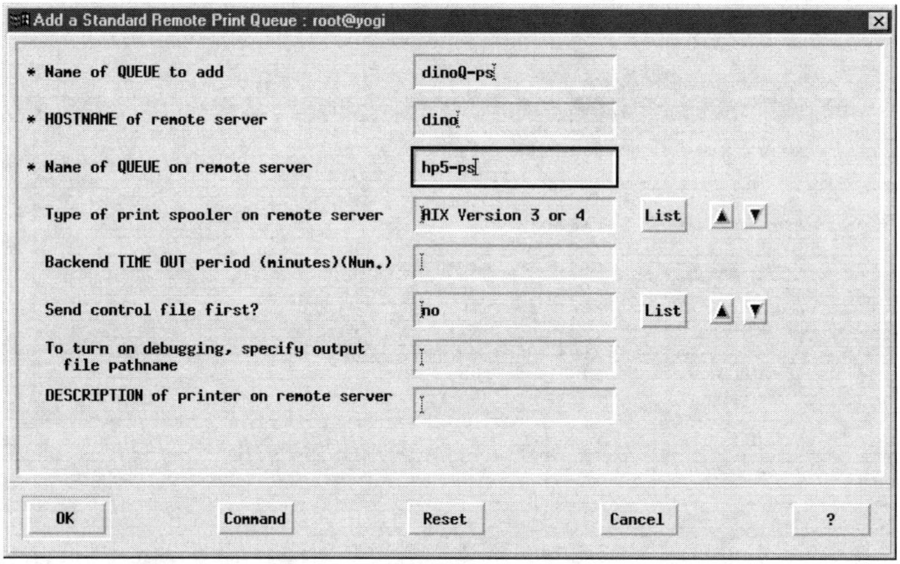

Figure 12-13.   Add A Standard Remote Print Queue SMIT panel

HP JetDirect

The HP JetDirect printers are widely used, and this section gives a short overview of the steps necessary to configure these printers in the landscape. The first step is to make sure that the driver for the JetDirect card is installed on the *local* AIX machine. To check for the fileset, enter the following command:

```
# lslpp -l printers.hpJetDirect.attach
```

The response should look something like the following output:

```
Fileset                    Level   State     Description
-----------------------------------------------------------------------
Path: /usr/lib/objrepos
    printers.hpJetDirect.attach
                           5.1.0.0  COMMITTED  Hewlett-Packard JetDirect
                                               Network Printer Attachment
```

If the `printers.hpJetDirect.attach` fileset is not installed on your system, then you need to install it from the AIX installation medium for the current operating system level of your machine. Use the SMIT FastPath **smit installp**.

The next step is to configure the remote printer. You can configure the remote queue with either WebSM or SMIT. To use WebSM, type **wsm** at the command prompt and select **Printers**. In the **Printer Queues** window, use the menu options to fill in all of the printer information and make sure that you select **HP JetDirect** attachment.

For SMIT, use the FastPath **smit mkpq**. Use the **Printer Queues** menu to configure the printer by selecting hpJetDirect and then selecting the model of the printer you are installing. If you do not see the exact printer listed, you may be able to find the driver on the installation CD-ROM. If you do not find the exact printer, do not panic. Just pick a similar model, and the printer will work fine. Of course, if the printer is in the predefined list but is not installed on your system, you will be prompted to install the driver.

In the next panel, you want to select **Do NOT Make This System A BOOTP/TFTP Server**. In the **Add A Print Queue** panel, fill in the queue name(s) for this new printer. You can enter any or all print queue types, PCL, PostScript, and HP-GL/2. Then fill in the hostname of the JetDirect card. You must use a hostname and not an IP address for remote print queues because the system would truncate the device name to the first octet of the IP address, causing two printers on the same subnet to have conflicting device names. Now you are ready to roll.

Custom Backends

You may wish to use your own custom shell scripts and programs as queue backends. If your backend application requires access to variables and data handled by the **qdaemon**, a library of routines is supplied in `/usr/lib/libqb.a` that will allow you to communicate with the elements of the queuing system. Normally your backend program should write to standard out.

Customizing Banner Pages

If you will be using header and/or trailer pages for a local queue, you can customize their format to match those used by other systems in your environment. The format templates for burst pages are stored in the /usr/lpd/pio/burst directory. For each format template, a filename prefix of H is used to indicate header definitions and T for trailers. Sample definitions are provided for ASCII, plotter, and PostScript banners. The templates consist of program, text, and variable sections. Variables are prefixed with a percent sign (%), as shown in Table 12-2.

The following is an example of an H.ascii banner:

```
*###################################################################
*###################################################################
*###################################################################
*###################################################################
*******************************************************************
*******************************************************************
%t   %T
%p   %P
%q   %Q
%h   %H
%s   %S
%d   =====> %D <=====
*******************************************************************
*******************************************************************
%a
%A
*******************************************************************
*******************************************************************
```

You may wish to add your own custom banner definitions to this directory. Use one of the existing header or trailer pages as a template. You can update the associated queue entry via the SMIT FastPath **smit chpq**.

Remember to conserve paper. Use burst pages only when they are needed. You may also specify that a single header and/or trailer page will be used for all of a particular user's queued files by grouping. Encourage your users to recycle, and keep recycle bins near your printers and plotters.

Variable	Meaning
%A	Formatting flag values
%D	Banner user name
%H	Machine name
%P	Time printed
%Q	Time queued
%S	Submitting user name
%T	Title
%%	Escape for percent sign

Table 12-2.   Banner Template Variables

TESTING AND MODIFYING PRINTER CONFIGURATION

You may test your virtual printer, queue, queue device, and print device combinations with the same tools used when testing the hardware interface and driver. Simply use the virtual printer, queue, or queue device name when using the **/usr/bin/cat** or **/usr/bin/lptest** commands.

```
# cat [FileName] | lp
# lptest [Columns] [Lines] | lp
```

It goes without saying that you must verify the operation of the AIX printing subsystem in the same way your end users will interoperate with it. Develop a short suite of print commands and options based on the environments used by your user community to validate the subsystem any time you have made any changes. Depending on your user base, you may need to test all of the AIX, BSD, and System V commands.

When you need to display or modify your configuration, it is helpful to remember that AIX uses a two-character command and SMIT FastPath prefix scheme with the unique suffixes that represent virtual printers (**virprt**), print queues (**pq**), and print devices (**prt**). These prefixes are usually **mk** to add, **ls** to list, **ch** to change, and rm to remove a component. For example, the FastPath names to make, list, modify, and remove a print queue are **mkpq**, **lspq**, **chpq**, and **rmpq** respectively. This is not always the case, but you may find it a helpful rule that will reduce the time you spend in DocSearch. In some cases, you will have to remove the entry and then read it to make the desired modification.

MANAGING AIX PRINTERS

Queue management and administration tasks in AIX can be handled by one command, **/usr/bin/enq**. AIX does provide wrapper programs for **enq** that may be easier to remember, but in most cases they use the same options. Once you have a handle on the option set, it will likely be easier to use **enq**. If you are familiar with the BSD or System V print management commands, you may use these in the AIX environment to provide uniformity in a heterogeneous environment. For the sake of this discussion, we will focus on **enq** and its wrapper counterparts. You can perform these functions using SMIT and WebSM. The SMIT FastPath for managing queues is **smit pqmanage**. The basic administrative responsibilities for the queuing subsystem include starting and stopping access, listing queue jobs and status, promoting jobs in a queue, removing jobs from a queue, and moving jobs between queues. The **enq** command and its associated wrapper programs may focus the action of each of these tasks to all jobs or queues, specific queues, specific users, or specific jobs using the options listed in Table 12-3.

Starting and Stopping Queues and Printers

From time to time, you may have to stop a queue due to a device malfunction or to let a backlog of jobs clear out before accepting additional print requests. Use the **disable, qadm,** or **enq** command to manipulate the availability of a queue or device. Note that these commands have no effect on remote queues. To stop **qdaemon** from sending more jobs to a queue and let the currently queued jobs print, use:

```
# qadm -D <queue_name>
# enq -D -P <queue_name>
# disable <queue_name>
```

To keep **qdaemon** from queuing more jobs and to kill the currently printing jobs, use:

```
# qadm -K <queue_name>
# enq -K -P <queue_name>
# disable -c <queue_name>
```

To bring the queue and printer back online, use:

```
# qadm -U <queue_name>
# enq -U <queue_name>
# enable <queue_name>
```

Option	Focus
−A	All queues
−P printer	Specific printer
−u user	Specific user
−# number	Specific job
-L	Long format output
−j	Report job number

Table 12-3.　enq Command Options

Listing Print Jobs

In order to manipulate jobs in the queuing subsystem or to review their status, you will need to display the contents of each queue. This is done using the **qchk**, **enq**, and **lpstat** commands. All have similar display formats. To list the print jobs in all queues, enter one of these commands:

```
# qchk -A
# enq -A
# lpstat
```

To list the jobs queued to a particular printer, use:

```
# qchk -P <queue_name>
# enq -q -P <queue_name>
```

```
Queue  Dev   Status    Job    Files       User   PP  Blks  Cp    Rank
-----  ---   ------    ---    ----------- ----   --  ----  --    ---
hp4    lp0   DOWN
             QUEUED    35     smit.script root   40        1     1
             QUEUED    36     payroll.rpt izar   20        1     2
```

The display will list the jobs by queue and device, status, job number, filename, submitting user, percent printed, size in blocks, copy count, and priority. You can use the information listed in these fields to manipulate the jobs in the queue. The status field provides feedback on the state of the queue, the device, and current jobs (see Table 12-4).

Status	State
READY	Printer accepting print requests
DOWN	Printer offline
UNKNOWN	Printer state unknown
OPR_WAIT	Printer waiting operator response
DEV_WAIT	Printer not ready
RUNNING	Print job being queued or printing
QUEUED	Print job ready for printing

Table 12-4. Printer States

Changing Priority

There are times when special circumstances require that you change the priority of jobs in a queue, overriding the default queuing discipline. It may be that you want to defer printing a large job, or an impatient user is leaning over your shoulder with that "I needed this yesterday" look. To change the standing of a job in the queue, use the **qpri** or **enq** command. To move a job up in priority, give it a higher number. You cannot change the priority of jobs in a remote queue. Once the priority is changed, you should see the position relative to other jobs in the queue change by the value in the rank field.

```
# qpri -#[JobNumber] -a[Priority]
# enq -P <queue_name> -#[JobNumber] -a[Priority]
```

Removing Print Jobs

To remove a print job from a queue, use the **qcan**, **enq**, or **cancel** command. If the job you wish to remove is printing, you will first have to stop the printer before removing the job:

```
# qcan -P[Printer] -x[JobNumber]
# enq -P[Printer] -x[JobNumber]
# cancel JobNumber [QueueName]
```

If circumstances require that you remove all jobs in a queue, use the **-X** flag.

```
# qcan -P[Printer] -X
# enq -P[Printer] -X
```

Holding a Job in a Queue

Sometimes you just want to hold a print job for a while and release it later to print. The **qhld** command is used to *temporarily* hold a print job in a queue. This command is also used to release the print job in the queue for printing.

Suppose you want to hold print job number 1555 in the queue. Since print job numbers are unique, you do not need to specify the queue name. The following command will hold job number 1555:

```
# qhld -P<Printer> -#1555
# enq -P<Printer> -h -#1555
```

The status of the 1555 print job will switch to **HELD**.

To release print job number 1555 in the queue for printing, use the following command:

```
# qhld -P<Printer> -r -#1555
# enq -P<Printer> -p -#1555
```

You can also use the SMIT FastPath **smit qhld**.

Moving Jobs Between Queues

Sometimes a queue gets hung or is unavailable for one reason or another. You can move print jobs between queues using the **qmov** command. The **-m** command parameter specifies which queue to move the job to. Again, using only job numbers we can use a command to act on a single print job. If I have a job with the job number 1557, which is currently queued on the hp9-ps print queue, and I want to move this job to the fl3hp4-ps print queue, then I issue the following command to accomplish the task:

```
# qmov -mflhp4-ps -#1557 -Php9-ps
# enq -Q'flhp4-ps' -#'1557' -P'ph9-ps'
```

Now the job is queued on the fl3hp4-ps print queue.

Keeping the Printers Printing!

If you have a large number of remote printers and a small network pipe, you may run into occasions when the print queues go into a DOWN state. Usually, queues go down because of a communications time-out. I worked at a hospital that had hundreds of remote printers at satellite clinics around town. If I had not written a shell script to query the print queues, I would have spent all day working on keeping the print queues up instead of doing any meaningful work.

To get around the DOWN print queue problem, you can put the following piece of code in a shell script and use a cron table entry to execute the script every 15 minutes:

```
QDOWN=$(enq -A | tail -3 | grep DOWN | awk '{print $1}')
[[ $QDOWN = '' ]] && exit 0
for Q in $(echo $QDOWN)
do
     qadm -U $Q
done
```

If you have a printer that cannot be brought online, then either the printer is turned off, the network connection is down (try to ping the remote print server), the printer and/or the print server may need to be rebooted, or the **qdaemon** and **lpd** daemons may not be running. If you work with developers, sometimes they unintentionally print a binary file instead of the source code, which will eat up a lot of paper and can cause the print queue to go down.

Being proactive stops a lot of phone calls and frees up your time for the fun stuff.

HIGHLY AVAILABLE PRINT QUEUES

For the high-availability crowd, the loss of a print job due to a system failure is not acceptable. Not only do people submit print jobs, but many applications spend a lot of time sorting and calculating data and then sending it to a printer. The loss of one of these print jobs is a major inconvenience and may even have a major negative impact on the business as a whole.

For these situations, your business may want to look at highly available print queues. For this to work, you need a HACMP cluster that has at least two nodes (for more information on HACMP, see Chapter 28). Any printer that is connected *directly* to a cluster node becomes unavailable if the system fails. However, attaching the printer to the LAN easily solves the unavailability problem.

There are at least four possible ways to connect the printer to the LAN:

1. Attach the printer to a *remote* RS/6000 or pSeries machine. This remote machine must have the **lpd** daemon running. Using this method will make the printer available to the entire cluster, but a print server failure causes the printer to be unavailable to the entire cluster.

2. Attach the printer to a terminal server on the LAN. Some terminal servers, such as the IBM 7318 Network Server, can connect both serial and parallel devices, such as printers and terminals.

3. Use a printer with a LAN adapter integrated into the printer. This method allows you to connect the printer directly to the LAN.

4. Use either an internal or external HP JetDirect print server to attach the printer directly to the LAN. This is similar to the third option.

Once the printer is attached to the LAN, the real fun starts. The major requirement of the highly available print queue is correct placement of the spooling directories. The trick is to place the spooling directories on the *shared* disks in the cluster, since internal spooling directories will become unavailable in a node failure. Using the shared disk scenario allows the backup server in the cluster to have the same view of the disk services, and the print jobs are saved.

The next step is to move the spooling directories, `/var/spool/qdaemon` and `/var/spool/lpd/qdir`, to the shared disks instead of the internal disks. The best way to do this is to create two filesystems that have mount points on the spooler directories. These new filesystems must *not reside* in rootvg. Select a volume group that is shared by the nodes in the cluster and place the mounting of these new filesystems under the control of HACMP.

In this configuration, if a node in the cluster fails, one of the surviving nodes in the cluster will take control of the shared disks, activate the shared disks, verify that the state of the disks is stable, mount the spooling filesystems, restart the **qdaemon**, and print the jobs.

ASCII TERMINAL PRINTERS

Many ASCII terminals support an auxiliary serial port or parallel port for screen printing and printing from connected computers. Routing a print job from the remote computer to the auxiliary port on the terminal requires sending a special sequence of characters before and after the print job to enable and disable connection to the terminal's auxiliary serial or parallel port. The particular control character sequences are terminal specific and may be configured in the **terminfo** database entry for the given terminal type. Consult your terminal documentation for the specific sequence. Some terminals also include the capability to temporarily ignore control character sequences to support sending non-ASCII data to a printer. Note that this requires that the data stream *not* contain the transparent mode on/off character sequence. The transparent mode on/off sequence can be included with the AUX port on/off sequence in terminfo.

terminfo AUX Print Variables

```
mc5=[ctl char sequence] ◀──────── AUX print on
mc4=[ctl char sequence] ◀──────── AUX print off
```

To configure a serial TTY printer:

1. Configure TTY port information.
2. Update the AUX port on/off control sequence for the TTY type in terminfo.
3. Create a virtual printer and print queue for the ASCII type using **smit mkpq**.

Dial-up modem ports may support a number of different terminal types. In order to identify the printer terminfo data for a dial-up printer connection, set the PIOTERM environment variable to identify the terminfo terminal type:

```
$ set PIOTERM=[Terminal-Type]; export PIOTERM
```

Pass-Through Mode

A number of public-domain applications exist that will send vt100 auxiliary port sequences to a remote terminal or terminal emulation program. Most of these programs use the following algorithm:

1. Save the TTY state.
2. Set the TTY to raw mode.
3. Send the start aux sequence.
4. Send the file.
5. Send the stop aux sequence.
6. Restore the TTY state.

Many terminal emulation packages for personal computers support vt100 pass-through mode sequences. These include **kermit** for direct connect and dial-up access and NCSA telnet for TCP/IP.

X STATION PRINTERS

Starting with AIX 5L, IBM no longer supports X Stations. I have several X Stations, and when I called IBM support after installing AIX 5L, they first said that X Stations were no longer supported, but then I kept on and on, and guess what? You can load the X Station filesets from your AIX 4.2.1–4.3.3 distribution and they work fine on AIX 5L, although technically not supported. The X Station code has not been modified since AIX 4.2.1. You will need to install three filesets:

```
X11.x_st_mgr.rte
X11.x_st_mgr.compat
X11.msg.{$LANG}.x_st_mgr.rte
```

where $LANG is the language environment installed on your system. For United States English, the language environment is en_US.

Additionally, if you installed AIX 5L using the migration path and you previously had X Stations installed and configured, you will need to uninstall and reinstall the X Station manager filesets and reconfigure each X Station. Check the functionality first, but you will most likely see that your X Stations no longer function. It is a good idea to go into SMIT and save the current configuration before uninstalling and reinstalling the filesets.

The X- Station filesets support printing to printers attached to IBM X Stations. You may also be able to support printing to other vendors' X terminals using either **lpd** or the pass-through mode printing technique described for ASCII terminals. When using the IBM X Station Manager, define an X station–attached printer to the queuing subsystem with the SMIT FastPath **smit mkvirprt** command.

```
# smit mkvirprt
```

Select option 3, **Printer Attached To X-Station**, from the SMIT menu and supply the X Station name.

You will be asked to supply the interface type, X Station model, printer baud rate, parity, bits per character, start/stop bits, and printer model. This is quite similar to the procedure for adding a standard locally attached printer. Refer to the previous sections on print devices and queue devices and queues.

The backend program used for IBM X Station printing is **/usr/lpp/x_st_mgr/bin/lpx**, which is a shell script. The stanza generated by SMIT for the /etc/qconfig file should look like the following entry:

```
*
* Xstation Queue Device
*
plab1:
    discipline = fcfs
    up = TRUE
    device = plabd
```

```
plabd:
   file = false
   header = never
   trailer = never
   backend = lpx plab1 -s 19200,n,8,1
```

When to Add Printers in a Large Environment

The problem in large shops that have a large number of active printers printing all day is finding a good time to add a printer without disrupting the flow of data to the printers. The problem is that when you add a new print queue to the system, the **qdaemon** must create a new qconfig.bin file, which is the binary version of the /etc/qconfig file. Sometimes this short period of time needed to compile the new config.bin file will hose up some of the printers in the landscape.

To avoid this problem, add printers during the period of least activity on the print queues. Our shop uses a shell script to add the printers, so we can schedule this event during off-peak hours. We take all of the new printers that need to be added and list them in a data file that the shell script reads in a loop. I suggest that you **ping** each remote print server to ensure that it is talking on the network. Also, check the return code of the **mkque** command and send notification of any errors indicating that creation of the queue failed.

CONFIGURING AND USING THE SYSTEM V PRINTER SUBSYSTEM

By default, both the classic AIX and System V printer subsystems are installed with AIX 5L. The AIX printer subsystem was created by combining features of the System V and the BSD print standards. On top of these standards, IBM added some features unique to the AIX print subsystem. These unique features that were added made the AIX print subsystem less compliant to the traditional standards. When IBM started developing AIX 5L, the designers wanted the printer subsystem to be compliant to traditional standards, so System V was selected because it the primary standard to most UNIX flavors. There are advantages to both printer subsystems, but IBM has a long-range goal of moving completely to the System V print subsystem, although, of course, the classic AIX print subsystem will be around as an option for many years. In upcoming releases of AIX 5L, you will see more System V features added, but the classic AIX print subsystem will remain the same.

System V Advantages

For Systems Administrators experienced with UNIX variants other than AIX, the System V print subsystem provides easy-to-manage printing. Since the classic AIX printer subsystem is proprietary, many of the interface programs written for other

UNIX variants will not run under the AIX print subsystem and must be completely rewritten. This situation has limited the number of printers that support the AIX print subsystem over the years. Additionally, under the AIX printer subsystem, you cannot control user access to the printers without customizing the backend program, as you can in the System V print subsystem.

Many companies use expensive preprinted custom forms. When these forms are loaded in a printer, it is important not to let just any user have access to the printer. The System V printer subsystem has a way of loading forms in the printer that either allows or denies user access to the printer, depending on the particular form that is mounted in the printer. To have this same type of functionality in the classic AIX print subsystem, you must create multiple print queues and control which print queues are enabled while the form is mounted in the printer.

System V Printing Administration

The command line is the primary interface for both printer subsystems. In the classic AIX printer subsystem, you can manage the printers using both SMIT and WebSM, as well as the command line. In System V printing, only the WebSM is available for graphical print management, but the command line is the primary interface for most Systems Administrators. IBM has plans to expand the System V print subsystem administration functionality with subsequent AIX 5L releases.

On Itanium-based systems, only the System V printer subsystem is supported, and it is installed as part of the BOS installation. On POWER systems, both print subsystems are supported and installed by default in AIX 5L.

The System V filesets that are installed by default include the following:

```
bos.msg.en_US.svprint      ◄──────────── System V Print Subsystem Messages
bos.svprint.fonts          ◄──────────── System V Print Fonts
bos.svprint.hpnp           ◄──────────── System V Hewlett-Packard
bos.svprint.ps             ◄──────────── System V Print Postscript
bos.svprint.rte            ◄──────────── System V Print Subsystem
bos.terminfo.svprint.data  ◄──────────── System V Printer Terminal
```

Switching Between Printer Subsystems

Since only one of the printer subsystems can be active at any time, you have a mechanism to switch between them. There are three methods of making the switch: SMIT, WebSM, and the **switch.ptr** command. To check which printer subsystem is currently active, you can use either SMIT, WebSM, or the **switch.prt -d** command. To switch between subsystems using the command line, use one of the following commands:

```
# switch.prt -s AIX       ◄──────────── Switch to the AIX printer subsystem
# switch.prt -s SystemV   ◄──────────── Switch to the System V printer subsystem
```

Optionally, you can use the SMIT FastPath **smit chprtsubsystem** or **smit spooler** to look at the print spooling characteristics. You can also use the Web-Based System

Manager (WebSM) to switch between subsystems. In either case, the **switch.prt** command is executed.

Eight steps are involved in switching between subsystems. To switch from the AIX print subsystem to the System V subsystem, use the **switch.prt** command.

1. Checks to see if any print jobs are currently active. If any printing is active, the **switch.prt** command exits with the following error message:

    ```
    All print jobs must be terminated.
    ```

2. Stops the following AIX print daemons: lpd, qdaemon, and writesrv.

3. Changes the /etc/inittab file to start only the System V print subsystem daemons on all subsequent reboots.

4. Clears the SMIT menus that control the AIX print subsystem. However, some are not removed, but if you attempt to use them, you will receive an error message.

5. Modifies the WebSM to use only the System V plug-ins.

6. Changes the lock files from AIX to System V.

7. Changes all links from AIX to System V.

8. Starts the System V print subsystem daemon, **lpsched**.

To switch from the System V print subsystem to the AIX subsystem, use the **switch.prt** command

1. Checks to see if any print jobs are currently active. If any printing is active, the **switch.prt** command exits with the following error message:

    ```
    All print jobs must be terminated.
    ```

2. Stops the System V print daemon, **lpsched**, using the **lpshut** command.

3. Changes the /etc/inittab file to start only the AIX print subsystem daemons on all subsequent reboots.

4. Enables the SMIT menus that control the AIX print subsystem.

5. Modifies the WebSM to use only the AIX plug-ins.

6. Changes the lock files from System V to AIX.

7. Changes all links from System V to AIX.

8. Starts the AIX print subsystem daemons, **lpd**, **qdaemon**, and **writesrv**.

After the printer subsystem has been switched, any disabled printers or print queues will remain disabled until you enable all of the print queues. Also, if a user tries to submit a print job using the **qprt** or **enq** command under System V control, an error message will be displayed:

```
Cannot awaken qdaemon (requested accepted anyway)
```

When, and if, the AIX printer subsystem is reestablished, the job will print.

Common AIX and System V Print Commands

The following commands are available in both print subsystems:

- **cancel**   Cancels a print job
- **disable**   Disables a print queue
- **enable**   Enables a print queue
- **lp**   Sends a print request to a line printer
- **lpq**   Examines the spool queue
- **lpr**   Queues a print job to the specified queue
- **lprm**   Removes a print job from spooling queue
- **lpstat**   Displays all print queue status information

Each of these commands is shared by both print subsystems, but the command options and behavior differ between print subsystems. There are two directories that are linked to the /usr/bin directory, /usr/aix/bin for the AIX print subsystem, and /usr/sysv/bin for the System V print subsystem.

When you look at the man pages for each of these commands, please notice that each man page has information about both print subsystems. Please read the man pages for each of the shared commands listed previously.

System V Printing Process

The **lpsched** daemon controls System V printing. This daemon is started during the boot process if the System V print subsystem is active. The **lpsched** daemon is not under the control of the System Resource Controller (SRC), so you *cannot* use the **startsrc**, **refresh**, or **stopsrc** command to control this daemon. However, you can stop the **lpsched** daemon using the **lpshut** command, and you can restart the **lpsched** daemon with the **/usr/lib/lp/lpsched** command.

Jobs are submitted using the **lp** or **lpr** command. The user can send the job to a specific printer, or class of printer, and can add attributes that will control how the print job is handled and printed.

When the **lpsched** daemon receives the print job, it first checks to see if the job is allowed to print. As we stated before, System V printing has the capability to control which users are able to print on any printer. This review process is called *job screening*. The **lpsched** daemon screens the job to see if the printer is capable of printing the job as requested, including the type of job and the attributes supplied when the job was submitted. The printer configuration file and data from the terminfo database are used to make this determination.

The printer configuration file contains information about each printer, including the device name, the banner and form feed setup, the path of the interface script, the printer type as listed in the terminfo database, and the content types that are accepted by the printer.

The terminfo database describes the characteristics for each different printer type. This database information is used by the **lpsched** daemon in the job screening process. Then the printer is initialized using the same information in the terminfo database.

If the job is not rejected in the job screening process, the job is given a unique ID by the **lpsched** daemon. Then a *request file* describing the print job is created in the print spooler directory. Each print job ID consists of two parts: the printer's name and the unique ID number. Printers are sometimes grouped into *classes* of printers. Using printer classes, a user can submit a print job to a class of printers, and the job will be queued to the first printer in the class that is capable of printing the job. This is more efficient if you have a pool of printers in a centralized location.

The System V printer subsystem uses two types of filters to perform three separate functions. The first filter function is used in converting file content, which may include adding carriage returns and line feeds or character mapping. The second filter function is used to decipher special user-requested printer modes, such as reversing the page order or changing between landscape and portrait modes. The third filter is used to detect printer faults. The two types of filters are *slow* and *fast* filters. The slow filters are run directly by the **lpsched** daemon in the background for file conversion. The slow filters are run in the background because of the high overhead they produce converting files. The fast filters act on the printer directly. The fast filters directly control the printer and in some cases run file conversions as slow filters do. Fast filters are executed by the interface program, but the interface program is controlled by the **lpsched** daemon. The **lpsched** daemon may use a combination of several different filters to get the desired result.

As a print job reaches the head of the print queue, the **lpsched** daemon passes control of the print job over to the interface program defined for the specific printer. The interface program, which is just a shell script, then takes direct control of the printer. The interface program then initializes the printer using the terminfo database information, then uses a fast filter to print the banner page (if a banner page has been defined), and finally uses a fast filter to print the specified number of copies of the file.

System V Printing Lingo

The System V print subsystem is confusing to the AIX specialists because of the terminology. For example, there are at least three different *types.* There are the *printer type,* the *interface type,* and the *content type.* Please refer to Table 12-5.

The *printer type* points the printer to an entry in the terminfo database. The **lpadmin** command is used to set the printer type. There are two default printer types, postscript (PS) and standard. The syntax to specify a printer type is

```
# lpadmin -T {PS, standard}.
```

The *interface type* is just a pointer to the interface program used for a particular printer.

Terminology	Term Description	Term Example
Printer type	Printer terminfo entry	PS, Standard
Interface type	Interface program	/usr/lib/lp/model/{PS, standard}
Content type	Types of files allowed	{postscript, standard}
Class	Group of printers	floor2
System V printer	Print queue	f2hp2-ps
Printer device	Printer device driver	/dev/lp05

Table 12-5. System V Print Terminology

The *content type* specifies the type of data or files that the printer can handle printing. Thus, the content type can specify postscript or standard text. Some printers can handle more than one content type. The command syntax to specify a content type is

```
# lpadmin -I {PS, standard}.
```

The *class* refers to a group of printers. If a user submits a job to a print class, then the first printer in the class that can handle the job will print the job. The syntax to add a printer to a printer class is

```
# lpadmin -c <print_class_name>.
```

A *System V Printer* refers to the print queue. The syntax to define a printer is

```
# lpadmin -p <printer_queue_name>.
```

The *printer device* refers to the device driver used by the printer. The syntax to associate a system device, such as /dev/lp01, to a device driver is

```
# lpadmin -p <queue_name> -v <system_device_name>.
```

Adding a System V Local Printer

Adding a System V printer is a two-step process. First the printer *device* is created. This is a system device. Then the System V printer is created. Devices can be displayed using the **lsdev** command. To show the currently *defined* printers, which are listed in the ODM customized database, use the following command:

```
# lsdev -Cc printer
lp0 Available 00-00-0P-00 Hewlett-Packard LaserJet 4,4M
```

To show all of the *supported* printer devices, which are listed in the ODM predefined database, use the following command:

```
# lsdev -Pc printer
  . . .
printer opp     parallel Other parallel printer
printer osp     rs232    Other serial printer
printer osp     rs422    Other serial printer
printer hplj-4 parallel Hewlett-Packard LaserJet 4,4M
printer hplj-4 rs232    Hewlett-Packard LaserJet 4,4M
printer hplj-4 rs422    Hewlett-Packard LaserJet 4,4M
  . . .
```

The output of both of the **lsdev** commands will vary, depending on how many printers are configured and which printer drivers have been installed on the system. You can ignore printer device attributes, since they are not used in printing through either AIX or System V subsystems. If the printer device driver is not currently installed on your system, you can install it using the SMIT FastPath **smit install_package**. To install an individual printer device, you can do a search of the installation CD-ROM by typing a forward slash, /, and entering the search pattern for the printer you want to add. Normally, it is not necessary to have an exact match between the printer driver and the printer model. For example, you can use the HP LaserJet II printer driver for most HP printers. An exact match may give you extra functionality, so I always try to match the driver to the printer model.

Once the printer driver is installed, you can proceed to add the System V printer to the system. There are three steps to enable the printer. The **lpadmin** command is used to add the printer:

```
# mkdev -c printer -t hp4V -s parallel -p ppa0 -w p
# lpadmin -p hp4V -v /dev/lp0 -D "Hewlett-Packard LaserJet 4/4M"
```

After the System V printer has been added to the system, you need to use the **accept** command to allow the printer to accept print requests:

```
# accept hp4V
```

The last step is to enable the new print queue using the **enable** command:

```
# enable hp4V
```

If you prefer using the *printer wizard*, you can use the Web-Based System Manager, WebSM. Start WebSM using the **wsm** command. From the main screen on the left side, select Printers (System V). Then select **Standard Overview And Tasks**. In the middle of the screen, select **New Printer** and fill in each field and the printer wizard will do everything for you, including allowing the printer to accept requests and enabling the queue. Figure 12-14 shows the WebSM menu for System V printer subsystem.

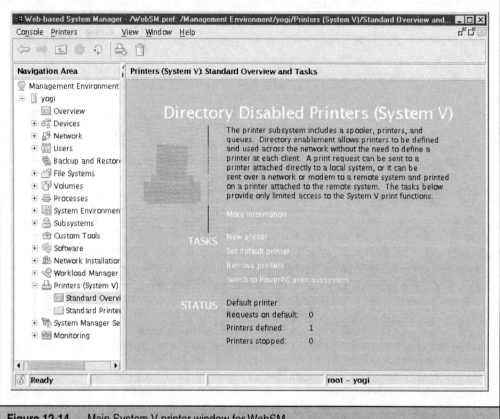

Figure 12-14. Main System V printer window for WebSM

Adding a Network System V Printer

Adding a network printer involves a few more steps than adding a local printer. You have to perform most of the following steps:

- Register each of the remote systems.
- Allow or deny user access.
- Set the parameters for the remote system.
- Configure the remote client.
- Define the print queue on the remote client.

To register the remote system with the System V print service, use the following command syntax:

```
# lpsystem [-T timeout] [-R retry_attempts] <system_name>
```

To define the print queue on the remote client, use the following command syntax:

```
# lpadmin -p <client_printer_name> -s
<remote_pr_server>!<remote_pr_queue>
```

After this step, be sure to **accept** and **enable** the print queue on the remote client.

To grant or deny user access to the remote printer, use the following command syntax:

```
# lpadmin -p <printer> -u allow:AIX_user_list
# lpadmin -p <printer> -u deny:AIX_user_list
# lpstat -p -l   ◄─────────────── The lpsched daemon must be running!
```

Managing System V Printers

Plenty of Administrative System V printer commands are available to accomplish any task. The **lpadmin** command can do most of the tasks you want to do when you select the appropriate command parameter. All the System V administrative commands are listed in Table 12-6.

System V Command	Duties Performed
accept	Allows the printer to accept print requests for the specified destination. The destination can be a printer or a class of printers.
reject	Stops all print queuing to the specified destination.
enable	Activates the specified print queue by enabling the queue to print requests queued by the **lp** command. For remote print queues, the **enable** command will allow the transfer of the request only to the remote print server.
disable	Disables all print requests from printing on the specified queue.
lpadmin	Allows you to add, remove, and change printers, as well as set default destinations, set up alerts, and define remote printers.
lpfilter	Used to add, delete, change, and list filters used with the **lp** print service.
lpforms	Used to provide administration for preprinted forms.
lpmove	Provides a mechanism to move print requests between printers and queues.
lpsched	The System V print service master control.
lpshut	Stops the System V print service.
lpsystem	Defines network parameters to the System V print service.
lpusers	Sets limits on the queuing priority levels for jobs submitted by users.

Table 12-6.   System V Print Services Administration Commands

Using Forms with System V Print Service

Using forms with the System V print service has seven possible steps. These are registering the form with the print service, requesting a form for a print job, alerting the user to mount the form in the printer, mounting the form, unmounting the form, controlling who can access the form, and displaying status information. Each of these steps is outlined in the following sections.

Registering a Form with the Print Service

A form needs a form definition file, which describes the form. Things like number of pages, character pitch, and page length and width need to be defined. Once you have created the form definition, register it with the System V print service using the following syntax:

```
# lpforms -f <form_name> -F <form_definition_file>
```

Requesting a Form to Submit a Print Job

A user can request a specific form by using the **lp -f** command using the following syntax:

```
# lp -f <form_name> -d <printer> <file_to_print>
```

The previous command will queue the print job, but the form must be mounted before the job will print.

Alerting Someone to Mount a Form

Before the job can print on the specified form, the form must be mounted. This is usually done by an operator or a print services administrator. To set up print services to notify the Print Services Operator when a user has requested a form, use the following syntax:

```
# lpforms -f <form_name> -A <alert_type> [-Q number] [-w interval]
```

where:

-f form_name is the name of the specific form.
-A alert_type can be either **mail**, **write** to the console, **shell_script** to run, **quiet** to stop messages, or **none** for no alert.
-Q number starts alerting when number of form requests have been queued. The default is one.
-w interval defines the number of minutes between resending the alert. The default is zero.

Procedure to Mount a Form

The following five steps are needed to let the print services know that the form is mounted:

1. Disable the print queue using the **disable** *<print_queue>* command.

2. Load the form into the printer.

3. Tell the print services that the form is mounted and ready to print on using the following command syntax:

   ```
   # lpadmin -p <printer> -M -f <form_name>
   ```

4. Align the form if necessary.

5. Enable the printer using the **enable** *<print_queue>* command.

Unmounting a Form From the Printer

The following four steps are necessary to unmount a form from the printer and inform the print service that the form is no longer mounted:

1. Disable the printer using the **disable** *<print_queue>* command.

2. Unload the form from the printer.

3. Tell the print service that the form is no longer available using the following command syntax:

   ```
   # lpadmin -p <print_queue> -M -f none
   ```

4. Reenable the print queue using the **enable** *<print_queue>* command.

Limiting Access to Forms

If you want to limit who can print on your expensive preprinted forms, you can use the following commands:

```
# lpforms -f <form_name> -u allow:AIX_user_list
# lpforms -f <form_name> -u deny:AIX_user_list
```

where *AIX_user_list* is a list of AIX users separated by commas.

Gathering Form Information

The following command is used to gather information about a particular form:

```
# lpforms -f <form_name> -l
```

The output of this command will vary, depending on who is running the command. The **root** or **lp** user will see the complete picture including the user allow and deny lists and the alignment pattern. Any other user who executed the command will see only the information that is in the form definition file.

CHECKLIST

The following is a checklist for the key points in printing:

- [ ] Each time you submit a job for local printing, the job goes through a queue. Users and applications submit jobs for printing using one of the following commands: **qprt, lp, lpr,** or **enq**.

- [ ] The **qdaemon** maintains the print queues by maintaining a list of all of the defined queues and is responsible for monitoring the queues for new print jobs.

- [ ] If a file is spooled, a copy of the file remains in the /var/spool/qdaemon until the job has completed printing. This allows you to change or edit the original file without affecting the printer output.

- [ ] When a file is queued, a pointer to the original file is placed in the /var/spool/lpd/qdir directory. If the original file is changed before the file is printed, then the updated file is printed.

- [ ] Any user can define a default printer that overrides the first entry in the /etc/qconfig file. The PRINTER environment variable is used to define a different default printer. This variable must be set by each user who wishes to define a default printer.

- [ ] You can start AIX printer configuration with the SMIT FastPath **smit spooler**.

- [ ] Inbound print requests from a TCP/IP-based network are managed by the **/usr/sbin/lpd** daemon.

- [ ] To configure a machine with a local printer attached to a print queue to act as a print server, add the client machines into the /etc/hosts.lpd file, and start the **lpd** daemon.

- [ ] To use a printer server from a remote client, you have to define the remote print queue.

- [ ] You can customize header and/or trailer pages for a local queue. The format templates for burst pages are stored in the /usr/lpd/pio/burst directory.

- [ ] Queue management and administration tasks in AIX can be handled by the **/usr/bin/enq** command.

- [ ] The SMIT FastPath for managing queues is **smit pqmanage**.

- [ ] Use the **disable, qadm,** or **enq** command to manipulate the availability of a local queue or device. These commands have no effect on remote queues.

☐ To display the contents of the queuing system, use the **qchk**, **enq**, and **lpstat** commands.

☐ To change the priority of a job in the queue, use the **qpri** or **enq** command. To move a job up in priority, give it a higher number. You cannot change the priority of jobs in a remote queue.

☐ To remove a print job from a queue, use the **qcan**, **enq**, or **cancel** command.

☐ Move print jobs between queues using the **qmov** command.

☐ If your environment requires high availability for print resources, consider highly available print queues. For this to work, you need a HACMP cluster that has at least two nodes.

☐ Starting with AIX 5L, IBM no longer supports X Stations. You can load the X Station filesets from your AIX 4.2.1–4.3.3 distribution, and they work fine on AIX 5L, although technically not supported.

☐ By default, both the classic AIX and System V printer subsystems are installed with AIX 5L.

☐ Only one of the printer subsystems can be active at any time. To switch between them you can use one of three methods: SMIT, WebSM, and the **switch.ptr** command.

☐ The **lpsched** daemon controls System V printing. This daemon is started during the boot process if the System V print subsystem is active. The **lpsched** daemon is not under the control of the System Resource Controller (SRC).

☐ Adding a System V printer is a two-step process. First the printer system device is created. Then the System V printer is created.

☐ After the System V printer has been added to the system, you need to use the **accept** command to allow the printer to accept print requests enable the new print queue using the **enable** command.

☐ To add a Network System V printer, you have to register each of the remote systems, allow or deny user access, set the parameters for the remote system, configure the remote client, and define the print queue on the remote client.

☐ You can use the **lpadmin** command can do most System V printer administrative tasks.

☐ The steps to use forms with the System V print service are registering the form with the print service, requesting a form for a print job, alerting the user to mount the form in the printer, mounting the form, unmounting the form, controlling who can access the form, and displaying status information.

PART V

Network Configuration and Customization

CHAPTER 13

TCP/IP

These days, virtually every business needs to access information from other systems or the Internet, whether for customer services, sales, marketing, or data analysis. It is imperative for a computer system to connect and communicate with other systems. TCP/IP provides the fundamental capabilities for systems to connect to a network and communicate with each other. This chapter will provide an overview of the TCP/IP network model and its protocols, and how to configure and manage TCP/IP on AIX 5L. If you are already familiar with the concepts, you may want to skip to the configuration sections later in the chapter.

TCP/IP NETWORK MODEL

It is difficult to get a one-to-one mapping between TCP/IP and OSI models. TCP/IP bundles much of the functionality defined in the OSI model into a smaller number of layers. Rather than attempt to define a TCP/IP-to-OSI mapping, it will be more pertinent to this discussion to present a model of the TCP/IP protocol suite (see Table 13-1). Each layer of the TCP/IP has its own set of protocols and services. The higher layer is designed to use the services of the lower layers.

The Interface Layer includes the network interfaces and protocols. It interfaces to the physical network. It sends IP packets over a specific hardware network adapter using the applicable protocol, for example, IEEE 802.3 over the Ethernet network.

The Internet Layer is responsible for moving and routing the packets over the network. This layer consists of a number of protocols. IP (Internet Protocol) version 4 and 6 are the most important ones. IPv4 and IPv6 are connectionless protocols that provide packet formatting, fragmentation, and routing.

There are several other protocols that are part of the Internet Layer, whose purpose is to help the IP protocols function. The ARP protocol handles translation between IP addresses and hardware addresses for IP version 4, while the NDP protocol performs this function for IP version 6. ICMP and ICMPv6 are also part of this layer, and are used to send error and control messages for IPv4 and IPv6, respectively.

The Transport Layer handles the communication between systems. It consists of the Transmission Control Protocol (TCP) and User Datagram Protocol (UDP). TCP ensures the reliable delivery of packets, whereas UDP provides a simpler service of delivering

Application Layer	Telnet, SMTP, FTP	TFTP, SNMP	X11	RPC	NFS
Transport Layer	TCP	UDP			
Internet Layer	IGMP, ICMP, IPv4, ARP, RARP		ICMPv6, IPv6, NDP		
Interface Layer	Ethernet, Token Ring, FDDI, SOCC, HiPPI				

Table 13-1. TCP/IP Architecture Stack

datagrams from one system to other system, but there is no guaranteed delivery. The reliable delivery in TCP usually comes at the cost of packet throughput.

The Application Layer implements the user interface. Client/server protocols are most often defined at the Application Layer. Common application-level services include Telnet, File Transfer Protocol (FTP), Simple Mail Transfer Protocol (SMTP), Network File System (NFS), and the X11 Window System.

NETWORK DEVICES AND INTERFACES

TCP/IP operates over different network adapters. AIX 5L supports IP over Token Ring, Ethernet, EtherChannel, FDDI, ATM, and serial link. For each of the network adapters, there is a corresponding network interface automatically created for it, except in the case of ATM. It is possible to have multiple interfaces for an ATM device. Hence it requires an interface to be added explicitly. For more information, see "Network Interface Configuration," later in this chapter.

To display existing network interfaces in an AIX system, use the following command:

```
# lsdev -Cc if
```

The AIX naming convention for the network interface is shown in Table 13-2.

Among these interfaces, Ethernet is the most well used, since it is relatively easier to implement and inexpensive to deploy. With the availability of Gigabit Ethernet and EtherChannel, Ethernet can address bandwidth or availability issues, which were addressed traditionally by ATM and FDDI by design. Token Ring is still being used in some legacy networks. However, with a transmission speed of 16 Mb/sec, Token Ring is unlikely to be used for a new network. The following sections will outline the attributes of each of the more common network interfaces along with cabling and support hardware. Please refer to IBM's Web site for information regarding technologies and support for other high-speed options such as high performance parallel interface (HiPPI) and Fiber Channel Standard.

Device Type	Device Name	Interface Name
Asynchronous Transfer Mode (ATM)	atm#	at#
Ethernet (IEEE 802.3)	ent#	et#
Ethernet (Standard, version 2)	ent#	en#
Fiber Distributed Data Interface (FDDI)	fddi#	fi#
Loopback	N/A	lo#
Serial line	N/A	sl#

Table 13-2.   Network Device and Interface Naming Convention

Device Type	Device Name	Interface Name
Token Ring	tok#	tr#
Virtual IP Address (VIPA)	N/A	vi#

The # sign denotes the index number of the device or interface.

Table 13-2.   Network Device and Interface Naming Convention *(continued)*

Ethernet

Ethernet was developed in the early 1980s by Xerox and represents the largest TCP/IP install base due to its low cost. It is a broadcast-based protocol that uses collision detection and avoidance to regulate network traffic. The Carrier Sense Multiple Access/Collision Detection (CSMA/CD) protocol allows any system to start transmission when the wire is clear, but requires it to back off and wait a pseudorandom period of time if it detects that it has a collision. If it detects a collision again after retransmission, it will wait for a random period of time before trying again.

Common network topologies for Ethernet are *bus* and *star*. In the bus topology, systems connect to the Ethernet segment using T-connectors. Both ends of the segments are terminated with 50 ohms terminators. The star topology (shown in Figure 13-1) is more common in today's environment, where systems are connected point-to-point to a hub or a switch using RJ-45 connectors for copper wire or SC connectors for fiber optic cable.

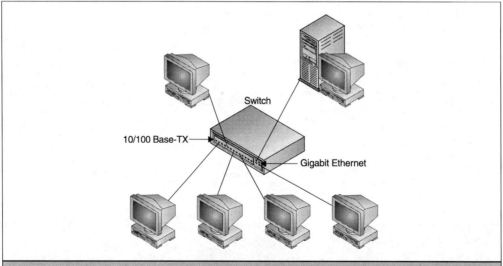

Figure 13-1.   Ethernet network star topology

The pSeries supports 10 and 100 Mb/sec, as well as Gigabit Ethernet adapters. The IBM 10/100 Ethernet TX PCI adapter supports connections to 100BaseTx and 10BaseT networks. It supports both full duplex and half duplex using RJ-45 connectors. The 10/100/1000 BaseT Ethernet PCI card provides operating speeds up to 1000 Mb/sec. At speeds of 10 or; 100 Mb/sec, it supports both full duplex and half duplex, while at a speed of 1000 Mb/sec, it supports only the full-duplex mode. The Gigabit-SX adapter attaches 1000BaseSX networks using 50 and 62.5 micron cables with SC connectors. The Gigabit-SX can only operate at full-duplex mode. See Table 13-3 for Ethernet Media. The standard for 10 Gigabit Ethernet (IEEE 802.3ae) is targeted to be IEEE approved in the second half of 2002, and there are several manufacturers that have unveiled their 10 Gigabit Ethernet adapters for limited server trials.

Configure your Ethernet adapter (see Figure 13-2) via the SMIT FastPath **smit chgenet**. You may want to increase the value of the TRANSMIT buffer. The value represents a queue of buffers for outgoing packets. Values may range from 20 to 150.

```
# smit chgenet
```

EtherChannel

EtherChannel is a technology created by Cisco Systems that can be used to aggregate multiple Ethernet adapters together for increased bandwidth or backup in case of adapter failure. A channel can consist of two to eight adapters, and will appear to the upper layers of the system to be a single network interface. Three modes are available. Standard mode uses the destination IP address to select the adapter that will be used to send the traffic. This is useful when traffic is being sent to many different IP addresses. Round-robin mode will alternate packets between the adapters in the channel. In netif backup mode, only one of the adapters will be active at a time; but if the active adapter were to fail, another would take over.

Type	Medium	Cable	Maximum Length	Nodes	Topology
10Base5	Thickwire*	RG 11	500 m	100/segment	Bus
10Base2	Thinwire†	RG 58	185 m	30/segment	Bus
10BaseT	Twisted pair	UPT Cat 3	100 m	16/segment	Star
100BaseT	Twisted pair	UPT Cat 5	100 m	+	Star
1000BaseT	Twisted pair	UPT Cat 5	100 m	+	Star
1000Base-SX	Fiber	62.5 Micron	260 m	+	Star

*Transceivers 2.3 m apart and segment lengths multiples of 23.4 m.
†Transceivers .5 m apart.
+ Limited by number of ports on a switch

Table 13-3.   Ethernet Media

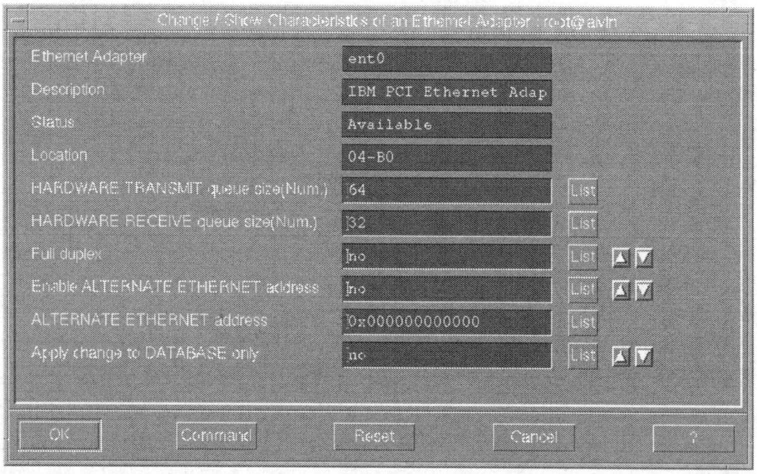

Figure 13-2. SMIT Ethernet Adapter panel

In order to use EtherChannel, it is required that the switches the Ethernet adapters use also support the EtherChannel technology. EtherChannel is configured using the following command (refer to Figure 13-3):

```
# smit etherchannel
```

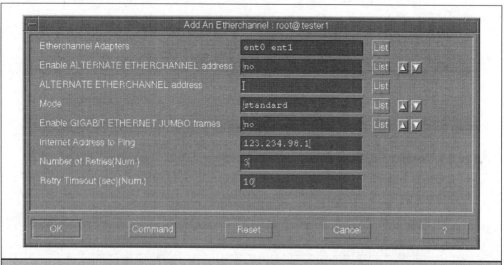

Figure 13-3. SMIT Add An EtherChannel panel

Token Ring

Token Ring was originally developed by IBM and later adopted by the IEEE as specification 802.5. Token Ring protocol uses a token-passing mechanism to regulate traffic on the ring. A particular workstation on the ring must gain control of a token before it can transmit data onto the ring. While data is being transmitted on the ring, a token is not available to other workstations. A dual ring topology will provide a degree of fault tolerance. If the ring is broken, the dual paths are used to form a new ring. Token Ring supports either 4- or 16-Mb/sec bandwidth. At the high end, Token Ring can sustain around 12 Mb/sec throughput. Figure 13-4 illustrates this ring topology.

The IBM Token Ring PCI adapter card for pSeries and RS/6000 supports 4 and 16 Mb/sec with either half duplex or full duplex. To modify attributes for the Token Ring adapter, use the SMIT FastPath **smit chgtok**.

Fiber Distributed Data Interface (FDDI)

Fiber Distributed Data Interface (FDDI), ANSI X3T9.5, is a token-passing protocol similar to Token Ring, but implemented using optical fiber rings. FDDI and its copper-based cousin, Copper Distributed Data Interface (CDDI), support data rates at 100 Mb/sec. FDDI was designed to be implemented for network backbones. It has been slow to gain acceptance due to high per-node cost.

FDDI, like Token Ring, operates with distributed control over all stations connected to the ring. Each station receives token or data frames from one neighbor and, if not the recipient, passes them on to the next neighbor. The media access control (MAC) layer of the FDDI specification supports tailoring of the token-handling time to reflect the data types generally transmitted over the ring. Low-time values provide better interactive response, whereas high values are better for moving large block data.

The pSeries and RS/6000 support both single-ring and dual-ring topologies. A single-attach station (SAS) is used for single-ring configurations. The dual-attach station (DAS) adapter provides the ability to support a primary and secondary ring topology. In this configuration, the secondary ring supports traffic flow in the opposite direction from the primary ring. This allows a failover ring to be formed in the event

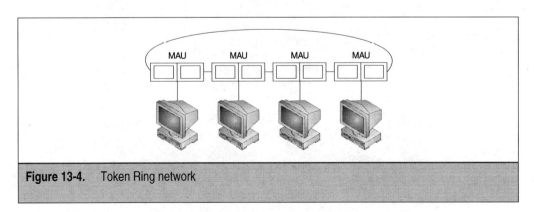

Figure 13-4.   Token Ring network

that the ring is segmented. Note that the secondary ring is available for fault tolerance only and may not be used as a separate network.

It is recommended that 62.5/125-micron multimode optical fiber be used for each ring. You can get away with using other popular fiber sizes, as long as you keep signal loss to a minimum. FDDI concentrators may be connected as lobes in a star ring topology. Fiber distribution panels can be located in wiring closets similar to Token Ring MAUs.

To change the attributes for FDDI devices, use the SMIT FastPath **smit chgfddi** and refer to Figure 13-5.

Asynchronous Transfer Mode (ATM)

Asynchronous Transfer Mode (ATM) is a full-duplex cell-switching protocol that supports end-to-end connections between participating ATM components. ATM systems segment TCP/IP packets (called protocol data units or PDUs in ATM) into 53-byte cells for transmission over the ATM network. Each cell identifies the source and next hop in a pair of header fields called the virtual path identifier (VPI) and the virtual channel identifier (VCI). The aggregate of VPI:VCI sets that define the path between the source and recipient define the virtual circuit. ATM switches bundle together cells that share the same next-hop destination. Cells are reassembled into a PDU at the receiving end of the virtual circuit. RFC 1577 defines the specification for supporting TCP/IP over ATM.

AIX 5L supports ATM adapters running at 25, 100, 155, and 622 Mb/sec over single or multimode fiber to an ATM switch. Up to 1024 switched or permanent virtual circuits are supported per adapter. Multiple adapters can be tied together using switches with multigigabit switched backplanes. Switch-to-switch communication is handled using one or more adapters running at 155 and 622 Mb/sec.

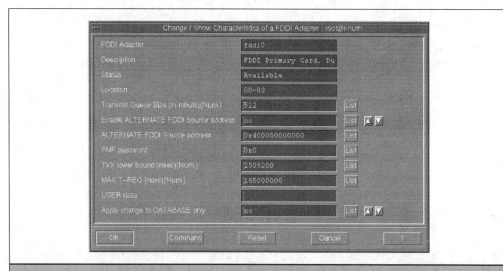

Figure 13-5. SMIT FDDI Adapter panel

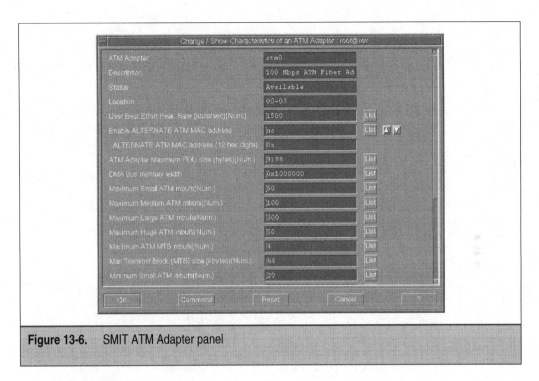

Figure 13-6.   SMIT ATM Adapter panel

To view or modify attributes for an ATM card, use the SMIT FastPath **smit chg_atm** and refer to Figure 13-6.

ADDRESSING

Each computer on the network must be known by a unique identifier. TCP/IP uses two different types of addresses: hardware addresses and IP addresses.

Hardware Addressing (MAC Address)

Manufacturers encode a unique hardware address into each adapter that they produce. You might think this should satisfy network uniqueness, so why are IP addresses also needed? Hardware addresses have different formats for different types of network adapters. An Ethernet hardware address has meaning only to an Ethernet adapter, but cannot be used to communicate with an ATM adapter in a different part of the network. These numbers are also a bit hard to remember, even when represented in hexadecimal.

IPv4 Addressing

IP version 4 is the traditional version of the Internet Protocol. This is the protocol that is commonly used in the Internet and most private networks. The IPv4 address is a 32-bit number represented as four 8-bit fields, referred to as octets, separated by dots. Each octet is an integer ranging from 0 through 255 enabling a complete address range of **0.0.0.0** to **255.255.255.255**. The address is split into two, representing a network address and a host address on that network. Historically, the IP address space was divided into three classes, class A, class B, and class C. Class A was made up of all addresses whose first bit was 0. In class A addresses, the first octet represented the network address and the last three octets represented the host address. The first two bits of an address in the class B range are 10. In class B addresses, the first two octets represent the network address and the last two octets represent the host address. Class C addresses begin with the three bits 110. Their first three octets represent the network address and their last octet represents the host address. Under this scheme, a very large organization with many hosts might be allocated a class A address, while small organizations could use a class C (see Table 13-4). See RFC 1166, "Internet Numbers," for a complete description of IP address definition.

Netmasks and Subnetting

Subnetting allows an organization to subdivide the address range it has been allocated. For instance, if a large organization with several departments has been allocated a class A address, that organization might wish to subdivide that class A network address and assign a class B–sized address to each of its departments. This requires a mechanism to allow routers and hosts to know how many bits of an address indicate the subnetwork address and how many bits indicate the host address. This mechanism is called a netmask. A netmask is most commonly written as a dotted decimal address such as 255.255.0.0. For each bit in the netmask that is set to 1, the corresponding bit in the address is part of the network address. For each bit in the netmask that is set to 0, the corresponding bit in the address is part of the host address.

A new terminology called Classless Inter-Domain Routing (CIDR) has expanded the concept of simple class A, B, and C networks. CIDR defines integer prefixes from /1 through /30 that can be used to allocate a block of addresses of whatever size is needed rather than always allocating addresses along class A, B, or C boundaries.

Class	Address	Hosts	Address Range
A	N.H.H.H	16M*	0.0.0.0–127.255.255.255
B	N.N.H.H	64K*	128.0.0.0–191.255.255.255
C	N.N.N.H	254*	192.0.0.0–223.255.255.255

N = network address; H = host address.
*Host and network addresses 0 and 255 are reserved.
Network address 127 is reserved.

Table 13-4. IP Address Classes

This results in fewer wasted addresses and more efficient routing. For a complete explanation, see RFC 1878.

Blocks of public IP addresses are obtained from an Internet service provider (ISP) who will have acquired them from their upstream registry. These public IP addresses must be unique so they will not conflict with any other address in the world. The details for administration and registration of Internet Protocol numbers can be found at these local sites:

http://www.arin.net/	North and South American, the Caribbean, and sub-Saharan Africa
http://www.ripe.net/	Europe, Middle East, and Africa
http://www.apnic.net/	Asia Pacific

You may not need to have public IP addresses for all the hosts at your site. Only hosts that are directly connected to the Internet need unique global addresses. A common plan is to configure public IP addresses on gateways or firewalls that will provide Network Address Translation (NAT) for your private internal IP networks. Three ranges of private IPv4 addresses are reserved, by the Internet Assigned Numbers Authority (IANA), for use by all enterprises for their internal network administration. This private IP space provides a safeguard to protect the internal network while conserving addresses in the public IP space of the Internet.

Private IP Range	CIDR	Addresses
10.0.0.010–255.255.255	10/8	16,000,000
172.16.0.0–172.31.255.255	172.16/12	1,024,000
192.168.0.0–192.168.255.255	192.168/16	64,000

ARP

ARP (Address Resolution Protocol) is used to perform the translation between IPv4 addresses and hardware addresses. Since network adapters only understand hardware addresses, the hardware address of the next adapter to receive a packet must be included in that packet, even though the final destination for which the packet is intended is identified by its IP address. ARP handles this translation. AIX 5L systems keep an ARP cache that contains mappings of IP address-to-hardware address for systems on all directly attached networks. When sending an IP packet, once the IP address of the next hop is known, AIX 5L will check its ARP cache to determine whether it has an existing mapping for that IP address. If it does not, it will send an ARP request. ARP requests are hardware-level broadcast packets that contain the IP address that the system needs the MAC address for. Each system on the local network will receive the request and examine it to see whether the request is for its IP address. The system that is configured with that IP address will send an ARP response containing its hardware address to the requestor. The requestor will add that entry to its ARP cache and can now send its packet.

IPv6 Addressing

IP version 6 is the new version of the Internet Protocol. Currently, it is used mostly for experimental purposes, either on private networks or on a global network called the 6bone. However, its popularity is increasing, and it is beginning to be used on production networks.

The IPv6 address is a 128-bit number represented as eight 16-bit hexadecimal fields separated by colons. A short syntax is allowed to represent multiple adjacent fields of zero as "::" only once in the address and to omit leading insignificant zeros within each field.

It is common for interfaces to have multiple IPv6 addresses—for example, one that is valid only for communication on the local network link and one that is global. This concept is called *address scope*.

IPv6 also defines two types of addresses that are used for compatibility with IPv4. The first type has a prefix of 0:0:0:0:0:0:ffff/96. The final 32 bits of the address will be an IPv4 address. This type of address is used simply to represent an IPv4 address in IPv6 format and is called an IPv4 mapped address. The other type of address has a prefix of 0:0:0:0:0:0:0/96. The final 32 bits will again be an IPv4 address. This is called an IPv4-compatible address and is used for IPv6 automatic tunneling. Automatic tunneling is used for IPv6 nodes that must send to other IPv6 nodes across an IPv4 network. If both systems have IPv4-compatible addresses, the sender can send the packet to the receiver's IPv4-compatible address and the packet will be automatically encapsulated within an IPv4 packet so that it can be sent across the IPv4 network.

For more details about IPv6 addressing, see RFC 2373.

NDP

Neighbor Discovery Protocol (NDP) is the IPv6 replacement for ARP. It performs the functions that ARP performed for IPv4, and also adds some more functionality.

The basic function of mapping IPv6 addresses to hardware addresses is performed using the Neighbor Solicitation and Neighbor Advertisement packets. These are very similar to ARP requests and responses. NDP also makes use of two other types of packets called router solicitations and router advertisements. Router solicitations are multicast by hosts to all routers on their local links. Routers respond with router advertisements, which can include information about prefixes the host should use and what destinations this router is able to route to. For more information about NDP, see RFC 2461.

IPv6 Autoconfiguration

One important feature of IPv6 is that it allows for automatic configuration of addresses on hosts. IPv6 uses the hardware address of each network adapter to derive a 64-bit identifier. Since hardware addresses for each media type are globally unique, this 64-bit identifier will be unique on its network link. The 64-bit identifier can then be used to create a link local address. Once each interface has been configured with a link local address, the system is able to send traffic on the local network. It can now send router solicitations on each of its local networks, and receive router advertisements telling it which prefixes it should use to configure its site local and global addresses. This allows new hosts to be added to a network without requiring each one to be configured manually. Only the routers require special configuration.

On AIX 5L, the **autoconf6** command can be used to configure interfaces with link local IPv6 addresses. The **ndpd-host** daemon, when run on a host, will send router solicitation packets and process any router advertisements that are received. The **ndpd-router** daemon should be run on IPv6 routers to cause them to send router advertisements. **ndpd-router** can be configured so that the router will advertise the correct prefixes and routers for the network it is on.

Aliasing

It is possible for a network interface to have multiple addresses associated with it. This is known as aliasing. An interface can have multiple IPv4 with multiple IPv6 addresses concurrently. Aliasing can be useful when renumbering a network; it may be desirable to assign the new address to the interface while keeping the old one during the transition time. When using IPv6, it is common for interfaces to have multiple addresses of different scopes, for example, a link local address and a global address.

Use the SMIT FastPath **smit inetalias** to configure aliasing on AIX 5L.

VIPA

A virtual IP address (VIPA) is an address that is not associated with a particular physical network adapter. VIPAs can be used in situations where network communications might need to continue even in the event of a network interface going down. AIX 5L allows an administrator to configure an interface called **vi0** and assign an address to it. This address will be used as the default source address for any packets sent unless the application is explicitly bound to a different address. Using this mechanism, if the interface that was used to send the traffic is deleted, communication can continue using a different interface as long as there is still a route that allows traffic to reach its destination. Using a VIPA requires that the neighboring routers in the network be configured to be able to route responses back to the correct host. This could be done either by manually configuring the routers or by running the **gated** application on the host with the VIPA. **gated**, when configured to use the OSPF protocol, will automatically advertise information about the VIPA to neighboring routers.

NETWORK ROUTING

In IP routing, a system sending packets does not need to have complete information about where in the network every destination resides. Instead, it only needs to know the next hop to send to in order to get the packet closer to its destination. The next hop system is then responsible for knowing where to send the packet next.

There are two different ways of managing routing. Routing information may be determined dynamically by querying the routers for a path from point A to point B or by the use of static routes configured by the Systems Administrator. Static routes work fairly well for small networks, but, as the network size gets large, they become increasingly difficult to manage.

Generally, dedicated routers are used to route IP traffic between networks, and an AIX 5L system needs to deal with IP routing only as a sender, not a forwarder. AIX and other UNIX systems have the capability to function as IP routers; but in network configurations where medium-to-large amounts of IP traffic need to be routed, a dedicated router will provide the best performance.

Kernel Routing Table

All routes, regardless of whether they are static or dynamic, are stored in the kernel routing table. The routing table can be displayed in AIX 5L with the **netstat -r** command. Each entry in the routing table consists of a destination, a gateway, and an interface, along with some auxiliary information. A destination could be a single host address, a network address, or a special destination called *default*, which will match any address that was not previously matched by a host or network address. When the IP layer is ready to send a packet, it will look up the address it is trying to send to in the routing table. If it finds a route to that host address, a network containing that host, or a default route, it will use the gateway field of that route as its next hop and the interface field of the route as the network interface to send the packet over. AIX 5L has two separate routing tables, one for IPv4 addresses and another for IPv6 addresses.

Static Routing

The Systems Administrator can add routes to the kernel routing tables using **route**, **chdev**, or SMIT FastPath **smit mkroute**. In simple network configurations, this works quite well. For instance, if there is only one gateway that connects a network with all outside networks, each host on the network need only have two routes—one for systems on the local network, and one default route that allows them to reach any other destination. On AIX 5L, a route is automatically added for each directly attached network when the interface on that network is configured—so, in this situation, the administrator would only need to add a default route on each host.

Dynamic Routing

Dynamic routing can also be used to manage the kernel routing table. Applications such as **gated** and **routed** run routing protocols, which exchange information with neighboring routers, and then add the correct routes to the kernel routing table based on the information they have learned. Although dynamic routing takes some effort to configure for the first time, it has several advantages over static routing. First, for large or complex networks where there are many routers, it saves the administrator the trouble of keeping track of which router is used to reach which networks. Another advantage is that it can adjust dynamically if a router goes down. In this case, the neighboring routers will adjust their routing tables to use an alternate path to the destination.

AIX 5L supports the RIP protocol using the **routed** or **gated** applications. **gated** also supports the RIPng, EGP, BGP and BGP4+, HELLO, OSPF, IS-IS, and Router Discovery protocols.

Multipath Routing and Dead Gateway Detection

AIX version 5L added two enhancements to the routing subsystem. The first of these is multipath routing, which allows the kernel table to have multiple routes to the same destination. This allows load balancing of outgoing traffic, either between multiple network interfaces on the same subnet or between multiple gateways. If multiple routes exist to a destination, AIX 5L will alternate between them round-robin style. Another enhancement is dead gateway detection, which allows an administrator to specify "backup" routes to a destination to be used if the primary router for that destination becomes unreachable. AIX 5L will then detect whether the primary router is reachable, either by actively sending probes or passively, using existing network connections, depending on the configuration. If the primary router for a destination becomes unreachable, the kernel routing table will be adjusted to use a backup route for that destination if one exists. This allows host systems to detect and adjust for the loss of a first-hop router without needing to run routing protocols on every host.

DOMAIN NAME SYSTEM

IP addresses are sufficient for sending and receiving packets or datagrams over the network. However, IP addresses are not as intuitive for people to remember, whereas symbolic names are. For a small network, cross-references between IP address and symbolic names are kept in an **/etc/hosts** file on each machine on the network. For large networks, TCP/IP applications use the Domain Name System (DNS), which is a client/server application with a distributed database for mapping IP addresses to names. The software part that is responsible for constructing a request is called the resolver. The part that manages and services the requests is called the name server daemon (**named**).

Domain Names

Computers and organizations in DNS are identified by a domain name. A domain name is a name tuple delimited by dots that represents the administrative hierarchy of the name space of which it is a member. Domain names are usually represented in two to four levels. Note that there is no implied mapping of subdomains to IP number octets!

```
Format: hostname.subdomain.subdomain.topdomain
Example: techsupport.services.ibm.com
```

For large networks, the DNS provides a more efficient and distributed name management and resolution. In the DNS hierarchy, upper-level domains (such as COM, ORG, and NET) need only record the names of the next lower level in the tree along with the IP numbers of the name servers that resolve addresses for that level.

A domain can be divided into subdomains. There is a concept of zones in DNS. Zoning has to do with the authority of managing naming resolution for hosts of the subdomains in the zone. A name-resolving protocol called DOMAIN is used to recursively query name servers until a domain name is resolved to an IP number. All name servers must know the addresses of the top-level Internet name servers. This system supports local management of the name space and ensures timely information to the network at large.

Name Servers

A name server is a host responsible for resolving names into IP addresses for other hosts in its zone authority. There can be more than one name server per zone. The server process, which actually controls the naming resolution, is called **named**. It listens to two well-known ports, UDP port 53 and TCP port 53. To improve the performance of the naming resolution process, as well as reduce the network traffic, all name servers cache query data they receive from remote name servers.

AIX 5L ships both compiled versions of Berkeley Internet Name Domain (BIND), version 4 and version 8. There are differences in configuration for BIND4 and BIND8, but generally the process is somewhat similar. You may also consider building BIND9 from source that you can obtain from the Internet Software Consortium at the following URL:

```
http://www.iso.org/products/BIND/
```

Installation and configuration of **named** is straightforward but beyond the scope of this chapter. For details, read the AIX Commands Reference, Volume 4, or DocSearch keywords named8 and named4. These documents will also list the location of sample configuration files and **awk** scripts.

Host Names

A host name is a special symbolic name, in that there is one host name per system regardless of how many network interface adapters are in the system. If you have more than one network adapter on your system, there can be a symbolic name associated with each of the network interfaces, but you only have one host name for your system. It is associated with the primary network interface.

To display or temporarily modify the host name on AIX, use the command **hostname**. To change the host name permanently, use SMIT FastPath **smit mkhostname**. The host name is not only written to the memory of the current running system, but also to the ODM configuration database to be used in the next system reboot.

Naming Resolution Process

Applications resolve names and IP addresses via two library routines, **gethostbyname()** and **gethostbyaddress()**. These routines are part of a name translation library, called *resolver*.

The default process used by the resolver subroutines on AIX depends on the configuration of the system. If the file /etc/resolv.conf exists, the resolver assumes there is a name server for the local area network; otherwise, it assumes that no name server exists. If there is no name server, the resolver uses the /etc/hosts file to resolve the request. With a name server, it first queries the DNS database on the first name server on the list. If the timeout period expires before an answer is received, the second name server is tried. If that query fails, the resolver will then check the /etc/hosts file.

Here is /etc/resolv.conf:

```
# cat /etc/resolv.conf
domain      mcgraw-hill.com    ; Use a semicolon for comments
nameserver  123.145.100.1      ; name server1
nameserver  123.145.100.2      ; name server2
```

The default order can be overridden by the order specified in the file /etc/irs .conf or /etc/netsvc.conf, or the environmental variable **NSORDER.** The precedence is **NSORDER**, /etc/netsvc.conf, then /etc/irs.conf.

TCP/IP SUBSYSTEMS

TCP/IP daemons run as subsystems under AIX. This means that they are under the control of the system resource controller (SRC). Daemons controlled by the master TCP/IP daemon **inetd**, like **ftpd**, are known as subservers. Subservers are enabled in the /etc/inetd.conf file and started as needed by **inetd**. All the subsystems associated with the TCP/IP group should be started from the /etc/rc.tcpip script. The **start()** function in this script will use the **startsrc –s** command to start each subsystem that has been uncommented. Never start all the TCP/IP subsystems using the **startsrc –g** command. The following are some helpful SRC commands:

```
# lssrc -T        ◄─────────────List all the inetd subservers
# lssrc -t ftp ◄───────────────List the status of the ftp subserver
# lssrc -g tcpip ◄─────────────List all the TCP/IP subsystems
# stopsrc -g tcpip ◄───────────Stop all the TCP/IP subsystems
# startsrc -s inetd ◄──────────Start the subsystems one by one
# refresh -s inetd ◄───────────Makes the daemon read configuration files
```

Further configuration of the TCP/IP subsystem can be completed from the menu bullets listed on the following SMIT FastPath **configtcp** panel:

```
# smit onfigtcpc   ←────   TCP/IP further
                           configuration
```
- Hostname
- Static Routes
- Network Interfaces
- Name Resolution
- Client Network Services
- Server Network Services
- Manage Print Server
- Select BSD style rc Configuration
- Start Configured TCPIP Daemons
- Stop TCPIP Daemons
- Authentication Configuration

Master Daemon inetd

Some of the TCP/IP service daemons, rather than running continuously, can be started when a request is made for the service and shut down when the service has been completed. This capability is supported by the **inetd** daemon.

Configuration for **inetd** is located in the /etc/inetd.conf and /etc/services files. Entries in the /etc/inetd.conf file indicate the service name and startup information. The /etc/service file lists the service name, whether it uses TCP and/ or UDP protocols, and the well-known port number associated with the service. Any time updates are made to either of these files; you will need to refresh **inetd**. This can be done with the SRC **refresh** command or by sending a hangup signal to the **inetd** process. Note that some daemons require that the **portmap** daemon be running.

```
# refresh inetd
# kill -HUP <inetd-pid>
```

Other Network Daemons

Not all TCP/IP server daemons run under the control of **inetd**. You may also choose to run an **inetd** subserver as a stand-alone daemon to service high-traffic loads. This eliminates the overhead involved in restarting the daemon for each service request. Start stand-alone service daemons using an entry in /etc/inittab or from a local /etc/rc.tcpip file.

Startup Configuration

The TCP/IP subsystem is normally started at system boot via an entry in /etc/inittab. The /etc/rc.net and /etc/rc.tcpip configuration files contain entries to enable the network interface, set the host name, set the default route, start **inetd**, and so on. If you do not want to start certain TCP/IP subsystems, comment out the entries for the subsystem in /etc/rc.tcpip.

DHCP

The Dynamic Host Configuration Protocol (DHCP) is a protocol that allows for automatic configuration of network hosts. Traditionally, each system must be manually configured by an administrator using an IP address and other information given out by a Network Administrator. As networks become larger, this manual configuration becomes increasingly difficult and error-prone. DHCP allows the configuration parameters for the entire network to be managed in one place, the DHCP server. All hosts on the network can then function as DHCP clients and retrieve their configuration information from the server.

AIX 5L's DHCP implementation consists of two application-space daemons; **dhcpcd** is the client daemon and **dhcpsd** is the server daemon. Multiple DHCP servers can be configured on the same network for redundancy. Most operating systems ship a DHCP client, and many also ship a DHCP server, so AIX 5L can serve as a DHCP server in a heterogeneous network or be a DHCP client on a network that uses a different DHCP server.

SLIP AND PPP

AIX supports TCP/IP over dial-up lines using the Serial Line Internet Protocol (SLIP) and Point-to-Point Protocol (PPP). The hardware employed by these protocols uses standard serial ports, modems, and switched lines. SLIP is a very simple protocol for framing IP packets on a serial line. It does not support packet addressing or type fields, data compression, or reliability. Only one protocol may be supported on a link at a time. SLIP links must be started manually.

PPP goes further than SLIP by including a link control protocol (LCP) for link control and a set of network control protocols (NCP) to support multiple protocols at a time. In addition, PPP also has stronger encapsulation and encryption (CHAP).

To set up a serial port for SLIP/PPP, use the SMIT FastPath **smit maktty** (see Figure 13-7). In most instances, you will want to use link speeds at or above 9600 bits per second. If the serial port will be used for dial-out only, set the LOGIN state to DISABLE. For dial-in support, use ENABLE. For dial-in and dial-out, use SHARE.

```
# smit maktty
```

   or

```
# mkdev -c tty -t tty -s rs232 -p sa1 -w s2 -s speed=38400
```

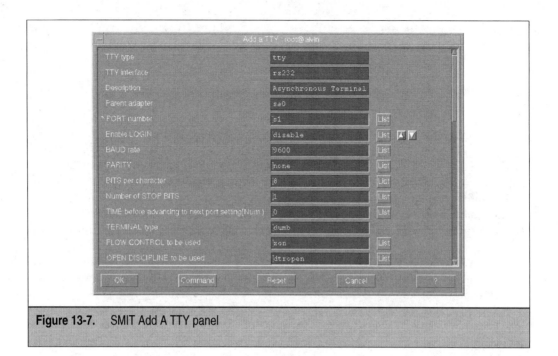

Figure 13-7. SMIT Add A TTY panel

Standard TCP/IP addressing and routing specifications apply to SLIP and PPP. In the following discussion concerning SLIP support, the configuration requirements have been split up into those used for dedicated SLIP links and those used for ad hoc SLIPLOGIN connections.

Dedicated SLIP

A dedicated SLIP link is a connection between two systems with the same IP and domain addresses. Since this type of link is not being used by multiple systems and users, the infrastructure to support it is not as complex. The AIX **slattach** command is executed to establish a SLIP link for both client and server connections. Command options include the TTY device to be used, line speed, and a Hayes-type dial string that will be used to establish the SLIP login session. The dial string is modem dependent and will be set for either dial-out or auto-answer for incoming connections. The format of the dial string is the same as is used by UUCP, for example,

```
"" ATZ OK ATDT123-4567 CONNECT""
     1.    ""       Null from modem
     2.    ATZ      Send reset to modem
     3.    OK       Response from modem
     4.    ATDT…    Send dial command to modem
     5.    CONNECT  Connection string
     6.    ""       Done
```

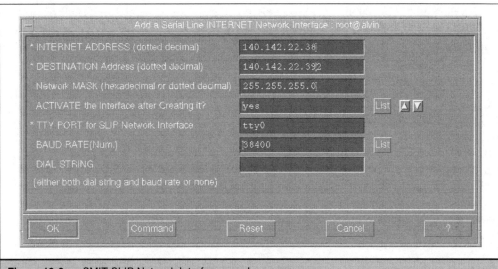

Figure 13-8. SMIT SLIP Network Interface panel

For either the client or server side of a SLIP link, configure the interface addresses by invoking the SMIT FastPath **smit mkinet** and select **Add A Serial Line Internet Network Interface** (see Figure 13-8).

```
# smit mkinet1sl
# mkdev -c if -s SL -t sl -w sl1 -a netaddr='192.168.1.10 \
  -a dest='192.168.1.151' -a metmask='255.255.255.0' \
  -a state='up' -a ttyport='tty1'
# slattach tty1 38400 '""ATHO OK \pATDT1234567 CONNECT""'
# slattch tty1   ◄─────────── From the answering node
```

You can also load the SLIP driver into the kernel and control the interface characteristics from the command line using the **strload** and **ifconfig** commands. Make sure you also add domain names for each IP address to be used in the appropriate name service tables.

```
# ifconfig sl[n] [options]   ◄──────────Set SLIP interface characteristics
# strinfo -m | grep "\'slip\'"  ◄──────────Check whether SLIP kernel extension is loaded
# strload -m /usr/lib/drivers/slip ◄────────Load SLIP kernel extension
```

On the system that will receive incoming connections, start SLIP using the **slattach** command with the **tty** option. The system will now listen on this TTY port for SLIP requests.

```
# slattach tty[n]
```

On the client dial-out system, start **slattach**. Note that you may include the baud rate and dial string on the command line.

```
# slattach tty[n] 19200 "" ATZ OK ATDT123-4567 CONNECT""
```

Once connected, you can control the SLIP interface using **ifconfig**.

```
# ifconfig sl0      Query sl0 interface
sl0: flags=30<POINTOPOINT,NOTRAILERS>
        inet 140.142.22.38 --> 140.142.22.39 netmask 0xffffff00
```

To disable a SLIP connection, send a hangup (HUP) signal to the **slattach** process. Do not use -9 (KILL), since this may cause system panics.

Nondedicated SLIP

A SLIPLOGIN configuration is used for ad hoc SLIP connections on interfaces, which may be shared between multiple users. This type of link may also support different IP and domain address pairs for each user.

On the server side (dial-in support), create AIX user accounts for each dial-in user with the shell **/usr/sbin/sliplogin**. You'll either have to log in to each of these accounts and reset the password or remove the ADMCHG flag from **/etc/security/passwd** to remove the prompt for password change at first login.

Next, edit the /etc/slip.hosts file to set the IP addresses to be used by each user connection. You will also need to add domain names for each IP address in the appropriate name service files, for example,

```
# format:    user  server-slip-ip    caller-slip-ip    hex subnet mask    options
      fred  7.9.8.1     7.9.8.2      0xffffff00   normal
      fred  7.9.8.3     7.9.8.4      0xffffff00   normal
     Jenny  7.9.8.1     7.9.8.2      0xffffff00   normal
```

Update /etc/uucp/Devices to include the options for the dial-out connection. This entry can be shared by both SLIP and UUCP.

```
Direct tty0 - 19200 direct
```

Make sure that the /etc/slip.login and /etc/slip.logout files exist and that the kernel extension is loaded.

```
# ifconfig sl[n] [options]      ◄─────────────── Set SLIP interface characteristics
# strinfo -m | grep "\'slip\'"  ◄─────────────── Check whether SLIP kernel extension is loaded
# strload -m /usr/lib/drivers/slip  ◄─────────── Load SLIP kernel extension
```

On the client side of a connection, you will need to add IP and domain addresses to your name resolution tables and update the TTY options in /etc/uucp/Devices as just described. Use the **slipcall** command to start the connection.

```
# slipcall [number] [tty] [baud] [user name] [password]
```

PPP

The Point-to-Point Protocol (PPP) goes beyond the simple encapsulation protocol used by SLIP. The Link Control Protocol (LCP) used in PPP can encapsulate and multiplex multiprotocol datagrams. PPP also provides additional session negotiation options, link-level error detection, compression, and authentication.

PPP is a subsystem managed by the system resource controller. The primary PPP control daemon **pppcontrold** is started as a subserver and is responsible for loading the PPP kernel extensions. One **pppattachd** subserver is started for each PPP connection. **pppattachd** binds the PPP and TTY STREAM. Configuration information for the PPP subsystem is stored in the /etc/ppp directory.

PPP uses both PAP (Password Authentication Protocol) and CHAP (Challenge Handshake Authentication Protocol) as the authentication methods for the client machines to authenticate to the server machines. The differences between them are that in PAP, the client name and password (shared secret) are sent in clear text, while in CHAP, the shared secret is not sent in clear text. Instead, the server sends a challenge, and the client must prove that it knows the secret by generating a hash value from the challenge and the shared secret and sending the value to the server. The server also generates its own hash value and compares with the value received from the client.

To configure the PPP subsystem, begin by invoking the SMIT FastPath **smitppp**. The first step will be to configure LCP (see Figure 13-9). You will need to choose a subsystem name for LCP. This can be any text string. It is not related to any TCP name service entry. Next, define the maximum number of server (inbound connections), client (outbound connections), and demand (sessions started when network traffic is detected) connections to be supported by LCP. You can throttle the mixture of server, client, and demand connections by the maximum number of IP interfaces and asynchronous high-level data link control (HDLC) attachments defined for the subsystem.

```
# smit ppplcp
```

Once the LCP subsystem is defined, you will need to set the IP addresses to be used when PPP connections are established. Invoke the SMIT FastPath **smit pppip** (see Figure 13-10). Identify the local machine's IP address, the base IP number for assigned addresses, the number of addresses to be assigned, and the subnet mask.

```
# smit pppip
```

If you chose to use authentication for establishing connections, invoke the SMIT FastPath **smit ppppap** or **smit pppchap**. Add each user, machine, and password that will be allowed to establish a PPP connection. These values are stored in clear text in the /etc/ppp/ppp-secrets file. Verify that permissions restrict access to this file.

When configuration has been completed, you can start the PPP subsystem using SMIT or the **startsrc** command.

```
# startsrc -s ppp     ◄──────── Start PPP subsystem
```

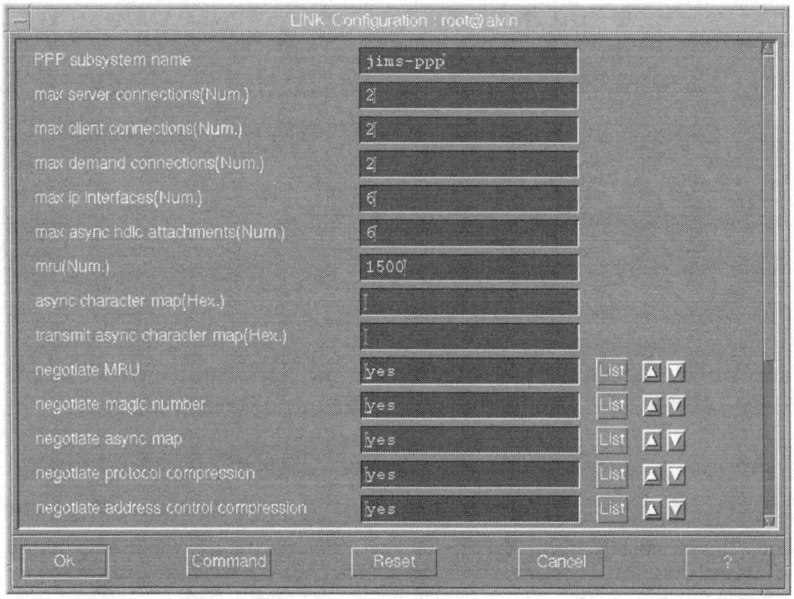

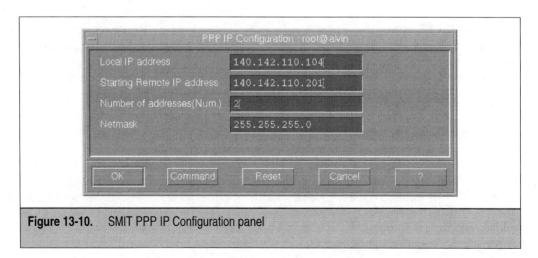

Figure 13-9. SMIT Link Configuration panel

To start a client PPP connection, use the **pppdial** command. Example client session ChatFiles (sign-on scripts) are available in the /etc/ppp directory. ChatFile format follows the conventions used for UUCP.

```
# pppdial -f [ChatFile]
```

Figure 13-10. SMIT PPP IP Configuration panel

PLANNING

Whether you are new to TCP/IP or sport a fair number of stars on your wizard's hat, installing or upgrading your network infrastructure will require some careful planning and plenty of homework. It is very important to carefully plan before beginning to configure your network. How many different networks are needed? How many hosts will you have on each of those networks? Make sure you allow room for growth—while 30 hosts per subnet may be enough now, will that still be the case several years down the road? Will you use DNS or an /etc/hosts file? DHCP or manual host configuration? Do you have a large enough range of global IP addresses, or should you use local addresses along with Network Address Translation? Does your network hardware have enough bandwidth to handle the expected load? Should you use a routing protocol or is static routing sufficient?

The answers to all these questions will depend on factors such as the size of your network, what it is used for, whether you have requirements for high availability, how often the network changes, and what your plans for future growth are. In a small, static network, it may be appropriate to use an /etc/hosts file and manual configuration. In a large complex network that often has new hosts added to it, DNS and DHCP will save a great deal of time and trouble for administrators. If you have high-availability requirements, redundant hardware along with the use of routing protocols and features such as Dead Gateway Detection and EtherChannel can help ensure that critical resources are always available. The bottom line is that a little planning now can save a lot of time and money later. Make sure you consider all the requirements for your network and design it to meet those requirements before you purchase hardware and begin configuration.

TCP/IP CONFIGURATION

Now that you are familiar with a number of important concepts and aspects of TCP/IP networking, the following sections are going to describe how to configure TCP/IP on AIX. This will allow your system to connect and communicate with other systems on the same network or on the Internet.

AIX provides different tools to configure different aspects of TCP/IP: the System Management Interface Tool (SMIT), Web-Based System Manager (WebSM), and command-line interface (CLI) commands. To invoke SMIT, type **smit**. **smit** invoked on a nongraphical window is the same as invoking **smitty**. To invoke Web-Based System Manager, type **wsm**. Web-Based System Manager is a GUI implemented using Java. In this chapter, we will use **smit** as the configuration tool. One notable thing is that if you use a configuration tool, **smit** or **wsm**, to configure TCP/IP, the configuration data is written to the ODM configuration database and is persistent across a system reboot. Commands such as **ifconfig** and **route** change only the currently running system and do not persist after a reboot.

Configure TCP/IP

The SMIT FastPath **smit tcpip** is for TCP/IP configuration. Select **Minimum Configuration & Startup** to configure a primary network interface, host name, IP address, domain name, subnet, default name server, default gateway, and whether or not you want to select dead gateway detection for your default gateway (see Figure 13-11). You can also specify if you want to start the TCP/IP daemons in the /etc/rc.tcpip file. SMIT will update the configuration files, such as /etc/hosts, /etc/resolv.conf, and so on, with appropriate information.

```
# smit tcpip
  * Minimum Configuration & Startup  ◄──────────── FastPath mktcpip
  * Further Configuration  ◄──────────── FastPath configtcp
  * Use DHCP for TCPIP Configuration & Startup ◄─── FastPath usedhcp
  * IPV6 Configuration  ◄──────────── FastPath configtcp6
  * Quality of Service Configuration & Startup ◄── FastPath configqos
  * Configure IP Security (IPv4)  ◄──────────── FastPath ipsec4
  * Configure IP Security (IPv6)  ◄──────────── FastPath ipsec6
```

For a simple configuration, this may be all you need to set up your system to connect to the network. However, if you have a need to communicate to multiple networks via multiple network interfaces or different routes to use for better throughput and so on, the following sections will provide additional configuration steps.

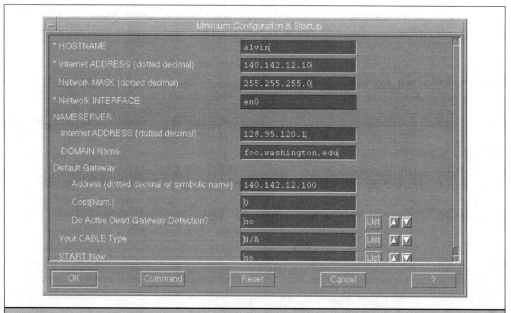

Figure 13-11. Minimum Configuration & Startup

Network Interface Configuration

As stated in the preceding section, if you use the **Minimum Configuration & Startup** SMIT panel to configure TCP/IP, the default interface is already configured for you. Additional network interfaces may be configured using SMIT FastPath **smit chinet** or by using the **ifconfig** command. The same command can be used to change the addresses or masks of an adapter, should you need to make changes to the network configuration. Please note that if you use the **ifconfig** command, your modification is in effect only for the current instance of the running system. In other words, it will not be persistent across a system reboot unless you add an **ifconfig** entry in the /etc/rc.net startup script. However, this is not the recommended method because, depending on the order of execution, you may get unexpected results.

The adapter interface can be brought up and down for maintenance or testing using SMIT or from the command line using the **ifconfig** command. Note that this will interrupt service to the target interface and may affect dependent applications.

```
# ifconfig en0 up      ◄─────────── Start Ethernet interface
# ifconfig en0 down    ◄─────────── Stop Token Ring interface
# ifconfig en0 detach  ◄─────────── Detach en0 before making changes to ent0
```

The following is an example of using **ifconfig** to assign address 123.145.100.18 to the Standard Network Interface with a netmask of 0xffffff00 and the broadcast address of 123.145.100.255.

```
# ifconfig en0 123.145.100.18 netmask 0xffffff00 broadcast
123.145.100.255
```

arp Command

The **arp** command can be used to view and configure the ARP table in AIX 5L. **arp -a** will display all entries in the ARP table. Incomplete entries will be shown for addresses for which ARP requests have been sent but no reply has yet been received. Normally, it is not necessary to edit the ARP table by hand; but in a few special circumstances, it may be necessary—for instance, if a system on the network does not respond to ARP requests, or if an adapter in the network has been replaced and it is necessary to delete an old ARP entry.

```
# arp -a
```

autoconf6 Command

Running the **autoconf6** command is the first step in configuring a system to use the IPv6 protocol. IPv6 requires that each network interface have a link local address that can be used to communicate with routers and other hosts on the local network link. **autoconf6** automatically generates and assigns a link local address on each interface that is already configured with an IPv4 address. In addition, it will create the **sit0**

interface, which is used for automatic tunneling. The **sit0** interface will be created using
the IPv4 address of the first configured IPv4 interface, unless a different interface is
specified using the **-m** flag of **autoconf6**.

ndpd-host Command

The **ndpd-host** daemon handles non-kernel Neighbor Discovery Protocol functions for
IPv6 hosts. It sends router solicitations and handles the router advertisements sent in
response. It should be started on IPv6 hosts from the `/etc/rc.tcpip` script.

ndpd-router Command

The **ndpd-router** daemon should be run on systems serving as IPv6 routers. It handles
the sending of router advertisements and can also exchange routing information with
other routers using the RIPng routing protocol. The daemon should be started on IPv6
routers from the `/etc/rc.tcpip` script.

The `/etc/gateway6` file is used to configure the **ndpd-router** daemon. The line

```
rtadv = y
```

will cause **ndpd-router** to send router advertisements and is the only configuration
needed in many cases. Other directives control which interfaces advertisements are
sent on and some characteristics of the advertisements, as well as the behavior of RIPng

Routing Configuration

The kernel routing table can be modified in two ways: the **route** command or the SMIT
panels. The shortcut to the routing SMIT panels is **smit route**. It is important to note
that the SMIT panels will modify the routing information in the ODM databases, causing
the changes to persist after a reboot, while the **route** command will make changes only
on the currently running system.

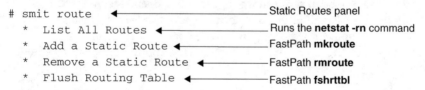

```
# smit route       ◄───────────────── Static Routes panel
   *  List All Routes ◄─────────────── Runs the netstat -rn command
   *  Add a Static Route ◄──────────── FastPath mkroute
   *  Remove a Static Route ◄───────── FastPath rmroute
   *  Flush Routing Table ◄────────── FastPath fshrttbl
```

Modifying Static Routes Using SMIT

The routing SMIT panel offers four options. List All Routes will display the routes
currently in the kernel routing table, but will not display the routing information in
the ODM database. The **Add a Static Route** SMIT panel allows additional static routes
to be added to the system since the system's default route was added in the **Minimum
Configuration & Startup** SMIT panel. This panel allows several characteristics of the route
to be specified, such as the **Destination Type**, which can be "host" or "net". The **Destination
Address** is the IP address or symbolic name of the host or network this route allows the

system to reach. The **Gateway Address** specifies the IP address or symbolic name of the next-hop gateway that should be used to reach the destination host or network. The **Cost** field is used by the **Dead Gateway Detection** functionality. The **Network Mask** field specifies the netmask to be used for this route. The **Network Interface** field is used to specify which network interface traffic sent to the destination network should be sent out. The **Enable Active Dead Gateway Detection** field determines whether periodic probes will be sent to this gateway to determine whether it is down. This is useful only if a backup route has been specified for this destination. Finally, the **Is This A Local (Interface) Route?** field allows administrators to add routes to the local network link. The base AIX 5.1 does not have this last field until you apply the latest maintenance level.

The third option offered by the routing SMIT panel is **Remove a Static Route**. This panel allows the **Destination Type**, **Destination Address**, **Gateway Address**, and **Network Mask** to be specified. This will delete the routes from both the current kernel routing table and the ODM databases.

The last option given by the routing SMIT panel is **Flush Routing Table**. This will delete all entries from the routing table on the running system with the exception of the interface routes. It does not remove the routes from the ODM configuration databases.

There is a separate SMIT panel for modifying the IPv6 routing table. It can be reached through the FastPath **smit route6**. This panel offers the same four options as the IPv4 panel. The parameters that can be set in each option are nearly identical to the IPv4 panels, except that netmask is replaced by prefix length.

The route Command

The current routing table can also be modified using the **route** command. Here is an example of the syntax used to add a route:

```
route add -net 10.1.1.0 10.2.0.1 -netmask 255.255.255.0
```

This command adds a route to network 10.1.1.0 through gateway 10.2.0.1. To delete the route, the subcommand **add** would be replaced with **delete**. To add and delete IPv6 routes using the **route** command, the flag **-inet6** must be used.

Dynamic Routing

AIX 5L includes two routing daemons that can be used for dynamic routing. The **routed** daemon is by far the simpler of the two, but runs only the RIP routing protocol, which has some limitations. The **gated** daemon supports many routing protocols; but as a result of its greater flexibility, it takes quite a bit more effort to configure. The **routed** and **gated** daemons should never be run at the same time. The **routed** daemon should be started as a system resource from the /etc/rc.tcpip script and can configured to do so with the SMIT FastPath **smit strouted** or the following **chrctcp** command:

```
# /usr/sbin/chrctcp -a routed -f supply='yes'
# grep /routed /etc/rc.tcpip         ◄─────── Configures routed to start on next reboot
start /usr/sbin/routed "$src_running" " -s"◄──── See how the new entry looks
```

The optional **-s** flag causes the routed daemon to send, not just receive, information about its routes. When **routed** is started, it will send RIP packets on each of its attached networks. In this way, it can inform all neighboring routers about the networks it can reach. When it receives RIP packets, it can add routes to the routing table about the routes that the neighbors can reach, and can then send RIP packets informing other neighbors about those routes. In addition to advertising routes to directly reachable networks, **routed** can be configured to advertise information about other routes. The /etc/gateways file is used for this purpose. The format of the file is

```
{ net | host } name1 gateway name2 metric { passive | active | external }
```

If a gateway listed in /etc/gateways exchanges RIP information, it should be marked as active. If it does not, it should be marked as passive. The **external** keyword is used to inform **routed** that the route will be added to the kernel routing table by other means, and **routed** should not install any other routes to the destination. **routed** will not send any RIP information about external routes.

The **gated** daemon, like **routed**, should be started from the /etc/rc.tcpip script and can be configured to do so with the SMIT FastPath **smit gated** or the following **chrctcp** commands:

```
# /usr/sbin/chrctcp -S -d routed    ◀─────────── This stops and un-configures routed
# /usr/sbin/chrctcp -S -a gated     ◀─────────── This starts gated now and next reboot
```

The **gated** daemon is configured using the /etc/gated.conf file. Since **gated** supports so many protocols, there are many options that can be configured, and an entire book could be devoted to **gated** alone. The /etc/gated.conf file itself contains quite a bit of information about the file format and gives sample stanzas for different routing protocols.

Network Options

Network options are used to tune various behaviors of TCP/IP on AIX 5L. They are set and displayed using the Network Options command, **no**. It is important to note that options set with **no** are not stored in the system's ODM database, and therefore are not persistent. If an administrator wants an option to be set on every reboot, it must be added to one of the system's configuration files such as /etc/rc.net.

A few network options are known as *load-time* options. These options take effect at the time that the networking kernel extension is loaded. Changing them after this time has no effect. The only way to change these options is to modify the /etc/rc.net file so that the options are changed at the *beginning* of the file. The other *runtime* options should always be changed at the end of the /etc/rc.net file, as many of them are not available until after this kernel extension is loaded. Read the Network Tunable Parameters section in IBM's *Performance Management Guide* for a complete explanation of the over 100 network options.

```
# no -a          ◄───────────────────── Display all network options and their current values
# no -o <option name> ◄──────────────── Display a single network option and its current value
# no -o <option name>=<value>◄──────── Set the value of a network option
# no -d <option name> ◄──────────────── Set a network option to its default value
```

NETWORK SECURITY

Network security is a topic about which many books have been written, and enough could be said about the subject to fill several volumes. This section does not intend to turn you into a network security expert. Rather, it is designed to give a brief overview of some of the issues you should consider when administering a network, and some of the different types of network security features offered by AIX 5L.

There are those who will say that network security is an oxymoron—that if you put a computer on a network, it is no longer secure. To some degree, this is true. There is no such thing as a perfectly secure network. However, by being aware of some of the issues and taking some fairly simple steps, you can choose an appropriate level of network security for your environment and greatly reduce your risk.

Network Trusted Computing Base

AIX supports a set of access control and auditing facilities called the Trusted Computing Base (TCB). The TCB system also encompasses network support and is known as the Network Trusted Computing Base (NTCB). Along with TCB user authentication mechanisms, NTCB supplies connection authentication, secure session, auditing of network configuration files and events, and an enhanced security TCP/IP operation mode.

Connection authentication is provided by defining which remote host addresses are allowed to connect to the local system. Security levels may be defined for each network interface to limit the activities that can take place over a given interface.

Secure sessions are enforced through the use of the trusted path, trusted shell (tsh), and secure attention key (SAK). The trusted path and shell limit the applications that may make use of a terminal session. The SAK establishes the environment necessary for a secure session.

The AIX auditing system records changes in permissions, modification times, checksums, and network events.

A full set of security features can be enabled using the **securetcpip** command. **securetcpip** disables untrusted commands and restricts access to interfaces that are not configured at specified security levels. The Berkeley **r** commands **rsh**, **rcp**, and **rlogin** are disabled along with **tftp**. The ftp, **telnet**, and **rexec** commands provide additional security checking. Once the **securetcpip** command is invoked, the **tcpip** filesets must be reinstalled to restore standard operation. Interface security levels are based on the IP security option described in RFC 1038.

IP Security

IP security is an IETF standard feature that is implemented in AIX 5L to provide security at the IP layer. IP security is used to create virtual private networks, or VPNs, which allow for secure communications between systems even on insecure networks. Since it functions at the IP layer, IP security is transparent and requires no changes to applications. There are three services that can be provided by IP security: authentication, integrity, and encryption. Authentication is used to verify the identity of a host involved in network communications. Integrity ensures that data has not been modified during transit. Encryption provides privacy by hiding the contents of the data while it is transmitted across the network.

The Authentication Header (AH) protocol is used to provide authentication and integrity, while the Encapsulating Security Payload (ESP) protocol provides encryption. AH can be used alone in cases where encryption of the data is not needed, or along with ESP when all three types of protection are needed.

Security Associations (SAs) are used to specify when IP security should be used. An SA specifies the security parameters, such as destination address, algorithms, key, and key lifetime, that should be used for a particular type of traffic.

AIX 5L supports two methods for managing SAs. IKE tunnels are used to exchange keys securely and dynamically create SAs. Manual tunnels are used with static keys and are provided for interoperability with systems that do not support the IKE standard.

See RFCs 2402 and 2406 for more details about the AH and ESP protocols.

Secure r Commands

It is important to note that traditionally, when using commands such as **telnet**, **ftp**, and **rlogin**, passwords are sent in clear text over the network, where they can be intercepted by anyone with a network sniffer. This creates an obvious security hole. In AIX 5L, the **rlogin**, **rcp**, **rsh**, **telnet**, and **ftp** commands, collectively known as the **r** commands, are enhanced to allow authentication methods that do not transmit a clear password on the network. The authentication method used is configurable on a system-wide basis, and three choices are available: Standard AIX, Kerberos V.5, and Kerberos V.4. Standard AIX is the traditional password-based method, which allows the password to be seen using a network sniffer. When Kerberos V.5 authentication is in use, the system gets a Kerberos V.5 ticket from a security server. This will be a set of credentials encrypted for the server the connection is being made to. The server will then be able to decrypt the ticket and verify the identity of the user without the use of a password. Kerberos V.4 authentication is very similar, but supports only **rsh** and **rcp** and is provided for backward compatibility only.

The acceptable configuration methods and the order they should be attempted in are configured using the **lsauthent** and **chauthent** commands.

Traditional Security Measures

There are also some traditional measures that you can take to secure your environment. The first is the judicious use of $HOME/.rhosts and /etc/hosts.equiv files. Using these files allows use of the Berkeley **r** commands without requiring a password. This eliminates passwords sent in the clear over the Net and limits the damage that may be done with PTY sniffer programs. It is true that if these files are compromised they can present a nasty security hole. Care must be taken when implementing their use. Basically, these files list the hosts and user names that are allowed to execute **r** commands without a password.

Connection authentication can be implemented on a service-by-service basis by implementing a wrapper program for **inetd**. A wrapper program validates and logs the connecting system's address based on an access table. The **tcpd** program available via anonymous FTP from cert.org is an example of this type of application. The **tcpd** system controls access by service class, as well as individual service.

Security Information

The Computer Emergency Response Team (CERT) based at Carnegie Mellon University tracks and disseminates vendor security information. CERT regularly posts information to the comp.security.announce Usenet group. They also support an anonymous FTP site containing security-related documents. Another Usenet security-related discussion group is alt.security.general.

TCP/IP TROUBLESHOOTING

There are a number of tools that are provided in AIX 5L to allow for network troubleshooting and debugging. The most important of these are probably the packet tracing tools, **iptrace** and **tcpdump**. These two tools perform similar functions, but their syntax and output format are different. Both tools provide methods to filter traffic so that only the specified packets are traced. This greatly reduces the size of the trace. The **tcpdump** command does its filtering within the kernel, while **iptrace** must copy every packet to user space and filter within the application. For this reason, when tracing packets on a busy network, **tcpdump** may be the better choice, as it is less likely to drop packets.

The **traceroute** command is another useful debugging tool included in AIX 5L. It can be used to diagnose network connectivity issues. The command will display the name or IP address of each router that packets pass through on their way to the destination host. If the host should be reachable but is not, **traceroute** allows the administrator to see which router is the last to receive the packets. The problem is then that either that router is not correctly forwarding the packets to the next hop, or the next hop is down or not functioning correctly (for instance, **ipforwarding** could be disabled). In the case where there are many routers between two hosts, **traceroute** can help pinpoint where in the network a routing problem is occurring.

The simple **ping** command can also be used to debug network problems. If **ping** is used with a destination's IP address rather than its name, this is a simple test for network connectivity.

The **netstat** command can be used to display interface statistics and connection status for a given workstation or host. The **-a** option will show all server connections on the system, including the port numbers. So if, for instance, **telnet** to a particular host will not work, check to see if **netstat -a** shows a connection in the TCP listen state on the Telnet port. If not, it may be necessary to modify /etc/inetd.conf or /etc/rc.tcpip to ensure that the correct server applications are started.

Sniffers

One good tool to have handy for medium-to-larger networks is a sniffer. A sniffer is a custom computer that attaches to the network to analyze packet traffic. These systems are compact so they can be taken anywhere and are tuned to keep up with packet rates. Packet types can be filtered and logged to provide statistics over time. For the budget minded, there are packages available for workstations and PCs that provide many of the same functions.

CHECKLIST

The following is a checklist for the key points in TCP/IP:

☐ Define TCP/IP.

☐ Identify the layers of the TCP/IP Network Model.

☐ Identify network devices and interfaces.

☐ Identify the different types of addresses TCP/IP uses.

☐ Manage routing.

☐ Manage TCP/IP applications by using the Domain Name System (DNS) to get the mapping between IP addresses and names.

☐ Identify how TCP/IP daemons run as subsystems under AIX.

☐ Define the Dynamic Host Configuration Protocol (DHCP).

☐ Define the Simple Network Management Protocol (SNMP).

☐ Show how AIX supports TCP/IP over dial-up lines using the Serial Line Internet Protocol (SLIP) and Point-to-Point Protocol (PPP).

PART VI

Networked Filesystems

CHAPTER 14

Networked Filesystems: NFS, NIS, and NIS+

Support for different types of filesystems on a UNIX system is made possible by the open interface called a virtual file system (VFS). A virtual file system provides an abstraction over the physical filesystem implementation and hence a consistent interface to different filesystems, such as JFS and NFS, as well as a consistent view of the directory regardless of the underlining filesystem.

Filesystem architectures supported by VFS are specified in the /etc/vfs file:

```
# name   vfs_number mount_helper filesystem_helper
%defaultvfs   jfs    nfs
#
cdrfs          5     none                              none
procfs         6     none                              none
jfs            3     none                              /sbin/helpers/v3fshelper
jfs2           0     /sbin/helpers/jfs2                none
dfs            7     /sbin/helpers/dfsmnthelper        none         remote
nfs            2     /sbin/helpers/nfsmnthelp          none         remote
nfs3          18     /sbin/helpers/nfsmnthelp          none         remote
cachefs       17     /sbin/helpers/cfsmnthelp          none         remote
autofs        19     /sbin/helpers/aufmnthelp          none
afs            4     none                              none
```

NETWORK FILE SYSTEM

NFS, developed by Sun, is based on a client/server architecture that enables applications to seamlessly interoperate with files and directories shared between networked machines without regard to their locale. NFS uses Remote Procedure Call (RPC) to support filesystem operations between systems with different hardware architectures and the External Data Representation (XDR) language to communicate different data formats among the systems (see the illustration).

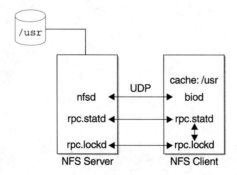

AIX supports both NFS version 3 and NFS version 2. Supporting both versions of the NFS enables AIX to be backward compatible with NFS version 2 clients and servers. In addition to supporting UDP as their transport layer, AIX versions 4.2.1 and later also support TCP. In fact, since AIX 4.3, TCP is a default transport protocol. You can specify which version of NFS or which transport protocol to use by using the options **vers** and **proto** of the **mount** command. This will be discussed in detail later in this chapter.

Configuring NFS

AIX provides both NFS server and NFS client packages. The packages are automatically installed in the system, but steps must be taken to start the daemons. You can start the NFS daemons using one of the following methods:

- The **wsm** command (Web-Based System Manager, WebSM)
- The SMIT FastPath **smit mknfs**
- The **mknfs** command

Any of these methods will place an entry in the /etc/inittab file to execute the /etc/rc.nfs script to start the NFS daemons.

```
rcnfs:23456789:wait:/etc/rc.nfs > /dev/console 2>&1 # Start NFS Daemon
```

The /etc/rc.nfs script begins by starting the NFS block I/O **biod** daemons. If the /etc/exports file exists, it is exported using **exportfs -a** before starting the **nfsd** and **rpc.mountd** daemons. The /etc/rc.nfs script finishes up by starting the **rpc.statd** and **rpc.lockd** daemons. The /etc/rc.nfs script also contains entries for starting NIS and HANFS subsystems and subservers.

NFS may be made the default remote filesystem type by defining it as the **defaultvfs** in /etc/vfs. Uncomment the following lines in the /etc/vfs table.

```
%defaultvfs jfs nfs
nfs 2 /etc/helpers/nfsmnthelp none remote
```

NFS also can be managed as a subsystem by the AIX **srcmstr**. Thus, NFS daemons may be started or stopped as a group using the **startsrc** and **stopsrc** commands. NFS operations may also be managed from the SMIT FastPath **smit nfs** submenus, and all the necessary subsystems will be started both now and at system startup by NFS configuration scripts like **mknfsexp**.

```
# lsssrc -g nfs    ◄──────── List daemons in NFS subsystem
# startsrc -g nfs  ◄──────── Start NFS subsystem
# stopsrc -g nfs   ◄──────── Stop NFS subsystem
```

NFS SERVER

The NFS server is designed as a stateless system. This should eliminate the need to support recovery operations in the event of a server or client failure. It turns out that this is not entirely true. NFS uses UDP as a transport, and we all know that UDP does not guarantee packet delivery or packet order. To overcome the deficiencies of UDP, NFS servers must maintain a volatile cache of recent RCP handshaking state to avoid duplicate, out-of-order, or lost I/O operation packets. This also means that the server must keep track of whom it is talking to. To keep the **nfsd** daemon stateless, additional daemons are used to track machine connections, RPC status, and file locks. IBM's High-Availability Network Filesystem (HANFS) makes use of the volatile cache state and lock daemon information to support backup NFS servers.

To ensure file integrity, NFS servers use a write-through cache, forcing file updates immediately to disk. Data integrity is maintained for the sake of performance. Asynchronous write support is available in some architectures to improve read performance when data integrity is not an issue.

NFS Server Daemons

NFS servers rely on a number of daemons to manage distributed filesystem services. I/O requests from multiple clients are multiplexed through multiple threads of the **nfsd**. The **nfsd** daemon manages file I/O operations. The number of **nfsd** threads is self-tuned and created in accordance with the client request to the server.

The **rpc.mountd** daemon is used by the server to manage and track client mount requests. Recent RPC operations between clients and servers are cached by the **rpc.statd** daemon. SYSV advisory file and record locking is supported by the server's **rpc.lockd** daemon.

The NFS server daemons are shown in Table 14-1.

Because NFS is RPC-based, the NFS server daemons must register themselves with the **portmap** daemon. The **portmap** daemon maintains the available set of RPC applications on a particular machine. Each application is represented as a tuple of

Daemon	Purpose
nfsd	NFS server daemon
portmap	RPC program to port manager
rpc.mountd	NFS mount manager
rpc.statd	RPC status manager
rpc.lockd	NFS lock manager
rpc.pcnfsd	PC authentication service

Table 14-1. NFS Server Daemons

application name, version, and port number. Servers register their application data with the **portmap** daemon. Client applications query the **portmap** daemon to learn the port number associated with a known server application name and version. The **portmap** listens to a well-known port number listed in /etc/services, thus avoiding the "chicken and egg" problem of determining what **portmap**'s port number is.

The **nfsd, rpc.lockd, rpc.mountd**, and **rpc.statd** NFS server daemons are started in the /etc/rc.nfs script, while the other NFS server daemons are controlled by the **inetd** super-daemon.

Exporting Server Filesystems

Each filesystem or directory available for remote mounting is identified by an entry in the server's /etc/exports file. Along with the directory path name, the /etc/exports entry controls which machine names are allowed root permissions and write access. If NFS root access is not enabled for a remote NFS client, the root UID of the server is mapped to a default UID of –2 (4294967294), user name **nobody**. This restricts access against the superuser UID on a remote machine.

The /etc/exports file is a flat ASCII text file that may be manually edited using your favorite editor or maintained using the SMIT FastPath **smit mknfsexp** (see Figure 14-1).

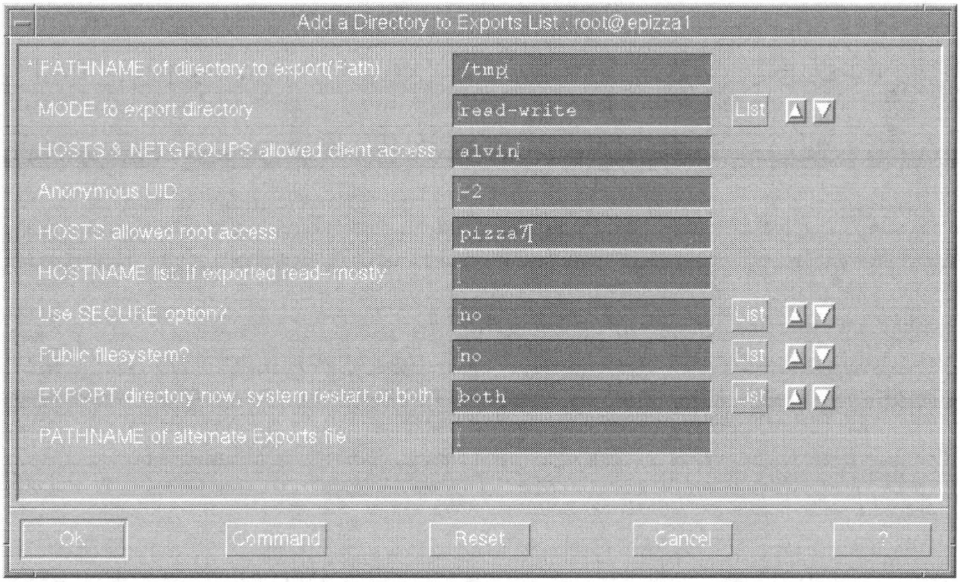

Figure 14-1.   Add A Directory To Exports List SMIT panel

Manual updates to the `/etc/exports` file must be made known to the server daemons by invoking the **/usr/sbin/exportfs** command.

The following is an example of `/etc/exports`:

```
/var/spool/lpd/pio/@local -ro
/scripts -root=bambam:dino:wilma,access=bambam:dino:wilma
```

```
# /usr/sbin/exportfs -a  ◄────────Exports all of the entries in the /etc/exports file
```

PC-NFS

PC-NFS is a program for PCs to mount filesystems exported by a NFS server and to request network addresses and host names from the NFS server. If the **rpc.pcnfsd** daemon is running on the NFS server, the PC can also access authentication and print-spooling services.

To start the **rpc.pcnfsd** daemon, uncomment the following line in the `/etc/inetd.conf` file:

```
pcnfsd sunrpc_udp  udp  wait    root /usr/sbin/rpc.pcnfsd pcnfs 150001 1-2
```

NFS CLIENTS

To improve performance, the NFS clients implement client-side data caching. This requires that some level of cache consistency be maintained between multiple NFS clients and the server. A time stamp expiration mechanism is used to allow the clients to update cache information when it becomes stale.

Each client runs a multithreaded NFS **biod** block I/O daemon. The number of threads created depends on the workload. NFS clients also run the **portmap** daemon. The **portmap** daemon is queried to identify RPC services and bind port connections to NFS servers.

NFS RPC mechanisms allow clients to block applications in the event of a server failure. I/O operations continue when access to the server is restored. A retry limit is provided so that client applications do not wait forever in the case of long-term server failures. Sun also added *hard* and *soft* mount options so that a client could be interrupted when server access is blocked. There are only two NFS client daemons required:

```
biod    ◄────────NFS block I/O daemon
portmap ◄────────RPC program to port manager
```

Importing Filesystems

There are three different way to import (**mount**) a network filesystem: predefined, explicit, and automatic.

Predefined Mounts

Predefined mounts are where the NFS filesystem definitions are configured as stanzas in the `/etc/filesystems` file. The stanza is similar to a local filesystem definition with the addition of the remote hostname listed in the `nodename =` parameter. The `dev =` parameter defines the directory path on the remote machine to be mounted. You can specify the mount options using the `options =` parameter. For example, to specify use of NFS version 3 and the transport protocol UDP for this mount entry in addition to other options, add `vers=3,proto=udp` to the end of the parameter list of the `options` attribute. If you do not specify the version or protocol, the **mount** command will try first to use version 3 with TCP, then version 3 with UDP, then version 2 with TCP, and then finally version 2 with UDP. The `/etc/filesystems` entries may be edited directly or managed using the SMIT FastPath **smit mknfsmnt** (see Figure 14-2). By default, the **mount** command will try to mount the entries with

```
# smit mknfsmnt
```

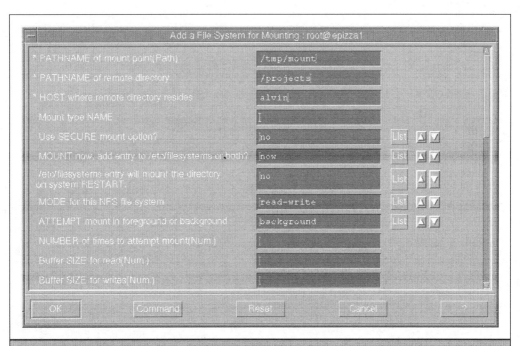

Figure 14-2.   Add A File System For Mounting SMIT panel

The following is an example of an /etc/filesystems NFS stanza:

```
/usr/local/common:
        dev             = "/usr/local/common"
        vfs             = nfs
        nodename        = yogi
        mount           = false
        type            = nfsfile
        options         = bg,hard,intr
        account         = false


/usr/sys/inst.images:
        dev             = "/usr/sys/inst.images"
        vfs             = nfs
        nodename        = bambam
        mount           = false
        type            = nfsfile
        options         = bg,hard,intr
        account         = false


/usr/share/man:
        dev             = "/usr/share/man"
        vfs             = nfs
        nodename        = dino
        mount           = false
        type            = nfsfile
        options         = bg,hard,intr
        account         = false


/sapmnt/help:
        dev             = "/sapmnt/help"
        vfs             = nfs
        nodename        = sapprod1
        mount           = false
        type            = nfsfile
        options         = ro,bg,hard,intr
        account         = false
```

The type = nfsfile parameter may be added to the stanza definitions to identify NFS filesystems as an **nfsfile** group. This way, they can be mounted or unmounted as a group using the **-t** option of the **mount** and **umount** commands.

```
# mount -t nfsfile
# umount -t nfsfile
```

Explicit Mounts

Explicit mounts are for mounting files or directories for a short period of time and are not required to persist across system reboots. You use the **mount** command on the command line with all needed mount options for this kind of mount. For example, to mount /tmp/STUFF from host **lobo** to /tmp/lobo using mount options of background, nfs version 3, transport protocol **tcp**, and retry up to three times, issue the following command line:

```
# mount -n lobo -o "bg,vers=3,proto=tcp,retry=3" /tmp/STUFF /tmp/lobo
```

A second option is to use the NFS mount defaults with the following command:

```
# mount lobo:/tmp/STUFF   /tmp/lobo
```

Automatic Mounts

AutoFS controls the *automatic* mounts. There are no explicit mounts for automatic mounts until a program or a user attempts to access the mount points. See AutoFS for details later in the chapter.

CacheFS

The Cache File System allows caching for NFS file systems on an NFS client system to improve performance for clients on a slow network. Files are stored in the cache when they are first accessed. The subsequent requests can be accessed locally in the Cache File System instead of over the network. CacheFS periodically checks the modification time against the previous modification time for files stored in the cache. If the modifications times are different, data for the files are flushed from the cache and updated data are retrieved from the filesystem.

Use the SMIT FastPath **smit cachefs** for CacheFS administration and mounting.

AutoFS

AutoFS includes a kernel extension, the **automountd** daemon, and the **automount** command. AutoFS will mount the NFS filesystem when a program or a user accesses it. The **automount** command is used to load the AutoFS map file, which contains the mapping information of the local directories to the server directories, into the AutoFS kernel extension. When users access the local directory listed in the map file, the kernel extension sends a mount request to the **automountd** daemon to mount the directory if it is not currently mounted. If the filesystem is not accessed within an appropriate interval (five minutes by default), the **automountd** daemon unmounts the filesystem.

The **automountd** daemon can be managed using the AIX **srcmstr** commands, **startsrc** and **stopsrc**.

```
# startsrc -g autofs ◄──────Start AutoFS subsystem
# stopsrc -g autofs ◄──────Stop AutoFS subsystem
```

NETWORK INFORMATION SERVICES: NIS AND NIS+

Sun developed the name services and originally called the services Yellow Pages (YP). Since YP was a registered trademark of British Telecommunications, Sun was forced to rename the service to Network Information Services. As the name implies, Network Information Services (NIS) was designed to centralize the information about systems and users in a network in order to simplify system administration.

NIS was implemented using a client/server model. Its components include server, client, maps, and a set of administration tools. The design assumptions for NIS were for a small network where most of the configuration data is static; network information was to be managed by a System Administrator. In today's computing environment, the need arises to decentralize administration and adapt to the hierarchical structure of an organization. NIS+ was developed to address these problems, as well as the security problem in NIS. Please note that NIS+ is replacement for NIS. There are a number of differences in terminology for similar concepts, as well as a number of new features in NIS+.

The following sections provide an overview for the components of NIS and NIS+ and how to configure them.

NIS

NIS uses domains, which share a set of configuration data using NIS services, to organize systems. An NIS domain consists of a master server, zero or more slave servers, and a collection of client machines. You will need the **bos.net.nis.server** or **bos.net.nis.client** file set installed for each respective NIS application. All the SMIT FastPath panels in the following NIS discussion are accessible from the main NIS configuration SMIT FastPath **smit yp**.

There is one master server in an NIS domain in which the main maps are maintained. Slave servers get the copy of the NIS maps from the master server. The slave servers can respond to the client's requests just as the master server does, thereby increasing the availability of the information. Slave servers can get updated maps automatically if the master server is running the **ypupdated** daemon, if the master server is stopped and restarted, or if **yppush** command is invoked at the master server. Both master and slave servers run the **ypserv** daemon to process requests from clients for information contained in the maps. The master server also runs the **yppasswdd** daemon to handle users' password change requests.

NIS clients make up the majority of hosts in the NIS name space. An NIS client runs the **ypbind** daemon to locate the closest NIS server and to query servers for such information as IP addresses or user data.

NIS Domain

The domain defines the area of administrative control available to the servers. Systems belonging to a domain share a common set of configuration and network information such as user, group, host name, and IP address. The domain name must be set on all systems in the domain. Use the following **chypdom** command to define the domain name now and at next reboot:

```
# chypcom -B <DomainName>
```

To display an NIS domain name use the **domainname** command without parameters.

```
# domainname
```

NIS Maps

NIS maps are built from the standard text files, for example, /etc/passwd, /etc/group, /etc/hosts, on the master server and converted to DBM database format using **makedbm** command. Essentially, a map record is a key-value pair. NIS provides a makefile, /var/yp/Makefile, which runs **makedbm** to create default NIS maps when you invoke **make all**. Collectively, the NIS maps make up the NIS database. An NIS database may be transferred to another domain using the **ypxfr** command. Before any maps can be created of transferred using any of these methods, the /var/yp/<DomainName> subdirectory must be created on the target NIS server.

Files	Maps	Files	Maps
/etc/passwd	passwd.byname	/etc/services	services.byname
	passwd.byuid	/etc/protocols	protocols.bynumber
/etc/group	group.byname		protocols.byname
	group.bygid	/etc/netgroup	netgroup
/etc/hosts	hosts.byaddr		netgroup.byhost
	hosts.byname		netgroup.byuser
/etc/ethers	ethers.byaddr	/etc/publickey	publickey.byname
	ethers.byname	/etc/bootparams	bootparams
/etc/networks	networks.byaddr	/etc/aliases	mail.aliases
	networks.byname		mail.byaddr
/etc/rpc	rpc.bynumber	/etc/netmasks	netmasks.byaddr
master & slave	ypservers	passwd & group	netid.byname

The ypservers map is a special map that contains the names of the master and slave servers in the domain. Clients use the ypservers map to find the nearest available server. The master server refers to it to determine the names of the slave servers to prompt to get updated copies of the NIS maps.

The NIS netgroup file, /etc/netgroup, defines network-wide groups that are identified for authentication purposes during the login, rlogin, remote mount, and remote shell processes. The /etc/netgroup file is used to build the netgroup.byuser and netgroup.byhost maps. The netgroup definition file, /etc/netgroup, identifies each netgroup name followed by participant tuples. Each tuple is enclosed in parenthesis and identifies the machine, user, and domain name of the netgroup participant.

The format for /etc/netgroup is as follows:

```
netgroupname1  (host,user,domain)  (host,user,domain)
netgroupname2  (host,user,domain)  (host,user,domain)
```

NIS Servers and Clients Configuration

To create an NIS master, slave, or client, invoke the SMIT FastPath **smit mkmaster**, **smit mkslave**, or **smit mkclient**, respectively after you have defined the domain name with **smit chypdom**. With AIX versions older than AIX 4.3.3 ML9, you may also have to manually create a domain name subdirectory in /var/yp/ for the map files.

The following is a quick list of SMIT options for each master, slave, and client panel.

```
# smit mkmaster ◄────────Configure this Host as an NIS Master Server
  HOSTS that will be slave servers              [slave1,slave2]
  Can existing MAPS for the domain be overwritten?   yes
  EXIT on errors, when creating master server?       yes
  START the yppasswdd daemon?                         no
  START the ypupdated daemon?                         no
  START the ypbind daemon?                           yes
  START the master server now,                       both
   at system restart, or both?


# smit mkslave ◄────────Configure this Host as an NIS Slave Server
  HOSTNAME of the master server                 [Master]
  Can existing MAPS for the domain be overwritten?   yes
  START the slave server now,                        both
    at system restart, or both?
  Quit if errors are encountered?                    Yes


# smit mkclient ◄────────Configure this Host as an NIS Client
  START the NIS client now,                          both
    at system restart, or both?
  NIS server - required if there are no         []
   NIS servers on this subnet
```

To stop, start, or check status of the NIS client **ypbind** daemon, run the following commands:

```
# lssrc -s ypbind ◀————————Will display active or inoperative
# stopsrc -s ypbind ◀————————Stops ypbind client when needed
# startsrc -s ypbind ◀————————Restarts the ypbind client as needed
```

To stop, start, or check status of the NIS server **ypserv** daemon, run the same **lssrc**, **stopsrc**, and **startsrc** commands with **ypserv** and the argument for the –s option on the target master or slave server. Other commands that will be helpful for managing you NIS environment are **ypwhich**, **ypcat**, **ypmatch**, **ypservers**, and **yppasswd** (if enabled).

Public Key Authentication

NFS authentication is implemented through the use of DES public key services. Each user in the NIS domain must have his own public and private encryption key entries in the /etc/publickey file. The system administrator defines new user entries in the file using the **newkey** command. Users update their public keys using the **chkey** command. The /etc/publickey file is then NIS-mapped to /var/yp/publickey.byname. Users' entries are identified in the files by their Net names.

```
# newkey -u username ◀————————Create user public key entry
# newkey -h hostname ◀————————Create root public key entry
# cd /var/yp; make publickey ◀————————Build NIS publickey.byname
```

The **keyserv** daemon encrypts the public keys and stores them as private keys in the /etc/keystore file. A separate file, /etc/.rootkey, is used to hold the superuser private key. This avoids problems when private keys are wiped clean during a system reboot following a crash. To initialize the keyserv server, invoke the following SMIT FastPath **smit mkkeyserv** or the **/usr/etc/yp/mkkeyserv** command.

```
# smit mkkeyserv ◀————————Start the keyserv daemon
# /usr/sbin/mkkeyserv -B ◀————————Optional command-line method
```

The **keylogin** command is used to decrypt a user's secret key, which is stored by the **keyserv** server for secure RPC operations. The **keylogin** can be added to the default system login profile. A **keyserv** entry is required to access filesystems flagged with the **-secure** option in /etc/exports and /etc/filesystems. Note that this mechanism requires synchronized clocks between participating machines. System time is used to create and expire keys stored in the server. The default secure NFS expiration is 30 minutes.

Starting NIS Services

Like NFS, NIS is managed as a subsystem under AIX. NIS daemons are started using the SRC **startsrc** and **stopsrc** commands. The /etc/rc.nfs script contains code to start up NIS services before bringing up NFS.

```
# startsrc -g nis ◀————————Start NIS
# stopsrc -g nis ◀————————Stop NIS
```

The NIS daemons are as follows:

`ypserv` ◀————————NIS server daemon
`ypbind` ◀————————NIS server binding manager
`yppasswdd` ◀————————NIS passwd update daemon
`ypupdated` ◀————————NIS map update invoked by **inetd**
`keyserv` ◀————————Public key server daemon
`portmap` ◀————————RPC program to port manager

Automounter

The **automount** daemon can be run in a large NIS network to simplify NFS filesystem access. The **automount** daemon will automatically mount a filesystem whenever a file or directory in the filesystem is opened. Files and directories associated with an **automount** filesystem are kept in an NIS map. The **automount** daemon forks child processes that appear as NFS clients that monitor filesystems drawing on the information in the maps. The daemons unmount filesystems that have not been accessed in the last five minutes. The master **automount** map file is `auto.master`.

`# /usr/sbin/automount` ◀————————Automount daemon

NIS+

NIS+ was not an enhancement to NIS. It replaced NIS. NIS+ was designed to address several shortcoming of NIS such as meeting the needs involved in managing a complex and big network, decentralizing the network administration tasks, and providing network security. You will still need both **bos.net.nis** server and client file sets installed as prerequisites for the NIS+ **bos.net.nisplus** file set.

An NIS+ namespace can be organized in hierarchical domains. Conceptually, you can think of an NIS+ namespace as like a UNIX filesystem structure, where you have a root directory and subdirectories below it. In NIS+, the root directory is called the root domain, while subdirectories are called subdomains. The depth in levels of subdomains depends on the size and complexity of your organization. The subdomains can be managed autonomously; however, clients can access information in other subdomains under the same root domain.

Another difference in NIS+ is that information for the domains is stored in NIS+ relational database tables instead of maps as in NIS. You must use a set of administrative commands provided by NIS+ to view and update the tables. The tables are kept in the directory `/var/nis/data`. Updates to the tables do not require the tables to be remade, and they are propagated to the replica servers incrementally.

NIS+ includes authentication and authorization for security. In order for a user, a host, or a process, called an NIS+ principal, to access NIS+ information, called an NIS+ object, it must be authenticated using DES (the Data Encryption Standard). After the authentication process, the principal is categorized in an authorization class (**owner**, **group**, **world**, or **nobody**) of the object. In each class, there are permissions to specify certain operations that can be done with an NIS+ object. The operations include **read**, **modify**, **create**, and **destroy**.

NIS+ provides the NIS-compatibility mode to allow NIS+ servers to response to requests from NIS clients. There are no required changes to NIS clients except in case of the domain name.

NIS+ Servers and Clients Configuration

To create NIS+ master servers and clients, invoke the SMIT FastPath **smit nisp_config** an you will see a the following menu structure much like the **smit yp** panel from the NIS configuration:

- Change NIS+ Domain Name of this host
- Configure this host as a NIS+ Master Server
- Populate the Root Master Server Tables
- Create client credentials on the server
- Configure this host as a NIS+ Client
- Remove NIS+ Server Configuration from this host
- Remove NIS+ Client Configuration from this host

AIX also provides setup scripts to set up NIS+: `nisserver`, `nispopulate`, and `nisclient`.

The `nisserver` script lets you to set up root master, non–root master, and replica NIS+ servers with level 2 security (DES). This script creates NIS+ directories and default system tables for new domains, but it does not populate them with information. You must use the `nispopulate` script to populate the tables with the files or NIS maps. These default tables are: `auto_master`, `auto_home`, `ethers`, `group`, `hosts`, `networks`, `passwd`, `protocols`, `services`, `rpc`, `netmasks`, `bootparams`, `netgroup`, `aliases`, and `shadow`. To initialize an NIS+ client, you can use the `nisclient` script, which can also be used to create credentials for hosts or users. Files that are being modified during the client initialization process are backed up as `files.no_nisplus`. The files that are usually modified during a client initialization are: `/etc/defaultdomain`, `/etc/nsswitch.conf`, `/etc/inet/hosts`, and, if it exists, `/var/nis/NIS_COLD_START`.

The following table contains a list of common NIS+ commands to manage different NIS+ components.

Command	Description
niscat	Displays object properties of an NIS+ table
nisls	Displays the contents of an NIS+ table
nisrmdir	Removes an NIS+ object from a namespace
nisrm	Removes NIS+ directories and subdirectories from a namespace
rpc.nisd	The NIS+ daemon; provides NIS+ services
nisinit	Initializes a workstation to be an NIS+ client

Command	Description
nis_cachemgr	Starts the NIS+ cache manager daemon
nisshowcache	Displays the contents of the shared cache file
nisping	Pings the replicas and prompts for updating
nislog	Displays the contents of the transaction log
nisgrpadm	Creates, deletes, and performs miscellaneous administration operations on NIS+ groups
nisdefaults	Displays the seven default values currently active in the namespace
nisaddent	Creates NIS+ tables from corresponding /etc files or NIS maps

Starting NIS+ Services

Like NIS, NIS+ is managed as a subsystem under AIX. NIS+ daemons are started using the SRC **startsrc** and **stopsrc** commands. The /etc/rc.nfs script contains steps to start up NIS+ services.

```
# startsrc -g nisplus    ◄──────── Start NIS+
# stopsrc -g nisplus     ◄──────── Stop NIS+
```

NIS+ daemons are as follows:

```
rpc.nisd         ◄──────────── NIS+ server daemon
rpc.nispasswd    ◄──────────── NIS+ passwd update daemon
nis_cachemgr     ◄──────────── NIS+ cache manager daemon
```

TROUBLESHOOTING

Complex distributed services like NFS and NIS present a real debugging puzzle when things run amok! Based on the symptoms and error messages associated with the problem, begin examining each component of the system. Refer to Chapter 13 for details on debugging network problems.

Begin troubleshooting problems by listing and verifying the current set of client mounts known to the server. The client mount list is recorded in /etc/rmtab and is displayed using the **showmount** command.

```
# showmount -a
asimov:/usr/local/gnu
asimov:/usr/local/bin
asimov:/usr/local/lib
softy:/n0
softy:/n1
```

The **showmount** command can also be used to verify the list of exported directories as recorded in the /etc/xtab file. This information should match up with the entries in /etc/exports. If the data doesn't match, invoke **exportfs -a** to refresh /etc/xtab.

```
# showmount -e
/usr/lpp/info/En_US alph, lisa
/n1    softy
/n0    softy
/usr/local/gnu    asimov
/usr/local/lib    asimov
/usr/local/bin    asimov
```

NFS I/O statistics can be reset and displayed using the **nfsstat** command. Statistics include the number and success of RPC and NFS calls for both servers and clients. Check to see if you have a high number of time-outs and retransmissions. You may need to increase the number of **nfsd** and **biod** threads on the server and client using **chnfs** command.

RPC errors like "Application Not Registered" are related to the **portmap** daemon. Check to see that the **portmap** daemon is running on both the local and remote systems. You can also verify the application, version, protocol, and port data maintained by local and remote **portmap** daemons using the **rpcinfo –p <hostname>** command.

Verify that the **srcmstr** daemon is aware of the current NFS and NIS subsystems' and subservers' states. Erratic behavior will occur if the SRC environment is out of sorts. Subsystem and subserver states can be displayed using the **lssrc** command.

```
# lssrc -g nfs
Subsystem         Group           PID      Status
 biod             nfs             9034     active
 nfsd             nfs             9296     active
 rpc.mountd       nfs             9554     active
 rpc.statd        nfs             10580    active
 rpc.lockd        nfs             10838    active
```

Since small deltas in client/server response times can add up quickly for large NFS environments, you may want to closely monitor traffic between systems. You can easily collect statistics with network sniffers or by using a public domain package like **nfswatch**.

To display and set the NFS options in the kernel, use the **nfso** command; **nfso –a** displays the configurable NFS options and their current values.

HIGHLY AVAILABLE SERVERS

If you have been dealing with IBM for any number of years, you have surely heard of "Reliability, Availability, and Serviceability" (RAS). To remain competitive in the glass-house environments, UNIX must provide the same 7×24 availability that has been the hallmark of operating systems like MVS. The proliferation of X stations and diskless workstations in departmental computing environments means that there are a whole lot of folks out there who are depending on those RS/6000 and pSeries servers to be ready wherever they are.

Like everyone else, I hate any system interruptions. Whenever a system or service drops out of sight, I want that service back as quickly as possible. The sooner it is back up and running, the happier I am going to be. A highly available system should be able to survive a single point of failure and impose only the minimum required delay while service recovery transitions occur. For more information on highly available server see Chapter 28 on HACMP.

High-Availability Network Filesystem

One of the problems with NFS is that when the NFS server goes down, so do all your applications and workstations that were depending on the server's filesystems. The High-Availability Network Filesystem (HANFS) provides an extension to standard NFS services that allows a second pSeries or RS/6000 machine to act as a backup NFS server should the primary NFS server fail. HANFS can be configured such that each machine may be acting as a primary NFS server for distinct filesystems while acting as a backup server for the other, the primary requirement being that the systems share physical connections to external SSA disks and additional network adapters (see the illustration). Note that the shared disks volume groups are online only to the primary NFS server and that internal disks are not supported.

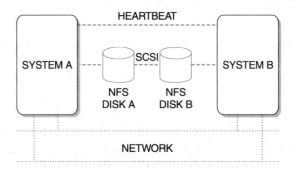

HANFS makes use of the server's RPC cache information and the journaled file system (JFS) logs to enable NFS server recovery on the backup system. The primary server's NFS RPC cache information is recorded in the JFS logs and is read by the backup server to reconstruct the cache.

During normal operation, the HANFS servers periodically exchange keep alive messages. When the primary NFS server fails, the backup server takes over the volume groups and checks their consistency. It rebuilds the duplicate cache from the information stored in the JFS logs and begins impersonating the failed server's network IP address. NFS locks are then resynchronized by stopping the **rpc.lockd** daemon from accepting new locks while the **rpc.statd** daemon requests all NFS clients to reclaim their locks. After a grace period, the **rpc.lockd** daemon begins to accept new lock requests. Other than the notification to reclaim filesystem locks, remote NFS clients experience only a short delay while server recovery procedures are completed. Recovery time after a server failure is somewhere in the neighborhood of 30 to 300 seconds.

HANFS also supports the automatic reintegration of the primary server once the problem failure has been rectified and the system is back online. Basically, the procedure described in the previous paragraph is reversed, and the servers go back to doing their old jobs. Note that no changes to standard NFS client software is required to make use of HANFS services. HANFS will work fine with your Sun, HP, DEC, and other standard (grain of salt here) NFS clients and servers.

CHECKLIST

The following is a checklist for the key points in Networked Filesystems: NFS, NIS, and NIS+:

- ☐ Define a virtual filesystem (VFS).

- ☐ Identify the client/server architecture that is the basis for NFS.

- ☐ Define the NFS server and identify its design.

- ☐ Improve performance by using the NFS clients to implement client-side data caching.

- ☐ Simplify system administration by using Network Information Services NIS to centralize the information about systems and users in a network.

- ☐ Begin troubleshooting problems by listing and verifying the current set of client mounts known to the server.

- ☐ Use the High-Availability Network Filesystem (HANFS) to provide an extension to standard NFS services that allows a second RS/6000 or pSeries to act as a backup NFS server should the primary NFS server fail.

- ☐ Share NFS server CPU cycles and memory between all operating system components.

CHAPTER 15

Distributed File System

In the late 1980s, the Open Software Foundation (OSF) went looking for a network-based filesystem architecture to overcome some of the limitations inherent in Sun NFS. The filesystem had to be stateful to support access control and locking better in a distributed environment. Improvements in caching, replication, and cloning were desired to improve performance and availability. A centrally managed directory structure was needed to enforce a common filesystem view between participating systems yet not restrict flexibility and access. All of these are features exhibited by the Andrew File System (AFS) architecture. So, the OSF selected AFS V4 from the Transarc Corporation as the basis for its Distributed Computing Environment (DCE) Distributed File System (DFS) technology.

Conceptually, DFS is enhanced AFS. The major differences involve the tight integration of DFS with the other DCE services, and the underlying DCE local file system (LFS). DFS requires a larger number of support daemons than are normally used with AFS and far more than with NFS. Users who are familiar with AFS will be able to adapt to the DFS semantics easily. Systems Administrators will require a little more homework in order to configure and activate all the DCE services on which DFS depends, as well as manage the DFS environment itself. My intent in this chapter is to provide a cursory overview of AIX DFS. Proper treatment of the subjects of AIX DFS and AIX DCE easily requires an entire book in itself. I hope to at least get you started. Here is a bit of history first.

Andrew File System

In order to impose additional levels of authentication and administration and to improve the scalability of NFS, Carnegie Mellon University developed the Andrew File System (AFS). AFS, now a product of the Transarc Corporation, uses a remote procedure call mechanism called RX to support client/server interactions. AFS uses the Kerberos V4 authentication system to validate client access to remote filesystems. AFS introduces the notion of a cell, which defines the administrative domain over filesystems in the shared space. A consistent view of the shared filesystem space is provided using a common root tree, /afs. Subtrees for each cell follow the root using the cell name /afs/cellname/. Note that no restriction is placed on mount points or naming under NFS. AFS cells are identified by a database called CellServDB.

AFS security is further enhanced through the use of Access Control Lists (ACLs). ACLs extend the standard UNIX file permissions to provide a finer degree of granularity on access rights. AFS uses the first four UNIX permission bits to define read, lookup, insert, write, delete, lock, and administer (rliwdka) permissions. Note that AFS ACLs apply to only the directory levels of a filesystem. AFS also uses a UserList to define access rights and mapping. Users gain access to the AFS shared file space via the **klog** command, which grants them a Kerberos ticket for access. They can release their rights via the **unlog** command. Under AFS, the standard path can no longer be used to access files on the server.

Another important enhancement for distributed filesystems is that AFS separates the logical filesystem structure from the disk blocks used to contain the filesystem. AFS volumes may contain one or many filesystem hierarchies. The volumes are made up of partitions that are collections of disk blocks identified by the special name, `vicepN` (`N=a,b,c,..`). AFS also improves client cache consistency using a callback mechanism to invalidate data blocks that have been modified. Release-level filesystem replication is also supported by AFS.

General Parallel File System

The General Parallel File System (GPFS) for AIX is a shared disk filesystem. It was released in 1998 as a software simulation storage area network under the name Virtual Shared Disk (VSD). GPFS is basically a parallel disk filesystem guaranteeing availability of the entire filesystem to all nodes within a cluster, allowing simultaneous write access to a single striped file from multiple nodes. This can provide major benefits for parallel and sequential programs. GPFS is distributed to all the nodes in a cluster, providing an extended kernel interface to AIX and the virtual filesystems. System calls to AIX, from the applications, are translated to GPFS, which uses local resources or transfers them to a daemon that completes the task with buffer and I/O management much like a filesystem. The primary environment for GPFS, which is highly scalable, is the RS/6000 SP with a high-speed switch network and HACMP with shared clusters of concurrent direct attached disks. Many high performance computing facilities use GPFS for temporary storage in large parallel computation workspace. DFS now provides the kernel extensions that enable GPFS data to be exported. With DFS consistency protocols, a filesystem may be exported from only one node, whereas NFS can export the same GPFS data from multiple nodes, possibly providing higher throughput.

Distributed File Service

The Distributed File Service, a distributed filesystem, takes the features offered by AFS and marries them with other OSF DCE services to compose a tightly integrated client/server computing environment. DFS relies on other DCE services to coordinate communication, access control, and synchronization. These services include the DCE Remote Procedure Call (RPC), DCE Security Service, DCE Global and Cell Directory Service, and DCE Distributed Time Service. These DCE servers must be configured and started before you can begin working with DFS. IBM's DCE V3.1 and DFS V3.1 are now sold separately and come with subtle packaging changes that were needed to synchronize the AIX and Solaris distributions. Table 15-1 breaks down the DFS file sets to show some of the packaging changes.

NOTE   Throughout this chapter are references to "file sets" that are Licensed Program Products as in Table 15-1 and "filesets" that are components of the DFS Local File System. This confusion will only persist in this chapter.

Application	DFS V3.1	DCE/DFS V2.2
DFS Client Services	dfs.client	dce.client.dfs.rte
DFS Server	dfs.server	dce.dfs_server.rte
Enhanced DFS with Local File System	dfs.server	dce.edfs.rte
NFS to DFS Authenticating Gateway	dfs.nfsauth	dce.dfsnfs.rte
DFS GPFS for AIX Support	dfs.gpfs.rte	N/A
DFS Storage Management Runtime	dfs.sm.rte	N/A
DFS Privacy Level Protection Feature	dfs.priv	dce.priv
DFS HTML Documentation	dfs.html.en_US	dce.doc.en_US.html

Table 15-1. DFS V3.1 vs. V2.2 File Sets

Access Control

Administrative domains called *DCE cells* delegate access control. Principals in a cell authenticate themselves via the DCE security service based on MIT Kerberos v5. Unfortunately, the AFS Kerberos v4 security service and the DCE Kerberos v5–based security service are not interoperable, making migration from AFS to DFS a bit of a chore. ACLs are used in DFS and apply to both directories and files. DFS modifies the standard UNIX file permission bits to support read, write, execute, control, insert, and delete permissions (rwxcid). The UNIX permission bits reflect the ACL permissions when viewed with standard commands like **ls -l**. DFS users are identified uniquely and globally to the DCE environment, so problems with UID and GID collisions are eliminated.

Filesystem Structure

DFS shared filesystem trees are also similar to AFS in that a common root is identified with the next lower level delimited by cell name. The DFS shared root is named / . . ., and cell subdirectories follow as / . . . / cellname /. The shorthand strings "/ . :" and "/ : " indicate the local cell and root fileset respectively. Clients need only mount root "/ . . ."–level DFS space to access all filesets exported by DFS file servers in the cell space. The following compares AIX and DFS path syntax that refers to the same relative home/username/ .kshrc file.

AIX	DFS
/home/username/.kshrc	/.../cellname/fs/home/username/.kshrc
	/.:/fs/home/username/.kshrc
	/:/home/username/.kshrc

A DFS filesystem mount point is similar in concept to a UNIX filesystem or NFS mount point. However, rather than using a directory as the mount point, DFS uses an object as the mount interface. To mount a DFS filesystem, use the **fts** *crmount* command.

```
# fts crmount -dir [PathName] -fileset [FilesetName | FilesetID]
```

As an end user, you will not be able to tell the difference between a mount point directory and a mount point object. Use the **fts** *lsmount* command to see if a directory serves as a mount point for a fileset.

```
# fts lsmount -dir /.:/fs/home
```

DFS is a cached filesystem. Frequently accessed files and directories are cached on the client either in memory or on disk. Client cache consistency is maintained via a token-passing mechanism complete with callback for synchronizing shared access to file metadata. DFS servers control the rights to file access tokens that must be acquired by a client before modifying data. DFS also supports both scheduled and release (manual) filesystem replication.

You can also export an AIX CD-ROM filesystem from a DFS File Server. The exported CD-ROM filesystem can be mounted into the DFS file space and accessed from DFS client machines.

Local File System

In order to gain the full benefit of DFS services and take advantage of access control lists, you must use the DCE Local File System (LFS) as the underlying physical filesystem for DFS. The LFS architecture consists of *aggregates* that are analogous to UNIX disk partitions and *filesets* that are collections of related files and directories. LFS directories are called containers, which hold other containers (subdirectories) and LFS objects, better known as files.

LFS is a log-based filesystem similar to the AIX Journaled File System (JFS). All filesystem metadata updates are grouped and logged as atomic transactions. Groups of transactions against a single object are also grouped into an equivalence class to facilitate recovery. The transaction equivalence class ensures that either all or none of the updates will be applied during system recovery.

DFS filesets may be moved between LFS aggregates while maintaining online access via a procedure called fileset cloning. Space must be available in the partition to build a copy of the fileset. The cloned fileset is marked "read only" and kept up to date via copy-on-write procedures until the move is complete. Filesets may also be replicated. Think of this as somewhat like cloning between computers over a network. Cloning and replication along with logging and dynamic aggregate sizing provide a highly available filesystem architecture that is quite easy to administer.

Table 15-2 is a comparison of Local File Systems and non-LFS.

Local File System	Non-LFS (Journaled File System)
rw/ro/backup for each fileset	Only rw filesets
Multiple filesets per aggregate	One fileset per aggregate (JFS)
DCE ACLs	

Table 15-2.   DFS Local File System vs. DFS Non-LFS

VFS Compatibility

Any virtual file system (VFS) that has been enhanced to support DCE VFS can be exported by DFS file servers. DFS also provides an NFS/DFS Authenticating Gateway to provide DFS filesystem access to NFS clients. An NFS client may have difficulty working with DFS ACLs in the exported filesystem because it does not have a way to get a DCE context. The following is what you can do to set default ACLs that open this security exposure:

```
# acl_edit /.:/[PathName] -m any_other:rwxcid
# acl_edit /.:/[PathName] -ic -m any_other:rwxcid
# acl_edit /.:/[PathName] -io -m any_other:rwxcid
# acl_edit /.:/[PathName]/[EachFile] -m any_other:rwxcid
```

The NFS to DFS Authenticating Gateway maintains DCE credentials on behalf of NFS clients to satisfy ACL permission restrictions. To use this feature, install the `dfs.nfsauth.rte` and `dfs.nfsauth.smit` file sets. AFS and NFS may also be used independently on a DFS file server. Given these capabilities, you should be able to easily integrate DCE DFS into existing NFS and AFS environments.

DFS COMPONENTS

As already mentioned, DFS requires a number of servers for coordinating filesystem activities in a cell. These servers can be distributed and in some cases replicated across a number of machines, or they can be run on a single computer. I would not recommend the latter unless you are running a very small cell. The cluster of DFS servers includes

- The System Control Machine (SCM) is responsible for housing and distributing the administration lists. These lists determine which principals (users and machines) can issue requests to the DFS servers. The group of servers managed by the SCM is called its *domain*. The SCM must be configured before any other DFS servers. Administrative lists managed by the SCM are stored in `/opt/dcelocal/var/dfs`. The two server processes that run on the SCM are **bosserver** and **upserver**. The **bosserver** process is the basic overseer server, which runs on all DFS machines. The **upserver** process distributes administration lists to other DFS machines.

- The Binary Distribution Machine distributes /usr/lpp/dce/bin executables to other server machines in the cell of the same architecture (CPU/OS). The binary distribution machine runs the same **upserver** process as used by the SCM. In this case, **upserver** distributes the DFS binaries. You can also use the binary distribution machine to distribute non-DFS binaries.

- The Fileset Database Machine (FLDB) runs the **flserver** process, which is responsible for maintaining information on all filesets available in a cell. All DFS file servers must register their filesets with the FLDB. The FLDB maps pathnames to the associated file server and make this information available to DFS clients. Since the FLDB is essentially a directory name server, it is a good idea to run multiple FLDB systems. Implement an odd number of FLDB servers because the machines vote to see who will be primary and who will be secondary. Primary servers are RW. Secondaries are RO copies. The vote from the server with the lowest network IP address carries more weight in case one of the servers is down. Like the other servers, the FLDB also runs **bosserver** and **upclient**.

- The File Server Machine runs the fileset exporter **fxd**, which makes filesets available to DFS clients. AIX filesets can include LFS, non-LFS, and CD-ROM types. Along with **fxd**, the file server also runs the fileset server **ftserver**, the directory and security process **dfsbind**, and **upclient** to receive administration lists and binaries. Principals and groups with fileset authority are listed in the admin.ft admin list. A token manager is associated with each file server to track access to metadata. A special server called the Private File Server can be run by a workstation user who would like to export his or her own filesets. This is handled independent of the SCM.

- The Fileset Replication Machine manages fileset replication in a domain. It is primarily responsible for handling scheduled replication. Replicas improve availability of critical filesets in a domain.

- The Backup Database Machine (BDM) manages the dump schedules of all the fileset families requiring backup services. The backup database machine interacts with the Tape Coordinators to access dump devices. This is a critical resource, so you should run more than one BDM. The **bakserver** process is responsible for maintaining backup information on the BDM. You guessed it: There is a **bosserver** and an **upclient**.

- The Tape Coordinator Machine (TCM) controls physically attached dump devices and makes them available for use by the BDM. The TCM may actually run on the same computer as a BDM. This would save you a **bosserver** and an **upclient**, for instance.

- DFS clients access filesets exported by the DFS file servers. A client contacts the FLDB to find the DFS file server that is exporting the desired fileset. Each client runs a copy of **dfsd**, which manages the cache on the client and synchronizes the cache against the DFS file servers. A client also runs the **dfsbind** process that interacts with the DCE cell directory service, security service, and FLDB to resolve path names to file servers.

- Aggregates are similar to UNIX partitions. Each aggregate can contain multiple filesets. Aggregates under AIX are logical volumes that have been formatted as a DCE LFS using the **newaggr** command.

- Filesets are collections of related files and directories administered as a unit under DCE/DFS. DCE quotas are applied at the fileset level. A fileset name and ID number identifies each fileset. The fileset ID number is two positive integers separated by two commas. Quotas in DFS are applied at the fileset level in 1K increments. Filesets can be RW, RO, or backup. A backup fileset is a clone (snapshot) of an active fileset used for backup purposes.

- The Local File System (LFS) is a log-based filesystem that supports all the features available under DFS. This includes DCE ACLs, replication, quotas, and multiple filesets per aggregate.

INSTALLATION AND CONFIGURATION

This discussion assumes that you have already installed and configured DCE services (this is described in Chapter 24). At a minimum, you will need a DCE Cell Directory Server, a DCE Security Server, and three Distributed Time Servers. Each DFS client or server must also be configured as a DCE client or server. The message "Cannot configure DFS components until a CDS clerk (cds_cl) is configured" is the first clue that DCE is not working. Chapter 24 covers important details and system considerations needed before installing DCE and DFS file sets as well as ongoing housekeeping.

You will need to install the following DCE clients in addition to one or more of the DFS file sets shown earlier in Table 15-1:

```
dce.client.rte           DCE Client
dce.client.smit          DCE SMIT Client Tools
dce.msg.en_US.client.rte  DCE Base Client Messages
dce.msg.en_US.client.smit DCE SMIT Base Messages
```

After installing the required DCE and DFS file sets, you can use SMIT to configure the base DFS servers by invoking the **mkdcesrv** FastPath. Command-line tools are available for administering DFS; however, their detailed explanations are beyond the scope of this chapter. The majority of the AIX online documentation concerning DCE and DFS may be accessed through SMIT Help or the F1 key from SMIT.

If you have already configured your Distributed Computing Environment (see Chapter 24 for details on doing this), then you will know and need the following information before you proceed:

```
Cell Name
Security Server Name
CDS Server Name (if in a separate network)
Cell Administrator's Account (and password)
LAN Profile
```

You will be prompted for the DCE cell administrator's password from time to time as you configure each service. This should have been set when you installed and configured the base DCE services (see Chapter 24 for assistance). The SMIT (or SMITTY) panels for DFS are organized into a menu tree hierarchy. The following list illustrates the SMIT FastPath associated with various SMIT panels needed to configure DFS as explained in this chapter.

```
FastPaths—Panel Menu Tree
 none      # System Management
 commo      # Communications Applications and Services
 dce         # DCE (Distributed Computing Environment)
 mkdce         # Configure DCE/DFS
 mkdcesrv       . # Configure DCE/DFS Servers
 mkdfsscm      . . # DFS (Distributed File Service) System Control Machine
 mkdfsfldb     . . # DFS Fileset Database Machine
 mkdfssrv      . . # DFS File Server Machine
 mkdfsrepsrv   . . # DFS Fileset Replication Server Machine
 mkdfsbkdb     . . # DFS Backup Database Machine
 mkdceclient   . # Configure DCE/DFS Clients
 dfsadmin      # DFS (Distributed File Service) Administration
 dfsjfs        . # Add / Delete JFS File Systems
 dfscdrom      . # Add / Delete CDROM File Systems
 dfslfs        . # Add / Delete LFS Aggregates and Filesets
 mkdfsaggr     . . # Export and Aggregate from the Local Machine
 mkdfsft       . . # Create a Fileset in an Aggregate on the Local Machine
 dfs_acl       . # ACLs (Access Control Lists) for DFS LFS Directories and Files
 dfsnfs        # NFS to DFS Authenticating Gateway Administration
```

System Control Machine

The first thing to do is to configure one or more SCMs. Each SCM will control an individual domain in the cell. Select "DFS (Distributed File Service) System Control Machine" from the SMIT menu list or use the FastPath **mkdfsscm**. If the DCE client has not been configured on this machine, then just enter the cell name, enter the machine's DCE hostname, select Yes for Start Components And Clean Up At System Restart, select the MASTER SECURITY server, select Yes to Synchronize Clock, and enter the hostname of the Timer Server. After verifying that the Cell Administrator account name is correct, press ENTER, and supply the *cell_admin* password when prompted. The minimum DCE clients will be started along with **upserver** and **bosserver**. Figure 15-2 highlights this important information needed with the following SMITTY panel:

```
# smitty mkdfsscm ◄————SMIT FastPath
```

Fileset Database Machine

Now configure the Fileset Database (FLDB) on the same Machine. Multiple FLDBs will improve availability and share the workload of client requests but will cause major configuration headaches for beginners. Select "DFS Fileset Database Machine" from the SMIT menu list or use the **mkdfsfldb** FastPath. The DFS System CONTROL machine identification field should be left blank if you want this machine to maintain its own administration list. This field is ignored if this machine is configured as SCM. The GROUP to administer filesets is where you may add other groups to administer this machine, in addition to the principals and groups listed in admin.ft, to administer all machines. After verifying that the Cell Administrator account name is correct, press ENTER and supply the *cell_admin* password when prompted. The minimum DCE clients will be started along with **flserver** and **bosserver** if needed. The following SMTTY panel will look just like Figure 15-1 with two more fields at the bottom.

```
# smitty mkdfsfldb  ◄────── FastPath for DFS Fileset Database Machine
```

File Server Machine

One or more DFS file servers will be required to export DFS aggregates and filesets. Choose the DFS File Server Machine option from the SMIT menu list or use the

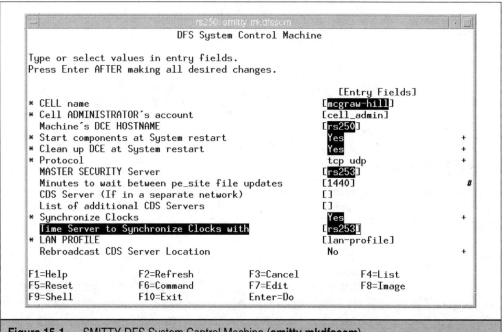

Figure 15-1. SMITTY DFS System Control Machine (**smitty mkdfsscm**)

FastPath **mkdfssrv**. After verifying that the information and Cell Administrator account name are correct, press ENTER and supply the *cell_admin* password when prompted. The minimum DCE clients will be started along with **ftserver**, **fxd**, **dfsbind**, and **bosserver** if needed. You should be able to accept all the defaults in the following SMITTY panel (see Figure 15-2):

```
# smit mkdfssrv       ◄────────FastPath for DFS File Server Machine
```

Start the DFS Client

At this point, you may want to start a DFS client on the local machine to help verify the results of the following filesets you will be creating. User the SMIT FastPath

Figure 15-2.   SMITTY DFS File Server Machine (**smitty mkdfssrv**)

mkdceclient, but select dfs_cl for "CLIENTS to configure" if the base DCE clients are already running on this machine. You may select both all_cl and dfs_cl on remote DFS client machines that do not have DCE clients configured. Use the following command and select Full when prompted, then refer to Figure 15-3 and take all the defaults not highlighted in the following SMITTY panel:

```
# smitty mkdceclient          ◄────────FastPath to Full DCE/DFS Client Configuration
```

You should now be able to see the DFS shared root with the following **df** command:

```
# df /...
Filesystem 512-block    Free %Used  Iused %Iused Mounted on
DFS         18000000 18000000   0%      0    0% /...
```

Creating and Exporting Aggregates

Create an aggregate logical volume to hold the LFS filesets. User the **mklv** command to create a logical volume with type set to lfs in the target volume group. This lfs type

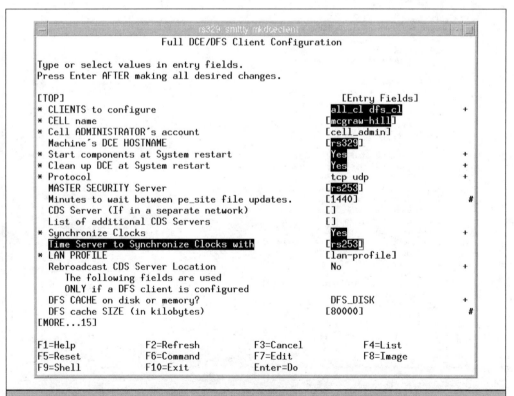

Figure 15-3.   SMITTY Full DCE/DFS Client Configuration (**smitty mkdceclient**)

definition instructs the **mklv** command to create an Episode File System, but that is just a small part of the aggregate processing. The following command will make a logical volume named **lvlfs01** of type lfs with 100 logical partitions and mirrored (**-c 2**):

```
# mklv -y lvlfs01 -t lfs -c 2 VolumeGroupName 100
```

Use the SMIT FastPath **mkdfsaggr** to format and export the aggregate. You may also want to tune the aggregate blocksize to match the intended use of the filesystem. For example, use a small blocksize for filesystems that will hold many small files. This SMIT processing will run **newaggr** and **mkdfslfs** with standard output listing their command-line arguments. User the following command, select Yes when prompted to INITIALIZE Device and refer to Figure 15-4 for details on naming, formatting, and exporting the aggregate:

```
# smitty mkdfsaggr          ◄───────── FastPath to Export an Aggregate from the Local Machine
```

A line entry is placed in the `/opt/dcelocal/var/dfs/dfstab` file for each new aggregate. Use the following **df** command to see the new device mounted for export:

```
# df /dev/lvlfs01
Filesystem  ... Mounted on
/dev/lvlfs01 ... /opt/declocal/var/dfs/aggrs/lfs01
```

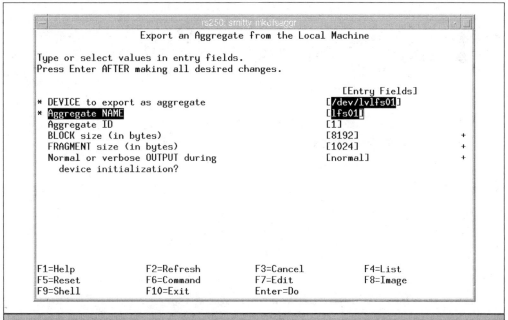

Figure 15-4.   SMITTY Export An Aggregate From The Local Machine (**smitty mkdfsaggr**)

Creating and Mounting Filesets

You are now ready to create the root fileset in your new aggregate. This first fileset created must be named `root.dfs`. User the SMIT FastPath **mkdfsft** as the interface to the `mkfilesys.dfs` script, and the fileset name `root.dfs` will appear by default if it has not been created. Refer to Figure 15-5 as you run the following command and press the F4 key in the AGGREGATE field for aid in selecting **lfs01**, which you exported earlier. Do not define a mount point for this first root.dfs fileset. It will be `/.:/fs` by default.

```
# smitty mkdfsft
```
◄──────── FastPath to Create a Fileset in an Aggregate on the Local Machine

Let us examine this new `root.dfs` fileset before we continue. After you press ENTER to create the `root.dfs` fileset in the **lfs01** aggregate, it will not become available until the next Cache Manager refresh. In the following example, we can use the **ls** command to show that `/.:/fs` does not exit until we manually refresh the Cache Manager with the **cm** command or wait until the next scheduled refresh.

```
# ls /.:/fs
```
◄──────── Examine mount point before the Cache Manager refresh
```
ls: 0653-341 The file /.:/fs does not exist.
```

```
# cm checkf
```
◄──────── Refresh the Cache Manager with checkfilesets option
```
All backup filesets checked.
l
# ls /.:/fs
```
◄──────── Examine the mount point after the Cache Manager refresh
```
ls: /.:/fs: The file access permissions do not allow the specified action.
```

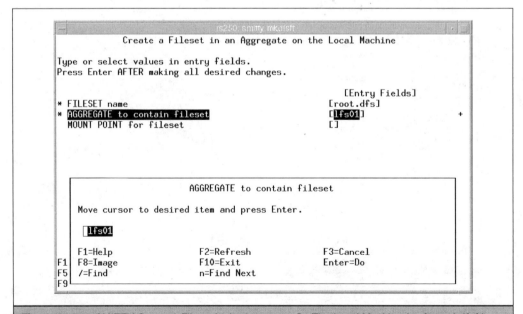

Figure 15-5. SMITTY Create A Fileset In An Aggregate On The Local Machine (**smitty mkdfsft**)

Now the mount point is there, and we just need permission to access it. Use the commands in the following example to examine, authenticate, and change the permissions before you try to create directories or files or to mount more filesets:

```
# ls -ld /.:/fs    ◄──────────Examine the original permissions
drwx------ 2 140 103   256 may 27 16:50 /.:/fs/

# dce_login cell_admin  ◄──────────Log in as the Cell Administrator (again if needed)
# klist | grep Prin  ◄──────────Check to make sure you are now cell_admin
# chmod 777 /.:/fs  ◄──────────Change permissions to open read-write access

# ls -ld /.:/fs  ◄──────────View the new permissions
drwxrwxrwx 2 140 103   256 may 27 16:50 /.:/fs/
```

You can export newly created aggregates and create filesets either from the SMIT dfslfs panels or with the `mkfilesys.dfs` script. Along with making the aggregate and fileset available to clients, this script will also register the exporter in the FLDB. Note that exporting an aggregate makes all the filesets it contains available to clients. Once a fileset has been exported, it can be mounted using **fts crmount**. Let's create and mount the home.dfs fileset with the following commands:

```
# mkfilesys.dfs -file_system_type lfs -fileset home.dfs \
      -aggregate_name lfs01 -mount_point /.:/fs/home
# fts delmount -dir /.:/fs/home  ◄──────────Unmount
# fts crmount -dir /.:/fs/home -fileset home.dfs  ◄──────────Remount
```

The default permissions for a fileset are `rwx------` (`700`). You may wish to modify these permissions using **acl_edit** after mounting. Also verify that the fileset quota is sufficient. Check and set the fileset quota with **fts lsquota** and **fts setquota**, respectively.

```
# acl_edit /.:/fs/home -l  ◄──────────List all the ACL object for the fileset
# acl_edit /.:/fs/home -m group_obj:rwxcid other_obj:rx  ◄──────────Modify
# fts lsquota -path [PathName]  ◄──────────Check quota
# fts setquota -path [PathName] -size [KB]  ◄──────────Set quota
```

Fileset Replication Server Machine

The Replication Server (**repserver**) stores read-only fileset replicas, keeps track of how current replicated data is, and updates it at the replication sites. Select **DFS Fileset Replication Server Machine** from the SMIT menu list or invoke the SMIT **mkdfsrepsrv** FastPath and supply the cell_admin password when requested. This is all that is required to start the replication server on the system.

```
# smitty mkdfsrepsrv  ◄──────────FastPath to Fileset Replication Server
```

Backup Database Machine

To perform periodic DFS backups, create one or more DFS backup database machines. You can select **DFS Backup Database Machine** from the SMIT menu list or invoke the SMIT **mkdfsbkdb** FastPath. After you complete the SMIT information and option execution, the system will be configured to run the **bakserver** process.

```
# smitty mkdfsbkdb  ◄────────FastPath to Backup Database Machine
```

Installation Verification

After completing configuration of the DFS service machines, verify the configuration from each participating system with the following **lsdce** and **lsdfs** commands:

```
# lsdce -r
        Component Summary for Host: rs250
      Component              Configuration State   Running State
Security client                 Configured            Running
RPC                             Configured            Running
Directory client                Configured            Running


# lsdfs -r
        Component Summary for Host: rs250
      Component              Configuration State   Running State
DFS client                      Configured
  dfsd                          Configured            Running
  dfsbind *                     Configured            Running
DFS File server                 Configured
  fxd                           Configured            Running
  dfsbind *                     Configured            Running
  bosserver *                   Configured            Running
  ftserver                      Configured            Running
DFS System Control Machine      Configured
  upserver                      Configured            Running
  bosserver *                   Configured            Running
DFS Fileset Database            Configured
  flserver                      Configured            Running
  bosserver *                   Configured            Running
 * - denotes daemons that are used by more than one component.
```

Next, verify aggregates, filesets, and exports using the following **fts** and **dfsexport** commands:

```
# fts lsaggr -server rs250
There is 1 aggregate on the server rs250 (rs250.mcgraw-hill.com):
```

```
              lfs01 (/dev/lvlfs01): id=1    (LFS)

# fts lsft -fileset root.dfs
_____

root.dfs 0,,1 RW LFS    states 0x10010005 On-line
  rs250.mcgraw-hill.com, aggregate lfs01 (ID 1)
  Parent 0,,0    Clone 0,,2    Backup 0,,3
  llBack 0,,0     llFwd 0,,0    Version 0,,1
    Infinite alloc limit;      9 K alloc usage
      5000 K quota limit;      9 K quota usage
  Creation Mon May 27 16:50:48 2002
  Last Update Mon May 27 16:50:48 2002
  11 reads, 0 writes in 36779 seconds since Mon May 27 16:50:48 2002
  0.000299084 reads per second; 0 writes per second.

root.dfs
    readWrite   ID 0,,1 valid
    readOnly    ID 0,,2 invalid
    backup      ID 0,,3 invalid
number of sites: 1
  server        flags   aggr  siteAge principal  owner
rs250.mcgraw-hill.com  RW   lfs01  0:00:00 hosts/rs250 <nil>
_____


# dfsexport
Aggregate Device  Name   Type  Aggr ID  Non-LFS fileset ID
/dev/lvlfs01    lfs01  lfs   1
```

OPERATION AND ADMINISTRATION

We have already covered a number of the commands used to administer DFS. Each of the DFS commands supports enough options and parameters that the permutations and combinations are well beyond what can be covered in a single chapter. Table 15-3 lists the base commands with a short description and the following command-line help syntax will provide brief listings of available options for most of those commands.

```
# CommandName help [option]  ◄────────Display command help
# CommandName option -help   ◄────────Handy alternative help
```

Command	Description
mkdfs	Create DFS components
rmdfs	Remove DFS components
lsdfs	List DFS components
bak	Manage backup system
bos	Bosserver access
cm	Cache manager control
dfsexport	Export aggregates and filesets
fts	Manage filesets
growaggr	Expand aggregates
newaggr	Create aggregates
salvage	Check LSF integrity
scout	Monitor exporters

Table 15-3.   DFS Administration Commands

STARTING DFS

All DCE and DFS services can be started from the /etc/inittab file at system boot. The clean_up.dce script should always run before any other DCE services. Then the rc.dce script should start before any remaining DCE or DFS services. DFS V3.1 comes with a dedicated SMIT panel to add all the needed entries to /etc/inittab except dceinuxd that must me added manually (dceunixd is detailed in Chapter 24). Unfortunately, the current release configures the clean_up.dce script to start in the wrong order. So until this problem is fixed, use the SMIT **mkdceitab** FastPath and select the services you want started at boot time. Just make sure you check the resulting /etc/inittab entries with the **grep** command that follows and edit the file to correct the order. Use the **who -d** command after reboot to check the return code from each /etc/inittab command (the *respawn* entries will not display).

```
# smit mkdceitab  ◄────────FastPath to Start DCE and DFS services
```

```
# grep -e dce -e dfs /etc/inittab
cleanupdce:2:wait:/usr/bin/clean_up.dce
rcdce:2:wait:/opt/dcelocal/etc/rc.dce all
dceunixd:2:respawn:/usr/bin/dceunixd -l 60 -d 1 >/dev/console 2>&1
rcdfsnfs:2:wait:/opt/dcelocal/etc/rc.dfsnfs
```

```
# who -d | grep -e dce -e dfs -e clean
  . . May 29 23:53   0:09   1994 id=cleanup term=0 exit=0
  . . May 29 23:56   0:09   1996 id=rcdce  term=0 exit=0
  . . May 30 00:00   0:09   13756 id=rcdfsnf term=0 exit=0
```

ACCESS CONTROL LISTS

Just a few words about DCE ACLs: They work a bit differently than what you may expect from dealing with standard UNIX permissions. ACLs are applied to containers and objects. DFS containers are directories that contain objects (files) or other containers. By default, directories and files inherit the container ACL of the directory under which they reside. You can set specific ACLs for users, groups and others using the **acl_edit** command. ACLs are very nice in that the owning user can set them up. You as a Systems Administrator only have to worry about system default ACLs that are required to ensure general security. Remember that ACLs apply only to LFS filesets.

ACLs are associated with object types **mask_obj**, **user_obj**, **group_obj**, and **other_obj**. The **mask_obj** entry is used to filter the maximum set of permissions that can be granted by object types. It cannot be used to increase or extend permissions (see Tables 15-4 and 15-5).

```
$ acl_edit [PathName] -m [ACL_obj:rwxcid]  ◄─────── Modify ACLs
$ acl_edit [PathName] -1  ◄─────── List ACLs
```

The **any_other** entry is used for users who are not authenticated to the local cell.

Token	Description
r	Read enabled
w	Write enabled
x	Executable or Directory accessible
c	Control Access
i	Insert: create new files in directory
d	Delete: remove files from directory
io	Initial object: default directory ACL for file creation
ic	Initial container: default subdirectory ACL for file creation

Table 15-4.   ACL Permissions and Defaults

Type	Effect
user_obj	The user who owns the object
user	The user "username" from the local cell
foreign_user	The user "username" from the foreign cell "cell_name"
group_obj	Members of the group who own the object
group	The group "group_name" from the local cell
foreign_group	The group "group_name" from the foreign cell "cell_name"
other_obj	Users from the local cell who do not match any preceding entries
foreign_other	Users from the foreign cell "cell_name" who do not match any of the preceding entries
any_other	Users from any foreign cell who do not match any of the preceding entries
mask_obj	Mask for maximum permissions that can be set, except for group_obj and other _obj

Table 15-5.   ACL Object Types and Effects

FILESET REPLICATION

DFS replication is a handy tool for managing common filesystem trees across a number of machines when availability requirements will not allow network mounting. A replicated fileset should be a group of files that are not modified often. Good candidates for replication include operating system commands and application binaries. Replicas are created from a RW master copy. Each replica fileset is RO. Replicas are updated either at scheduled intervals or at manually called releases. To create a replica, begin by setting the replication information and site list on the machine with the master copy of the fileset.

```
# fts setrepinfo [-release | -scheduled]  ◄────── Source replica type
# fts addsite  ◄────── Source sitelist update
```

On the target machine(s), first create an aggregate large enough to hold the replica and update the site list.

```
# fts addsite  ◄────── Client sitelist update
```

If you chose scheduled replication, then the fileset will be replicated at the interval you indicated. For release replicas, you can manually start replication using the fts release option.

```
# fts release  ◄────── Manual replication
```

Note that replication improves availability by making multiple copies of a fileset available to clients. The client cache manager will select RO replicas when acquiring a mount point unless RW is specified.

DFS BACKUP

DFS has its own backup system that keeps track of tapes, dump dates, backup sets, and other types of fileset recovery information. You cannot perform dumps using standard UNIX dump commands due to DFS specific metadata like ACLs. A non-LFS fileset mounted on the local system can be backed up using standard UNIX tools, since non-LFS filesets do not have ACLs. Note that you can use standard UNIX tools in a DFS environment to create archives like **tar** and **cpio**; however, no ACL information is stored in the archive.

The DFS dump process begins by taking a snapshot of an active filesystem called a *clone*. The clone is not a copy of the data, but rather a set of pointers to the data blocks that made up the filesystem at the time the clone was made. Users may continue to actively use the filesystem while the clone is traversed for backup purposes. This eliminates the problem of backing up an active filesystem where an inode may be invalid due to updates in progress.

```
# fts clone -fileset [FilesetID]   ◄————————Clone a fileset
# bak dump -family [FilesetFamily] -tcid [DevID]  ◄————————Start a dump
```

The **bak** command is used to configure, dump, and track dump status. DFS backup supports both full and incremental dumps. The DFS **bak** command is another one of the commands that is best left to more extensive documentation concerning its vast number of options. Run **bak help** to see all the options.

CHECKLIST

The following is a checklist for the key points in Distributed File System:

- ☐ Define DFS.
- ☐ Identify the DFS Components.
- ☐ Obtain a DCE Cell Directory Server, a DCE Security Server, and three Distributed Time Servers.
- ☐ Configure each DFS client or server as a DCE client or server.
- ☐ Identify the DFS commands.
- ☐ Start all DCE and DFS services from the /etc/inittab file at system boot.
- ☐ Apply ACLs to containers and objects.
- ☐ Define DFS replication.
- ☐ You cannot perform dumps using standard UNIX dump commands due to DFS specific metadata like ACLs.

PART VII

Linux Affinity

CHAPTER 16

Linux Affinity with AIX

IBM embraces the open source and GNU movement by adding the capability to run many Linux applications on the highly scalable AIX operating system. The *AIX Toolbox for Linux Applications* is a collection of software that will run on AIX 4.3.3 and AIX 5L systems installed on IBM pSeries and RS/6000 models. Linux application developers are comfortable working with the AIX Toolbox for Linux Applications. The tools are easy to install using the RPM format. With the addition of the software and development tools, IBM has introduced a bold affinity between Linux and AIX applications. In most cases, it is easy to rebuild your Linux applications on the AIX platform.

RUNNING LINUX APPLICATIONS ON AIX 5L

IBM uses a two-phase approach for the implementation of Linux affinity into AIX. The first phase came with the release of the AIX Toolbox for Linux Applications, which was released with AIX 4.3.3 at maintenance level 8. The second phase is to provide additional application program interfaces (APIs) and header files with each subsequent AIX 5L release. These additional APIs allow you to bring your Linux source code over to your AIX 5L machine and recompile the program to create an AIX application. Each recompiled Linux application is treated as an AIX 5L application, which comes with the additional reliability, availability, and scalability that AIX provides.

You can get the latest installation procedure and download the latest version of the Toolbox packages at the following URL:

```
http://www.ibm.com/servers/aix/products/aixos/linux/
```

There is an excellent IBM Redbook called *Running Linux Applications on AIX* that goes into great detail about installing the Linux Toolbox and compiling and running Linux code on AIX. This Redbook can be downloaded for printing in either an HTML or PDF format at this URL:

```
http://www.redbooks.ibm.com/redbooks/SG246033.html
```

Contents of the AIX Toolbox for Linux Applications

Not only can you compile Linux applications on AIX, but you can also install a large variety of Linux native applications from the AIX Toolbox for Linux. You can change the user interface to run GNOME and KDE, instead of CDE or the command line. The list of native Linux applications that reside on the CD-ROM is too large to cover here; a sample is given in Table 16-1.

The list in Table 16-1 displays a few of the tools and programs in the AIX Toolbox for Linux. In the next section, we cover installing the Toolbox on an AIX machine.

Installing the AIX Toolbox for Linux Applications

Before you install the toolbox, you must ensure that you have enough disk space for the installation. Unlike when using SMIT or **installp**, you do not have the option when

Package	AIX Platform	Description
bison	Power/IA-64	GNU parser generator
cdrecord	Power/IA-64	Command-line CD/DVD recording program
cvs	Power/IA-64	A version control system
emacs	Power	The emacs editor
enscript	Power/IA-64	ASCII-to-PostScript converter
flex	Power/IA-64	Tool to create scanners for pattern recognition
gcc	Power	GNU gcc C compiler
g++	Power	GNU gcc C++ compiler
gbd	Power	GNU gcc debugging tool
ghostscript	Power	PostScript interpreter and renderer
gnome	Power	GNOME GUI desktop environment
gnuplot	Power/IA-64	For plotting mathematical expressions and data
jabber	Power	Instant messaging system
kde	Power	K desktop environment
lsof	Power	Lists open files
php	Power/IA-64	The PHP scripting language
python	Power/IA-64	Interactive object-oriented programming language
rpm	Power/IA-64	Red Hat package management tool
samba	Power/IA-64	Samba client and server package
sudo	Power/IA-64	Allows restricted root access for defined users
tk	Power/IA-64	tk toolkit with the shared libraries
wget	Power/IA-64	Retrieves files using FTP and HTTP protocols
xfig	Power	Tool for drawing vector graphics
zsh	Power	Shell based on ksh with enhancements

Table 16-1.   Short List of the Linux Toolbox for AIX

installing the Toolbox to automatically extend the filesystem on the fly. On AIX 5L, the Toolbox is installed in the /opt filesystem. Table 16-2 shows the space requirements for the various components of the Toolbox.

The space requirements listed in Table 16-2 may expand with new releases of the Toolbox. If you want to change your desktop to either GNOME or KDE, make sure that three additional AIX filesets are installed: **X11.adt.lib**, **X11.apps.xdm**, and **X11.samples.apps.clients**. The quickest method to check for these installed filesets is to use the **lpp -L** command.

```
# lslpp -L X11.adt.lib  X11.apps.xdm  X11.samples.apps.clients
```

Description	Group for ezinstall	Space Requirement
Base Linux support	base	12MB
Common programs for the desktop	desktop.base	15MB
GNOME base	gnome.base	80MB
GNOME applications	gnome.apps	80MB
KDE base	kde.base	170MB
KDE applications	kde.opt	80MB
GNU application development		200MB
Total Space Requirement		**637MB**

Table 16-2. AIX Toolbox for Linux Space Requirements

If any of the listed products are missing, you need to install the packages from the AIX installation media. Do not forget to reinstall the patch set for the current maintenance level in case modifications have been made. The maintenance-level code is installed by using the SMIT FastPath **smitty update_all**.

On the next screen, you are prompted for the location of the maintenance code; for example, if it is located on a CD-ROM inserted in /dev/cd0, then enter the device name. If the code is located in /usr/sys/inst.images, then enter the system path. If you do not want to commit the software updates, but instead install the patch set in an applied state, follow this procedure: in the SMIT panel set the **COMMIT Software Updates?** field to **No**, and set the **SAVE Replaced Files?** field to **Yes**. Then press the ENTER key twice to install the software.

Red Hat Package Manager (RPM)

Before installing the whole AIX Toolbox for Linux, you must first install the Red Hat Package Manager (RPM). This fileset must be installed as a traditional AIX fileset using **installp**, SMIT, or WebSM. The quickest method is to use **installp** on the command line. First, change directory to the CD-ROM mount point, for example, /cdrom. In this case, you need to change directory to the installation directory /cdrom/INSTALLP/ppc. Use the following **installp** command:

```
# cd /cdrom/INSTALLP/ppc
# installp -qacXg -d . rpm.rte
```

or use the SMIT FastPath **smitty install_latest**

On the first SMIT screen, you are prompted for the location of the code to install. If your CD-ROM is mounted as /cdrom, use the path /cdrom/INSTALLP/ppc. You can leave the **Software To Update** field set to **_update_all**, since the RPM package is the only fileset in this directory.

This installation will take several minutes because the installation will query the system for information about currently installed shared libraries on the system. If you want to download the latest `rpm.rte` fileset, go to the following FTP site:

```
ftp://ftp.software.ibm.com/aix/freeSoftware/aixtoolbox/INSTALLP/ppc
```

The user ID is *anonymous* if you need one; and, if a password is needed, it will be your e-mail address. The download method is binary. You can also get the latest versions of the prebuilt RPM packages from this web site.

The man page directory for the Toolbox is located in `/opt/freeware/man`. To add this path to the MANPATH variable, use the following syntax:

```
# export MANPATH=$MANPATH:/opt/freeware/man
```

Or, you can add this MANPATH to your `$HOME/.profile` or to the system profile located in `/etc/profile`.

Installing the Toolbox Base Filesets

Now that RPM is in place, we can install the remaining packages. The first step is to see which packages are already installed on the system. The following RPM command will give you the installed package list:

```
# rpm -qa
```

At this point, you will probably see only three RPM packages. Before installing the rest of the packages, ensure that you have provided adequate disk space; space requirements are listed earlier in Table 16-2. To install all of the base RPM packages, perform the following steps:

```
# cd /cdrom/ezinstall/ppc
# rpm -hiv */*
```

or

```
# rpm -hiv base/* desktop*/* kde*/* gnome*/*
```

The preceding commands install all the RPM packages. The ezinstall packages include **base**, **gnome.apps**, **kde2.all**, **kde2.opt**, **desktop.base**, **gnome.base**, and **kde2.base**. If you are not planning to change your desktop to either KDE or GNOME, then you can save a lot of disk space by installing only the **base** ezinstall package.

Installing the Toolbox Utilities and Programs

In the preceding section, we installed only the Toolbox base filesets. To install the rest of the Toolbox Linux utilities and programs, use one of the following commands:

```
# cd /cdrom/RPMS/ppc   ◄─────── For AIX 5L
```

or

```
# cd /cdrom/RPMS/ppc-4.3.3   ◄──────── For AIX 4.3.3
```

Now you are in the directory containing all of the programs and utilities for your AIX version. To install *everything,* issue the following command:

```
# rpm -hiv *
```

However, if you want to install individual programs and utilities, you can use the following technique.

To install all of the **apache** filesets, issue the following command:

```
# rpm -hiv apache*
```

To install all of the filesets for **emacs** and **samba**, issue the following command:

```
# rpm -hiv emacs* samba*
```

You can also install individual filesets you find in this directory. To install the **gzip** program, issue the following command:

```
# rpm -hiv gzip-1.2.4a-5.aix4.3.ppc.rpm
```

In most cases, you can also install other RPM packages that you find for PowerPC (ppc) Linux. Each of the programs and utilities on the CD-ROM has a man page associated with it. So, if you have any questions, there is a lot of documentation in the man pages.

Desktop Environments

Within the AIX Toolbox for Linux Applications, you have the ability to change the desktop environment to either KDE or GNOME, both of which are standard Linux desktops. With the ability to change desktops, any user who is comfortable with Linux can feel at home.

GNOME Desktop   The GNOME desktop environment is designed to run on any UNIX-like operating system. The GNOME desktop provides an easy-to-use Windows-based user environment with a rich set of applications, libraries, and tools. The GNOME project has also produced the GNOME Office suite of office programs.

Once you install GNOME, using the Red Hat Package Manager (RPM), you need to follow these steps to start using GNOME. The first step is to edit the .xinitrc file in your $HOME directory. If you do not have one, then copy the default file to your $HOME directory using the following command:

```
# cp /usr/lpp/X11/defaults/xinitrc  $HOME/.xinitrc
```

The second step is to edit the $HOME/.xinitrc file. Remove the last three lines of the file, which look like the following:

```
xsetroot -solid grey60
aixterm =80x25+0-0 &
exec mwm -multiscreen -xrm "ShowFeedback: -quit"
```

In place of these three lines, insert the following line:

```
exec /usr/bin/gnome-session
```

If your default desktop environment is CDE, then from the **CDE Desktop Login Panel**, select **Command Line Login** as the login type. At the command line, type the following command:

```
# xinit -- -T    # This will only work from the Low Function Terminal (lft)
```

To start your desktop on a remote X server that allows access, use the following commands:

```
# DISPLAY=X.SERVER.IP.ADDRESS:0
# export DISPLAY
# startx
```

For more information on using and configuring GNOME, see the man page:

```
# man gnome
```

Also see the GNOME and GNU Web sites at the following URLs:

```
http://www.gnome.org/
http://www.gnu.org/
```

KDE Desktop   Like GNOME, the K Desktop Environment (KDE) is a free desktop environment for all UNIX-like operating systems. The desktop has a look and feel similar to the desktops you see with Mac OS, Windows 95/NT, and (to some extent) the Common Desktop Environment (CDE). With the KDE installation comes an excellent set of office applications known as the KOffice suite. This office suite combines word processing, spreadsheets, and presentation programs into a single package.

KDE is installed using the Red Hat Package Manager (RPM), as all of the Toolbox tools and applications are installed. Once the KDE desktop is installed, there are two ways to start it. You can start KDE from the command line or edit the /etc/initab file to start KDE as the default user interface.

From the command line, edit the $HOME/.xinitrc file to add the following block of code to replace the last three lines of the file:

```
 [[ -z "$SESSION" ]]  && SESSION=failsafe
case $SESSION in
  kde)
        export PATH=/opt/freeware/kde/bin:$PATH
```

```
        exec /opt/freeware/kde/bin/startkde ;;
   CDE)
        exec /usr/dt/bin/Xsession ;;
   gnome)
        exec /opt/freeware/bin/gnome-session ;;
   failsafe|*)
        aixterm -geometry 80x35+0-0 -ls &
        exec mwm ;;
esac
```

If your system is running CDE, from the **Desktop Login Panel**, select **Command Line Login** as the login type. Then enter the following command:

```
# export SESSION=kde
# xinit -- -T     # This will only work on the Low Function Terminal (lft).
```

The second option is to start KDE from the display manager. First, kill any CDE sessions on the system, making sure that there are no users currently using the sessions, and then start the KDE display manager (**kdm**). Use the following two commands:

```
# ps -ef | grep dtlogin | grep -v grep | awk '{print $2}' | xargs kill -9
# /opt/freeware/kde/bin/kdm
```

If you want the system to always use KDE on each system reboot, replace the dt entry in the /etc/inittab file as follows.

Remove this entry:

```
dt:2:wait:/etc/rc.dt
```

Add this entry:

```
kdm:2:wait:/opt/freeware/kde/bin/kdm
```

Now KDE is the default desktop environment each time the system reboots. For more information on KDE, check out the following URL:

```
http://www.kde.org/
```

Instant Messaging for AIX

With the AIX Toolkit for Linux comes Jabber. Jabber is an instant messenger program that is similar to Yahoo! Messenger, AOL Instant Messenger, MSN Instant Messenger, and ICQ. Jabber is different in that it expands into wireless communications, Internet infrastructure, and embedded systems.

Jabber is an XML-based open source system and protocol that enables real-time communications between logged-on users and can be used to notifify you of other messenger users who are currently logged on. The Jabber project was started in 1998 by Jeremie Miller. The Jabber.org project continues with about a dozen main contributors and many more doing testing and writing code for new clients.

Jabber server software is licensed under the Jabber Open Source License. Jabber clients are licensed with the vendors of the various client software packages. Please refer to the documentation for licensing details.

The Jabber software is installed in the `/opt/freeware/jabber` directory. To start the Jabber server, use the following command:

```
# /opt/freeware/jabber/jabberd/jabberd -h host.domain.name &
```

You can also edit the `jabber.xml` file and, in the `<host>` section, change the `<localhost>` to your machine's fully qualified hostname. By adding the local hostname in the `jabber.xml` file, you avoid having to specify the name on the command line using the **-h** parameter. To see debugging output while troubleshooting, use the **-D** switch when you start the Jabber daemon.

I must leave the details of using Jabber to you. The documentation for Jabber can be found at the following URL:

```
http://docs/jabber.org/
```

STRONG LINUX AFFINITY WITH AIX

IBM's move into the Linux and System V worlds evinces a broader-based approach to UNIX as a whole. In AIX 5L, as another example, the System V printer subsystem is available as a replacement for the classic AIX printer subsystem. Linux affinity, too, is just a natural progression in IBM's plan to be a major player in every market. The evolution in e-business is responsible for this first push toward a more centralized platform for information sharing and intercommunications. In the present phase, IBM has acknowledged the emergence of Linux into the mainstream and embraced the movement into the open source and GNU world.

With AIX 5L, IBM has expanded Linux affinity to include Linux application source compatibility. These efforts expand on emerging Linux standards that allow for deployment of Linux applications on AIX. All of these efforts allow Linux programs to be easily recompiled into native AIX applications.

The topic of Linux affinity with AIX is too broad to expect complete coverage in one chapter in one book. The Redbooks at `http://www.redbooks.ibm.com/` provide the latest information for the Linux tools available under AIX. The list keeps expanding, and you are invited to bring all of your Linux source code to your AIX machine and make each Linux program into a native AIX application.

I wish I could go into more detail in this chapter, but the most complete and up-to-date information on this topic is to be found at the IBM Web site. Please refer to each of the URLs presented in this chapter for a more comprehensive look at recompiling and running Linux applications on AIX 4.3.3 and AIX 5L, and configuring your AIX machine to use the KDE and GNOME desktops.

CHECKLIST

The following is a checklist for the key points in Linux on AIX:

☐ You can compile Linux applications on AIX, and you can also install a large variety of Linux native applications from the AIX Toolbox for Linux. You can change the user interface to run GNOME and KDE, instead of CDE or the command line.

☐ Before installing the whole AIX Toolbox for Linux, you must first install the Red Hat Package Manager (RPM). This fileset must be installed as a traditional AIX fileset using **installp**, SMIT, or WebSM.

☐ Once you have installed RPM, check to see which packages are already installed on the system with the command **rpm-qu**.

☐ Before you install the AIX Toolbox for Linux, you must ensure that you have enough disk space for the installation. Unlike when using SMIT or **installp**, you do not have the option when installing the Toolbox to automatically extend the filesystem on-the-fly.

☐ If you are not planning to change your desktop to either KDE or GNOME, then you can save a lot of disk space by installing only the **base** ezinstall package and not **gnome.apps**, **kde2.all**, **kde2.opt**, **desktop.base**, **gnome.base**, and **kde2.base**.

☐ If you install the GNOME package using RPM, before you can use GNOME, you need to edit the `.xinitrc` file in your `$HOME` directory, remove the last 3 lines, and replace them with `exec/usr/bin/gnome-session`.

☐ If you install the KDE desktop, there are two ways to start it. You can start KDE from the command line or edit the `/etc/initab` file to start KDE as the default user interface.

☐ The AIX Toolkit for Linux comes with Jabber, an instant messenger program similar to Yahoo! Messenger, AOL Instant Messenger, MSN Instant Messenger, and ICQ.

PART VIII

Distributed Services

CHAPTER 17

Mail and Sendmail

Electronic mail is one of the most popular features of the Internet. For corporate users, e-mail is often considered the most critical service of the information technology department. If a backup server fails, someone might notice; if the e-mail system fails, everyone will notice. Immediately. This chapter will review the way e-mail is transported on the Internet, describe the e-mail software and services available for AIX, and explain how to configure, debug, and use this software.

The electronic mail or e-mail system is conceptually if not physically divided into three components: the mail user agent (MUA), the mail delivery agent (MDA), and the mail transfer agent (MTA).

```
/bin/mail or /usr/ucb/mail ◄──────── Mail user agent
/usr/bin/bellmail ◄──────────────── Mail delivery agent
/usr/sbin/sendmail ◄─────────────── Mail transfer agent
```

Almost all hosts on a network will need to implement these. Even special-purpose systems without end users will require them if the server, and its applications, will use e-mail to communicate on the network. The MTA configuration section emphasizes this multifunctional nature of mail transportation. We will examine five key MTA roles: a spoke, a client, a hub, a gateway, and a fallback server. In addition to traditional MUAs, MDAs, and MTAs, many network environments support an additional mail remote delivery protocol; the most common are the Post Office Protocol (POP) and the Internet Message Access Protocol (IMAP). These hosts are referred to in configuration examples throughout this chapter.

Mail Transfer Agents

The *mail transfer agent* is responsible for receiving and delivering mail. At a minimum, the MTA must be able to accept mail from MUAs and the network, decipher addresses, and deliver the message to a local user mailbox or to a remote MTA. Better MTAs will be able to detect e-mail loops, route a single mail message for multiple recipients at the same site, support privacy, and route problem mail to a site postmaster. Common MTAs include **sendmail**, **qmail**, **smail**, and **exim**. The following sections cover **sendmail** configuration and administration; **sendmail** is the MTA shipped by IBM with the base AIX operating system.

Mail User Agents

The *mail user agent* provides the user interface to the mail system. The MUA presents incoming mail to the user for reading and archiving. Editor facilities for composing, forwarding, or replying are managed by the MUA. The ATT and BSD **mail** programs are the classic UNIX command-line MUAs to send and receive mail. For many end users, full-screen and graphical user interfaces like Netscape Navigator, Pine, or Ximian Evolution have replaced these utilities in everyday use. In addition to an intuitive interface, these GUIs often directly support mail delivery protocols such as POP and IMAP. However, command-line MUAs remain important, even in an environment where end users have advanced graphical interfaces, because they can be used easily in shell scripts to automate system reporting. Command-line utilities are also handy for debugging MTA configuration issues.

In the following sections, where reference is made to an MUA, assume basic UCB mail functionality and options. Default configuration options for this program are defined via the /usr/lib/Mail.rc file. Each user may override the global defaults by resetting the options in a local $HOME/.mailrc file. The following is a configuration file for MUA:

```
# /usr/lib/Mail.rc
# Options
set ask askcc dot save keep crt
# Don't display the following header lines
ignore Received Message-Id Resent-Message-Id
ignore Status Mail-From Return-Path Via
```

Mail Delivery Agents and Protocols

While **sendmail** will queue mail for delivery and route mail to other systems, it does not actually deliver the mail to the end user. For this task, **sendmail** relies on a *mail delivery agent (MDA).* Using an external program for delivery allows for greater flexibility in supporting both legacy systems and evolutionary change. In this way, **sendmail** supports UUCP users (a legacy system) and **procmail** users (a newer delivery agent that supports greater user customization). Although not included in the AIX base operating system, **procmail** is provided free from IBM on the *AIX Toolbox for Linux Applications* CD-ROM detailed in Chapter 16. In the **sendmail** configuration file, the MDA is referred to as a MAILER, and **bellmail** is the default MDA for local delivery.

Additional remote mail delivery protocols, POP and IMAP, have become very popular. These protocols allow mail users the potential to access their mailboxes from any computer on the network, regardless of hardware architecture or operating system. The difference between them lies in how they treat the mailbox: POP implements a distributed mailbox, pulling new messages from a central server; IMAP implements remote access to a centralized mailbox. IMAP makes the central mailbox available to the users, keeping both read and unread messages in the central location. POP typically allows the user to download new messages to whatever computer that user happens to be using at that moment, never to be available again from any other computer. For this reason, IMAP is more popular in open campus environments. POP and IMAP daemons are distributed with recent versions of the AIX base operating system.

SENDMAIL COMPONENTS

The standard MTA on AIX is **sendmail** (version 8.11 as of AIX 5.1). The **sendmail** program was originally written by Eric Allman at the University of California, Berkeley, in the 1970s. At the time, networking at UCB was heterogeneous and evolving, as it likely was everywhere. This evolution has left **sendmail** rich with features for delivering mail in such an environment, and these features have added to the complexity in configuring **sendmail**. Fortunately, the Simple Mail Transport Protocol (SMTP) has emerged as a standard on the Internet, making many of these features obsolete. The **sendmail** MTA is probably still the most common MTA in use today. The `/etc/mail/sendmail.cf` file is the primary location of configuration data.

Sendmail Files

The **sendmail** MTA uses the following files for configuration and data:

```
/etc/mail/sendmail.cf  ◄─────── Sendmail configuration file
/etc/mail/aliases  ◄─────── Mail aliases
/etc/mail/aliases.db  ◄─────── Compiled alias file
/etc/mail/sendmail.pid  ◄─────── PID of sendmail daemon
/etc/sendmail.pid  ◄─────── Link to sendmail.pid file
/etc/mail/statistics  ◄─────── Mail statistics
```

The **sendmail** configuration file, `/etc/mail/sendmail.cf`, contains the majority of the options and rules required by **sendmail** to deliver e-mail. The `sendmail.cf` file maintains three sets of configuration data:

- Options, variables, and parameters
- Address rewriting rule sets
- Mailer identification and delivery

AIX V5 supplies a boilerplate `sendmail.cf` file that can be used with minimal changes if your e-mail environment is not complex. By complex, I mean that you have a number of mail gateways to other networks or a hierarchy of MTAs. You should not use this default configuration if your server is connected directly to the Internet, because it allows promiscuous relaying. Specific configuration examples are covered in a later section.

Commands and definitions begin in column 1 in the `sendmail.cf` file. Comments begin with a number sign (#). Blank lines are ignored. Due to the number of special characters used, you need to be careful when adding address types like DECNETS "::" node delimiters. A set of predefined character symbols are used to indicate the definition of new symbols, classes, options, macros, or rules. Using a dollar sign ($) with a macro or variable name indicates the value of the variable or macro. A question mark (?) indicates a Boolean test. In the following discussion, I'll define the symbols used in each section of the `sendmail.cf` file and provide an example.

Options and Definitions Section

The first section of the `sendmail.cf` file identifies the runtime options and variables. These include definition of the host or domain name, the status of name service mail exchange support, message precedence, and so on. Option symbols are as follows.

"D" defines a symbol from text or a built-in variable:

`DSfoo.bar.com` ◄─────── Define subdomain as variable S

"C" defines a class from a list:

`CFhost1 host2 host3` ◄─────── Define a host list as variable F

"F" defines a class from a file:

`FF/usr/local/lib/hosts` ◄─────── Obtain list F from hosts file

"H" defines header formats:

`H?P?Return-Path: <$g>` ◄─────── Define return-path format

"O" sets **sendmail** runtime options:

`OA/etc/aliases` ◄─────── Define alias file path
`OK ALL` ◄─────── Support all nameservice mail exchange records and host table lookups

"T" sets trusted users:

`Tusername1 usernamer` ◄─────── Users trusted to invoke sendmail and
                                    masquerade as other users

"P" sets message precedence:

`Ppriority=100` ◄─────── Indicate delivery priority if precedence:header field is found.
`Pjunk=100`   Negative numbers do not return mail on error

Address Rules Section

The **sendmail** daemon uses rule sets to parse the address lines from the mail header to determine how the mail message should be delivered. Each rule set is made up of three parts: left-hand side (LHS), right-hand side (RHS), and optional comment (C). Any two parts are separated by a tab. In general, if an address matches the LHS rule, then the RHS rule is applied to the address. The rule sets are applied in order until a failure occurs. Any number of rule sets can be defined (see Tables 17-1 and 17-2).

Rule	Description
3	Applied first and is responsible for making the address canonical to internal form.
2	Rewrites recipient address.
1	Rewrites sender address.
0	Applied last and determines delivery. Address must be resolved to a (mailer, host, user) tuple.
4	Final rewrite of canonical internal form to external form.

Table 17-1.   Default sendmail.cf Rule Sets

To deliver a mail message, the rule sets must resolve to a (mailer, host, user) tuple. The following example shows a rule set of a seven-parses domain string:

```
S7
#Domain addressing (up to 6 level)
R$+@$-.$-.$-.$-.$-.$-  @$2.$3.$4.$5.$6.$7
R$+@$-.$-.$-.$-.$-     @$2.$3.$4.$5.$6
R$+@$-.$-.$-.$-        @$2.$3.$4.$5
R$+@$-.$-.$-           @$2.$3.$4
R$+@$-.$-              @$2.$3
R$+@$-                 @$2
```

Mailer Delivery Section

The last section of the `sendmail.cf` file identifies the mailers to be used to deliver the mail message. Each mailer is identified by a name, a program used to transfer the

LHS Tokens		RHS Tokens	
$*	Match 0 or more tokens	$n	Use token *n* from LHS
$+	Match 1 or more tokens	$>n	Call rule set *n*
$-	Match exactly 1 token	$#mailer	Resolve to mailer
$=X	Match any token in class X	$@host	Specify host to mailer
$~X	Match any token not in X	$:user	Specify user to mailer
		$[host$]	Get host from resolver
		$@	Terminate rule set
		$:	Terminate current rule

Table 17-2.   Rule Set Symbols

messages to the mailer, the set of program flags, the send and receive rules, and the argument set. The mailer identification format is as follows:

```
M<mailer> P=<prog> F=<flags> S=<send-rule> F=<receive-rule> A=<arguments>
```

The following is an example of a local and X.400 RFC 987 mailer definition:

```
Mlocal, P=/bin/bellmail, F=lsDFMmn, S=10, R=20, A=mail $u
M987gateway, P=/usr/lpp/osimf/etc/x400mailer, F=sBFMhulmnSC, S=15, R=25,
        A=gateway -f/etc/x400gw.cfg $f$u
```

The **sendmail** program accesses configuration file information from a compiled version of the /etc/sendmail.cf table. To compile a new version of the database, use **sendmail** with the **-bz** flag.

```
# /usr/lib/sendmail -bz  ◄───────── Compile a new sendmail.cf database
```

Configuration with m4

The authors of **sendmail** have devised another means of configuring **sendmail**, m4 macros. While **sendmail** permits almost limitless flexibility in rule writing, in practice, the same few rules are used repeatedly across most installations. The **bos.net.tcp.adt** fileset includes a repository of these common configurations stored as m4 macros, allowing mail administrators to simply include the prepared definition when building a sendmail.cf file. To follow this methodology, you first edit a sendmail.mc file located in the /usr/samples/tcpip/sendmail/cf directory, adding the features and rules that you wish to use. Then simply compile the file.

```
# m4 sendmail.mc > sendmail.cf
```

This method was actually used by IBM in creating the default sendmail.cf, as indicated by the comments in the file. One advantage of this approach is the simplicity of the sendmail.mc file. While a sendmail.cf file might be 20 pages long, the associated sendmail.mc file is usually less than 20 lines. The m4 approach allows multiple administrators to maintain a mail system without each needing to study a 20-page configuration. The m4 approach even supports local rules sets. Documentation of all of the defined m4 macros is located in /usr/samples/tcpip/sendmail/README.

Sendmail Databases

The **sendmail** configuration file uses resource files when routing and addressing mail messages. A few of the more important ones are

```
/etc/mail/aliases  ◄─────── Mail aliases
/etc/mail/local-host-names  ◄─── ── Domains accepted as local
/etc/mail/mailertable  ◄─────── Domain to MDA map
```

```
/etc/mail/virtusertable  ◄——————— Virtual user to real user map
/etc/mail/genericstable  ◄——————— Real user to virtual user map
```

Aliases Database

The **sendmail** aliases database provides a mechanism for forwarding mail to one or more users when mail is addressed to the alias name. In particular, you will want to set up aliases for the site postmaster and MAILER-DAEMON IDs. The postmaster account is a standard used by the network at large for requesting mail help and information for a site. The MAILER-DAEMON account is used by **sendmail** to route problem mail. The following is an example of /etc/aliases:

```
##
#  Aliases in this file will NOT be expanded in the header from
#  Mail, but WILL be visible over networks or from /bin/mail.
#
#       >>>>>>>>>>  The program "sendmail-bi" must be run after
#       >> NOTE >>  updating this file before any changes
#       >>>>>>>>>>  show through to sendmail.
##
# Alias for mailer daemon
MAILER-DAEMON:root
#
# The Following alias is required by the new mail protocol, RFC 822
postmaster:root
#
# Aliases to handle mail to msgs and news
msgs: "|/usr/ucb/msgs -s"
nobody: "|cat>/dev/null"
#
# Alias for uucp maintenance
uucplist:root
#
### These are local aliases ###
trouble:    root
root:  deroest
```

    sendmail accesses alias information from a **dbm** version of the /etc/aliases table. To compile a new version of the /etc/aliases table, use **/usr/lib/sendmail -bi**.

```
# /usr/lib/sendmail -bi  ◄——————— Create new alias database
```

STARTING AND STOPPING SENDMAIL

IBM ships a working configuration file with **sendmail**. While this configuration is sufficient to start **sendmail** as a stand-alone system on a network, it is strongly discouraged if the server has a direct connection to the Internet. Do *not* use this configuration on systems that connect directly to the Internet without disabling promiscuous relaying of mail. Promiscuous relaying will be exploited by third parties who wish to send bulk junk mail at your expense.

The **sendmail** program is invoked as a subsystem from the /etc/rc.tcpip script. The AIX **sendmail** automatically compiles the /etc/mail/aliases and /etc/mail/sendmail.cf files when it is started. If you are running a non-IBM-supplied **sendmail**, you may need to force a compile of these files as part of the start-up.

If you update any of the configuration information while **sendmail** is running, refresh the **sendmail** subsystem by issuing an SRC **refresh** command or by sending the daemon a SIGHUP.

```
# refresh -s sendmail
# kill -1 'head -1 /etc/sendmail.pid'
```

The basic startup flags for **sendmail** should invoke **sendmail** as a daemon and specify the time in minutes between mail queue scans for postponed messages. These flags are **-bd** and **-q<time>**.

```
# /usr/lib/sendmail -bd -q30m   # Start and scan mail queue every 30 minutes
```

To stop the **sendmail** daemon, use the SRC **stopsrc** command or send a SIGABORT to the daemon.

```
# stopsrc -s sendmail
# kill -6 'head -1 /etc/sendmail.pid'
```

To restart the stopped server, use the SRC **startsrc** command. (Note that starting **sendmail** with **startsrc** requires an additional parameter.)

```
# startsrc -s sendmail -a'-bd -q30m'
```

To check the status of the **sendmail** daemon, use the SRC **lssrc** command.

```
# lssrc -s sendmail
```

MAIL LOGS

It's a good idea to keep logs of **sendmail** activity. They are very helpful in diagnosing problems, identifying slow mail loops, and sleuthing connections from remote sites. Note that **sendmail** logs activities using **syslogd**. The default log file location per /etc/syslog.conf is the /var/spool/mqueue/syslog file. The following is a sample excerpt from **syslog**:

```
Aug 9 13:19:01 daffy sendmail[146022]: AA146022:
  message-id=<9308092018.AA05836 @mx1.cac.washington.edu>
Aug 9 13:19:01 daffy sendmail[146022]: AA146022:
  from=<MAILER@UWAVM.U.WASHINGTON.EDU>, size=1731, class=0,
  received from mx1.cac.washington.edu (140.142.32.1)
Aug 9 13:19:02 daffy sendmail[51047]: AA146022:
  to=<deroest@daffy.cac.washington.edu>, delay=00:00:02, stat=Sent
```

Because the log file tends to grow rapidly, you need to periodically close it and archive it. This procedure can be handled via **cron** and the /usr/lib/smdemon.cleanu script. The script closes the syslog file and copies it to a log.<n> file for archiving. The default root crontab contains an entry for smdemon.cleanu. However, it is commented out. Remove the comment and replace the crontab to activate log file clean-up:

```
45 23 * * * ulimit 5000; /usr/lib/smdemon.cleanu > /dev/null
```

CONFIGURATION EXAMPLES

This section demonstrates various **sendmail** configurations that meet specific roles across several computers on a network. The scenario is as follows:

Wine University would like to offer mail to all of its staff and students. The campus is broken down into departments, and the departments have many of their own computing resources. The university would like everyone to have an e-mail address of the form user@wine.edu. These users will access their mailboxes remotely using the IMAP protocol. The only exception to this policy is the computer science and engineering department. The computer scientists have lobbied to run their own mail server and have e-mail addresses of the form user@cse.wine.edu. For security reasons, no server on the campus network will connect directly to the Internet except gateway.wine.edu; all mail servers are required to relay outbound mail through the gateway system. Wine's sister university, Whiskey, has agreed to act as a fallback mail host for the wine.edu domain. Figure 17-1 details this network topology.

Hosts on the campus network use the following DNS configuration:

```
192.168.100.3          english.wine.edu
192.168.100.4          biology.wine.edu
192.168.100.5          cse.wine.edu
```

```
192.168.100.6          hub.wine.edu
192.168.200.10         gateway.wine.edu
wine.edu    MX    10   hub.wine.edu
```

Hosts on the Internet see only the following:

```
10.12.100.10           mail.wine.edu
10.10.100.11           smtp.whiskey.edu
wine.edu    MX    10   mail.wine.edu
wine.edu    MX    20   smtp.whiskey.edu
```

This "split-horizon" DNS configuration prevents Internet mail hosts from attempting mail delivery to `hub.wine.edu`, or from knowing about any of the systems behind the wine.edu firewall. Both schools run exclusively on **sendmail** and AIX.

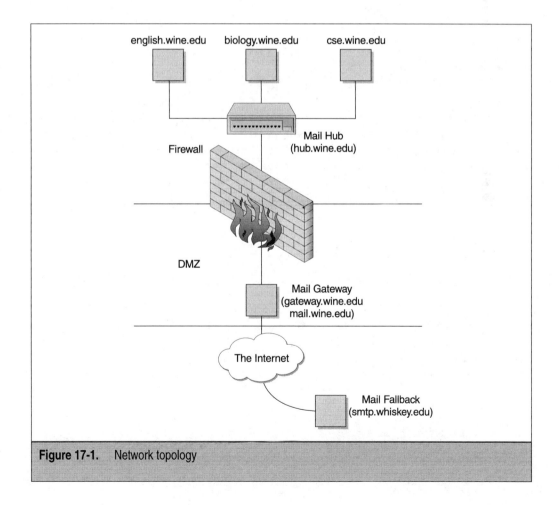

Figure 17-1. Network topology

For this example, addresses in the 10.x.x.x range have been used to represent real Internet routable IP addresses. In reality, this address, too, is private. Be sure to use proper IP addresses as assigned by your Internet service provider.

Spoke Configuration

The "spoke," as I'm calling it, is very much like the client configuration except that it will receive mail from remote hosts—namely, the mail hub. It is a spoke in the sense that it relies on the mail hub to relay all outbound mail to the gateway. It would be possible to simply configure two hubs, and allow `cse.wine.edu` to forward mail directly to the gateway. However, there are two reasons you might not want to do that: an extra load is placed on the gateway, as mail destined for `wine.edu` users is routed back to the hub; and the security configuration of the network firewall may not permit it.

Define the smart host in the `sendmail.cf` file:

```
DShub.wine.edu
```

Client Configuration

The client system does not receive any mail from remote systems. If the mail is intended for a local user, **sendmail** calls the MDA and it is delivered. Otherwise, it is relayed to the smart host for delivery. In this configuration, it is unnecessary to run the **sendmail** daemon; the mail user agent will start **sendmail** on a case-by-case basis. It is still necessary to have a working `sendmail.cf`. This configuration is useful when users or applications on the system wish to send notification messages to other hosts on the network but don't want to receive responses or don't want to receive responses locally.

Define the smart host in `sendmail.cf`:

```
DShub.wine.edu
```

Comment out the following rule in `sendmail.cf`:

```
#R$* < @ $* .$=m. > $* $#esmtp $@ $2.$3. $: $1 < @ $2.$3. > $4
```

Hub Configuration

The mail hub accepts mail for delivery from any host in its domain. It verifies the users and locally spools the mail to them. The one exception is for users on `cse.wine.edu`; their mail is relayed to the `cse.wine.edu` mail server. For all other domains, the mail hub forwards the mail to the gateway for final delivery.

The hub enables support for `/etc/mail/local-host-names`:

```
Fw/etc/mail/local-host-names
```

This file contains the names of hosts that should follow local delivery rules, in this case, `biology.wine.edu` and `english.wine.edu`. Note that `cse.wine.edu` is specifically excluded from this list. Then, the hub sets DM to masquerade as the host `wine.edu`.

```
DMwine.edu
```

and defines gateway as the relay host:

```
DSgateway.wine.edu
```

Relaying all outbound mail through `hub.wine.edu` reduces the number of direct connections maintained with untrusted hosts. It also provides an opportunity to centrally archive all e-mail, as a site's audit policy might require. Finally, the hub runs an IMAP daemon (**imapd**) to give users access to their mailboxes. This will work out-of-the-box if users are defined in `/etc/passwd` (or in a map such as NIS) with home directories available on the hub system and **imapd** enabled in the `/etc/inetd.conf` file.

Gateway Configuration

The gateway server relays mail. For hosts in the `wine.edu` domain, it relays mail to `hub.wine.edu`. For all other hosts. it relays mail to the host with the best available MX record. Split-horizon DNS ensures that the gateway recognizes `hub.wine.edu` as the best MX for the wine domains. All other hosts on the Internet recognize `gateway.wine.edu` as the best host. By forcing all Internet mail destined for the `wine.edu` domain to be relayed through the gateway, the number of vulnerabilities is minimized, allowing security patches to be applied more quickly. Support for this gateway function is now included in most commercial firewalls.

To avoid the open relay defined in the default AIX `sendmail.cf`, build a new configuration using the following m4 macros in `gateway.mc`:

```
# cat gateway.mc
divert(-1)
include('/usr/samples/tcpip/sendmail/m4/cf.m4')dnl
OSTYPE('aixsample')dnl
DOMAIN('generic')dnl
undefine('UUCP_RELAY')dnl
undefine('BITNET_RELAY')dnl
MAILER(local)dnl
MAILER(smtp)dnl
```

To create a new `sendmail.cf`, simply issue the following command:

```
# m4 gateway.m4 > sendmail.cf
```

Finally, add support for relaying to the resulting `sendmail.cf`:

```
CRwine.edu cse.wine.edu
```

Fallback Configuration

The fallback server must run a **sendmail** daemon to accept mail from remote systems. It probably serves several functions: fallback server for one mail domain, gateway server for another. To make a system receive mail as the fallback, simply add the fallback domain to the R class of `sendmail.cf`, verify that the server is listed in DNS as a low-priority MX host for the domain, and restart **sendmail**. If the host `smtp.whiskey.edu` is our fallback mail host for `wine.edu`, the administrator there should add the following to the `sendmail.cf`. The `gateway.mc` creates a good base configuration.

```
CRwhiskey.edu cse.wine.edu wine.edu
```

CAUTION   The use of fallback hosts is controversial when the server providing this service is not locally administered. The specific configuration options chosen for this system affect whether received messages are properly forwarded, rewritten, and queued. Failure to configure the fallback server consistently can cause mail to be lost.

DELIVERY AGENTS AND PROTOCOLS

Once a message is received by a mail host, it must be delivered, transferred, or queued. If the user is local, mail is delivered to their local spool. Mail that has been delivered to the local user's mail spool is then available for user access by either a MUA or a remote delivery protocol. If the user is remote, the message is either routed to the best available mail exchange host or queued for later transfer.

MDAs bellmail and procmail

The default local delivery agent for AIX is **bellmail**. It delivers new mail by appending the message to the end of a user's mail spool, usually located in the file `/var/spool/mail/userid`. A mail user agent will read this file and transfer saved messages to a user's home directory, typically in a file named `mbox`. Unread messages are held in the mail spool. Mail spools and `mbox` files can become quite large. It is important to plan for enough disk space in the `/var` and `/home` filesystems to accommodate this.

A popular alternative, or addition, to **bellmail** is **procmail**, which is a filtering MDA capable of sorting incoming mail by sender, recipient, content, or other criteria. The **procmail** program can even perform junk mail filtering. This sorted mail can then be directed to different delivery locations, even remote locations. To configure **procmail** as an alternative to **bellmail**, make sure the program is installed on the system, and then add the associated m4 macro to `sendmail.mc` and rebuild `sendmail.cf`.

```
define('PROCMAIL_MAILER_PATH','/usr/bin/procmail')dnl
feature(local_procmail)dnl
MAILER(procmail)dnl
```

More simply, **procmail** can be called by the user using the `.forward` file.

```
"|exec /usr/bin/procmail"
```

In either case, **procmail** configuration is controlled via `/etc/procmailrc` and the `.procmailrc` file in a user's home directory.

POP

One of the oldest and best-known solutions to the distributed mail problem is the Post Office Protocol (POP) version 3, defined in RFC 1725. POP clients connect to a POP server, which is the repository for incoming mail. The client downloads the entire contents of the user's inbox to the client machine. The inbox is then processed on the local client. POP works very well for those users who run from a single client over a fast connection. If you operate from a number of clients, then you still have the problem of scattering your inbox folders between machines. A basic POP daemon is included with the AIX base operating system for POP version 3. It is run from **inetd** and can be enabled by simply uncommenting the entry in `/etc/inetd.conf`:

```
# pop3      stream      tcp nowait root    /usr/sbin/pop3d    pop3d
```

The daemons will serve POP mail for locally defined users. POP uses a password for authentication, although newer implementations make use of Kerberos security services. You shouldn't have any difficulty locating more advanced public domain, shareware, and vendor POP implementations for just about any operating system. This includes both POP clients and servers.

IMAP

The Internet Message Access Protocol (IMAP), defined in RFC 2060, solves the problem of centralizing the processing of mailboxes accessed from multiple distributed mail clients. The Internet Message Support Protocol (IMSP) extends the IMAP protocol to include administration of address books and clustering multiple IMAP servers. A complete solution requires a friendly IMAP-based user agent that is available for most popular operating systems. An **imap** daemon is also included with the AIX base operating system. To enable IMAP support for remote users that are defined in the local /etc/passwd file, uncomment the associated entry in /etc/inetd.conf.

```
# imap2   stream      tcp nowait root   /usr/sbin/imapd  imapd
```

IMAP was designed as a follow-on to POP to address the issues of shared access, resource localization, and low-bandwidth connections to a remote mail server. IMAP is a client/server protocol similar to NNTP. The IMAP protocol is used by a mail user agent to transfer mail header information or individual mail messages between the client and the server. Destination folders may reside on either the local client or the mail server. This makes IMAP ideal for low-bandwidth connections such as dialup access. IMAP can be used to transfer complete mailboxes from a server to a client to mimic POP services. Other IMAP facilities include searching mailboxes for text strings, accessing news servers, and managing MIME (Multipurpose Internet Mail Extensions) attachments. MIME is used to attach multimedia files to a mail message using a seven-bit encoding of eight-bit data. IMAP news support provides a means for integrating user mail and news interfaces under a single client. The IMAP API library called the C-client is used to integrate IMAP support into existing mail user agents. IMAP server and C-client software is available from the University of Washington. IMAP-based mail user agents may be obtained from a number of public and vendor sources.

MAIL CLIENTS

A number of Web browser and desktop mail vendors are adding the IMAP protocol to their e-mail suites—most notably, Netscape Communicator.

/usr/bin/mail

AIX 5 has done away with the two different mail user agents and now uses just one: the UCB mail program. If invoked without command-line arguments, this simple MUA will read the user's mail spool and display some message header information: sender, date, time, size, and message subject. A series of one-letter commands allow the user to read, delete, and compose messages. A list of these options can be viewed by typing **help** at the ? prompt.

Netscape Communicator

AIX 5 ships with Netscape Communicator version 4.7. In addition to a Web browser, this bundle includes a GUI mail client. The client supports IMAP, POP 3, and movemail, the local UNIX mailbox format. From the GUI, it is possible to read, delete, compose, and organize mail and mail folders.

Pine

Pine provides a simple hot-keyed menu interface for processing both locally delivered and IMAP-managed mailboxes. Local mail queue support allows Pine to work in non-IMAP environments like other popular mail user agents. Onscreen message management keeps you informed of the arrival of new mail and system warnings without interrupting work in progress. The Pine menu hierarchy includes address book management, mail and news folder lists, sorted message indexes, message composition, and configuration. Online help is available everywhere in the system. Message composition is aided by a basic editing tool called Pico and an integrated spelling checker.

Although Pine's goal is to provide a basic "meat and potatoes" interface to electronic mail processing, it also includes a number of sophisticated facilities for power users: choose your own text editor and spell checker, custom-sort message indexes, tag messages for batch operation, tailor message header display, and manage MIME attachments. These are just a few of the advanced features available in Pine.

DEBUGGING

Mail configurations can be debugged at numerous stages in the delivery process. Both **sendmail** and **mail** have useful built-in features for verbose output and interactive sessions. In addition, the **sendmail** program can also be used to interactively test rulesets.

Addressing and Headers

In order for a mail message to traverse the space from user A to user B, an addressing mechanism that is understood by the MTAs must be used. From the discussion in Chapter 13 concerning the domain name space, you might think that this is a simple issue. However, e-mail gateways to other networks involving other addressing protocols can make the address resolution problem as hard as artificial intelligence.

The most common UNIX mail formats involve Internet domain addressing and UUCP addressing.

```
user@domain-address     ◄──────── Internet address
host1!...!destination!user ◄──────── UUCP address
```

Two types of mail headers are attached to each mail message that define the attributes of the message. The Simple Mail Transfer Protocol (SMTP RFC 821) provides a command syntax that MTAs use to negotiate mail transfer from one MTA to the next. The following example contains an SMTP header:

```
HELLO smtp.whiskey.edu   ◄──────── Introduce yourself to the MTA
MAIL From: raphael@english.whiskey.edu ◄──────── Indicate the originator
RCPT To: rachael@wine.edu ◄──────── Announce the recipients
DATA ◄──────── Supply the data of the e-mail message
QUIT ◄──────── Exit
```

The second type of mail header is the RFC 822 header. It is used by both the MTA and the MUA. The RFC 822 header identifies the path the mail message has traveled, date, originator, recipients, subject, and so on.

```
Received: from gateway.wine.edu
        by hub.wine.edu id AA03037;
        Sun, 10 Nov 02 15:07 PST
Received: from smtp.whiskey.edu
        by mail.wine.edu id  AA10255;
        Sun, 10 Nov 02 15:04 PST
Received: from english.whiskey.edu
        by smtp.whiskey.edu id AA12242;
        Sun, 10 Nov 02 15:01 PST
Date: Sun, 10 Nov 02 14:59:10 PST
From: raphael@english.whiskey.edu
To: rachael@wine.edu
Subject: Meeting Wednesday
Rachael:
I enjoyed that seminar last Wednesday. What was
the name of that professor who kept falling asleep?
Raphael
```

The ordering of the received lines indicates the MTA path that the mail message has traveled. This path can be used to debug routing problems and loops.

How Mail Is Sent

When a user composes a mail message, the MUA attaches a header envelope to the message separated by a blank line. The MUA then hands the message off to the **sendmail** MTA. A new **sendmail** daemon is forked to process the new message. It passes each of the addresses associated with the mail message through address translation rule sets. The rule sets parse the address line and determine whether the message destination is local or remote. If the message is destined for a remote site, a name service may be queried to determine whether a preferred mail exchange site is requested for the remote site (name service MX record). If the remote site is running a **sendmail** MTA, the message is transferred to the remote site using the SMTP protocol described previously. At the remote site, **sendmail** runs the addresses through the rulesets again to determine whether the recipient is local or remote. If the recipient is local, the headers are rewritten and the message is spooled to the recipient's mail inbox.

A Verbose /usr/bin/mail Session

The simplest way to test **sendmail** is to use the **-v** verbose flag with /usr/bin/mail. It provides feedback on the interaction between MTAs. The following example also uses the **-s** option to include a subject heading:

```
$ echo "Happy birthday Judith" | mail -v -s "Birthday" judith@wine.edu
judith@wine... Connecting to wine.edu. via esmtp...
220 AIXadm.org ESMTP Sendmail AIX5.1/8.11.0/8.11.0; Sat, 8 Jun 2002
>>> EHLO McGraw-Hill.com
250-wine.edu Hello McGraw-Hill.com (may be forged), pleased to meet you
250-ENHANCEDSTATUSCODES
250-EXPN
250-VERB
250-8BITMIME
250-SIZE
250-DSN
250-ONEX
250-ETRN
250-XUSR
250 HELP
>>> MAIL From:<terry@McGraw-Hill.com> SIZE=57
250 2.1.0 <terry@McGraw-Hill.com>... Sender ok
>>> RCPT To:judith@wine.edu
250 2.1.5 <judith@wine.edu>... Recipient ok
>>> DATA
354 Enter mail, end with "." on a line by itself
>>> .
250 2.0.0 g592WdN15290 Message accepted for delivery
judith@wine... Sent (g592WdN15290 Message accepted for delivery)
Closing connection to wine.edu.
>>> QUIT
221 2.0.0 wine.edu closing connection
```

Testing Alternative Mail Hosts

It is possible to specify an alternate host to receive and process the test message. This is particularly useful when checking the proper configuration of the fallback mail host. The alternative mail host is specified with an e-mail address of the form `user%host.domain@another.host.altdom`. Here is another example based on `/usr/bin/mail`:

```
# /usr/bin/mail -v bart%wine.edu@smtp.whiskey.edu
Subject: help  ◄──────── Enter a subject here or enter
Sideshow Bob did it!  ◄──────── Enter a message or just enter
.  ◄──────── Enter "." Indicates the end of message
Cc:  ◄──────── Enter to bypass Cc
```

For this to work properly, the message should originate from a mail host known to the receiving MTA. This is because most mail hosts are configured to deny connections from hosts that fail a reverse lookup. Another way to achieve this result is to telnet directly to the mail host's **sendmail** port and converse with the server through an interactive SMTP session.

Testing Sendmail Rulesets

Test rule sets by invoking **sendmail** with the **-bt** flag. The **sendmail** program will prompt for the rule sets to be invoked and the desired address. Separate every two rule set numbers with a comma.

```
# sendmail -bt -C/etc/mail/sendmail.cf
ADDRESS TEST MODE (ruleset 3 NOT automatically invoked)
Enter <ruleset> <address>
> 2,4,0 user.name@node.dept.wine.edu
2                     input: user . name @ node . dept . wine . edu
2                   returns: user . name @ node . dept . wine . edu
final                 input: user . name @ node . dept . wine . edu
final               returns: user . name @ node . dept . wine . edu
parse                 input: user . name @ node . dept . wine . edu
Parse0                input: user . name @ node . dept . wine . edu
Parse0              returns: user . name @ node . dept . wine . edu
ParseLocal            input: user . name @ node . dept . wine . edu
ParseLocal          returns: user . name @ node . dept . wine . edu
Parse1                input: user . name @ node . dept . wine . edu
Parse1              returns: $# local $: user . name @ node . dept . wine . edu
parse               returns: $# local $: user . name @ node . dept . wine . edu
> /quit
```

The **sendmail** command supports a number of debugging and trace levels. They can be activated using the start-up option **-d<nn>.<mm>**, where **nn** and **mm** define the debug and trace levels. You'll want to redirect the output to a file, since it can be *very* verbose. The IBM AIX **sendmail** daemon supports only a value of 21.<mm>, where <mm> can be any positive integer. If you are running a current copy of **sendmail**, refer to the source code for debug and trace values.

```
# /usr/lib/sendmail -bd -q30m -d21.1
```

Check the logs, mail queue, and stats files periodically for stalled mail or loops. You can list the pending delivery queue using the **mailq** command.

```
# mailq
----Q-ID---- --Size-- -----Q-Time----- ----Sender/Recipient----
g592WdN15290*       5 Sat Jun  8 18:04 terry   judith@wine.edu
```

The following **ls** command lists the files queued to the /var/spool/mqueue/ directory:

```
# ls -l /var/spool/mqueue
total 2
-rw-------   1 root     system          5 Jun 08 18:04 dfg592WdN15290
-rw-------   1 root     system        481 Jun 08 18:04 qfg592WdN15290
-rw-------   1 root     system          0 Jun 08 18:04 xfg592WdN15290
```

QID	Queue File Type
d	Message data file
l	Lock file
n	Backup file
q	Control file
t	Temp file
x	Transcript file

Table 17-3.   Mail Queue File Types

Files in the mail queue are identified by a QID. The first character of the QID designates the type of queue file. Table 17-3 lists the file types.

The /etc/mail/statistics file can be checked using the **/usr/lib/mailstats** command. You will need to create the statistics file with the **touch** command if it does not exist.

```
# mailstats
Statistics from Sat Jun  8 20:51:29 PDT 2002
 M   msgsfr  bytes_from    msgsto   bytes_to  msgsrej msgsdis  Mailer
 3       18         18K         0         0K        0       0  local
 5        0          0K        18        18K        0       0  esmtp
=============================================================
 T       18         18K        18        18K        0       0
 C       18                     18                   0
```

To output the same information in a program-readable format and reset the **statistics** file, use the following **-p** option:

```
# mailstats -p
1023594689 1023594773
 3       18          18         0         0         0       0  local
 5        0           0        18        18         0       0  esmtp
 T       18          18        18        18         0       0
 C       18          18         0
```

MANAGING MAIL QUEUES

As Administrators, it's our responsibility to inform users when mail arrives and pester them to get rid of old unwanted mail. Since the latter is a difficult job at best, I'll start with the easy part of informing users when mail arrives.

The **comsat** daemon, when prompted by **sendmail**, informs users that new mail is waiting. This feature is supported by the MAIL and MAILMSG variables defined in the default /etc/profile.

```
MAIL=/var/spool/mail/$LOGNAME    ◄————————Path to incoming mail
MAILMSG="[YOU HAVE NEW MAIL]" ◄————————Mail waiting message
```

The **comsat** daemon must also be defined and uncommented in /etc/inetd.conf.

```
comsat dgram  upd  wait  root  /usr/sbin/comsat  comsat
```

It's also a good idea to inform users when mail is waiting at login time. This can be accomplished by checking the mail from the default login scripts for each shell. See Chapter 20 for details on setting up system-wide default login scripts. Here is a sample login mail check to add to the default user /etc/security/.profile before creating new user accounts:

```
if [ -s "$MAIL" ]
  then echo "$MAILMSG"
fi
```

Without being heavy-handed with your user community, it is difficult to encourage users to keep up with incoming mail. The best policy is to use regular reminders and track queue usage with disk utilization commands like **du**.

```
# du -sk /var/spool/mail ◄————————Disk usage for mail queue
# du -sk /var/spool/mail/* ◄————————Mail queue usage by user
```

CHECKLIST

The following is a checklist for the key points in Mail and Sendmail:

- ☐ Identify the components of the electronic mail, or e-mail, system.
- ☐ Identify the **sendmail** components.
- ☐ Do *not* use the IBM working configuration on systems that connect directly to the Internet without disabling promiscuous relaying of mail.
- ☐ Keep logs of **sendmail** activity.
- ☐ Identify the various **sendmail** configurations that meet specific roles across several computers on a network.
- ☐ Identify delivery agents and protocols.
- ☐ Identify the Mail Clients.
- ☐ Define debugging.
- ☐ Inform users when mail arrives and pester them to get rid of old unwanted mail.

CHAPTER 18

Apache Web Service

IBM ships the Apache HTTP Server with the base operating system. Although several other Web servers run under AIX, Apache is now the Internet standard. The server's job is to provide a common access interface to multimedia data and common Internet services. It does this via a combination of the Hypertext Transport Protocol (HTTP) and the Hypertext Markup Language (HTML). HTML data pages residing on the server are transmitted to Web clients via HTTP. The Web server is responsible for maintaining access control to secured information and negotiating secure channels with Web clients.

The HTTP implementation resembles SMTP, the Internet mail protocol, in that it is a command/response-driven protocol that sends commands, data, and error codes on the same bidirectional socket connection. It also relies on MIME encoding documents to overcome self-imposed character set restrictions. These simple design choices aided in rapid implementation, widespread deployment, and the general popularity of the platform. Beyond simple HTML, the functionality of HTTP has been extended through the use of companion technologies, such as the programming languages JavaScript and Java. Extensible Markup Language (XML) and Extensible Stylesheet Language XSL are also helping transform the interworkings of the Web by differentiating between data and presentation elements.

Apache Server Configuration

AIX includes a Web-based configuration system, which is accessible from the default server Web page. This configuration utilities run from an additional instance of the **httpd** daemon listening on network port 8008. This instance of the server must be started manually:

```
# /usr/HTTPServer/bin/httpd -f /usr/HTTPServer/conf/admin.conf
```

This configuration tool uses both Java and JavaScript for user interaction and can be helpful for quick installation of simple server configurations. However, the long chain of software and network dependencies that it requires makes it difficult to rely on. It is highly recommended that the competent Web administrator actually understand the details of Apache configuration.

The IBM-supplied binary distribution installs Apache into /usr/HTTPServer and organizes these resources into subdirectories (see Table 18-1).

Directives Configuration

Apache contains a rich set of configuration options, controlled via "directives" that set either global or local values. Example 18-1 contains a listing of the first few directives in the httpd.conf file. Apache historically divided the configuration into three files: srm.conf, access.conf, and httpd.conf. The directives and data contained in these three files are now combined into httpd.conf. Support for srm.conf and access.conf is disabled by default by setting the AccessConfig and ResourceConfig directives to /dev/null (any number of arbitrarily named configuration files may be

Directory	Contents
conf/	Configuration files
ssl/	Secure Socket Layer keys and certificates
bin/	Executable binaries
libexec/	Dynamic shared object modules
cgi-bin/	Default location of CGI scripts
htdocs/	HTML content
proxy/	Proxy request cache
logs/	Log files
icons/	Image library
man/	Manual pages
admindocs/	Web-based administration documentation
apachesrc/	Apache source code
include/	Apache C header files
example_module/	An example module

Table 18-1.   Apache HTTP Server Directory Structure

added with the Include directive). The Apache HTTP Server documentation provides a complete reference for available directives.

Example 18-1

```
##
## httpd.conf -- Apache HTTP server configuration file
##

# This is the main server configuration file. See URL
http://www.apache.org/
# for instructions.

# Do NOT simply read the instructions in here without understanding
# what they do, if you are unsure consult the online docs. You have been
# warned.

# Originally by Rob McCool

# These two directives are used to combine the three config files into one.
# The three config files are a legacy setup and are not needed.

AccessConfig /dev/null
ResourceConfig /dev/null
```

Several directives control the scope of other directives (e.g., <Location /location ></Location>, <Directory /directory></Directory>, and <VirtualServer IP address></VirtualServer>). Directives encountered within one of these tags are scoped within the associated namespace, with the exceptions of a few server-wide directives.

Server-Wide Directives

Server-wide configuration options affect server identification, network configuration, file locations, process control, and resource usage for the whole server. Apache was designed to handle a high volume of HTTP traffic with a high level of reliability and securability. Preforking, self-expiring processes are important to achieving reliability. On start-up, the parent **httpd** process will bind and listen to a network socket, and it will prefork several child processes to respond to requests in accordance with certain server-wide directives. Requests are tracked, and after a period of time the child processes will expire and the parent will spawn new children. Preforking allows the server to respond to multiple requests quickly, and expiration helps to limit the potential for memory leaks that could disable the server. Example 18-2 contains a listing of many of the server-wide configuration directives that control this behavior. Most of these directive names are effective in describing their purpose.

Example 18-2

```
# ServerRoot: The directory the server's config, error, and log files
# are kept in.
ServerRoot /usr/HTTPServer
# ServerType is either inetd or standalone.
ServerType standalone
# Port: The port the standalone listens to. For ports < 1023, you will
# need httpd to be run as root initially.
Port 80
# Listen: The Listen directive is required only if the server will
# be listening on more than 1 port.
#Listen 80
# HostnameLookups: Log the names of clients or just their IP numbers
HostnameLookups off
# User/Group: The name (or #number) of the user/group to run httpd as.
User nobody
Group nobody
# ServerAdmin: Your address, where problems with the server should be
# e-mailed.
ServerAdmin you@your.address

# PidFile: The file the server should log its pid to
PidFile /usr/HTTPServer/logs/httpd.pid
# ScoreBoardFile: File used to store internal server process information.
ScoreBoardFile /usr/HTTPServer/logs/httpd.scoreboard
# ServerName allows you to set a host name which is sent back to clients for
```

```
# your server if it's different than the one the program would get (i.e. use
# "www" instead of the host's real name).
#ServerName new.host.name
Timeout 300
KeepAlive On
MaxKeepAliveRequests 100
KeepAliveTimeout 15
MinSpareServers 5
MaxSpareServers 10
StartServers 5
MaxClients 150
MaxRequestsPerChild 10000
#Listen 3000
#Listen 12.34.56.78:80
```

Modular Extensions

The modular design of Apache allows for the extension of the base functionality, providing new logic and directives when needed. This also helps to manage the potentially large memory requirement for the **httpd** daemon. Modules are implemented as dynamic shared objects linked into the process memory space at runtime via the **dlopen()** system call. Even the Apache core is linkable at runtime. Because DSOs are shared between the parent and all child processes, only enough memory to load one instance of each module is required. Example 18-3 contains a selection of common Apache modules, as used in the httpd.conf file.

Example 18-3

```
#LoadModule proxy_module      libexec/libproxy.so
LoadModule userdir_module    libexec/mod_userdir.so
LoadModule alias_module      libexec/mod_alias.so
LoadModule rewrite_module    libexec/mod_rewrite.so
LoadModule access_module     libexec/mod_access.so
LoadModule auth_module      libexec/mod_auth.so
#AddModule mod_proxy.c
AddModule mod_userdir.c
AddModule mod_alias.c
AddModule mod_rewrite.c
AddModule mod_access.c
AddModule mod_auth.c
```

LoadModule inserts the additional code into the addressable memory space of **httpd**. AddModule makes the directives defined within the module available to the server. Until AddModule is called, the new module is not usable. It is important to place all references to module-defined directives after the associated LoadModule and AddModule lines. Additional modules may be compiled and installed at runtime using the header files in the include/ subdirectory, along with the **apxs** program.

Access Control

After data transfer, access control is probably the most important function of the Web server. Access control limits the capabilities of both Web clients and Web page publishers primarily according to location and identity. In the example shown in Example 18-4, access control is first strictly limited in one scope and then relaxed in another to meet administrative objectives. One directive scope can be a subset of another, which effectively overrides the former for some branch of the uniform resource identifier (URI) tree.

Example 18-4
```
DocumentRoot /usr/HTTPServer/htdocs/en_US/
<Directory />
Options FollowSymLinks
Allowoverride none
</Directory>
<Directory /usr/HTTPServer/htdocs/en_US>
Options Indexes FollowSymLinks
AuthType basic
AuthName "Web Server Access Control"
AuthUserFile conf/UsersAndPasswords
Require valid-user
</Directory>
```

The first `Directory` block sets the default access rules for the default document root: Publishers are permitted to map objects from the filesystem into the URI space recognized by the server; they are, however, unable to override any subsequent access control via `.htaccess` files. The second `Directory` block enables basic user authentication for the whole document tree. The `AuthUserFile` directive defines the user database file location.

The simple AuthUserFile database is a colon-delimited text file of user IDs and hashed passwords, similar to the UNIX `/etc/passwd` file. On servers with many users, searching this file can become a performance problem. The `AuthDBUserFile` directive can be used instead to speed up this process. The **htpasswd** and **dbmanage** utilities are used to populate the respective user files.

Both of these authorization schemes offer minimal real security, because the passwords are passed across the network as "cleartext," readable by anyone capable of sniffing the network connection. Keep this in mind when implementing a basic authentication scheme for your Web site; a least make sure the server is outside of a firewall and otherwise isolated on the network from sensitive systems. For more serious security, use the Secure Sockets Layer (SSL) protocol, also supported by Apache HTTP Server.

Access may also be limited in terms of the host, or network, where the user is logically located. This is accomplished via the `Order`, `Allow`, and `Deny` directives. For example:

```
Order deny, allow
Allow from 10.10.120,
Deny from cse.froth.edu
```

This example gives `Deny` directives preference over `Allow` directives, then explicitly allows connections from users on the 10.10.120 network and denies users coming from `cse.froth.edu`. These directives are typically scoped to a specific directory tree or virtual host.

URI Mapping Directives

When a document root is set, this implies a valid URI tree for the host rooted at the `DocumentRoot` directory: any valid file or directory below the `DocumentRoot` directory becomes part of a valid URI. However, it is often desirable to map other files and directories into this space. Two such mapping directives are `Alias` and `ScriptAlias`. Enabling aliases simply maps one valid subtree into another space. Optional directives like `Indexes` and `FollowSymLinks` will still need to be activated for the new directory for these features to work properly (see Example 18-5).

Example 18-5
```
<Directory /usr/local/myhtdocs/>
Options Indexes
Allowoverride none
</Directory>
Alias      /mydocs/     /usr/local/myhtdocs/
```

MIME Types

The Web is a multimedia service capable of incorporating any arbitrary data format. Because of the design of the HTTP protocol, many data types cannot be transferred without conversion to another format. This is accomplished using MIME format headers. MIME allows the Web server to convert the document to a format supported by HTTP and the Web client to convert it back to the original format, all without input from the Web client user. Conversion and display of many data types, such as JPG images, are often supported directly by the browser. When the browser encounters a MIME type that it does not support, it relies on helper applications to display or otherwise process the data. Apache uses the `mime.types` file to determine the MIME type headers to send to a client requesting data, so that the client knows how to format the data. Additional types can be added by either editing this file, or by using the `AddType` directive in the `httpd.conf` file.

Support Programs

Apache includes a number of additional programs to support the Web administrator. These binaries are installed in the `bin/` subdirectory of the server root directory. The most important of these is **apachectl**, which controls the manual stopping and starting of the **httpd** daemon, as well as validation of the `httpd.conf` configuration file. Apache may be stopped and started with

```
# /usr/HTTPServer/bin/apachectl stop
# /usr/HTTPServer/bin/apachectl start
```

Additionally, after making modifications to the configuration file, it is a good idea to validate the changes:

```
# /usr/HTTPServer/bin/apachectl configtest
```

A bad configuration file will prevent a running server from restarting, causing unwanted downtime while the error is researched and corrected. After a successful validation, it is safe to restart a running server:

```
# /usr/HTTPServer/bin/apachectl restart
```

The **rotatelogs** program is another helpful tool. As the name suggests, it helps to manage what can be voluminous Web logs. The most common way to use this program is by calling it from within the `httpd.conf` file itself. The details of how to do this are discussed in the section "Managing Logs" later in this chapter.

Virtual Server Configuration

Virtual hosts are a popular feature of Apache that allows the administrator to run multiple Web sites from one server. Virtual hosts come in two types: name based and IP address based. IP-based virtual hosts require a separate IP address for each host. This can usually be achieved with IP aliases on one physical network interface. In contrast, name-based virtual hosts may share one IP address; all DNS records for these hosts refer to the same IP address. The name-based virtual host relies on the client to send an HTTP/1.1 header identifying the name of the host it is trying to contact. Most browsers now support HTTP/1.1, making name-based virtual hosts a viable and practical option. The exception to this is secure servers; secure servers require matching reverse DNS lookups. Example 18-6 shows a name-based virtual host configuration. An example of an IP-based virtual host appears in the next section.

Example 18-6
```
NameVirtualHost *
<VirtualHost *>
ServerName accounting.wine.edu
DocumentRoot      /var/data/accounting.wine.edu
```

```
</VirtualHost>
<Directory /var/data/accounting.wine.edu>
Options Indexes
Allowoverride no
</Directory>
<VirtualHost *>
ServerName chemistry.wine.edu
DocumentRoot      /var/data/chemistry.wine.edu
</VirtualHost>
```

Secure Server Configuration

Apache supports the Secure Sockets Layer protocol through the *mod_ibm_ssl* DSO module, which is installed with the **http_server.ssl.128** fileset. A secure server requires a certificate that will be presented to the browser client. If the certificate is signed by a certificate authority (CA) recognized by the browser, a secure session key will be negotiated and the requested data will be sent by the server. If the certificate is not recognized, the user will be prompted about how to proceed. AIX 5L includes **ikeyman** for generating keys, self-signed certificates, and certificate authority requests. The **ikeyman** program is an X desktop application written in Java. To generate a self-signed certificate, first create an initial personal key database (key.kdb by default) specifying the hostname of the system that will run a secure server. Then click the Self-Signed Certificate icon. When that step is completed, create an IP-based virtual host and reference the key.kdb file with the KeyFile directive (see Example 18-7).

Example 18-7
```
LoadModule mod_ibm_ssl        libexec/mod_ibm_ssl_128.so
AddModule mod_ibm_ssl.c
Listen 443
<VirtualHost 10.10.120.25:443>
ServerName secure.wine.edu
DocumentRoot /secure/document/location
Options Indexes
SSLEnable
KeyFile /usr/HTTPServer/ssl/keys/server.kdb
</VirtualHost>
```

It is a common mistake to connect to the secure server using an insecure HTTP URI. The connection succeeds without error, but the data is of an unknown MIME type. The browser usually attempts to save the data without reporting any error. This URI will not return the expected data if a secure virtual server is listening on port 443:

```
http://secure.wine.edu:443
```

The correct form is https://secure.wine.edu:433.

Managing Logs

Apache logs are of two types, error logs and access logs. The error log records internal server events with a variable level of specificity. The directives to name the error log and define message level are respectively `ErrorLog` and `LogLevel`. The access log records every request made to the Web daemon and has configuration options to control logged data type, format, and location. The `LogFormat` directive defines a template, similar to the C language `printf` function. The template is enclosed in double quotes and contains predefined tokens like `%h` for hostname and `%u` for user ID. Refer to the HTTPServer documentation for a complete list of custom log format tokens. The template definition is followed by an optional second parameter, the log format name or alias. Aliased formats allow the administrator to define multiple access logs.

CAUTION   A group-writable logging directory can be a security risk. The logging directory should be owned by the user that starts the daemon, and only that user should be able to write to it.

The access logs are defined with the `CustomLog` directive (see Example 18-9). Rather than log to a file, the `CustomLog` directive can specify a pipe and program to handle the data. The **logrotate** program included with Apache serves this purpose, and it is designed to limit how large the logs are allowed to become. Note that **logrotate** may be called from the command line, from the `httpd.conf` file, or from `crontab`, truncating the log daily by default.

Example 18-9

```
# ErrorLog: The location of the error log file. If this does not start
# with /, ServerRoot is prepended to it.
ErrorLog /usr/HTTPServer/logs/error_log
# LogLevel: Control the number of messages logged to the error_log.
# Possible values include: debug, info, notice, warn, error, crit,
# alert, emerg.
LogLevel warn
# The following directives define some format nicknames for use with
# a CustomLog directive (see below).

LogFormat "%h %l %u %t \"%r\" %>s %b \"%{Referer}i\" \"%{User-Agent}i\"" combined
LogFormat "%h %l %u %t \"%r\" %>s %b" common
LogFormat "%{Referer}i -> %U" referer
LogFormat "%{User-agent}i" agent

CustomLog /usr/HTTPServer/logs/access_log common
CustomLog /usr/HTTPServer/logs/referer_log referer
CustomLog "|usr/HTTPServer/bin/logrotate >>/usr/HTTPServer/logs/agent_log" agent
```

CAUTION   Truncating the a log file with **rm** can yield unexpected results. If another process has the file open, the file size will be zero, but the data blocks will not be freed. Eventually this course of events can invisibly fill the filesystem. Manual log truncation should be done with `# > logfile`.

CREATING WEB CONTENT

Configuring the Web server is the first step in running a Web site. The second step is to create useful and meaningful content. The default content in the Apache document root is documentation written by the Apache Group and IBM.

There are as many, or more, options for creating content than there are options available for configuring Apache. The first of these is simple files containing HTML. HTML is useful for sharing static information in an intuitive way. When the data to be displayed is dynamic, server-side includes, the Common Gateway Interface, JavaScript, Java, or another server-side language extension must be employed. The subject of Web content can be only briefly touched on here, but the following chapter sections should give you a basic framework for deciding what is possible.

HTML Documents

Begin by creating a hypertext document as the focal point to your service. This document, called a home page, can be created using a standard editor. The format, links, and programmatic characteristics of the document are specified using Hypertext Markup Language (HTML). HTML tags are special ASCII character sequences that are embedded within the text of the document. HTML tags take on one of three basic forms:

```
<tag-name> text </tag-name>
<tag-name attribute-name=args> text </tag-name>
<tag-name>
```

HTML tags are not case sensitive; thus, `<TITLE>` is equivalent to `<title>`. A sampling of HTML tags is listed in Table 18-2.

A basic HTML document will have a title, one or more headings, text paragraphs, and optionally programmatic interfaces like links, lists, images, or input/output fields. The title field identifies the purpose of the document and is usually displayed separate from the document by most browsers. This means you will want to echo the title information using a heading within the document body. Six levels of heading fields are available. Text within the document is contained by paragraph tags. If you want custom formatting within a paragraph, you must use additional tags to honor the formatting. Generally, line breaks and spacing are ignored.

It's very easy to build and test HTML documents. Create a document using an editor of choice and save it with the file extension `.html`. (The `.html` extension is a convention rather than a requirement.) Use the Open Local or Open File option of a browser such as Netscape or Mosaic to display the document on the screen. Repeat the process until the document has been refined to meet your expectations. It's a good idea to review your document with a couple of different browsers to validate that it has a common look and feel. You can make things even easier by using one of the WYSIWYG HTML editors or tool sets. These tools will validate and/or display HTML information during the edit process. Example 18-10 shows HTML code for a test page, `test.html`.

Tag Function	Start Field	End Field
Title	`<TITLE>`	`</TITLE>`
First-level head	`<H1>`	`</H1>`
Paragraph	`<P>`	
Line breaks	` `	
Preformatted text	`<PRE>`	`</PRE>`
Anchor/link	`<A HREF=pathname>`	`</A>`
Lists:		
Numbered	`<OL>`	`</OL>`
Unnumbered	`<UL>`	`</UL>`
Entry	`<LI>`	`</LI>`
Definition list	`<DL>`	`</DL>`
Term entry	`<DT>`	`</DT>`
Definition entry	`<DD>`	`</DD>`
Image	`<IMG SRC=image-uri>`	
Text style:		
Bold	`<B>`	`</B>`
Italic	`<I>`	`</I>`
Typewriter	`<TT>`	`</TT>`

Table 18-2. Sample HTML Tags

Example 18-10

```
<HTML>
<TITLE>AIX 5L: Apache HTTP Server test page</TITLE>
<BODY BACKGROUND="./images/bigblue.jpg">
      <H1>test 1</H1>
      <H2>test 2</H2>
      <H3>test 3</H3>
      <IMG SRC=foo.gif> A picture of foo.
      <BR>
      Take a look around but <I>don't stay too long.</I>
      <P>
      <B>Please send</B><A HREF=address.html>money!<A>
      <P>
</BODY>
</HTML>
```

Dynamic Data

HTML itself is just static data displayed by the Web browser, but there are several useful standards for making the Web more dynamic. Standards are more important for client-side processing, where the dynamic elements are executed on the browser. The basic server-side dynamic data methods are server-side includes (SSI) and Common Gateway Interface (CGI) scripts. In addition, a bevy of advanced language extensions have emerged as server-side standards.

Server-Side Includes

Server-side include syntax was defined by the National Center for Supercomputing Applications, and support was included in the NCSA **httpd**. This server is no longer supported by the developers, but SSI functionality is available now in many commercially maintained Web servers, including Apache.

```
<!--#echo var="hello world" -->
if, else, elif
<!--#if expr"$HTTP_USER_AGENT" -->
<B>output something</B>
<!--#endif -->
<!--#include file="footer.html" -->
```

Common Gateway Interface

CGI is another early method for providing dynamic Web content that was developed at NCSA and is in wide use today. An HTML form passes data to a server, which processes the data with the associated CGI script and returns another HTML page.

```
<html><title>script.cgi</title><body>
<form method="post" action="script.cgi">
<select name="instance_name">
<option selected>opt1
<option> opt2
</select>
<input type="submit" value="submit">
</form></body></html>
```

The following is an example of what `script.cgi` might look like:

```
#!/bin/ksh
read myline;
echo "Content-type: text/html\n"
echo '<HTML><TITLE>script.cgi</TITLE><BODY>'
```

```
echo 'You chose: '
echo $myline | awk -F'=' '{print $2}'
echo '</BODY></HTML>'
```

Finally, the Options directive must enable ExecCGI within the proper URI scope. CGI scripting should only be employed with extreme caution because of its potential for security vulnerabilities.

Server Language Extensions

The modular nature of Apache spawned a vast industry in server language extensions. The most popular of these are PHP, mod_perl, and Java Server Pages (JSP). Server language extensions allow the programmer almost infinite flexibility to generate content, interact with the user, and modify the functionality of the HTTP server itself.

JavaScript

JavaScript is an interpreted language for distributed programming logic. JavaScript is sent from the Web server and executed on the client browser. Because JavaScript is interpreted by the browser, it is less than optimal for computationally intensive programming tasks. It is, however, widely used in the Internet for simple operations.

JavaScript can be wholly embedded in an HTML document using the <SCRIPT> tag (see Example 18-11). It does not require JDK for development, only a Java-aware browser. For pre–Java period browsers, you need to hide the script in order to keep from confusing the browser. You can hide JavaScript by using the tags shown in Example 18-12. Again, the reader is referred to the books and online tutorials for more information on JavaScript programming.

Example 18-11

```
<HTML>
<TITLE> JavaScript Example</TITLE>
<SCRIPT LANGUAGE="JavaScript">
      function hello Web() {
      document.write('Hello World Wide Web')
      }
</SCRIPT>
<BODY>
      ...HTML STUFF...
<SCRIPT>
      helloWeb()
</SCRIPT>
</BODY>
</HTML>
```

Example 18-12

```
<SCRIPT LANGUAGE="JavaScript">
<!-- [Start hiding.]
document.write('Hello World Wide Web')
//[Stop hiding.]
</SCRIPT>
```

In a Web environment, Java-aware browsers act as middleware between applets and the user. These browsers include a number of predefined classes and objects that you can reference to obtain details about the page, history, and referenced URIs. Predefined classes include

- **Window**   Window properties (multiple for frames)
- **Location**   Current URI properties
- **History**   Visited URI properties
- **Document**   Current document properties

When building your Java- or JavaScript-enhanced Web page, try to keep in mind how the page is loaded by the browser. If you are referencing multiple applets, try to keep them small. Sequence page loading to keep your audience entertained while applets are being transferred to the client. This is especially important for slow modem connections. The recommendation here is to locate your JavaScript entries in the top section of your HTML document. This will limit interruptions when the user clicks on the page before the script has completed loading.

Java

Another advanced option for dynamic Web data is Java applets. Java is a full-featured programming language that promises cross-platform compatibility through the use of bytecode compilation and virtual machine architecture. The following is an example of a simple java applet.

```
import java.applet.Applet;
import java.awt.Graphics;
public class HelloWorld extends Applet {
  public void paint(Graphics g) {
    g.drawString("Hello World!", 150, 25);
  }
}
```

Java is a compiled language, but it is not compiled to a machine architecture–specific form. It is compiled to *bytecode*. This design is what permits Java to claim cross-platform superiority; the same bytecode can be run on any system that has the supporting Java virtual machine. It is the JVM's responsibility to convert the bytecode to a machine-specific form. To compile the example into bytecode, **javac** must be installed:

```
# /usr/java130/bin/javac HelloWorld.java
```

The output of this command should be a `HelloWorld.class` file,which can be called from a web page as in the following example:

```
<HTML><HEAD>
<TITLE>Hello World as a Java Applet</TITLE></HEAD>
<BODY>Java applet HelloWorld says:
<APPLET CODE="HelloWorld.class" WIDTH=150 HEIGHT=25></APPLET>
</BODY></HTML>
```

Applets have not gained widespread popularity, partially because of early performance problems and partially because of the lack of universal support for the Java Virtual Machine. Applets are probably most popular in relatively homogeneous large corporate computing environments.

XML and Style Sheets

XML is a standard for describing structured data. XML tags define the relationships between the data elements and say nothing about how to present the data. To effectively display content on the Web with XML, it is necessary to separately describe how to display the data. XSLT fills this role. XSLT is similar in concept to cascading style sheets: it describes how to display data. Because only newer browsers are able to parse XML and apply XSLT rules to the data tree, the server must do the parsing if older browsers are going to be supported. Example 18-13 shows an XML document containing information about institutions. Only three tags are used, and the tag names are arbitrary but descriptive.

Example 18-13
```
<institutions id="schools">
<name>Wine
    <dept>English</dept>
    <dept>Science</dept>
    <dept>Theater</dept>
<name>Whiskey
    <dept>Literature</dept>
    <dept>Math</dept>
    <dept>Science</dept>
</name></institution>
```

WEB BROWSERS AND HELPER APPLICATIONS

AIX ships with Netscape Communicator that, like any browser, relies on MIME-type headers, sent from the Web server, to properly display images and other nontext data. Browsers handle many common MIME data types internally or through browser plug-ins. When the browser is unable to handle the MIME type, either internally or via a plug-in, the browser usually asks the user how to handle the data.

CHECKLIST

The following is a checklist for the key points in Apache Web Service:

- ☐ Configure the Web server.
- ☐ Define DSO modules.
- ☐ Define access control.
- ☐ Define virtual servers.
- ☐ Define configuration directive scooping.
- ☐ Define HTML tags.
- ☐ Identify the standards that make the Web more dynamic.
- ☐ Include server-side syntax.
- ☐ Provide dynamic Web content by using CGI.
- ☐ Generate content, interact with the user, and modify the functionality of the HTTP server itself through the use of server language extensions.
- ☐ Create useful and meaningful Web content.

CHAPTER 19

X11 Administration

T he UNIX display system of choice is simply known as X. The formal name for this basic staple is the X Window System, Version 11, usually referred to as X11. AIX 5L now provides a selection of graphical user interfaces (GUI) to make the display colorful if not more productive. With the introduction of Linux-rooted desktop environments like KDE and GNOME, the default Common Desktop Environment (CDE) may not be so common any more. Before delving into these desktop environments, I will examine the background and workings of X and IBM's port, known as AIXwindows. Welcome to X11.

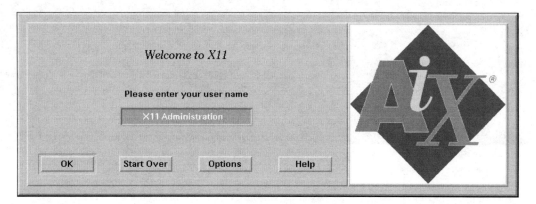

OVERVIEW

The X Window System was developed by a group of vendors and researchers at the Massachusetts Institute of Technology, collectively known as the MIT X Consortium. The consortium was formed in 1988 to evolve a window system from X10 developed by the MIT Computer Science department and Project Athena. A new independent X Consortium, now part of The Open Group, was formed in 1993 to continue with X development.

X11 uses a client/server protocol for presenting display windows. The client pieces are applications with graphics to be displayed, and the server part is an application that renders those graphics. GUI widget and toolkit libraries are linked by applications and used to manipulate networked or locally attached displays via remote procedure calls.

More information on X11, X Consortium membership, freely available source code, and other open source efforts may be obtained from the following sites:

```
http://www.x.org/
ftp://ftp.x.org/
http://www.xfree86.org/
ftp://ftp.xfree86.org/
```

COMPONENTS

The fundamental components of the X11 environment include: the X-server, which controls the display; a window manager, which manages objects on the display and integrates the mouse and keyboard; a font library for displaying pretty text strings; widget libraries for adding things like buttons and pointers; and a set of X-clients that give you everything from bouncing balls to graphical editors. The names of the basic X components are as follows:

- **X** X Window System controls a local display device
- **mwm dtwm** Window managers for the display environment
- **aixterm xterm** Emulated terminals for system using PTY devices
- **xrdb** Manager for X resources like color map, font paths, and client attributes
- **xdm dtlogin** Display manager that manages local and remote X-server access

AIXwindows is included and installed with the AIX base operating system. It is built from the X11R6 code base and comprises all the fundamental X components listed previously, including an extensive X-client and library set. The X11R4 fonts and commands have been removed from the current release of AIXwindows. Compatibility libraries supporting legacy X11R5 applications still ship with AIX 5L, but X11R3 and X11R4 support last shipped with AIX 4.3.3.

Symbolic links are provided from the standard MIT directory locations to the various AIX subdirectory and file targets listed in Table 19-1.

List the installed X11 filesets with the following **lslpp** command (refer to the listing at the end of this chapter):

```
# lslpp -l "*X11*"   ◄─────── The X must be capitalized
```

Symbolic Links	AIX Repository Target	Comments
/bin	/usr/bin	Root link
/lib	/usr/lib	Root link
/usr/bin/X11	/usr/lpp/X11/bin	Executables
/usr/lib/X11	/usr/lpp/X11/lib/X11	Libraries, defaults, and fonts
/usr/include/X11	/usr/lpp/X11/include/X11	Include files and bitmaps
/usr/lib/libX*.a	/usr/lpp/X11/lib/R6/libX*.a	Tool and widget libraries
/usr/lib/libX*.a	/opt/freeware/lib/libX*.a	Tool and widget libraries

Table 19-1.   AIX Symbolic Links and Tagets

Linux Applications

New Linux-rooted Open Source applications such as the KDE window and display managers, **kwin** and **kwm**, are packaged as RPM binaries and installed in the `/opt/freeware` directory. Figure 19-1 shows KDE applications at work. Many of these applications have AIXwindows counterparts and function in a similar manner. I will include references to these new applications as we continue, but be aware that these applications are available from IBM on an "as-is" basis. For more information on the Open Source binaries and source code for AIX 4.3.3 and AIX 5L, refer to Chapter 16 and visit the following IBM Web site:

```
http://www.ibm.com/servers/aix/products/aixos/linux/download.html
```

MANAGEMENT

The following sections describe X11 functionality as it pertains to desktop environment support in order to build a fundamental understanding for those systems administrators

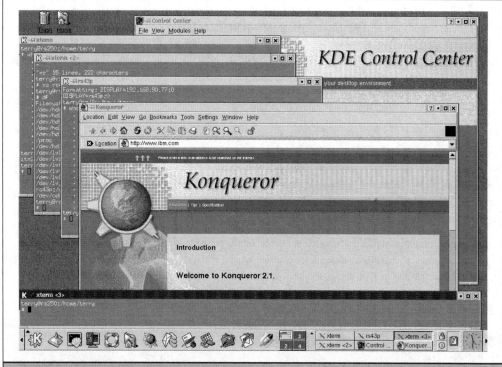

Figure 19-1. The K Desktop Environment on AIX 5L

new to X. AIXwindows is a stable implementation of X with a fully integrated and configurable Common Desktop Environment (CDE), including development tools and samples. Since most hard-core AIX programmers are accustomed to this IBM integration, the main focus of this chapter will be on the CDE desktop and basic X11 functionality as it pertains to desktops in general. For more in-depth information, search the Internet for "x.window.system.administration" from your favorite search engine.

Xinit and Application Defaults

The **startx** script is a front end to the more complicated **xinit** program that starts an X-server, if needed, and the first X-client. When **startx** runs, it first searches for xserverrc in the same manner it searches for the environment file $XINITRC, $HOME/.xinitrc, or xinit in the default system locations. All X11 application default resource files needed by different client applications are located in various app-defaults or app-custom directories. These application defaults can be overridden by custom settings in a user's $HOME/.Xdefaults file. X11 resources include things like foreground and background colors, fonts, and behavior. Here is a list of some AIX 5L locations for these files:

```
/usr/lpp/X11/defaults/  ◄────────── System xserverrc and xinitrc
/usr/lib/X11/app-defaults/  ◄──────── X11 application defaults
/usr/dt/app-defaults/  ◄──────── CDE application defaults
/opt/freeware/lib/X11/app-defaults/  ◄────────── Open source application defaults
/opt/freeware/kde/share/apps/kdisplay/app-defaults/ ◄──KDE application defaults
/usr/lib/X11/app-custom/  ◄──────── Custom resource defaults
```

Fonts

Default AIXwindows fonts are located in the /usr/lpp/X11/lib/X11/fonts directory. The symbolic link /usr/lib/X11 provides access using the standard X11 font path. Bitmap distribution format (*.bdf) and server normal format (*.snf) are X11R4 formatted fonts. The AIXwindows X11R6 distribution uses the portable compiled font (*.pcf) format. The pcf fonts take up less space and are readable across different machine architectures. The conversion program **bdftopcf** can be used to interchange formats.

The /usr/lib/X11/fonts directory, as well as each subdirectory, contains index (fonts.dir) and alias (fonts.alias) files, both of which are referenced by X-clients and servers to locate particular font files. The alias files are installed with each font fileset, and the index files are created by the **mkfontdir** command during install or manually. The fonts.dir file maps the compressed font file to the logical name. The fonts.alias file is used to reference long logical font names using a short alias. The logical font name is created from the font attributes, which include: foundry, font family, weight, slant, width, style, pixels, points, horizontal dpi, vertical dpi, spacing, average width, owner, and code set.

To rebuild the font directory index for the `misc` fonts after adding a new font file, run the following command:

```
# mkfontdir /usr/lib/X11/fonts/misc
```

You must manually edit the `/usr/lib/X11/fonts/misc/fonts.alias` file to add the new alias.

An Example of Logical Name Mapping in fonts.dir

Font File and its Logical Name

```
7x13.pcf.Z       -misc-fixed-medium-r-normal--13-120-75-75-c-70-iso8859-1
7x14.pcf.Z       -misc-fixed-medium-r-normal--14-130-75-75-c-70-iso8859-1
clR8x12.pcf.Z    -schumacher-clean-medium-r-normal--12-120-75-75-c-80- iso8859-1
6x9.pcf.Z        -misc-fixed-medium-r-normal--9-90-75-75-c-60-iso8859-1
clR8x13.pcf.Z    -schumacher-clean-medium-r-normal--13-130-75-75-c-80- iso8859-1
clR8x10.pcf.Z    -schumacher-clean-medium-r-normal--10-100-75-75-c-80- iso8859-1
5x7.pcf.Z        -misc-fixed-medium-r-normal--7-70-75-75-c-50-iso8859-1
clR8x16.pcf.Z    -schumacher-clean-medium-r-normal--16-160-75-75-c-80- iso8859-1
```

Alias Mapping in fonts.alias

Alias and its Logical Name

```
fixed      -misc-fixed-medium-r-semicondensed--13-120-75-75-c-60-iso8859-1
variable   -*-helvetica-bold-r-normal-*-*-120-*-*-*-*-iso8859-1
5x7        -misc-fixed-medium-r-normal--7-70-75-75-c-50-iso8859-1
5x8        -misc-fixed-medium-r-normal--8-80-75-75-c-50-iso8859-1
6x9        -misc-fixed-medium-r-normal--9-90-75-75-c-60-iso8859-1
6x10       -misc-fixed-medium-r-normal--10-100-75-75-c-60-iso8859-1
6x12       -misc-fixed-medium-r-semicondensed--12-110-75-75-c-60-iso8859-1
6x13       -misc-fixed-medium-r-semicondensed--13-120-75-75-c-60-iso8859-1
```

Window Managers

As the name implies, you use a window manager to dynamically arrange the layout of windows and objects on your display. It stylizes frame and title decoration, imparting a common look and feel to all the objects displayed, as illustrated in Figure 19-2. It is the window manager that allows you to click and drag objects on the screen, shuffle windows up and down, and customize pull-down menus. Without a window manager, you have no way to manipulate or move overlapping objects or alter their size. It is quite easy to see just how much you depend on a window manager by running an **xterm** without using one. If another **xterm** is started, it will overlay and block access to the first.

Table 19-2 lists the window managers shipped with AIX 5L. I will briefly cover the Motif-style window managers as a fundamental example for desktop management.

Figure 19-2. GNOME Desktop with Sawfish window manager on AIX 5L

Motif

The Motif window manager (**mwm**) is what most AIX users are familiar with from all previous releases of AIXwindows. The default configuration file used by **mwm** is /usr/lib/X11/system.mwmrc. Your local copy is $HOME/.mwmrc. In the example

Binary	Default Configuration File	Install Fileset	Description
mwm	/usr/lib/X11/system.mwmrc	X11.motif.mwm	Motif window manager
dtwm	/usr/dt/config/C/sys.dtwmrc	X11.Dt.rte	CDE window manager
kwin	undocumented	kdebase*ppc.rpm	KDE window manager
sawfish	undocumented	sawfish*ppc.rpm	GNOME window manager

Table 19-2. Window Managers for AIX 5L

that follows, I define a primary menu called *RootMenu* that will be displayed when button 1 on the mouse or the SHIFT-ESC key combination is pressed with the cursor on the root window. I can also restart or quit **mwm** from the menu or select a submenu called Applications. From the Applications menu, I can start an **xterm** window.

```
# SAMPLE .mwmrc
# Menus and Functions
Menu RootMenu
{
     "Root Menu"      f.title
     no-label         f.separator
     "Appls"          f.menu Applications
     "Restart?"       f.restart
     "Exit mwm"       f.quit_mwm
}
Menu Applications
{
     "Applications"   f.title
     no-label         f.separator
     "Xterm"          f.exec "xterm -fg white -bg steelblue &"
}
# Key and Button Bindings
Keys DefaultKeyBindings
{
  Shift<Key>Escape root    f.menu RootMenu
}
Buttons DefaultButtonBindings
{
     <Btn1Down>      root    f.menu RootMenu
}
```

CDE window manager resources are essentially **mwm** resources, so a short example is in order. I have specified the use of the icon box, defined menus to use black lettering on a light blue background, and set rom14 as my default font. Add the following lines to your sample $HOME/.Xdefaults file:

```
Mwm*useIconBox: true
Mwm*menu*foreground: black
Mwm*menu*background: lightblue
Mwm*fontList: rom14
```

Figure 19-3 shows what this example should look like after starting your X-server (**startx**) and the Motif window manager (**mwm**). See the next sections for more details on starting X.

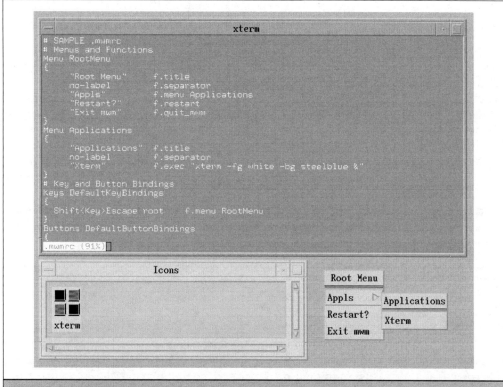

Figure 19-3.   Motif window manager RootMenu example on AIX 5L

User Configuration Files

The window manager is usually started last in your X-startup configuration file. It may be started in either the foreground or the background depending on the particular window manager. Starting the window manager last allows you to configure your environment so that you can exit the X-server when you exit the window manager. If you start your X session with the **startx** command or from the **xdm** display manager, then the window manager or desktop environment is usually the last entry in your $HOME/ .xinitrc file. The X display manager (**xdm**) is the only display manager shipped with AIX 5L that will execute your $HOME/.xinitrc file by default. Add the following lines to the end of your $HOME/.xinitrc file and uncomment the desktop you want started from your **xdm** login. The **startx** command will have problems when a display manager is running.

```
#exec /opt/freeware/kde/bin/startkde  ◄──────── For KDE desktop
#exec /opt/freeware/bin/gnome-session  ◄──────── For GNOME desktop
#exec /usr/dt/bin/Xsession  ◄──────── For CDE desktop
```

```
## For MWM uncomment the following lines.
#xsetroot -solid grey60
#xterm -geometry 80x24+0+0 -fg white -bg black -name MWM_Session &
#exec mwm -multiscreen -xrm "ShowFeedback: -quit"
```

Window managers, like all well-behaved X-clients, provide a mechanism to allow users to customize the appearance, interaction, and behavior of their sessions via resource files. A start-up configuration file used in conjunction with the X-resource information defined in the $HOME/.Xdefaults file can be modified to tailor the window manager to meet your needs. I typically use the style manager to control the look and feel of my desktop and find maintaining a personal Xdefaults file cumbersome for my computer work style. But if you are interested, there is an unlimited amount of documentation and example files on the Internet. Just search for *xdefaults*.

The dtwmrc configuration file will generally allow you to define actions and menus, which are bound to a mouse button or key for activation. Although formats do differ for each window manager, they tend to follow the following format:

LABEL/TITLE, FUNCTION ◄———————— Define menus and actions

KEY/BUTTON, CONTEXT, FUNCTION ◄———————— Bind keys/buttons to actions

The context describes where the button or key action is active. For example, you may want to use a button to display a menu only when the cursor is on the root window. Window manager functions are called by defining the *f.function_name* in the configuration file entry. Table 19-3 lists common function names. Read the man pages of dtwmrc for more details.

Function	Purpose
f.exec	Start a command or shell script
f.kill	Kill the selected client
f.menu	Display a menu
f.title	Display a menu title
f.separator	Display a separator bar in menus
f.raise	Bring client to the front
f.resize	Resize a client
f.move	Move a client
f.minimize	Reduce the client to an icon
f.maximize	Restore icon to an open client
f.restart	Restart the window manager

Table 19-3. Window Manager Functions

Display Manager

Authentication is important in any distributed client/server environment. The X display manager provides a protocol for user-based access control to X11 session logins. An unfortunate common practice in many X11 environments is to use the **xhost** command to disable access control to a display. The **xhost** command authenticates only at the host level. This means that anyone logged into that host has **xhost** access to your X-server. The display manager already has a better access control mechanism called an MIT-MAGIC-COOKIE-1, which is secured by file access permission. The display manager writes a random 128-bit code (the magic cookie) into your $HOME/.Xauthority file and shares this number with your X-server. X-clients must then authenticate themselves to the server by presenting this code when connecting to the server. This magic cookie is shared with the other machines in the network using the **xauth** command. A simpler method is to use a secure shell to push your $HOME/.Xauthority file to your $HOME directory on the machines that need it. If you are using a distributed file system like NSF or DSF for your home directory, then the file will already be accessible to the X-clients.

Table 19-4 lists the three display managers shipped with AIX 5L. Both **xdm** and **dtlogin** have login authentication methods that will force a user to change their password if the system requires it. Unfortunately, they both have configuration tasks in order to allow desktops other than their defaults. Now **kdm**, seen in the following illustration, has simple configuration tasks to allow different desktops; by default it is configured for KDE, GNOME, CDE, failsafe, and **xterm**.

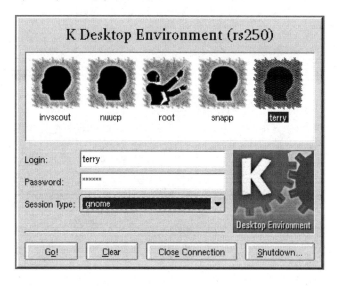

The one big problem with **kdm** is that it currently has no provision that will force users to change their passwords if the system requires it. This must be rectified in future releases before **kdm** can replace **dtlogin** or **xdm**. The **dtlogin** display manager ignores the $HOME/.xinitrc file, making it difficult for users to configure for

Binary	Configuration Directory	Install Fileset	Description
xdm	/usr/lpp/X11/lib/X11/xdm/	X11.apps.xdm	X display manager
dtlogin	/usr/dt/config/	X11.Dt.rte	CDE display manager
kdm	/opt/freeware/kde/share/config/kdm	kdebase*ppc.rpm	KDE display manager

Table 19-4.   Display Managers for AIX 5L

desktops other than CDE. So that leaves the reliable **xdm** as the only display manager I can recommend for all the new AIX 5L desktops.

This illustration shows the login GUI for **xdm**.

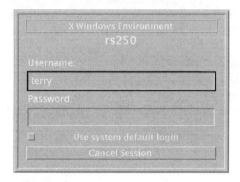

Display Manager Configuration

The display managers in use similar configuration files stored in their respective configuration directories (refer to Table 19-4).

The xdm-config file must have a *DisplayManager*userPath* definition added, or **xdm** will use a hard-coded PATH variable to overwrite the one from the /etc/ environment file, where most systems administrators define it. The user can still overwrite or add to the path from his $HOME/.xinitrc or $HOME/.profile files. Add the following line to the existing definitions in the xdm-config file:

```
DisplayManager*userPath:   /bin:/usr/ucb:/usr/dt/bin:/usr/local/bin:\
/opt/freeware/bin:/opt/freeware/kde/bin
```

I did not add /bin/X11 because **xdm** adds /usr/lpp/X11/bin to the end of the PATH variable by default. Remember, /bin/X11 is a symbolic link to /usr/lpp/ X11/bin.

The Xservers file defines where to force the display manager's login GUI. You may want to comment out the default last line that forces the display on the local console, particularly if it has no graphic adapter display. You can also force a login GUI to display on an X-server that does not support the X Display Manager Control Protocol (XDMCP) by adding the following line to the `Xservers` file:

```
<hostname_of_xterminal>:0 foreign /usr/lpp/X11/bin/X -T -force
```

The `Xaccess` file can limit what hosts have access to directly or indirectly access the login GUI. To limit only *MyXterminal* access to the display manager, comment out the following two lines that begin with an asterisk (*) and add the two *MyXterminal* lines to replace them in the `Xservers` file:

```
#*          ◄──────────Grant service to all
MyXterminal.DomianName
#*                  CHOOSER  BROADCAST  ◄──────────Any indirect host can get a chooser
MyXterminal.DomianName          CHOOSER  BROADCAST
```

The display managers invoke the `Xsession` file to set up the desktop environment and resources. The **dtlogin** display manager treats the `Xsession` file as an executable script and stores it in a different location from the configuration files as `/usr/dt/bin/Xsession`. The **xdm** and **kdm** display managers provide for sourcing the `/etc/profile`, `$HOME/.profile`, and `$HOME/.login` files, whereas **dtlogin** provides no sourcing of `/etc/profile` from the Xsession file and only a hook from `$HOME/.dtprofile` that allows users to source their own `.profile` or `.login` files when DTSOURCEPROFILE is *true*. The `Xsession` file for the **kdm** display manager will source the profile files before calling the `/usr/dt/bin/Xsession` script if you select CDE as your desktop.

START AND STOP DISPLAY MANAGERS

Each of the three display managers can be started by an entry in the `/etc/inittab` file at system boot time or from the command line, and if that is how you started the one you use, then you may stop it, if needed, by simply killing the PID found in the appropriate `xdm-pid` file. I like to keep a line for each display manager in the `/etc/inittab` file with only the one I use, at system boot, uncommented. My entries look like this:

```
xdm:2:wait:/usr/lpp/X11/bin/xdm        # Starts XDM as daemon
:kdm:2:wait:/opt/freeware/kde/bin/kdm  # Starts KDM as daemon
:dt:2:wait:/etc/rc.dt                  # Starts dtlogin as daemon
:dt_nogb:2:wait:/etc/rc.dt             # Starts dtlogin as system resource
```

To stop them after system boot has started your preferred display manager, use one of the following commands:

```
# kill -term $(cat /usr/lpp/X11/lib/X11/xdm/xdm-pid) ◄──────────Stops xdm
# kill -term $(cat /opt/freeware/kde/share/config/kdm/xdm-pid) ◄─Stops kdm
# kill -term $(cat /var/dt/Xpid) ◄──────────Stops dtlogin
```

If you make changes to the configuration files, then refresh the display manager with

```
# kill -HUP <PID>
```

To start a display manager manually from the command line, use *only one* of the following commands:

```
# /usr/lpp/X11/bin/xdm ◄────────── Starts xdm
# /opt/freeware/kde/bin/kdm ◄────────── Starts kdm
# /usr/dt/bin/dtlogin -daemon ◄────────── Starts dtlogin
```

If you start **dtlogin** from the command line with `/etc/rc.dt`, as the `/etc/inittab` file does, then the script tests to see if the system is booting; if not, it starts **dtlogin** with the system resource controller (**srcmstr**). So if you want to start and stop **dtlogin** as a system resource, use the following commands:

```
# startsrc -s dtsrc ◄────────── Starts dtlogin as a system resource
# lssrc -s dtsrc ◄────────── Lists the status (active or inoperative)
# refresh -s dtsrc ◄────────── Makes dtlogin reread the configuration files
# stopsrc -s dtsrc ◄────────── Stops dtlogin as a system resource
```

Another custom feature for **dtlogin** is the **dtconfig** script and SMIT panel to add or remove the `inittab` entry with the **mkitab** and **rmitab** commands. The following are four optional methods of using the **dtconfig** command:

```
# smit dtconfig ◄────────── SMIT fast path to dtconfig
# dtconfig -e ◄────────── Enable dtlogin on next
# dtconfig -enograph ◄────────── Enable dtlogin as system resource
# dtconfig -d ◄────────── Disable dtlogin on next reboot
```

Access Control

You must have guessed by now that all these display managers are enhanced **xdm** servers. That gives us the `/dev/xdm` devices that can be defined as valid *ttys* in the `/etc/security/user` file to help limit user access through *only* the display manager. If you also disable **rlogin**, the user will be able to log in only from the display manager running on the local graphics console. Please note that if the **rshd** is active on the system, the users may still have `hosts.equiv` and `.rhosts` access. To limit a user to remote access only through the display manager login, disable **rshd** access (not explained here) and run the following **chuser** command:

```
# chuser ttys='/dev/xdm/MyXterminal_0' terry
```

Read `/usr/lpp/X11/lib/X11/xdm/README` for more details.
To see the status of the remote shell resource, run the following **lssrc** command:

```
# lssrc -t shell
Service   Command        Description   Status
 shell    /usr/sbin/rshd  rshd          active
```

If this resource is active, the user may still be able to **rsh** commands to circumvent the display manager limit. In most development environments, **rsh** access is required, although you might want all the desktops running on a trusted and secure server with **rsh** disabled. These desktops might then be trusted to a large development environment.

THE DESKTOP ENVIRONMENT

Everyone likes software that is intuitive and has a common look and feel across all the applications they use. Nobody enjoys spending time reading manuals. All of us want to be able to install an application and begin using it immediately. This means that each application must behave and interact with the user in ways that are already familiar. This capability can be realized only if the operating environment provides application interface specifications that can easily be incorporated into new software products, enabling them to exhibit similar traits even if developed by different vendors. For developers, the proper path to successfully implementing a common look and feel in your product is through a specification agreement between the software vendors. To implement this idea, a group of vendors got together at Uniforum in 1993 and formed the Common Open Software Environment (COSE). The COSE initiative proposed to assist in the development of open systems standards through technology sharing between the member vendors. The focus of much of the COSE effort was on user interface infrastructure. This eventually led to a set of specifications called the Common Desktop Environment (CDE) based on windowing and object technologies from Hewlett-Packard, IBM, OSF, Novell, and SunSoft.

Commercial UNIX vendors quickly adopted this new, reasonably licensed product from The Open Group (X/Open) as their default desktops or sold it as an option. Then Linux came along, and users wanted an open source desktop solution that was free. Today there are more open source desktops and window managers than we ever imagined. Two of these robust desktops, KDE and GNOME, are now included as free options to AIX 4.3.3 and AIX 5L.

PLiG Ltd has a wonderful Web site with a wealth of information on desktops and window managers, past and present, at the following URL:

```
http://www.plig.org/xwinman/
```

DESKTOP COMPONENTS

A display manager presents a login GUI on your X-server display and authenticates your identity as detailed in the Display Manager section. A session manager then restores your last running applications and window environment to your display.

Window managers facilitate the manipulation of multiple workspaces and manage your windows and menu layout. The style manager provides the means for tailoring fonts, color, and wallpaper for each workspace. File, application, and help managers make up the interface to the UNIX file system, commands, and application set. These tools are accessed using the main panel launcher.

Session Manager

The session manager is responsible for setting up the user's desktop environment after login processing has completed. The session managers can restore either the user's initial desktop configuration, called the home session, or a snapshot of the running desktop saved by the session manager during the last logout, called the current session. This option is configurable in CDE from the Style Manager–Startup (key) icon (see Figure 19-4). The user can select either home or current or to be asked at logout. Select **Set Home Session** from the same Startup panel to create the `home` snapshot subdirectory. The environment and resources for `home` and `current` desktop sessions are stored in `$HOME/.dt/sessions/` subdirectories as shown in Table 19-5. Users may also elect to have the session manager execute applications and scripts at login and logout times by placing the command strings in the `sessionetc` and `sessionexit` files.

File and Application Managers

The CDE file and application managers work jointly to provide a graphical interface to the UNIX file system. These tools assist you in navigating directories, managing files, and accessing applications using a *file-and-folder, point-and-click* paradigm. Files and applications are represented and manipulated as objects. This means that each object has an associated name, type, and behavior. Type and behavior attributes can include executable paths, passed parameters, prompts, and associated files. Object linking via type and behavior is how the file and application managers work together. For example, a C language source file may be branded as a type that would automatically invoke the

Location and Filename	Description
$HOME/.dt/sessions/<current,home>/dt.resources	X-resources
$HOME/.dt/sessions/<current,home>/dt.session	Running applications
$HOME/.dt/sessions/<current,home>/dt.settings	Desktop custom
$HOME/.dt/sessions/<current,home>/dtxxxxx	Application state
$HOME/.dt/sessions/sessionetc	Run after startup
$HOME/.dt/sessions/sessionexit	Run at logout
$HOME/.dt/errorlog	Error messages

Table 19-5.   Session Manager Files

lpex source code editor when it is clicked from the file manager. CDE object capability also extends to *drag-and-drop* behavior and associating particular icons by object type. Figure 19-4 shows the Install icon for the Mail subpanel where I dragged and dropped the Calculator icon from the application manager.

Main Panel

Now that login processing has completed and desktop resources have been restored, the CDE main panel will be displayed on the screen. This panel is basically an application launcher. Clicking icons displayed on the main panel will expand selection drawers, open menus, and start applications. Like other CDE services, the main panel display can be personalized to support particular application sets and user preferences. Attributes that make up the main panel are stored in database files identified by a .fp suffix and stored in the .dt/types/fp_dynamic/ subdirectories. Do not worry about the how the files are created, because CDE will create them after you drag and drop program icons from the application manager to the install icon and then copy them to the main panel (see Figure 19-4).

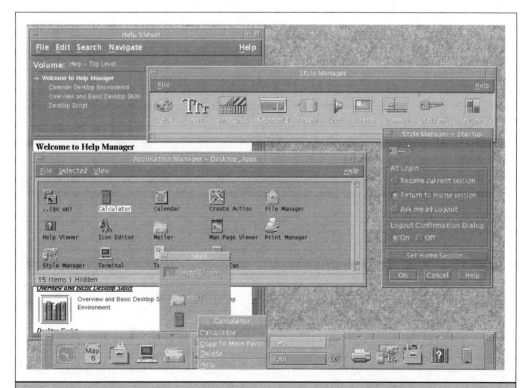

Figure 19-4.   The Common Desktop Environment application and style managers

Along with launching other CDE tools and UNIX applications, the CDE main panel also provides an interface to the printer subsystem. Clicking the printer icon slides out a drawer that allows you to access the print manager and default printers. Once a printer and queue are identified, clicking its icon will access the printer.

Style Manager

The CDE style manager's job is to make your life easier when customizing your desktop. It can be started from the main panel and provides a nice GUI interface for doing things like setting colors, fonts, wallpaper, keyboard layout, and screen savers, and for configuring window manager options. It greatly simplifies tailoring X-resources (see Figure 19-4). The style manager is also used to set your login session preferences for the session manager. Style manager resources are stored in the Dtstyle file.

Window Manager

The window manager, sometimes referred to as workspace manager, manages windows, menus, and key bindings on the desktop. CDE's **dtwm** window manager design is based on the Motif Window Manager (**mwm**). The configuration syntax for **dtwm** is very similar to **mwm**. Copy the /usr/dt/config/C/sys.dtwmrc file to $HOME/.dt/dtwmrc as a starter file for your personal window manager mouse button–activated menus. Let's add the **xterm** command to the middle mouse button. Edit your new $HOME/.dt/dtwmrc file and add the next line to the existing *DtButtonBindings* description group:

```
<Btn2Down>    root      f.menu   DtMidRootMenu
```

Now go back to the top of the file and add the following new menu after the *DtRootMenu* description group:

```
Menu DtMidRootMenu
{
    "Middle Menu"     f.title
     no-label         f.separator
    "Local Xterm"     f.exec "xterm -fn 10x20 -title `hostname`"
}
```

Click **Restart Workspace Manager** from the right mouse Workspace Menu and then test your new middle mouse button "Local Xterm" application.

Help Manager

The help manager (see Help View in Figure 19-4) provides a hypertext help and documentation environment. Information is organized in a hierarchy by volume and subtopic. You navigate documents using index and search tools. The key here is that this system behaves just as you have come to expect from other desktop help interfaces.

DESKTOP SUMMARY

All the desktops can be customized, as seen in the following illustration, with the KDE panel, but the Common Desktop Environment (CDE) seems to be a few years ahead when it comes to ease of customization. I set up new users all the time and enjoy their amazement as I start pointing and clicking, opening windows, editing `.dtprofile` then `.xinitrc`, and copying over a custom `dtwmrc` file before dragging the best little X calculator in the world to their main panel as I say: "there you are, all set up." Just remember to make a snapshot of all the new configurations before you log off.

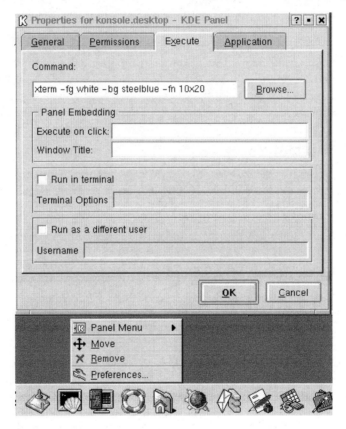

IBM X STATION ADMINISTRATION

Most software X-server solutions and third party X-terminals support XDMCP out of the box, and the preceding detail and configurations should be all you need. This section applies only to IBM X Stations model 120 through 160. IBM no longer supports this hardware with AIX 5L. However, the version of IBM's X Station Manager software shipped with AIX 4.3 and AIX 4.2 should work fine. I was able to install the following filesets on AIX 5L, but make no guarantees:

```
X11.x_st_mgr.rte        4.2.1.0
X11.x_st_mgr.compat  4.2.0.0
X11.msg.en_US.x_st_mgr.rte    4.3.0.0
```

X stations provide an effective alternative to providing fully equipped disk workstations as platforms for X Window. Using one or more workstations as servers, X stations provides all the functionality of a complete X Window–based workstation. X stations also reduces the administration headaches for both the system administrator and end user.

Most environments support a number of different vendor X stations, and it is useful to manage them as a group from central servers under **xdm**. At EPROM level 1.5 for the X Station 120 and using the IBM X Station Manager at version 1.3 or above, all models of the IBM X Station can be supported alongside the rest of your X station menagerie with **xdm**.

Configuration and Boot

When you flip on the power switch, the X station performs a power-on self-test (POST). Once POST is passed, it will optionally direct or broadcast a bootp request packet in an attempt to find a boot server. Once contact is made, the information received determines the IP addresses of the X station and the server and the name of the boot configuration file. Since this information can be configured into the X station, you may opt to bypass the bootp step for normal operation. To configure address information into the X station, access the network configuration menu by pressing the F12 key after POST has completed. These configuration screens enable you to set the IP address information for the terminal, server, and gateway, and disable the bootp process. Similar information may be configured for token ring connections. The models 130, 150, and 160 also support IP over a serial link using SLIP. To configure the model 130, 150, or 160 for a serial TTY connection, press the F11 key after POST has completed.

Once the boot server has been contacted, the X station will **tftp** a copy of the boot file `/usr/lpp/x_st_mgr/bin/bootfile` from the server. The boot file and configuration file downloaded inform the X station which fonts, keymap, rgb database, and server code should be requested from the server. During the bootp and tftp steps, the X station display provides some diagnostic information concerning the terminal/server packet exchanges. The two lines of interest are

```
BOOTP    0000 0000 0000 0000
TFTP    0000 0000 0000 0000 0000
```

The first group of numbers indicates the number of packets sent from the X station. The second group indicates the number of packets received from the server. The third group is the count of bad packets received. The fourth group displays the number of timeouts that have occurred. The fifth group on the TFTP line displays the final error code for the transaction. You may access further diagnostic and test information by pressing CTRL-BREAK after POST has completed.

AIX X Station Manager Configuration

Again, remember that IBM does not support the X Station Manager on AIX 5L. The AIX X Station Manager program provides the boot services for IBM X Stations. Once the X Station Manager is installed, verify that its services are defined in the proper configuration file with the following **grep** commands:

```
# grep x_st_mgr /etc/rc.tcpip
/usr/lpp/x_st_mgr/bin/x_st_mgrd -b/usr/lpp/x_st_mgr/bin/x_st_mgrd.cf -s x_st_mg

# grep -e bootp -e x_st_mgr /etc/services
bootps    67/udp    # bootp server port
bootpc    68/udp    # bootp client port
x_st_mgrd 7000/tcp  # ibm X terminal

# grep bootps /etc/inetd.conf
bootps dgram udp wait root /etc/bootpd bootpd /etc/bootptab
```

You may then define your network type, boot file, and boot file directory via the X Station selection from the SMIT Devices menu. You may also specify whether the server is a primary or secondary server. It is a good idea to support two boot servers if possible. The X stations may then be configured to try each server in sequence at startup time.

```
# smit x_config  ◄──────── Configure X Station Manager
```

The X Station Manager's x_st_mgrd.cf Configuration File

```
xam.foo.edu DISPLAY=xam.foo.edu:0; export DISPLAY;\
XSTATION=xam.foo.edu; export XSTATION;\
LANG=En_US; export LANG;\
/usr/lpp/x_st_mgr/bin/pclient\
-p /usr/lpp/X11/defaults/xmodmap/En_US\
-l keyboard\
-s 5\
-m /usr/lpp/X11/bin/xmodmap\
-a "/usr/lpp/X11/bin/aixterm -fn Rom14 -geometry 80x25+0+0\
-W -e/usr/lpp/x_st_mgr/bin/login"
```

The X Station Manager's Boot File

```
/usr/lpp/x_st_mgr/nls/keymap
/usr/lpp/x_st_mgr/nls/msg
/usr/lpp/x_st_mgr/bin/x11xor3.out
/usr/lib/X11/fonts,/usr/lib/X11/fonts/ibm850
/usr/lpp/x_st_mgr/bin/rgb.txt
```

Once you have defined your network type, you may define each of the X stations being supported. You need to identify each X station's network type, the hardware address of the adapter, whether **xdm** services will be used, and the initial application to be started. You may also define local printer support for X stations equipped with printers via the SMIT printer/plotter menu.

X11 LPP Filesets

```
X11.Dt.ToolTalk    AIX CDE ToolTalk Support
X11.Dt.bitmaps     AIX CDE Bitmaps
X11.Dt.helpinfo    AIX CDE Help Files and Volumes
X11.Dt.helpmin     AIX CDE Minimum Help Files
X11.Dt.helprun     AIX CDE Runtime Help
X11.Dt.lib         AIX CDE Runtime Libraries
X11.Dt.rte         AIX Common Desktop Environment (CDE) 1.0
X11.adt.bitmaps    AIXwindows Application Development Toolkit Bitmap Files
X11.adt.ext        AIXwindows Application Development Toolkit for X Extensions
X11.adt.imake      AIXwindows Application Development Toolkit imake
X11.adt.include    AIXwindows Application Development Toolkit Include Files
X11.adt.lib        AIXwindows Application Development Toolkit Libraries
X11.adt.motif      AIXwindows Application Development Toolkit Motif
X11.apps.aixterm   AIXwindows aixterm Application
X11.apps.clients   AIXwindows Client Applications
X11.apps.config    AIXwindows Configuration Applications
X11.apps.custom    AIXwindows Customizing Tool
X11.apps.msmit     AIXwindows msmit Application
X11.apps.pm        AIXwindows Power Management GUI Utility
X11.apps.rte       AIXwindows Runtime Configuration Applications
X11.apps.util      AIXwindows Utility Applications
X11.apps.xdm       AIXwindows xdm Application
X11.apps.xterm     AIXwindows xterm Application
X11.base.common    AIXwindows Runtime Common Directories
X11.base.lib       AIXwindows Runtime Libraries
X11.base.rte       AIXwindows Runtime Environment
X11.base.smt       AIXwindows Runtime Shared Memory Transport
X11.compat.lib.X11R5       AIXwindows X11R5 Compatibility Libraries
X11.fnt.coreX              AIXwindows X Consortium Fonts
X11.fnt.defaultFonts       AIXwindows Default Fonts
X11.fnt.iso1               AIXwindows Latin 1 Fonts
X11.fnt.util               AIXwindows Font Utilities
X11.help.en_US.Dt.helpinfo AIX CDE Help Files and Volumes
X11.loc.en_US.Dt.rte       CDE Locale Configuration
X11.loc.en_US.base.lib     AIXwindows Client Locale Config
X11.loc.en_US.base.rte     AIXwindows Locale Configuration
X11.man.en_US.Dt.adt       AIX CDE Toolkit Man Pages
X11.man.en_US.Dt.rte       AIX CDE Man Pages
X11.motif.lib              AIXwindows Motif Libraries
X11.motif.mwm              AIXwindows Motif Window Manager
X11.msg.en_US.Dt.helpmin   AIX CDE Minimum Help Files
```

```
X11.msg.en_US.Dt.rte          AIX CDE Messages
X11.msg.en_US.adt.ext         AIXwindows X Extensions Messages
X11.msg.en_US.adt.imake       AIXwindows imake Messages
X11.msg.en_US.apps.aixterm    AIXwindows aixterm Messages
X11.msg.en_US.apps.clients    AIXwindows Client Application Msgs
X11.msg.en_US.apps.config     AIXwindows Config Application Msgs
X11.msg.en_US.apps.custom     AIXwindows Customizing Tool Msgs
X11.msg.en_US.apps.pm         AIXwindows Power Mgmt GUI Msgs
X11.msg.en_US.apps.rte        AIXwindows Runtime Config Messages
X11.msg.en_US.apps.xdm        AIXwindows xdm Messages
X11.msg.en_US.base.common     AIXwindows Common Messages
X11.msg.en_US.base.rte        AIXwindows Runtime Env. Messages
X11.msg.en_US.fnt.util        AIXwindows Font Utilities Messages
X11.msg.en_US.motif.lib       AIXwindows Motif Libraries Messages
X11.msg.en_US.motif.mwm       AIXwindows Motif Window Mgr Msgs
X11.msg.en_US.vsm.rte         Visual System Mgmt. Helps & Msgs
X11.msg.en_US.x_st_mgr.rte    X Station Manager
X11.samples.apps.clients      AIXwindows Sample X Consortium Clients
X11.samples.common            AIXwindows Imakefile Structure for Samples
X11.samples.lib.Core          AIXwindows Sample X Consortium Core Libraries
X11.vfb                       Virtual Frame Buffer Software for AIXwindows
X11.vsm.lib                   Visual System Management Library
X11.x_st_mgr.compat           X Station Manager Compatibility
X11.x_st_mgr.rte              X Station Manager Runtime Environment
bos.rte.X11                   AIXwindows Device Support
devices.*.X11                 AIXwindows Graphics Adapter Software
devices.*.X11.com             AIXwindows Graphics Adapter Common Software
```

CHECKLIST

The following is a checklist for the key points in X11 Administration.

- ☐ Identify the complete X Window System, Version 11.
- ☐ Present display windows by using the X11 client/server protocol.
- ☐ Identify the fundamental components of the X11 environment.
- ☐ Describe X11 functionality as it pertains to desktop environment support.
- ☐ Start and stop display managers.
- ☐ Define the Common Desktop Environment (CDE).
- ☐ Identify the desktop components.
- ☐ Customize the desktops.
- ☐ Identify the complete IBM X Station Administration environment.

PART IX

Managing Users and Resources

CHAPTER 20

Managing the User Environment

Uer is a four-letter word! If you administer multiuser systems and haven't taken care to define default environment policies or streamline account management, there are likely many other four-letter words in your vocabulary. A large user base can dominate a Systems Administrator's time with trivial tasks like adding and expiring accounts, setting passwords, juggling home directories, fixing UID collisions. . . the list goes on and on, and so do the requests. Just remember that it's users that keep us employed!

The default environment policies can be thought of as a contract for basic services and resources. Whether it is formally stated or implied, your user base assumes some level of support. There will be less confusion for both your users and user support communities if the basic rules of the road are formally stated and documented. A simple way to disseminate this type of information is to make it available as a man page or help file. You can also provide a default policy statement as a `msg` file that is displayed the first time a user logs in to the system.

First you need to define what the policies are and how they will be implemented. What are the requirements for establishing an account? What basic resources are provided with an account? What does the default shell environment look like? How long does an account last?

Resources policies must take these basic factors into account:

- Physical resources
- Resource limits
- Account access rights
- Account environment

PHYSICAL RESOURCES

Let's start out by making sure we don't promise more than we can deliver. What are the workload characteristics of your user base? How much in the way of disk, tape, memory, and CPU resources will be required to support your expected total number of users and the expected concurrent user sessions? In an existing environment, you can construct a fairly good profile by sifting through old accounting information. It's also worthwhile to benchmark your application mix. Push the system to the limit. Stress the CPU, paging, and I/O subsystems. This will give you a feel for what to expect during spikes in load.

User Filesystems

After you have determined the resource level you can offer, structure the physical resources such that they can be managed easily under software control. If your user base is continually changing, you may want to segregate your user `/home` filesystem from the rest of the operating system. This isolates these filesystems from operating system upgrades and maintenance. Set up user filesystems on different physical disks and volume groups. This will facilitate moving them between machines if circumstances require. Use a naming convention for user file-system mount points that makes them easy to remember and easy to identify. A possible method would be to use the /home<number> scheme on AIX. In a distributed or clustered environment, you might use the first character of the machine name that owns the filesystem followed by an integer. Don't make them too long!

To reduce the impact of managing user home directories in multiple user filesystems, use symbolic links to link the top-level user directories in each filesystem to a common /home directory. No matter where a particular user's home directory physically resides, it can be accessed via the /home/<user name> path. Specify the symbolic link path name for the home directory field in the /etc/passwd file too. This will allow you to move user directories around in your user filesystems to balance utilization without requiring each user to learn a new home directory path.

```
# ln -s /home6/stimpy /home/stimpy
stimpy:!:1234:30:Stimpson_Cat:/home/stimpy:/bin/ksh
```

You will also need to size your user filesystems. If large files are not heavily used, then multiple small filesystems *may* be preferred. Small filesystems (less than 1GB) reduce backup and restore times. They can be easily moved and will partition your user community such that a filesystem catastrophe won't affect your entire user base.

If you do not have a large distributed user base, then the default /home filesystem is all that is needed. Depending on what the users are doing and storing in their home directories, /home can grow quickly, especially in a development and production support environment. Occasionally the user community needs a review of what is appropriate to store in /home. As you know, most computer users are pack rats that have to keep a backup copy of everything, but they use /home more often than not for this storage. Of course, disk space is cheap, so you may just want to make /home into a huge filesystem and let users have all of the disk space that they want. This need varies by environment.

UID SPACE AND GROUPS

User account names are in fact a matter of human convenience in identifying users under UNIX. The AIX operating system identifies a particular user by an unsigned long integer called the UID. The UID is mapped to the user name in the /etc/passwd file. UIDs are used on other UNIX systems but may be represented under other integer formats.

It's a good idea to segregate your user UID space from the UIDs used by system daemons' administrative accounts. This simplifies the task of identifying privileged accounts for accounting and security applications. Pick a number like 1000 to define the bottom of your user UID space for allocation. The consistency of UIDs is extremely important in environments where users have accounts on multiple machines. Some examples include HACMP clusters (HACMP stands for High Availability Cluster Multi-Processing; see Chapter 28 for details); in distributed environment environments, or if you are using Network File System (NFS), you must ensure that UIDs are consistent across all of the systems. By *consistent,* I mean that if user "stimpy" is UID 1234 on host A then the same UID is reserved for stimpy on any other system. Ownership and permission problems can arise if the same UID represents different users in clustered, distributed, and NFS environments. Remember, the operating system identifies users by UID, not by user name.

While you define your UID space, it's also a good idea to plan your Group ID (GID) space. Groups provide a coarse mechanism for sharing information between users. File and directory permissions offer read, write, and execute permissions for world, group, and owner. AIX and other UNIX flavors assume a limited group set to implement access privileges. What needs to be decided is whether you want to implement other GID sets for specific workgroups or collaborators. If your user base is small, this can be done relatively easily. For large numbers of users, managing GID sets can be a big chore.

The /etc/group and /etc/security/group Files

All GID mapping is maintained in the /etc/group and /etc/security/group files. The /etc/group file lists each group name and GID followed by the list of members, or user names. The /etc/security/group file contains a stanza for each group name in the /etc/group file, indicates whether the group may be administered by users other than root, and identifies the administrators by user name. Groups and their associated attributes are managed through SMIT or WebSM, or else from a series of group management commands listed here:

mkgroup ◄──────── Create a new group
chgroup ◄──────── Change group attributes
lsgroup ◄──────── List groups and attributes
chgrpmem ◄──────── Change administrators or members of a group
setgroups ◄──────── Reset the current groups set for a user
newgrp ◄──────── Set the group ID for session
rmgroup ◄──────── Remove a group

Now for a few examples. The first file is a sample /etc/group; the second file is a sample /etc/security/group.

A Sample /etc/group File

```
system:!:0:root,ops
daemon:!:1:
bin:!:2:root,bin
sys:!:3:root,bin,sys
adm:!:4:bin,adm,kenm,root
```

```
uucp:!:5:uucp
mail:!:6:
security:!:7:root
cron:!:8:root
staff:!:10:root,ren,stimpy,daffy,huey,dewey
user:!:30:luge,acadmus,gwyneira,bungi
```

A Sample /etc/security/group File

```
system:
        admin = true
daemon:
        admin = true
bin:
        admin = true
sys:
        admin = true
adm:
        admin = true
uucp:
        admin = true
mail:
        admin = true
security:
        admin = true
cron:
        admin = true
staff:
        admin = false
        adms = ren,stimpy
user:
        admin = false
```

RESOURCE LIMITS

How much of the pie are you going to give each user? How do you make sure each user gets no more than his or her fair share? Profiling the application mix with estimated concurrent users will give you some ballpark figures. AIX provides the capability to enforce limits on each user's slice of the available system resources through operating system controls. Limits can be defined for CPU, memory, and disk utilization on a per-process basis. The total number of concurrent processes per user is capped by the kernel configuration parameter. Aggregate filesystem usage can be governed through activating disk quotas at user and group levels.

The /etc/security/limits File

The kernel manages per-process limits using the **setrlimit()**, **getrlimit()**, and **vlimit()** system calls. Each process has an associated `rlimit` structure that indicates soft and hard ceilings for each resource type. The `rlimit` structure is defined in `/usr/include/sys/resource.h`. Default and resource limits for the system and users are specified in the `/etc/security/limits` file. Each user defined to the system is represented by a stanza identified by user name. System defaults are active for each user that does not have an overriding parameter under the user's stanza. When a process exceeds one of the specified limits, it is killed. Check out the sample `/etc/security/limits` file here:

A Sample /etc/security/limits File

```
*
* Sizes are in multiples of 512 byte blocks, CPU time is in seconds
*
* fsize       - soft file size in blocks
* core        - soft core file size in blocks
* cpu         - soft per process CPU time limit in seconds
* data        - soft data segment size in blocks
* stack       - soft stack segment size in blocks
* rss         - soft real memory sage in blocks
* fsize_hard - hard file size in blocks
* core_hard  - hard core file size in blocks
* cpu_hard   - hard per process CPU time limit in seconds
* data_hard  - hard data segment size in blocks
* stack_hard - hard stack segment size in blocks
* rss_hard   - hard real memory usage in blocks
*
* The following table contains the default hard values if the
* hard values are not explicitly defined:
*
*    Attribute          Value
*    ==========    =============
*    fsize_hard    set to fsize
*    cpu_hard      set to cpu
*    core_hard         -1
*    data_hard         -1
*    stack_hard        -1
*    rss_hard          -1
*    ==========    =============
*
* NOTE:  A value of -1 implies "unlimited"
*
```

```
*
* The following table contains the default hard values if the
* hard values are not explicitly defined:
*
* Attribute          Value
* ==========         ==========
* fsize_hard         set to fsize
* cpu_hard           set to cpu
* core_hard             -1
* data_hard             -1
* stack_hard            -1
* rss_hard              -1
*
* NOTE: A value of -1 implies "unlimited"
*
default:
        fsize = 2097151
        core = 2048
        cpu = -1
        data = 262144
        rss = 65536
        stack = 65536
root:
daemon:
bin:
sys:
adm:
uucp:
guest:
nobody:
lpd:
stimpy:
        fsize_hard = 10240
        cpu_hard = 3600
nuucp:
```

The kernel limits the maximum number of processes per user as specified by the kernel configuration parameter maxuproc. The default value of 40 indicates that up to 40 processes may be running concurrently for a given user. The value may not be exceeded by logging into the system multiple times. The maxuproc value may be altered using SMIT, WebSM, or the **chdev** command (see the SMIT panel in Figure 20-1).

```
# chgdev -1 sys0 -a maxuproc=80
# smit chgsys
```

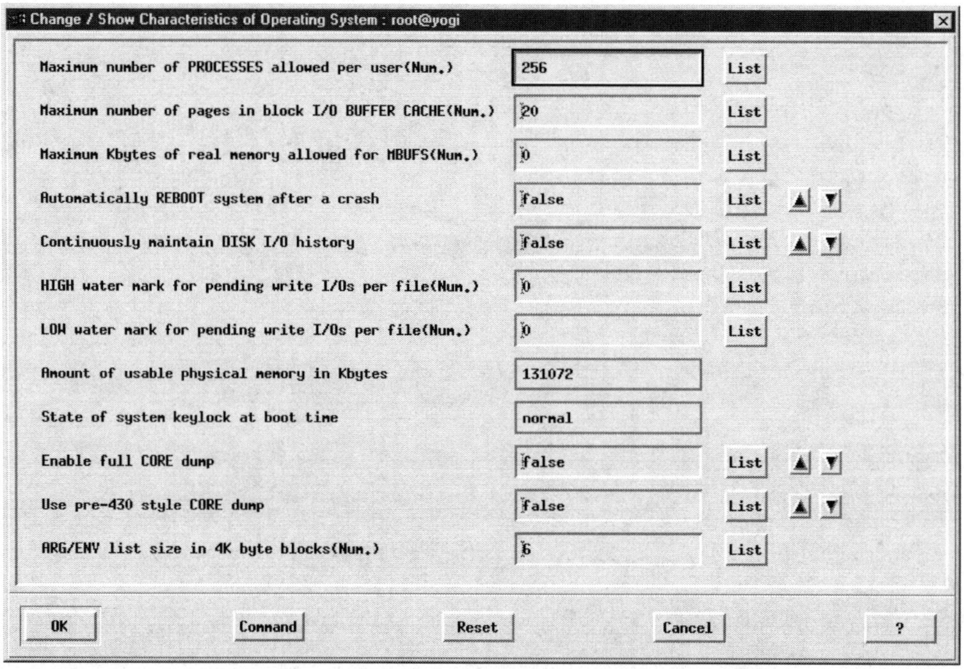

Figure 20-1. Change / Show Characteristics of the Operating System SMIT panel

Disk quotas limit the maximum number of blocks a user or group may consume in quota-participating filesystems. The AIX implementation of disk quotas is based on BSD quotas. User and group quota limits are set by the Systems Administrator using the **edquota** command. Quota limits for disk blocks and i-nodes are specified by three parameters: soft limit, hard limit, and grace period. A user may exceed the soft limits for a default grace period of one week. When the grace period expires, the soft limits become hard limits.

The value of the soft limit indicates at what point the user or group begins receiving warnings that the soft limit has been exceeded, and that the hard limit is being approached. Warnings are delivered at login time and at each close that exceeds the specified limit. The hard limit specifies at what point the user or group will no longer be able to allocate additional disk space or i-nodes. The grace period defines a period of time that the user or group has to reduce utilization below the soft limit value. If utilization is not reduced before the grace period expires, the soft limit is enforced as a hard limit.

To implement disk quotas on a filesystem, use the **chfs** command to edit the stanza entry in /etc/filesystems associated with the filesystem name. Add the parameter quota=<userquota>,<groupquota> to the stanza. The userquota and groupquota values indicate the quota types to be enforced. The quota limits for each user or group are recorded in files in the top-level directory named quota.user or quota.group, respectively. You may override these filenames with your own by including userquota=<pathname> and groupquota=<pathname> parameters in the filesystem stanza.

Add the stanza entries to /etc/filesystems with the following command:

```
# chfs —a 'quota=userquota' —a 'userquota=/home1/user.quota' /home1
```

Check the /etc/filesystems stanza using the following **more** command:

```
# more /etc/filesystem
/home1:
        dev = /dev/lv43
        vfs = jfs
        log = /dev/loglv00
        mount = true
        check = true
        options = rw
        quota = userquota
        userquota = /home1/user.quota
```

If the quota limit files do not exist in the filesystem, you can create them using **touch**.

```
# touch  /home1/quota.user
```

Use the **edquota** command to create a user quota for one of the users on the system. These values can be used as a template for setting the limits for other users on the system. The **edquota** command will invoke the default editor, specified by the EDITOR environment variable, and display the quota values for update.

```
# edquota stimpy
Quotas for user stimpy:
/home1: blocks in use: 50, limits (soft = 80, hard = 100)
        inodes in use: 11, limits (soft = 120, hard 150)
/home2: blocks in use: 0, limits (soft = 80, hard = 100)
        inodes in use: 0, limits (soft = 120, hard 150)
```

After setting the soft and hard limits for the default user, invoke **edquota -p** *<default-user> <new-user>* to clone the default limits for each additional user in the system.

```
# edquota -p stimpy ren
```

To enable the quota systems, execute the **quotaon** command. As part of the nightly system housekeeping, update the information in the quota files by running the **quotacheck** command. You can use the **-a** flag to indicate *all* quota filesystems. The following are quota update commands:

```
# quotaoff -a  ←————————Turn quotas off for all filesystems
# quotacheck -a  ←————————Updates quota information for all filesystems
# quotaon -a  ←————————Turn quotas on for all filesystems
```

The quota limits for a user or a summary can be displayed using the **quota** and **repquota** commands, respectively, as shown here:

```
# quota ren
Disk quotas for user ren (uid 4084):
Filesystem  blocks    quota limit grace files quota limit grace
/home1      11836*     5120  6144  none   363  1000  2000

# repquota —u -a
                Block limits              File limits
User         used  soft  hard  grace  used soft  hard  grace
root    --  31448     0     0          700    0     0
bin     --  57700     0     0         2037    0     0
sys     --      4     0     0            1    0     0
bilbro  --     16     0     0            4    0     0
```

USER ACCOUNT ACCESS RIGHTS

Who gets an account and how long can they keep it? Access and expiration policies might not seem like a big deal for small workgroups; however, the less ambiguity, the better. There are also legal implications that can be avoided if these policies are formalized and made public. Expiring and cleaning up accounts on large user base systems can be automated easily if expiration policies are clearly defined. AIX provides a mechanism for expiring accounts and performing the cleanup housekeeping. By providing both facilities, AIX allows you to implement grace periods between when an account expires and when it is actually removed from the system. This can be incorporated into a last-use policy.

USER ACCOUNT ENVIRONMENT

What face will the system present to new users? As a Systems Administrator, you are charged with setting up the default environment for each new account. You want to maintain some level of control over environment parameters, yet you want to allow users the freedom of tailoring their own work space. Shells, editors, terminal definitions, and the like are religious issues best left to the faithful! You can't keep everyone from shooting themselves in the foot. You also don't want to open the floodgates to more shell environments than you can support. You can provide a simple, modular login environment that simplifies recovery for the adventurous user when shell experimentation goes awry.

Begin by defining the default environment variables that will be set for all users. Environment variables are *name=value* pairs that are read by shells and commands to set values or determine behavior. For example, the environment variable EDITOR indicates what editor is to be invoked by applications. Environment variables may be command or shell specific, and they may be modified by the end user. See Table 20-1 for a list of some common environment variables.

To view the current values of environment variables, use **echo** or **print** and precede the variable name with a dollar sign, as shown here:

```
# echo $MANPATH
# print $MANPATH
```

The /etc/environment and /etc/profile Files

AIX provides two files that are used to set default environment variables for the system. The /etc/environment file contains default variables set for each process

Variable	Use
PATH	List of directory paths to search for commands and files
LIBPATH	List of library paths to search for binding
MANPATH	List of directory paths to search for man page files
PAGER	Default full-screen pager
EDITOR	Default editor
TZ	Time zone
TERM	Terminal type
MAIL	Incoming mail path
MAILMSG	Message text prompt when new mail arrives
LANG	Locale name in effect for NLS
LOCPATH	Directory containing locale file
NLSPATH	Full path to NLS catalogs
USER	User name
LOGNAME	User name
HOME	Home directory path

Table 20-1. Common Environment Variables

by the **exec()** system call. The /etc/profile file contains the set of environment variables and commands that will be invoked when a user logs into the system. The contents of these files are read before local shell start-up files, and they are best kept non-shell-specific. The AIX-supplied /etc/environment and /etc/profile files provide a good base for tailoring your own defaults. See the default /etc/environment file here.

The Default System /etc/environment File

```
# @(#)18      1.21   src/bos/etc/environment/environment, cmdsh, bos430,
9737A_430 5/13/94 15:09:03
# IBM_PROLOG_BEGIN_TAG
# This is an automatically generated prolog.
#
# bos430 src/bos/etc/environment/environment 1.21
#
# Licensed Materials - Property of IBM
#
# (C) COPYRIGHT International Business Machines Corp. 1989,1994
# All Rights Reserved
#
# US Government Users Restricted Rights - Use, duplication or
# disclosure restricted by GSA ADP Schedule Contract with IBM Corp.
#
# IBM_PROLOG_END_TAG
#
# COMPONENT_NAME: (CMDSH) Shell related commands
#
# ORIGINS: 27
#
# (C) COPYRIGHT International Business Machines Corp. 1989, 1994
# All Rights Reserved
# Licensed Materials - Property of IBM
#
# US Government Users Restricted Rights - Use, duplication or
# disclosure restricted by GSA ADP Schedule Contract with IBM Corp.
#
################################################################
# System wide environment file.  This file should only contain
#      1.  comment lines which have a # in the first column,
#      2.  blank lines, and
#      3.  Lines in the form name=value.
#
# WARNING: This file is only for establishing environment variables.
#          Execution of commands from this file or any lines other
#          than specified above may cause failure of the initialization
#          process.
#
# Searching the current directory last is usually a BIG time saver.
```

```
# If /usr/ucb is at the beginning of the PATH the BSD version of commands will
# be found.
#
PATH=/usr/bin:/etc:/usr/sbin:/usr/ucb:/usr/bin/X11:/sbin:/usr/local/bin
TZ=EST5EDT
LANG=en_US
LOCPATH=/usr/lib/nls/loc
NLSPATH=/usr/lib/nls/msg/%L/%N:/usr/lib/nls/msg/%L/%N.cat
LC__FASTMSG=true
MANPATH=/opt/freeware/man

# ODM routines use ODMDIR to determine which objects to operate on
# the default is /etc/objrepos - this is where the device objects
# reside, which are required for hardware configuration

ODMDIR=/etc/objrepos
DOCUMENT_SERVER_MACHINE_NAME=saptst1
DOCUMENT_SERVER_PORT=80
CGI_DIRECTORY=/usr/HTTPServer/cgi-bin
DOCUMENT_DIRECTORY=/usr/HTTPServer/htdocs
DEFAULT_BROWSER=netscape
# IMNSearch DBCS environment variables
IMQCONFIGSRV=/etc/IMNSearch
IMQCONFIGCL=/etc/IMNSearch/dbcshelp
ITECONFIGSRV=/etc/IMNSearch
ITECONFIGCL=/etc/IMNSearch/clients
ITE_DOC_SEARCH_INSTANCE=search
```

The Default /etc/profile File

```
# @(#)27       1.20  src/bos/etc/profile/profile, cmdsh, bos430, 9737A_430 8/9/94
12:01:38
# IBM_PROLOG_BEGIN_TAG
# This is an automatically generated prolog.
#
# bos430 src/bos/etc/profile/profile 1.20
#
# Licensed Materials - Property of IBM
#
# (C) COPYRIGHT International Business Machines Corp. 1989,1994
# All Rights Reserved
#
# US Government Users Restricted Rights - Use, duplication or
# disclosure restricted by GSA ADP Schedule Contract with IBM Corp.
#
# IBM_PROLOG_END_TAG
#
# COMPONENT_NAME: (CMDSH) Shell related commands
#
# FUNCTIONS:
```

```
#
# ORIGINS: 3, 26, 27
#
# (C) COPYRIGHT International Business Machines Corp. 1989, 1994
# All Rights Reserved
# Licensed Materials - Property of IBM
#
# US Government Users Restricted Rights - Use, duplication or
# disclosure restricted by GSA ADP Schedule Contract with IBM Corp.
#
################################################################

# System wide profile.  All variables set here may be overridden by
# a user's personal .profile file in their $HOME directory.  However,
# all commands here will be executed at login regardless.

trap "" 1 2 3
readonly LOGNAME

# Automatic logout, include in export line if uncommented
# TMOUT=120

# System Added Path
PATH=$PATH:/usr/local/sbin:/usr/local/netscape

# The MAILMSG will be printed by the shell every MAILCHECK seconds
# (default 600) if there is mail in the MAIL system mailbox.
MAIL=/usr/spool/mail/$LOGNAME
MAILMSG="[YOU HAVE NEW MAIL]"

# If termdef command returns terminal type (i.e. a non NULL value),
# set TERM to the returned value, else set TERM to default lft.
TERM_DEFAULT=lft
TERM='termdef'
TERM=${TERM:-$TERM_DEFAULT}

# If LC_MESSAGES is set to "C@lft" and TERM is not set to "lft",
# unset LC_MESSAGES.
if [ "$LC_MESSAGES" = "C@lft" -a "$TERM" != "lft" ]
then
        unset LC_MESSAGES
fi
export LOGNAME MAIL MAILMSG TERM

trap 1 2 3
```

The /etc/security/environ File

Individual user environment variables may also be defined in the /etc/security/
environ file. This file contains a stanza for each user in the system, identified by user

name, followed by a list of environment variables and associated values. The environment `variable=value` pairs are separated by commas. Those variables specified as `usrenv` are set at login. To protect environment variables from being reset by unprivileged applications, use the `sysenv` specification.

An /etc/security/environ Stanza

```
stimpy:
        usrenv = "TNESC=35,PAGER=/bin/more,EDITOR=/bin/vi"
        sysenv = "HOME=/home/stimpy"
```

Next, define the default shell and shell environment variables. The default shell and start-up files are set by the `/usr/lib/security/mkuser.sys` script and `/usr/lib/security/mkuser.default` file. The `mkuser.sys` script reads the `mkuser.default` file and creates the home directory, sets permissions, and copies the default shell start-up file from `/etc/security` into the new home directory. The `mkuser.sys` script is invoked each time the **mkuser** command is executed by SMIT or from the command line to add a new account.

A /usr/lib/security/mkuser.default File Listing

```
user:
        pgrp = staff
        groups = staff
        shell = /usr/bin/ksh
        home = /home/$USER
admin:
        pgrp = system
        groups = system
        shell = /usr/bin/ksh
        home = /home/$USER
```

Shell Startup Files

```
sh      $HOME/.profile
ksh     $HOME/.profile, $HOME/.kshrc (if indicated by ENV)
csh, tcsh   $HOME/.login, $HOME/.cshrc, $HOME/.logout
```

The default behavior of `mkuser.sys` is to copy a complete shell start-up file into the user's home directory. This can be a problem should you decide to change some part of the default shell environment later on. You will need to incorporate the change into each user's start-up files without destroying any customizations added by the user.

The /etc/security/login.cfg File

Even with simple schemes like this, many of us don't want to have to support every shell that might be built by a user. You can restrict the shells supported on the system by specifying the shell path in the `/etc/security/login.cfg` file. Edit the usw:

stanza and list the path name of each supported shell, separating the names by commas after the `shells=` parameter.

Shells Supported by /etc/security/login.cfg
```
usw:
        shells =/bin/sh,/bin/bsh,/bin/csh,/bin/ksh,/bin/tsh,/bin/ksh93,
/usr/bin/sh,/usr/bin/bsh,/usr/bin/csh,/usr/bin/ksh,/usr/bin/tsh,
/usr/bin/ksh93,/usr/sbin/uucp/uucico,/usr/sbin/sliplogin,/usr/sbin/snappd
```

The `/etc/security/login.cfg` file also defines the default login heralds and password profile. Stanzas associated with these facilities will be discussed in Chapter 23.

MANAGING USER ACCOUNTS

Systems Administrators can't escape the ongoing stream of account management requests that come from an active user community. The good news is that AIX automates the task of adding, updating, and removing user accounts by providing a set of tools that take care of updating all the appropriate tables and filesystems. It's still not perfect, but it beats doing it by hand!

Adding a User Account

To add a new user to the system, execute the **mkuser** command either from the command line or using SMIT or WebSM. Due to the number of parameters involved, I suggest using SMIT or WebSM unless you are accepting system defaults. In the event that you are adding a large number of users, you can add the first using SMIT and then duplicate the **mkuser** command in the `smit.script` file for each subsequent account to be created. Figure 20-2 shows the SMIT panel to add a user.

```
# smit mkuser
```

For most general user accounts, you can select a user name and accept the supplied defaults. Table 20-2 lists the option fields available for configuring account resources.

See Chapter 23 for more information concerning primary and secondary authentication methods as well as password support.

Updating User Accounts

You can modify existing user accounts by invoking the **chuser** command from the command line or with SMIT and WebSM. In most cases, only a small number of fields are changed, so using **chuser** from the command line does not involve a large number of arguments. You may also update system account tables directly with an editor in some cases. Care should be taken that stanza format and permissions are not compromised. As a Systems Administrator, you need to learn how to manage large

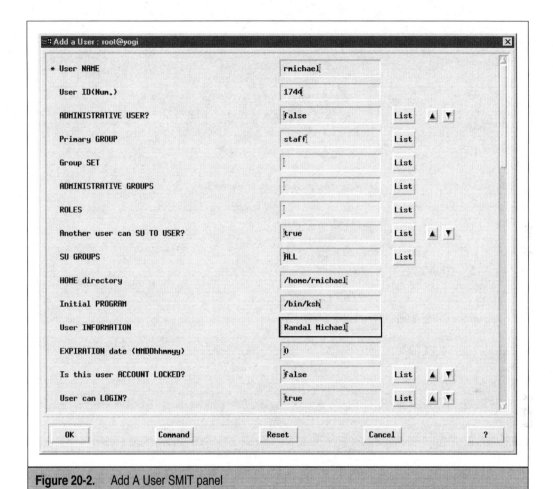

Figure 20-2.   Add A User SMIT panel

Field	Use
UserNAME	Up to eight characters; no uppercase or special characters
User ID	Unique integer; may need to be altered if you are using unique UIDs across multiple systems
ADMINISTRATIVE user	Administrative privileges
PRIMARY group	Default group at login
Group SET	Other group membership
ADMINISTRATIVE groups	User is an administrator of these groups

Table 20-2.   **mkuser** Fields

Field	Use
Another user can SU TO USER?	True/false
SU GROUPS	What groups may **su** to this user?
HOME directory	Home directory path `/home/<user name>`
Initial PROGRAM	Login shell program, for example `/bin/ksh`
User INFORMATION	User full name, phone, etc. for GECOS field in `/etc/passwd` file
EXPIRATION date	Account will expire on this date
Is this user ACCOUNT LOCKED?	Is the user restricted from logging in?
User can LOGIN?	Can the user use **login** to access the system?
User can LOGIN REMOTELY?	Can the user use **rlogin** to access the system?
Allowed LOGIN TIMES	Restrict access to these times
Number of FAILED LOGINS	Number of failed login attempts before user account is locked. [0] means never lock.
Login AUTHENTICATION GRAMMAR	Authentication method
Valid TTYs	TTY ports that may be used to log in to this UID
Days to WARN USER before password expires	Number of days to warn user with message at login
Password CHECK METHODS	Rules for validating proper passwords
Password DICTIONARY FILES	Word dictionaries used to validate password
NUMBER OF PASSWORDS	How many passwords before reuse
WEEKS before password reuse	How long before reuse of the same password
Weeks between password EXPIRATION and LOCKOUT	How long after expiration before restricting access
Password MAX AGE	Maximum time before requiring a password change
Password MIN AGE	Minimum time before a password can be changed
Password MIN LENGTH	How short can a password be
Password MIN ALPHA	Minimum number of alphabetic characters
Password MIN OTHER	Minimum number of non-alpha characters
Password MAX REPEATED	Maximum repeated characters allowed
Password MIN DIFFERENT	Minimum number of different chars required
Password REGISTRY	Authentication mechanism
Soft FILE size	Soft resource limits changeable by user
Soft CPU time	Soft CPU limit
Soft DATA segment	Soft DATA segment limit
Soft STACK size	Soft STACK size limit
Soft CORE file size	Set a soft limit for CORE file size

Table 20-2. mkuser Fields *(continued)*

Field	Use
Soft physical MEMORY	Sets the soft MEMORY limit
Hard FILE size	Hard resource limits for the user
Hard CPU time	Hard CPU time limit
Hard DATA segment	Hard DATA segment limit
Hard STACK size	Hard STACK size limit
Hard CORE file size	HARD CORE file size limit
Hard physical MEMORY	Hard setting for physical memory limit
File creation MASK	Default `umask` for the user
AUDIT Classes	Audit classes representing this UID
TRUSTED PATH	Trusted path status
PRIMARY authentication method	Authentication program used to validate this user to the system; default SYSTEM represents standard user name and password
SECONDARY authentication method	Secondary authentication program; if it fails, it does not deny access

Table 20-2.   **mkuser** Fields *(continued)*

numbers of users using the command line and scripts, or you will be lost when you have to manage a large environment.

See Figures 20-3 and 20-4 for the change user SMIT panels.

```
# smit chuser
```

The SMIT panel in Figure 20-3 prompts for a user name to change. Clicking the List button gives you a listing of all users defined on the system. When you enter or select a

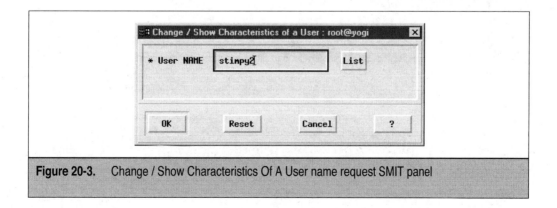

Figure 20-3.   Change / Show Characteristics Of A User name request SMIT panel

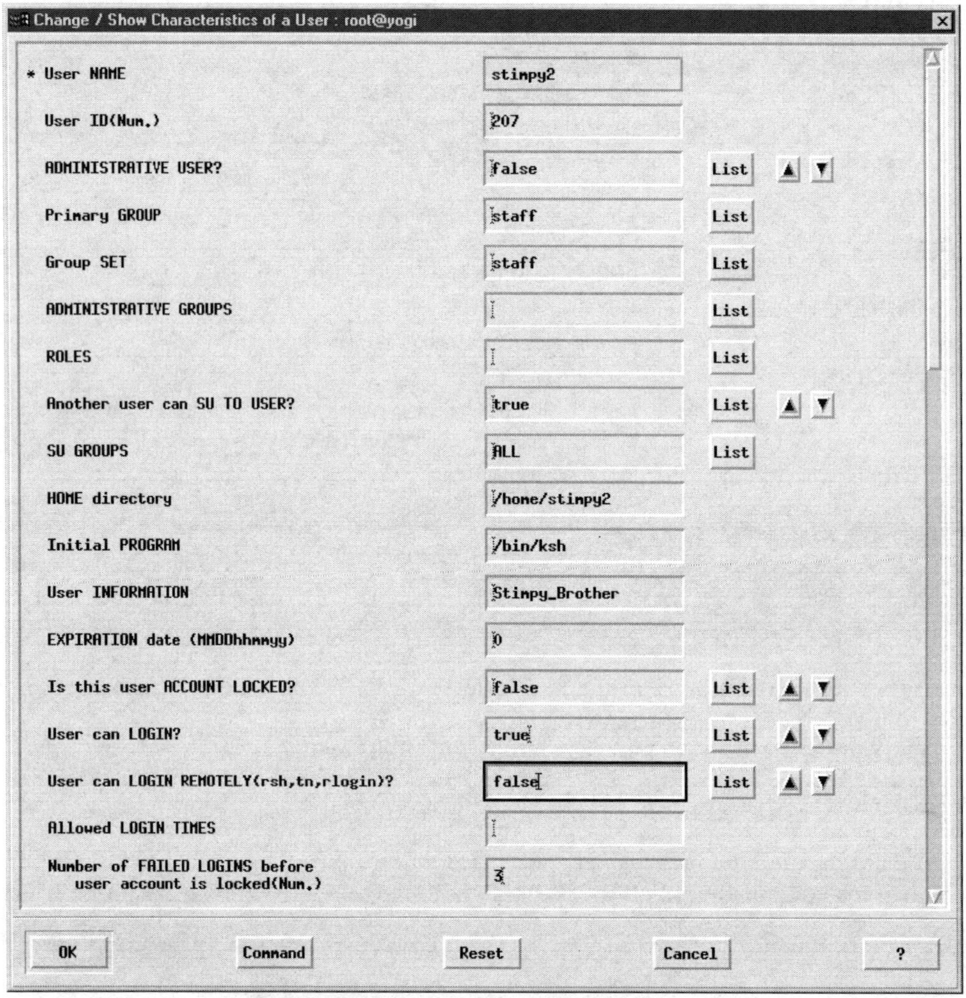

Figure 20-4.   Change / Show Characteristics Of A User SMIT panel

user from the list, you are next presented with the SMIT panel shown in Figure 20-4. This panel is where you can change specific user attributes in SMIT.

You can list the current set of attributes defined for a user on the command line using the **lsuser** command as shown here:

```
# lsuser stimpy

stimpy id=17742 pgrp=uadmin groups=uadmin,staff,printq,ecotools
```

```
home=/home/stimpy shell=/usr/bin/ksh gecos=Stimpy - AIX System Admin
login=true su=true rlogin=true daemon=true admin=false sugroups=ALL
admgroups= tpath=nosak ttys=ALL expires=0 auth1=SYSTEM auth2=pad_meth
umask=22 registry=files SYSTEM=compat logintimes= loginretries=5
pwdwarntime=49 account_locked=false minage=0 maxage=7 maxexpired=-1
minalpha=3 minother=1 mindiff=0 maxrepeats=2 minlen=6 histexpire=0
histsize=8 pwdchecks= dictionlist= fsize=-1 cpu=-1 data=-1 stack=-1
core=2048 rss=-1 time_last_login=1021398808
time_last_unsuccessful_login=1021141628 tty_last_login=/dev/pts/4
tty_last_unsuccessful_login=/dev/pts/4 host_last_login=10.10.10.10
host_last_unsuccessful_login=167.105.28.110 unsuccessful_login_count=0
roles=
```

Removing User Accounts

To remove users from the system, use the **rmuser** command. It can be invoked from the command line or using SMIT and WebSM. The **rmuser** command takes care of removing the user from the system tables. You also have the option of retaining user data in the `/etc/security/passwd` file. The SMIT Panel to remove a user from the system is shown in Figure 20-5.

```
# rmuser -p stimpy
# smit rmuser
```

To automate the process of removing accounts from the system, you can use cron to run a nightly process that looks for expired accounts and invokes **rmuser**. See Chapter 21 concerning using cron.

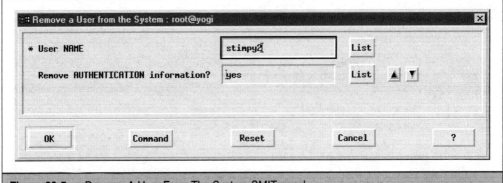

Figure 20-5.   Remove A User From The System SMIT panel

Restricting Access

If it is required to restrict access to the system for a particular user, you may deny access from a number of mechanisms depending on the situation. Setting the **LOGIN User** and **User Can RLOGIN** fields to false can restrict login access. You may also restrict access by resetting the date in the **EXPIRATION** field. The simplest method is to **LOCK** the account. If you wish to send the user an informative message concerning account status, create a script or program to write the message to stdout and add the program name to the **Initial PROGRAM** field for the user. After the user supplies a user name and password at login time, the message is displayed and the user is logged off. Use the **chuser** command to enable the desired level of access restriction.

PASSWORD FILES

All the information created by the AIX account management tools end up as entries in a number of user accounts support tables. I have discussed the structure that some of these files provide in the previous sections. There are three other files that are primarily responsible for identifying an account to the operating system and application set. These are the /etc/passwd, /etc/security/passwd, and /etc/security/ user files.

The /etc/passwd File

The /etc/passwd file uses the standard password file format available on most UNIX systems, the only exception being the use of a shadow password file. Shadow password support removes the encrypted password from the world-readable /etc/passwd file and places it into another file with restricted access. A placeholder, the exclamation point (!), is inserted into the password field in /etc/passwd. Fields in the /etc/ passwd file are separated by a colon as shown here.

A Sample /etc/passwd File

```
# USER NAME:!:UID:GID:GECOS:HOME DIRECTORY:SHELL
root:!:0:0:System Overseer:/:/bin/ksh
daemon:!:1:1::/etc:
bin:!:2:2::/bin:
sys:!:3:3::/usr/sys:
adm:!:4:4::/usr/adm:
uucp:!:5:5::/usr/lib/uucp:
stimpy:!:4084:30:Stimpson Cat:/home/stimpy:/bin/ksh
```

AIX commands and applications that must resolve user information query /etc/ passwd through the use of library calls like **getpwnam()**. Parsing large password files can cause significant delays in command response time. The **mkpasswd** command is used to create indexed security files. These indexes are used by the library subroutines `getpwnam`, `getpwuid`, `getuserattr`, and `putuserattr`. The result is a significant increase in performance for systems with a large user base. The indexes are defines in the `/usr/include/usersec.h` file. By default, the following indexes are created:

```
/etc/passwd.nm.idx  ◄──────── Index /etc/passwd with the username as the key
/etc/passwd.id.idx  ◄──────── Index /etc/passwd with the userID as the key
/etc/security/passwd.idx  ◄──────── Indexed /etc/security/passwd file
/etc/security/lastlog.idx  ◄──────── Indexed /etc/security/lastlog file
```

Here are some samples of using the **mkpasswd** command:

To Create and Enable Indexed Read for Security Files
```
# mkpasswd -f
```

To Create and Enable Indexed Read for only the /etc/security/passwd file
```
# mkpasswd /etc/security/passwd.idx
```

To Check, and Rebuild if Necessary, All Indexes
```
# mkpasswd -c
```

To Delete All Indexes
```
# mkpasswd -d
```

The /etc/security/passwd File

Shadow password support is provided by the `/etc/security/passwd` file. Each user account is represented by a user name stanza. The stanza contains the encrypted password, the time of last update, and the update flag. The update flag contains either the null value or one of the following:

- **ADMIN**   Only root may change this password.
- **ADMCHG**   A member of the security group reset this password, so it must be changed at next login.
- **NOCHECK**   None of restrictions set in the `/etc/security/user` file are enforced for this account.

An Example /etc/security/passwd Stanza
```
stimpy:
       password = dWe3asfZpuoJ6
       lastupdate = 722287867
       flags = NOCHECK
```

The /etc/security/user File

The /etc/security/user file contains the extended attributes defined for the user. Each user is identified by a user name stanza followed by each attribute and value. A default stanza follows the header comments in the file. Each user entry may override a default attribute by specifying a local value. See the following example:

```
default:
        admin = false
        login = true
        su = true
        daemon = true
        rlogin = true
        sugroups = ALL
        ttys = ALL
        auth1 = SYSTEM
        auth2 = NONE
        tpath = nosak
        umask = 022
        expires = 0
stimpy:
        login = false
        rlogin = false
```

Salting Group and Passwd Files

In large environments, there may be a need to synchronize the user and group space for system and applications across all new installs. This means that the *mqm, cics,* and *kmem* groups, as well as the *cics* and *mqm* user ID numbers, must be defined before the *TXSeries, MQSeries,* and *freeware.lsof.rte* applications are installed. When the applications are installed, they will create their user and group with different results if they do not already exist. The solution is to create a minimum installed image from the AIX 5L base install CD and then add, or salt, the entire list of future group and user IDs that your enterprise may ever need. The image can be salted with your own script that adds groups and users with native commands, or the system can pull over the master files from the control workstation if there are no ID conflicts. Here is a list of some of the files you may want to pull or push from the master repository workstation:

```
/etc/passwd
/etc/passwd.nm.idx
/etc/passwd.id.idx
/etc/group
/etc/security/passwd
/etc/security/passwd.idx
```

```
/etc/security/group
/etc/security/user
/etc/security/login.cfg
/etc/security/
/etc/resolv.conf
/etc/netsvc.conf
```

CHECKLIST

The following is a checklist for the key points in "Managing the User Environment."

- ☐ Define default environment policies.
- ☐ Streamline account management.
- ☐ Identify physical resources.
- ☐ Manage UID space and groups.
- ☐ Identify resource limits.
- ☐ Define the user account access rights.
- ☐ Set up the default environment for each new account.
- ☐ Manage user accounts.
- ☐ Identify the password files.
- ☐ Synchronize the user and group space for system and applications across all new installs.

CHAPTER 21

Process Management

A group of processes executing under AIX is analogous to the generations of a family tree. *Parent* processes beget *child* processes. Processes are born, live out their vocations, and then pass away. Process ID 1, **init**, is the great-grandparent to which all process generations trace their origins. Like a loving grandparent, **init** takes in the orphan processes that have lost their parents. Each process gets its turn to execute on the CPU. Like little children, they require the guidance of the scheduler so that everyone is ensured a fair share of the CPU. The systems administrator represents the grand overseer over the process universe, wielding ultimate control over the lives of all processes. A benevolent and all-seeing systems administrator will learn the ways of process life in the AIX world so that he may conduct his work in tranquility and peace.

PROCESS ATTRIBUTES

A process consists of an executing program and its address space. Each process is named by a positive integer number called the process identifier (PID). The PID is a vector index in the kernel process table. PIDs are unique and are allocated in a somewhat random fashion. Process table entries point to per-process kernel data structures. The `proc` data structures defined in `/usr/include/sys/proc.h` in turn define the attribute values associated with the process. The global AIX process table can support up to 131,073 processes per user. You can set the maximum number of processes per user by using the SMIT FastPath **smitty system** and then selecting **Change/Show Characteristics Of The Operating System**. The top entry in the list of options is **Maximum Number Of Processes Allowed Per User**. The valid range is displayed when you press F4. In most system environments, a value of 200 to 2000 is adequate, but not all environments are the same. The value you select will depend on the applications and databases your systems are running.

Here is a small sampling of process attributes that can be observed:

- Process identifier
- Process group identifier
- Process parent identifier
- Process owner
- Effective and real user and group identifiers
- Priority
- Controlling terminal
- Address space
- Size in pages
- Paging statistics

- Resource utilization
- Process state

Displaying Process Attributes

The **ps** command is your friend when you need to look at processes in the system. The **ps** command options are many, and as with many AIX commands, you can use either System V or BSD command switches. The System V personality is used when the command-line arguments are preceded by the hyphen character (-); otherwise, the BSD format is used. You can also use SMIT and the Web-Based System Manager to invoke **ps**, but you may find using **ps** from the command line to be faster.

The **ps -elk** SYSV command displays processes using the following format:

```
     F S  UID    PID  PPID   C PRI NI ADDR    SZ  WCHAN TTY   TIME CMD
   303 A    0      0     0 120  16 -- 2412    12          -   6:51 swapper
200003 A    0      1     0   0  60 20 142a   836          -   1:13 init
   303 A    0    516     0 120 255 -- 2613     8          - 775:05 wait
   303 A    0   1032     0   0  37 -- 1028    64        * -  21:01 gil
   303 A    0   1290     0   0  16 -- 1229    16  6ae818  -   0:00 lmsched
 40201 A    0   2080     0   0  60 20 2472    16          -   0:00 lvmbb
 40401 A    0   2672     1   0  60 20 194c   572  14b774  -   0:00 errdemon
240001 A    0   2918     1   0  60 20 1b4d   780          -   0:00 rcmstr
 40303 A    0   3128     1   0  39 -- 1f2f    16          -   0:00 ioserver
240001 A    0   3392     1   0  60 20  663   320 309eb298 -   5:06 syncd
```

The **ps auxw** BSD command displays processes using the following format:

```
USER     PID %CPU %MEM   SZ   RSS  TTY STAT   STIME   TIME COMMAND
root     516 98.8  8.0    8 10520    - A    Feb 04 788:38 wait
root   22036  0.6  1.0 1512  1424    - A   4:24:01   0:18 /usr/dt/bin/dtterm
root    1032  0.2  8.0   64 10576    - A    Feb 04  21:03 gil
root       0  0.1  8.0   12 10524    - A    Feb 04   6:51 swapper
root    3392  0.1  0.0  320   240    - A    Feb 04   5:06 /usr/sbin/syncd 60
root       1  0.0  0.0  836   288    - A    Feb 04   1:13 /etc/init
root   13936  0.0  0.0 1372   344    - A    Feb 04   1:00 /usr/dt/bin/dtlogin
root   17098  0.0  2.0 2484  2016 pts/1 A   Feb 04   0:54 dtwm
root    5160  0.0  1.0 1368  1212    - A    Feb 04   0:27 /usr/sbin/snmpd
```

The COMMAND and CMD columns represent the program being run in the process address space. You may have noticed the COMMAND with PID number 516 from the preceding **ps auxw** command output. This PID is always the first **wait** (or **kproc**) process. The **wait** process collects CPU time when there are no threads to run for a given time slice. This is no cause for alarm. A **wait** process is assigned to each CPU so that the scheduler has somewhere to put the idle time. Since the AIX operating system must always be doing *something*, if the CPU is idle the **wait** process just keeps the clock ticking. The **wait** process is the AIX 5L replacement for the **kproc** process that is seen in the process table of AIX 4.3.3 and earlier.

Process Identifiers

Along with its PID, each process records the integer ID of its parent and its group membership, parent process identifier (PPID), and process group identifier (PGID). Process groups are collections of one or more processes. The group leader has a PGID equal to its PID, and each member has a PGID that matches the leader. Unless reset by a **setpgrp()** call, a process inherits the PGID of its parent. Process groups provide a mechanism for signaling all processes within the group using the PGID. This eliminates the need to know each member's PID. The PID, PPID, and PGID are the primary handles used by the system administrator for controlling process behavior.

A nifty GNU tool written by Fred Hucht called **pstree** will graphically map process relationships on a text terminal screen. His latest **pstree** source code is available under the GNU public license from the Gerhard Mercator University. A fix was added to the source code starting with **pstree.c** version 2.17 that made the code compatible with AIX 5L.

```
http://freshmeat.net/projects/pstree/
ftp://ftp.thp.Uni-Duisburg.DE/pub/source/
```

Effective and Real UID and GID

Processes are associated with an owning user identifier (UID) and group identifier (GID). The UID and GID name spaces are maintained as part of the system account management and are recorded in the `/etc/passwd` and `/etc/group` files (see Chapter 23). The real UID and real GID numbers identify process owners for accounting and process control purposes. An effective UID (EUID) and an effective GID (EGID) are assigned to each process and represent the permissions and privileges available to the process during its lifetime.

Controlling Terminal

Processes other than system daemons are usually associated with a *control terminal*. The control terminal represents the default device for standard input, output, and error channels and for sending signals via keyboard control characters. The control character–to–signal mapping is user-customizable and recorded in the `termio` structure. The controlling terminal is identified in the **ps** TTY column.

You can reassign the system console to a different TTY, pseudo-terminal or file using the **chcons** command; however, the redirection will not take place until the next system restart. Additionally, you can mirror a console, tty, or pseudo-terminal if you need to by using the **portmir** command. Details on the **chcons** and **portmir** commands and on the **mirrord** daemon can be found both in the man pages and in the DocSearch documentation library. There are two SMIT FastPaths for the console assignment and tty port mirroring:

```
# smitty console
# smitty portmir
```

Resource Utilization and Priority

AIX uses a priority-based set of run queues to allocate CPU resources among active processes. Priorities values range from 0 to 127, each of which is represented by a run queue. Lower-numbered queues are scheduled more often than higher-numbered queues. Processes in a run queue level are scheduled in a round-robin fashion. Each process's queue priority is calculated from the sum of its short-term CPU usage (0 to   100), its nice value (0 to 40), and the minimum user process level (40). The priority value increases for processes that execute frequently and decreases for those that are waiting for execution. Processes with a priority value exceeding 120 will execute only when no other process in the system requires CPU resources. A process's short-term CPU usage, priority, and nice value are displayed in the PRI, C, and NI fields using the SYSV **ps -l** option.

The nice value is an integer that represents coarse priority differences between processes. AIX supports both the BSD nice value range of 20 to –20 and the SYSV range of 0 to 39. The *larger* the number, the *lower* the priority. The two value ranges are mapped such that BSD –20 corresponds to SYSV 0 for highest priority and BSD 20 corresponds to SYSV 39 for lowest priority.

New processes inherit the nice value of their parents. The nice value may be altered dynamically during the process lifetime. The owning UID for a process can lower the process nice value. Only the superuser can improve nice priority. The nice value can be set from the command line using the **nice** command when starting a process.

```
# nice -n <value> <command>
```

Process owners and the superuser can modify existing process nice values by using the **renice** command.

```
# renice <value> -p <PID>
```

Be aware that the BSD %CPU field represents the percentage of CPU resources that a process has used in its lifetime. You may see short-lived processes shoot up to very high %CPU numbers. A better gauge for identifying CPU crunchers or runaway processes is the TIME column. When using the **ps -elf** command, you want to pay particular attention to the PRI and NI columns. The smaller the PRI value, the higher the process priority. An average process runs at a process priority of around 60. The nice value, specified by NI, is used to adjust the process's priority. The higher the nice setting, the lower the priority is for the process. The default nice value is 20.

Process State

The scheduler parcels out CPU time slices at a frequency that makes it appear as if all processes are executing at the same time. In fact, they are being scheduled one at a time, except in the case of multiprocessor systems. When a process isn't executing on the CPU, it may be waiting on a resource or lock, sleeping on an event, being suspended, or moving through some dispatch or scheduler state. The process state is maintained as part of the `proc` structure information. The process state is displayed by the **ps aux** command in the STAT column (see Table 21-1). When the BSD l or SYSV -l flag is used, **ps l** or **ps -l**, processes that are flagged as waiting can be viewed in the **WCHAN** column. The **WCHAN** column identifies the address of the event being waited on.

Listing the Top CPU Hogs

There are several techniques to discover who is hogging the system. In AIX 4.3.3 and 5L, IBM added the **topas** program, which has a nice set of monitoring tools, including one to show the top CPU users. Also, if you like the freeware **monitor** program, you will find that it is still available at the UCLA web site.

A couple of **ps** commands will do the job with very minimal load. I like to set up aliases to these commands in my `$HOME/.kshrc` file, so that they are always available. Both of the following commands produce the desired result:

```
alias topprocs="ps aux | tail +2 | sort -k 1.15,1.19nr | head -n 15"
alias top15="ps -ef | grep -v STIME | sort +3 -r | head -n 15"
```

To view a list of the top 15 most CPU-intensive processes (in descending order) that are not owned by you user ID, enter the following command:

```
# ps -ef | egrep -v "STIME|$LOGNAME" | sort +3 -r | head -n 15
```

Binding Kernel Threads to a Processor

The **bindprocessor** command enables you to bind and unbind kernel threads to or from a particular processor or lists all of the available processors. You need to understand that the actual process is not bound, but the kernel threads are bound.

STAT Value	Meaning
A	Active
O	Nonexistent
S	Sleeping
W	Waiting
R	Running
I	Intermediate
Z	Cancelled
T	Stopped
K	Available kernel process
X	Growing

Table 21-1.   Process States Displayed by the **ps** Command

After the kernel threads are bound to a particular processor, they will always be scheduled to run on the bound processor. You can later unbind the kernel threads by using the **-u** command switch.

The **bindprocessor** command is valid only on multiprocessor machines. The available command switches include these:

- **-q** Displays all available processors
- **-u** Unbinds the threads of the specified process

To bind the threads of the process identified by the PID 12345 to processor 2, we can use the following command:

```
# bindprocessor 12345 2
```

To display the processes and the CPU each binds (BND) to (if any), run the following command:

```
# ps -e -F comm,pid,user,thcount,bnd | more
```

To later unbind the threads of PID 12345, we use the following command:

```
# bindprocessor -u 12345
```

Using the Web-Based System Manager with Processes

The Web-Based System Manager allows you to manage processes in a graphical manner. From the main navigation screen, select **Processes**. From the next window, you have two options to control and view processes, **All Processes** and **Overview And Tasks**, as shown in Figure 21-1.

From the window in Figure 21-1, you can change the priority of a process, delete a process, and list the top 10 CPU processes. As always, the **wsm** is a fun tool to have around.

PARENT CHILD INHERITANCE

A parent process creates a new child process by invoking the **fork()** system call. The kernel reserves a vacant PID for the child and copies the attribute data associated with the parent into the child's `proc` structure. The child is a clone of the parent until either the child, the parent, or a privileged authority modifies the child's attributes by way of a system call. The most common method for modifying a child's `proc` attributes is by invoking a new program using the **exec()** system call.

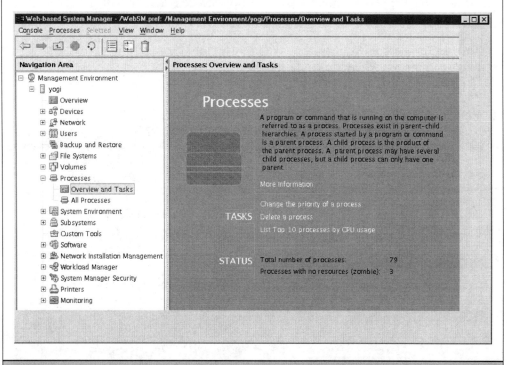

Figure 21-1. Web-Based System Manager for Processes Overview And Tasks

CONTROLLING PROCESSES

In an earlier section, "Resource Utilization and Priority," I talked about using the **nice** and **renice** commands to control the scheduling priorities of processes. What do you do when process management requires a heavier hand? If you really need to get rid of a process, you use the **kill** command!

The command name "kill" sounds much more ominous than in fact it is. What **kill** does is send a specified signal to a process. The signal does not necessarily cause process termination. Note that **kill** is a built-in command for some shells, /bin/csh, for example. The behaviors of the shell version of **kill** and of **/usr/bin/kill** may be different.

```
# kill [-Signal] [PID PID PID …]
```

The value range of the PID directs **kill** where to send the specified signal. If the PID integer is positive, the signal is sent to the process with that PID value. If the PID value is zero (0), the signal is sent to all the processes that have the same process group ID (PGID) of the sender. If the PID value is negative one (–1), the signal is sent to all the processes with the effective user ID(EUID) of the sender. No signal will be sent to the processes with the ID of zero or one.

- **PID > 0**   Sends signal to specified PID integer
- **PID = 0**   Sends signal to PIDs that have PGID equal to the sender
- **PID = –1**   Sends signal to all PIDs with EUID equal to the sender
- **PID < –1**   Sends signal to all PIDs with a PGID equal to the absolute integer specified

If you want to send a signal to all your processes except the sending process, use the **killall** command. Of course, if you are logged in as root, then the **killall** command will kill all processes except for the very basic processes that are needed to keep the system running. Everything else goes to the bit bucket.

```
# killall [-signal]
```

To display the set of supported signals, use the **-l** argument of the **kill** command:

```
# /bin/kill -l
 1) HUP        14) ALRM       27) MSG        40) bad trap   53) bad trap
 2) INT        15) TERM       28) WINCH      41) bad trap   54) bad trap
 3) QUIT       16) URG        29) PWR        42) bad trap   55) bad trap
 4) ILL        17) STOP       30) USR1       43) bad trap   56) bad trap
 5) TRAP       18) TSTP       31) USR2       44) bad trap   57) bad trap
 6) ABRT       19) CONT       32) PROF       45) bad trap   58) bad trap
 7) EMT        20) CHLD       33) DANGER     46) bad trap   59) CPUFAIL
 8) FPE        21) TTIN       34) VTALRM     47) bad trap   60) GRANT
 9) KILL       22) TTOU       35) MIGRATE    48) bad trap   61) RETRACT
10) BUS        23) IO         36) PRE        49) bad trap   62) SOUND
11) SEGV       24) XCPU       37) bad trap   50) bad trap   63) SAK
12) SYS        25) XFSZ       38) bad trap   51) bad trap
13) PIPE       26) bad trap   39) bad trap   52) bad trap
```

AIX signals are based on the SYSV implementation; however, some BSD signals are mapped to their SYSV counterparts, and BSD signal system calls are available. When writing or porting programs that use BSD signals and calls, be aware that signals are not automatically reset after being caught. They must be specifically reset to the required behavior in the signal handler routine. You can also write into your shell scripts the capability to **trap** exit signals. You can **trap** any signal except for **kill -9**.

Rules of Thumb

It seems to be a common practice to use the **kill -9** signal to terminate a process. I recommend that you do this only as a last resort after first trying HUP (**kill -1**) and ABRT (**kill -6**). The latter two signals allow a process to terminate gracefully. In the case of ABRT, a `core` file is produced that may be used for debugging. The **kill -9** signal basically attempts to yank the process out of the process table without permitting any cleanup activities.

- **kill -1 <*PID*>** First try HUP
- **kill -6 <*PID*>** Then try ABRT
- **kill -9 <*PID*>** KILL if all else fails

Occasionally a user may try out some ingenious bit of C code that contains a statement along the lines of this:

```
while(1) fork();
```

I'm not insinuating that this is done on purpose, but it can be a pain in the neck to stop. New processes are being created as fast as you can kill them. One little trick you can try is to kill them by PGID. Use the formatted output (**-o**) option with SYSV **ps** command to display the PGID. Then send a signal to the *negative* PGID.

```
# ps -e -o pgid,ppid,pid,ruser,comm=XYZ | grep -i xyz

PGID   PPID   PID    RUSER XYZ
6968      1   6968     root xyzdaemon
6968   6968   7224     root xyz001
6968   6968   7482     root xyz002
6968   6968   7740     root xyz003
6968   6968   8004     root xyz004
6968   6968   8264     root xyz005
6968   6968   8520     root xyz006

# kill -6 -6968    # 6968 is from the PGID column
```

Ignoring hangup

A common problem is starting a command in the background or as a daemon from the command line of a login shell only to find that the command exits when you log out. This is because a hangup (HUP) signal is sent to the process when your terminal connection has been broken. You can specify that these commands are to ignore HUP by using the **nohup** command.

- **nohup <*command*> &** Background process ignoring hangup

THE /proc FILESYSTEM

New to AIX 5L is support for the /proc filesystem. The /proc filesystem is a pseudo-filesystem used to map processes and kernel data structures to the process files. Previous to AIX 5L, this type is information was hidden under the covers, but now that it has been made available to snoop into, extreme caution should be used at all times! This is not the place to ever try to store information or attempt to *fix* anything.

You can look at the statistics of the /proc pseudo-filesystem with either the **df** command or the **mount** command.

```
# df -k

Filesystem    1024-blocks      Free  %Used     Iused %Iused Mounted on
/dev/hd4           32768       3972    88%      1783    11% /
/dev/hd2         1212416      37544    97%     37638    13% /usr
/dev/hd9var        53248      25328    53%       596     5% /var
/dev/hd3          106496      99768     7%       168     1% /tmp
/dev/hd1            4096       3904     5%        42     5% /home
/dev/hd10opt      638976      22388    97%     15603    10% /opt
/proc                  -          -     -         -      - /proc
```

```
# mount

   node        mounted        mounted over    vfs       date          options
-------- --------------- --------------- ------ ------------ ---------------
         /dev/hd4        /               jfs    Feb 04 10:55 rw,log=/dev/hd8
         /dev/hd2        /usr            jfs    Feb 04 10:55 rw,log=/dev/hd8
         /dev/hd9var     /var            jfs    Feb 04 10:55 rw,log=/dev/hd8
         /dev/hd3        /tmp            jfs    Feb 04 10:55 rw,log=/dev/hd8
         /dev/hd1        /home           jfs    Feb 04 10:56 rw,log=/dev/hd8
         /dev/hd10opt    /opt            jfs    Feb 04 10:56 rw,log=/dev/hd8
         /proc           /proc           procfs Feb 04 10:56 rw
```

Notice that in both **df** and **mount**, the /proc filesystem really has no statistics. This pseudo-filesystem does not have a size, a percentage used, or inodes. In the **mount** command output, /proc has a filesystem type of procfs, as opposed to a jfs filesystem. The entry in the /etc/vfs file for procfs is shown here:

```
# lsvfs procfs
procfs    6           none         none
```

Each process on the system is assigned a directory in /proc with a name equal to the PID of the process. Under each one of these process directories are several files and subdirectories that relate the corresponding internal control data structures of the process. Most, but not all, of these files are read-only, but some are available for process control and can be written to. The tools that are used to work with these files are the standard C language subroutines **open()**, **read()**, **write()**, and **close()**. A description of each of the data structures can be found in the /usr/include/sys/procfs.h file. All of the files in /proc are owned by the PID owner, a fact that allows regular users to access only the processes that they own.

To show the structure of the /proc filesystem, let's look at a particular process on my machine. I am currently running **docsearch**. The PID of the **docsearch** command on my machine is 19898. Use the **ls -l** command to show the contents of the directory.

```
# ls -l /proc/19898

total 0
-rw-------   1 root     system          0 Feb 16 14:42 as
-r--------   1 root     system        128 Feb 16 14:42 cred
--w-------   1 root     system          0 Feb 16 14:42 ctl
dr-xr-xr-x   1 root     system          0 Feb 16 14:42 lwp
-r--------   1 root     system          0 Feb 16 14:42 map
dr-x------   1 root     system          0 Feb 16 14:42 object
-r--r--r--   1 root     system        448 Feb 16 14:42 psinfo
-r--------   1 root     system       1024 Feb 16 14:42 sigact
-r--------   1 root     system       1520 Feb 16 14:42 status
-r--r--r--   1 root     system          0 Feb 16 14:42 sysent
```

As this process executes, there is a lot of process information that is constantly changing. As Table 21-2 shows, each of these pseudo-files has a specific function.

The object directory contains files that correspond to the files mapped in the address space of the process. Looking further into the /proc structure, the **ls -l /proc/19898/object** command output is listed here:

```
# ls -l /proc/19898/object

total 14504
-r-xr-xr-x   4 bin      bin        240404 Apr 08 2001  a.out
-r-xr-xr-x   2 bin      bin       6411106 Jul 30 2001  jfs.10.5.2071
-r--r--r--   1 bin      bin        118685 Apr 08 2001  jfs.10.5.2179
-r-xr-xr-x   4 bin      bin        240404 Apr 08 2001  jfs.10.5.4207
-r-xr-xr-x   1 bin      bin         11059 Apr 08 2001  jfs.10.5.4372
-r--r--r--   1 bin      bin        377654 Apr 08 2001  jfs.10.5.4438
-rwxr-xr-x   1 bin      bin         14342 Apr 08 2001  jfs.10.5.8459
```

The a.out file is the C language executable binary file that represents the program from which the process originates.

The lwp directory contains subdirectories for each kernel thread running in the process. IBM uses the term "lwp" to mean a lightweight process; it means the same thing as the term "thread" as used in AIX documentation. The name of each of the lwp subdirectories is a thread ID (TID) associated with the process. My **docsearch** process

Pseudo-File	Function
as	Allows access to the address space of the process. You can read and write to memory belonging to the process
cred	Shows the credentials associated with the process
ctl	Allows you to control the process, for example, to stop and resume the process
lwp (directory)	Contains kernel thread information for the process
map	Allows access to the virtual address map of the process
object (directory)	Contains map filenames
psinfo	Contains the same information provided by the **ps** command
sigact	Shows the current statuses of all of the signals associated with the process
status	Contains process state information such as address and heap size
sysent	Shows system calls available to the process

Table 21-2. Functions of the Pseudo-Files in /proc/<PID>

has only one thread ID, 29059, which can be seen in the process table using the following command:

```
# ps -mo THREAD -p 19898

  USER    PID  PPID   TID ST CP PRI SC WCHAN      F    TT BND COMMAND
  root  19898 15518    - A   0  76  1     -  200001 pts/2  0 /usr/bin/docsearch
     -      -    - 29059 S   0  76  1     -   10400     -  0 -
```

In the /proc/19898/lwp/29059 directory, we have the following three files:

```
# ls -l /proc/19898/lwp/29059

total 0
--w-------  1 root      system            0 Feb 16 16:08 lwpctl
-r--r--r--  1 root      system          120 Feb 16 16:08 lwpsinfo
-r--------  1 root      system         1200 Feb 16 16:08 lwpstatus
```

The lwpctl, lwpsinfo, and lwpstatus files contain all of the thread-specific information needed to control the thread. Their contents are similar to the information found in the files in the /proc/19898 directory in our example. Using the credentials information, we can offer a better example of the data that can be retrieved from these files. We use the **od** (octal dump) command to show the contents of the /proc/19898/cred file as shown here:

```
# ls -l /proc/19898/cred
-r--------  1 root   system  128 Feb 16 16:29 /proc/19898/cred
```

Now do an octal dump on the /proc/19898/cred file:

```
# od -x /proc/19898/cred
0000000 0000 0000 0000 0000 0000 0000 0000 0000
```

```
*

0000160 0000 0000 0000 0007 0000 0000 0000 0000
0000200 0000 0000 0000 0002 0000 0000 0000 0003
0000220 0000 0000 0000 0007 0000 0000 0000 0008
0000240 0000 0000 0000 000a 0000 0000 0000 000b
0000260
```

In the far left column, the octal byte offset of the file is displayed. All of the other information is the actual content of the file in hexadecimal notation.

For more information on the /proc filesystem, refer to the IBM Redbook sg245765, *AIX 5L Differences Guide Version 5.1 Edition*. An index of all of the pSeries and UNIX Redbooks can be found at the following URL: http://publib-b.boulder.ibm.com/ Redbooks.nsf/Portals/UNIXRedbooks.

The *AIX 5L Differences Guide Version 5.1 Edition* Redbook is located at following URL: http://www.redbooks.ibm.com/pubs/pdfs/redbooks/sg245765.pdf.

SCHEDULED PROCESSES (CRON)

The UNIX **cron** utility provides a basic means for scheduling jobs to be run at a particular time of the day, or on a periodic basis. A **cron** job can be used to take care of regular system housecleaning tasks like synchronizing disk writes, cleaning out /tmp, and running accounting programs. These types of periodic tasks may be tailored through the use of *crontabs*. A crontab is a list of commands and scripts with designated runtimes that will be invoked by **cron** under the EUID of the owner. A **cron** job reports any errors or output information to the owning user after the commands are executed by way of e-mail. Additionally, **cron** logs errors to a log file, /var/adm/cron/log, and, if AIX auditing is enabled, produces audit records.

crontab

To create a **crontab**, use your favorite editor to create a table with the following format:

```
minutes hours day month weekday command
```

Table 21-3 lists valid values for each entry.

Each of the time-associated fields may be represented as a comma-separated list, a hyphen (-) separated range, or an asterisk (*), which may be used to represent all possible times. For example, if I wanted to display uptime statistics every half hour on the system console, I would add the following line to my crontab file.

```
0,30 * * * * /bin/uptime > /dev/console 2>&1
```

Field	Valid Values	Notes
Minutes	0–59	0 = On the hour
Hours	0–23	0 = Midnight
Day	1–31	
Month	1–12	
Weekday	0–6	Sunday = 0, Saturday = 6
Command	Full pathname of the file to execute	

Table 21-3. Valid Crontable Values

Once you have your `crontab` file tailored to your liking, hand it off to the **cron** daemon by invoking the **crontab** command.

```
# crontab <YourCrontabFile>
# crontab —e # As the cron table owner
```

All crontabs are stored in the `/var/spool/cron/crontabs` directory under the owning user's name. The listing that follows is from the **adm** user's crontab, which is used to gather system statistics:

```
#=================================================================
#       SYSTEM ACTIVITY REPORTS
#  8am-5pm activity reports every 20 mins during weekdays.
#  activity reports every an hour on Saturday and Sunday.
#  6pm-7am activity reports every an hour during weekdays.
#  Daily summary prepared at 18:05.
#=================================================================
0 8-17 * * 1-5 /usr/lib/sa/sa1 1200 3 &
0 * * * 0,6 /usr/lib/sa/sa1 &
0 18-7 * * 1-5 /usr/lib/sa/sa1 &
5 18 * * 1-5 /usr/lib/sa/sa2 -s 8:00 -e 18:01 -i 3600 —ubcwyaqvm &
#=================================================================
#       PROCESS ACCOUNTING:
#  runacct at 11:10 every night
#  dodisk at 11:00 every night
#  ckpacct every hour on the hour
#  monthly accounting 4:15 the first of every month
#=================================================================
#10 23 * * 0-6 /usr/lib/acct/runacct 2>/usr/adm/acct/nite/accterr > /dev/null
#0 23 * * 0-6 /usr/lib/acct/dodisk > /dev/null 2>&1
#0 * * * * /usr/lib/acct/ckpacct > /dev/null 2>&1
#15 4 1 * * /usr/lib/acct/monacct > /dev/null 2>&1
#=================================================================
```

Any user can create a `crontab` file unless the systems administrator enforces the access controls on who may use the cron services by listing user names, one per line, in the `/usr/adm/cron/{cron.allow,cron.deny}` files. Any time a user attempts to create or edit a cron table, the **cron** daemon checks the authorization of these files before invoking a user's `crontab` file. The default is to allow access to all users.

Be careful! If you create a `/var/adm/cron/cron.deny` file, then this file takes precedent over the `cron.allow` file. Also, if a `cron.allow` file exists and an entry has not been made for the root user, then not even root can edit a cron table!

Ad Hoc Jobs

Suppose you want to run a job off hours but don't want to create a crontab entry for it. It may be a one-time-only run. You can do this using the **at** and **batch** commands. Note that **batch** is just a script that invokes **at**. Execute **at**, specifying the time and the input stream of commands. The job stream is copied to the `/usr/spool/cron/atjobs` directory. When the time comes, **cron** executes the job stream at the specified time. Authorization to run jobs with **at** is controlled, as in the case of **crontab**, by listing user names in the `/usr/adm/cron/{at.allow,at.deny}` files. The default is to allow access to all users.

```
# at <time> input <Ctrl-D> ◄──── Start a job at <time>
# echo "shutdown -Fr" | at 11 pm sat ◄──── Reboot the system at 11:00 PM on the next
                                             Saturday. Do not forget the echo or the
# atq <username> ◄──── List scheduled jobs   system will reboot now from the current shell
# at -r jobnumber ◄──────── Remove a job
```

If a more sophisticated batch scheduling system is required, you can create a "batch queue" using the printer subsystem.

Managing cron Activities

In active batch environments, you might want to place some limits on **cron** scheduling. The `/usr/adm/cron/queuedefs` file can be configured to limit the number of concurrent jobs by event type, set the default nice value, and set the retry limit. Event controls are listed one per line in the `queuedefs` file. A sample of the `queuedefs` file is listed here:

```
# cron values for each queue of batch jobs:
#
#        queue.xxjxxnxxw
#
# queues:
#  a - sh jobs          d - sync event
#  b - batch jobs       e - ksh jobs
```

```
#  c - cron event        f - csh jobs
#
#  xxj - maximum number of jobs in this queue (deafult 100)
#  xxn - nice value at which these jobs will run at (default 2)
#  xxw - wait time till next execution attempt (default 60 seconds)
#
#
# here is an example of a low prority (nice 20), 50 entry batch queue
# b.50j20n60w
```

The `queuedefs` file is shipped empty. Default values for all event types (which are shown in Table 21-4) support 100 concurrent jobs at nice value 2 with a 60-second retry limit. Here is a sample `queuedefs` entry:

`c.2j2n90v` ◄───────── Two crontab jobs, nice value 2, retry every 90 seconds

SYSTEM RESOURCE CONTROLLER

AIX provides a mechanism for controlling and managing sets of programs that function collectively as a unit. This mechanism is called the *System Resource Controller (SRC)*. SRC provides simple command interfaces to display the status of, refresh, start, and stop system services as a single entity. These interfaces reduce the operational and administrative complexity of managing all the daemons and programs that make up a particular service.

The collection of programs that comprises an SRC service unit is called a subsystem. The daemons that make up a subsystem are known as subservers. Subsystems may be grouped by the overall service they provide and are identified as subsystem groups. For example, the **ftpd** daemon is a subserver of the **inetd** subsystem. The **inetd** subsystem is a group member of the TCP/IP subsystem group. SRC allows the operator or administrator to operate on a service at the subserver, subsystem, or subsystem group level.

Type	Class of Events
a	at events
b	batch events
c	crontab events
d	sync events
e	ksh events
f	csh events

Table 21-4. `queuedefs` Event Types

SRC components

Overall, SRC is provided by the **srcmstr** daemon. The **srcmstr** daemon is started at boot time by an entry in the /etc/inittab file.

```
srcmstr:23456789:respawn:/usr/sbin/srcmstr   # System resource controller
```

The **srcmstr** daemon identifies subsystem components from definition in ODM object classes /etc/objrepos/{SRCsubsys,SRCnotify}. Subsystems and subserver configuration information are managed through the use of the {**mk,ch,rm**}**ssys** and {**mk,ch,rm**}**server** commands. In most cases, the subsystems and subservers are predefined for each product at installation time, so you will rarely if ever have to work at this level.

Once a subsystem group, subsystem, or subserver is configured into the ODM, it may be operated on using the following commands:

- **startsrc**   Start a subsystem
- **stopsrc**   Stop a subsystem
- **refresh**   Restart or refresh a subsystem
- **trace -a, trcon, trcoff, and trcstop**   Turn on/off tracing of a subsystem
- **lssrc**   Display subsystem status

Subsystems may be started at boot time after **srcmstr** is loaded by invoking the **startsrc** command as part of a boot **rc** script or directly from /etc/inittab. Some SRC command examples include these:

- # **startsrc -g tcpip**   Start the TCPIP subsystem group
- # **refresh -g nfs**   Refresh the NFS subsystem group
- # **stopsrc -s qdaemon**   Stop the **qdaemon** subsystem

To display the status of all defined subsystems, use the **lssrc** command. Note that subsystem control may also be invoked using the **smitty subsys** and **smitty subserver** SMIT FastPaths or through the Web-Based System Manager.

```
# lssrc -a
```

Subsystem	Group	PID	Status
syslogd	ras	3670	active
sendmail	mail	4144	active
portmap	portmap	3878	active
inetd	tcpip	4388	active
xntpd	tcpip	4644	active
snmpd	tcpip	5160	active
dpid2	tcpip	4904	active
hostmibd	tcpip	5418	active

qdaemon	spooler	7224	active
writesrv	spooler	7484	active
dtsrc		9550	active
ctrmc	rsct	11106	active
IBM.ERRM	rsct_rm	11876	active
i4llmd	iforls	12128	active
IBM.AuditRM	rsct_rm	11362	active
biod	nfs		active
nfsd	nfs		active
rpc.statd	nfs		active
rpc.lockd	nfs		active
rpc.mountd	nfs		active
lpd	spooler		active
clvmd			inoperative
gated	tcpip		inoperative
named	tcpip		inoperative
routed	tcpip		inoperative
rwhod	tcpip		inoperative
iptrace	tcpip		inoperative
timed	tcpip		inoperative
dhcpcd	tcpip		inoperative
dhcpsd	tcpip		inoperative
dhcprd	tcpip		inoperative
ndpd-host	tcpip		inoperative
ndpd-router	tcpip		inoperative
tftpd	tcpip		inoperative
mrouted	tcpip		inoperative
rsvpd	qos		inoperative
policyd	qos		inoperative
llbd	iforncs		inoperative
glbd	iforncs		inoperative
i4lmd	iforls		inoperative
i4glbcd	iforncs		inoperative
i4gdb	iforls		inoperative
wsmrefserver			inoperative
pppcontrold	uucp		inoperative
pxed	tcpip		inoperative
binld	tcpip		inoperative
ypserv	yp		inoperative
ypupdated	yp		inoperative
yppasswdd	yp		inoperative
dfpd	tcpip		inoperative
i4conmgr	iforls		inoperative
secldapclntd	secldap		inoperative

```
automountd       autofs              inoperative
keyserv          keyserv             inoperative
ypbind           yp                  inoperative
nis_cachemgr     nisplus             inoperative
rpc.nisd         nisplus             inoperative
rpc.nispasswdd   nisplus             inoperative
```

CHECKLIST

The following is a checklist for the key points in process management:

- [ ] A process consists of an executing program and its address space. Each process is named by a positive integer number called the process identifier (PID).

- [ ] You can set the maximum number of processes per user by using the SMIT FastPath **smitty system** and then selecting Change/Show Characteristics Of The Operating System.

- [ ] Use the **ps** command to look at processes running on the system.

- [ ] The nice value is an integer that represents coarse priority differences between processes. The *larger* the number, the *lower* the priority.

- [ ] Only the superuser can improve nice priority. The nice value can be set from the command line using the **nice** command when starting a process.

- [ ] Process owners and the superuser can modify existing process nice values by using the **renice** command.

CHAPTER 22

System Accounting

L et me see . . . that is 22 minutes on 12 CPUs, 3GB of disk space, and 3 hours of connect time. Will that be cash or check? Nothing in life is free! Especially if you are crunching numbers at a large High Performance Computer Facility. Even if you do not charge back for system resources, it is a good idea to regularly monitor utilization. By collecting accounting data, you get a reasonable profile of how your system is being used. Who are the big resource hogs? How soon will you need that extra 10GB of disk space? Maybe you need to justify resources to a higher authority.

The AIX accounting system is System V in flavor. There is, however, a set of the standard BSD accounting system management commands bolted onto the System V environment. Sites that write their own accounting programs and scripts will find that AIX provides the tools and accounting data formats that will facilitate porting an existing system from other UNIX environments. For the less adventurous, AIX supplies all the commands and scripts required to manage system accounting data. The accounting system is based on a set of three components:

- Data collection
- Management and reporting commands
- Periodic data management scripts

Data collection takes place automatically when accounting is enabled. Management and commands enable you to start and stop the accounting system, manage the data files, and generate reports. Periodic data management scripts are invoked by **cron** (see later section, "Crontab Entries") to automate closing out data and generating general summary information.

DATA COLLECTION

Data collection begins when system accounting is turned on and stops when it is turned off. AIX samples and records process utilization and session data for each user in the system. The collected information represents connect time, process resources, commands, disk usage, and print queuing utilization.

Connect Time

Connect-time data is accumulated in the /var/adm/wtmp and /etc/utmp files. Each time you log in to AIX, the login process writes a record to wtmp and utmp. The data indicates the user name, date, time, port, and connecting address. The **init** process writes a similar record when you exit the system. This data represents the duration time of your connection to the system.

Combinations of **rsh** and X11 clients may circumvent the connection data accounting in environments where there is X11 usage. The **xterm** terminal emulation client provides a flag indicating whether or not an /etc/utmp record should be written. The **xterm** terminal emulation also has a history of corrupting the /etc/utmp file. You may want to use a wrapper command that forces the users of remote client applications to comply with connection accounting.

Corruptions or errors in both wtmp and utmp files may be corrected by translating the target binary file to a temporary ASCII file with the **fwtmp** command, manually editing the suspect entries, and then translating the temporary file back to the binary target. The new file will overwrite connection data logged during this edit process.

```
# last -f /var/adm/wtmp | more        ◄───────── To find the problem data field
# /usr/sbin/acct/fwtmp < /var/adm/wtmp > temp.file  ◄── Make ASCII file
# vi temp.file    ◄──────────────────────── Edit the problem field
# /usr/sbin/acct/fwtmp -ic < temp.file > wtmp.new  ◄── Make binary file
# last -f wtmp.new | more    ◄────────────── To review the corrected field
# cp -pi wtmp.new /var/adm/wtmp   ◄────────── To overwrite to problem target
```

Process Resource Usage

Resource utilization information for each process run by the operating system is recorded in the /var/adm/pacct file at process exit. No information is recorded for processes that do not exit. A process accounting record indicates the UID, GID, user name, elapsed wall clock time, CPU time, memory use, character I/O total, and disk block I/O totals.

Command Usage

A nice side effect of process data is an audit trail of command and application usage. This data provides a profile of application use and may assist in tracking security problems. Be aware that experienced hackers tend to fix up accounting information before leaving the scene. See Chapter 23 for secure audit details.

Disk Usage

You can periodically collect disk usage information for the system and store it in the /var/adm/dtmp file. Collecting disk usage data with the dodisk script may cause a load on the system, so schedule the cron job during an off-hour shift. AIX assigns disk usage data to users according to the files they own in the file system and any links to files they may have created. The usage statistics for a file are distributed evenly between the users with links to the file.

It is also possible to track disk usage and regulate limits on usage by user and/or group. This is done through the disk quota system. See Chapter 20 concerning details on the disk quota system.

Print Usage

The **enq** command and the **qdaemon** process record print queuing system utilization statistics. The **enq** command writes a record for each print job it handles. The record indicates the print job owner, the job number, and the filename. When the file is printed, **qdaemon** writes another record that includes this information plus the number of pages that were printed. There are public domain backends for PostScript queues that will supply accounting records for PostScript conversion and attributes.

Accounting Files

Accounting records are stored in a set of files located in the /var/adm directory. Table 22-1 lists the files and data collected.

ACCOUNTING CONFIGURATION

The accounting system will create most data collection files as needed if the startup script runs from the **adm** user account before any other user runs it (see section "Starting and Stopping Accounting" in this chapter). This will not always be the case, so you will need to know how to change or create the files manually. This should be done with **adm** authority but may have to be done as **root** to correct file ownership. Make sure the bos.acct fileset has been installed as you walk through this configuration section. See Chapter 6 for details on installing missing filesets.

```
# lslpp -l bos.acct
```

Setting Up Collection Files

I usually have to fix or create at least one data collection file (Table 22-1) even when I remember to start up the accounting system properly from the **adm** user shell. The most common problem to fix is the permissions on the pacct file that collects the process data. Touching the filename or running **nulladm** can create a missing file stub.

Filename	Data Collected
pacct	Active process data
Spacct.<mmdd>	Daily active process data (runacct)
qacct	Print usage data
utmp	Connect session data
dtmp	Disk usage data
wtmp	Active process data

Table 22-1. List of Accounting Records

The **nulladm** command creates or overwrites the arguments supplied as zero-length files and sets the correct permissions.

```
# touch /var/adm/pacct   ◀─────────Only changes the time stamp if the file exists
# chown adm /var/adm/pacct
# chgrp adm /var/adm/pacct
# chmod 644 /var/adm/pacct
```

or

```
# /usr/sbin/acct/nulladm /var/adm/pacct   ◀─────────This will overwrite the file
```

The qacct file to collect the print usage data must be manually created (see section "Print Accounting (/etc/qconfig)" later in this chapter).

Identifying Shifts

Configure the /etc/acct/holidays file to reflect your prime-time shift and scheduled holidays. The first uncommented line in the file must indicate the year and the starting and ending time of the prime shift. Subsequent lines indicate the data and description of each holiday scheduled over the year. Each holiday entry indicates:

- Integer day of the year
- Three-character month name
- Integer day of the month
- Text string holiday description

You may want to just update the year for the first uncommented line and comment out all the holiday lines to keep the **runacct** crontab job (see section "Crontab Entries" later in this chapter) from reporting that the file is out of date. A good source for holiday schedules is a Web page published by the United States Office of Personnel Management (http://www.opm.gov/fedhol/). Your /etc/acct/holidays file might read something like this:

```
* Prime/Nonprime Table for AIX Accounting System
*
* Curr   Prime   Non-Prime
* Year   Start   Start
*
  1990   0800    1700    * The year in this line must be updated
*
* Day of      Calendar    Company
* Year        Date        Holiday
    1         Jan 1       New Year's Day
   50         Feb 19      Washington's Birthday (Obsvd.)
```

```
148        May 28       Memorial Day (Obsvd.)
185        Jul 4        Independence Day
246        Sep 3        Labor Day
326        Nov 22       Thanksgiving Day
327        Nov 23       Day after Thanksgiving
359        Dec 25       Christmas Day
365        Dec 31       New Years Eve
```

Disk Accounting (/etc/filesystems)

Disk accounting may be toggled *true* or *false* for a filesystem by changing the accounting attribute for that filesystem. Use the **chfs** command to set the `account` stanza to `true` for each file system you intend to monitor. Do not edit the `/etc/filesystems` file directly. The **lsfs** command lists the characteristics of each filesystem, and the last column, which usually word-wraps on a standard terminal, is the `account` stanza.

```
# lsfs
# chfs -a account=true /home
# lsfs /home
```

Print Accounting (/etc/qconfig)

Print usage records may be saved if an accounting collection file is identified by the `acctfile` parameter of each queue stanza in the `/etc/qconfig` file. You may also need to create the target collection file first with the following **nulladm** command (see section "Setting Up Collection Files" later in this chapter for details).

```
# ls -l /var/adm/qacct
# nulladm /var/adm/qacct   ◄────── This will overwrite any existing file
```

Use following **chque** command to add this stanza to `/etc/qconfig` and refresh the **qdaemon**.

```
# chque -q 'quename' -a 'acctfile = /var/adm/qacct'
```

Report Directories

Manually create the report subdirectories `nite`, `fiscal`, and `sum` with **adm** ownership in the `/var/adm/acct` directory.

```
# su - adm
# cd /var/adm/acct
# mkdir nite fiscal sum
```

If you miss this step, the `/var/adm/pacct` data file will remain empty after the accounting system has started. See the `/usr/adm/acct/accterr` error file that is specified in the **adm** cron table, located on the **runacct** line, in the following section for detailed errors.

Crontab Entries

Remove the comments from the `adm` crontab. Edit the crontab using the **crontab -e** command.

```
# su - adm
# crontab -e    ◄──────── This will open vi to edit the crontab.
```

The `adm` crontab should look like this:

```
#===================================================================
#       SYSTEM ACTIVITY REPORTS
# 8am-5pm activity reports every 20 mins during weekdays.
# Activity reports every hour on Saturday and Sunday.
# 6pm-7am activity reports every hour during weekdays.
# Daily summary prepared at 18:05.
#===================================================================
0 8-17 * * 1-5 /usr/lib/sa/sa1 1200 3 &
0 * * * 0,6 /usr/lib/sa/sa1 &
0 18-7 * * 1-5 /usr/lib/sa/sa1 &
5 18 * * 1-5 /usr/lib/sa/sa2 -s 8:00 -e 18:01 -i 3600 -ubcwyaqvm &
#==========================================================
#       PROCESS ACCOUNTING:
#  dodisk at 11:00 nightly will run diskusg and acctdisk.
# runacct at 11:10 nightly to process connect, fee, disk, printer
#         and system accounting data.
# ckpacct every hour checks the size of /var/adm/pacct, free space
#         in /var and will turn off accounting if limits are exceeded.
# monacct Monthly accounting at 4:15 the first of every month.
#==========================================================
0 23 * * 0-6 /usr/lib/acct/dodisk >/dev/null 2>&1
10 23 * * 0-6 /usr/lib/acct/runacct 2>/usr/adm/acct/nite/accterr >/dev/null
5 * * * * /usr/lib/acct/ckpacct >/dev/null 2>&1
15 4 1 * * /usr/lib/acct/monacct >/dev/null 2>&1
#==========================================================
```

If you change **runacct** to run only one or two times per week, then also change **dodisk**. More space will be used in the `/var` filesystem. One noticeable affect of **runacct** is that the `/var/adm/wtmp` file will be reset. I always add **alias olast="last -f /var/adm/acct/ nite/owtmp"** to my `$HOME/.kshrc` file so that I can easily check user connections from the previous `wtmp` file. See Chapter 20 for details on **crontab**.

Work Unit Fees

The `chargefee` script can be used to add work unit entries for each user on the system into the `/var/adm/fee` file. This data is later merged with other accounting files by the **acctmerg** program to produce reports, and the `fee` file is reset if the permissions allow it. The **chargefee** command can be incorporated into the system accounting scripts to implement a chargeback system. To append a fee of five units for username to the `/var/adm/fee` file, enter

```
# /usr/sbin/acct/chargefee username 5
```

ACCOUNTING COMMANDS

As I mentioned in the introduction, AIX offers both SYSTEM V accounting commands and a subset of the BSD commands. These commands enable you to display, manage, generate reports from, and record charge fees from the collected accounting information.

Starting and Stopping Accounting

The main command for starting and stopping the accounting system is **accton**. The front-end shell script `turnacct` provides a more logical syntax with simple `on` and `off` arguments. A `startup` script is provided to start the accounting system at boot time by appending boot data to `/var/adm/wtmp` with the **acctwtmp** command, running the **turnacct on** command, and then executing the **remove** command to clean up previous session files. Add the following two lines to the `/etc/rc` script after the `sadc` dummy record command line:

```
# Start Process Accounting
/usr/bin/su - adm -c /usr/sbin/acct/startup
```

Now uncomment or add this `sadc` dummy record command line in the same file:

```
/usr/bin/su - adm -c /usr/lib/sa/sadc /usr/adm/sa/sa`date +%d`
```

Note that `/usr/adm` is a backward-compatible link to `/var/adm`.

The `shutacct` script is called from the system `shutdown` script to append shutdown data to `/var/adm/wtmp` with the **acctwtmp** command and turn off accounting with **turnacct off**.

Start the accounting system manually by invoking the **turnacct** or **accton** command.

```
# su - adm
# /usr/sbin/acct/turnacct on
```

or

```
# su - adm
# accton /var/adm/pacct    ◄────────────This will not check permissions of pacct
```

Stop system accounting manually by using the **turnacct** or **accton** command.

```
# su - adm
# /usr/sbin/acct/turnacct off
```

or

```
# su - adm
# accton
```

Displaying Statistics

At any time, you can take the pulse of your system or look back through accounting history from the command line. You can also create ad hoc reports by directing standard output to a file. A general summary of data stored in /var/adm/pacct can be displayed using the **sa** command. The **sa** command supports a number of flags that can be used to filter and restrict the output. Two of the most useful flags are the **-m** flag, which summarizes by user, and the **-s** flag, which summarizes by command. The **-s** flag can also be used to merge the summary with an existing history file.

```
# sa -m
root            766      0.75cpu    77743653tio      11532k*sec
daemon            8      0.02cpu      663334tio        848k*sec
adm              75      0.07cpu     1242340tio        747k*sec
ops              36      0.29cpu     3810811tio       7740k*sec
nobody           15      0.14cpu     4890509tio      26791k*sec

# sa -s | head -7  ◄────────Print first seven lines
    900     17008.96re    1.28cpu      98167avio     6k
      6         0.39re    0.39cpu   10289152avio     3k   egrep
      6      2060.74re    0.23cpu     471744avio     5k   xterm
      3         0.15re    0.13cpu    1566208avio    33k   ds_rslt
     17      2850.94re    0.13cpu      51588avio     3k   ksh
     47      2944.44re    0.07cpu      44948avio     3k   ***other
     30         0.07re    0.03cpu      13452avio     3k   awk
```

Connection histories can be displayed using the BSD **ac** and **last** commands. The **ac** command can tally connection times by day or for the interval of time covered by the

/var/adm/wtmp file. The **last** command can be used to display the login times for all users or an individual user.

```
# /usr/sbin/acct/ac -p | awk '{print $1"    "$2}'
duane    0.46
deroest   264.16
donn    487.54
noyd    9961.55


# /usr/sbin/acct/ac -d
Sep 01  total    269.68
Sep 02  total    613.75
Sep 03  total    914.32


 # last -4
ops      pts/92    xtreme.sar.washi   Fri Sep 17 10:41 still logged in
don      pts/86    tlab1.bnn.washin   Fri Sep 17 10:07 still logged in
kenm     pts/75    192.168.90.125    Fri Sep 17 10:00 - 10:22 (00:21)
davidw   pts/56    redy.aal.washing   Fri Sep 17 08:23 still logged in
```

Exhaustive command usage information can be generated using the BSD **lastcomm** command. Like **ac**, this command supports a large number of flags to filter the output. Be aware that it will also use significant system resources when invoked!

```
# lastcomm | sed "s/                              //g"  ◄────────28 spaces
acctwtmp     S    root          __    0.02 secs Fri Sep 17 23:44
httpd        F    nobody        __    0.05 secs Fri Sep 17 13:50
tftpd        S    root          __    0.69 secs Fri Sep 17 11:28
tftpd        F    nobody        __    0.01 secs Fri Sep 17 11:28
nfssync_kpro  DX root          __    0.01 secs Fri Sep 17 23:44
ksh          F    root      pts/0     0.01 secs Fri Sep 17 23:44
whoami       S    root      pts/0     0.03 secs Fri Sep 17 23:44
termdef      S    root      pts/0     0.03 secs Fri Sep 17 23:44
sh           S    adm       pts/1     0.28 secs Fri Sep 17 22:02
```

Summary Reports

A standard set of reports is produced at intervals by the **runacct** and **monacct** commands. These commands should be run by the adm crontab. The summaries and reports are recorded in the following directories:

```
/var/adm/acct/nite   ◄──────────── Daily files used by runacct
/var/adm/acct/sum    ◄──────────── Daily summaries created by runacct
/var/adm/acct/fiscal ◄──────────── Monthly summaries created by monacct
```

Reports and data files include:

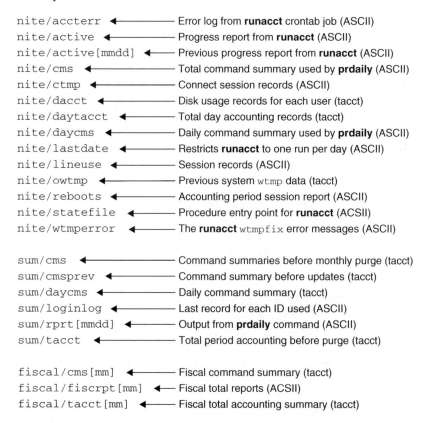

```
nite/accterr    ◄──────── Error log from runacct crontab job (ASCII)
nite/active     ◄──────── Progress report from runacct (ASCII)
nite/active[mmdd] ◄─────── Previous progress report from runacct (ASCII)
nite/cms        ◄──────── Total command summary used by prdaily (ASCII)
nite/ctmp       ◄──────── Connect session records (ASCII)
nite/dacct      ◄──────── Disk usage records for each user (tacct)
nite/daytacct   ◄──────── Total day accounting records (tacct)
nite/daycms     ◄──────── Daily command summary used by prdaily (ASCII)
nite/lastdate   ◄──────── Restricts runacct to one run per day (ASCII)
nite/lineuse    ◄──────── Session records (ASCII)
nite/owtmp      ◄──────── Previous system wtmp data (tacct)
nite/reboots    ◄──────── Accounting period session report (ASCII)
nite/statefile  ◄──────── Procedure entry point for runacct (ACSII)
nite/wtmperror  ◄──────── The runacct wtmpfix error messages (ASCII)

sum/cms         ◄──────── Command summaries before monthly purge (tacct)
sum/cmsprev     ◄──────── Command summary before updates (tacct)
sum/daycms      ◄──────── Daily command summary (tacct)
sum/loginlog    ◄──────── Last record for each ID used (ASCII)
sum/rprt[mmdd]  ◄──────── Output from prdaily command (ASCII)
sum/tacct       ◄──────── Total period accounting before purge (tacct)

fiscal/cms[mm]      ◄──────── Fiscal command summary (tacct)
fiscal/fiscrpt[mm]  ◄──────── Fiscal total reports (ACSII)
fiscal/tacct[mm]    ◄──────── Fiscal total accounting summary (tacct)
```

Performance Tools

Here are some tools shipped with Accounting Services that will help evaluate performance, along with short examples of their use.

The **vmstat** command reports information about kernel threads, memory, disk I/O, traps, and processor activity. New command-line options as of AIX 5L add I/O-oriented output with three new fields and a time stamp per line. To view two summaries of five-second system slices with new AIX 5L arguments, enter

```
# vmstat -It 5 2
```

The **timex** command will display the elapsed, user, and system execution times for a command. Command-line options allow total system activity reports with data items similar to the **sar** command. To display the system activity created by the **ps -ef** command, enter

```
# timex -s ps -ef >/dev/null
```

The **iostat** command reports processor statistics and all system input and output device statistics. New command-line options shipped with AIX 5L add new adapter and system throughput header fields and reports. You must have the **iostat** attribute for **sys0** set to *true* before this command may collect data. Use the **lsattr** and **chdev** commands to list and change this attribute.

```
# lsattr -El sys0 -a iostat  ◀─────────── Check the iostat attribute
# chdev -l sys0 -a iostat=true  ◀──────── Change the iostat attribute
```

Use the following command lines to collect I/O performance data from three test drives while copying a large file to the target filesystem /fstest striped across those three drives.

```
# echo '/bin/cp ./largefile /fstest\n/usr/sbin/umount /fstest' > a.out
# iostat -d hdisk2 hdisk3 hdisk4 5 >/tmp/iostat.out &
# timex sh a.out
# jobs  ◀─────────── To see what background jobs to stop
# kill %1  ◀─────────── To kill the background iostat command
```

Unmounting the filesystem ensures that all the data was written to the target drive for the test, and the **timex** command will give you a gauge for reference. Please do not use, test, or unmount a production filesystem for this example.

The **sar** command is particularly adept at collecting CPU statistics from symmetric multiprocessor systems. It calls the **sadc** command and accesses many of the data collection files already activated by the accounting system and the adm crontab. Actually, /usr/lib/sa/sa2 is a wrapper script for **sar** that was configured to run once a day from the adm crontab (see the section "Crontab Entries" in this chapter). To make an ad hoc report that can be used as an ASCII input file for a spreadsheet to illustrate the day's performance of CPU number four (the report will track %usr, %sys, %wio, and %idle over the course of a day), enter

```
# sar -P 4 >/tmp/cpu4_data.txt
```

PERIODIC HOUSECLEANING

Turning on system accounting is a little like opening the floodgates. On an active multiuser system, accounting can generate a large amount of data that must be filtered and archived as part of your regular housecleaning activities. The default accounting procedures specified in the adm crontab periodically close and rename accounting files to assist in managing the data. It is left up to the systems administrator to implement procedures to archive and clean up the old data files. What information should be saved for posterity? You can take the conservative approach and save all the reports and data files, or you can throw caution to the wind and create crontab scripts to delete old reports and data files on a daily basis. Moderation suggests that it might be wise to periodically compress and archive the summary files and keep a copy of the previous day's data files online for short-term history queries.

CHECKLIST

The following is a checklist for the key points in System Accounting:

- [ ] The AIX system accounting system is based on data collection, management and reporting commands, and periodic data management scripts, and it supplies all the commands and scripts required to manage system accounting data based.

- [ ] Data collection begins when system accounting is turned on and stops when it is turned off. The collected information represents connect time, process resources, commands, disk usage, and print queuing utilization.

- [ ] Connect-time data is accumulated in the /var/adm/wtmp and /etc/utmp files.

- [ ] Combinations of **rsh** and X11 clients may circumvent the connection data accounting in environments where there is X11 usage.

- [ ] Resource utilization information for each process run by the operating system is recorded in the /var/adm/pacct file at process exit. No information is recorded for processes that do not exit.

- [ ] Process data also provides is an audit trail of command and application usage which can help profile application use and might assist in tracking security problems. However, experienced hackers tend to fix up accounting information before leaving the scene.

- [ ] You can periodically collect disk usage information for the system and store it in the /var/adm/dtmp file.

- [ ] The **enq** command and the **qdaemon** process record print queuing system utilization statistics.

- [ ] Accounting records are stored in a set of files located in the /var/adm directory.

- [ ] The accounting system will create most data collection files as needed if the startup script runs from the **adm** user account before any other user runs it.

- [ ] If you have to manually change or create accounting system data files, do it with **adm** authority. It is possible you might have to use **root** authority to correct file ownership.

- [ ] When manually configuring accounting files, configure the /etc/acct/holidays file to reflect your prime-time shift and scheduled holidays. The first uncommented line in the file must indicate the year and the starting and ending time of the prime shift. Subsequent lines indicate the data and description of each holiday scheduled over the year.

☐ When manually configuring disk accounting, toggle disk accounting true or false for a filesystem by changing the accounting attribute for that filesystem. Use the **chfs** command to set the account stanza to true for each file system you intend to monitor. Do not edit the /etc/filesystems file directly.

☐ When manually creating accounting files, create the report subdirectories nite, fiscal, and sum with **adm** ownership in the /var/adm/acct directory, or the /var/adm/pacct data file will remain empty after the accounting system has started.

☐ The main command for starting and stopping the accounting system is **accton**.

☐ A startup script is provided to start the accounting system at boot time.

☐ The shutacct script is called from the system shutdown script to append shutdown data to /var/adm/wtmp.

☐ Stop system accounting manually by using the **turnacct** or **accton** command.

☐ You can display a general summary of data stored in /var/adm/pacct using the **sa** command.

☐ Display connection histories with the BSD **ac** and **last** commands.

☐ A standard set of reports is produced at intervals by the **runacct** and **monacct** commands. These commands should be run by the adm crontab.

☐ The **vmstat** command reports information about kernel threads, memory, disk I/O, traps, and processor activity.

☐ The **timex** command will display the elapsed, user, and system execution times for a command.

☐ The **iostat** command reports processor statistics and all system input and output device statistics.

☐ The **sar** command also collects CPU statistics from symmetric multiprocessor systems.

☐ The default accounting procedures specified in the adm crontab periodically close and rename accounting files to assist in managing data. The systems administrator must implement procedures to archive and clean up the old data files.

PART X

Security

CHAPTER 23

Auditing and Security

The amazing growth of the Internet and increase in the number of computers have changed the way many people operate their businesses and live their lives. Few would deny the great benefits that have been reaped from the technology explosion over the past decade. Unfortunately, with these great benefits has come an equally great burden: the world is filled with new and valuable targets for computer hackers and others who wish to do damage to a company's infrastructure. The need for computer security has never been greater, and the responsibility of providing that security falls squarely on the shoulders of the systems administrator.

What Is Security?

The word "security" will often mean different things to different people: A user may expect that the e-mails and files that he or she creates on a computer are kept private from unauthorized eyes. A business could be destroyed if the customer information stored in a database was stolen or corrupted. If a critical system becomes unavailable due to a denial of service attack, everyone who depends on that system will be impacted.

For a Systems Administrator, any of the preceding problems constitutes a security violation. Proactive measures are required to ensure that as many scenarios as possible are thought out, planned for, and protected against.

Defining a Security Policy

While it is true that the most secure computer is the one that is powered off and locked in a bank vault, that computer will probably not serve any useful purpose. Before taking such drastic measures, consider the benefits of defining and implementing a formal security policy. By publicizing some simple rules and enforcing those rules through the auditing and the controls provided by AIX, you can protect yourself from the majority of attacks.

In defining this security policy, it is important to understand the trade-off between protection and usability. Restrictions that are too strict can impede the use of the system and cause users to look for "shortcuts" around the policy. Ensure that the policy is distributed to the user community, and that users understand their role in keeping the system and data secure. When developing a security policy, consider, at a minimum, the following points:

- User privacy
- System integrity
- Availability and authorized access
- Ease of use
- Auditing and accountability

PASSWORDS

According to the **System Administration, Networking, and Security (SANS) Institute**, default and weak passwords constitute one of the most common security vulnerabilities. Few things are more unpopular with users than restrictive password policies. Unfortunately, without rigorous controls, people will often use simple, easily guessable words that are no match for the power of password cracking programs.

What makes a good password? It must be easy to remember, but it should not be a word found in the dictionary or one based upon easy-to-discover personal data. Passwords should be changed frequently; but if users are forced to change their passwords too often, they will often resort to using weaker passwords, defeating the original security goal.

Some of these issues can be resolved only by having a well-publicized password policy and by educating the user community on the danger of weak passwords. Fortunately, AIX 5L provides a number of tools and facilities that help to address some of these problems and enforce your defined policies.

/etc/passwd and /etc/security/passwd

All UNIX-based operating systems store information about user accounts in the file /etc/passwd. Each user account on a system is represented by one line in this file, with individual fields separated by colons. The fields represent

- The username
- The user's encrypted password
- The user identification number (UID)
- The user's primary group identification number (GID)
- The user's full name
- The user's home directory
- The user's shell

Several of the fields may be blank, as seen in this excerpt from an /etc/passwd file:

```
root:!:0:0::/:/bin/ksh
daemon:!:1:1::/etc
...
jdoe:!:210:1:John Doe:/home/jdoe:/usr/bin/ksh
jane:!:211:1:Jane Plain:/home/jane:/usr/bin/ksh
```

Astute readers will notice that the second field, which should contain the user's encrypted password, contains either an asterisk or an exclamation point. The reason for this concerns the solution to one of the biggest problems with the UNIX password scheme.

The `/etc/passwd` file must be readable by all system users; it is how programs on the system get information about users, including their usernames and their home directories.

```
# ls -l /etc/passwd
-rw-r--r--  1 root    security   989 Apr 21 11:24 /etc/passwd
```

Though the password stored in the file is encrypted, the encryption is done via an algorithm that is easily cracked through the power of today's computers. AIX solves this problem by putting a placeholder character in the password field and storing the actual encrypted password in another file, readable only by root. This file is `/etc/security/passwd`.

```
# ls -l /etc/security/passwd
-rw-------  1 root    security   508 Apr 21 11:24 /etc/security/passwd
```

The entries in this file for the preceding user accounts are

```
root:
    password = m1lzn0OisArdw
    lastupdate = 1015529254
    flags =

daemon:
    password = *
...

jdoe:
    password = LW94qD/8zKd.c
    lastupdate = 1019416125
    flags =

jane:
    password = QVyvzV3vkSwcY
    lastupdate = 1019416076
    flags = ADMCHG
```

There are several items of note in the preceding `/etc/security/passwd` excerpt:

- The password for the daemon account is a single asterisk. Since it is impossible for the encrypted value of any password to ever be a single asterisk, this account has a password that cannot be typed and can never be logged into (though root can **su** to the account).

- The flag **ADMCHG** is indicated for **jane**. This flag signifies that the most recent password change for the user **jane** was performed by root, and so **jane** will have to immediately enter a new password upon her next login. No one, including root, should ever know the unencrypted password of a user.

Password Restrictions and Aging

Rarely are users inclined to use strong passwords, and they do not, in general, like to change their passwords more than once in a lifetime. These inclinations break the golden rules of account security. Fortunately, AIX provides a mechanism both for forcing users to change their password and for guiding them in the creation of strong passwords.

Table 23-1 presents the options that are available for enforcing the quality of user passwords, and the frequency with which they must be changed. These options can be set on a per-user basis when creating the account (SMIT FastPath **mkuser**) or at any point after, via the SMIT FastPath **passwdattrs**. They can also be set on a system-wide basis by editing the following fields in the `default` stanza of the `/etc/security/ user` file. Table 23-1 shows a quick map of these user attributes to the SMIT options. Use SMIT Help for a complete description of each attribute.

ALTERNATIVE AUTHENTICATION METHODS

In addition to the standard local username/password combination, there exist a number of additional methods for authenticating users. Some of these methods are designed to improve the security of the login process, while other methods have as

User Attributes	SMIT mkuser or passwdattrs Options
pwdwarntime	Days to warn user before password expires
pwdchecks	Password check methods
dictionlist	Password dictionary files
histsize	Number of passwords before reuse
histexpire	Weeks before password reuse
maxexpired	Weeks between password expiration and lockout
maxage	Password maximum age
minage	Password minimum age
minlen	Password minimum length
minalpha	Password minimum alpha characters
minother	Password minimum other characters
maxrepeats	Password maximum repeated characters
mindiff	Password minimum different characters

Table 23-1. User Attributes to SMIT Options Map

their goal to create a common authentication service for multiple systems spread out over different networks. AIX 5L provides several facilities for incorporating these alternative authentication schemes.

Adding Custom Authentication Methods

The file /usr/lib/security/methods.cfg contains a block of text, commented out by default, that allows the system administrator to define an alternative authentication method:

```
* auth_method:
*        program = /any/program
```

By specifying the path to a custom authentication program on the program line, the administrator enables that program to be used to validate the user. The most common use for this is NIS and DCE (already present in this file with AIX 5L). The following trivial example of an **auth_method** will request from the user a secret word. If the user enters the proper word, the program exits with a zero code. If the correct word is not entered, the program exits with a nonzero code.

```
#!/bin/ksh -
# trivial alternate auth_method

read secret?"Who goes there? "
if [[ $secret = "itsme" ]]; then
    exit 0
else
    exit 1
fi
```

If the preceding program is saved as /usr/local/auth/whogoesthere, the following stanza should be added to /usr/lib/security/methods.cfg:

```
whogoesthere:
    program = /usr/local/auth/whogoesthere
```

To use the new authentication method, it must be specified in the /etc/security/user file. If listed in the default stanza, the new method will apply to all users:

```
default:
    auth1 = SYSTEM,whogoesthere
    auth2 = NONE
```

When the user **nancy** tries to log in, she will be presented with

```
login: nancy
nancy's Password: <nancy's password>
Who goes there? Idontknow
3004-007 You entered an invalid login name or password.
```

If she then enters the proper secret word, the login process continues successfully.

Kerberos

Kerberos is the name of a system designed by MIT and provided by IBM on the AIX 5L for POWER V5.1 Expansion Pack CD. Kerberos is a network authentication protocol, designed to provide strong authentication for client/server applications by using secret-key cryptography.

In a "Kerberized" environment, all systems and applications are assumed to be untrustworthy, except for the authentication server itself. Users obtain an authentication credential, called a *ticket*, from the authentication server, and that ticket is presented to other systems and applications. By using this system, the transmission of the user's password over the network is minimized. A ticket is valid for a limited amount of time, and so even if it is captured and cracked, it contains no information that might be useful to someone trying to break into a system.

Kerberos requires a significant amount of setup before it is useful, and any application that wishes to use this authentication method must be written to support Kerberos. Kerberos is used extensively as the authentication method for the distributed computing environment (DCE) and the Andrew File System (AFS), as well as with IBM SP systems.

Installing Kerberos

The implementation of Kerberos included with AIX 5L is called the "IBM Network Authentication Service", and can be found on volume one of the AIX 5L for POWER V5.1 Expansion Pack. Each system that will be using Kerberos authentication must have the fileset **krb5.client.rte** installed. This fileset contains the Kerberos libraries and the user commands. On the system that has been designated as the Key Distribution Center (KDC), and on any "slave" KDCs, you must also install the **krb5.server.rte** fileset.

Note that the preceding filesets install the commands into /usr/krb5/bin and /usr/krb5/sbin. This is done to avoid the mixing and possible overwriting of commands already installed into the standard locations. These commands are also used in the DCE, but are incompatible implementations. Therefore, if you want to use the Network Authentication Service, ensure that the /usr/krb5 directories are before /usr/bin and /usr/sbin in the PATH. Also, since Kerberos is highly dependent on the accurate time synchronization of all client and server systems, it is recommended that either **xntpd** or **timed** be used to ensure the proper clock settings.

Configuring the Server

To configure the master KDC and Kerberos administration server, use the command **/usr/sbin/config.krb5**, with the following flags and arguments:

Flag	Example Argument	Meaning
-S	none	Indicates that the configuration is for a server.
-d	domain.tld	Specifies the DNS domain containing this realm.
-r	REALM.DOMAIN.TLD	Specifies the name of the Kerberos realm being defined.
-s	hostname.domain.tld	Specifies the fully qualified domain name of the host being configured. Not currently supported.

So, to set up the KDC and administration server on the host named **kdcsrv**, located in the domain osborne.com, for the realm BOOKS.OSBORNE.COM, you would execute this command:

```
# /usr/sbin/config.krb5 -S -d osborne.com \
    -r BOOKS.OSBORNE.COM
```

The most overlooked part of the Kerberos configuration is synchronizing the system clock. The following **setclock** command will be sufficient for this example but you may need to give this more thought for an enterprise solution:

```
# setclock timeserver.osborne.com   ◄────────Synchronize the system clock
```

Configuring the Clients

Each client must be configured as a member of the Kerberos realm; this is also done with the **config.krb5** command, with the following flags and arguments:

Flag	Example Argument	Meaning
-C	none	Indicates that the configuration is for a client.
-c	hostname.domain.tld	Specifies the fully qualified domain name for the realm's KDC.
-d	domain.tld	Specifies the DNS domain containing this realm.
-r	REALM.DOMAIN.TLD	Specifies the Kerberos realm.
-s	domain.tld	Specifies the fully qualified domain name for the realm's administration server.

Thus, to configure a client to use the Kerberos realm defined in the previous section, execute this command:

```
# /usr/sbin/config.krb5 -C -c kdcsrv.osborne.com \
    -d osborne.com -r BOOKS.OSBORNE.COM \
    -s kdcsrv.osborne.com
```

```
# setclock timeserver.osborne.com   ◄────────Synchronize the system clock
```

Now let's create a host key, a host key table file, and a user on the KDC with the following commands:

```
# kinit admin/admin  ◄────────Authenticate as the admin account
# kadmin  ◄────────Start the kadmin interactive shell
kadmin: list_principals
kadmin: add_principal -randkey -clearpolicy host/kdcsrv.osborne.com
kadmin: ktadd host/kdcsrv.osborne.com
kadmin: add_principal UserName
kadmin: exit
```

Now test your new UserName principal from the client and KDC server.

```
# kinit UserName  ◄────────Authenticate as the new UserName principal
# klist  ◄────────List your new Kerberos ticket
```

Additional Information

The preceding sections provide only a brief introduction to the deployment of the Network Authentication Service. Implementing Kerberos can take a great deal of planning and resources to ensure the security, reliability, and scalability of the system. Fortunately, IBM provides extensive documentation in both PDF and HTML format, in the fileset **krb5.doc.en_US**, also found on the Expansion Pack CD-ROM. Another excellent source of information is the M.I.T. Kerberos website, at `http://web.mit.edu/kerberos/www/`.

CONTROLLING SUPERUSER ACCESS

Great care should be taken with the root password, how it is used, and who has access to it. In general, root should never log in to the system directly; users with access to the superuser account should log in to their own accounts first, and then use the **su** command to become root. This way, all attempts to become root, whether they succeed or fail, are logged to `/var/adm/sulog`. To prevent direct logins to the root account from the network, run the command

```
# chuser rlogin='false' root
```

AIX provides additional protection by defining the groups who may use the **su** command to switch to a particular account, and by refusing to permit the use of **su** to switch to an account. These controls are set in the `/etc/security/user` file, on a per-user basis:

```
root:
   sugroups = system,security
```

The preceding stanza states that only members of the system or security group may switch to root via the **su** command.

SECURING NETWORK ACCESS

Securing network access is perhaps the most important part of ensuring a safe and protected computing environment. A large portion of security violations occur through improperly configured network services or poorly designed applications. It is thus imperative to make sure that the network "footprint" of your systems is as narrow and secure as possible.

Security issues related to the various networking protocols, services, and applications are covered in detail in those chapters related to networking. In brief, there are three cardinal rules for network security:

- If a running service is not necessary, disable it.
- Restrict access to remaining services so that only those systems and networks that need to connect are able to.
- If an application uses an insecure protocol for its communications, it should be replaced with a secure alternative.

For detailed information, refer to the networking chapters in this book, and the sources listed at the end of this chapter.

SECURING FILE ACCESS

AIX 5L, like all UNIX-based operating systems, uses permissions to determine who can read, modify, and execute the objects (regular files, directories, and special device files) on a system. Permissions may be set individually for the owner of the object, for the members of a group listed in /etc/group, and for all other users ("other").

Basic File Permissions

The traditional, or basic, file access permissions are those assigned through the use of the **chmod** command. A user can use **chmod** to modify the permissions on any file that the user owns. Permissions may be specified using either octal or symbolic notation.

```
$ chmod 640 a_file

$ ls -l a_file
-rw-r-----  1 jdoe   staff      0 Apr 20 14:54 a_file
```

In the preceding example, the permissions on `a_file` are set to read and write for the owner, **jdoe** (the "6", in the first position), read-only for members of the **staff** group (the "4" in the second position), and no access for other users (the "0" in the third position).

To set the same permissions using symbolic mode:

```
$ chmod u+rw,g+r,o-rwx a_file
```

The umask

The default permissions for files and directories created by a user account can be set by using the **umask** command (often in the user's shell profile), via the SMIT FastPath mkuser (when creating the account), or via the SMIT FastPath chuser (to modify an existing account.)

```
# smit chuser
...
  File creation UMASK                    [22]
```

Note that the **umask** value is removed (but not subtracted!) from the default permissions of 777 (for newly created directories) or 666 (for newly created files.) Thus, a **umask** value of 022 results in

```
$ umask 022

$ mkdir a_new_directory ; ls -ld a_new_directory
drwxr-xr-x  2 jdoe    staff    512 Apr 20 15:26 a_new_directory

$ touch a_new_file ; ls -l a_new_file
-rw-r--r--  1 jdoe    staff      0 Apr 20 15:26 a_new_file
```

Set-UID and Set-GID

The root user can also make a file or directory set-UID or set-GID. Normally, when a file is executed, it runs with the UID and GID of the user running the program. However, when a file has been made set-UID, that program is run with the effective user ID of the owner of the file.

In AIX, only compiled programs can be made set-UID or set-GID; if those permissions are applied to a shell script, they are ignored when the shell script is executed, for security reasons.

A copy of `/usr/bin/ksh` is made in `/tmp`, and the owner of that copy is set to "root."

```
# cp /usr/bin/ksh /tmp/ksh
# chown root /tmp/ksh
# ls -l /tmp/ksh
-r-xr-xr-x  1 root    system  243374 Apr 20 15:10 /tmp/ksh
```

The user **jdoe** runs the **id** command through the **/tmp/ksh** shell. Because that shell is executable by all users ("other"), the command succeeds and prints **jdoe**'s UID and GID.

```
# su - jdoe

$ /tmp/ksh -c "id"
uid=210(jdoe) gid=1(staff)
```

The root user then changes the permissions on **/tmp/ksh** to be set-UID.

```
$ exit

# chmod u+s /tmp/ksh

# ls -l /tmp/ksh
-r-sr-xr-x  1 root    system  243374 Apr 20 15:10 /tmp/ksh
```

The user **jdoe** again executes the **id** command through the **/tmp/ksh** shell. Because the shell is now set-UID root, any user who uses that shell has the effective UID of root.

```
# su - jdoe

$ /tmp/ksh -c "id"
uid=210(jdoe) gid=1(staff) euid=0(root)
```

This example demonstrates the inherent danger in set-UID and set-GID programs. Extreme caution should be used when setting these modes on programs. Be sure you remove the **/tmp/ksh** copy when you have finished with this example.

```
# rm /tmp/ksh
```

Access Control Lists (ACLs)

In addition to the basic access permissions, AIX 5L provides a more fine-grained method, using access control lists, or ACLs. Three commands are used to display and manipulate access control lists:

aclget	Prints the ACL set on the specified file
acledit	Edits the ACL in the editor specified by the EDITOR environment variable
aclput	Assigns the ACL to the file specified, reading from standard input of a separate file

To determine whether a file has an ACL associated with it, you can either use **aclget** to display the information or use the **ls** command with the **-e** flag, which will display an additional field to the right of the base permissions. If the field contains a plus sign (+), then the file has an ACL set.

Setting ACLs

An ACL consists of three sections: attributes, base permissions, and extended permissions:

```
$ aclget /home/datafile
attributes:
base permissions
  owner(jdoe): rw-
  group(staff): r--
  others: ---
extended permissions
  disabled
```

The preceding ACL is for a file created with a **umask** of 022, and without any extended permissions assigned.

Attributes   The attributes section of an ACL details any special modes on the file, such as set-UID (SUID), set-GID (SGID), or "sticky" (SVTX). These modes should be set using the **chmod** command with symbolic notation (for reasons explained later in this section).

Base Permissions   The base permissions section shows the standard permissions set on the file, also set via the **chmod** command or per the user's **umask** value.

Extended Permissions   The extended permissions section contains a list of access control entries (ACEs). An ACE consists of three fields: a keyword, the permission in symbolic notation, and a list of users and/or groups to which this ACE applies. The keyword is one of **permit**, **deny**, or **specify**.

```
$ aclget /home/datafile
...
extended permissions
  enabled
  specify   rw-   u:jane
  specify   rw-   g:payadmin
  deny      rw-   u:fred
  permit    r--   g:payroll
```

The preceding lines in the extended permissions section specify that

- Extended permissions are enabled (note that the word "enabled" must appear as indicated, or the ACL will not be active).
- The user **jane** may read and write to the file.
- Any member of the group **payadmin** may read and write to the file.
- The user **fred** may not read or write the file, even if he is a member of the **staff** or **payadmin** group.
- Any member of the **payroll** group may read the file.

Caveats in Using ACLs

There are several important points to keep in mind before using access control lists on your systems:

- There is no standard for ACLs. Thus, the implementation of ACLs in AIX 5L is different from that in other UNIX-based operating systems, including Sun Solaris and HP-UX, and those used in the AFS filesystem.

- ACLs will be honored on an NFS-mounted filesystem only if the NFS server is AIX.

- If an ACL is set on a file, any subsequent use of the **chmod** command with octal notation will *disable* the ACL. The ACL must then be reset via the **acledit** command. Therefore, use only symbolic notation with the **chmod** command on files that may have ACLs set.

- It is important to know if the backup program that you are using supports ACLs; if it doesn't, any files restored from it will have their ACLs removed. The **backup** and **restore** commands used with **mksysb** support ACLs, while **tar**, **pax**, and **cpio** do not.

TRUSTED COMPUTING BASE

It is an almost impossible task to constantly monitor a system's files and directories, looking for unfamiliar programs, incorrect permissions, and unauthorized changes to important files. Fortunately, AIX 5L has an integrated security system called the Trusted Computing Base (TCB) to help you automate the critical task of making sure that there are no *surprises* that may lead to a compromise of the system.

The components of the TCB work together to monitor and report on changes to the software on a system, and to provide a *trusted* subset of commands whose integrity can be relied upon in untrustworthy computing environments.

TCB Installation

The Trusted Computing Base may be installed only during a new installation of the operating system. It cannot be installed after installation or during a migration upgrade. This restriction is important because it provides assurance that none of the programs and files monitored by the TCB have been altered.

To check whether the Trusted Computing Base is installed onto a system, execute **/usr/bin/tcbck** as root. If TCB is installed, a usage statement will be printed. If not, the following error message will be displayed:

```
3001-101 The Trusted Computing Base is not enabled on this machine.
    To enable the Trusted Computing Base, you must reinstall and
    set the 'Install Trusted Computing Base' option to YES.
    No checking is being performed.
```

TCB Configuration

The configuration file for the Trusted Computing Base is /etc/security/sysck.cfg. For each trusted item, there is a stanza in sysck.cfg containing various attributes of the application or file.

```
# cat /etc/security/sysck.cfg
...
/usr/bin/ps:
    owner = bin
    group = system
    mode = TCB,SGID,555
    type = FILE
    class = apply,inventory,bos.rte.control
    size = 64506
    checksum = "02845  63 "
```

The preceding stanza is for the **/usr/bin/ps** command. For this command, the TCB will monitor the owner and group, permissions, and file size. It will also compute a checksum to ensure that the program hasn't been replaced by another file with the same size and attributes.

By default, over 4000 programs and files are included in the TCB configuration. You may add your own files to this, and change or remove any of the predefined stanzas, depending on the security needs of your particular situation.

Using the TCB

The Trusted Computing Base is accessed via the **/usr/bin/tcbck** command. Through **tcbck**, items can be added to the TCB for monitoring; attributes of objects can be changed; items can be removed from the TCB; and, most important, checks for inconsistencies and problems can be run.

The following table details the attributes and options that can be specified or checked for items under TCB monitoring:

acl	The access control list (ACL) for the file. If this does not match the actual file ACL, **tcbck** will set the file's ACL to this value.
checksum	The checksum of the file, generated via the **sum –r** command.
class	The class or classes that this entry is in.
group	The GID or name of the file's group. If this does not match the actual file, **tcbck** will set the file's group to this value.
links	A list of hard links to the file. If the links specified do not exist, **tcbck** will create them.
mode	A comma-separated list containing the file permissions and special modes (SUID, SGID, SVTX, and TCB). If this does not match the actual file's values, the file's mode will be changed.
owner	The UID or name of the file's owner. If this does not match the actual file, **tcbck** will set the file's owner to this value.

program	The path, name, and flags to the program used to check this file entry. If the program exits with a nonzero code, **tcbck** will print an error for this entry but will take no further action.
size	The size of the file.
source	The source for the file. If specified, **tcbck** will copy over the file being checked with the item specified.
symlinks	A list of symbolic links to this file. If the links specified do not exist, **tcbck** will create them.
target	Used only for sysck.cfg entries that are symbolic links; contains as a value the file that the entry is linked from.
type	The type of the entry; can be one of FILE, DIRECTORY, FIFO, BLK_DEV, CHAR_DEV, or MPX_DEV.

Checking for Problems

To perform a scan of the TCB, execute the command **/usr/sbin/tcbck** with one of the following arguments:

-n	Reports problems but takes no action
-t	Reports problems and prompts user to take suggested corrective action
-y	Reports problems and automatically takes corrective action
-p	Silently corrects problems without reporting the problem or the action taken

You must also specify the path and name of the file to check, the name of the class to be checked, all entries in the /etc/security/sysck.cfg file, or all files on the system. Note that the latter two options can take a significant amount of time.

The following examples show the syntax and results for each of the types of checks.

Example 1   To check all of the attributes of the **/usr/sbin/backup** command, without fixing any problems, execute

```
# /usr/bin/tcbck -n /usr/sbin/backup
3001-024 The file /usr/sbin/backup has the wrong file owner.
3001-023 The file /usr/sbin/backup has the wrong file mode.
```

The output of the command indicates that the permissions and ownership of **/usr/sbin/backup** are incorrect.

Example 2   To silently fix the problems in the **/usr/sbin/backup** program, run the command

```
# /usr/bin/tcbck -p /usr/sbin/backup
```

The preceding command will reset the ownership and permissions of **/usr/sbin/backup** to those indicated in the /etc/security/sysck.cfg file but will not report on any of the problems or corrective actions taken.

Example 3   To check all of the attributes of all of the files included in the TCB configuration, and to be prompted for each inconsistency found, execute the command

```
# /usr/bin/tcbck -t ALL
3001-024 The file /usr/bin/df has the wrong file owner.
3001-073 Change the file owner for /usr/bin/df? (yes, no) yes
3001-031 The link from the file /usr/sbin/lsvfs
     to /usr/sbin/chvfs does not exist.
3001-066 Create the link for /usr/sbin/chvfs? (yes, no) yes
```

In the preceding example, **tcbck** reported problems with the **df** and **lsvfs** commands and asked the user if the problems should be fixed.

Changing the TCB

Adding a file to the TCB for monitoring is also done with the **tcbck** command. For example, after installing OpenSSH, the administrator of a system wants to add both the server and client programs to the TCB.

```
# ls -l /usr/local/bin/ssh /usr/local/sbin/sshd
-rws--x--x  1 root    system  1032156 Mar 07 09:34 /usr/local/bin/ssh
-rwxr-xr-x  1 root    system  1028207 Mar 07 09:34 /usr/local/sbin/sshd

# /usr/bin/tcbck -a /usr/local/bin/ssh checksum owner group mode size type
class=local

# /usr/bin/tcbck -a /usr/local/sbin/sshd checksum owner group mode size type
class=local
```

The preceding commands add **ssh** and **sshd** to the `/etc/security/sysck.cfg` file; indicate that the checksums, ownership, permissions, file sizes, and types should be monitored; and specify that both files should be added to the TCB class `local`. The following two stanzas are added to `/etc/security/sysck.cfg`:

```
/usr/local/bin/ssh:
    class = local
    checksum = "64052 1008 "
    group = system
    mode = SUID,rwx--x—x
    owner = root
    size = 1032156
    type = FILE

/usr/local/sbin/sshd:
    class = local
    checksum = "12079 1005 "
    group = system
```

```
mode = rwxr-xr-x
owner = root
size = 1028207
type = FILE
```

To remove a file from the TCB database, execute the **tcbck** command with the **-d** flag and the name of the file to be removed.

Secure Attention Key

The Secure Attention Key (SAK) feature of the Trusted Computing Base ensures that only trusted commands are available to a user logging in to the system over a serially attached terminal. Note that SAK is not available for sessions over the network.

To set up SAK, root must modify the /etc/security/login.cfg file and add sak_enabled=true to the entry of each TTY port that SAK is to be available on. Once that is done, a user who is authorized to use SAK and is logging on via that TTY can invoke the trusted communication path by entering the key sequence CTRL-X CTRL-R. That key sequence should be typed before the user name and password are entered.

After the user invokes SAK and then logs in to the system as usual, the trusted shell (**tsh**) is started for that user instead of the usual shell. The trusted shell is similar in syntax to the Korn shell (**ksh**), with a few key differences:

- Only trusted programs (those marked as trusted by TCB) may be executed.
- Functions and alias definitions are not supported.
- The IFS and PATH environment variables cannot be redefined.
- The history mechanism is not available.
- The only profile executed is **/etc/tsh_profile**; shell configuration scripts in the user's home directory are not run.

THE AUDITING SUBSYSTEM

When discussing security, it is often not sufficient to check periodically to see if someone left the barn door open. It is much better to be actively notified that the door has been opened. AIX 5L includes an auditing subsystem that can track and log any number of predefined or custom system activities. By enabling auditing, you can easily monitor a wide range of security-related events. Note that, by default, auditing is disabled. The log files associated with auditing can grow rapidly, and the overhead created by the auditing process can have a slight but measurable impact on system performance.

Audit Categories

The AIX auditing subsystem provides four general categories that may be monitored and logged.

Events

An *event* is a system activity, usually defined at the system call level. Every time a command is executed, a number of system calls are made. Each of those system calls corresponds to an event and will be recorded by the auditing process. The name of the event, the command that caused the event, the user executing the command, the date and time, and the success or failure of the event will all be logged.

Classes

A *class* is simply a group of events. There can be one or more events in a class, and grouping related events makes administration and interpretation of the auditing logs easier. Note that AIX is limited to 31 classes (plus the ALL class, which includes all system events).

Objects

An *object* is a file. When a specific file is defined as an audited object, all attempts at reading, writing, and executing the file will be recorded.

Users

The *user category* defines the specific events and classes to be audited for a particular user account. The number of events recorded can be increased or decreased in accordance with the perceived trustworthiness of a user.

BIN Versus STREAM

The auditing subsystem can be run in two modes, BIN or STREAM. Each mode has its advantages, and both can be used if desired.

The BIN, or binary mode, sends auditing data to two alternating "bins" and writes its data to the file /audit/trail in a compact, binary format. It is best suited for long-term storage of auditing records.

To convert this file into a readable format, the **auditpr** command must be run.

```
# /usr/sbin/auditpr < /audit/trail
```

The STREAM mode writes audit records to the file /audit/stream.out, processing the audit information as it is generated. This file is in plain text and can be read as it is written. Note, though, that this file is erased each time auditing is restarted. Thus, STREAM mode is best suited for real-time monitoring of audited events.

Auditing Configuration

All configuration files for the auditing subsystem are located in the /etc/security/audit directory.

```
# ls -l /etc/security/audit
total 56
-rw-r-----  1 root    audit       37 Sep 30 1997   bincmds
-rw-rw----  1 root    audit     2116 Nov 06 16:37  config
-rw-rw----  1 root    audit    12236 Nov 06 22:00  events
-rw-r-----  1 root    audit      340 Sep 30 1997   objects
-rw-r-----  1 root    audit       54 Sep 30 1997   streamcmds
```

The /etc/security/audit/config file is arranged into stanzas, each defining an aspect of the auditing subsystem's behavior. The start stanza sets the mode that auditing will run in when started—BIN, STREAM, or both:

```
start:
    binmode = on
    streammode = off
```

The next two stanzas define locations and other behaviors of each of the two modes. For the BIN mode, the names and locations of the two bins and the output file may be defined. The STREAM stanza contains only the location of the file containing the audit stream processing command.

```
bin:
    trail = /audit/trail
    bin1 = /audit/bin1
    bin2 = /audit/bin2
    binsize = 10240
    cmds = /etc/security/audit/bincmds


stream:
    cmds = /etc/security/audit/streamcmds
```

The various classes are detailed in the next stanza. By default, ten classes are defined in the following format; you are free to modify these existing classes or add your own.

```
classes:
    general = USER_SU,PASSWORD_Change,FILE_Unlink,FILE_Link,FILE_Rename,FS_Chdir,
FS_Chroot,PORT_Locked,PORT_Change,FS_Mkdir,FS_Rmdir
```

The final stanza, users, contains the names of users that are to be audited, with the specific classes to audit for those users.

```
users:
    root = general
```

Users may be selected for auditing by manually adding them to this file, or by selecting the audit classes to monitor in appropriate fields of the SMIT **mkuser** or **chuser** screens:

```
# smit chuser
```

```
AUDIT classes              [general,objects,files] +
```

Audit classes assigned to files must be defined in the `/etc/security/audit/objects` file. Each stanza in this file lists the name of the object to be audited, the operation to be audited (read, write, and/or execute), and the event associated with that operation.

```
/etc/security/passwd:
    r = "S_PASSWD_READ"
    w = "S_PASSWD_WRITE"
```

Starting and Stopping Auditing

The auditing subsystem is controlled by the **/usr/sbin/audit** command. After performing the necessary configuration, execute this command:

```
# /usr/sbin/audit start
```

The preceding command will start system auditing. If auditing in STREAM mode is requested, note that any previous data in the `/audit/stream.out` file will be cleared. If you want to have auditing active at each system start-up, IBM recommends that the **audit start** command be placed in the `/etc/rc` file, so that events are monitored early in the start-up process.

To query the status of the auditing subsystem, run the command

```
# /usr/sbin/audit query
```

If auditing is not active, the following information will be printed:

```
auditing off
bin processing off
audit events:
    none

audit objects:
    none
```

If auditing is active, the PID of the auditing process will be displayed, along with a list of the events, classes, and objects being monitored. To stop auditing, execute the command

```
# audit shutdown
```

This command should be added to your /etc/rc.shutdown script to ensure a clean termination of the auditing process. Auditing can be paused and restarted by specifying off and on as arguments to the **audit** command.

ADDITIONAL SECURITY TOOLS

A tremendous number of open source and free software tools are available for AIX. These tools can help secure your systems and ensure the integrity of the data stored within. Several of the more popular tools are listed in the following sections.

Note that while many of the tools listed are available in a compiled, ready-to-install format, it is a good policy to build programs from the source when possible.

John the Ripper

One of the most important things that you can do to protect your systems is to help your users develop good password habits. Users may not want this help, but it is critical that they understand the need for it and for the creation of strong passwords to protect their accounts.

John the Ripper is a password-cracking tool. It takes as its input a list of encrypted passwords and tries to determine their unencrypted values. If John the Ripper can determine a user's password, that password is probably not very strong.

The homepage for John the Ripper is http://www.openwall.com/john/. The latest release of John can be downloaded in source form from that site, or in a compiled LPP format from http://www.bull.de/pub/.

Swatch

Swatch, "The Simple WATCHer," is a Perl application that continually monitors log files, looking for patterns defined in a configuration file. When the pattern is detected, swatch can perform a number of actions, such as executing a program or e-mailing the detected error to a specified address. Swatch automates the tedious process of constantly reading log files, separating the important entries from the noise.

Swatch can be downloaded from http://www.oit.ucsb.edu/~eta/swatch/. It requires Perl, which is included with AIX 5L.

Tripwire

Tripwire is a file integrity monitoring tool, available both free and in a commercial version. Along with the features provided by the TCB, Tripwire offers a number of additional features and reporting capabilities. It is also available for a wide variety of platforms, and is thus an excellent solution for heterogeneous data centers. The commercial version provides centralized configuration, monitoring, and reporting. For more information about Tripwire, see http://www.tripwire.com/. Instructions for building the free version of Tripwire on AIX can be found at the IBM eServer

Developer Domain Web site, `http://www-1.ibm.com/servers/esdd/ pseries.html`, in the "Tutorials" section.

SOURCES OF INFORMATION

There are a number of free information sources that can help you keep up-to-date on the latest security vulnerabilities. IBM posts security advisories and patch announcements to a mailing list, which can be subscribed to at the Web page `http://techsupport. services.ibm.com/server/listserv/`.

The SANS Institute, in conjunction with the FBI, maintains a list of the 20 most critical Internet security vulnerabilities at `http://www.sans.org/top20.htm`. Many of the vulnerabilities occur in all UNIX systems, not just AIX, and following the guidelines provided will greatly reduce your system's exposure.

The IBM Redbooks Web site, `http://www.redbooks.ibm.com/`, has several books on the subject of AIX system security. These guides are an excellent resource and help provide an in-depth understanding of the tools and facilities available to you in making your systems as secure as possible.

CHECKLIST

The following is a checklist for the key points in auditing and security:

- ☐ Define security.
- ☐ Change passwords frequently.
- ☐ Identify the alternative authentication methods.
- ☐ Control the superuser access.
- ☐ Secure network access.
- ☐ Secure file access.
- ☐ Identify the components of the TCB.
- ☐ Use the TCB to monitor and report on changes to the software on a system.
- ☐ Use the TCB to provide a trusted subset of commands whose integrity can be relied upon in untrustworthy computing environments.
- ☐ Monitor a wide range of security-related events.
- ☐ Identify all of the open source and free software tools available for AIX.
- ☐ Identify all of the free information sources that can help you keep up-to-date on the latest security vulnerabilities.

CHAPTER 24

Distributed Computing Environment (DCE)

D CE sites are springing up everywhere. DCE technology has matured over the last few years. Testimony to this fact is the pervasive use of DCE for open distributed security in most vendor operating systems. DCE's newfound popularity stems from the infrastructure requirements of the highly distributed computing world we find ourselves in. DCE may not have all the answers, but it is the best game in town for binding legacy computing environments with newer distributed technologies under a single security and communication framework.

In May 1990, the Open Software Foundation (OSF) announced the specification for DCE, which was based on vendor technologies provided by Hewlett-Packard, Digital Equipment Corporation, Siemens Nixdorf, Massachusetts Institute of Technology, Sun, Transarc, and Microsoft (see Table 24-1). DCE is basically a set of remote procedure call (RPC) hooks, routines, and servers that facilitate the development of distributed services across a network of heterogeneous systems. DCE provides the layer of glue to bind distributed applications onto the underlying operating system and network services.

At the top level, DCE defines a decentralized hierarchy of administrative domains called *cells* (see the following illustration). Cells identify administrative domains of DCE services and objects for naming, security, and management purposes. Cells are hierarchical in the global DCE name space and interoperate on the basis of levels of trust. Table 24-2 contains a list of the DCE components we will detail.

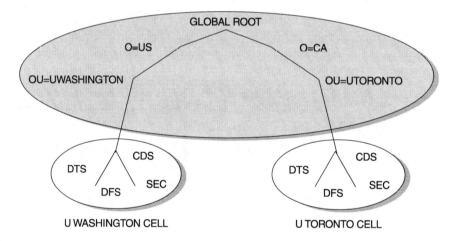

DCE RPC

At the lowest level, DCE clients and servers communicate via remote procedure calls (RPCs). An Interface Definition Language (IDL) is provided to build DCE interfaces into applications, hiding the RPC intricacies and architecture dependencies from the programmer. The **idl** compiler produces a language-dependent interface called a stub that can be incorporated into the target application client and server software. Stubs are

Vendor	Technology
HP/DEC	Remote Procedure Call (RPC)
DEC	Concert Multithread Architecture (CMA)
	Distributed Time Service (DECDTS)
	Distributed Naming Service (DECDNS)
Siemens Nixdorf	X.500 (DIR.X) Directory Service
MIT Project Athena	Security (Kerberos)
Microsoft/Sun/HP	PC Integration Services
Transarc	Distributed File System (DFS)
Transarc/HP	Diskless Services

Table 24-1.   DCE Technology Selections

uniquely identified in the name space and are responsible for maintaining client/
server context and state information (see the following illustration). For a list of the
idl command options, run the following command:

```
# /usr/bin/idl -confirm
```

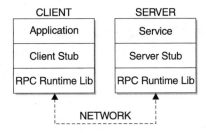

DCE Component	Description
Remote procedure call	Routines for building distributed services
Directory services	Global and cell name service
Security service	Authentication, authorization, and access control services
Distributed time service	Cell time synchronization service
Thread services	POSIX thread service for multiplexing RPC interfaces
Distributed file system	Distributed file service based on AFS

Table 24-2.   DCE Components

Cell Directory Service

Objects within and between cells are located and identified via queries to directory
name services (DNS). DCE Global DNS is based on X.500 and the X/Open Directory
Service (XDS) API. Name service with a cell is based on Internet DNS and the Cell
Directory Service (CDS). DCE objects may include people, organizations, systems,
resources, services, and so on. Directory services are hierarchical and decentralized
to support worldwide and local cell name spaces. Replication and caching are used to
guarantee local access performance levels.

Syntax for Global Directory Service (GDS), Cell Directory Service (CDS), and
Internet Domain Name Service (DNS) can be a bit confusing. The following syntax
examples illustrate the naming convention used by GDS and DNS. The "/..."
symbols represent the GDS and DNS root level. /.../CellName and "/.:" symbols
represent the local cell root.

```
GDS X.500    C=[Country]/O=[Organization]/OU=[Org Unit]/CN=[Common Name]
       /.../C=US/O=University of Washington/ \
       OU=Computing & Communications/CN=DeRoest


DNS     /.../[CellName]/[SubClass]
        /.../cac.washington.edu/sec/principal/deroest
        /.:/sec/principal/deroest
```

The real unit of binding within DCE directory service is a 128-bit number called a
universal unique identifier (UUID). Each RPC interface in the name space is represented
by a UUID. Directory services provide the mapping of object name to UUID for DCE
applications. The **uuidgen** utility is used to create UUIDs for new interfaces.

Security Service

DCE security service is based on Kerberos version 5. The encryption mechanism
uses private or secure keys versus public keys. The private key is the first level of
authorization and authentication in the cell. Keys are generated for each account/
password and are stored in a key table on the master server. The master security
server checks the private key at **dce_login** time. Once the user is validated, the
security server will issue session keys (tickets) for use with each service as the client
requests them. The security server distributes session keys using key-within-a-key
encryption. A ticket may also include a privilege authorization certificate (PAC).
The PAC describes the client's authorization level for a particular service. The ticket
exchange interaction can be quite confusing. You can find a short description of
Kerberos ticket passing in Chapter 23.

Finer-grained access control is provided using access control lists (ACLs). ACLs
may be associated with any object. They are similar to standard UNIX permissions but
provide additional levels of access control. ACLs may be defined at the user or group
level by both the end user and the Systems Administrator. The ACL is basically a list
that says who can do what to an object. ACLs also represent another level of complexity

beyond the initial security authorization and access control. You need to give careful thought into how ACLs and groups will be defined for your cell.

Distributed Time Service

DCE's Distributed Time Service (DTS) is pretty straightforward. Time service is implemented as a hierarchy of servers that synchronize timing in the cell. At the top level, a time provider obtains standardized time from a standards body or hardware device. Global time servers distribute the time reference from the provider to the clients and servers in the cell. If the cell contains multiple LANs, each LAN may require a local time server. All nodes within the cell synchronize local system time via a time clerk. The clerks obtain the reference time from the servers via time couriers.

The DCE time standard is based on Coordinated Universal Time (UTC). Like Greenwich Mean Time (GMT), UTC is based from 0 degrees longitude. Time zones are calculated by adding a positive or negative time differential factor (TDF) to the UTC time. UTC is formatted as a 128-bit time stamp with 100-nanosecond resolution. The DTS protocol is interoperable with the Network Time Protocol (NTP). Clock correction routines manage skewing, communication delay, and leap seconds between machines and cells.

Threads

Threads support parallelism and pipelining between DCE clients and servers. A thread can be thought of as a single task or flow of control. Threads share the process address space and do not necessarily require special interprocess communication (IPC) mechanisms to share data. Facilities are available to implement synchronization and locking between process threads and to manage scheduling.

Distributed File Service

Data sharing is facilitated by the Distributed File Service (DFS, see Chapter 15), which was derived from the Andrew File System (AFS) technology developed by Transarc and Carnegie Mellon University. The major differences between DFS and AFS involve the integration of DFS with the other DCE services and the underlying DCE Local File System (LFS) architecture. LFS is a dynamic, log-based filesystem that is very similar to the AIX Journaled File System (JFS). LFS structures also map quite closely to AFS constructs. For example, DFS filesystem trees are similar to AFS in that a common root is identified with the next level delimited by cell name. The DFS shared root is named `/...` and cell subdirectories follow as `/.../cellname/`. Local and remote access transparency is maintained using a token passing mechanism and POSIX semantics to mediate updates and locking. A high level of filesystem availability is maintained through replication and local caching. DFS supports both scheduled and release filesystem replication. DFS can export any virtual file system (VFS) that has been enhanced to support the DCE VFS extensions.

Table 24-3 should help explain some of the basic terminology used with DCE.

Terminology	Description
binding	Process through which a client establishes contact with a server.
cell	Collection of nodes and resources to be administered as a unit.
client	An entity that requests a service.
clerk	Similar to a client but is autonomous; clerks are used for maintenance purposes.
courier	Requests time information from a global server on behalf of a clerk.
local DTS	Time server for a LAN within a cell.
global DTS	Time server for a cell.
provider DTS	Obtains standardized time information for DTS servers.
principal	Any entity involved in a security interaction with the DCE security service.
server	A service provider.
UUID	Universal unique identifier; a bit string that uniquely identifies all DCE entities.

Table 24-3.   Basic DCE Terminology

DCE Versions

The Open Software Foundation (OSF) released DCE V1.0 way back in 1991. Until recently, the third release of version 1, DCE V1.0.3, was the basis of most vendor offerings, including AIX V3. DCE V1.1 hit the streets in November 1994. DCE V1.1 addressed many of the complaints levied by users of the previous code base. Specifically, V1.1 reduced much of the complexity in administering DCE. A single administrator interface, **dcecp**, was introduced; it simplifies the cumbersome command-line interface. A DCE master daemon, **dced**, provides remote administration access to DCE services. Cell aliasing allows you to change or reference your cell by different names without requiring a complete rebuild. Hierarchical cell administration was implemented with DCE V1.2. New programmatic features were added, including extended registry attributes (`xattrschema`) and Generic Security Service Application Program Interface (GSS-API). Using extended registry attributes, you can map DCE and legacy security systems together to support *single sign-on*; for example, you can map a DCE principle to an MVS RACF 2.2 identity.

IBM's current DCE V3.1 and previous DCE V2.2 are both based on the OSF DCE 1.2.2 release. DCE V3.1 and DFS V3.1 are now sold separately and come with subtle packaging changes that were needed to synchronize both of IBM's AIX and Solaris distributions. These include new **dcecp** enhancements, DFS improvements, and IDL C   support.

AIX AND DCE

The DCE layer between the application and the operating network is thicker than one might have thought! However, you do not need the full set of DCE services on every node in a cell. IBM has packaged DCE so that you can make the DCE layer only as thick as required for each node. For example, each DCE client does not need the full set of directory services code. A client needs only a sufficient set of routines to contact a directory server. Table 24-4 breaks down the DCE file sets to show the packaging changes.

DCE Base Services for AIX provides DCE client support for RPC, CDS, DTS, and SS functions. The DCE base services can be integrated into AIX authentication services. Other components in the base include documentation; a SMIT interface; and directory service access using API, X/Open Directory Service (XDS), and abstract data manipulation (XOM).

DCE Security Services is a separate security service from standard AIX security features. The DCE security server **secd** and database management tools are included in the product. Authentication via the security server requires that client users invoke the DCE login facility **dce_login**. Authentication via the security server is required to create a DCE context used to gain access to other DCE services and satisfy ACL permissions in DFS. As mentioned in the DCE overview, these security features are based on the Kerberos V5 authentication algorithm.

DCE directory service is provided by the AIX DCE cell directory service. DCE DNS is interoperable with both Bind DNS and X.500 protocols. The server consists of a cell directory server (CDS) and a global directory agent (GDA). The CDS manages the database of resources within a cell. The GDA communicates between cells to access global resources.

Table 24-5 lists the different DCE daemons with the related service.

Table 24-6 lists a few of the DCE commands you will want to become familiar with.

Application	DCE V3.1	DCE V2.2
DCE Base Services	dce.client.rte.*	dce.client.core.rte.*
DCE Security Services	dce.security.rte	dce.security.rte
DCE Cell Directory Services	dce.cds.rte	dce.cds.rte
Online Documentation	dce.doc.*	dce.doc.*
Messaging	dce.msg.*	dce.msgs*
DCE Threads Libraries	dce.client.rte.pthreads	dce.pthreads.rte
DCE X.500 API Library	dce.xdsxom.rte	dce.xdsxom.rte
DCE for Application Developers	dce.tools.*	dce.tools.*
DCE System Management	dce.sysmgmt.*	dce.sysmgmt.*
Distributed File Service (see Chapter 15)	dfs.*	dce.dfs*

Table 24-4.   DCE V3.1 vs. V2.2 File Sets

Service	Daemon	Description
SS	**secd**	Security server
	dced	Client security/rpc server
	dceunixd	DCE/AIX security integrator
CDS	**cdsd**	Cell directory server
	cdsadv	CDS advertiser—help clients access CDS
	cdsclerk	Interface between CDS client and server
	gdad	Global directory agent—intercell access
DTS	**dtsd**	DTS client/server
DFS	**dfsd**	See Chapter 15 for client/server list

Table 24-5.   AIX DCE Clients and Servers

Command	Description
mkdce	DCE configuration setup script
lsdce	DCE script displays state
rmdce	DCE configuration removal script
dcecp (interactive)	DCE control program for management task objects
rpccp (interactive)	RPC control program for endpoint map and RPC application
cdscp (interactive)	CDS control program manages name space
dtscp (interactive)	Time service administration
rgy_edit (interactive)	Security server administration
uuidgen	Creates Universal Unique Identifiers
rmxcred	Removes stale credentials
chpesite	Updates the `pe_site` file
rc.dce	Start-up script for DCE services
dce.clean	Shutdown script for DCE services
passwd_import	Populates registry from AIX group and password files
passwd_export	Creates AIX group and password files from registry
cdsli	CDS recursive list
cdsdel	CDS recursive delete
sec_create_db	Initializes security database
dfs	See Chapter 15

Table 24-6.   AIX DCE Administration Commands

DCE PLANNING

It is critical that you carefully plan out your overall DCE cell topology before getting too far into the installation process. Once your configuration is in production, it is extremely difficult to change. Something as simple as a cell name is not easily changed, although new, unsupported cell alias commands provide alternatives.

Cell Topology

Begin by projecting your expected population growth over the next couple of years. You should take into account increases in numbers of users, computers, applications, and administrative groups. If you expect rapid growth, it may be prudent to start with a number of cells that map to the administrative roles in your organization. Combine groups of users and systems that function as a unit, share resources, and exhibit a common authentication base. Keep in mind that the principal name space that identifies all users, computers, and services in a cell must be unique. Network topology might also dictate the boundaries chosen for a cell. Try to stay away from single points of failure and network bottlenecks between clients and critical services. Multiple cells may scale better over the longer term compared with putting everything in one cell. Cell hierarchies will assist in managing multiple cells.

Once you have identified your cell layout, choose unique cell names that will assist in identifying your workgroups and simplify intercell communication. Keep in mind the formats used for intercell (X.500) and intracell (DNS) identification. If you already have existing Internet DNS domain names that represent departments in your organization, consider using these as cell names. Map each DNS domain level to an X.500 level. If you will be operating with existing cells outside your organization, you may need to follow cell naming conventions used in the external environment. Choose carefully!

Server Topology

Now decide how you will distribute DCE servers in your cell. Decisions here are going to be based on computer and network hardware topology. Each server type can coexist with other DCE servers on the same computer or reside on a dedicated system. If you can afford the hardware, the latter is preferred. You should also consider replicating the servers for availability. There is a trade-off to be made between availability and performance. More replicas mean more time spent in synchronizing and for checkpoint copies. DCE supports two kinds of name space replication between servers: immediate and skulk. Immediate replication occurs each time the master server is updated. Periodic updates are performed using skulk replication. You may also prioritize access to servers via profiles. Default profiles are created as part of the base install and configuration. You can customize your own server profiles, but it means keying in UUID information by hand. You should deploy an odd number of replicas to simplify server voting to determine master and slave roles.

A minimum DCE configuration requires the following three servers:

- Security Server
- Cell Directory Server
- Distributed Time Server

Use the hard key procedure for architecting your security server environment. This means, dedicate a machine and lock it in a closet! If you plan to use DFS for sharing data in your cell, refer to Chapter 15 for details on planning, installation, and administration.

Principals and Security

Every user, computer, and service in your cell is identified as a principal and associated with a UUID number. As the number of principals in your cell grows, it will be easier to identify roles if you allocate UUID ranges to each principal type. You should also consider defining additional groups to facilitate access control early on.

Before beginning the installation process, choose a cell administrator ID and password. This account will be used to administer the DCE security service and registry. You might also restrict use of the cell administrator account to a particular machine or secure subnet if you use the administrator password in clear text for administration functions.

You will also need to decide how to keep AIX and DCE security information synchronized. User password information must be added to the local AIX databases and also to the DCE security registry. To batch updates to either database, the **passwd_export** and **passwd_import** tools can be used. Invoke **passwd_import** to read your existing AIX password information and initialize your DCE registry after installing DCE. The **passwd_export** tool reads from the registry and creates AIX password files.

To integrate DCE in the AIX authentication process at login time, you must use the **dceunixd** service. This will keep users from having specifically to invoke **dce_login** after logging into AIX.

Test Cell

It is a very good idea to set up a test cell for validating and stress-testing your DCE configuration. A test cell is also an excellent learning tool for new DCE systems programmers, administrators, operators, and end users. If you can afford the machines, keep the test cell in place after deploying your production system. It will give you a chance to try out new configurations without disrupting production service and assist in tuning and debugging. Use the test cell for checking interoperability for phased migration and implementation.

DCE INSTALLATION AND CONFIGURATION

Starting with new installations of AIX 5L, the /opt directory is now a filesystem. Administrators of AIX 4.3.3 systems may want to create this dedicated filesystem for the Linux affiliated applications available from IBM or to prepare the system for an AIX 5L migration. Please be aware that the DCE install creates a symbolic link to **/usr/lpp/dce** named **/opt/dcelocal**. Even though DCE installs to the /usr, /var, and /etc filesystems and directories, applications will expect DCELOCAL=/opt/dcelocal as set in the /etc/rc.dce start-up script.

The IBM documentation recommends making separate filesystems of 30MB each for /var/dce and /var/dce/directory (for CDS) to protect them if /var fills up. If you are running multiple DCE services on a machine, you should make /var/dce twice that size and monitor it carefully for possible expansion. You will regularly need to clean out expired credentials, logs, and audit files from this filesystem, so consider adding these housekeeping tasks to cron.

Refer to Chapter 6 for instructions on installing the AIX DCE packages that will be used on each computer in the cell. Install only the DCE packages required for the services you intend to support on each machine.

You may want to limit what network interfaces may bind to CDS and endpoint mapping by defining the RPC_UNSUPPORTED_NETIFS variable. This is a valuable tool that can be extremely disruptive if incorrectly implemented. RPC will bind through all network interfaces if this variable is not set by default. To disable RPC from binding to the network interfaces en2 and en3, thus still allowing bind to en0 and en1, add the following line to the /etc/environment file before logging in to configure or start DCE:

```
RPC_UNSUPPORTED_NETIFS=en2:en3   ◀──────── Now these interfaces will not RPC bind
```

Use the following **rpccp** command to display all map elements after DCE is configured:

```
# rpccp show mapping
```

Configure DCE in two steps. First configure and start the base cell services: a master security server, a cell directory server, and a time server. After these services have been configured and started, configure additional DCE services and replica servers. Use SMIT FastPath **smit dce** or **mkdce** to configure these services and register the cell name. Note that you will need to completely remove a service if a failure occurs during configuration or if you wish to make changes. You can remove a service by selecting the Unconfigure option in SMIT (Figure 24-1) or by invoking **rmdce**. Use the **lsdce** command to verify the configuration status.

```
# smit dce   ◀────────SMIT DCE configuration (Figure 24-1)
# mkdce [Options]  ◀────────Create DCE clients and servers
# lsdce [Options]  ◀────────List DCE services
# rmdce [Options]  ◀──────── Remove DCE services
```

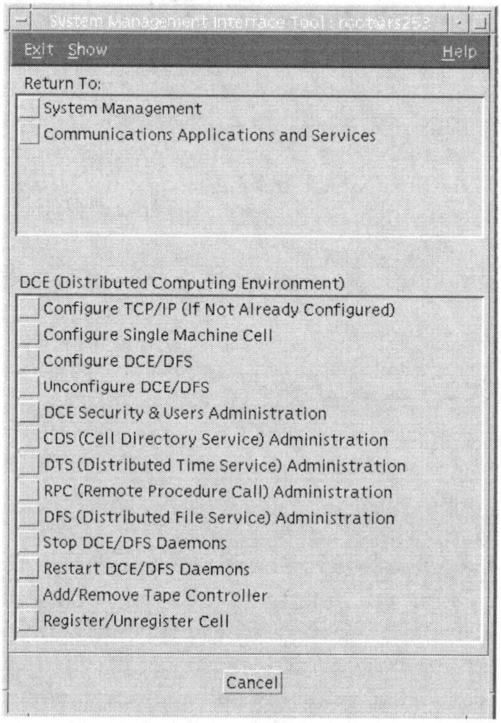

Figure 24-1.   SMIT DCE panel

Security Service

You begin by defining the master security server using the SMIT FastPath **smit mkdcesecsrv**. Select "primary" from the list when prompted. You will be asked to define the cell name, the security server host name, the cell administrator's account, and whether to enable or disable certificate-based login. Leave the default *NO* here because defining the *Entrusted Profile* is beyond the scope of this chapter. Choose the starting and maximum UID range you will use for principals. Once completed, SMIT will start the **dced** and **secd** daemons on the machine (see Figure 24-2).

```
# smit mkdcesecsrv  ◄────── Create security server
```

Directory Service

Configure the master cell directory server by invoking the SMIT FastPath **smit mkcdssrv**. You will be prompted for the cell name and security server name

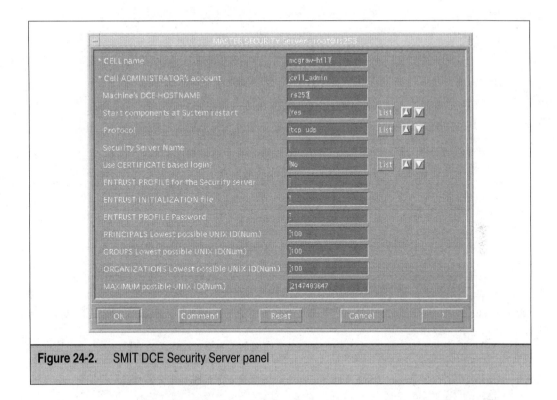

Figure 24-2.   SMIT DCE Security Server panel

configured in the previous section. Verify that the other DCE fields are correct and select a host name for the CDS. Once completed, the master CDS server (**cdsd**), a CDS client (**cdsadv**), and a CDS clerk (**cdsclerk**) are started. SMIT will also create an initial clearinghouse for the CDS (see Figure 24-3).

```
# smit mkcdssrv ◄─────────Create cell directory server
```

Distributed Time Service

Next create a distributed time server for the base cell by executing SMIT FastPath **smit mkdtssrv**. You will be prompted to select the DTS type for this machine. Note that a DTS server cannot coexist with another DTS server or client. If the DTS is on a separate subnet from the security server, which inhibits broadcasts, enter the security server host name. When completed, the host will be configured as a CDS client, and the DTS (local or global) time service (**dtsd**) will be started (see Figure 24-4).

```
# smit mkdtssrv ◄─────────Create distributed time server
```

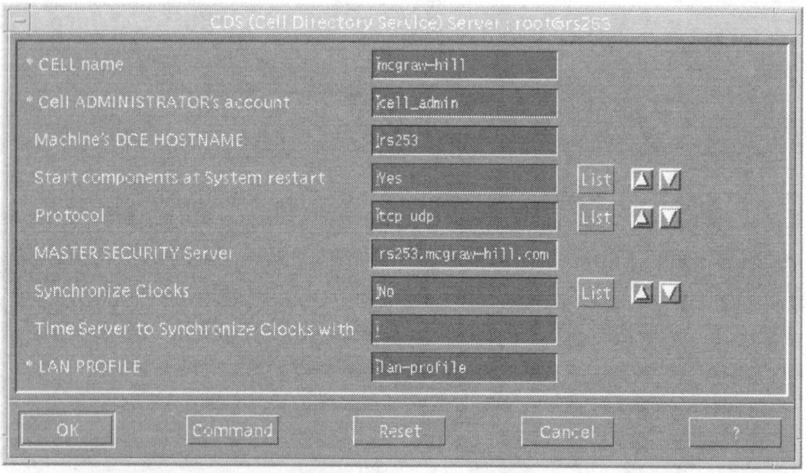

Figure 24-3. SMIT DCE CDS panel

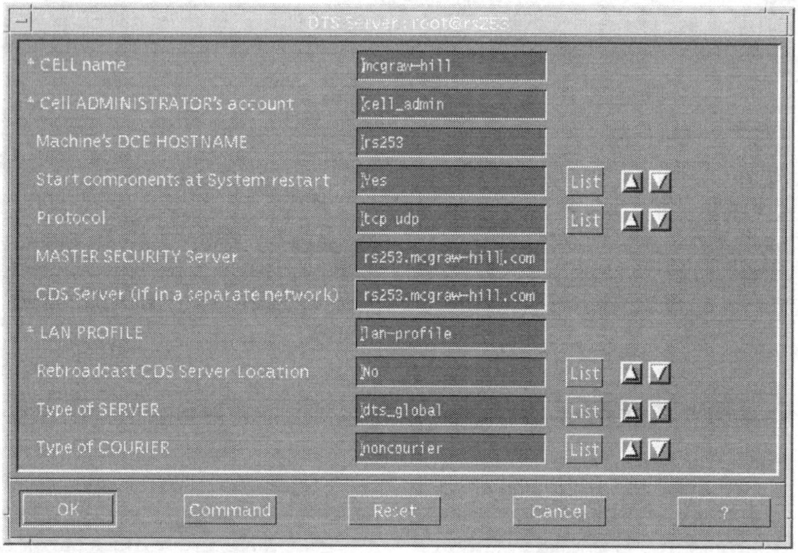

Figure 24-4. SMIT DCE DTS panel

Clients and Servers

Now you are ready to configure additional server replicas, other DCE servers like DFS (Chapter 15), and DCE clients. Clients can be created with full or local administrator access. In the latter case, the cell administrator does not have root access to the local client, and the local client does not have cell administrator access. In this case, DCE client setup is a two-step process. First, the admin portion is executed on a cell machine with cell administrator access. The local portion follows this on the local client machine. Both steps can be completed on the local machine if full access is selected. Invoke the SMIT FastPath **smit mkdceclient** to create a DCE client. Note that one of the first clients you create should be the security server client process if you do not select all_cl for all clients (see Figures 24-5 and 24-6).

```
# smit mkdceclient  ◄────────Create a DCE client
```

Verifying DCE Configuration

After completing configuration of the DCE client and server machines, verify the configuration from each participating system. Run the **lsdce** command.

```
# lsdce -r
Gathering component state information...


                Component Summary for Host: rs253
            Component          Configuration State    Running State
Security Master server            Configured            Running
Security client                   Configured            Running
RPC                               Configured            Running
Initial Directory server          Configured            Running
Directory client                  Configured            Running
DTS Global server                 Configured            Running
```

Use **dcecp** to list the hosts you have configured in the cell:

```
# dcecp -c host catalog
/.../mcgraw-hill/hosts/rs250
/.../mcgraw-hill/hosts/rs253
```

You can also use the **dcecp** catalog option to list other principals and resources configured in the cell.

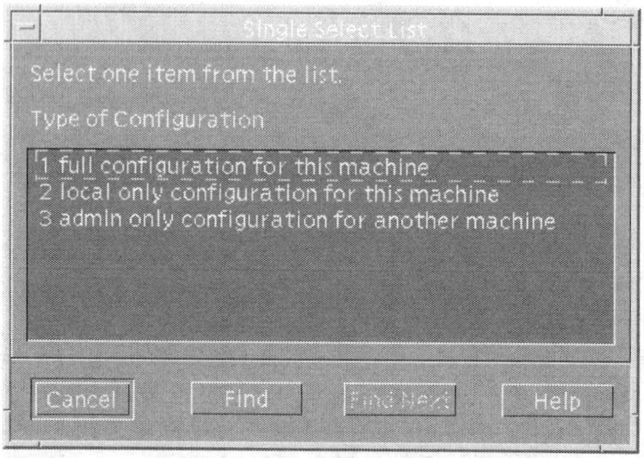

Figure 24-5. SMIT DCE Client Type panel

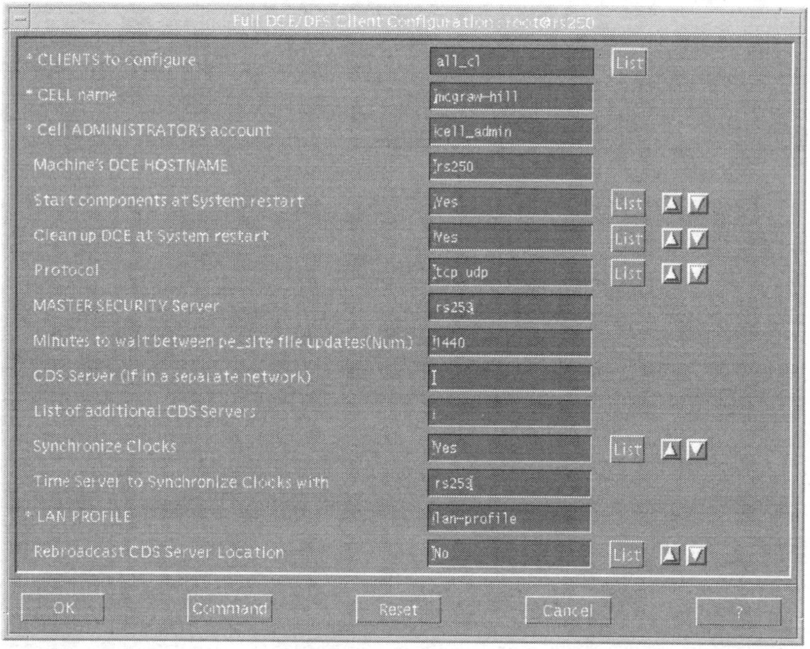

Figure 24-6. SMIT DCE Client panel

Account Configuration

Continue to configure the machines to allow DCE authentication logins by synchronizing the DCE registry with the local AIX user database using the following commands:

```
# dce_login cell_admin  ◄——————You must log in as your defined administrator
# klist | grep Principal ◄——————Check to see if you are really cell_admin
# passwd_import ◄——————Answer "no" to all the questions
```

Users with no user or group identification conflicts now have DCE registry accounts. You may list, examine, enable, and set the password for these accounts with the following command line and interactive **dcecp** commands:

```
# dcecp —c account catalog ◄——————Lists all the accounts
# dcecp —c account show UserName ◄——————Lists the details of an account
# dcecp ◄——————Starts the interactive mode needed to modify accounts
dcecp> account modify UserName —acctvalid yes ◄——————Enables an account
dcecp> account modify UserName —password T3mP ◄——————Sets temporary password
```

At this point, any user on the system should be able to acquire Kerberos authentication as the new *UserName* principal with the following commands:

```
# dce_login UserName ◄——————This authenticates you
# klist ◄——————This will display your Kerberos ticket information
```

This may be all the authentication your applications need, but the rest of this section describes how to configure the system to allow a user to **telnet** in and acquire the authentication from one AIX/DCE login process. The most common need for this is to access a Distributed File Service. Other applications for this single login process are beyond the scope of this chapter.

Start the **dceunixd** daemon at boot time from /etc/inittab after DCE services have started. This must run on servers or clients that will allow a single AIX/DCE login (**telnet**, **rexec**, and **rlogin**). Otherwise, the users will have to use **dce_login** to acquire their authentication tickets. The following **mkitab** command will add **dceunixd** to the /etc/inittab file:

```
# mkitab —i rcdce \
"dceunixd:2:respawn:/bin/dceunixd —l 60 —d 1 >/dev/console 2>&1"
```

The **dceunixd** daemon must be started without DCE context, so the easiest way to start it is to reboot the system at this point.

Starting with AIX 4.3.3, the following DCE authentication method is included in the /usr/lib/security/methods.cfg file and the auth_method stanza in

/etc/security/login.cfg is no longer supported. Check the methods.cfg file with the following **tail** command:

```
# tail /usr/lib/security/methods.cfg
DCE:
        program = /usr/lib/security/DCE
```

Edit /etc/security/user to set the default user SYSTEM stanza or user the **chuser** command to change this stanza for individual users.

```
# vi /etc/security/user
default:
                SYSTEM = "DCE OR DCE[UNAVAIL] AND compat"
```

or

```
# chuser SYSTEM='DCE OR DCE[UNAVAIL] AND compat' user_name
```

You should now be able to **telnet** to this server with the account *UserName* you enabled with the preceding **dcecp** commands and use **klist** to see your new Kerberos tickets. You will get the following error message at login if **dceunixd** is not running:

```
3004-007 You entered an invalid name of password.
```

DCE IMPLEMENTATION CONSIDERATIONS

In most cases, you will want to use replicated servers and dedicate separate machines for CDS and security servers. If your name space is large, say 100,000 principals or larger, you are going to need large memory spaces on these servers. Most of the server name space has to be held in virtual memory, so that means RAM and swap. You can reduce some of the memory hold on your primary servers by distributing the CDS name space between the replica servers. This way, your primary CDS server will not get bogged down with infrequently accessed data. Resource consumption by the CDS and security servers grows linearly with the size of the name space. The good news is that the data access profiles are pretty much flat, even with large name spaces. The database size does not seem to adversely affect queries. Get the latest patches for your version of AIX DCE. Some patches help reduce the memory requirements for your CDS and security servers, along with increasing the size limit of the name space.

When determining machine configurations for servers, remember that DCE randomly selects systems among replicas. This means your overall throughput is going to be affected by your slowest server. You also need to be aware of service interruptions during replica checkpoints. You can tune the frequency of checkpoints to limit service outages during prime time. Note that the CDS servers are cached but not validity based. This means that data can become inconsistent between replicas. This is not good for frequently changing data. You will need to remember this when determining checkpoint frequency and what information you decide to store in the CDS.

Try to limit the CDS lookup frequency when building applications and configuring your environment. The CDS is referenced each time an application requires the address of a service. For example, the location of a security server must be obtained at DCE login time. When coding an application, you might cache a server's address when feasible rather than doing a lookup for each access. You can also distribute a `pe_site` file to your DCE clients. This file lists the addresses of frequently used servers like the security servers. Clients will look up addresses in the site file before going to the CDS. This will reduce the load on your CDS server but will require that you keep the site files up to date.

DRIVING DCE

A number of large enterprise applications require DCE in at least a local RPC configuration like the TXSeries part of the IBM WebSphere Enterprise Edition and HP's MeasureWare and OpenView. Some may even ship with the required thin DCE client products with their own custom configuration script. The important thing to remember is that applications usually will drive your need for DCE. When you start to see more applications painting you into the DCE corner, then you may need to get serious about the direction you are going. Alternatively, you may be interested in just Kerberos as a local or enterprise security layer. Keep in mind that Kerberos version 5 is shipped with AIX 4.3.3 and AIX 5L on the Bonus Pack, and you may want to take a close look at it before you start testing DCE and all it entails. For more information on Kerberos, please refer to Chapter 23.

CHECKLIST

The following is a checklist for the key points in Distributed Computing Environment (DCE):

- ☐ Define DCE technology.
- ☐ Identify the DCE layer.
- ☐ Plan out your overall DCE cell topology before getting too far into the installation process.
- ☐ Install and configure DCE.
- ☐ Use replicated servers and dedicate separate machines for CDS and security servers.
- ☐ Use DCE for large enterprise applications.

PART XI

System Recovery and Tuning

CHAPTER 25

Backup and Copy Utilities

How much are your time and data worth to you? How many times have you erased what you thought was an unnecessary file only to discover a week later that it contained some vital piece of information? Even the most meticulously maintained system will be subject to disk failures. A regular schedule for system backups will significantly reduce the cost and frustration related to data loss problems. Believe me, you will rest easier at night!

The data on the machines can make or break a business, and some companies have gone out of business because of failed disaster recovery efforts. How much does downtime cost your organization? Do you even know? I doubt that many Systems Administrators can give a realistic number to the cost of downtime. These *real* numbers for the cost of downtime have to be determined by the business managers, not Systems Administrators. The business managers can bring in the total cost numbers by analyzing the end-to-end business costs. For example, if the systems are down, the business may have to resort to a different pay scale or method, and downtime adds in the cost of lost Internet sales and lost materials that cannot be tracked when the computer systems are down. The total cost of downtime can easily top $1,000,000 per hour, or $5000 per second!

Tools Included with AIX 5L

AIX brings with the operating system many mechanisms to perform system backups, restores, and copy services. In the following sections, you will be introduced to the many services available under AIX 5L.

Bootable System Image: mksysb

The **mksysb** is your friend! The **mksysb** command, whose name stands for *make system backup,* is used to create a *bootable* system image of the rootvg volume group. Notice that I said *rootvg*! If your system has more volume groups than rootvg, then you must consider additional backup steps (see the following discussion of the **savevg** and **restvg** commands). All of the rootvg filesystems must be mounted to be included in the **mksysb** backup. The **mksysb** command can save you in a catastrophic failure and get you back up and running in a very short period of time. The section "Creating a Bootable Operating System Image: mksysb," later in this chapter, has full details on using **mksyb**.

Saving and Restoring Volume Groups: savevg and restvg

The **savevg** is equivalent to a **mksysb** for non-rootvg volume groups. Actually, the **savevg** command is a symbolic link to the **mksysb** command. The **savevg** command will save an entire volume group and its structure in an easily restorable format using the **restvg** command. Full details on the **savevg** and **restvg** commands are found in the section "Use savevg for Non-Root Volume Groups," later in this chapter.

The backup and restore Facility Commands

IBM has also added the **backup** and **restore** facility to AIX, which allows you to back up by filename or by i-node. The **backup** utility is the most common way of backing up filesystems using a rotating backup schedule. The command is intuitive to use, and restoration of data is easier than with some other methods found on the system. The section "Backup Schedules and Rotation," later in this chapter, details the use of the **backup** command.

The mkcd Command

The **mkcd** command was new to AIX starting with 4.3.3. The requirements to make system backups using the **mkcd** command are quite extensive. First of all, you must have enough disk space to hold the contents of the CD-ROM or DVD on disk, which is 645MB for a CD-ROM and 8.8GB for a DVD. Additionally, IBM uses a proprietary DVD case that has an angled slot for the write-protect hole. I found this out the hard way when the DVDs that I bought would not let me write on them because the drive insisted they were write-protected. So just be aware that you will have to buy your DVDs from an IBM source. For more details on the **mkcd** command, see "Requirements for Writable CD and DVD Drives," later in this chapter.

The tar Command

The **tar** command is as old as UNIX. Tar (the name stands for *tape archive*) is a very flexible tool. This is the most widely used archiving tool because it is easy and intuitive to use and it has few failures. "Network Backups," later in the chapter, has more information on using the **tar** command.

The cpio Command

Backups made using **cpio** are among the more difficult backups to restore back on the system if the exact command parameters are not known. The **cpio** command stands for *copy input/output*. I mostly use **cpio** when I move data around within the machine. The section "Other Backup Utilities," later in this chapter, shows some of the more common uses for the **cpio** command.

The pax Command

The **pax** utility now supports files larger than 2GB under AIX 5L, yet **tar** and **cpio** do not. IBM now uses **pax** with the **snap** command for gathering system information for IBM support. The nice thing about **pax** is that it can read both **tar** and **cpio** archives. See "Other Backup Utilities," later in the chapter, for more on using the **pax** command.

The dd Command

The **dd** command works on data at the byte level. This command has conversion capabilities that no other command on the system can perform. One of the more common uses for the **dd** command is to convert between EBCDIC and ASCII. The **dd** command also allows you to set the block size, making it a valuable tool for working with raw data. For more information on using the **dd** command, refer to "Network Backups," later in this chapter.

Network Backup with rdump and rrestore

The **rdump** and **rrestore** commands allow you to perform a local backup using a remote tape drive on another machine. If your shop is like mine, you have a lot of small AIX workstations that do not have a tape drive and you do not want to spend money on a license for a network backup solution or a tape drive. This is where **rdump** and **rrestore** work great. You get cheap backups that are easy and reliable to restore. See "Network Backups," later in the chapter for details.

Sparse Files

A *sparse file* is created with a greater length than the data it contains to reserved space for future data. These files are difficult to manipulate and archive because the **cp**, **mv**, **tar**, and **cpio** commands may not preserve the sparse allocation. The **backup**, **restore**, and **pax** commands are documented as able to preserve sparseness or actively make a file sparse.

BACKUP STRATEGIES

When defining a backup strategy, trade-offs must be made between the time and cost of performing the backups and the level of data recovery that is required. For single-user workstations, the workstation owner has a good idea when a backup should be made to protect critical data. Even in the single-user environment, it's a good idea to develop a discipline for performing regular backups. Large multiuser systems have very dynamic file update characteristics, which make it difficult to perform backups on an as-needed basis. Careful thought must be devoted to implementing backup policies that meet the needs of a large and diverse user base.

Here are some important backup policy considerations:

- Which filesystems are backed up and how often
- Whether to back up while filesystems are mounted or unmounted
- Full and incremental backup schedules
- Sizes of filesystems
- Media types
- Media rotation schedule
- Backup verification schedule
- Off-site storage

- Bandwidth considerations for network-based backups
- Backup program and format to be used
- Restore procedures
- Data protection and privileges

What and When

With the price of storage at record-breaking low levels and falling, it is awfully easy to keep throwing disk packs at storage bottlenecks. The problem is that you end up spending all your time backing up this proliferation of disks. Vendors don't want you to stop buying disks, so you need to take a harder look at which filesystems actually need to be backed up.

Root volume group filesystems, such as /usr and /, tend to be static in nature and may be replicated on a number of machines. Thus, they may not require dumping as often as dynamic filesystems such as those containing user home directories and work areas.

Mounted or Unmounted

To guarantee data integrity, a filesystem should be synched and unmounted during backup. Users in environments that require 24 × 7 availability may find this procedure difficult to live with. You can perform backups while a file system is mounted and in use; however, you run the risk of missing data block updates in progress during the backup. A number of shops, including my own, run dumps on live filesystems. For the most part, we have not experienced a large number of problems. As a rule, it is not a good practice to back up a live filesystem if you can avoid it. There are some commercial backup packages available that perform a checksum on each file during a live backup to ensure data integrity. Advanced filesystems like DFS (Chapter 15) and the Enterprise Storage Server (ESS in Chapter 29), more commonly known as the Shark, enable you to copy or mirror a filesystem, take the copy offline, and then back it up. High filesystem availability requirements mean that either you spend a little more money for duplicate storage or you cross your fingers and hope that a missed block isn't yours.

Full and Incremental Backups

Time and money always being the deciding factor, it's not practical to run a full filesystem backup every day. There are two types of incremental backup strategies. The first method is to run a full backup once a week, probably on Sunday; then, for the rest of the week, back up only the changes from the previous day. The advantage to this method is that the backups run very quickly; on the other hand, there are a lot of tapes involved in a restore procedure. Also, if you have problems with one of the tapes, you will have trouble restoring the remaining tapes.

The second method still uses a weekly full backup every Sunday. However, the rest of the week, an incremental backup runs that will back up everything that has changed since the last full backup instead of just the previous day. Using this method, the restore effort is greatly simplified because you need only the full backup tape and the last incremental backup tape. As you go through the week, the backups will get longer as the data is updated; and toward the end of the week, if a lot of the data has changed, the backup could be almost as long as a full backup.

Most UNIX backup commands implement the full/incremental backup feature using a set of dump levels, 0–9. A level 0 dump represents a full dump. Levels 1–9 are the incremental dumps that represent filesystem changes against the previous less-than or equal-to dump level.

- **Level 0**   Full dump
- **Levels 1–9**   Incremental dumps

The many backup options are available both through the Web-Based System Manager, which is started by entering the **wsm** command, and by using SMIT. The top-level backup and restore window for the WebSM is shown in Figure 25-1.

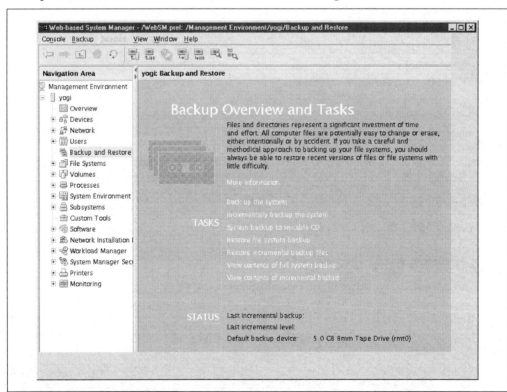

Figure 25-1.   Web-Based System Manager backup and restore main window

Backup Schedules and Rotation

There are many strategies you can use to rotate between full and incremental dumps to optimize media utilization and dump wall clock time. The trade-off here is media utilization and complexity. On the simple side, daily level 1 backups can follow a weekly level 0 full backup. When a restore operation is requested, the level 0 is consulted followed by the most recent level 1. Simple, but not very elegant.

To optimize media utilization and dump time, one of the more complex rotation strategies like the *Towers of Hanoi* sequence may be used. I must admit I have always hated the Towers of Hanoi sequence after having to sweat over the algorithm in Computer Science 101. Nevertheless, it provides a very good rotation mechanism and saves on tapes.

The Towers of Hanoi sequence involves a new level 0 dump for each filesystem followed by five sequences of levels 1–9. Four sets of level 1 tapes are used for each filesystem. Tapes for levels 2–9 are reused, and it is assumed that levels 2–9 will fit on one tape.

Towers of Hanoi Dump Level Sequence

The Towers of Hanoi uses the following backup types for the dump level sequence.

- **Backup type**   Backup level number sequence
- **Full**   0
- **Incremental**   3 2 5 4 7 6 9 8

Complex backup sequences can be tracked through the use of the /etc/dumpdates file. The dumpdates file records the filesystem, backup level, and time stamp. The **-u** flag provided by the **backup** and **rdump** commands will update the time stamp each time a backup is run.

```
# cat /etc/dumpdates
/dev/rhd11   Fri Feb 22 02:10:56 2002
/dev/rhd2    1 Mon Feb 25 02:04:25 2002
/dev/rhd2    0 Sun Feb 24 03:23:12 2002
/dev/rhd9var     0 Sat Feb 23 02:30:59 2002
/dev/rhd4    1 Mon Feb 25 02:00:04 2002
/dev/rhd9var     1 Mon Feb 25 02:09:33 2002
/dev/rlv00   0 Sun Feb 24 04:24:41 2002
/dev/rlv00   1 Mon Feb 25 02:17:25 2002
```

The sequence of dump levels can be automated using **cron**.
The following is the backup level **crontab**:

```
0 2 * * 1 /usr/sbin/backup -0 -u -f/dev/rmt0 /home
0 2 * * 2 /usr/sbin/backup -3 -u -f/dev/rmt0 /home
```

```
0 2 * * 3 /usr/sbin/backup -2 -u -f/dev/rmt0 /home
0 2 * * 4 /usr/sbin/backup -5 -u -f/dev/rmt0 /home
0 2 * * 5 /usr/sbin/backup -4 -u -f/dev/rmt0 /home
0 2 * * 6 /usr/sbin/backup -7 -u -f/dev/rmt0 /home
0 2 * * 7 /usr/sbin/backup -6 -u -f/dev/rmt0 /home
```

You can also use either SMIT or the WebSM, **wsm**, to perform backups. The SMIT FastPath for a filesystem backup, **smitty backfilesys** is shown in Figure 25-2.

Disaster Recovery and Validation

It follows that, while you are safeguarding your filesystems, you will also want to safeguard the backups themselves. First and foremost, you should periodically test your backup sets by performing a restore operation. Verify that the backup media is good and that the data is valid. This will eliminate the problem of backing up bad data.

Periodically rotate a full set of backup media off-site. Disasters can range from the file level to the building and city level. Regularly cycle the media through a physical cleaning and validation check. This will include periodic maintenance and cleaning of the backup devices.

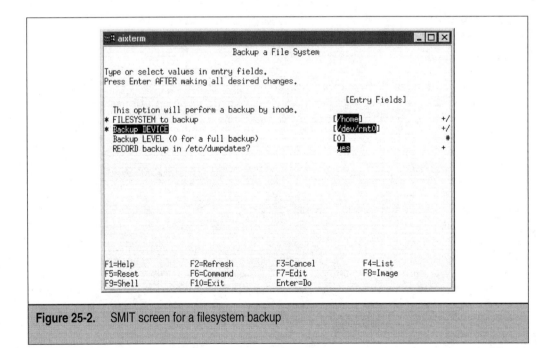

Figure 25-2. SMIT screen for a filesystem backup

Backup Media

Choose backup media that fit your environment. I think we all agree that it doesn't make much sense to back up 500 megabytes of filesystem space using diskettes. Careful consideration must be given weighing media cost, transfer rate, and storage capacity. Larger shops might opt for optical storage or robotic jukeboxes. See Chapter 7 for information on the various tape media characteristics.

Requirements for Writable CD and DVD Drives

New to AIX 5L is the capability to back up data onto either DVD or CD-ROM drives. The problem is that the drive is not treated as a filesystem type of data write. As you know, you can mount a CD-ROM in a CD reader and read the data on the disc as if it is a typical filesystem. The CD-ROM and DVD writers are not as intuitive to use. You have to have actual hard disk space defined to use a CD writer. For a CD-ROM, you need 645MB, and for a DVD, you need 8.8GB of filesystem space. The default filesystem is /mkcd. When you make an image, it is stored in the /mkcd filesystem and then this newly created image is copied to the optical media.

Only the CHRP processor systems allow booting from the DVD device. However, any machine type—RSPC, RS6K, or CHRP systems—may create a backup image. For Itanium-based systems, a backup performed on one machine may or may not install on another system due to the wide variety of devices and device drivers that IBM has no control over in the Itanium platforms.

BACKING UP A FILESYSTEM

The AIX **backup** and **restore** commands are similar to their BSD **dump** and **restore** counterparts. The **backup** command can be used to dump entire filesystems, as well as support a backup by name for dumping subdirectory trees. The following examples demonstrate a filesystem full dump and backing up a subdirectory tree by name:

```
# backup -0 -u -f/dev/rmt0.1 /usr
# find /usr/local -print | backup -i -f/dev/rmt0.1
```

CREATING A BOOTABLE OPERATING SYSTEM IMAGE: mksysb

To back up AIX rootvg filesystems, consider using the **mksysb** command. The **mksysb** command creates a filesystem image in backup-file format for each of the root filesystems complete with filesystem descriptions that can be used to restore from the stand-alone maintenance system. Invoke the **mkszfile** command to create a new /image.data file that describes the rootvg filesystems, or just add the **-i** flag to the **mksysb** command to accomplish the same task. You can edit the /image.data file to include only those filesystems to be used for restoration purposes. Run the **mksysb** command to create the backup image.

To create a bootable backup copy of the root volume group to the rmt0 tape device and create a new /image.data file, use the following syntax:

```
# mksysb -i /dev/rmt0
```

To create a bootable system image complete with disk map files, use the following command syntax:

```
# mksysb -m /dev/rmt0
```

To create a new /image.data file and exclude the files listed in the /etc/exclude .rootvg file, use the following syntax:

```
# mksysb -i -e /dev/rmt0
```

You can also perform a **mksysb** system image backup using SMIT or the WebSM, **wsm**. The SMIT FastPath **smit mksysb** is shown in Figure 25-3.

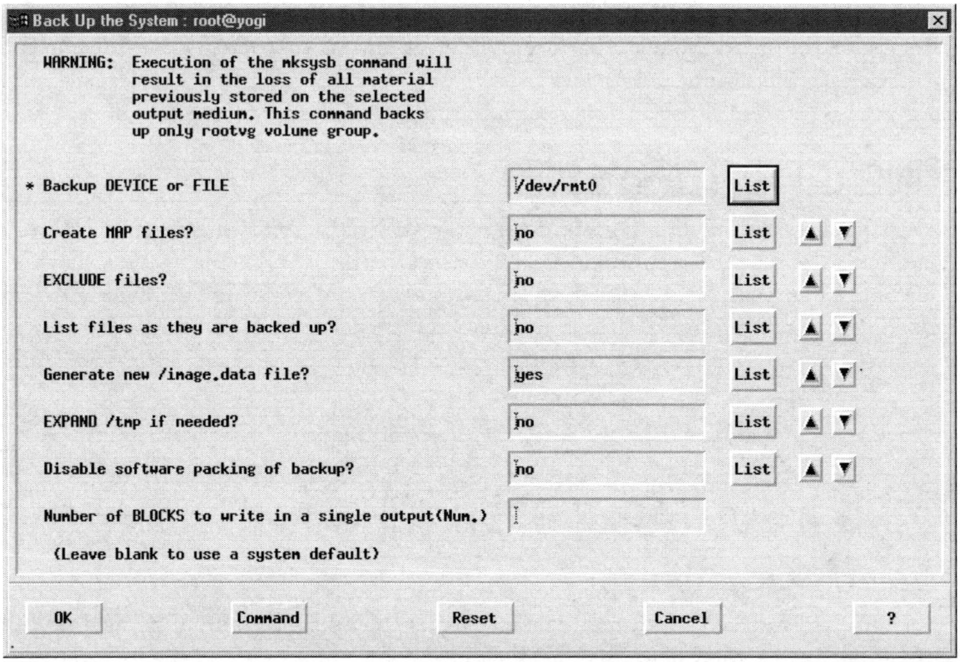

Figure 25-3. SMIT FastPath **smit mksysb**

Extracting Individual Files from a mksysb System Backup

At times, you may want to extract some individual files from the **mksysb** system images tape. Since a **mksysb** is not a direct backup tape, there is a process to step through to get files off a **mksysb** tape. Let's assume that you want to extract the /etc/hosts file from the tape using the /dev/rmt0 tape drive and you want to restore it into the /tmp filesystem. Follow the following steps:

```
# cd /tmp          ◄──────────────── Change directory to /tmp
# mt -f /dev/rmt0 rewind  ◄───────── Rewind the tape
# tctl -f /dev/rmt0.1 fsf 3 ◄─────── Fast-forward the tape 3 records in no-rewind mode
# restore -xvqf /dev/rmt0.1 ./etc/hosts ◄──── Restore the /etc/hosts file
# mt -f /dev/rmt0 offline  ◄──────── Eject the tape
```

There are several things to note in this procedure. In the first step, I change directory to /tmp. The **mksysb** command backs up all files by relative pathnames. This means that /etc/hosts was backed up as ./etc/hosts. That "**.**" (dot) specifies the archived file was backed up using relative pathnames, and allows me to restore the files in /tmp. In the next step, I just rewind the tape. The third step in this process is critical. First, note that I use /dev/rmt0.1 when I specify the tape device to the **tctl** command. The last .1 specifies no-rewind to the tape device. The **fsf 3** in the next part of the command will fast-forward the tape *three tape records*, which is where the data on a **mksysb** tape actually resides. Since the no-rewind option was specified, **rmt0.1**, the **restore** command can now extract the /etc/hosts file from the tape. The result of this restore procedure is that the /etc/hosts file is extracted from the **mksysb** tape and placed in /tmp/etc/hosts. You could have also restored the file back into /etc by starting the **restore** command while sitting in the root directory /.

USE savevg FOR NON-ROOT VOLUME GROUPS

Using **savevg** does the same type of full volume group backup that **mksysb** does for the rootvg volume group. In fact, the **mksysb** shell script calls **savevg** to perform its rootvg backup. To perform a backup of a volume group called appvg to the tape drive, use the following command syntax.

```
# savevg -i -f /dev/rmt0 appvg
```

This command creates a new /tmp/vgdata/appvg/appvg.data file and then backs up the entire appvg volume group to the /dev/rmt0 tape device. You can also execute a **savevg** through the SMIT FastPath **smit savevg**, as shown in Figure 25-4.

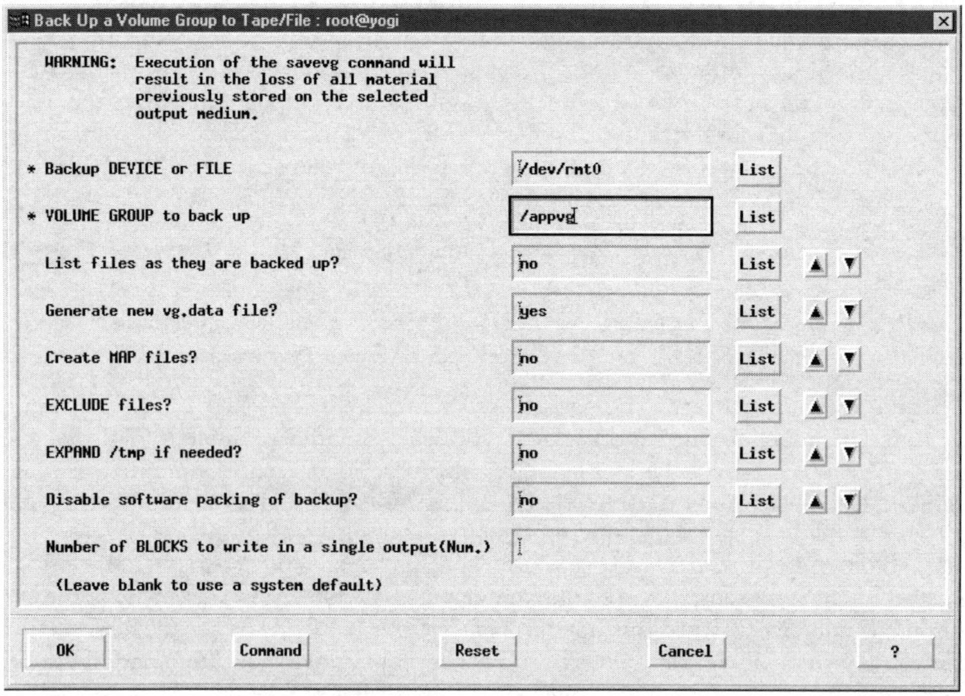

Figure 25-4. SMIT FastPath smit savevg

TIVOLI STORAGE MANAGER (TSM)

Tivoli Storage Manager (TSM) is far beyond the scope of this book. However, I want to mention it here because most large shops running AIX use TSM as the main backup and disaster recovery tool. IBM offers numerous different classes at sites all over the world on different aspects of using TSM in the enterprise. For a list of IBM training sites and classes in the United States, go to the following Web sites:

```
http://www.ibm.com/training/us
http://www.tivoli.com/
```

The next site offers some very good Red Books that are free to download and print:

```
http://ibm.com/redbooks
```

IBM'S SYSBACK UTILITY

If Tivoli Storage Manager is overkill for your site, then SysBack may be your answer. The SysBack license is pretty cheap compared to TSM. The SysBack utility allows you to do network backups of filesystems and also to create network bootable system images of your system comparable to a **mksysb** bootable system image. The nice thing about restoring a system from a SysBack image is the speed of the restore over the network in comparison with the time to run the tape. SysBack includes extensive documentation and is relatively easy to set up and use. You can either use shell scripts or a scheduling tool such as Maestro to perform the backups.

RESTORING FILES AND FILESYSTEMS

The **restore** command options are similar to those used by **backup**. If you have problems remembering the path name of a particular file you wish to restore, you can use the **-T** flag to output an index of the files on the tape. You can also use the **-i** flag to run **restore** in an interactive mode for filesystem i-node dumps. This allows you to move around to directories stored on the tape much as you would to directories on a disk.

```
# restore -T -f /dev/rmt0.1     ◄────────Display media index
# restore -r -f /dev/rmt0.1     ◄────────Restore full filesystem
# restore -f /dev/rmt0.1 -xdv bin ◄──────Restore file in bin directory
# restore -i -f /dev/rmt0.1     ◄────────Start interactive restore from i-node backup
```

You can also use the Web-Based System Manager or SMIT to perform most restores. The SMIT FastPath to restore a filesystem, **smitty restfilesys**, is shown in Figure 25-5.

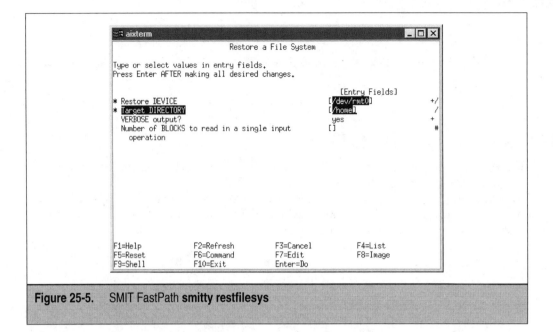

Figure 25-5. SMIT FastPath **smitty restfilesys**

OTHER BACKUP UTILITIES

The **tar**, **pax**, and **cpio** utilities can be used when portability is an issue. Either **pax**, **tar**, or **cpio** will allow you to copy files and directory trees between systems, preserving UIDs and permissions. In some cases, **tar** will not span multiple volumes. Use **cpio** on SYSV UNIX machines where **tar** is not available.

```
# tar -cvf /dev/rmt0.1 ./source        ◄——————Copy to tape
# tar -xvf /dev/rmt0.1 ◄—————————————— Restore tar archive
# find . -print | cpio -ov > /dev/rmt0 ◄——Copy to tape
# cpio -idmv < /dev/rmt0.1 ◄——————————Restore cpio archive
```

If you have the disk space to spare, you can copy a logical volume using the **cplv** command. This mechanism could be used to create a filesystem copy for backup, leaving the primary copy online.

```
# cplv -e <ExistingLV> <SourceLV> ◄————Copy a logical volume
```

As I stated before, **pax** now supports files larger than 2GB. Here are some typical uses for **pax**:

- To copy an entire directory structure from one directory to another:

```
# pax -rw /my_original_dir /my_new_directory
```

- To copy the current directory to the /dev/rmt0 tape drive:

  ```
  # pax -w -f /dev/rmt0
  ```

- To extract the pax archive on the /dev/rmt0 tape drive:

  ```
  # pax -r -f /dev/rmt0
  ```

- To list the contents of the pax archive on the /dev/rmt0 tape drive:

  ```
  # pax -f /dev/rmt0
  ```

The **pax** utility has many more command options. For more information on **pax**, refer to the man page and DocSearch.

NETWORK BACKUPS

What about using the network to back up remote workstations onto machines equipped with high-capacity tape drives? You can do this by using the **rdump** and **rrestore** commands. Both **rdump** and **rrestore** are very similar to the **backup** and **restore** commands described previously. They share many of the same flags and parameters. The primary difference is that they use a remote_host:device argument to the **-f** flag, which designates the host name of the machine equipped with the backup device. It is important to understand that both **rdump** and **rrestore** support backup only by i-node. This means that all files have a relative path, so Mike's home directory cannot be restored as /home/mike; you must **cd** to /home and restore it as ./mike. The IBM documentation for **rrestore** that is shipped with AIX 5L still shows the wrong examples for restoring /home/mike, so do not let it confuse you.

```
# umount /home          ◄──────────────────────────── If you want a clean backup of /home
# rdump -u -0 -f yogi:/dev/rmt0 /home ◄──────────────── Here, /home must be a filesystem
# rrestore -f yogi:/dev/rmt0 -t ◄────────────────────── To list the contents of tape
# cd /home              ◄──────────────────────────── You may need to remount /home first
# rrestore -f yogi:/dev/rmt0 -x ./mike/file2 ◄──────── Restore Mike's file
# rrestore -i -f fogi:/dev/rmt0 ◄────────────────────── Restore from interactive shell
# rrestore -x -f fogi:/dev/rmt0 ◄────────────────────── Restore all to current directory
```

Another network-based option is to use the remote shell command **rsh** with one of the local backup or copy commands. You can use **rsh** with pipes and redirection to obtain results similar to those obtained with **rdump** and **rrestore**.

```
# tar cvf - ./home | rsh judy "dd of=/dev/rmt0 obs=1024"
# rsh judy "dd if=/dev/rmt0 ibs=1024" | ( cd /home; tar xvf - )
```

In either of these cases, if you do not wish to be prompted for a password on the remote system, create an .rhosts file in the $HOME directory of the remote user ID being used for the remote shell. On each line of the `.rhosts` file, enter the names of each machine and user ID that are allowed to connect without providing a password.

VERIFYING THE BACKUP IS SUCCESSFUL

The only real way to ensure that a backup was successful is to actually restore the data back on the system. Some people like to list the table of contents of the tape. If you are using shell scripts to run your backups, then *always* check the *return code* of the backup command (specified by `$?`)! If the return code is not 0, then the backup was *not* successful. A technique that I like to use is to create a dummy file on the system just prior to initiating the backup. When the backup is complete, I remove the dummy file, rewind the tape, and restore the dummy file back onto the system. Using this method ensures that the tape is good and that data can be extracted from it. This, of course, is not a full restore of the data, but it is better than a table of contents listing. Should you ever have any backup or restore fail, you should *always* check the error log (`errpt`) for any **rmt** errors.

MAKING A COPY OF A TAPE

The **tcopy** command is used to make a copy of a magnetic tape. The source tape must have the normal EOF double tape markers to specify the end of tape. The EOF markers tell the **tcopy** command to stop copying. The **tcopy** command takes as input source and destination tape devices as command parameters. As an example, to copy from the streaming tape device `/dev/rmt0` to the tape device `/dev/rmt4`, you use the following command:

```
# tcopy /dev/rmt0 /dev/rmt4
```

If only the source tape device is specified on the command line, then the **tcopy** command prints information about the size of the tape records and the tape files. If that tape is empty or full, you will not get the tape or command line back until **tcopy** gets to the physical end of the tape.

WHAT'S ON THAT TAPE?

Have you ever had a backup tape for which you had no clue how the archive was made? This is a typical problem, but there is a way to determine not only the archive format but also the tape drive block size that was used to make the tape.

The first step is to save the current tape block size using the **lsattr** command:

```
# lsattr -El rmt0 | grep block_size
```

This command assumes the tape drive is /dev/rmt0. The second column in the output is the current tape drive block size. If it is 0, then the tape is set to variable length, which is what we want for this procedure. If the block_size is anything other than zero, then write down the value for future reference. To set the block size to variable length, issue the following command:

```
# chdev -l rmt0 -a block_size=0
```

assuming the tape drive is /dev/rmt0. The next step is to extract the first 128K block of data from the tape. To accomplish this, use the **dd** command and set the block size to 128K:

```
# dd if=/dev/rmt0 bs=128k of=/tmp/tape.out count=1
```

Using the output file that we created, /tmp/tape.out, we can determine the block size that was used to make the tape by doing a long listing of the file. The size of the file is the tape block size:

```
# ls -l /tmp/tape.out
-rw-r--r--   1  root      system      1024  Fed 21  10:08    tape.out
```

In this example, the tape block size is 1024. To find the format of the data on the tape—for example, **tar**, **backup**, or **cpio**—you use the **file** command.

```
# file /tmp/tape.out
tape.out:      tar archive
```

This archive is a **tar** archive and was backed up with a tape block size of 1024.

If you changed the tape block size to variable length before, you can now change it the desired tape density using the following command:

```
# chdev -l rmt0 -a block_size=new_value
```

CHECKLIST

The following is a checklist for the key points in system backup:

- ☐ The **mksysb** command is used to create a bootable system image of the rootvg volume group. However, this command doesn't back up other volume groups that might exist on your system.

- ☐ For non-rootvg volume groups, use the **savevg** command to save an entire volume group and its structure in a format that can be easily restored with the **restvg** command.

- ☐ Use the **backup** and **restore** facility to back up by filename or by i-node.

☐ Even in the single-user environment, it's a good idea to develop a discipline for performing regular backups.

☐ When creating a backup policy, some items you must consider are which file-systems to back up and how often, whether to back up while filesystems are mounted or unmounted, full and incremental backup schedules, media types and media rotation schedules, bandwidth considerations for network-based backups, the backup program and format, and restore procedures.

☐ Root volume group filesystems, such as /usr and /, tend to be static in nature and may be replicated on a number of machines. Thus, they may not require dumping as often as dynamic filesystems such as those containing user home directories and work areas.

☐ To guarantee data integrity, a filesystem should be synced and unmounted during backup. If your environment requires 24 × 7 uptime, you can perform backups while a filesystem is mounted and in use, but you run the risk of missing data block updates in progress during the backup.

☐ An efficient full/incremental backup strategy is to run a full backup once a week, and on the other days run an incremental backup to back up everything that changed since the last full backup.

☐ Complex backup sequences can be tracked through the use of the /etc/ dumpdates file. The dumpdates file records the filesystem, backup level, and time stamp.

☐ Periodically test your backup sets by performing a restore operation. Verify that the backup media is good and that the data is valid.

☐ Periodically rotate a full set of backup media off-site.

☐ Regularly cycle the media through a physical cleaning and validation check. This includes periodic maintenance and cleaning of the backup devices.

☐ AIX 5L adds the ability to back up data onto DVD or CD-ROM drives. However, for a CD-ROM, you need 645MB available actual filesystem space, and for a DVD, you need 8.8GB of filesystem space.

☐ The **tar**, **pax**, and **cpio** utilities can be used when portability is an issue. Either **pax**, **tar**, or **cpio** will allow you to copy files and directory trees between systems, preserving UIDs and permissions.

☐ Use **cpio** on SYSV UNIX machines where **tar** is not available.

☐ If you have the disk space to spare, you can copy a logical volume using the **cplv** command. This mechanism could be used to create a filesystem copy for backup, leaving the primary copy online.

☐ You can use the network to back up remote workstations onto machines equipped with high-capacity tape drives with the **rdump** and **rrestore** commands, which are similar to the **backup** and **restore** commands.

☐ You can also perform network-based backups using the remote shell command **rsh** with one of the local backup or copy commands.

☐ Use the **tcopy** command to make a copy of a magnetic tape.

CHAPTER 26

System Monitoring
and Tuning

Performance monitoring and tuning could be the phrase that sends more systems administrators into hysterics than any other. Trying to figure out why a system is suddenly performing poorly is not a particularly enjoyable task. There are so many different places to begin looking for trouble; you can ask yourself "Do I need more memory?" or "Do I need more processor power" or "Are my disk drives working too hard?" Fortunately for us, AIX 5L has many tools available to assist us in answering these questions.

KNOW YOUR WORKLOAD

Knowing your workload is one of your most important duties as an AIX systems administrator. What we mean by this is that you know the system, its hardware configuration, and what applications are running on it better than anyone else. Therefore, it will be your responsibility to know what events are running at particular times of the day that could affect the performance of the system. For example, let's say you are in the distribution business, and you have a system that is running some type of warehouse or inventory control software. It would be logical to assume that the system will be busier early in the morning and late in the evening, as distribution trucks leave the warehouse at the beginning of their delivery routes and return at the end. During other times of the day, the system would probably not be under as heavy a workload.

AIX OPERATING SYSTEM CHARACTERISTICS

The basic characteristics of the operating system that we can most easily monitor and adjust are the CPU load, the system memory, disk input and output, and the network the system is attached to.

CPU Scheduling

CPU scheduling refers to the act of assigning priorities to processes on the system. The process of accomplishing this can be as simple as using the **nice** command to raise or lower the priority of a single process, or as complex as using the **schedtune** command to tune the CPU scheduler itself. In service level 2 of AIX 4.3.3, and continuing on in AIX5L, IBM has incorporated a new performance-tuning feature known as Workload Manager. This allows for a policy-based approach to resource management. Using Workload Manager, like tasks are grouped together into classes, and priorities for system resources are assigned to those classes. If you are interested in taking this type of approach to system performance, IBM has a Redbook on the subject, *AIX 5L Workload Manager (WLM)*. The catalog number for this Redbook is SG245977, and it is available online at http://www.redbooks.ibm.com/.

Virtual Memory Management

The role of the virtual memory manager is to manage the allocation of real-memory page frames and to resolve references by the program to virtual-memory pages that are not currently in real memory or do not yet exist (for example, when a process makes the first reference to a page of its data segment). The amount of virtual memory that is in use at any given time may very easily exceed the amount of physical memory on the system. When this occurs, the virtual memory manager stores the surplus memory pages on disk. The action of writing those memory pages to disk and reading them from disk is called *paging*. The virtual memory manager deals with two types of memory pages, computational and file memory. Computational memory is used to hold working storage, such as 2 + 2 = 4, and executable program segments, such as a shell script. File memory is used to hold data from files stored on disk.

The vmstat Command

To examine the virtual memory statistics, use the **vmstat** command. To tell **vmstat** to take a snapshot of the system at two-second intervals, and repeat five times, we would enter the following command:

```
# vmstat 2 5

kthr    memory         page              faults      cpu
-----  -----------  ------------------------  ------------  -----------
 r b   avm  fre   re pi po fr   sr cy  in   sy  cs  us sy id wa
 1 3 113726  124   0 14  6 151  600  0 521 5533 816 23 13  7 57
 0 3 113643  346   0  2 14 208  690  0 585 2201 866 16  9  2 73
 0 3 113659  135   0  2  2 108  323  0 516 1563 797 25  7  2 66
 0 2 113661  122   0  3  2 120  375  0 527 1622 871 13  7  2 79
 0 3 113662  128   0 10  3 134  432  0 644 1434 948 22  7  4 67
```

The output from the **vmstat** command is divided into the following sections:

- **kthr** Kernel thread state changes per second over the sampling interval
  - **r** Number of kernel threads placed in run queue
  - **b** Number of kernel threads placed in wait queue (waiting for resources or I/O)
- **memory** Information about the usage of virtual and real memory
  - **avm** Active virtual memory pages
  - **fre** Size of the free list
- **page** Information about page faults and paging activities. These are averaged over the sample interval and given in units per second.
  - **re** Reclaimed. Since AIX Version 4, reclaiming is no longer supported

- **pi**   Pages paged in
- **po**   Pages paged out
- **fr**   Pages freed by page replacement algorithm
- **sr**   Pages scanned by page replacement algorithm

NOTE   Pages are considered over-committed when the ratio of **fr** to **sr** is high. What could be considered high will depend on the individual application and/or workload.

- **cy**   Number of cycles per second of the clock algorithm. The Virtual Memory Manager uses a technique known as the clock algorithm to select pages to be replaced. This technique takes advantage of a referenced bit for each page as an indication of what pages have been recently used (referenced).
- **faults**   Trap and interrupt rate averages per second over the sampling interval
  - **in**   Device interrupts
  - **sy**   System calls
  - **cs**   Kernel thread context switches
- **cpu**   Breakdown of percentage usage of CPU time
  - **us**   User time
  - **sy**   System time
  - **id**   CPU idle time
  - **wa**   CPU idle time during which the system had outstanding disk or NFS I/O requests (I/O wait)

The vmtune Command

The memory management algorithm tries to keep the size of the free list and the percentage of real memory occupied by persistent segment pages within specified bounds. These bounds can be altered with the **vmtune** command, which can be run only by the root user. Changes made by this tool remain in effect until the next reboot of the system. To determine whether the **vmtune** command is installed and available, run the following command:

```
# lslpp -lI bos.adt.samples
```

NOTE   The **vmtune** command is in the samples directory because it is very VMM-implementation dependent. The **vmtune** code that accompanies each release of the operating system is tailored specifically to the VMM in that release.

The **vmtune** command is located in the `/usr/samples/kernel` directory. Running the **vmtune** command with no options will display the current configuration as follows:

```
vmtune: current values:
 -p    -P    -r     -R     -f    -F    -N     -W
minperm maxperm minpgahead maxpgahead minfree maxfree pd_npages maxrandwrt
 52190  208760    2        8       120    128    524288      0


 -M    -w    -k    -c     -b     -B      -u     -l   -d
maxpin npswarn npskill numclust numfsbufs hd_pbuf_cnt lvm_bufcnt lrubucket defps

209581  4096  1024    1     93       96        9     131072    1


    -s          -n      -S       -h
sync_release_ilock nokillroot v_pinshm strict_maxperm
    0           0       0        0


number of valid memory pages = 261976   maxperm=79.7% of real memory
maximum pinable=80.0% of real memory   minperm=19.9% of real memory
number of file memory pages = 19772   numperm=7.5% of real memory
```

Remember that changes made with **vmtune** stay in effect only until the next system reboot. If you want these changes to be permanent, you will need to put a **vmtune** command in `/etc/inittab`.

Disk Input/Output

Disk input and output management can be a very frustrating process. As disk drive technology advances, the storage capacity of a disk drive can double every six months. However, just because we can now store 72 gigabytes of data where we once could store only 36 gigabytes does not necessarily mean that we would want to, or at the very least we want to be careful about where we store it. The goal of disk I/O management is to spread the data around multiple disks, so that each disk is accessed an equal amount of the time. This is something that we will want to constantly monitor, so that heavily used files do not reside on the same physical disk.

In managing our disk I/O, it is very important that we understand what our disk layout strategy is. How we configure the disk will have a great impact on our I/O performance. If we are using RAID 5 disks, then the data will be automatically striped across multiple disks, thus improving read access. However, there is a slight performance degradation with write access in a RAID 5 configuration, as the parity bit must be calculated before the write actually completes. In a RAID 1 configuration, AIX will automatically balance read requests between the mirrored disks. Again, there is a slight performance hit with write access if we have mirror write consistency turned on for that logical volume, as the mirrors must be synched before the write operation completes. In a storage area network, such as an IBM Enterprise Storage Server or an EMC Symmetrix, the storage system itself has software that tunes the disk I/O automatically.

The iostat Command

One of the more useful commands in diagnosing disk I/O problems is the **iostat** command. The system maintains a history of disk activity since the last reboot, and the **iostat** command is used to report that history.

CAUTION   If you run the **iostat** command and see the message "Disk history since boot not available," this is an indication that the disk activity history is not being retained. To change this, enter the following command:

```
# chdev -l sys0 -a iostat=true
```

Once the system has been configured to retain **iostat** history, a sample **iostat** report would look like this:

```
tty:    tin       tout   avg-cpu: % user   % sys    % idle  % iowait
        0.0       1.3              0.2      0.6      98.9     0.3

Disks:    % tm_act    Kbps    tps   Kb_read   Kb_wrtn
hdisk0      0.0       0.3     0.0    29753     48076
hdisk1      0.1       0.1     0.0    11971     26460
hdisk2      0.2       0.8     0.1    91200    108355
cd0         0.0       0.0     0.0     0         0
```

From this report, we can see that the system is mostly idle. Any time that we see a disk that is running greater than 50 in the % Time Active column, we might want to start thinking about relocating some of the data that is on that disk to some other disk. To find out what data is on a given disk, run the **lspv -l hdisk#** command against that disk. This will show all of the logical volumes that reside on that disk.

Network Performance

There are times when everything will appear to be running fine on the system as far as we can tell, yet the end users are still complaining about poor performance. These are the times when we would want to examine the network as being a possible culprit. In most medium- to large-sized organizations, it is very common to have a separate group in the department that handles network management. In the companies that I have worked with, it is not uncommon for the network to get blamed for any unresolved performance problems. The typical scenario involves a perplexed systems administrator throwing the problem at the network group with the comment, "The network performance is bad." After some period of time passes, they will throw the problem back with the comment, "The network is fine, there must be a problem with your server." If you really do suspect there is a network problem, document exactly what you are seeing that makes you suspect the network, and provide that information to the network group to assist them in narrowing down what the true problem is.

The no Command

One very important command to know in AIX networking is the networking options, or **no**, command. As more and more networks are upgraded to gigabit Ethernet, as well as high-performance 100 megabit Ethernet networks, it is important to set the TCP send and receive spaces to 65535 in order to accommodate "jumbo frames." Whenever the TCP send or receive space parameters are changed, remember that the **inetd** daemon must be refreshed in order for the changes to take effect. An example of setting those parameters is as follows:

```
# no -o tcp_sendspace=65535
# no -o tcp_recvspace=65535
# refresh -s inetd
0513-095 The request for subsystem refresh was completed successfully.
```

For a detailed explanation of all the options available with the **no** command, please refer to the *AIX 5L Version 5.1 Commands Reference* that shipped with your copy of AIX 5L.

The netstat Command

Traditionally, the network statistics, or **netstat,** command is used more for problem determination than for performance monitoring. It can, however, be used to determine the amount of traffic on the network to determine if performance problems are due to network congestion. To see the statistics for all configured interfaces on a system, enter the following command:

```
# netstat -I
```

Name	Mtu	Network	Address	Ipkts	Ierrs	Opkts	Oerrs	Coll
lo0	16896	link#1		144834	0	144946	0	0
lo0	16896	127	localhost	144834	0	144946	0	0
lo0	16896	::1		144834	0	144946	0	0
en0	1500	link#2	8.0.5a.d.a2.d5	0	0	112	0	0
en0	1500	1.2.3	Lazarus	0	0	112	0	0

- **Name**   The name of the network interface. In our example system, there are only two network interfaces configured, lo0, which is the loopback device, and en0, a 10MB Ethernet card
- **MTU**   The Maximum Transmission Unit size for the interface
- **Network**   What network the interface is attached to
- **Address**   The hardware address and name of the adapter. If the **-n** flag is specified, this will show the IP address of the interface instead of the name
- **Ipkts**   Number of packets received (input) on the interface
- **Ierrs**   Number of receive errors for the interface
- **Opkts**   Number of packets sent (output) to the interface

- **Oerrs** Number of transmit errors for the interface
- **Coll** Number of collisions for the interface

From this report, we can see that this system does not have very much network traffic, since everything seems to be going through the loopback interface.

AIX TUNING TOOLS

Up to this point, we have discussed tools that will offer a snapshot of exactly what the system is doing now. These tools are great for reacting to a bad situation and correcting it, also known as putting out fires, but our goal is to be proactive, not reactive, to our systems. We want to be able to know what direction the system is heading and to be able to anticipate changes that should be made before performance degrades to the point that the user community notices. In order to do that, we will need some tools to help us record and analyze trends.

Traditional UNIX Tools

We have already discussed many of the traditional UNIX tools, such as **vmstat**, **vmtune**, **iostat**, and **netstat**. Without having to do too much work, it would be easy to create a script that could be run by **cron** that would collect data from these commands at regular times into a file that could be examined by a Systems Administrator for trend analysis. Just be sure to schedule a job to clean up old entries in the file; we don't want to fill up a filesystem with performance data!

The topas Command

Another traditional tool that captures much of the same data as these commands, and formats it into one easy-to-use screen, is the **topas** command. Running **topas** with no options produces the following screen:

```
Telnet - Lazarus
Connect  Edit  Terminal  Help
Topas Monitor for host:    Lazarus           EVENTS/QUEUES      FILE/TTY
Wed Jun 12 02:34:49 2002   Interval:  2      Cswitch    204     Readch   209.9K
                                             Syscall    951     Writech     189
Kernel   19.7   |######            |         Reads       18     Rawin         0
User     35.7   |##########        |         Writes       0     Ttyout        0
Wait     44.4   |##############    |         Forks        0     Igets         0
Idle      0.0   |                  |         Execs        0     Namei        25
                                             Runqueue   1.0     Dirblk       48
Network  KBPS    I-Pack  O-Pack   KB-In  KB-Out   Waitqueue  1.0
en0       0.2     0.4     0.4      0.0     0.2
en1       0.0     0.0     0.0      0.0     0.0     PAGING             MEMORY
                                             Faults     105     Real,MB      64
                                             Steals     131     % Comp     79.2
Disk     Busy%    KBPS     TPS KB-Read KB-Writ   PgspIn       0     % Noncomp  21.0
hdisk0    52.9    429.8    68.4   359.9    69.9   PgspOut     17     % Client    0.5
hdisk1    23.4    133.8    12.4    63.9    69.9   PageIn     105
                                             PageOut     17     PAGING SPACE
Name         PID CPU% PgSp Owner              Sios        88     Size,MB     128
ds_rslt     8000 42.0  6.8 imnadm                                 % Used     33.1
netscape_  15514  4.0  9.1 root                                   % Free     66.8
topas      16534  2.0  0.8 root               NFS (calls/sec)
X           3638  1.5  3.7 root               ServerV2     0
gil         1032  1.0  0.0 root               ClientV2     0      Press:
httpdlite  16270  0.0  0.2 imnadm             ServerV3     0       "h" for help
                                             ClientV3     0       "q" to quit
```

Here, in one screen, is a view of everything that we need to be concerned with: CPU performance, network interfaces, disk I/O, NFS I/O, and what the largest processes running on the system are. This screen will automatically refresh itself every two seconds, until you exit **topas**. While **topas** is a great tool, again it is only a snapshot of the system as it is right now; it will not help us to look for trends on the system.

The sar Command

The **sar** command is used to gather statistical data about CPU usage. One of the nice features of **sar** is that it can break out the statistics for each processor in a multiprocessor system. Earlier in this chapter, we looked at using the **vmstat** command to view the percentage of CPU time that was being consumed by system, user, idle, and wait times. When using **vmstat** to report this, we are looking at an average of all the processors in the system. Using **sar**, we can break those numbers out by processor, as seen in the following example:

```
# sar -u -P ALL 1 5

AIX Lazarus 1 5 000031037500   04/20/02

13:33:42 cpu    %usr   %sys   %wio   %idle
13:33:43   0      0      0      0     100
           1      0      0    100
           2      0      0    100
           3      0      0    100
           -      0      0      0     100
13:33:44   0      2     66      0      32
           1      0      1      0      99
           2      0      0      0     100
           3      0      1      0      99
           -      0     17      0      82
13:33:45   0      1     52     44       3
           1      0      1      0      99
           2      0      4      0      96
           3      0      0      0     100
           -      0     14     11      74
13:33:46   0      0      8     91       1
           1      0      0      0     100
           2      0      0      0     100
           3      0      1      0      99
           -      0      2     23      75
13:33:47   0      0      7     93       0
           1      0      0      0     100
           2      0      1      0      99
           3      0      0      0     100
```

```
   -      0    2    23    75

Average   0    1    27    46    27
   1      0    0     0   100
   2      0    1     0    99
   3      0    0     0   100
   -      0    7    11    81
```

Using the combination of the **-u** and **-P** flags, along with the **ALL** processors keyword, gave us the per-processor statistics sampled at one-second intervals and repeated five times. Two other important flags we should be familiar with are the **-o** and **-f** flags. The **-o** flag is used to output **sar** data to a binary file, and the **-f** flag is used to read from that file. Using these two flags, we could transfer the **sar** data to another system, and report on it there, thus minimizing the performance impact on the system we are analyzing.

If we take a look at the file `/var/spool/cron/crontabs/adm`, we will see that entries have already been made to allow `/usr/lib/sa/sa1` and `/usr/lib/sa/sa2` to collect performance data but are commented out. These two programs are special versions of **sar** that have been modified to be run by the **cron** daemon. See Chapter 28 for complete details on configuring system accounting and **sar**.

Performance Diagnostic Tool

The Performance Diagnostic Tool (PDT) is an optionally installable tool within AIX that collects performance and configuration information and attempts to identify potential problems. It is installed via the file set **bos.perf.diag_tool**. After installation, it is activated by running the command **/usr/sbin/perf/diag_tool/pdt_config**. This command will cause appropriate entries to be placed into the **adm** crontab file that will allow the tool to begin periodically collecting data. By default, PDT will keep approximately one month's worth of performance data on the system and will e-mail a daily report to the *adm* user. This report is broken down into five sections: Header, Alerts, Upward And Downward Trends, System Health, and Summary. The following is an example of a PDT report:

```
Performance Diagnostic Facility 1.0

 Report printed: Wed Apr 17 17:54:50 2002

Host name: Lazarus
 Range of analysis includes measurements
 from: Hour 12 on Tuesday, April 16th, 2002
 to: Hour 17 on Wednesday, April 17th, 2002
```

```
Notice: To disable/modify/enable collection or reporting
     execute the pdt_config script as root
----------------------- Alerts ---------------------
```

I/O CONFIGURATION
 - Note: volume hdisk1 has 872 MB available for allocation
   while volume hdisk0 has 148 MB available
 - Physical volume hdisk2 is unavailable; (in no volume group)

PAGING CONFIGURATION
 - Physical Volume hdisk2 (type: SCSI) has no paging space defined
 - Paging space paging00 on volume group rootvg is fragmented
 - Paging space paging01 on volume group uservg is fragmented

I/O BALANCE
 - Phys. volume hdisk2 is not busy
   volume hdisk2, mean util. = 0.00 %

PROCESSES
 - First appearance of 20642 (cpubound) on top-3 cpu list
   (cpu % = 24.10)
 - First appearance of 20106 (eatmem) on top-3 memory list
   (memory % = 8.00)

FILE SYSTEMS
 - File system hd2 (/usr) is nearly full at 100 %

NETWORK
 - Host ah6000e appears to be unreachable.
   (ping loss % = 100) and has been for the past 4 days

```
--------------------- Upward Trends ----------------
```

FILES
 - File (or directory) /usr/adm/wtmp SIZE is increasing
   now, 20 KB and increasing an avg. of 2163 bytes/day
 - File (or directory) /var/adm/ras/ SIZE is increasing
   now, 677 KB and increasing an avg. of 11909 bytes/day
FILE SYSTEMS
 - File system hd9var (/var) is growing
   now, 17.00 % full, and growing an avg. of 0.38 %/day
 - File system lv00 (/usr/vice/cache) is growing
   now, 51.00 % full, and growing an avg. of 4.64 %/day
   At this rate, lv00 will be full in about 9 days

```
PAGE SPACE
 - Page space hd6 USE is growing
   now, 81.60 MB and growing an avg. of 2.69 MB/day
   At this rate, hd6 will be full in about 29 days
ERRORS
 - Software ERRORS; time to next error is 0.958 days


-------------------- Downward Trends --------------
PROCESSES
 - Process 13906 (maker4X.e) CPU use is declining
   now 1.20 % and declining an avg. of 0.68 % per day
 - Process 13906 (maker4X.e) MEMORY use is declining
   now 13.00 and declining an avg. of 0.98 % per day
FILES
 - File (or directory) /tmp/ SIZE is declining
FILE SYSTEMS
 - File system hd3 (/tmp) is shrinking


--------------------- System Health ---------------


SYSTEM HEALTH
 - Current process state breakdown:
   75.00 [ 100.0 %] : active
   0.40 [ 0.5 %] : swapped
   75.00 = TOTAL
   [based on 1 measurement consisting of 10 2-second samples]


-------------------- Summary ------------------------
This is a severity level 3 report
No further details available at severity levels > 3
```

Options related to the severity of problems collected and reported on, as well as who the report is e-mailed to, can be modified using the **pdt_config** tool. By default, the following entries will be placed in crontab for the *adm* user:

```
0 9 * * 1-5  /usr/sbin/perf/diag_tool/Driver_daily
0 10 * * 1-5  /usr/sbin/perf/diag_tool/Driver_daily2
0 21 * * 6   /usr/sbin/perf/diag_tool/Driver_offweekly
```

The cronjob **Driver_ *daily*** handles data collection, while **Driver_ *daily2*** handles reporting. The **Driver_ *offweekly*** cronjob handles data retention, which defaults to 35 days. Changes to the scheduling of these scripts can be handled directly through **cron**, and the retention period can be modified by changing the value in the /var/perf/cfg/

diag_tool/.retention.list file. All of the thresholds that PDT reports on are specified in the /var/perf/cfg/diag_tool/.thresholds file. The list of filesystems that PDT monitors for growth is found in /var/perf/cfg/diag_tool/.files. By default the following filesystems are monitored:

```
/usr/adm/wtmp
/var/spool/qdaemon/
/var/adm/ras/
/tmp/
```

PDT has the ability to track average ping delay to hosts whose names are listed in the /var/perf/cfg/diag_tool/.nodes file. It is important to note that this file is not created by default when PDT is enabled, the systems administrator will have to create it manually. The format of the file is quite simple, one hostname per line.

One final note on PDT: If you wish to run a PDT report on demand instead of waiting for the scheduled **cron** job, simply execute the script /usr/sbin/perf/diag_tool/pdt_report, passing it the severity number (1, 2, or 3) of the errors you wish to report on. Running the report this way will in no way modify the normally scheduled report.

Performance Toolbox for AIX

Performance Toolbox for AIX (PTX) is a separate licensed program product from IBM. As such, it must be purchased separately. It is a very powerful performance monitoring and collecting tool that is highly configurable to individual system requirements. Besides its own set of tools for recording, playback, and graphing of just about every performance metric imaginable, it also has tools that will export its data into generic files that can be imported into your tool of choice, such as a spreadsheet. PTX is broken down into two main components, the PTX agent, **xmservd**, which collects data on individual hosts, and the PTX manager, **xmperf**, which receives that data and manages the display graphs. Because of this two-tiered approach, you can very easily configure one PTX manager to handle reporting on the performance of many systems.

The PTX Agent

The PTX agent that runs on the host being monitored is the **xmservd** daemon. The daemon provides for real-time monitoring of the host via the PTX manager, as well as recording of performance metrics locally. The metrics that **xmservd** monitors and records are controlled through the xmservd.cf file, usually found in /etc/perf. An example of the configuration file is as follows:

```
retain 8 1
frequency 600000
start 0-6 00 00 0-6 23 50
CPU/gluser
```

```
CPU/glkern
CPU/glwait
CPU/glidle
Proc/runque
Proc/swpque
Proc/pswitch
Mem/Real/%free
Mem/Real/%comp
Mem/Virt/pagein
Mem/Virt/pageout
Mem/Virt/pgspgin
Mem/Virt/pgspgout
PagSp/%totalused
LAN/ent0/framesout
LAN/ent0/framesin
LAN/ent0/xmitdrops
LAN/ent0/recvdrops
LAN/ent0/xmitque
Disk/hdisk0/busy
Disk/hdisk1/busy
Disk/hdisk2/busy
Disk/hdisk3/busy
Disk/hdisk4/busy
Disk/hdisk5/busy
```

The *retain* line of this example is configured to keep eight days' worth of performance data, one day per file. The next line, *frequency*, is set to capture data once every 600,000 milliseconds, or once every 10 minutes. The *start* line is used to instruct **xmservd** when to collect data, in this example Sunday (day 0) through Saturday (day 6), from Midnight until 23:50. All of the remaining lines in the file are which performance metrics to collect. These metrics are collected in files named azizo, which are located in /etc/perf. With this example of the retain line, we could expect to see files in /etc/perf named azizo.1 (today) through azizo.8 (one week ago).

During installation of the agent, the **xmservd** daemon is configured as an **inetd** daemon, with the proper line added to /etc/inetd.conf. In order to have **xmservd** start automatically at system boot time, the following lines should be added to the end of /etc/rc.tcpip:

```
/usr/bin/sleep 10
/usr/bin/xmpeek
```

The **sleep** command is necessary to allow all the other TCP/IP processes to complete initializing, and the **xmpeek** command is used to initialize the **xmservd** daemon. After being initialized, the **xmservd** daemon will respawn itself as configured by the *frequency* and *start* lines in the configuration file.

The PTX Manager

The PTX manager, **xmperf**, is a graphical X Window–based program. The **xmperf** program is used to define monitoring environments to supervise the performance of the local system and remote systems. Each monitoring environment consists of a number of consoles. Consoles show up as graphical windows on the display. Consoles, in turn, contain one or more instruments, and each instrument can show one or more values that are monitored. There are two types of instruments, recording instruments and state instruments. Recording instruments are used to show values over a period of time. This does not imply that the values are being stored on disk somewhere, just that they show changes over time. State instruments, on the other hand, do not show any history, only the current value of what is being measured. Each of the two types of instruments can be configured in the following graph styles:

- Recording Graphs:
  - Line Graph
  - Area Graph
  - Skyline Graph
  - Bar Graph
- State Graphs:
  - State Bar
  - State Light
  - Pie Chart
  - Speedometer

To demonstrate this, here is a sample console:

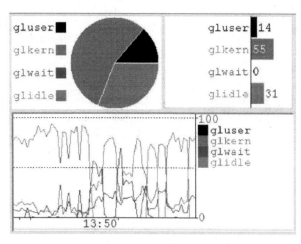

Here we see the same data, CPU utilization, displayed in three different instrument styles: in the upper left as a pie chart, in the upper right as a bar chart, and at the bottom as a line graph. The configuration of instruments and consoles is saved in the file xmperf.cf, which is located in the user's /home directory. By storing the configuration in the /home directory, different administrators can view the instruments in the style they prefer, or they could be looking at entirely different systems.

For more information on Performance Toolbox for AIX, please see the *Performance Toolbox for AIX Guide and Reference* that is included on the AIX 5L Documentation CD.

AIX MONITORING TOOLS

Monitoring tools are used to alert the Systems Administrator when a situation arises that requires attention. These tools can be simple scripts that perform various periodic checks of the system or complex packaged software that can monitor the entire enterprise. While it would be possible for a Systems Administrator to write scripts to monitor for various situations, it would not be advisable to take this approach, because the scripts would need to be constantly maintained as the system changes, and the possibility of something being overlooked would be significant. Instead, we will take a look at some of the packaged software available to assist in monitoring systems. Both of the packages we will look at are graphical X Window displays. This makes it very easy to tell the status of a system at a glance.

Tivoli NetView

Tivoli NetView is a graphical monitoring tool that is based on the Simple Network Management Protocol (SNMP). The concept behind SNMP is quite simple. Once an event happens on a system, it sends a TCP/IP alert to the system responsible for monitoring SNMP. You will often hear this monitoring system referred to as the enterprise console, since it has the capability of seeing systems across the entire enterprise. SNMP is a nearly universal protocol for sending alerts; AIX, SUN, Windows, and virtually every other operating system can generate SNMP alerts, as can many types of hardware, such as network routers. An SNMP alert is often referred to as a *trap*.

Using NetView, when a trap is received, it is passed through a set of filters, known as a ruleset, to determine what action to take. Using a GUI programming interface, actions can be set up to execute either a script or a command to try to correct the problem, change the color of an icon representing the system from green to red, or even send a text page to the systems administrator alerting him to the situation. For an example of this GUI programming interface to handle traps, see the following illustration:

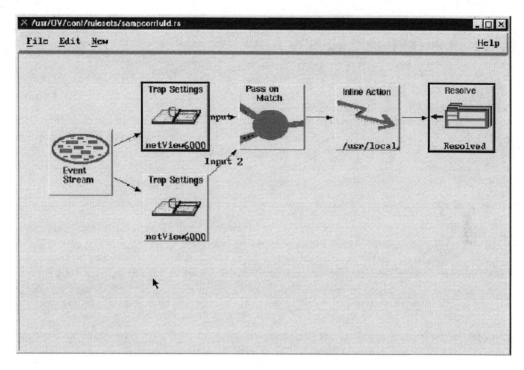

Here, we can see two different traps being compared for a match, and if they do match, a script is executed and the event is marked as resolved. Traps can be generated from many types of events, such as a disk drive failing, or from inside a custom-written script. Many packaged applications, such as an Oracle database, also have the ability to generate SNMP traps.

There are a few things we want to keep in mind when relying on a package like NetView. The first is that if we are relying on this product to notify us when events happen, we want a separate method to notify us if something happens to NetView itself. That means we may want to have NetView on a system that is protected by HACMP to give the NetView application some high availability capability. Another thing to keep in mind is that if we are relying on the paging daemon inside of NetView to alert us via text pages, we will want to keep a close eye on the **nvpagerd** process, which is the pager daemon. It is not uncommon for the modem to go offline and need to be power-cycled, which will cause the pager daemon process to die. Here is an example of a script that monitors this process and uses an alternate route to get a text page out. In this example, the text pager can also receive e-mail via the Internet, so we will use the mail program to route the e-mail to the pager:

```
#!/bin/ksh
ps -ef|grep nvpagerd|grep -v grep
RC=$?
if [[ $RC -ne 0 ]]
then
 print nvpagerd has died on 'hostname'|mail -s "ALERT"
4045551212@messaging.<some-telecom>.com
fi
```

This script could then be scheduled via **cron** to run periodically to check the status of the pager daemon and alert someone when it has died. If the pager daemon has died, check the /usr/OV/logs/nvpagerd.alog file. If you see messages about the modem not responding, simply power the modem off and back on, and run the two commands **/usr/OV/bin/nvstop** and **/usr/bin/nvstart** to recycle NetView and the pager daemon.

One of the advantages to using a product like NetView is how well it integrates into other packages from Tivoli. Tivoli also makes software to handle backup and recovery of data (Tivoli Storage Manager), as well as job scheduling (Tivoli Workload Scheduler), that all integrate into the SNMP framework monitored by NetView. While Tivoli is certainly not the only software company to produce integrated packages like this, they are very close to IBM and have a greater understanding of AIX and the pSeries and RS/6000 servers. For more information on Tivoli NetView, please contact your IBM account representative, or check online at http://www.tivoli.com/. There are also a number of Redbooks about NetView available at http://www.redbooks.ibm.com/.

Big Brother

Another graphical tool to assist in monitoring systems is Big Brother. Big Brother has several advantages as a monitoring tool, not the least of which is the price. Big Brother is free for noncommercial use and very inexpensive for commercial use. The Big Brother server that performs the actual monitoring functions can reside on either an AIX- or NT-based host. It serves its informational displays up in HTML format, which means that a Systems Administrator can check on the status of the servers from anywhere on the network. Plus the HTML displays offer drill-down access, and they are read-only displays, so nontechnical personnel, possibly even managers, could open them up for use. An example of a top-level Big Brother display, showing several functions being monitored on several servers, is as follows:

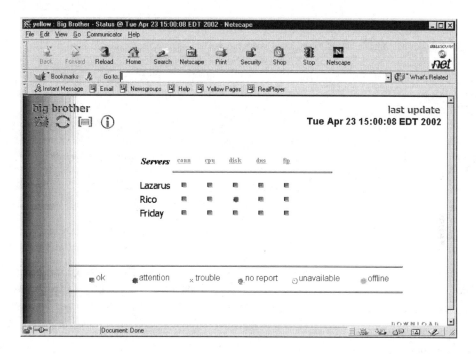

Here we see three servers being monitored for connectivity, CPU utilization, disk utilization, dns daemon, and ftp daemon. Note the yellow attention marker under the disk utilization for the Rico server. Clicking that marker brings up the following screen:

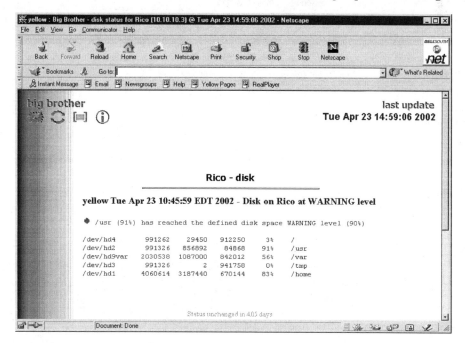

Now we can see a detailed listing of the filesystems being monitored on Rico, and which one is calling for attention. We can also see, according to the message at the bottom, that the status has not changed in the last four days.

Like NetView, Big Brother has the ability to send out text pages as well. The only drawback to Big Brother is that installing and configuring it can be a large undertaking. Big Brother ships as source code, which means that after downloading the code, it will have to be compiled. Also, Big Brother will require a Web server in order to display the status pages, so a Web server should be in place and functioning before attempting the installation process. Fortunately, the Apache Web server is available on AIX free of charge.

For more information on Big Brother, look at `http://www.bb4.com/`. Also, there is a lot of helpful information about Big Brother at `http://www.deadcat.net/`.

The following is a brief description of the terms and commands used in this chapter:

CPU Tuning

`nice`	Command to change to priority of a process
`sar`	Command used to collect, report, and save system activity information
`schedtune`	Sets parameters for CPU scheduler and Virtual Memory Manager processing
`Workload Manager (WLM)`	A tool to give systems administrators more control over how the CPU scheduler and Virtual Memory Manager (VMM) allocate resources to processes

Memory Tuning

`Virtual Memory Manager (VMM)`	Manages the allocation of real-memory pages and resolves references to virtual memory pages not currently in real memory
`vmstat`	Command used to report virtual memory statistics
`vmtune`	Command used to change the operational parameters of the Virtual Memory Manager

Disk Tuning

`iostat`	Command used to report input/output statistics for the entire system
`lspv -l`	Command to display what logical volumes are stored on a given disk

Network Tuning

`netstat`	Command used to report network statistics
`no`	Command used to set network options

Performance Monitoring

`Performance Diagnostic Tool (PDT)`	Tool to automatically identify performance problems
`Performance Toolbox for AIX (PTX)`	Set of graphical tools for collecting and reporting performance data
`xmpeek`	Command used to spawn the xmservd daemon
`xmperf`	Command used to monitor and supervise the performance of local and remote systems
`xmservd`	The Performance Toolbox data collection daemon

`Big Brother`	A Web-based systems and networks monitor
`NetView`	A graphical tool for monitoring and reporting systems and networks
`SNMP`	Simple Network Management Protocol
`Trap`	An event alert sent out via SNMP

CHECKLIST

The following is a checklist for the key points in system monitoring and tuning:

- ☐ Identify your workload as an AIX Systems Administrator.
- ☐ Monitor and adjust are the CPU load, the system memory, disk input and output, and the network the system is attached to as part of the basic characteristics of the AIX operating system.
- ☐ Identify the AIX tuning tools.
- ☐ Identify the AIX monitoring tools.

CHAPTER 27

*Problem Analysis
and Recovery*

D o you ever wonder if there isn't a little gremlin lurking just behind the front cover of your RS/6000? From time to time, you just catch a glimpse of two beady little eyes peering out of the diskette slot. You do a double take, and nothing is blinking except one of the tape or diskette lights. With a nervous shrug you go ahead and fire up that high-priority application you have put off until the very last minute. Just at the critical point in your timeline, you notice an eerie flickering in the room. With a sinking feeling in your stomach, you look at the front panel, and there it is: the dreaded flashing 888. Fingers trembling, you press the Reset button and stare at the play of glowing numbers after each touch. Your luck continues to fail as the dump LED reads 0c5. System dump attempted and failed. You power down, pause to wipe the sweat off your brow, and power-cycle back up. The numbers dance across the LED window. Is that a malevolent giggling you hear? It can't be. You tell yourself that it's only too many hours of overtime or one too many lattes. With bloodshot eyes, you wince at the glare from the LEDs, and they pound into your head: 888, 888, 888. . . Too bad you can't have the same fun with some PowerPC models; they have no LEDs (sigh)!

Gruesome, isn't it? The only thing missing is "It was a dark and stormy night." Don't get me wrong; I'm not insinuating that system failures and panics are particularly commonplace on the POWER or PowerPC systems. Failures do happen, however, and they usually occur at the most inopportune times. The trick is to make sure that you have your system logging and recovery homework done before the gremlins begin playing with your sanity.

BACKUPS AND BOOTABLE MEDIA

Backups. If you don't have them, then none of the rest of this information is going to do you much good. It's surprising how many calls I get from users who are hoping for a miracle, one that will recover a bad disk because they never took the time to do backups. See Chapter 25 for details on system backups.

Next, make sure you have multiple copies of stand-alone bootable media that reflect the new system's install and maintenance level. Notice I said *multiple copies*. I must admit that I have been bitten more than once by having only a single copy of some crucial bit of data. Create a backup image of the new rootvg on tape using the **mksysb** command. These tapes can be used to recover from a disk failure or be used to install additional machines. When booting from the stand-alone tape, the AIX Install/Maint shell is executed. This will guide you through the restoration process.

To Create a Backup Copy of the Root Volume Group

```
# tctl -f /dev/rmt0 rewind  ◄──────Rewind tape
```

Use the **-f** flag in the **tctl** command to specify which tape drive to use.

```
# mksysb -i -X /dev/rmt0  ◄──────Create backup
```

Please note the **-i** flag in the **mksysb** command; it will automatically invoke the **mkszfile** command to generate the /image.data file. This file contains information about volume groups, logical volumes, physical volumes, filesystems, and paging space that is used in the restore process. The **-X** flag is used to allow the /tmp filesystem to be expanded if necessary. This filesystem is used to hold the boot image used to make a bootable tape. If you do not want the /tmp filesystem to be automatically expanded, run the following command to see what space will be needed in /tmp for the boot image:

```
# bosboot -qa
```

The **-qa** flag is used in the **bosboot** command to query how much space is needed for a complete boot image. If you do not wish to include certain files or directories in the backup, list them in the /etc/exclude.rootvg file, and include the **-e** flag in the **mksysb** command.

Make certain that you test the media after creating it. Doing so will bring you peace of mind and familiarize you with the restore procedure.

Restoring from a mksysb

Before beginning the restore process, ensure either through the **bootlist** command or the **System Management Services (SMS)** menu that the tape drive is indeed in the boot list. Then follow these steps:

1. Set the system key to the service position (if present).
2. Insert the **mksysb** tape.
3. Power on the system.
4. When prompted, select the console display.
5. Select the primary language.
6. Select **Start Maintenance Mode For System Recovery**.
7. Select **Access Advanced Maintenance Mode Functions**.
8. Select **Install From A System Backup**.
9. Select the proper tape device, and the restore will begin.

Restoring from a SysBack Backup

If you are fortunate enough to have installed the System Backup and Recovery for AIX licensed program from IBM, then there are many more options available to you in how to handle your restore. Many of these options will be dictated by how you used SysBack to do the backup, such as: did you back up to tape, or did you place the backup image on another server on the network? For the purpose of this example, let's assume you created an installation image backup to tape. As in restoring from a **mksysb** tape, ensure that the tape device is in the boot list before following these steps:

1. Set the system key to the service position (if present).
2. Insert the SysBack tape.
3. Power on the system.
4. When prompted, select the console display.
5. At the **Main** menu, select **Change Volume Group And Logical Volume Information**.
6. Select **Select Physical Volumes For Volume Groups** and select the proper physical volumes.
7. Select **Change Logical Volume Information** and enter the proper number of copies for each logical volume.
8. Select **Select Physical Volumes For Logical Volumes** and select which physical volumes you want each logical volume, and its copies, to reside on.
9. Press ESC to return to the **Main** menu.
10. Select **Install The System With Current Settings**, and the restore will begin.

LED STATUS INFORMATION

If you don't have LEDs on your computer front panel, go grab a cup of coffee and then skip down to the "Checking the Service Processor Error Log" section.

The story always begins with the dreaded flashing 888 on the LED front panel. Before deciding to punt and hitting the Power switch, press the Reset button to cycle though the set of four halt status numbers. These numbers indicate the current system state, the reason for the halt, and the dump state. Write them down. You're going to need them later in the analysis processes. Here is the sequence of codes listed each time you press the Reset button.

```
888 – bbb – eee – ddd
```

The first number following 888 on the LED display, represented by bbb in the example, indicates the hardware built-in self-test (BIST) status. In most cases, the BIST status will read 102, which indicates that BIST has started following a system reset. Other values may indicate a hardware problem. The next number, represented by eee, indicates the cause of the system halt (see Table 27-1).

20x	Machine checks
300	Storage interrupt: processor
32x	Storage interrupt: I/O channel controller
38x	Storage interrupt: Serial link adapter
400	Storage interrupt: instruction
500	External interrupt: DMA, bus error
52x	External interrupt: IOCC checks/timeout
53x	External interrupt: IOCC timeout
700	Program interrupt
800	Floating point unavailable

Table 27-1.   LED Halt Reason Codes

The last number in the sequence, represented by ddd, indicates the status of any dump associated with the failure (see Table 27-2).

One final note about LED error codes: If you see more than a three-digit code in the panel, you will need to reference the Service Guide for that particular model of RS/6000, or rSeries machine, as these codes and the corresponding actions to take are model specific.

0C0	Dump successful
0C2	User dump in progress
0C4	Partial dump successful
0C5	Dump device not accessible
0C6	Prompt for secondary dump device
0C7	Remote dump in progress
0C8	No dump device defined
0C9	Dump in progress

Table 27-2.   LED Dump Status Codes

CHECKING THE SERVICE PROCESSOR ERROR LOG

Whenever a firmware-related problem occurs, the Service Processor logs it. To view this log, the system must be in a powered-down state. From the system console, or an ASCII terminal attached to the S1 or S2 ports, press the ENTER key twice rapidly. If a Service Processor password has been set, you will be prompted for it. After verification, the following menu is displayed:

```
    GENERAL USER MENU
1. Power-on System
2. Power-off System
3. Read VPD Image from Last System Boot
4. Read Progress Indicators from Last System Boot
5. Read Service Processor Error Logs
6. Read System POST Errors
99. Exit from Menus
```

Select option 5 to view the **Service Processor Error Log**, which displays a screen like this:

```
Error Log
1. 11/30/99 19:41:56 Service Processor Firmware Failure
B1004999


Enter error number for more details.
Press Return to continue, or 'x' to return to menu.
Press "C" to clear error log, any other key to continue. >
```

It is important to note that all times and dates in the Service Processor error log are in Coordinated Universal Time (UTC), also known as Greenwich Mean Time (GMT). Enter the error number and the system will display nine words of System Reference Code (SRC) data, such as this:

```
Detail: 6005
SRC
- - - - - - - - - - - - - - - - - - - - - - - - - - - - - - -
word11:B1004999 word12:0110005D word13:00000000
word14:00000000 word15:00001111 word16:00000000
word17:B1004AAA word18:0114005D word19:A4F1E909
B1004999
Press Return to continue, or "x" to return to menu.
```

If you press ENTER on this screen, the contents of NVRAM will be dumped starting at address 0000, 320 bytes at a time.

WHAT'S IN THE SYSTEM ERROR REPORT?

Whenever an operating system module detects an error, the **errdaemon** is notified via the /dev/error special device file and writes the information to the error log. This information is accessed via the **errpt** command. Entering the **errpt** command with no flags produces the following summary error report:

```
IDENTIFIER TIMESTAMP  T C RESOURCE_NAME DESCRIPTION
EAA3D429   0430145602 U S LVDD          PHYSICAL PARTITION MARKED STALE
EAA3D429   0430145502 U S LVDD          PHYSICAL PARTITION MARKED STALE
EAA3D429   0430145502 U S LVDD          PHYSICAL PARTITION MARKED STALE
EAA3D429   0430145402 U S LVDD          PHYSICAL PARTITION MARKED STALE
EAA3D429   0430145402 U S LVDD          PHYSICAL PARTITION MARKED STALE
EAA3D429   0430145402 U S LVDD          PHYSICAL PARTITION MARKED STALE
EAA3D429   0430145402 U S LVDD          PHYSICAL PARTITION MARKED STALE
EAA3D429   0430145402 U S LVDD          PHYSICAL PARTITION MARKED STALE
EAA3D429   0430145402 U S LVDD          PHYSICAL PARTITION MARKED STALE
EAA3D429   0430145402 U S LVDD          PHYSICAL PARTITION MARKED STALE
0BA49C99   0430145402 T H scsi0         SCSI BUS ERROR
0BA49C99   0430145402 T H scsi0         SCSI BUS ERROR
0BA49C99   0430145402 T H scsi0         SCSI BUS ERROR
0BA49C99   0430145302 T H scsi0         SCSI BUS ERROR
0BA49C99   0430145302 T H scsi0         SCSI BUS ERROR
0BA49C99   0430145302 T H scsi0         SCSI BUS ERROR
0BA49C99   0430145302 T H scsi0         SCSI BUS ERROR
0BA49C99   0430145302 T H scsi0         SCSI BUS ERROR
0BA49C99   0430145302 T H scsi0         SCSI BUS ERROR
2BFA76F6   0430144802 T S SYSPROC       SYSTEM SHUTDOWN BY USER
9DBCFDEE   0430145402 T O errdemon      ERROR LOGGING TURNED ON
192AC071   0430144602 T O errdemon      ERROR LOGGING TURNED OFF
```

Here we see a unique identifier for each entry, the date and time that it occurred, what type (Pending, Performance, Permanent, Temporary, Unknown, or Informational) of event it was, what class (Hardware, Software, Informational, or Undetermined) of event, the resource that logged the event, and a brief description of the event. It is helpful to know that the timestamp of the event is in MMDDhhmmYY format. From looking at the summary report here, we can see that at 14:53 on 4/30/02 something happened as the system was booting to *scsi bus 0* that appears to have caused a lot of logical volumes to get marked stale. In order to drill down and get more information on what is going on, enter the **errpt** command with the **-a** flag to display details of all entries, or with the **-a** and **-j** [*identifier*] flags to get the specifics on a particular error ID.

Using our preceding summary report, if we enter **errpt -aj EAA3D429**, we get the following detailed report:

```
--------------------------------------------------------------------------
LABEL:      LVM_SA_STALEPP
IDENTIFIER: EAA3D429

Date/Time:    Tue Apr 30 14:57:51 EDT
Sequence Number: 97
Machine Id:   000031037500
Node Id:      Lazarus
Class:        S
Type:         UNKN
Resource Name: LVDD

Description
PHYSICAL PARTITION MARKED STALE

Detail Data
PHYSICAL VOLUME DEVICE MAJOR/MINOR
0000 0000
PHYSICAL PARTITION NUMBER (DECIMAL)
    306
LOGICAL VOLUME DEVICE MAJOR/MINOR
000A 0005
SENSE DATA
0000 3103 0000 7500 0000 00EC FD8E 82D3 0000 0000 0000 0000 0000 0000 0000 0000
--------------------------------------------------------------------------
```

In the detailed report, we see information such as the device major and minor numbers for the physical and logical volume(s) that were marked stale. This particular example was produced by pulling one of the (mirrored) disks out of a system while it was powered off, so every logical volume on that physical volume was marked stale at the same time when the system rebooted.

The AIX Error Logging Facility

AIX has several commands to help us manage the error log. The simplest of these is the **errlogger** command. This command is used to log operator messages to the error report. Using our preceding examples, we could execute the following command to make an entry that we replaced the disk drive:

```
# errlogger 'disk drive replaced'
```

The next time we ran the **errpt | head -4** command, we would see the following four lines:

```
IDENTIFIER TIMESTAMP T C RESOURCE_NAME DESCRIPTION
AA8AB241  0430185102 T O OPERATOR      OPERATOR NOTIFICATION
```

```
EAA3D429   0430145602 U S LVDD          PHYSICAL PARTITION MARKED STALE
EAA3D429   0430145502 U S LVDD          PHYSICAL PARTITION MARKED STALE
```

In the summary report, all we see is that an Operator Notification event was logged. By executing **errpt -aj AA8AB241**, we can see the actual message logged:

```
--------------------------------------------------------------------------
LABEL:     OPMSG
IDENTIFIER:  AA8AB241

Date/Time:    Tue Apr 30 18:51:39 EDT
Sequence Number: 115
Machine Id:   000031037500
Node Id:    Lazarus
Class:      O
Type:       TEMP
Resource Name:  OPERATOR

Description
OPERATOR NOTIFICATION

User Causes
ERRLOGGER COMMAND

      Recommended Actions
      REVIEW DETAILED DATA

Detail Data
MESSAGE FROM ERRLOGGER COMMAND
Disk drive replaced
--------------------------------------------------------------------------
```

One other useful command in managing the error log is the **errclear** command, which is used to clean up old entries in the log. To clear all entries older than seven days from the log, enter the following command:

```
# errclear 7
```

SYSTEM MEMORY DUMPS

When a system fault occurs, an automatic dump of selected kernel address regions is recorded on the dump device as defined in the master dump table. The primary dump device is a dedicated storage area for holding dumps. A shared secondary device that requires operator intervention may be defined. The default primary dump device is /dev/hd6, and the secondary device is sysdumpnull by default. Dump devices are defined and managed using the **sysdumpdev** command or using the SMIT FastPath **smit dump**. Make certain that your dump device is assigned and is large enough to contain at least one full dump.

```
# sysdumpdev -L ◄─────── List current dump status
# sysdumpdev -l ◄─────── List primary dump device location
# sysdumpdev -P ◄─────── Assign dump device
# sysdumpdev -e ◄─────── Estimate the size needed to dump
# smit dump   ◄─────────── Smit FastPath to System Dump
```

The following commands will create and configure two dedicated dump devices (primary and secondary) for a mirrored root volume group (never mirror a dump device!):

```
# mklv -y hd7 -t sysdump -x 5 rootvg 2 hdisk0 ◄─ This hd7 will be 2 partitions
# mklv -y hd71 -t sysdump -x 5 rootvg 2 hdisk1 ◄─ The -x limits the size
# sysdumpdev -P -p /dev/hd7 ◄─────────── Assign primary dump device
# sysdumpdev -P -s /dev/hd71 ◄─────────── Use /dev/sysdumpnull for no secondary
# sysdumpdev -K ◄─────────── Always allow system dump
# sysdumpdev -d /var/adm/ras ◄─────── Set forced copy flag to FALSE
# chdev -l sys0 -a autorestart=true ◄─── Enable auto REBOOT after crash
```

If the dump device is configured, you can force a system panic dump by using the **sysdumpstart** command, using SMIT, or turning the key to the service position and pressing the Reset button once. On PCI machines with no key or Reset button (6015–7248), try CTRL-ALT-NUMPAD 1 or just press Reset if possible. The larger machines all have different methods, so check the hardware guide for your machine before you try. Remember, you get only one try at getting a good system dump, and if you do it wrong, the system may just reboot.

Although it is acceptable to interrogate kernel dumps residing in the primary dump area, it's a good idea to copy them onto an AIX filesystem or removable media type. You can manage dump files using SMIT or the following **snap** and **tar** commands to secure a snapshot of the system and free up the dump area for problems lurking in your future.

```
# snap -gfkD -d /tmp/snap
# tar cvf /dev/rmt0 /tmp/snap
```

In this example, we use the **snap** command to interrogate the system environment. The **-g** flag is used to gather licensed program information, the **-f** flag gathers filesystem information, the **-k** flag gathers kernel information, and the **-D** flag gathers the information from the primary dump device. After **snap** copies this information to various subdirectories under /tmp/snap and stores compressed images of /unix and the dump to the /tmp/snap/dump directory, we **tar** the information to tape before examining the image from the dump device.

SYSTEM LOGS

The **syslogd** daemon receives messages via **datagram** sockets created by applications that use the **syslog** subroutine. The **syslogd** daemon directs the incoming messages to files or other systems as described by entries in the /etc/syslog.conf file. This file is read each time **syslogd** is started or receives a HUP signal. Due to the application-specific nature of **syslogd**, AIX provides an example `/etc/syslog.conf` template that must be configured to your application requirements. Each line in `/etc/syslog.conf` contains message selectors separated by semicolons followed by a field indicating where the message is to be sent. Incoming messages specify a facility code that represents one of the selectors. (See `/usr/include/sys/syslog.h` for a list of codes and selectors.) In the following example, mail messages are sent to a central repository on another system called **daffy**; all debug messages to `/var/adm/debug.log`; kernel critical and emergency messages to `/var/adm/kernel.log`; and alert messages to the **ops** user ID. The `debug.log` file is limited to 100K in size and has the four previous files saved as `debug.log.0` through `debug.log.3`. The `kernel.log` file also has four previous files saved, but they are not limited in size; instead, they are rotated once daily.

```
/***********Example /etc/syslog.conf************/

mail   @daffy
*.debug      /var/adm/debug.log    rotate size 100k files 4
kern.crit;kern.emerg     /var/adm/kernel.log     rotate time 1d
*.alert     ops
```

Remember that for real-time debugging, you can always use the system trace for even finer detail.

```
# trcon   ◄────── Start trace
# trcstop ◄────── Stop trace
# trcrpt  ◄────── Generate trace report
```

AIX KERNEL STRUCTURE

With the error log and LED status information in hand, we are ready to examine the dump. First, let's lay a little groundwork concerning the characteristics of the AIX kernel. AIX is based on a preemptible kernel. The kernel is divided into pinned and pageable regions. The pinned low region of the kernel contains the interrupt handler, the kernel text and data areas, the process table, and the page map. Pageable kernel regions include the file table; v-node, g-node, and i-node structures; and kernel extensions. It is important to remember that activities and services in the pageable kernel region are synchronous, whereas the pinned region activities are asynchronous. For example, an external I/O interrupt may be serviced by the pinned region long after the process initiating the request has completed its time slice and has been paged out.

Interrupts are divided into processor and external interrupt classes. All I/O-type interrupts are multiplexed into one external interrupt. External interrupts include I/O bus and system board devices. External interrupts are the only interrupt class that can be masked. Processor interrupts include system reset, machine check, storage, program, alignment, floating-point, and SVC interrupts.

Memory addresses are based on a 32-bit (POWER) or 64-bit (PowerPC) effective address and a 24-bit segment address. The first four most significant bits of the effective address represent one of sixteen segment registers. The remaining 28 bits of the effective address are used along with the 24-bit segment address to indicate a position in virtual memory.

Kernel and application address spaces are somewhat similar. For debugging purposes, it is important to understand the general layout of kernel regions. The exact addresses of kernel boundaries will be dependent on the AIX release you are running.

Kernel Symbols and Addresses for V5.1.0

```
0x00000000   ◄──────── Beginning of kernel
pin_obj_end  ◄──────── End of pinned kernel
TOC          ◄──────── Table of contents
Endcomm      ◄──────── End of kernel
0xe3000000   ◄──────── Process table offset
```

It's a good idea to generate a complete listing of kernel symbols and addresses for use when analyzing a dump. Use the **nm** command on the kernel object file associated with the dump.

```
# nm -vfx /unix
```

In this example, we use the **-v** flag to sort the symbols by value, instead of alphabetically. The **-f** flag specifies full output, and the **-x** flag gives us the hexadecimal value of the symbols.

crash COMMAND IS REPLACED BY kdb IN AIX 5L

The **kdb** command replaces the **crash** command from earlier versions of AIX. The Kernel Debugger (**kdb**) command is an interactive utility for examining an operating system image or the running kernel. It interprets and formats control structures in the system and provides miscellaneous functions for examining a dump. For a complete listing of the subcommands available for **kdb**, please refer to *Subcommands for the KDB Kernel Debugger* and **kdb** Command chapter in the *AIX5L Kernel Extensions and Device Support Programming Concepts*, available via **docsearch**.

HARDWARE DIAGNOSTICS USING diag

The RS/6000 and pSeries machines are very good about checking their hardware during the built-in self-test (BIST) at power-up time. Keeping track of the LED information during system power-up will assist you in debugging hardware problems. If you suspect hardware problems or the system won't boot, use the diagnostic programs to assist in determining the failure. The diagnostic programs may be run in stand-alone mode from

CD or in concurrent mode with AIX online using the **diag** command. For concurrent mode operation, as superuser enter the **diag** command and follow the menu instructions.

CALLING FOR HELP

Once you have determined that a software or hardware problem exists, collect all the pertinent log, dump, and LED information before contacting IBM support. You might also want to run the **snap**, **lslpp -hac >filename**, and **perfpmr** commands for a snapshot of the maintenance level and configuration of your system.

You can review the problem and service database yourself if you have network access to IBMLink or Support Line sites. If you don't have network access to these sites, IBM provides periodic snapshots of the IBMLink question and service databases on CD-ROM. You are now ready to contact IBM support. The following are the contact numbers for IBM support and the Web site for IBMLink:

1-800-CALL-AIX (software support)

1-800-IBM-SERV (hardware support)

```
http://www.ibmlink.ibm.com/
```

OPERATING SYSTEM FIXES

IBM now packages fixes for AIX 4.1 to AIX 5L in clean **gzip** files for the different maintenance releases. The main access for these is `http://techsupport.services.ibm.com`. Use the following **instfix** and **oslevel** commands to display your current maintenance levels and refer to these IBM sites for more details and downloads:

```
# instfix -i | grep AIX_ML
# oslevel -r
http://techsupport.services.ibm.com/rs6k/ml.fixes.html
http://techsupport.services.ibm.com/rs6k/fixdb.html
http://techsupport.services.ibm.com/servers/aix.CAPARdb
```

IBM may continue FixDist support for AIX 4 only. FixDist is an FTP interface that allows users to select and retrieve maintenance from anonymous FTP servers at IBM. You can select maintenance by PTF and APAR numbers. FixDist will take care of ensuring that all requisite fixes are included in the set. A companion tool called TapeGen can then be used to stack the fixes onto a tape that can be read by SMIT. This is handy if you are maintaining a large number of machines that don't have access to a network install service. These tools and the documentation on how to download and use them are available at the following IBM sites:

```
http://techsupport.services.ibm.com/rs6k/tools_FixDist.html
ftp://service.boulder.ibm.com/aix/tools/fixdist/fixdist.html
```

If you have access to a Usenet news service, check out the comp.unix.aix discussion and archives. The best help information comes from peers who are using AIX in the field. IBM support personnel and developers also watch these groups and may lend assistance.

It's always a good plan of action to read the required texts as part of the homework. Take a look at *RISC System/6000 Diagnostic Programs: Operators Guide*, SA23-2631-05; *RISC System/6000 Problem Solving Guide*, SC23-2204-02.

CHECKLIST

The following is a checklist for the key points in problem analysis and recovery:

☐ Perform system backups.

☐ Make sure you have multiple copies of stand-alone bootable media that reflect the new system's install and maintenance levels.

☐ Make sure you have LEDs on your computer front panel.

☐ Check the Service Processor Error Log.

☐ Identify what's in the System Error Report.

☐ Make sure that your dump device is assigned and is large enough to contain at least one full dump.

☐ Identify what's in the system logs.

☐ Identify the AIX kernel structure.

☐ Kernel Debugger (**kdb**) command.

☐ Use the **diag** command to run the diagnostic programs in stand-alone mode from CD or in concurrent mode with AIX online.

PART XII

High Availability

CHAPTER 28

HACMP and Clustering

Iigh Availability Cluster Multiprocessing (HACMP) for AIX is IBM's clustering software for AIX, linking multiple IBM server pSeries or IBM RS/6000 servers into highly available clusters. HACMP automatically detects system or network failures and eliminates single points of failure by managing failover to a recovery processor with a minimal loss of end-user time.

OVERVIEW

We'll start with a brief overview of the key concepts before moving on to how HACMP works and how to use it. (Sections of this chapter are copyright IBM and are quoted with permission of IBM.)

Fault Tolerance vs. High Availability

Until recently, the only avenue for achieving high availability in the UNIX realm was through fault-tolerant technology. *Fault tolerance* relies on specialized hardware to detect a hardware fault and instantaneously switch to a redundant hardware component. Although this cutover is apparently seamless and offers non-stop service, it's expensive, because the redundant components do no processing. More importantly, the fault-tolerant model does not address software failures, by far the most common reason for downtime today.

High availability views availability not as a series of replicated physical components, but rather as a set of system-wide, shared resources that cooperate to guarantee essential services. High availability combines software with industry-standard hardware to minimize downtime by quickly restoring essential services when a system, component, or application fails. While not instantaneous, services are restored rapidly, often in less than a minute.

The difference between fault tolerance and high availability, then, is this: *no service interruption* in a fault-tolerant environment versus a *minimal service interruption* in a highly available environment. High-availability systems are an excellent solution for applications that can withstand a short interruption should a failure occur, but that must be restored quickly. Some industries have applications so time-critical that they cannot withstand even a few seconds of downtime. Most industries, however, can withstand small periods of time when their database is unavailable. For those industries, HACMP-controlled clusters can provide the necessary continuity of service without the cost of total redundancy.

HACMP

IBM's tool for clustering on AIX is the High Availability Cluster Multiprocessing software, or HACMP. The HACMP software ensures that critical applications and the components that support them are available for processing.

The HACMP umbrella covers several products: High Availability Subsystem (HAS) is the basic clustering software for AIX and can be referred to as "HACMP Classic"; Enhanced Scalability (HACMP/ES) uses IBM's Reliable Scalable Cluster Technology

(RSCT) features to extend the basic clustering capability; Concurrent Resource Manager (CRM) in conjunction with HAS or HACMP/ES allows concurrent access; High Availability Geographic Cluster (HAGEO) offers high availability for cluster nodes in separate, geographically distant sites, aiding in disaster recovery.

PLANNING A CLUSTER

Planning for high availability starts with deciding what it is you want highly available, and then sketching out a good diagram of how your cluster will look with as many points of possible failure remedied as possible.

What Do You Want to Protect? ("Need to Have" vs. "Nice to Have")

So, you want to build a cluster. Your boss has assigned you to make your site "highly available." As a trip of a thousand miles starts with an all-important first step, so a cluster starts.

Start by making a list of all applications that run on your system. Then indicate whether each process is a "need to have" (critical to your business operation) or a "nice to have." You might evaluate the importance of each process by asking yourself, "How much money do I lose while this process is not operational?" This can quickly narrow down the list of truly critical applications. While making this list, identify any supporting processes required by each critical process.

Next, make a list of your current hardware, including servers, disks, and network connections. This is a good time to make an initial diagram of your current site, as in this sample diagram:

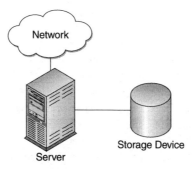

By now, you should have a fairly good idea of *what* resources you want to make highly available. Now you move on to *how* you will make them highly available. Write down a short statement about what you would like to happen to each application in case of a failure. Which server it should move to? Which IP address should be maintained? What will happen when the original server returns to normal service? Identifying these desired behaviors will help to determine the right cluster configuration for your environment.

What Hardware Do You Need?

Now is the time to identify the hardware you will need to implement the cluster. A basic cluster contains at least two nodes (servers), an IP network, and a serial (non-IP) network. If you want your data to attach to the current server running the application, you will want to use shared disks. A cluster may require more nodes for more complex failover conditions; HACMP clusters can have up to 8 nodes (HACMP Classic) or 32 nodes (HACMP/ES). Start thinking of where your site may have *single points of failure* (SPOFs). By ensuring a backup for all the components that may fail, you can eliminate or minimize downtime: you have another node to take over if a node fails; if a critical adapter card fails, you have a backup; if your network fails, you have another network to use. You might go so far as to have a remote site to go to if your primary site becomes unreachable in a disaster. You may not eliminate *all* single points of failure—after all, you have a budget to stick to—but you can minimize or eliminate the most obvious ones.

It's a good idea to draw a diagram of your proposed installation, as it can help you to visualize the project, as in Figure 28-1. After you make your initial drawing, continue to examine it, and you may be surprised at the SPOFs you've missed. Keep adding to your diagram until you reach what the configuration will look like once it becomes highly available. The highly available system shown here has two servers, each with two interfaces (service and standby) to the IP network and two disk adapters connecting to the shared disks. In addition, the servers are physically connected with an RS-232 serial network cable.

HOW HACMP WORKS

What does HACMP actually do? This section covers the basic functionality of HACMP and how it works to keep your cluster resources highly available. Some of the features introduced here are described in greater detail later in this chapter.

Resources and Resource Group Policies

The concept behind any high-availability product is to keep business-critical applications available to your users, even in the event of a network adapter, network, or node failure. This is accomplished by grouping these critical applications and the resources they depend on into an entity called a *resource group.* A resource group can contain such resources as the application itself, the IP address that a user connects to when running or accessing an application, the volume group used by the application to store data, the JFS and NFS filesystems that must be mounted (in the case of NFS, either exported or mounted). In an HACMP cluster, HACMP moves a resource group to another cluster node in the event of a node failure or other predefined condition. This *failover* action allows the resources to continue to be operational on the takeover node. When the failed node is repaired and rejoins the cluster, the original "owner" node may reacquire its resources, or the resources may remain on the takeover node, depending on the resource group policy you have specified.

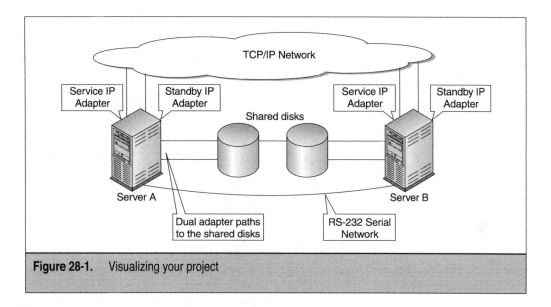

Figure 28-1. Visualizing your project

The *resource group policy* determines how HACMP reacts to a node failure or a node rejoin. The default resource group policies currently supported by HACMP are *cascading, rotating,* and *concurrent,* and these are defined here.

Cascading

With a *cascading* resource group (see Figure 28-2), one node is specified as the primary node; other cluster nodes are considered to be secondary nodes. By default, the resource group always resides on the primary node in the resource group. When the primary node fails, an available secondary node temporarily takes over the failed node's resources, and the critical application is restarted on the secondary node, along with all resources necessary for users to reconnect to the application.

When the failed node is repaired and rejoins the cluster, the secondary (takeover) node releases the resources, and the primary node reacquires them. The secondary node returns to its role as a standby node for the resource group. The cascading configuration also supports *cascading without fallback*, which allows you to schedule the reintegration of the primary node.

Rotating

With *rotating* resource groups (see Figure 28-3), there is no concept of a primary node. With a rotating policy, whichever node joins the cluster first acquires the resource group and starts the highly available application. All remaining nodes specified in the rotating resource group's definition join the cluster as standby nodes for this resource group. If the node that currently owns the resource group fails, the first standby node in an ordered list acquires the rotating resource group, including its corresponding IP address, and starts the critical application.

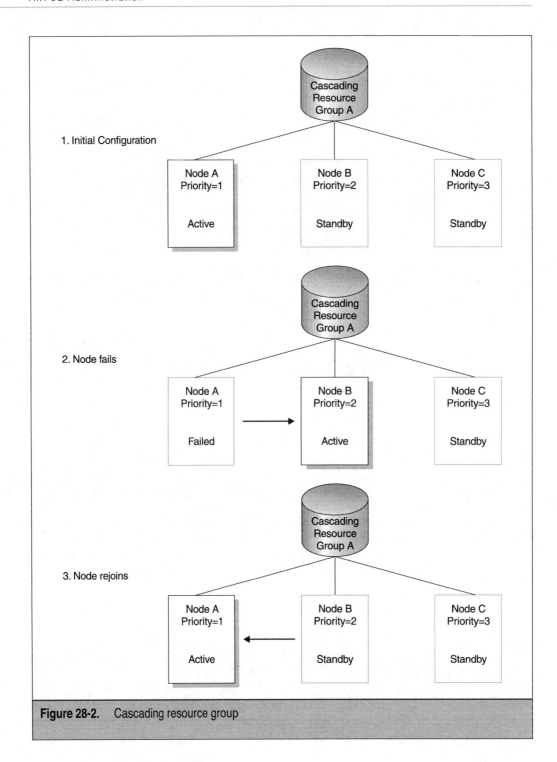

Figure 28-2. Cascading resource group

When the failed node has been repaired and rejoins the cluster, the resource group remains on its takeover node; the failed node joins as a standby node ready to take over the resource group if the node currently holding the resource group fails. Figure 28-3 displays this.

Concurrent

A *concurrent* access resource group is shared simultaneously by multiple nodes. All nodes concurrently accessing a resource group acquire that resource group when they join the cluster. There are no priorities among nodes, and no failover or fallback—and therefore no interruptions in service.

The only resources included in a concurrent resource group are volume groups with raw logical volumes, raw disks, and application servers that use the disks. The device on which these logical storage entities are defined must support concurrent access. For more information, see the manuals for the devices and for HACMP.

Basic Cluster Configuration Options

Another consideration for high availability is your basic configuration choice. The two basic types of cluster configurations are *standby* and *takeover*.

Standby configurations are the traditional redundant hardware configurations where one or more standby nodes stand idle, waiting for a server node to leave the cluster.

In *takeover configurations,* all cluster nodes do useful work, each processing part of the cluster's workload. There are no standby nodes. Takeover configurations use hardware resources more efficiently than standby configurations because there is no idle processor. Performance can degrade after node detachment, however, since the load on remaining nodes increases. A failover with two cascading resource groups that can both be run on the takeover node is referred to as *mutual takover.*

Takeover configurations that use concurrent access use hardware efficiently and also minimize service interruption during failover because there is no need for the takeover node to acquire the resources released by the failed node—the takeover node already shares ownership of the resources.

These configurations can have many variations, depending on your hardware and what resource group types you select. The configuration options are described in detail in the HACMP manuals.

The Cluster Manager

Each active node in an HACMP cluster has a *cluster manager* running that communicates with the cluster managers running on other cluster nodes. Using UDP packets called *keepalives*, or heartbeats, HACMP monitors the status of all configured network adapters, networks, and nodes. Missing keepalives cause the cluster manager to initiate problem determination to investigate what type of failure has occurred. The results of the problem determination trigger a series of primary and secondary events. Primary events are called by the cluster manager; secondary events are called by the primary events.

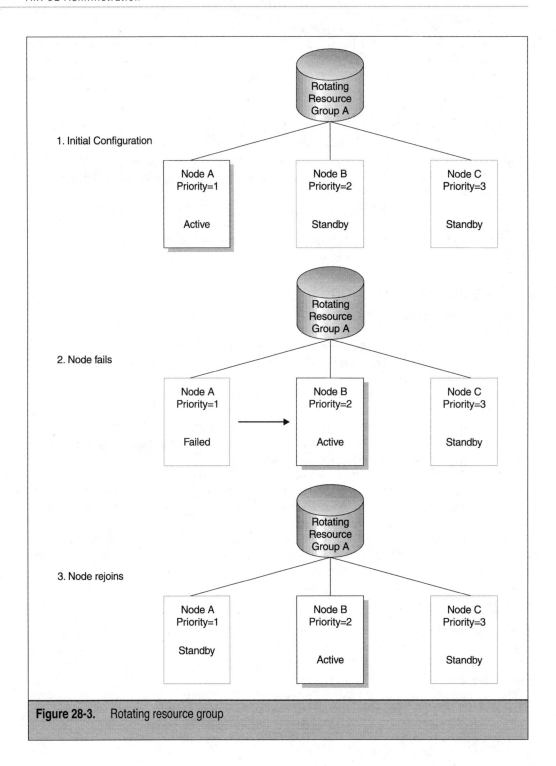

Figure 28-3. Rotating resource group

Event Scripts

Whenever the cluster manager detects a failure, or a node joins or leaves the cluster, the cluster manager calls an event script. Event scripts control all actions until the cluster returns to a normal state. These actions include calling other scripts and releasing or acquiring resources when a node leaves the cluster or joins the cluster.

What Happens in a Failover

The basic HACMP system (HAS) protects against the failure of a network adapter, network, or node. HACMP/ES offers additional protections against local network failure and application error. HACMP/ES also has more sophisticated policy-based failover behavior; for example, at the time of a failure, resources can be directed to the node with the lowest processor load at that moment, and only the affected resource group is moved, rather than all the resource groups on a node unselectively. These advanced failover policies give HACMP/ES much more functionality and flexibility than basic HACMP.

Although HACMP and HACMP/ES are two distinctly different products, much of their basic functionality is the same. The differences are primarily in the monitoring methods used and the additional configurable features that are available with HACMP/ES. Monitoring of cluster activity is handled by the cluster manager (**clstrmgr**) in HACMP and by Topology Services (**topsvcs**) and Group Services (**grpsvcs**) in HACMP/ES.

All clusters with HACMP and HACMP/ES version 4.4.1 and earlier are configured with service adapters, standby adapters, and boot adapters. As of version 4.5, HACMP/ES clusters may be configured for IP aliasing, in which case standby adapters are not used. IP aliasing uses only the service adapter and the boot adapter, the boot adapter having a stationary address.

Let's discuss how a failure of each of the protected resources is detected and how HACMP reacts to such a failure.

Network Adapter Failure

When a network adapter failure occurs, the failure is detected by a disruption of keep-alive packets on a service or standby adapter. If a failure is on the service adapter, the cluster manager causes a `swap_adapter` event to be executed. The `swap_adapter` event causes the IP address assigned to the service adapter to be exchanged with the IP address assigned to the standby adapter on the same node. This forces the IP address of the service adapter to now reside on the standby adapter. The failed adapter now has the address of the standby adapter assigned to it, and a `fail_standby` event is executed. If the failed adapter becomes available for use again, a `join_standby` event is executed, which returns the cluster to a normal state.

If the failure is detected on the standby adapter, no action is taken other than the execution of a `fail_standby` event. The results of the `fail_standby` event are displayed on the console and logged. (Log files and troubleshooting are discussed in a later section.)

Network Failure

With both a TCP/IP network and a non–IP based serial network, HACMP is able to differentiate between a network failure and a node failure. If a failure occurs on the IP network, it is first detected as a disruption of keepalives on both the service and standby adapters associated with a specific IP network. After a specified period of problem determination, the `network_down` event is executed. A message is displayed on the console and logged. With HACMP Classic, no other action is taken unless additional pre- and post-event processing has been configured; the cluster manager continues to monitor the failed network, and if it returns to service, the `network_up` event executes and a message is displayed on the console and logged. With HACMP/ES, when it has been determined that the failure is localized to the node with an assigned IP resource, a local network failure is determined, and the *selective failover* capability moves only the affected resource group to a surviving node.

Node Failure

A node failure is detected when there is a loss of keepalives on all configured networks. The failure is first detected on the fastest IP network as a `network_down` event. In a two-node cluster, for example, the cluster manager attempts to inform the cluster manager running on the other cluster node, via a TCP/IP-based message packet, that there has been a `network_down` event. This message packet must be acknowledged. When the failed node does not respond to the network down message packet, the remaining node escalates the failure to a `node_down` event.

The cluster manager on an available takeover node in the cluster executes the `node_down` event. The `node_down` event calls the `node_down_remote` event, and the takeover node acquires all of the resources of the failed node and starts the application locally.

Any event that causes the application to be stopped or started requires that the user reestablish a connection with the application.

Advanced Failover Behavior in HACMP/ES

In versions 4.4.1 and 4.5, HACMP/ES has been enhanced with more sophisticated policies to handle failures. Some of these are described here.

Selective Failover

Selective failover is an automatically launched functionality of HACMP/ES that attempts to selectively move only a resource group that has been affected by an individual resource failure to another node in the cluster, rather than moving all resource groups.

HACMP/ES utilizes selective failover in the case of failures of applications, service adapters, communication links, and volume groups. For example, in cases of application failures, if an application monitor is configured, the application monitor informs the cluster manager about the failure of the application, causing the failover of only the affected resource group to another node. In cases of volume group failures, the occurrence of the AIX error label LVM_SA_QUORCLOSE (for a specific `hdisk` that belongs to a volume group in a resource group) indicates that a volume group went offline on a node in the cluster. This causes the selective failover of the affected resource group.

Look-Ahead for Moving Resource Groups and Choosing Takeover Nodes

In releases prior to HACMP/ES 4.4.1, when a node attempted to acquire a resource group being released by another node during a failover, if there were no available standby adapters on the designated takeover node, the acquiring process failed. With HACMP/ES 4.4.1 and up, the calculation to determine the takeover node is modified from the highest-priority node to the *highest-priority node with available standby or boot adapters.*

If no nodes in the resource group participating node list have standby or boot adapters available, the resource group remains offline. This result is clearly indicated in the event summary in the `/tmp/hacmp.out` log file. To view this log file in real time issue the following command:

```
# tail -f /tmp/hacmp.out
```

Dynamic Node Priority Policy

Dynamic node priority allows you to use a system resource such as "lowest CPU load" to select the takeover node. With this option enabled, the order of the takeover node list is determined by the state of the cluster at the moment of the event, as measured for the selected RSCT resource variable. You can set different policies for different groups or the same policy for several groups. The default node priority policy is the order of the node list.

Three policies are preconfigured: highest percentage of free memory, node with the most idle time, and disk that is least busy. You can set these up using the **Configure A Dynamic Node Priority Policy SMIT** screen, reached by the FastPath **smitty cm_def_npp_menu**.

CREATING A CLUSTER: HARDWARE SETUP

These sections provide an overview of what hardware must be set up for your HACMP cluster.

Nodes

Since you need multiple adapters to ensure the availability of your critical processes, one of the biggest limiting factors is the number of I/O slots available in your server. You also want to make sure that your nodes have enough memory and processing power to properly run all of your critical processes *in addition to* their current workload. Keep in mind that because the node will not be running this heavy workload unless you are in a failover condition, it may not be obvious—until a failure and resulting failover of resources occurs—that it does not have the necessary processing power for high availability.

Disks and Volume Groups

In a cluster environment, an application moves from a failed node to a surviving node. Since you want your application to use only the most current data, you'll want to share the disk subsystem between nodes. This can be done with SCSI-2, SSA, or RAID technology. See the diagrams that follow for various cable connections. SCSI-2 has a limit of four initiators per bus, which limits you to a maximum of four nodes per cluster. SSA configurations vary from two to eight nodes per loop. An IBM Shark can have as many as 32 nodes sharing the same volume group.

Here is a SCSI-2 "twin-tailed" configuration with a special "Y" cable to put the terminators on the external bus:

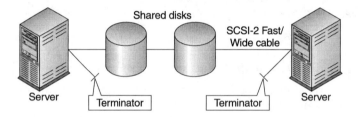

Here is an SSA configuration with serial cables wired in a loop:

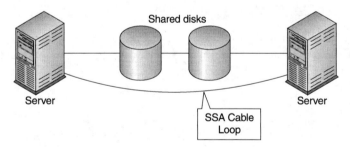

This configuration shows RAID using SCSI-2 (RAID is also supported with SSA and FIBRE connections):

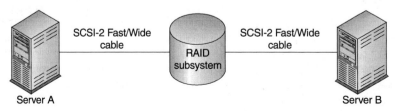

Here are the basic steps you take to get the disk hardware ready for HACMP:

1. First, set up the shared disks. The ODM (Object Data Manager) requires unique names for all devices configured. Using your design, identify the volume groups, logical volumes, and filesystems that will reside on the shared disks. Assign unique and meaningful names to all logical volumes (including the *shared* jfs log).

2. If you will be using NFS, select the major number for your volume group. Run **lvlstmajor** on each server to identify a common unused value on all systems. Assign the major number to the volume group when you create it using the **-V** option

3. Make sure the volume group has `autovaryon` set to no so that HACMP, not the AIX boot process, controls the varyon of the volume group. Then create all the logical volumes in your volume group.

4. Run the **logform** command on the **jfslog** logical volumes before creating any filesystems. Then create each filesystem on a previously defined logical volume.

5. Finally, varyoff the volume group and run **importvg -V** <major number> **-y** <volume group name> **hdiskx** to get the volume group definitions on the other nodes.

6. After importing, run **chvg -a n** (volume group name) to change the auto varyon setting to no.

7. Run **varyoffvg** and **importvg** on the next server until all of the cluster nodes have the same volume group definitions.

Proper operation of the shared filesystems can be checked by simply running a **varyonvg** of the volume group to the node and mounting the filesystems. If this test works without any errors, then unmount the filesystems and **varyoffvg** the volume group. When all nodes pass this test successfully, you are ready to set up the networks.

Networks

HACMP uses two different networks to eliminate SPOFs. The public IP network attaches the clients to the server nodes. The private "serial" network is used by the cluster nodes to verify and troubleshoot network/node problems. A two-node cluster with traditional IP address takeover requires six IP addresses and two subnets. Each node requires a boot address (the address that AIX stores in the ODM and initially assigns to the adapter when booting AIX), a service address (commonly known to clients when the node is active), and a standby address (the backup "spare tire" that is used if the service adapter fails). In this configuration, the *boot* and *service* address must be on the *same* subnet and the *standby* adapters must be on *different* subnets to ensure that packets are sent and received on particular adapters.

Note that in HACMP/ES version 4.5, the same two-node cluster can use IP aliasing for better performance on failover. In this case, the configuration requires boot addresses (each pair on a separate subnet) and a service address on a different subnet from the boot addresses. (No standby adapters are used.) Therefore the aliased network configuration requires six addresses and three subnets.

See the diagram in Figure 28-4 for a typical nonaliased IP network using Ethernet adapters. Notice they are connected to the same physical network; this makes the failover between adapters transparent to the client systems. This is an Ethernet network design with one service address and one standby address per node. The lower network cable is the RS232 serial network.

The serial network ensures that the nodes do not become isolated if the IP network fails. Traditionally, RS232 was used as a point-to-point serial connection between nodes for cluster messaging. If the RS-232 ports are not available, target mode SCSI (TMSCSI), or target mode SSA (TMSSA), can be used. Target mode functionality has been extended to SSA with a TMSSA device driver.

TUNING AIX FOR HACMP

To ensure that AIX works as expected in an HACMP cluster, several default AIX settings and files must be altered. In addition, certain AIX settings may be tuned for better performance.

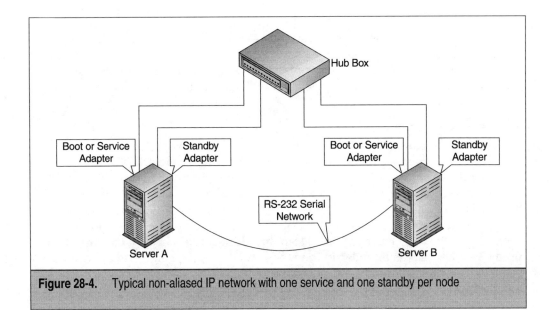

Figure 28-4.   Typical non-aliased IP network with one service and one standby per node

Changing Default AIX Settings

Here are some of the AIX settings that must be changed to run HACMP.

Network Option Settings

HACMP/ES requires that the `nonlocsrcroute`, `bcastping`, `ipsrcroutesend`, `ipsrcrouterecv`, and `ipsrcrouteforward` network options be set to 1; this is automatically changed during `clstrmgrES` initialization.

The /etc/rc.net File

By default, AIX 5.1 NFS clients do not respond to a ping on the broadcast address. Therefore, on any clients that use NFS, you need to edit the `/etc/rc.net` file to set the network option `bcastping` to 1.

Placing IP Addresses in /etc/hosts and /.rhosts Files

The `/etc/hosts` file on each node in the cluster must include the IP address and an "IP label" for all service, standby, and boot adapters for all cluster nodes. The IP label is a name associated with an IP address. Your naming convention for these labels might include the AIX interface name (as in *node1en0*) or might identify the adapter function (as in *node1svc, node1boot,* and so on). Here is an example of `/etc/hosts` file entries for a service and a standby adapter:

```
100.100.50.1      node1svc
100.100.51.1      node1stdby
```

The `/.rhosts` file on each cluster node must list, for *all* nodes, the hostname and the IP labels for the service and boot adapters. (If you are using Kerberos security, this is not necessary.)

Tuning I/O Pacing

By default, AIX is installed with high- and low-water marks set to `zero`, which disables I/O pacing. For an HACMP cluster to behave correctly during large disk writes, enabling I/O pacing is required. Although the most efficient high- and low-water marks vary from system to system, an initial high-water mark of 33 and a low-water mark of 24 provide a good starting point. These settings only slightly reduce write times and consistently generate correct failover behavior from the HACMP software.

Further Tuning for HACMP

Cluster nodes sometimes experience extreme performance problems, such as large I/O transfers, excessive error logging, or lack of memory. When this happens, the cluster manager can be starved for CPU time. Misbehaving applications running at a priority higher than the cluster manager can also cause this problem.

Setting tuning parameters correctly helps avoid such performance problems. It is recommended to adjust the AIX high and low watermarks for I/O pacing and the AIX `syncd` frequency rate first. Then, if further tuning proves necessary, you can adjust certain HACMP network tuning parameters such as failure detection rate and grace period for each type of network. See the HACMP manuals for complete information on these tasks.

CREATING A CLUSTER: DEFINING AND CONFIGURING RESOURCES

After configuring the cluster topology, you configure the highly available resources. Planning for and configuring resources takes careful thought and implementation. The many resource types and their individual configuration instructions are discussed in detail in the HACMP manuals.

SYNCHRONIZING THE CLUSTER

Synchronizing the cluster sends the entire cluster information contained on the local node to the remote nodes. You must synchronize cluster *topology* after defining or changing the cluster's node, disk, network, and adapter configuration. You must synchronize cluster *resources* after defining or changing the cluster's resource configuration.

During synchronization, a cluster verification utility runs; **clverify** checks that the configuration is valid and presents error or warning messages for any invalid or missing configuration information. This verification ensures that the AIX environment can support the cluster configuration, and that all nodes agree on the cluster topology, the network configuration, and the ownership and takeover of HACMP resources. You can add your own custom verification checks in addition to the ones HACMP automatically runs. When you make a change, or when you are first configuring HACMP, always work from the same node, and do the synchronization from the same node. If you make a change on one node and do the synchronization from a different node you overwrite the changes that you just made.

TRADITIONAL IP ADDRESS TAKEOVER AND IPAT VIA IP ALIASING

Traditional IP address takeover (IPAT), in all HACMP Classic versions and in HACMP/ES prior to version 4.5, moves the IP address of an adapter on one node to an adapter on another node, should the adapter on the first node fail. IPAT ensures that an IP label placed in an HACMP resource group is accessible through its IP address, no matter which physical network adapter this IP label is currently on. Remember that an IP label is a name that corresponds to an IP address, and that all cluster IP addresses and their corresponding labels are defined in the /etc/hosts file. It is the IP label that is defined as a resource in an HACMP resource group.

In conjunction with traditional IPAT, you can configure *hardware address takeover* (HWAT) to ensure that the mappings in the ARP cache are correct on the target adapter. However, moving the IP address *and* the hardware address takes considerably longer than simply moving the IP address.

In version 4.5, in HACMP/ES only, you can also configure IPAT on certain types of networks using the IP aliasing network capabilities of AIX 5L 5.1. Defining IP aliases to adapters allows creation of more than one IP label and address on the same network interface. IPAT through IP aliasing utilizes the Gratuitous ARP capabilities available on certain types of networks (Ethernet, Token Ring, FDDI, and SP Switch 1 and 2).

IPAT through IP aliasing is faster than standard IPAT with HWAT, and it simplifies network configuration, as you need only service and boot addresses and no standby adapters. With IPAT through IP aliasing, the boot IP label is never removed from the adapter on the takeover node. Instead, service IP labels are added (and removed) as alias addresses on that adapter. Unlike traditional IPAT, this allows a single boot adapter to support more than one service IP label placed on it as an alias. Therefore, a single adapter can host more than one resource group at the same time.

Here is a description of how a two-node cluster behaves with IPAT through IP aliasing. If Node A fails, Node B acquires Node A's service IP label and IP address. This service label is placed as an alias onto the appropriate adapter on Node B, and any other existing labels remain intact on Node B's adapter. Thus, an adapter on Node B now enables client requests directed to Node A's service address. Later, when Node A is restarted, it comes up on its boot address and attempts to reintegrate into the cluster on its service address by requesting that Node B release Node A's service address.

When Node B releases the requested service address, the alias for the service label and IP address is deleted on Node B, and Node A reclaims it and reintegrates into the cluster.

The key advantage, then, of having resource groups configured with IPAT through IP aliasing is that, on failover, more than one service IP label can be aliased onto the same boot adapter. Compared with the traditional IPAT, having such a configuration increases the availability of resources because more than one resource group containing service IP labels can be serviced by a node with a single physical interface (boot adapter).

Keep these points in mind when planning for IPAT through IP aliasing:

- Unlike in the traditional IP address takeover configuration, with IPAT through IP aliasing a service address must be defined on a different subnet from ALL boot addresses defined on the cluster node. This requirement enables HACMP/ES to comply with the IP route striping functionality of AIX 5L 5.1, which allows multiple routes to the same subnet.

- If you have configured IPAT through IP aliasing, then to enable NFS cross-mounting it may be necessary to add static routes between cluster nodes.

- Although the IPAT through IP aliasing facility allows having more than one service IP label on a boot adapter, each additional service IP label consumes part of the bandwidth for that adapter. Therefore, careful planning is required so that different resource group failover scenarios do not overload a single adapter.

For complete information on how IPAT through IP aliasing works and how to configure IP aliases, see the HACMP/ES 4.5 manuals.

CHOOSING A RESOURCE GROUP POLICY

HACMP's main purpose is to keep critical resources available to your system and your end users. These resources—for example, IP addresses, application servers, filesystems, and communication links—are placed in *resource groups,* which can be taken over by another cluster node in the event of a failure.

Different resource group types are handled differently during failover. Depending on a number of factors, including how long an outage can be tolerated in your environment and whether you want a specific resource to reside on a specific machine, you will choose to configure rotating, cascading, or concurrent resource groups.

Why Use Rotating Resource Groups?

If it is important to avoid downtime associated with fallbacks and keep resources distributed across the cluster, a *rotating* policy may be the best choice. Application availability is not disrupted during node reintegration because the reintegrating node rejoins the cluster as a standby node only and does not attempt to reacquire its resources.

Note that rotating resource groups require a standby node and that you configure IP address takeover.

In HACMP version 4.5, the new IPAT through IP aliasing capability allows a single adapter to host multiple service addresses. This provides more flexibility in configuring your resource groups and failover policy choices. For more information on IP aliasing, see the HACMP 4.5 manuals and the section on IPAT earlier in this chapter.

Why Use Cascading Resource Groups?

If it is essential to specify a preferred node for a critical application, a *cascading* configuration may be the best resource group choice—if you can live with the trade-off of a small disruption in service after a failover of a standard cascading configuration. Use cascading resource groups when you have a strong preference for which cluster node you want to own a resource group, for example, if you want the cluster node with the highest processing capabilities to control a critical application.

In a cascading resource group, when a node fails, its resources are taken over by the available node with the next highest priority and then returned to the preferred node when it is available again, except for the *cascading without fallback* configuration, which allows you to schedule the primary node's reintegration. However, there is always a temporary disruption in application availability when the failed node reintegrates into the cluster and takes back its "own" resources.

Cascading configurations do not require IP address takeover.

Cascading Without Fallback Attribute

Cascading resource groups have an attribute *cascading without fallback (CWOF)* that allows you to alter the traditional cascading behavior. When CWOF is set to `true`, an owner node does *not* reacquire its resource groups when it rejoins the cluster. It is thus similar to a rotating resource group, except that it does not require IP address takeover.

Using cascading resource groups with CWOF set to `true` avoids interruptions of service caused by fallbacks. However, without IPAT, there are some conditions under which CWOF resource groups can "clump" on a single node (unlike rotating groups, which usually distribute themselves appropriately). If you use CWOF, you must be prepared to sometimes manually redistributed clumped resource groups. For more information on CWOF, see the HACMP manuals.

Inactive Takeover Attribute

Inactive takeover is an attribute that allows you to fine-tune the *initial acquisition* of a cascading resource group by a node. If inactive takeover is set to `true`, then the first node in the resource group to join the cluster acquires the resource group, regardless of the node's designated priority. This brings the resource group up quickly but may cause a disruption when the highest priority node joins and acquires its resources. If inactive takeover is `false` (the default setting), each node joining the cluster acquires only those resource groups for which it has been designated the highest priority node.

Why Use Concurrent Resource Groups?

If it is crucial to have constant shared access with no time lost to failovers or fallbacks, you may want to choose a *concurrent* configuration.

A concurrent access resource group is shared simultaneously by multiple nodes. All nodes concurrently accessing a resource group acquire that resource group when they join the cluster. There are no priorities among nodes, and no failover or fallback— and therefore no interruptions in service.

To define a concurrent configuration, you must have the Concurrent Resource Manager (CRM) software installed, and the application must support concurrent access.

HACMP CLUSTER ADMINISTRATION

This section provides a list of tasks you perform to start and shut down cluster services, maintain shared LVM components, make dynamic changes, and monitor the cluster. The following administrative tasks for an HACMP system are described here:

- Starting and stopping cluster services
- Maintaining shared LVM components with C-SPOC
- Dynamic reconfiguration
- Monitoring cluster activity

Starting the Cluster

You can start HACMP on each of the cluster nodes or use the Cluster Single Point of Control (C-SPOC) utility, which starts (or stops) cluster services on *all* nodes that you specify.

Starting cluster services starts the HACMP daemons that enable the coordination required between nodes in a cluster and trigger the execution of certain HACMP scripts that acquire the highly available resources. Before starting cluster services, you must have a thorough understanding of the node interactions it causes and the impact on your system's availability.

To start HACMP on a single node, you can type **smit clstart** or use the **Start Cluster Services** SMIT menu. You have the following cluster start-up options:

- Start now
- Start on system restart
- Start now *and* on system restart (both options together)
- Start and reacquire resources that were manually changed or taken offline after the cluster has been forced down

---

NOTE When starting HACMP on system restart, the `/etc/inittab` entry for HACMP *must* be the very last entry in this startup file, since it takes over control of the system resources.

Stopping the Cluster

Stopping cluster services stops the HACMP daemons on a node that enable the coordination required between nodes in a cluster and may or may not cause the execution of additional HACMP scripts, depending on the type of shutdown you perform. Before stopping cluster services, you must have a thorough understanding of the node interactions it causes and the impact on your system's availability. Next we briefly describe when you may need to shut down the cluster and what are the different cluster shutdown options.

When to Stop Cluster Services

You must stop cluster services before performing the following tasks:

- Making any hardware and some software changes

- Shutting down or rebooting a node in the cluster

- Changing the name of the cluster, the name of the node, or the name of an adapter

Cluster Shutdown Options

To stop cluster services on a single cluster node, you type **smit clstop** or use the **Stop Cluster Services** SMIT menu. When you stop cluster services, you must decide when to stop (now, on system restart, or both). You must also decide how to handle resources that were owned by the node you are removing from the cluster. For this, you have the following options:

- In a *graceful* stop, the HACMP software shuts down its applications and releases its resources. The other nodes *do not* take over the resources of the stopped node.

- In a *graceful with takeover* stop, the HACMP software shuts down its applications and releases its resources. The surviving nodes take over these resources. This is also called *intentional failover*.

- In a *forced* stop, HACMP shuts down immediately. The node that is shutting down retains control of all its resources. Applications that do not require HACMP daemons continue to run. Typically, you use the forced option so that stopping the Cluster Manager does not interrupt users and clients. As no cluster agent is running on the node after a *forced* down, failures are not detected. This applies to hardware resources such as disks and adapters, as well as any monitored applications. If any resources defined to HACMP are disrupted, they should be restored to their prior state before restarting cluster services.

If you use an AIX shutdown command, HACMP services are stopped with the forced option. If you want resources to be taken over, you stop HACMP using the graceful with takeover option before performing the AIX shutdown.

Cluster Single Point of Control (C-SPOC)

HACMP provides the Cluster Single Point of Control (C-SPOC) utility, which simplifies maintenance of shared LVM components. C-SPOC commands provide comparable functions in a cluster environment to the standard AIX commands that work on a single node. For example, the C-SPOC utility includes a command called **cl_chlv** that provides similar functions to the AIX **chlv** command. (The C-SPOC command calls the AIX command.) By automating repetitive tasks, C-SPOC eliminates a potential source of errors and speeds up the process. You can use C-SPOC to perform the following LVM maintenance tasks:

- Create, import, extend, reduce, mirror, and unmirror shared and concurrent volume groups.
- Synchronize volume group mirrors.
- List all active shared or concurrent volume groups.
- Display characteristics of a shared (or concurrent) volume group.
- Create, make a copy of, and remove a copy of a logical volume.
- List all shared logical volumes by volume group.
- Change or view the characteristics of a shared logical volume (name, size).
- Remove a shared logical volume.
- Create, list, change, and remove shared filesystems.
- Add, replace, and remove a physical volume.

NOTE C-SPOC commands operate only on shared and concurrent LVM components that are defined as part of an HACMP resource group.

When you execute a C-SPOC command, the utility determines on which node to perform the operation and then executes the required commands on that node. Typically, C-SPOC executes the command on the node that owns the LVM component (has it varied on). However, you can use C-SPOC commands (on the command line, not from SMIT) on an LVM component that is not currently activated on any cluster node. In this case, C-SPOC determines which node will own the LVM component when it is activated, as specified for the HACMP resource group, and performs the operation on that node. Using C-SPOC simplifies the steps required for all tasks. Moreover, you do not have to stop and restart cluster services in order to do the tasks.

Dynamic Reconfiguration and Resource Group Management

When you configure an HACMP cluster, configuration data is stored in HACMP-specific object classes in the ODM. The AIX ODM object classes are stored in the default system configuration directory (DCD), `/etc/objrepos`. You can make certain changes both to the cluster topology and to the cluster resources while the cluster is running (dynamic reconfiguration).

Dynamic Cluster Reconfiguration (DARE)

At cluster start-up, HACMP copies HACMP-specific ODM classes into a separate directory called the Active Configuration Directory (ACD). While a cluster is running, the HACMP daemons, scripts, and utilities reference the ODM data stored in the ACD.

If you synchronize the cluster topology or cluster resources definition while the Cluster Manager is running on the local node, this action triggers a dynamic reconfiguration (DARE) event. In a dynamic reconfiguration event, the ODM data in the Default Configuration Directories (DCDs) on all cluster nodes is updated and the ODM data in the ACD is overwritten with the new configuration data. The HACMP daemons are refreshed so that the new configuration becomes the currently active configuration.

You can make many changes to the cluster topology and resources in an active cluster, dynamically, such as adding or removing nodes and adapters, changing network tuning parameters, swapping adapter cards, adding or removing resources from resource groups, and making changes to the configuration of many types of resources.

Some changes require stopping the cluster, such as changing the cluster name or changing a node name. For details on exactly which tasks can be performed dynamically and which cannot, see the HACMP manuals.

DARE Resource Migration

Additionally, you can use the DARE Resource Migration utility to move resource groups to other cluster nodes to perform system maintenance on a particular cluster node. DARE Resource Migration allows you to change the status (online or offline) or location of a cascading or rotating resource group without stopping cluster services. You can perform DARE resource migrations from the command line and through SMIT.

You can also disable resource groups dynamically, preventing them from being acquired during a reintegration. This disabling option allows a "swap" of resources in certain situations.

Tools for Monitoring the HACMP Cluster

By design, failures of components in the cluster are handled automatically by HACMP, but you still need to be aware of all such events. You can use several tools to check the status of an HACMP cluster; the nodes, networks, and resource groups within that cluster; and the daemons that run on the nodes. HACMP provides the following tools for monitoring a cluster:

- The *HAView* utility extends Tivoli NetView services so that you can monitor HACMP clusters and cluster components across a network from a single node.

- *Cluster monitoring with Tivoli* allows you to monitor clusters and cluster components and (in version 4.5) also perform cluster administration tasks through your Tivoli Framework console.

- *clstat* (the **/usr/[es/]sbin/cluster/clstat** utility, or **xclstat** for the X version) uses the HACMP Cluster Information Program (**clinfo**) API to retrieve and display the status of key cluster components—the cluster itself, its nodes, network interfaces, and resource groups—and can be viewed in an X Window, an ASCII display, or (in version 4.5) a Web browser. The **clinfo** daemon is a cluster monitor based on the Simple Network Management Protocol (SNMP).

- *Application Monitoring* allows you to monitor specific applications and processes and define action to take upon detection of process death or other application failures.

- The *Application Availability Analysis* tool measures uptime statistics for applications with application servers defined to HACMP/ES in version 4.5.

- The *Show Cluster Services* SMIT screen shows the status of the HACMP daemons.

- The *Show A Network Module* SMIT screen shows the attributes of a specific network.

- *Log files* allow you to track cluster events and history: The `/usr/[es/]adm/cluster.log` file tracks cluster events; the `/tmp/hacmp.out` file records the output generated by configuration scripts as they execute; the `/usr/[es/]sbin/cluster/history/cluster.mmddyyyy` file logs the daily cluster history; the `/tmp/cspoc.log` file logs the status of C-SPOC commands executed on cluster nodes.

- The *custom pager notification* utility can be configured to issue a customized page in response to a cluster event.

TROUBLESHOOTING

Both HACMP and AIX provide utilities to help determine the state of an HACMP cluster and the resources within that cluster. Using certain commands, you can gather information about volume groups or networks; examining log files helps you trace the behavior of resources after cluster events. Thorough knowledge of the HACMP system is essential for effective troubleshooting; you must be familiar with the characteristics of a normal cluster and be on the lookout for deviations from the norm as you examine the cluster components.

The following sections provide a very brief summary of some of the troubleshooting aids built in to HACMP. For further details, see the HACMP manuals, particularly the *Troubleshooting Guide*.

Error Handling

HACMP has many error handling routines built into the event scripts. User customized scripts should handle all common error within the customized script. However, if an event script fails to complete within six minutes, the console displays the message "In configuration too long...." This may be normal, as the cluster failover may require more than six minutes, or this may be the first indication of a problem with the failover. This is where knowing your cluster configuration is most important. The better you understand the cluster, the quicker you will be able to find and fix the problem. The first place to check is the error logs.

In version 4.5, you can change the default six-minute interval through SMIT to avoid getting the "configuration too long" message unnecessarily.

Error Logs

The most frequently used log for troubleshooting is the `/tmp/hacmp.out` log. It contains detailed output of all the event scripts run on the node. This information supplements and expands upon the information in the /usr/[es/]adm/cluster.log file.

Reported resource group acquisition failures (failures indicated by a nonzero exit code returned by a command) are tracked in `/tmp/hacmp.out`, and a summary is written near the end of the listing for each top-level event.

Checking this log is important and helps to identify problems in the cluster. Use **tail** (**tail -f /tmp/hacmp.out** for real time viewing) or **vi** to check the log file to quickly locate the ERROR location. You might want to scan the pages above the error condition to see if another condition caused the error. For example, if a filesystem didn't mount, further checking may indicate that the volume group did not varyon. This was probably caused by a difference between the VGDA on the volume group and the ODM copy on the system that was attempting to varyon the volume group. So instead of troubleshooting a filesystem problem, you need to troubleshoot the volume group problem.

The `/usr/adm/cluster.log` contains a good overview of the event scripts called by the cluster manager. Keep in mind the cluster manager does not start event scripts unless an event has occurred, that is, something has failed.

In HACMP/ES, Topology Services and Group Services have additional log files useful in troubleshooting network problems. See the HACMP/ES manual for details.

Event Summaries

In HACMP/ES only, event summaries appear at the end of each event's detailed output in the `hacmp.out` log. A good way to get a quick overview of what has happened in the cluster lately is to use the Display Event Summaries option, which compiles and displays all of the event summaries from the `hacmp.out` log file. In addition, resource group location and state information is reported at the bottom of the display, reflecting output from the **clfindres** command. The summary display is updated once per day with the current day's event summaries.

To view a compiled list of event summaries on a node or to save the event summaries to a specified file, navigate to the **Display Event Summaries** options under **Cluster System Management** in SMIT, or use the FastPath **smitty cm_dsp_evs**.

Note that event summaries can be seen in the `hacmp.out` file in HACMP/ES 4.4.1. The Display Event Summaries feature was added in version 4.5.

Deadman Switch

With HACMP Classic, a timer ensures that keepalives (heartbeats) are processed in a timely manner. If they are not, then you can have false failovers when no error condition exists. This timer is called the *deadman switch*. The deadman switch is a kernel extension loaded when HACMP starts. The duration of the timer is determined by the formula *time of the slowest IP network minus one second*. If the deadman switch fires, the kernel panics and a system dump occurs, indicated by the flashing 888 in the LEDs. If this happens, you should investigate why the cluster manager did not get processor time to process the keepalives. This is where AIX tuning comes into play, to minimize the possibility of the cluster manager not getting processor time.

Partitioned Clusters

In the event that the cluster managers lose communication with other cluster managers—that is, all network, IP, and serial communications are lost—you can end up with a "partitioned" cluster. That is, Node A thinks Node B is dead and vice versa. This is a very serious condition, as each node is programmed to do something if the other fails. HACMP/ES allows global networks that prevent this problem. For details on how to avoid cluster partitioning, or what to do in the event that partitioning occurs, see the HACMP manuals.

ADDITIONAL FEATURES IN HACMP

In addition to the cluster configuration, dynamic reconfiguration, monitoring, problem determination, and AIX tuning functionality described previously, HACMP has many other features, some of which we'll cover briefly here.

Customization of Events

The HACMP system is event driven. An *event* is a change of status within a cluster. When a cluster manager detects a change in cluster status, it executes the designated script to handle the event and initiates any user-defined customized processing.

HACMP allows the user considerable customizing power in this area. We'll list some examples here; for more detail, see the HACMP user manuals.

Customized Pre-Event, Event, and Post-Event Scripts

You can define multiple pre- and post-events for each of the events defined in the HACMPevent ODM class.

Customization for an event could include notification to the Systems Administrator before and after the event is processed, as well as user-defined commands or scripts for other actions before and after the event processing.

Custom User-Defined Events

In HACMP/ES only, users can add their own events. To define a customized cluster event script, write your own script for the event, then add it to your cluster configuration, using the **Define Custom Cluster Events** menu under **Cluster Custom Modification** in SMIT or the **smit cladd_event.dialog** FastPath.

Event Recovery and Retry

You can specify a script or AIX command to execute to attempt to recover from a cluster event command failure. If the recovery command succeeds and the retry count is greater than zero, the cluster event command is rerun. The arguments passed to this command are the event name and the arguments passed to the event command.

You can also specify the number of times to run the recovery command. Set the Recovery Counter field to one (1) or greater if a recovery command is specified.

Customized Event Duration

In HACMP 4.5, you can use SMIT to customize the time period allowed for a cluster event to complete before HACMP issues a system warning for it. Prior to HACMP 4.5, the timeout period was set to six minutes by default and could be changed only using the command line. If a cluster event lasted longer than six minutes, then every 30 seconds HACMP automatically issued a `config_too_long` warning message that was logged in the `/tmp/hacmp.out` file.

Automatic Error Notification

HACMP builds on the AIX error notification feature by providing a means of automatically turning on prespecified error notification methods for certain failures. This can be done in one step through the SMIT interface, saving the time and effort normally spent defining each notify method manually. The predefined notify methods are automatically enabled on all nodes in the cluster for the following devices:

- All disks in the rootvg volume group
- All disks in HACMP volume groups, concurrent volume groups, and filesystems. (To avoid single points of failure, the JFS log must be included in an HACMP volume group.)
- All disks defined as HACMP resources
- SP switch adapter

Custom Pager Notification

You can define a notification method through the SMIT interface to issue a customized page in response to a cluster event. In version 4.5, you can send a test message after configuring a pager notification method to confirm that the configuration is correct. You can configure any number of notification methods, for different events and with different text messages and telephone numbers to dial. The same notification method can be used for several different events, as long as the associated text message conveys enough information to respond to all of the possible events that trigger the page.

NFS Capability

Extended NFS capability, formerly included only in the HANFS product, has been added to the basic HACMP architecture and is included in both HAS and HACMP/ES products, allowing you to do the following:

- Make use of reliable NFS server capability that preserves locks and dupcache (2-node clusters only).
- Specify a network for NFS mounting.
- Define NFS exports and mounts at the directory level.
- Specify export options for NFS-exported directories and filesystems.

Highly Available Print Queues

In the event of a failover, the print jobs currently queued can be saved and moved over to the surviving node. The print spooling system consists of two directories: `/var/spool/qdaemon` and `/var/spool/lpd/qdir`. One directory contains files containing the data (content) of each job. The other contains the files consisting of information pertaining to the print job itself. When jobs are queued, there are files in each of the two directories. In the event of a failover, these directories do not normally fail over and thus the print jobs are lost.

In HACMP/ES, the plug-in **cluster.es.plugins.printserver** fileset provides scripts to start and stop the print server process, a script to verify that configuration files are present and stored in a shared filesystem, and scripts called by the monitoring functions of HACMP/ES that check on print server process life. You can also move all of the print services directory structures to the shared disks so that the queued jobs are always available, even with HACMP classic.

Highly Available WAN Communication Links

As of version 4.5, HACMP can provide high availability for three types of communication links:

- SNA configured over a LAN adapter
- SNA over X.25
- Pure X.25

With earlier HACMP releases, users could configure only SNA-over-LAN. (These links were termed CS/AIX communication links.) Support of the other protocols was previously available through the add-on HAWAN product.

LAN adapters are Ethernet, Token Ring, and FDDI adapters; these adapters are configured as part of the HACMP cluster topology.

X.25 adapters are usually, though not always, used for WAN connections. They are used as a means of connecting dissimilar machines, from mainframes to dumb terminals. Because of the way X.25 networks are used, these adapters are treated as a different class of devices that are *not* included in the cluster topology and *not* controlled by the standard HACMP topology management methods. This means that heartbeats are not used to monitor X.25 adapter status, and you do not define X.25-specific networks in HACMP. Instead, an HACMP daemon, **clcommlinkd**, takes the place of heartbeats. This daemon monitors the output of the **x25status** command to make sure the link is still connected to the network.

Making a communication link highly available in HACMP involves these general steps: Define the communication adapters and links in the operating system (AIX), then define the adapters and links in HACMP, and finally add the defined communication links as resources in HACMP resource groups. Each of these steps must be carefully thought out and implemented; the communication link should be tested thoroughly outside of HACMP before you add it to the cluster resource group. For full information and instructions, see the HACMP user manuals.

Highly Available Workload Manager Classes

AIX Workload Manager (WLM) is a systems administration resource included with AIX 4.3.3 and above. WLM allows users to set targets for and limits on CPU time, physical memory usage, and disk I/O bandwidth for different processes and applications; this provides better control over the usage of critical system resources at peak loads. As of version 4.5, HACMP allows you to configure WLM classes in HACMP resource groups so that the starting, stopping, and active configuration of WLM can be under cluster control.

For complete information on how to set up and use Workload Manager, see the AIX 5L Workload Manager (WLM) Redbook at `http://www.ibm.com/redbooks/`. For complete information on making WLM classes highly available resources in an HACMP cluster, see the HACMP user manuals.

Highly Available Tape Drives

HACMP 4.5 allows you to configure highly available tape drives. To make a tape drive highly available, you first define it as a resource, including specifying start and stop scripts, and then you add the resource to a cluster resource group. Sample scripts are available in the `/usr/[es/]sbin/cluster/samples/tape` directory. These sample scripts rewind the tape drive explicitly.

After adding a resource to a resource group, verify that the configuration is correct and then synchronize shared tape resources to all nodes in the cluster.

Emulation Tools

HACMP includes emulation capability for running cluster event emulations and for testing error notification methods.

Event Emulation

The HACMP Event Emulator is a utility that emulates cluster events and dynamic reconfiguration events by running event scripts that produce output but that do not affect the cluster configuration or status. The Event Emulator follows the same procedure used by the Cluster Manager given a particular event, but it does not execute any commands that would change the status of the Cluster Manager; thus it allows you to test a cluster's reaction to a particular event just as though the event actually occurred. You can run the Event Emulator through SMIT or from the command line.

NOTE The Event Emulator requires that both the Cluster SMUX peer daemon (**clsmuxpd**) and the Cluster Information Program (**clinfo**) be running on your cluster.

Error Emulation

HACMP provides a utility for testing your error notify methods. After you have added one or more error notify methods with the AIX Error Notification facility, you can test your methods by emulating an error. By inserting an error into the AIX error device file (/dev/error), you cause the AIX error daemon to run the appropriate prespecified notify method. This allows you to determine whether your predefined action is carried through, without having to actually cause the error to occur.

When the emulation is complete, you can view the error log by typing the **errpt** command to be sure the emulation took place. The error log entry has either the resource name EMULATOR or a name as specified by the user in the Resource Name field during the process of creating an error notify object. You can then determine whether the specified notify method was carried out.

More Information

For more information and the latest manuals for HACMP and other high-availability products, see the following Web pages from IBM:

```
http://www.ibm.com/servers/aix/products/ibmsw/high_avail_network/hacmp.html
http://www.ibm.com/servers/eserver/pseries/library/hacmp_docs.html
```

CHECKLIST

The following is a checklist for the key points in HACMP and clustering:

- ☐ Show how HACMP works and how to use it.
- ☐ Plan a cluster.
- ☐ What does HACMP actually do?
- ☐ Setup the hardware to create a cluster.
- ☐ Tune AIX for HACMP.
- ☐ Define and configure the resources to create a cluster.
- ☐ Synchronize the cluster.
- ☐ Define traditional IP address takeover (IPAT).
- ☐ Choose a resource group policy.
- ☐ Identify the administrative tasks for an HACMP system.

PART XIII

Storage Area Networks and Network Attached Storage

CHAPTER 29

SAN, NAS, and iSCSI
Consolidated Storage

The key concepts for storage these days are smaller, denser, and faster. In the forty-plus years of disk storage, one constant has remained the same. The rate at which you can read or write data on a disk is still dependent on how fast the disk platters spin. No electronics, adapters, or drivers can overcome the spindle speed dilemma. However, by making the platters smaller and denser while spinning the platter faster, IBM has achieved extraordinary results. As of this writing, the spindle speed has reached 15,000 RPM and the storage capacity of a single disk drive is up to 200GB and 290GB, with 400GB drives expected soon. In addition to these advancements in disk storage, write performance is enhanced by a large write cache available in many disk subsystems, and sequential data read performance is enhanced by a read-ahead cache. However, the read-ahead cache does not help for random disk reads.

At the other extreme are the micro-drives, which are about the size of a U.S. quarter. Currently, these drives have a storage capacity of 1GB or so. These micro-drives are coming to the market to replace flash memory cards for digital cameras and camcorders. But what is the key to all of this increased storage capacity on such a small footprint? Well, there are really two keys at work. The first is the advancement in drive head technology with Giant Magneto-Resistive technology heads. These new drive heads are made of layered metallic coatings of magnetic material capable of reading and writing up to 40GB of data per square inch. The second area of advancement is in the material used to coat the disk platter. New breakthroughs by IBM and their business partners have made the disk platters more dense and able to store more data per square inch. With this combination, how can you lose?

Compare these advancements with the past. For example, in 1956 the largest disk drive was 5MB. But this is not amazing part, this 5MB disk drive was three *feet* long and weighed *over* 200 pounds! These were the days when the IBM Customer Engineer (CE) could drive to your shop and fix the disk drive before it had a chance to *spin down.* Those were the days!

Leaving that aside, let's look at the latest in storage. If you have not noticed lately, storage is moving away from the server and onto networks. The old approach of each server having its own dedicated *attached* disk storage is gone. The new conception is that there will be no more wasted storage dedicated to a single server. The new storage paradigm is to have storage pools, managed by a vendor/OS-neutral network storage manager. This trend, called Enterprise Data Management, aims at consolidating the data into an environment that is more compatible with data sharing across a large variety of servers and operating systems.

STORAGE CONSOLIDATION

Consolidation of data involves some new techniques to handle all of the copies of the same data that are required for the business. The production data is gold, so it must be protected at all cost. This is where the first copy comes in, the backup copy. A typical night usually consists of producing a split mirror backup. This is where the gold data is synced to a backup copy of the data, which is a mirror image. Then the mirror is broken so that the now static point-in-time backup copy can be copied to tape for off-site storage. Different shops have different options for what to do with the backup copy until the next backup. Some shops want to resync the copies to within a few minutes of each other at a remote site, just in case.

However, what about the dev/test group? They need a copy of "real" data to do testing against, so there is the third copy. Then comes the audit group that wants to run reports against production data during normal business hours! When production has a fit about the slow response time, you get the privilege of keeping one more copy of the production data just for reporting. Now the storage requirements for this production data have quadrupled in size, but the original data has not grown. I think you get the picture of the storage problem that has been created.

Everyone has been talking about this "explosion of data!" There is no explosion of data that I see, but an explosion of *copies* of the same data! With UNIX seeing a 78 percent increase in market share, this consolidation of data is looking better all the time. With the focus moved away from the server, the new buzz words include: disaster recovery, data security, data availability, and data management. You may be surprised to find that storage management is much easier in a consolidated environment. The tools available with the new storage products are easy and fast to use, but they do detract from the Systems Administrator's normal ability to have full control. Now change requests are needed for everything, including allocating more disk space "on the fly."

Today's systems have a multihost attachment to storage, where any host can conceivably get to any part of the storage pool. This is the main focus of storage manufacturers today. To handle the multihost attached storage, the control of the data flow has moved away from the server to the controllers and adapters that make up the storage subsystem. On the server side, the disks are still represented as local disks by the operating system.

Storage Attachment Types

Most UNIX storage is attached to the system using SCSI attachments, but SCSI is slow compared to some other protocols on the market. Some UNIX vendors prefer SCSI; others would rather work with Serial Storage Architecture (SSA) disk subsystems. Still others like to use Fibre Channel or arbitrated loops. Then we have the new entry into the storage attachment arena, *iSCSI*. What is *iSCSI*? We will get to this concept, as well as the others. We really need to look at these one at a time.

SCSI

If you have been around machines, you know about SCSI protocol devices and connection requirements. SCSI speeds are going up, but you are still restricted to the speed of the slowest device on the SCSI chain. Now SCSI speeds reach 640 MB/sec, but the cable length is limited to only eight meters.

SSA

IBM implemented the Serial Storage Architecture (SSA) disk subsystem as a means of gaining multipath high-speed disk performance. SSA works like this: You have IBM model 7133, disk storage *trays,* or drawers. Each 7133 can hold up to 16 SSA disks. On the server, the SSA adapters have two *loops,* with each loop having two adapter connections. Most SSA adapters can support two independent loops. Each SSA loop has two paths that are bidirectional and high speed, up to 100 MB/Sec. This SSA subsystem has a multitude of disk configurations including JBOD (just a bunch of disks) and RAID 1, 3, 5, and 1+0. Depending on the disk layout and configuration, SSA disks have the fastest throughput to date.

iSCSI

With *i*SCSI, you have an emerging protocol for which the standard is just being settled on by the Internet Engineering Task Force (IETF). The *i*SCSI protocol is just what you would expect, a SCSI protocol over the IP network. Basically, the SCSI information is sent as packets over the IP network; at the destination, the IP packet header is removed, and the content is sent to the storage device as normal SCSI protocol traffic. The result is the ability to send SCSI block I/O protocol data over the network using the TCP/IP protocol.

Since this SCSI storage traffic is now traveling over the IP network, you may see a real need for a separate, *i*SCSI IP traffic–only, network. Some of the benefits of *i*SCSI include extended distance, ease of connectivity, and a standard TCP/IP transport protocol. Keep an eye on this protocol, it may take over the world!

NETWORK ATTACHED STORAGE (NAS)

Network attached storage (NAS) uses the IP local area network (LAN) to access remote storage. A SAN is different from NAS in that the SAN uses a storage network connected through Fibre Channel switches, routers, bridges, and directors as a "storage area network" completely independent of the "IP network," but NAS uses *storage appliances* on a network. The best term that I have heard to describe NAS is "NFS on steroids." The idea of NAS is file sharing across the IP LAN network. The data is transported between the server and the NAS over the LAN using the TCP/IP protocol. This allows for an any-to-any connection using the LAN as a fabric.

The data is accessed using common network access protocols such as NFS for UNIX servers and CIFS for Windows systems. With this technology, you can also detach the tape libraries from the servers with tools such as Tivoli Storage Manager (TSM). This allows sharing of tape devices and provides a better return on investment.

However, you cannot just throw some disk drives on the network and expect any communication to take place. Some smarts must be built in to manage the data communications and storage. Thus a NAS system includes a server, which has an operating system with attached storage, making it a storage server or a network appliance, not part of the network infrastructure. The key difference between NAS on the one hand and SAN and *i*SCSI on the other is that client I/O to NAS is done using *file* I/O, as opposed to the *block* I/O operations used in *i*SCSI and SANs. File I/O means that the only thing that is known is the filename, but not *where* the file resides. Only the remote NAS internal server knows where the file is located. NAS and SAN are contrasted in Table 29-1.

Storage	I/O Type	Characteristics
NAS	File I/O	Uses the existing TCP/IP LAN infrastructure as a transport mechanism
SAN	Block I/O	Uses Fibre Channel, a transport mechanism utilizing a serialized SCSI protocol over fibre

Table 29-1.   NAS Versus SAN

Using NAS, not only can you access the storage from the network, but by setting up a NAS gateway, you can also have connectivity to the SAN, which uses Fibre Channel. This is the wave of the future for networked storage. Some of the benefits of NAS include ease of implementation (NAS uses the existing LAN network), scalable pooled storage, and heterogeneous file sharing.

STORAGE AREA NETWORK (SAN)

A storage area network (SAN) is a centralized storage array in which you remove most of the local host storage management in favor of centralized storage management. A SAN has a specialized high-performance network that is dedicated to SAN traffic. The benefits are consolidation of disk storage capacity (servers and storage can be placed at different locations, offering better utilization of storage across platforms), lower overall storage cost, better control of storage resources, and lower cost to manage the infrastructure. With all of this comes more flexibility for the enterprise as a whole, which gains the ability to dynamically allocate storage as required to any of the servers in the SAN environment. This approach contrasts with the one server–one storage device conception, which results in wasted disk space because the storage cannot be shared.

Another great benefit of the SAN is extended and remote storage capabilities that allow for remote mirrored sites. Wow! Disaster recovery testing just got easier; we just need a remote site to mirror to. Well, before we get too far along, let's first look at the components of the SAN.

Three Type of SAN Topologies

To suit different application requirements, a SAN can be configured in any of three topologies, plus some combinations. For a two-node configuration, a *point-to-point* topology can be used. For a dual-path, multinode configuration, an *arbitrated loop* can be used. For maximum flexibility, a SAN *fabric* can be constructed.

Point to Point

A *point-to-point topology* can be used when there are exactly two nodes. This is a SAN topology in its simplest form, which provides for full bandwidth between the two nodes. However, it does not allow for any expansion of the SAN.

Fibre Channel Arbitrated Loop

In a *Fibre Channel Arbitrated Loop (FC_AL)*, the nodes/ports (server and storage nodes and devices) are configured in a loop configuration, using a hub or a switch, which looks eerily similar to a Token Ring configuration. Communications within the loop are accomplished by one node initiating a link with another, and data frames are transmitted in one direction around the loop. As more nodes are added to the loop, the bandwidth available to each node in the loop is reduced because nodes share the loop's bandwidth.

The reason that we call these "arbitrated loops" is that a node must arbitrate access to the loop when it wants to communicate with another node within the loop. When the node wins arbitration, it may then open a communications link with another node and maintain control of the loop until another node wins arbitration to take control of the loop. When communication is completed, the link is dropped, and the loop is available for a new communications link to be established. For this configuration to work, a set of protocols is used to control the interloop communications. These must include means to

- Assign node, or port, addresses within the loop
- Add new nodes/ports to the loop
- Open arbitration to gain access to the loop
- Open a communications link between two nodes in the loop
- Close the communications link when the nodes have finished talking
- Implement a policy whereby all nodes in the loop have a fair chance to gain access to the loop

As you can see, this is a tricky way of doing business, and if the nodes in the loop are at a distance, it can be slow because of communications latency. So this is not the best option in a large environment.

There are two types of loops. A *private loop* talks only to other private nodes and loops and does not connect to a SAN fabric. A *public loop* allows communications to a SAN fabric, thus extending the loop. A loop type is defined by the two upper bytes of its address. If they are zero, it is a private loop. If they are nonzero (positive integers), it is public. An example of using a public arbitrated loop is allowing access to a group of tape devices, which must reside on a public loop, from the SAN fabric. You need to take care that your public and private loops remain separate when a SAN fabric is involved.

Addressing is done at the port level. The port address is 24 bits and has the capability of addressing a total of 127 ports. These are called *arbitrated loop physical addresses (AL_PS)*. The loop priority is determined by the numeric value of the address; lower-numbered addresses have greater priority, and so, as you would expect, the disk arrays will have lower addresses. When two nodes in the loop communicate, a *port login* must first take place. A port login is nothing more than the swapping of information between the two nodes attempting to create a communications link. Once this takes place then a communications link can be opened between the two nodes and can be maintained until another node wins arbitration to gain control of the loop.

Fibre Channel Switched Fabric

The Fibre Channel Switched Fabric (FC_SW) consists of one or more Fibre Channel interconnecting components as defined by ANSI Technical Committee X3T11. This ANSI standard was originally used for fiber optics, but the spelling was changed from *fiber* to the French spelling *fibre* because it now uses both fiber optic cable and copper cables. However, Fibre Channel on the Enterprise Storage Server (ESS) is always based on fiber optics rather than copper cables.

The first things that we want to look at are the Fibre Channel switch and Fibre Channel directors. I have seen these terms used interchangeably, and in some sense this is justified. At present they are both multiport Fibre Channel components that use 100 MB/Sec for internal transport and gigabit external transport of data frames. Both fiber optic and copper cable can use gigabit transport, but copper has a 30-meter cable length limit, and optical fiber has a 10-kilometer limit. Unlike in an arbitrated loop where bandwidth is shared, in a Fibre Channel switched fabric, bandwidth actually *increases* as more devices are added. This is because these are multiport devices, and as you add devices you add bandwidth with the increased port paths.

Addressing in the Fibre Channel switched fabric is done using a Simple Name Server (SNS). This is needed because two addressing schemes must coexist, the 24-bit port address and a 64-bit World Wide Port Name (WWPN) address. The 64-bit WWPN is similar a network MAC address and is assigned, or burned in, when the device is manufactured. The switch assigns the 24-bit port address. The SNS, which resides inside the switch, keeps track of this two-tier addressing for you. The port address is broken into three parts: *domain, area,* and *port.* The domain is the address of the switch and has 239 possible values (256 minus some overhead addresses), so you can have 239 switches in the SAN fabric. The area is used to point to a group of one or more ports on a device as well as ports to public arbitrated loops. So each multiport device has a different area number, for a total of 256 areas. The port part of the address refers to the actual port on the device. When you multiply all of these together, you get a maximum number of ports equal to 15,663,104 port addresses. This should be more than enough in a typical Fibre Channel SAN fabric installation.

As in the arbitrated loop scenario, a login must occur between nodes. In the case of a Fibre Channel switched fabric, a *fabric login* must take place. This too opens up a communications link for the nodes to talk. When a node initiates a fabric login, it uses a port address of all zeros, thus signaling the SNS in the switch to assign an address using the domain, area, and port addressing scheme. At least you do not have to keep up with all of this! A public loop goes through the same process when accessing the fabric, but the loop address is used in assigning the port address. At this point, the address is entered into the SNS database.

On connection, the same process of switching and routing is used as in an IP network. In this case, the destination part of the frame packet is read, and the frame packet is routed through the fabric to the correct destination node. Note that the switch needs to have a buffering mechanism and alternate routes to the destination. This not only increases performance but also avoids dropped frame packets. Also take note of the routing mechanism used. Most switches use a *spanning tree*, which is defined in the IEEE 802.1 standard, in determining the route to take. This is needed to ensure that the packets do not get out of order in transmission between nodes when frame packets take different routes. The spanning tree approach does dynamic route determination and opens and closes, or locks, certain routes, thus keeping frame packets in order by forcing all packets to take the same path. This also increases the performance throughout the SAN fabric. Static routes can also be defined; should a static route go down, a new dynamic route through the fabric will be determined and used. Another nice thing about the fabric is that devices can be added to, and removed from, the fabric dynamically. This dynamic functionality is accomplished through a process of device state change notification and includes devices going offline.

ZONING

Zoning is used to limit access to areas in the fabric and can be thought of as a private virtual network. Since we are talking about an AIX environment in this book, it is fair to assume that you know not to mix UNIX and Windows environments! This is the cause of a lot of problems. We can separate the UNIX and Windows systems within the SAN fabric using zoning. You must zone out the Windows components because Windows will take every bit of the storage space that it sees for itself by writing header, or label, information on each disk. Major problem!

In another sense, we want to segregate our AIX environments too. We want separation between machines and between production and test environments. We can also make a backup by splitting the mirror, or zoning out the backup. So as you can see, zoning is a powerful tool in keeping everything in the fabric organized, but zoning usually does not go to this extreme. Devices within a zone can communicate only with other devices within the same zone. However, devices can belong to more than one zone. We can zone the fabric via hardware or software zoning. Hardware zoning acts by granting or denying access at the port address level, or the physical port level. This can include any port device or group of devices. Hardware zoning is done at the routing level through a filtering process and has a low performance impact. Software zoning accomplishes the same result but does so using the SNS in the switch. Within the SNS, you can zone at the device or port level, gaining somewhat more flexibility. Any device within a zone may belong to other zones, or zone members, so this process can get quit complex, and careful consideration must be given when *cross zoning*.

There is a security concern with software zoning, and every aspect of the hardware and software used in the fabric must be considered. In particular, consideration must be given to the ability of a device to bypass the SNS zoning table and make a direct connection to a device through new hardware discovery techniques. For this reason, it is recommended that you use only hardware zoning. Of course, as these products mature, this security concern should be resolved, and with the added flexibility of software zoning, it will become the preferred method. Another option for protecting from unauthorized access to a storage device is through logical unit number (LUN) masking. A LUN is nothing more than a *logical disk.* When a node requests access to a storage device, it is given through the LUN. The storage device can either accept or reject the request to this logical disk. The access control list is user defined but maintained through the device control access program. You will see this later in this chapter, as we consider the StorWatch Specialist that is used in the IBM Enterprise Storage Server, also known as the Shark. Most shops use one large zone and LUN masking for segregation.

When the Fabric Fills Up

As your infrastructure expands, you need to expand the fabric to accommodate the new devices. (Remember that new ERP project!) Adding more Fibre Channel switches is the easiest method and has many benefits. Adding more switches is referred to as *switch cascading.* You can add switches to the fabric dynamically without powering off anything, but extreme caution must be used, so follow the manufacturer's instructions carefully. With switch cascading comes increased bandwidth with the added Inter-Switch Links (ISLs), and extended high availability of the fabric because more switches mean more device ports. You sometimes just need more distance in the fabric, and switch cascading can make this an easy task. As you add switches, you also end up with a distributed name server across the fabric, which adds to the fault tolerance of the fabric itself. However, you still have a limit of 239 total switches in the fabric. Be careful, as you add to the SAN fabric, that you do not create a bottleneck of traffic through the fabric and that the hop count maximum is not exceeded. The hop count maximum varies, depending on the hardware and software used in the fabric.

SAN Enterprise Storage Management Standards

With the mix of SAN hardware vendors, you would hope that every company is not doing its own thing. If this were the case, you would see incompatibility across the SAN, LAN, and WAN, actually across the entire enterprise. The good news is that vendors are working to come up with some standards for SAN hardware, software, and control mechanisms to make everything work together as one cohesive unit. The vendors group called the Storage Network Management Working Group (SNMWG) is working to come up with industry standards for the management and reliability of the SAN as an entire environment, which extends to the application level, where there must be a standard for APIs as well.

Management of the SAN infrastructure involves a consolidation of all of the available tools into one management application. This must encompass data, resource, and network management, and you need to think of the SAN as one entity. We have all heard that *data* is the driver that makes or breaks a business, and Quality of Service (QoS) is always at the heart of the discussion. So it should come as no surprise that the *quality of the data* must be maintained, or we can all just go home. Centralized management of the SAN is usually accomplished through some kind of control workstation using a central SAN management tool. This is a must because of the explosion of servers and copies of data. Now one Systems Administrator is expected to manage three terabytes of data. Automation is the key to making this possible, and the SAN management tools provide it. We do not want to manage everything one server at a time!

The SAN management tool must be able to handle all of the follow SAN pieces:

- SAN resources
- SAN data
- SAN elements
- SAN network
- SAN fabric performance monitoring/correction
- SAN error monitoring/correction

Industry standards are being focused on the combination of these elements. We often hear the terms *inbound* and *outbound* in connection with management of SAN elements. Inbound refers to the internal communication between elements within the SAN fabric. This communication uses the SCSI Enclosure Services (SES) protocol, also known as SCSI-3 Enclosure Services. This is totally internal to the SAN and does not have any LAN connectivity. Other inbound standards are in the works. Outbound refers to the external communications of the SAN internals using TCP/IP. This is normally done using the Simple Network Management Protocol (SNMP) and the Management Information Base (MIB). These are both widely used protocols supported by most LAN and WAN vendors. Both of these methods provide a monitoring path for the SAN internals.

Tivoli SANergy

Another aspect of a SAN is the capability for file sharing among machines. With file sharing, you have more control and better consolidation of data. IBM uses Tivoli SANergy for this purpose. Some of the benefits of Tivoli SANergy include file sharing at the speed of a SAN, LAN-free and serverless data movement, and heterogeneous file sharing. I recommend the following Redbook for details on installing, configuring, and using SANergy: *A Practical Guide to Tivoli SANergy,* `http://www.redbooks.ibm.com/pubs/pdfs/redbooks/sg246146.pdf`.

ENTERPRISE STORAGE SERVER (ESS) A.K.A. THE SHARK

The Enterprise Storage Server (ESS), code name Shark, is a consolidated storage device that consists of two tightly coupled RS/6000 or pSeries machines that have full failover capability. The internal storage uses SSA disk subsystems, which are attached in loops. The disks can be configured as RAID or non-RAID, known as JBOD (just a bunch of disks). As of this writing, only RAID 5 is supported. However, in the next release support for RAID 0+1 is to be added. Some people call this RAID 10, but there is really no such standard. RAID 0+1 will add more options to get faster I/O capability. RAID 5 will perform better than JBOD when your load is mainly reads and sequential operations because the data is striped across all of the drives, which translates into more spindles and read/write heads in action. This allows more I/O to be performed in parallel. When RAID 0+1 is added, you will see a huge increase in write capability, too. See Table 29-2 for a description of the different RAID levels.

There is a potential problem with the LVM's locking mechanism when you have multiple paths from the server to the Shark. Here is an example of what can happen:

A colleague and I were adding a long list of logical volumes using a shell script before we realized that the volume group was not configured as a "Big" volume group. So, we just entered the command to change the VG on the fly, **chvg -B** *<vg_name>*, expecting that whenever the VG lock got a break, it would change the characteristic of the VG, but it blew up in our face! The lock was on a single path, so the command just went down another path and attempted to change the VG to a big volume group while the LVs were being created. You know what we had to do: stop the LV-creating script, remove all of the previously configured LVs, make the VG a Big VG, and restart the LV creation script. I never tried that again! So the LVM needs a better handle on controlling multipaths during VG locks. The Austin Development Center is aware and is working on a solution.

The ESS allows for storage consolidation and high-performance data solutions. The ESS supports all of the major platforms, including UNIX, Windows, and mainframes. Another huge benefit of the ESS lies in the areas of disaster recovery and data availability. The ESS design has no single point of failure and allows for failover servicing, which eliminates downtime.

RAID 0	Disk striping without fault tolerance
RAID 1	Disk mirroring with duplexing and fault tolerance
RAID 2	Disk striping with error correction using an algorithm
RAID 3	Disk striping with parity information on a single disk
RAID 4	Disk striping with large data blocks and one disk reserved for parity
RAID 5	Disk striping with parity information distributed evenly among the drives
RAID 0+1	Disk mirroring of RAID 0 arrays. Highest data transfer performance

Table 29-2. Disk RAID Levels

How the ESS Got Here

The first ESS was introduced in the first quarter of 1999. This was a major step into enterprise storage for IBM. This first model of the Shark was the 2105 Model E10/E20. The storage capacity was an impressive 420GB up to 11.2TB using 9GB and 18GB 10,000 RPM drives or the 7,500 RPM 36GB drives. With a storage cache of 6GB, this model was offered for the S/390 and open systems using the following attachment types:

- ESCON
- Ultra SCSI
- FICON (using a bridge)
- Fibre Channel (using a bridge)

The only copy service offered in the first quarter of 1999 was concurrent copy, which maintained mirrored copies of data. In the third quarter of 1999, IBM upgraded the E10/E20 models to F10/F20, which added the power of a pair of four-way RS/6000 Model H70 machines in a tightly coupled cluster. The existing Sharks received a brain transplant with the new machine models, and the cache was upped with an option of either 8GB or 16GB. With this upgrade, customers gained up to a 50 percent increase in performance.

In the first quarter of 2000, copy services were expanded to include FlashCopy for the S/390. Native Fibre Channel was introduced with an option for either direct or fabric attachment. Later in the second quarter of 2000, copy services were expanded again to include FlashCopy for open systems and added PPRC into the mix.

In the third quarter of 2001, IBM added Native FICON for direct or fabric attachment through McData and INRANGE model switches and directors. Longwave and shortwave Fibre Channel and FICON host adapters were added, along with an enhanced ESCON host adapter. The cache was upgraded to a maximum of 24GB, and CLI (Client Interface) was introduced. In the fourth quarter of 2001, 73GB 10,000 RPM drives were released, increasing to the storage capacity of a single ESS to 22TB. The Licensed Internal Code (LIC) was upgraded to allow the mixing of drive sizes, of course in different arrays within the Shark. Additional Linux support was added, in conjunction with the AIX Toolbox for Linux Applications, to include new application program interfaces (APIs) to AIX so that recompiled Linux applications using these APIs would not have to reference their own libraries.

In the second quarter of 2002, IBM introduced the 15,000 RPM drives in 18GB, 36GB, and 72GB sizes. The distance limits for Peer-to-Peer Remote Copy (PPRC) were extended, and the copy services command-line interface (CLI) for Tru64 UNIX was released.

The next generation of the ESS has the brains of a six-way 668 MHz pSeries 660 model 6H1. Did you get that? This pSeries 660 has six processors and runs at a clock speed of 668 MHz. Up to 32GB of cache is supported, and the Non-Volatile Storage (NVS) write cache has grown to 2GB.

The most interesting part of this Shark is that support for RAID 0+1 is added to the RAID 5 disk configuration options in coming releases. The result of the enhancements made to the ESS is twofold. For heavy storage requirements, a performance boost of up to two times is seen. This value will not be so great if you storage demands are not stressing the current model. I am guessing that this model will be called the G10/G20, since the last models were E and F, but I may be wrong.

Host Bus Adapters

Communications between the servers and the ESS is done through *host bus adapters (HBAs).* You have four choices in HBA adapters, ESCON, FICON, Fibre Channel, or SCSI. Each server can have multiple connections spread across the host adapter bays. This not only provides better availability to the server in case you lose an HBA bay, but it also spreads the I/O across all of the adapters. This is done automatically if you install the *Data Path Optimizer / Subsystem Device Driver* on the server. Up to 16 HBAs can be installed, except for Fibre Channel, which can support up to 8 dual-port HBAs.

Data Path Optimizer / Subsystem Device Driver (SDD)

The Data Path Optimizer / Subsystem Device Driver (SDD), for the open systems environment, enables multiple Fibre Channel and SCSI paths from the server to the target LUN group. The SDD optimizes the workload across all of the available HBA paths. This improves the server I/O by allowing parallel access to the same data, which balances the load. The SSD is a pseudo–device driver that resides on the server and provides the following functions:

- Dynamic load balancing of I/O across multiple paths
- Enhanced data availability
- Failover protection in multipath environments

The SDD adds another layer to the protocol stack and provides dynamic path protection by path monitoring and selection for data flow and load balancing, which eliminates data-flow bottlenecks between the server and the ESS.

The SDD supports AIX tracing. The **trace** ID for SDD is 2F8 and is used in the following manner:

To Start SDD Tracing
```
# trace -a -j 2F8
```

To Stop the Tracing
```
# trcstop
```

To Read the Trace Report
```
# trcrpt | more
```

The AIX trace function requires the **bos.sysmgt.trace** fileset.

The SDD provides a set of **datapath** commands that are used to display the status of adapters and devices, in addition to setting path conditions. The **datapath** commands are shown in Table 29-3.

The SDD works only with SDD `vpath` devices. Refer to the product documentation for the installation and configuration instructions.

ESS Configuration

I want to start with a word of caution. You can dig yourself into a hole very quickly at any time when working with a Shark. Everyone needs to download "Jesse's" document from IBM. Jesse Adams III wrote this document to help out the field engineers who were encountering some strange problems with varied configurations. The document is called "Data Path Optimizer on an ESS—Installation Procedures/Potential Gotchas." You can download this document for printing in PDF format. You will save yourself a lot of time and trouble if you read this document and keep a hard copy next to your terminal. You can download and print Jesse's document from the following URL:

```
ftp://ftp.software.ibm.com/storage/subsystem/tools/sdddpo-v120.pdf
```

Once you receive your ESS, install the hardware, power on the storage system, and see blinky lights, you are ready to watch the CE begin to configure the Shark. You may be surprised that not a whole lot of configuration is required initially. You do want to configure the network, serial, and storage communications; configure the StorWatch Master Console; call home and remote support; and cover any of the options for which the CE is going to ask you for configuration information.

One of the first things to check is the version of the Licensed Internal Code (LIC). Make sure that you are at the latest, most stable version of code. You can think of the LIC as a type of system microcode. LIC controls what the Web browser looks like, the disk drive configuration capabilities, and everything else that you see when interacting with the ESS.

The ESS consists of two RS/6000 or pSeries machines in a tightly coupled cluster configuration. Data is stored in cache, which is installed in the cluster nodes. The write

`datapath query adapter`	Displays information about adapters
`datapath query adaptstats`	Displays performance information for adapters
`datapath query device`	Displays information about devices
`datapath query devstats`	Displays performance information for devices
`datapath set adapter`	Sets device paths attached to an adapter online and offline
`datapath set device`	Sets the path of a device online or offline

Table 29-3. Datapath Commands

data to the disks is stored in the NVS (nonvolatile storage) in the *opposite* cluster node. Each of the two cluster nodes has a high-performance cache that can be configured with 3GB, 4GB, 8GB, 16GB, or 32GB of Synchronous Dynamic RAM (SDRAM) that provides single-bit, double-bit error detection. The ESS realizes full redundancy with dual power supplies, dual cooling fans, dual battery backup, and dual machines controlling the ESS. Communications are handled to the servers through host bus adapters (HBAs) and to the disk storage through device adapters (DAs) pairs. The clustered configuration allows for failover in the event of a cluster node failure. In this event, the ESS takes corrective action and transfers control to the surviving node in the cluster. The result is no interruption in service and no data loss.

The ESS supports using mixed drive sizes (intermix) in 8-packs. These 8-packs must be added to the ESS in pairs. Intermix support is available on all ESS models and provides for many different configuration options.

The ESS requires careful configuration planning. It is extremely important that you take your time planning the layout of data and give careful consideration of LUN sizes. The LUNs can be configured to just about any size that you want to use. Depending on your application and platform, this decision will vary. These are the basic steps to start your configuration:

- Draw a map that represents a logical view of how you want the ESS laid out.

- Use the logical view to map to the physical devices within the ESS.

- Ensure that you have done your homework for the required store capacity for current and future storage needs.

- Document your layout so that it is easy to understand when you configure the ESS using the StorWatch Specialist.

Let's go on to look at what the StorWatch Specialist and Expert can do.

ESS StorWatch Specialist

The ESS StorWatch Specialist is a Web browser–based interface for configuring and controlling the ESS. In fact, you can control many Sharks from a single Specialist session. The capabilities of the StorWatch Specialist and its look and feel are completely dependent upon the LIC. If you have a back level of the Licensed Internal Code, you may not be able to exercise some options. An example is the ability to mix different drive sizes within the same ESS. With the ESS Specialist, you can conduct the following tasks:

- Show the status of the ESS

- Monitor the ESS error logs

- Create and modify RAID and JBOD (just a bunch of disks) ranks

- Show the Licensed Internal Code (LIC) version level

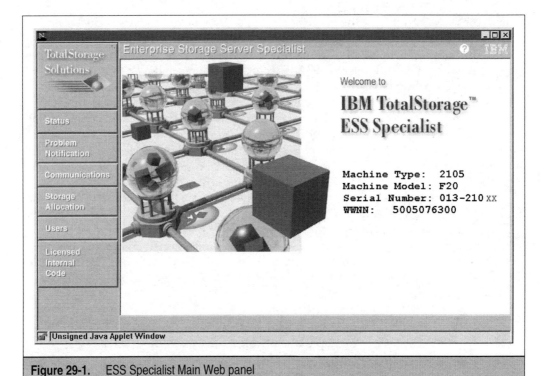

Figure 29-1. ESS Specialist Main Web panel

- Create users at various authorization levels
- Add and reassign disk volumes to hosts
- Show and modify the ESS configuration
- Configure SCSI and Fibre host ports
- Change and show communications settings

The ESS Specialist main Web panel is shown in Figure 29-1.

Configuring Call-Home and Remote Support

You may not like getting a phone call in the middle of the night. However, you may want to wake up some of the IBM support staff. The ESS call-home feature allows automatic notification to IBM service. Then IBM support team can log in remotely to access and service the ESS. You can also set up e-mail notifications. A typical call-home e-mail looks like the following sample.

Sample E-Mail Notification from Phoning Home with a Bad Disk

```
root@yogi.bear.na.cave.abc on 05/07/2002 09:55:20 AM
To:  rmichael@booboo.na.cave.abc
```

```
cc:
Subject:

# Begin of call home record.............= BEGIN OF FILE (2480)
# Product Manufacturer ID and Date......= 0752642001
# Business/Company Name.................= DINO-BooBoo Enterprises
# Product Machine type and model number.= 2105F20
# Product serial number.................= 7520220
# Call back expander port ID............= 1
# Outside line prefix...................= 9,
# Customer voice phone number...........= 5552321212
# Customer offshift voice phone number..=
# LIC level of local complex............= 1.3.3.37
# LIC level of remote complex...........= 1.3.3.37
# Reporting Cluster Number..............= 1
# Record type...........................= 1
# Report time/date stamp................= 05/07/02 09:55:18 EDT
# Host system type(s)...................= escon, fibre
# Level_CPSS information................= shark/R6.CPSS/engr/build/sint0821
# Possible FRUs to replace:
#
# Engineering     FRU          Likely FRU Location
# FRU Name        Name         to fix Description
#------------------------------------------------------------------------------

  rsDDM0202     36.4GB 10K DDM     100%  R1-U1-W3-D2
#------------------------------------------------------------------------------
# Additional Information
#
# Engineering FRU Name ... = rsDDM0202
#   Part Number ......... = 18P2199
#
# Primary Failing Unit ... = 2105-F20    75-20220
# Reporting Unit ......... = 2105-F20    75-20220
#
# Problem ID ............. = 42
# ESC .................... = E100
# SRN .................... = 10265
# Problem Status ......... = PENDING
# Description ............ = SSA subsystem detected error
# Additional Message ..... = NONE
# Failing Cluster ........ = 1
# Reporting Cluster ...... = 1
# Failing Resource ....... = rsDDM0202
# First Occurrence ....... = Tue May 7 09:54:28 2002
# Last Occurrence ........ = Tue May 7 09:54:28 2002
# Failure Count .......... = 1
# Re-presentation Interval = 28800
# Remaining Presentations. = 0
# Isolation Procedure .... = NONE
```

```
# Failure Actions ........ = 0000 "PERFORM PROBLEM DETERMINATION PROCEDURES"
# Probable Cause ........ = 6310 "DASD DEVICE"
# Failure Cause ......... = 6310 "DISK DRIVE"
# User Actions .......... = FFFF "NONE"
# End of record flag ..... = END OF FILE
```

From this e-mail, you can see that there was a disk failure. The FRU name is rsDDM0202, which is a 36.4GB 10,000 RPM disk drive. The location of the failed drive is also known to be R1-U1-W3-D2, and the part number is 18P2199.

This tells the whole story; now all that is needed is a CE to come and replace the drive. This is also automatic. The disk is ordered and sent to your site. The CE shows up at about the same time and replaces the drive, or he/she may call and make an appointment. At any rate, you always know if the ESS detects a problem.

Establishing LUNs and Assigning Storage to Specific Hosts

Now that you have carefully planned the storage layout in the ESS, you are ready to configure the storage for a particular host. This "host" does not have to be an actual host; it can just be a placeholder that you defined as a host, which is another nice thing about configuring the ESS. The first step is to go into the Storage Allocation panel, as shown in Figure 29-2.

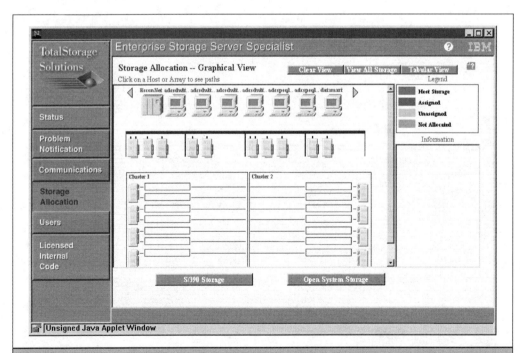

Figure 29-2. ESS Specialist Storage Allocation panel

Next click the Open System Storage button on the lower-right side of the ESS Storage Allocation panel in Figure 29-2. The next screen to appear has all of the information on the currently allocated storage in the ESS cluster. To add more storage to the storage pool, which is our task, click the **Add Volumes** button at the bottom of the **Open Systems Storage** panel, as shown in Figure 29-3.

The Open Systems Storage panel shows the current configuration and attachments of the ESS and the LUNs attached to each host. You can also modify the host/storage attachments here, as you will see in the section, **Moving Storage** "Attachment" from one AIX Server to Another. Our task is to add more storage, so let's keep going. From the ESS Specialist Open Systems Storage panel, you want to click the **Add Volumes** button, at the bottom-left side of the panel. This selection places you in a graphical view of the ESS storage allocation. The green area is storage that has not been allocated, as you can see in the legend on the top right as shown in Figure 29-4.

I have already selected the storage I want to use, so I want to point out the items of interest in the panel. To add storage, you *must* select one or more hosts to attach the new storage to. For a first-time configuration, I set up a dummy placeholder host, or hosts. Then as I create the new storage, I select the dummy placeholder *and* the actual

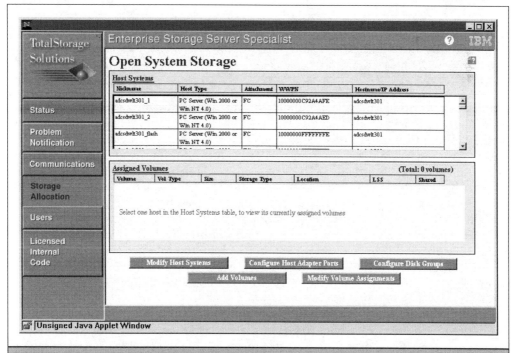

Figure 29-3.   ESS Specialist Open System Storage panel

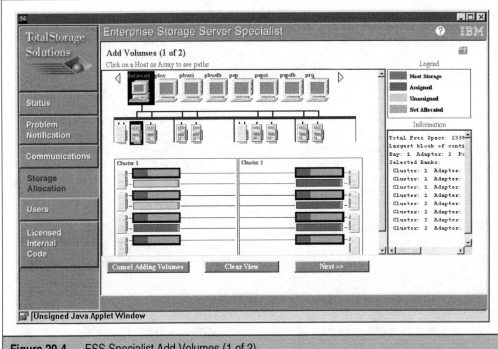

Figure 29-4. ESS Specialist Add Volumes (1 of 2)

host I want the storage attached to. Using this method allows me to detach the storage from one host and attach it to another without loosing every host definition on the LUNs in the process. This is just a placeholder, so make the dummy host names descriptive of what the storage is used for. An example is a VG and host name combination.

After we select the host, the next step is to highlight the storage arrays that you want to use. This is where your excellent storage planning will be seen by everyone. To select multiple arrays, just hold down the CTRL key and click each array you want to select. I have selected every A loop array in the ESS, as shown in Figure 29-4.

When you click **Next**, you move to the **Add Volumes (2 of 2)** panel, as shown in Figure 29-5. Now you have to make some actual configuration decisions.

In your planning, you decided on a LUN size for this group of storage. For my demonstration, I like to use a 64GB LUN size. I want to add 32 LUNs, each having a LUN size of 64GB, but there is still one more major decision to make. Do you want to add the LUNs sequentially, or does spreading the LUNs across all of the arrays make more sense? This decision varies, depending on what you are doing. For this example, I want to spread the partitions across all of the arrays. At the bottom of the panel, you

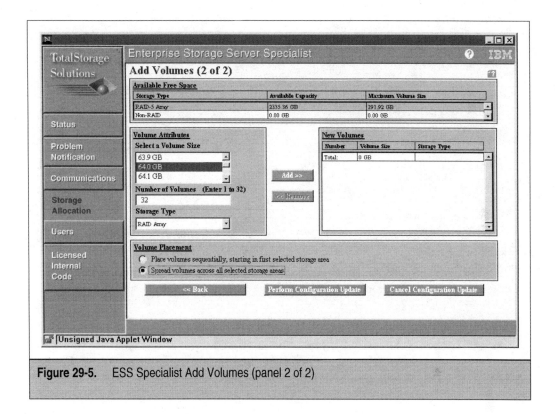

Figure 29-5.   ESS Specialist Add Volumes (panel 2 of 2)

can see a box named **Volume Placement**. I selected the second option to spread the volumes across all of the arrays.

When you are happy with the selections, click the **Perform Configuration Update** button at the bottom of the panel. The next panel, shown in the illustration, gives you an estimated time for the configuration task to complete.

Click **Yes** to continue with the configuration. As the configuration is being performed, the ESS gives you status of the progression as a percentage.

During this time, the ESS is setting up all of the pointers that are needed to format the disk set. The actual formatting can take many hours, depending on how much storage is being configured. When the configuration update is complete, you see another panel telling you that the task is complete but that the formatting continues.

After you click **OK**, you are again presented with the **Add Storage (2 of 2)** panel, as shown in Figure 29-6. However, this time you can see the new storage allocations on the right side in the **New Volumes** box. Each of the new 64GB LUNs is listed in this box.

To exit the panel in Figure 29-6, click **Cancel Configuration Update**. This will take you back to **Storage Allocation**.

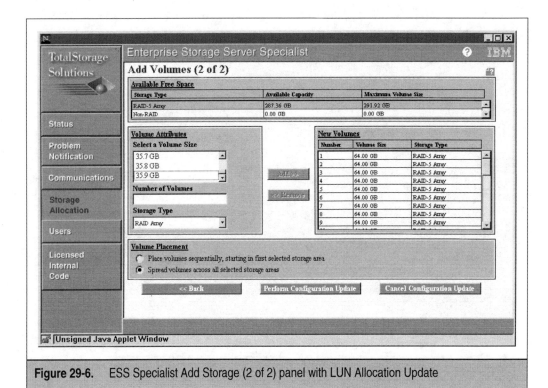

Figure 29-6. ESS Specialist Add Storage (2 of 2) panel with LUN Allocation Update

To check on the formatting status you click the **Refresh Status** button on the **Modify Volume Assignments** panel, as shown in Figure 29-7.

In the first column, under **Volume**, you will see a percentage for each volume that is being formatted. Notice that all but the last entries are 30GB LUNs. I started these earlier, and they are still formatting. When you create multiple volumes in a short period of time, you may end up with a lot of ESS activity, which is not a problem for the horsepower of the ESS. However, if one set of volumes has a lock on the disks, then the configuration submission is refused. Don't worry! This will free up in a minute or two. I get this problem mostly when I configure a lot of small LUNs in a series. Just wait a couple of minutes and try again.

This is about it for configuring new volumes in the ESS. The look and feel of these panels will change over time, especially since IBM has put out a free MES to replace all of the Windows NT ESS Master Consoles with the new Linux Master Consoles. With the new consoles, you have serial communication, as well as TCP/IP communications. With the serial link, the ESS is not dependent on the TCP/IP network to talk to the Linux Master Console.

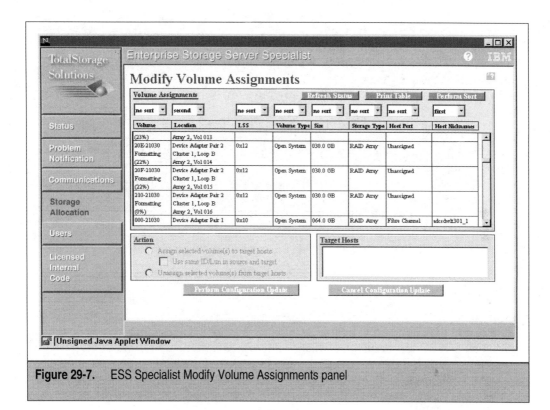

Figure 29-7. ESS Specialist Modify Volume Assignments panel

Moving Storage "Attachment" from one AIX Server to Another

This is not a physical attachment, but an attachment through the storage area network. The example here is a typical situation. You have an application and database that you need to move from one server to another server for testing or QA. This is not rocket science. The steps involved are shown in the following scenario.

Scenario   The disks in the ESS are currently attached to the host **yogi**. A ruling by management requires the QA group to test the application load on a smaller, lower-cost machine, which is known as **booboo**. There are two volume groups, called **appvg** and **dbvg**. The **appvg** VG has journaled filesystems, and **dbvg** contains raw logical volumes only. The task is to move the application and database from **yogi** to **booboo**.

On yogi   The first step is to save the current configuration on **yogi** in a file. Execute the following commands:

```
# datapath query device > /tmp/data-path-query-[$HOST].mmddyy
# lsvgcfg > /tmp/lsvpcfg-[$HOST].mmddyy
```

Running these commands *often* will same you a lot of time when you need to reconfigure the storage again on the same host.

Now we can remove the **appvg** and **dbvg** volume groups from **yogi**. First, unmount all of the filesystems associated with the appvg volume group. To get a list of the filesystems to unmount, enter the following command.

```
# lsvg -l appvg | grep open | grep -v N/A | awk '{print $7}'
```

For each mount point listed, use the **umount** command to unmount each filesystem. If you have a problem unmounting a filesystem, then it is in use. Use the **fuser** command to find the cause of the activity. If a user is sitting anywhere in the filesystem or a process is active that is using that filesystem, you will not be able to unmount it until the activity is removed. Repeat this step for each volume group that has mounted filesystems.

For the **dbvg** volume group, which has raw logical volumes, ensure that all of the logical volumes are *closed*. You can check the LV state using the following command:

```
# lsvg -l dbvg
```

You want the LV state, listed in the sixth column, to show `closed/synced`. If the LVs in the volume group are not closed, then the database must be active. Stop the database and look at the state again.

When all of the target filesystems are unmounted and the raw logical volumes are closed, you are ready to vary off the **appvg** and **dbvg** volume groups using the **varyoffvg** command.

```
# varyoffvg appvg
# varyoffvg dbvg
```

Next export the volume groups from **yogi** using the **exportvg** command.

```
# exportvg appvg
# exportvg dbvg
```

At this point, yogi's association with **appvg** and **dbvg** no longer exists. However, the hdisk and vpath definitions are still in yogi's ODM. To clean the system up and get rid of these ODM entries, run the following commands:

Remove All of the Old vpath Definitions
```
# lspv | grep vpath | grep None | awk '{print $1}' | xargs rmdev -dl
```

Remove All of the Old hdisk Definitions
```
# lspv | grep hdisk | grep None | awk '{print $1}' | xargs rmdev -dl
```

On the ESS   Go into **Storage Allocation**, as shown in Figure 29-10. From this panel, you can sort the output. In the pull-down menu above the **Host Nickname** column heading, select First, to sort first on this column. In the pull-down menu above the

Volume column heading, select Second from the pull-down list. Next click **Perform Sort**. Now the volumes are grouped together by host and ESS volume. Using this method makes it is easier to find the LUNs associated with each host.

From this list, select *all* of the LUNs that belong only to the **appvg** and **dbvg** volume groups that are still allocated to **yogi**. This is where you see how well you documented everything. For multiple LUNs, hold down the CTRL key.

CAUTION   Remember that you are the carbon-based life form in charge! The ESS Specialist assumes you know exactly what you are doing. No checks are performed, and whatever you specify will happen! If you make a mistake and tell the ESS Specialist to detach LUNs from a production database that is currently running, it will detach the disks. No checking! This is when you see all of these heads popping up over the cubicles, saying "I just lost the production database." Just a word to the wise: double-check the LUNs you want to attach or detach.

When you are sure that you have the entire set of **appvg** and **dbvg** volume group LUNs, go down to the bottom of the screen in the **Action** box. Select the following option:

```
Unassign selected Volume(s) from target hosts
```

Now moving to the box on the lower right, **Target Hosts**, select **yogi**. Depending on your configuration, you may encounter multiple entries for each HBA on the target host. Select all of them if you are utilizing multipaths.

Then just click **Perform Configuration Update**.

At this point, all of the disks are detached from **yogi**. Now it's time to configure attachments to booboo.

Once again, on the same ESS Specialist **Storage Allocation** panel, select the same group of LUNs that you just detached from yogi by highlighting each one. In the lower-left box, **Actions**, click the following selection:

```
Assign selected Volume(s) to target hosts
```

As this selection is made, available hosts are listed in the lower-right box, **Target Hosts**. From this list, highlight **booboo**. If **booboo** has multiple HBAs defined, select all that apply to each path if you want to utilize multiple paths. Now click **Perform Configuration Update**.

Now we are finished on the Shark. Move over to a **booboo** terminal session.

On Booboo   On booboo, you have to discover and configure the new storage. The first step is to run the configuration manager. Do not just enter **cfgmgr** and run with it. You want to discover the disks in **serial mode**, so use the following command:

```
# cfgmgr -S -v
```

The **-S** mean to walk the bus serially, instead of in parallel mode, and the **-v** allows you to see what is going on in verbose mode. After the configuration manager is finished, you can run **lspv** to see all of the new hdisks and vpaths. Each new hdisk and vpath will show up with no PVID and no volume group assignment.

To import the **appvg** and **dbvg** volume groups, we need to know the disk serial numbers in the ESS. To get the disk serial numbers, look at the `datapath query device` output from **yogi** that we made before we started. In the **yogi** output, you are looking for the serial number of *one* disk in each volume group.

To find the local hdisks on booboo that have the same serial number, run the following command:

```
# lsvpcfg | grep <serial number>
```

Repeat this command for each serial number that you have. Remember, you only need one hdisk per volume group to import the volume group.

With these newly gained hdisk numbers, you can import the **appvg** and **dbvg** volume groups using the following commands.

Assume hdisk10 Belongs to appvg

```
# importvg -y appvg hdisk10
```

If you need to specify the major number for the VG, then use the **-V** command option followed by the specific major number you need to use. Otherwise, you can omit it and the system will use the next available number.

Assume hdisk15 Belongs to dbvg and the Major Number Is 32

```
# importvg -y dbvg -V 32 hdisk15
```

After both volume groups are imported, run the following command to ensure that the volume groups are imported and varied online:

```
# lsvg -o
rootvg
appvg
dbvg
```

So far, so good. If you run the **lspv** command again, you should see both hdisks and vpaths. However, the vpath definitions show none for the PVID and None for the volume group.

The next task is to convert the hdisk-based volume groups into vpath-based volume groups using the following hdisk-to-vpath commands:

```
# hd2vp appvg
# hd2vp dbvg
```

At this point, the **lspv** command reveals that each vpath has a PVID and a VG assignment and that all of the hdisks have none for the PVID and None for the volume group.

Run the **df** command to ensure that all of the **appvg** filesystems are mounted. Everything should be varied on and mounted, except for the raw logical volumes in **dbvg**.

Verify that everything looks good before turning the system over to the QA group for testing.

Copy Services

With the ESS, you have two copy services for open systems and a third solution for the zSeries machines. For open systems you have FlashCopy and Peer-to-Peer Remote Copy (PPRC). FlashCopy is a solution for local copy services, and PPRC allows for extended disaster recovery capabilities. Extended Remote Copy (XRC) is a disaster recovery solution for zSeries machines.

Flash Copy

With FlashCopy, you make a point-in-time backup copy. It is important to know that a FlashCopy produces an exact *disk* copy. There are two ways to do a FlashCopy. The first method uses the *no-copy* option. The no-copy option sets up logical pointers to create a bitmap of the FlashCopy data. This takes about 3–6 seconds to create, and the flashed copy is ready to use. This is the most common way to create a point-in-time backup copy for tape archiving.

The second FlashCopy option is to actually copy the data. The data is again available in 3–6 seconds, when the bitmap is complete. However, in the background the copy is taking place inside the ESS and independently of the server. While the copy is taking place, any change to the original data causes the copy process to get an interrupt to copy the original data to the flashed copy before the data change takes place on the original data, which preserves the point-in-time data integrity of the data. The actual copying of the data in the background may take many hours to complete, so you need to consider this in your ESS planning effort.

A FlashCopy can be used to create the many images of the data that are required for backup, development, and testing, and for running reports against production data. This is part of the data explosion that everyone is talking about. You can detach a FlashCopy disk set from one server and attach the FlashCopy to one or more other servers, but be careful.

I want to warn you of a common mistake using a FlashCopy image. To understand the mistake, you need to remember what FlashCopy does. FlashCopy creates an identical *disk copy*, down to the PVID. Therefore, *never* import a flashed copy to the same system that has the original set of disks "attached"! This is scary!

Here is what can happen: You make a FlashCopy of a database. Now you have the currently attached master copy of the database and a second copy of the database that is currently not owned or attached by any host. Then, for some stupid reason, you are required to attach and import the *copy* to the same host as the master copy is attached to. You need to understand that you may have made this FlashCopy six months ago and never cleaned it up and now you need some additional storage! When you reconfigure the ESS to point the FlashCopy disks to the same host as the master (only PVIDs need to be the same!) and you run the configuration manager (**cfgmgr**), you are hosed! You do not even need to import the volume group, because the system will read the FlashCopy PVID of each disk and say, hey, you belong in this volume group that is already varied on; and Wham! you have *overlaid* production with whatever data is on the FlashCopy disks. Now you just have a bunch of trash. There is nothing you can do but restore everything. This is nonrecoverable most of the time.

This overlay problem is not the fault of the ESS or the LIC. This is a problem with the AIX configuration manager *allowing you* to have duplicated PVIDs within the same system. A modification to the configuration manager is needed to stop immediately if a duplicate PVID is found. The IBM Austin Development Team is aware of this problem, and a fix is in the works.

To make a FlashCopy, you need to set up a task in the **Copy Services** section of the StorWatch Specialist. Currently a FlashCopy is supported only within the same LSS, which consists of a set of disk arrays that make up a Device Adapter (DA) pair. In the next release of LIC, this LSS requirement will change.

Creating a Flash Copy Task   Before you can do a FlashCopy, you need to create a task. The nice thing about creating tasks is that you can pick and choose to get a list of previously created tasks and group all of the small tasks into a single large task. Then to run all of the tasks, you only need to kick off one task.

To create a FlashCopy task, you only need to do some pointing and clicking in the **Copy Services** menus. Now let's create a simple FlashCopy. From the main ESS Specialist panel, select **Copy Services**. This will bring up the main **Copy Services** panel. Next click **Volumes**. Use the pull-down menus in this panel to select the disk set that you want to set up for FlashCopy. As you can see in Figures 29-8 and 29-9, the selected disk sets depend on how you laid out the ESS.

In Figure 29-8, the FlashCopy is being configured in the same array. However, this will vary, depending on how the ESS is laid out. In Figure 29-9, the FlashCopy is being set up in separate arrays. This does not matter as long as the disks are in the same LSS.

You start by using the left mouse button to select the *source* LUN and use the right mouse button to select the *target* LUN. The source will be highlighted in blue, and the target is highlighted in red. In this case, I selected only one LUN, but you can select more, depending on the ESS layout. When you click the right mouse button again, you see the Task Wizard panel shown in Figure 29-10.

Click **Establish A FlashCopy Pair** and then click **Next**. The next step is to give the new task a name and a description.

When you click **Save**, the FlashCopy task is saved and you are presented with the Tasks panel, where you can see all of the previously defined tasks, as shown in Figure 29-11.

Now this is the interesting part. After you create all of the FlashCopy pairs, you have a bunch of separate FlashCopy tasks. Each task does an individual FlashCopy of data in a single LSS, but if they are all part of the same overall data, then you can roll up all of the little FlashCopy tasks into one big task by grouping them together. To group the tasks together, hold down the CTRL key and click each task to highlight the

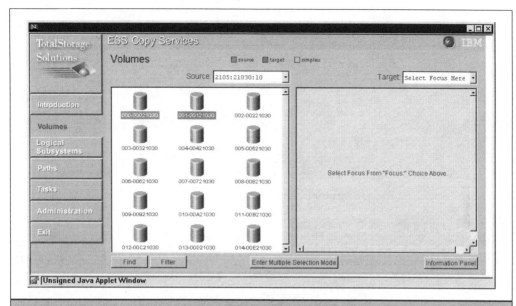

Figure 29-8.   ESS Copy Services Volume PANEL with FlashCopy in the same array

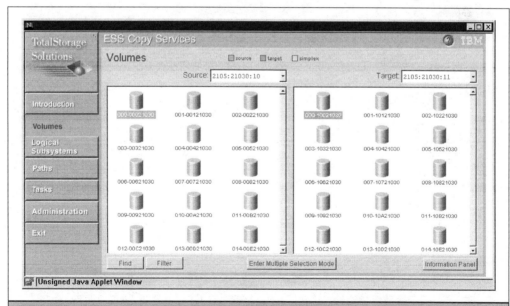

Figure 29-9   ESS Copy Services Volume panel with FlashCopy in the separate array

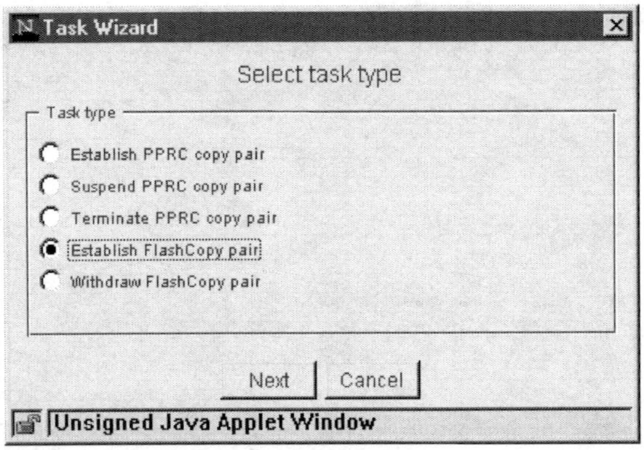

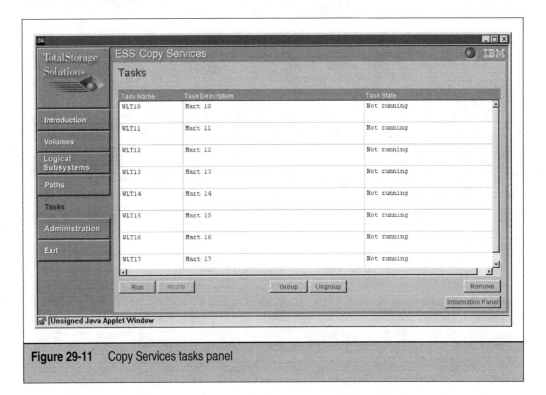

Figure 29-10.   Copy Services Task Wizard Function panel

entire group of tasks that you want to group. With the individual tasks highlighted, click **Group**. Then you will see the tasks rolled up into one task as shown in Figure 29-12.

Figure 29-11   Copy Services tasks panel

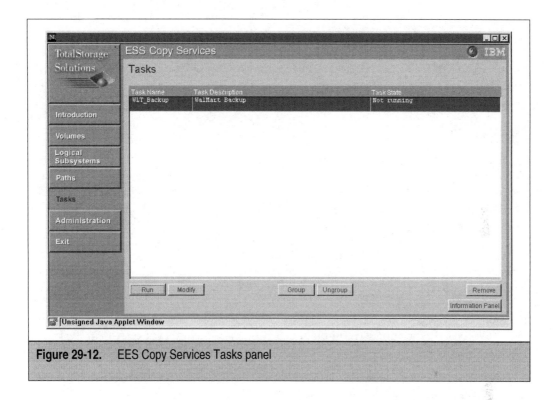

Figure 29-12.   EES Copy Services Tasks panel

If you ever need to ungroup the tasks, just highlight the task and click **Ungroup**. To look at the task definition, highlight the task and click the Information Panel button in the lower-right corner of the panel.

The **Information Panel** shows the details of the selected task. Here you can verify that you have selected the correct LUNs for each FlashCopy pair.

To execute the FlashCopy task, you can either run the task from the ESS Copy Services panel or use the command-line interface (CLI) and create a shell script to schedule the task from a remote machine using a cron table entry or other scheduling program.

Peer-to-Peer Remote Copy (PPRC)

Peer-to-Peer Remote Copy (PPRC) is a hardware solution that allows you to keep a synced copy of your data in another ESS at a remote site, in a process that is called shadow mirroring. When updates are made to the primary production copy, the remote copy of the data is shadowed to keep both copies in sync. PPRC is set up using the StorWatch Specialist Web interface. The primary and remote ESS machines are connected through an ESCON connection. PPRC is configured in a similar manner as a FlashCopy. You can use either the ESS Specialist Web interface or the command-line interface (CLI) to start and manage PPRC functions.

Extended Remote Copy (XRC)

Extended Remote Copy (XRC) is a combination of hardware and software that provides a solution to disaster recovery for the zSeries machines. XRC has the highest level of availability for disaster recovery at very long distances and allows for disk migration and moving the workload between zSeries systems.

ESS Expert

Another important component of the ESS TotalStorage software is the ESS Expert. The ESS Expert is a separate software package that you have to purchase but is a valuable tool for performance, capacity, and asset management. With the information gathering ability of the ESS Expert, you have the ability to discover all of the storage systems and identify them by name, serial number, and model. You can track the microcode levels in each of the clusters as well. With the ESS Expert, it is easy to do capacity planning by using past trends gathered by the Expert software.

The performance data collected allows you to view the disk utilization, read and write hit ratios, and read and write response times, as well as see the I/O requests for each array. With this information, the Storage Network Administrator can make informed decisions about where to add disk space and show trends of peak heavy disk utilization. With ESS Expert, you can also compile reports of all of the data collected. An IBM Redbook that I highly recommend is the *IBM StorWatch Expert Hands-On Usage Guide,* which can be downloaded and printed at the following URL:

```
http://www.redbooks.ibm.com/pubs/pdfs/redbooks/sg246102.pdf
```

To get started, you need to log in to the StorWatch Expert, which resides on a server, not on the ESS itself. The login screen is shown in Figure 29-13.

You need a valid user ID and password to use the ESS Expert. When you log in, the first screen is the Introduction, as shown in Figure 29-14. The left side of the panel has a navigation tree for direct access to any of the features in StorWatch Expert.

As you can see in Figure 29-14, the three most commonly used functions, which include data collection for capacity and performance and data preparation for performance data, are hyperlinked directly from this page.

Some of the features to look at include the current status of the ESS as shown in Figure 29-14. In the left navigation panel, click the **Manage ESS** folder.

To set up a schedule to collect data on the ESS, you click the **Manage Assets** folder. This panel allows you to create, edit, view, and delete data collection and to review

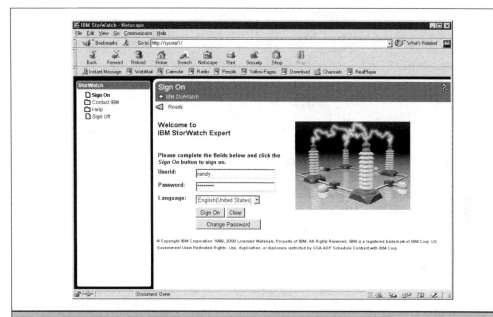

Figure 29-13. ESS Expert login screen

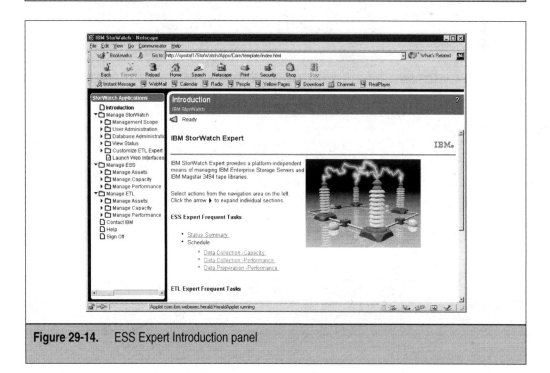

Figure 29-14. ESS Expert Introduction panel

data collected on the storage servers. If you click the **View Recent Data** hyperlink, you see the panel shown in Figure 29-15.

On the panel shown in Figure 29-16, I have two entries to select from. When you click the hyperlink in the **Nickname / Serial Number** column, you see a panel like the one shown in Figure 29-17. This shows recent data collected for disk utilization.

You can also view reports for the storage servers. There are three report options. The reports are broken down into the **Disk Utilization Summary**, the **Disk<>Cache Summary**, and the **Cache Report Summary**. The **Disk Utilization Summary** is shown in Figure 29-17.

The final part of the StorWatch Expert that I want to show you is a database summary. StorWatch Expert uses an internal DB2 database. Since this database can grow, you need to keep an eye on the status of the DB2 database. Under the Database Administration folder, click the Monitor Database folder. This brings up the panel shown in Figure 29-18.

As you can see in Figure 29-18, I still have plenty of room to grow. Notice on the right side of the panel that you can set the threshold limits for warnings and critical values.

There is much more to ESS Expert than I can cover here, but you can play around without doing any harm.

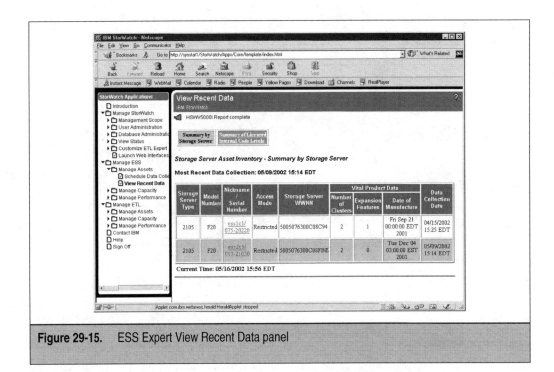

Figure 29-15. ESS Expert View Recent Data panel

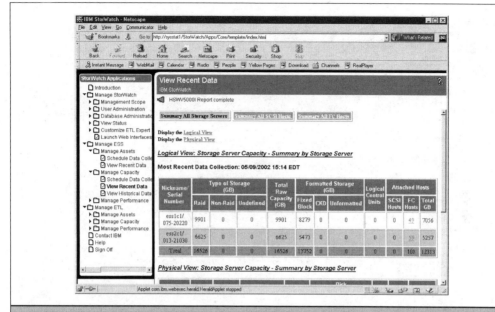

Figure 29-16. ESS Expert Data Summary for all storage servers

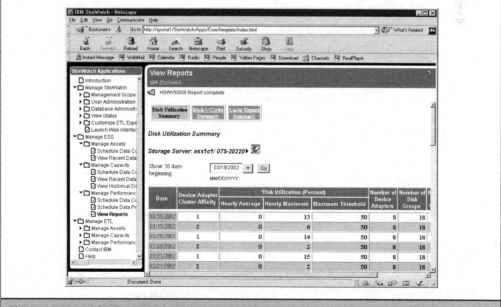

Figure 29-17. ESS Expert Disk Utilization summary

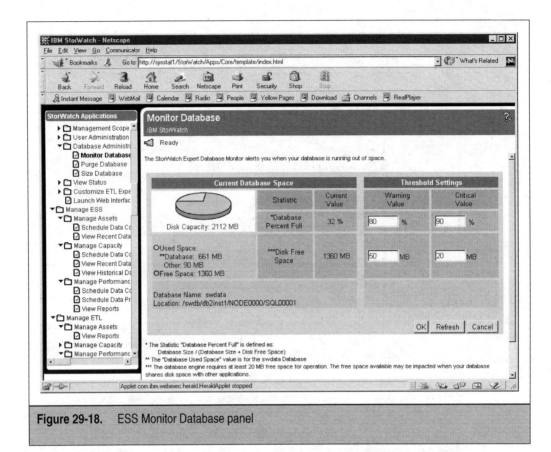

Figure 29-18. ESS Monitor Database panel

Since it is impossible to fully cover networked storage in a single chapter in a single book, I want to show you a list of Redbooks that are available for download and printing in PDF format from IBM. New Redbooks come out all of the time, so keep a close watch for new books at the IBM Redbook web site.

IBM RedBook Web site

```
http://www.redbooks.ibm.com/
```

Practical Guide for SAN with pSeries

```
http://www.redbooks.ibm.com/pubs/pdfs/redbooks/sg246050.pdf
```

IBM TotalStorage Enterprise Storage Server: Implementing the ESS in Your Environment

```
http://www.redbooks.ibm.com/pubs/pdfs/redbooks/sg245420.pdf
```

Fault Tolerant Storage Multipathing and Clustering Solutions for Open Systems for the IBM ESS `http://www.redbooks.ibm.com/pubs/pdfs/redbooks/sg246295.pdf`

Introducing Hosts to the SAN Fabric

`http://www.redbooks.ibm.com/pubs/pdfs/redbooks/sg246411.pdf`

IP Storage Networking: IBM NAS and iSCSI Solutions

`http://www.redbooks.ibm.com/pubs/pdfs/redbooks/sg246240.pdf`

Introduction to SAN Distance Solutions

`http://www.redbooks.ibm.com/pubs/pdfs/redbooks/sg246408.pdf`

IBM StorWatch Expert Hands-On Usage Guide

`http://www.redbooks.ibm.com/pubs/pdfs/redbooks/sg246102.pdf`

IBM SAN Survival Guide Featuring the IBM 2109

`http://www.redbooks.ibm.com/pubs/pdfs/redbooks/sg246127.pdf`

IBM SAN Survival Guide

`http://www.redbooks.ibm.com/pubs/pdfs/redbooks/sg246143.pdf`

CHECKLIST

The following is a checklist for the key points in SAN, NAS, and *i*SCSI consolidated storage:

- ☐ Define consolidation of data and what it involves.
- ☐ Identify how network attached storage (NAS) uses the IP local area network (LAN) to access remote storage.
- ☐ Define a storage area network (SAN).
- ☐ You can use *Zoning* to limit access to areas in the fabric and as a virtual private network.
- ☐ Define the Enterprise Storage Server (ESS).
- ☐ You can monitor the communications between the servers and the ESS through *host bus adapters (HBAs)*.

APPENDIX

Not all RS/6000 models support use of the **bootlist** command. The older RS/6000 machines that do support setting a service mode boot list have two separate boot lists, default and custom. The default boot list is for normal booting. This default boot list is used when you press **F5** or **F6** on a graphics terminal and **5** or **6** on a **tty** terminal just after the keyboard is initialized and the beep is sounded. The custom boot list is a device list created by using the **bootlist** command, **diag** facility or the SMS menu during boot.

All other PCI-Bus machines have an additional customized service boot list. You set up this boot list using the **bootlist** command with the **-m service** option. After you set up the service boot list, you use the **F5** and **F6** functions keys during the boot process. Use **F5** to use the default service boot list; use **F6** to boot from the customized service boot list. You will see some differences with various models. As always, refer to the User's Guide for your particular model. You can find this information online at this URL:

www.ibm.com/servers/eserver/pseries/library/hardware_docs/

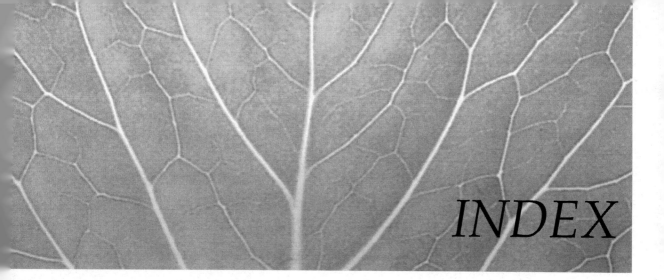

INDEX

C

D

INTERNATIONAL CONTACT INFORMATION

AUSTRALIA
McGraw-Hill Book Company Australia Pty. Ltd.
TEL +61-2-9415-9899
FAX +61-2-9415-5687
http://www.mcgraw-hill.com.au
books-it_sydney@mcgraw-hill.com

CANADA
McGraw-Hill Ryerson Ltd.
TEL +905-430-5000
FAX +905-430-5020
http://www.mcgrawhill.ca

**GREECE, MIDDLE EAST,
NORTHERN AFRICA**
McGraw-Hill Hellas
TEL +30-1-656-0990-3-4
FAX +30-1-654-5525

MEXICO (Also serving Latin America)
McGraw-Hill Interamericana Editores S.A. de C.V.
TEL +525-117-1583
FAX +525-117-1589
http://www.mcgraw-hill.com.mx
fernando_castellanos@mcgraw-hill.com

SINGAPORE (Serving Asia)
McGraw-Hill Book Company
TEL +65-863-1580
FAX +65-862-3354
http://www.mcgraw-hill.com.sg
mghasia@mcgraw-hill.com

SOUTH AFRICA
McGraw-Hill South Africa
TEL +27-11-622-7512
FAX +27-11-622-9045
robyn_swanepoel@mcgraw-hill.com

**UNITED KINGDOM & EUROPE
(Excluding Southern Europe)**
McGraw-Hill Education Europe
TEL +44-1-628-502500
FAX +44-1-628-770224
http://www.mcgraw-hill.co.uk
computing_neurope@mcgraw-hill.com

ALL OTHER INQUIRIES Contact:
Osborne/McGraw-Hill
TEL +1-510-549-6600
FAX +1-510-883-7600
http://www.osborne.com
omg_international@mcgraw-hill.com